Sheffield United Football Club

THE BIOGRAPHY

ONE OF THE FEATURE BOOKS OF THE CENTURY REFLECTING ON CHARACTERS AND EVENTS
WHICH MAKE SHEFFIELD UNITED RATHER SPECIAL AND UP AMONGST THE ELITE OF
FOOTBALL ORGANIZATIONS IN THE UNITED KINGDOM

KEVIN MCCABE
CHAIRMAN, SHEFFIELD UNITED FOOTBALL CLUB

SHEFFIELD UNITED FC

The Biography

REVISED EDITION

GARY ARMSTRONG WITH JOHN GARRETT

FOREWORD BY SEAN BEAN

Cover design by Mark Fickling of Synkronize

The opinions expressed in this book are those of the authors and are not necessarily those of the publisher or Sheffield United Football Club.
Where possible every effort has been made to obtain permission to reproduce photographs which are not in the ownership of Sheffield United Football Club.

©2006 Sheffield United Football Club
First Published in hardback 2006
Revised edition in paperback 2008

Published by The **Hallamshire** Press
for and on behalf of **Sheffield United Football Club**

Typesetting and design
Hallamshire Publications Limited

The publishers would like to thank Janet Davies and Christopher Cross of Snowdonia Press for their help in the production of this book

Printed in Great Britain by
Cromwell Press, Trowbridge

British Library Cataloguing in Publication Data:
    A catalogue record for this book is available from the British Library

ISBN 978-874718-68-0

Contents

Foreword

Like most football fans, I have vivid memories of my introduction to the game and the club I follow. It was the mid-60s and I would have been five or six when my dad, Brian, and my grandad, Harold, first took me to Bramall Lane, home of Sheffield United. It was an evening kick-off and a chilly February night. A cracking crowd made for an awesome atmosphere. The night sky was bathed in the eerie illumination provided by the floodlights, acting like beacons in the night to Blades followers, leading them to Sheffield's great football theatre. As we hurried down the street with other latecomers, a huge roar went up from inside the ground—Alan Woodward had just put United in front and we'd missed it. Over the years, missing early goals became a bit of a theme. From my late teens it was usually in the company of mates wanting to spend a bit longer in the pub.

Looking down from the Kop that night on my heroes in the red, white and black, the magical glow of a night match in the company of hordes of Blades munching pies and downing Bovril was something I will never forget. I was hooked. In a great city like Sheffield, an equal to any place in the world that calls itself a football hotbed, the club you support is rarely a matter of choice. Support is passed from generation to generation. My grandad was a Blade, my dad was a Blade—there was no way I was going to end up at Hillsborough, was there?

As a teenager in the 70s I became a regular on the Kop. I loved the pushing and swaying the terraces provided. I was never frightened or alarmed; why should I be? Surrounded by family, friends and Bladesmen any unwelcome visitors would soon be cleared off. When United scored, a young man could end up tossed around in the frenzy, finding himself miles from his original spot. When the joy died down we all looked around to see where we'd come from. Sometimes it was yards and yards away—but what a beautiful journey. Sheffield United had a good side in the early 1970s. Like many Blades I loved Tony Currie—his flair, his vision and his amazing talent. When able to grow my hair long and get my sideburns going, I wasn't a bad Currie look-alike. Alan Hodgkinson was a big favourite of mine, as were many other United keepers through the decades; Mel Rees, Simon Tracey, Alan Kelly, John Burridge and now Paddy Kenny. Great keepers and great characters all of them.

Local rivalry has always been a big part of being a Blade. In the 60s and 70s Leeds United was a prestigious club with money to buy our best players. Their fans had the strange idea they were the top team in Yorkshire. But they were formed 40 years after United and are just one club in a city the size of Sheffield. After their years of picking off our best players, the boot is now on the other foot. Sheffield Wednesday, are of course, our nearest and dearest rivals. Respect where it is due, they do have tremendous support. Sheffield derbies are fierce and vociferous; such occasions are a credit to our city. The authorities rarely permit the clubs and fans to engage at 3 o'clock on a Saturday these days. A new correctness around the game allied with Thatcherite legislation has ended some of the rivalry between Sheffield's two great clubs. What we're left with will be never-ending arguments over status. But I do know that, statistically, games won between the two weigh heavily in our favour. Anyway, what my grandad called 'The Parsons Cross Rangers' are usually out-sung at derby matches and have generally been unable to compete with Blades in terms of charisma and coolness. We are different to them.

Over the years filming has taken me all over the world. I have missed more United games than I would have liked. I have found myself making long distance calls in odd locations seeking the Blades' fortunes. A memorable match day for me was in Rajasthan, India, when I had to buy four pairs of sandals from a bloke in a cobbler's shop before he would switch on his Internet access and let me listen to the Radio Sheffield match commentary. Radio Sheffield was also received down the telephone line when I was in the Crimea—somehow this makes these matches all the more memorable.

Wherever United play, a Blades presence is evident, be it a boozer in Millwall or a Working Men's Club in Barnsley. Such a meeting of minds is a joy to behold for me. Blade away days are occasionally bizarre and always unscripted. I remember (as a young 31-year-old) swinging on the crossbar at Plough Lane, Wimbledon, scarpering off the pitch, then getting into a chauffeured car that took me to Heathrow before flying to Los Angeles to finish filming *Patriot Games* with Harrison Ford. They were good times. The film wasn't bad either.

My grandad passed away a few years ago. His ashes were scattered on the pitch at Bramall Lane. My dad still stands with my nephew near the young Blades at the back of the Kop. These youngsters are spirited and alive, they sing and dance. They make me proud. Their presence bodes well for the club's future. I will never forget the turnout when filming *When Saturday Comes* in 1995 at Bramall Lane, and the heart-splitting reception tens of thousands of Blades gave me when filming on the pitch. For that I am eternally thankful—I drank a double gallon of lager that night to bring me back down to earth.

It was an honour for me to be asked in 2001 to join the board of directors at Sheffield United. I have since enjoyed the comfort of padded seats in the Directors' Box. But status brings responsibility and club President Derek Dooley has had to tell me off for swearing, and occasionally causing a scene, so I tend to mix my seating arrangements up a bit these days—that way I can annoy a variety of people! I love the company of Blades followers, from the strongholds of Handsworth, Woodhouse, Darnall and Manor, amongst others. Even today when I socialise in Sheffield, the pubs and clubs I go to are always Blade dominated. Such places and people will be part of my life forever.

I've attended United games with Gary Armstrong for the past 16 years. A lifelong Blade and like me a Handsworth lad, he moved to London in the same month and year as me some 26 years ago. He is a prolific author and has contributed to a number of books that examine football, its nuances and what keeps us addicted to this thing. He is also one of my dearest friends.

There are some great stories and fascinating insights into the history of our club in this book.

Enjoy his story.

Keep the faith

Sean Bean with the author Gary Armstrong

I would like to dedicate my part in this work to my late father, Jack Garrett,
for making sure that the family affliction known as Sheffield United was passed on to me.
Also to my mother Audrey and brother Keith for ensuring that, in my father's absence, the finances
were there to ensure that my addiction to the Blades could be fed. Finally thanks to my wife Ellen
for her support and my sons Liam and Daniel for carrying on the Blade tradition.

John Garrett

I would like to thank the following for their invaluable assistance and support
throughout the Hall of Fame project:

**Len Badger, the family of Bobby Barclay, Sean Bean, Ted Burgin,
the family of Eddie Boot, John Bramall, Bill Brearley, Irene Brook,
Jim Brown, Robert Burns, Steve Cammack, Denis Clarebrough,
Kevin Cookson, Tony Currie, Ken Cotterill, the family of Albert Cox,
Ephraim 'Jock' Dodds, Derek Dooley, Mick Dudley, Keith Edwards,
John English, Dominic Field, Mark Fickling, Fred Furniss,
the Gilder family, The family of Billy Gillespie, Derek Goodison,
David Hagan, the Hague family, Handsworth Blades, Alan Hodgkinson,
the family of Walter Hardinge, Gary Hamson, Ted Hemsley,
Harry Hooper Jnr, Steve Jackson, Phil Jagielka, Alan Johnson,
Alan Kelly, Paddy Kenny, Jeremy Masterman, Kevin
McCabe, Suzie MacCagnan, Eric Needham, Andy Pack,
the family of Harold Pantling, the family of Gil Reece,
Jean Ringstead, The Sampy family, Beryl Shaw, Joe Shaw,
David 'Shred' Spencer, Jackie Stewart, the family of Jack Smith,
Chris Steer, the family of Charles Sutcliffe, Peter Thickett,
Martin Utley, Fred White, Dane Whitehouse,
Dora and Martin Winter.**

8

For my wife, Hani, and our children Lennie and Phoebe

Gary Armstrong

Acknowledgements

This book started life in a conversation in a pub in 1999. Like so many ideas in Sheffield its origins lie in two men drinking beer and putting the world to rights. Typical of Sheffield men and beer drinking, the top of the mountain, whilst promised over beers, had not been reached the following morning. As a consequence of further beers, the birth of children and something called Life interfering with grand intentions, the text was not completed until August 2006. The book is a life story of a football club. Like all stories, what a reader receives is the end of the journey. Many people were met en route, a few were side stepped but the stories and memories, some first hand others passed down, of those dead and alive became an integral part of the long hours encapsulated in the twelve months it took to write this text.

The end product is the outcome of a meeting of two minds and two projects. For me, it is the continuation of research that examines the social and political history of Sheffield United. This enquiry encompasses the people who ran the club, the players who represented it and the life and times of the City of Sheffield. For John Garrett, the book in places condenses his years of research which culminated in the magnificent Sheffield United Hall of Fame display which opened at the club's Bramall Lane ground in late 2001. The book attempts to mediate between the two intellectual processes. In any collaboration of this kind, one individual necessarily takes the lead and, implicitly, responsibility for what follows. I thus declare that any mistake or misrepresentation is down to me. My sincere thanks are due to John Garrett. The book would not have started life or be completed without him.

The book would not have happened either without the authorisation of Kevin McCabe, Sheffield United chairman. Integral to this idea becoming a reality was a meeting between the chairman and myself in the summer of 2005 wherein the idea of a club biography was prompted further by Sheffield United director Sean Bean, and friend of the club Suzie MacCagnan. The pair were convinced the project was needed. A wave of the hand from the chairman saw the deal finalised. The liaison throughout the production of the book was Sheffield United's Chief Operations Officer, Mark Fenoughty. His interest in the project ensured that time schedules were kept and at times textual sensibilities refined. My thanks are due to all concerned. To the credit of all at Sheffield United, no-one specified the content and no attempt was made by anyone at the club to airbrush the controversial low points in the club's history.

Those who were instrumental in the production of this text are listed below in alphabetical order, and so I thank: Len Badger, Dave Bassett, Ian Benjamin, Reg Brealey, David Capper, Cecil Coldwell, Albert Cox, Colin Collindridge, Ken Cotterill, Tony Currie, Andy Daykin, Brian Deane, Jock Dodds, Derek Dooley, Keith Edwards, Fred Furniss, Ken Furphy, Ted Hemsley, Alan Kelly, Andrew Kirkham, Joe McElligot, Billy McEwan, Ken Naylor, Ian Porterfield, Tony Pritchett, Ian Ramsey, Antonio Rattin, Mick Rooker, Alex

Sabella, Jimmy Sirrel, Graham Shaw, Joe and Hettie Shaw, Mick Speight, Pete Stone, Fred and Margaret White, Dane Whitehouse, and Alan Woodward. I am indebted to Nick Wilde for the contacts established on my behalf when visiting Argentina. Grateful thanks are due to Fernando Dr Tomasso and Romina Papierman for their hospitality and assistance whilst in Buenos Aires. The story of Jimmy Hagan was a product of many pleasant visits to the home of his daughter, Jackie Stewart. Of course thanks are due to the Reverend Tony Frain for taking me to Bramall Lane for the first time in September 1969 and my Mum and Dad for never seeking to dampen my enthusiasm for the game and Sheffield United FC over the past 35 years.

I am thankful for the assistance this text received from Professor David Russell and Thomas Tor. Their brilliant histories of Association Football should be read by anyone enthused by this book. More specifically, what follows would not have been possible without the generosity and lifelong scholarship of Denis Clarebrough, Sheffield United's official historian. His knowledge of Sheffield United and his collection of Sheffield United memorabilia is unparalleled. Many thanks are also due to Maureen Clarebrough who made my many visits to the Clarebrough household the most enjoyable of occasions and whose understated knowledge of British social history was occasionally crucial in my curiosities. Special thanks are also due to Matthew Bell whose willingness to share his vast knowledge of footballing details is an example to everyone involved in this game. Peter Sharpe's knowledge was similarly invaluable and provided with great generosity of spirit. A football club is blessed by the scholarship of such individuals.

The book was completed on top of my 'normal' job. I am however grateful to Professor Steve Hodkinson, Pro-Vice Chancellor of Brunel University, and Professor Ian Campbell, Subject Leader in Sport Sciences for permitting me the time away from the office that this text required. I thank you for the trust shown and hope it was repaid. Thanks are also due to School of Sport and Education Administrator, Carol Bark for facilitating so many things on my behalf over the last five years and especially during the last twelve months.

Last but not least are the people who made this book a reality. Pauline Climpson of Hallamshire Publications had the confidence to run with the idea and has published with characteristic excellence. The proofing was conducted with polite authority by Richard Whitehead and Pat Whitehead. The excellent images contained herein and the image technology such a process requires were provided in part by Mark Fickling and Mark Rogers. The images come mainly from the Hall of Fame collection. Some came courtesy of private collections, others arrived courtesy of both Denis Clarebrough and Andy Pack, Sheffield United's Media Officer. Sincere thanks are due to you all.

Finally a very special thanks is due to both Irmani Darlington and Karen Kinnaird for their IT and editing abilities. Without their dedication to the script and tolerance of my foibles, this book would not have made the deadline.

Gary Armstrong September 2006

The point about football in Britain is that it is not just a sport people take to, like cricket or tennis or running long distances. It is inherent in the people. It is built into the urban psyche, as much a common experience to our children as are uncles and school. It is not a phenomenon; it is an everyday matter. There is more eccentricity in deliberately disregarding it than in devoting a life to it. It has more significance in the national character than theatre has. Its sudden withdrawal from the people would bring deeper disconsolation than to deprive them of television. The way we play the game, organise it and reward it reflects the kind of community we are.

No player, manager, director or fan who understands football, either through his intellect or his nerve-ends, ever repeats that piece of nonsense trotted out mindlessly by the fearful every now and again which pleads, 'After all, it's only a game.' It has not been only a game for 80 years: not since the working classes saw it as an escape from drudgery and claimed it as their own. It has not been a sideshow this century. What happens on the football field matters, not in the way food matters but as poetry does to some people and alcohol does to others: it engages the personality. It has conflict and beauty, and when those two qualities are present together in something offered for public appraisal they represent much of what I understand to be art. The people own this art in the way they can never own any form of music, theatre, literature or religion because they can never be fooled in it as they can be in these other things, where intention can be deliberately obscured and method hidden beyond their grasp. Football does not ask for faith; it compels examination. Phoney footballers are simply booted aside. The crowds can be vindictive and brutal, but they can seldom be deceived. They know about their football intuitively, as they know about their families.

Arthur Hopcraft 1968: *The Football Man*

Sheffield United 2006

Prologue

Remembrance of Things Past

Football was never just a sport. The game and the clubs that facilitate it are statements about place and life; some are profound, some uncomplicated. Football since the mid-nineteenth century was and remains, for tens of thousands of Sheffield-born, the focal point of their heritage. The two professional football clubs which the city hosts and the population follow are integral to the city and its people's self-identity, bound up as they are with buildings, people, and recollections. Because football is made of memories, supporters are curious about their club's past—they have a tendency towards the nostalgic. There are a variety of ways of representing the past. What this book seeks to provide is a chronology of occasionally glorious footballing days, alongside commemoration of the people and places that have provided for a variety of events and moments in the history of Sheffield United. Integral to these objectives is the recognition of the idiosyncrasy of character. Attempting to account for and explain the procedures and processes of a football club from its chairmen through to its managers, players and supporters is not an easy task. Excuses made, a reader is presented with a book which is the extended version of a display of football antiques and memorabilia contained within the Sheffield United Hall of Fame housed in the interior of what is popularly known as the 'South Stand' of United's Bramall Lane stadium.

The Hall of Fame and this book are a consequence of a meeting of minds. For one, the catalyst was the authorship of the book, *Blade Runners: Lives in Football*, published in 1999, which examined the lives of 24 players and directors who were instrumental in the recent history of Sheffield United. Selling out in 12 months brought a realisation that recollection and revelation was something sought by thousands of United's supporters. Around the same time, one man, employed by Sheffield United, had his job description changed. One of his new duties was the care of match-day mascots and their families. This responsibility saw a change in approach to previous procedures and brought access to the Bramall Lane family treasures, then lying dormant under lock and key. Discovering a variety of memorabilia he was particularly taken by the 1925 FA Cup Winners' medal which had been bought by the club a decade before. The new approach to mascot tours would henceforth include pitch-side revelations of the medal to awestruck children and parents. Further enquiries discovered similar souvenirs belonging to a wide variety of sons, daughters and grandchildren of past players, many of whom proved willing to either donate or lend these items to the club for display purposes. When United's only living 1936 FA Cup finalist donated his runners-up medal to the club, the die was set for the idea of a Sheffield United museum.

A museum project was proposed in 1999 and struck a chord with the Sheffield United directors. Given a blank canvas to develop such an idea, a public launch in early 2000 attracted wide media attention and within days people began ringing in with both information and the offer of memorabilia. Not working to a template, or even seeking a role model, the project was left to its own devices. The outcome after a year of building and negotiation around appropriate displays was the Sheffield United Hall of Fame, which was opened in December 2001, thereby making it one of the first of its kind in English football. Meanwhile, research continued for the second edition of 'Blade Runners'.

Around 150 years ago, the City of Sheffield invented two products that were exported to worldwide acclaim and which changed the world. One was steel; the other was the game of Association Football. We could argue forever as to which was more consequential for the planet. Significantly, however, the curious have been able to learn about Sheffield's steel industries since the mid-1970s by visiting Abbeydale Industrial Hamlet. This was supplemented in the early 1980s by the opening of Kelham Island Visitors Centre, which illustrates in a variety of ways the industrial heritage of the city. A few years ago, the splendid Magna Centre was opened on the site of the former Templeborough Rolling Mills steelworks in nearby Rotherham. By contrast, football had nothing by way of display or representation.

The idea of commemorating the game and its Sheffield founders has a long history. In February, 1898, less than a decade after the club's founding, the Sheffield United match-day programme stated:

> *We are thinking of establishing a museum for the collection of various anonymous epistles, articles etc, not to mention leather medals.*

Nothing became of this idea and no further mention of such a display is evident in the match-day programme until 1999. It remains a mystery as to why no football museum was established in Sheffield. The National Football Museum opened in 2000 was housed in Preston, not in the city that gave football to the world.

Football is integral to the heritage of Sheffield. The city and its region have always produced footballers and managers. It is a world hotbed of the game and it has an unparalleled history. The world's oldest football club is Sheffield FC founded in 1857. The world's oldest 'derby' is played every Boxing Day between Sheffield FC and Hallam FC. The Bramall Lane stadium has a unique claim to footballing history. When in May 2002, Northwich Victoria FC played their last game at the Drill Field ground they could rightly argue that the ground had seen 125 uninterrupted years of football. At one time the club president claimed that the ground was the oldest in the world. In 1989 the Football Association substantiated this claim. Counter-claims appeared; one was from Bramall Lane. Historians subsequently found that the original Northwich club had folded and merged with another to form Northwich Victoria in 1890. Bramall Lane was thus, by one year, the oldest stadium for football in the world where one club has played continuously.

The influence of the city of Sheffield on the English game both by birth and association remains. In early 1999 the England manager, albeit a caretaker, was Sheffield-born Howard Wilkinson, whilst the acting chairman of the FA was Sheffield-born Geoff Thompson. The Sheffield-born Dave Richards was chairman of the International Committee and was later to succeed Thompson as head of the FA. The head of the League Managers' Association, John Barnwell, had in the early 1970s played for Sheffield United, as had England under-18s coach Nigel Spackman in the 1990s. A former Sheffield schoolteacher, Dick Bate, was coach of England under-16s. The Sheffield-based Labour MP Joe Ashton was chair of the Parliamentary All-Party Football Group as well as a director of Sheffield Wednesday. The New Labour Government Minister of Sport between 2001 and the date of publication is Sheffield MP and former Sheffield United director Richard Caborn. The man in charge of elite level referees (via the Professional Game Match Officials Board) between 2001 and the present day, Keith Hackett, is also a son of the city. In 2005, United stood 14th of all English clubs in providing players for the English national team—34 in total. In 8th place providing 45 players was Wednesday.

A reader might reflect as to why displays of football memorabilia and books are so popular. The answer seems to be that we tend to like and collect things we have grown up with, but why we do so is perplexing. A plausible argument is that it is an act of defiance against an ever-impending death. To collect is human, classification is embodied in fears of oblivion and hopes for eternity. To have and to hold is to be alive. Collectors of things are overwhelmingly male; psychologists tell us that men collect sets of things and ensure that they are well presented and kept in a special place. Women collect things that have particular memories for them, then display them around the home, usually in no particular order. Men tend to collect things as boys, then resume collecting in their late 30s and 40s. In between they may grow out of it and then, when their parents die and their children grow up and leave the home, resume collecting. This can be seen as a return to childhood only this time with time and money to be able to complete the collection. The behaviour of collecting has produced remarkable commentary from academics, some have argued that possession and collection are discreet forms of sexual perversion. Others take a more political viewpoint, arguing that collectors typify the passive bourgeoisie mentality of late capitalism. That's the theory. We might ask however; can we ever understand the events that made us what we are or do the things we do?

Sports enthusiasts have long memories and some sports have a long history of museums—Lord's Cricket Ground has collected artefacts for over 100 years. By contrast, UK athletics has little by way of collection and representation. Until recently, the same could be said of British football. Since the 19th century football-related paraphernalia has been collected, treasured and exchanged. Items range from international caps to the more commonplace football cigarette cards and match programmes. Private collections of football memorabilia compiled by individual enthusiasts have existed for decades. In the 1950s one man in Hitchin, Hertfordshire, claimed his collection made him the founder-curator of the first football museum. Sports journalist Harry Langton's collection of 4,000 football-related objects was even purchased by FIFA in 1998. The private collections of football memorabilia owned by footballers themselves mimic museums. Professional clubs similarly held collections of memorabilia behind cabinets in designated rooms, sometimes grandiosely described as 'trophy rooms'. Many collections only came to light when clubs made public appeals in the late 1990s for proposed museums.

For some 15 years the game in the UK has entered the era of retro-chic wherein the collectable is infinite. A marketing ethos, evidenced in most football clubs today, sees some offer club heritage tours which invariably end in newly built museums. Aware of the value of football memorabilia, specialist publications now exist for connoisseurs. Esteemed and high-class auction houses have joined the boom. The commercial value of football nostalgia was demonstrated in 2001 when the Professional Footballers' Association paid £1.92 million for the 1953 L.S. Lowry painting *Going to the Match*, an evocative depiction of fans making their way to watch Bolton Wanderers take on Sheffield United at Burnden Park. The growth in football-related nostalgia may well be a consequence of the game's confusing recent past, particularly its over-concern with finance and its unprecedented global dimensions. Such changes in the game intertwine with the rise of the individual's search for 'roots' in a transient world and the construction of 'sacred geographies' in a variety of identity politics.

Perhaps inevitably in a land that loves heroes, the USA built sporting 'Halls of Fame' as far back as the 1920s. America has always seen the value of celebrating its sporting heroes as a way of cementing national unity. Whilst football is a minor sport in the USA they were 25 years ahead of Britain in terms of honouring their footballing (soccer) heritage. The US Soccer Hall of Fame, founded in 1975, resides in Cooperstown in upstate New York. The Sheffield United Hall of Fame, whilst borrowing its title from the American concept, could equally be called a museum or a visitor centre. A museum does not have any agreed-upon definition, but we all know that a museum is involved in the processes of preserving, collecting and interpreting for now and the future and exists for the benefit of the public. Museums are institutions that safeguard and make accessible artefacts and specimens which they hold in trust for society. By this definition the United Hall of Fame is also a museum in that it aims to inspire and provide both learning and enjoyment. Museums are products of prejudice; selection is usually by the unelected and unaccountable. We ask readers not to judge us as experts on the politics of display, but as two informed fans well disposed to Sheffield United FC.

History by definition has gone. What remains are memories, photos, archives and sometimes film footage. History is a distillation of rumour, and in this journey we travel fitful, ever on the lookout for cool memories and anecdotes that might be crucial to an epoch. Our techniques of selection, be it in the Hall of Fame or in this book, were not subject to objective scrutiny. We accept that both written representation and visual display are intellectual acts of borrowing, assimilating, quoting and imitation. Our backgrounds encapsulate our notion of 'heritage' and thereby might attract criticism. In both display and storytelling we seek to locate and present the intricacies of motivation and memory; ambiguity is inevitable. Storytelling exists to create legends, and is a form of ancestor worship. Like all ancestors some need unloading, others should be locked away. The men herein existed, they did not hand us notions of 'tradition', they just were.

Sheffield United FC in its 117 years of existence has framed a million occasions of drama, friendship, love, hate, joy, jubilation, disappointment and memories. Dutch travel writer Cees Nooteboom evocatively stated that memory is like a dog that sits down where it pleases. Wherever it is found, the past ideally should assist in a more critical engagement both with what happened and its relationship to the present. The years should teach much which the days never knew.

1936 FA Cup runners-up medal
Awarded to Ephraim 'Jock' Dodds, who in 2006 is the oldest surviving FA Cup Finalist
Dodds donated this medal to Sheffield United in 2000 and inspired the Hall of Fame

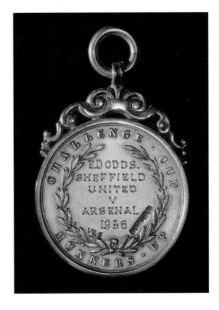

Gary Armstrong

Gary Armstrong is a Senior Lecturer in the School of Sport and Education, Brunel University, London. For ten years he lectured in Criminology at the University of Westminster and the University of Reading. Amongst the many projects he was involved in the two best known publications are Images of Control: The Rise of the Maximum Surveillance Society, *(Berg, 1998) (co-authored with Clive Norris) and* Surveillance, CCTV and Social Control, *(Ashgate 1999), co-edited with Clive Norris and Jade Moran. His research into sports related matters has produced the following publications:* Football Hooligans: Knowing the Score, *(Berg, 1998) and* Blade Runners: Lives in Football, *(Hallamshire Press, 1999). He has also co-edited, alongside Richard Giulianotti,* Entering The Field, New Perspectives in World Football, *(Berg, 1997),* Football Cultures and Identities, *(MacMillan 2000),* Fear and Loathing in World Football, *(Berg 2001) and* Football in Africa: Conflict, Conciliation and Community, *(Palgrave 2003). From 1998–present he has researched the role of football in the reconstruction of Liberia and the role that football has played in the politics of Malta.*

John Garrett

John Garrett is currently employed by Sheffield United FC on the Hall of Fame redevelopment project. An early career in financial advice and retail saw him join Sheffield United in 1998 as a Promotions Sales Representative. Seconded to the Sheffield United Hall of Fame project between 2000 and 2002 he then worked for two years at the Sheffield United academy. Returning to the Promotions Department, his matchday duties include the care of mascots and organised tours of the Hall of Fame.

Introduction

Sheffield United?

Stadiums produce common-sense meanings and understandings. That said, there is not a consensus on conventional or appropriate behaviour at a football match. If there were, then the segregation of stands and terracing would not have been evident from the game's beginnings. Neither would some favour the sidelines over the terracing behind the goals. Those who for decades have visited football grounds will understand, as the Romans did, that there exists in such enclosures a genius loci (a spirit of a place) because the ground is all about memory. By itself, the stadium, be it in its architecture or its function, is mundane. To exist it needs quantities of people, quality of exhibitions and the emotional investment of the former in the latter. Stadiums are, thus, spaces of representation and are defined by levels of disruptiveness; active participation produces such spectacle. The Bramall Lane stadium, both in origin and today, provides different experiences for those within it. For the athlete, it is the home of dreams and glory or, possibly, failure and physical pain. For the mass of spectators, it is a place that provides for admired aesthetic qualities and degrees of emotion. To the club owners and the City Fathers, the Bramall Lane football ground is an asset and part of the fabric of the city. Things are no different at Sheffield Wednesday's Hillsborough ground.

It cannot be easily argued that footballing success is the reason for the large number of fans in Sheffield who flock to watch Sheffield United and Sheffield Wednesday. Historically neither side has been superior to the other for very long, and neither has won an FA Cup or League Championship for over 50 years. Recently Wednesday won the League Cup in 1991 and were beaten finalists in that cup and the FA Cup in 1993. Overall, however, the city has not seen much silverware and United have not won a thing for 80 years. Considering this, the loyalty manifest in attendance figures is staggering. From a population of half a million people, the two clubs attracted a combined average of 50,000 per game when both were in the top division of English football in 1991–94. Needless to say, they had no problems packing Wembley Stadium to its 76,000 capacity in 1993 for an FA Cup semi-final tie. In the season that we finish this text (2005–06) the two Sheffield teams, playing in a division lower than they were in 1994 still attract a combined total of 50,000 spectators.

Fans of the two clubs do not hold a high opinion of each other. There is no obvious 'good' social or historical reason why the United–Wednesday rivalry should be so strong. The bitterness often shown by fans of both sides can be remarkable. One possible explanation comes from the Sheffield-based journalist, Jonathan Foster:

> *Sheffield is a uniquely insular city, the least cosmopolitan of all the large cities in Britain, with little apart from football in which jealousy or passion can be invested.*
>
> (Independent, *April 1993.)*

The history of the two clubs provides some clues as to the strength of the later rivalry. The Wednesday team was founded in 1867 out of a cricket club consisting of traders whose day off was a Wednesday. The football team was established to keep members together through the winter. United came into being

22 years later after a member of the Sheffield United Cricket Club ground committee at Bramall Lane saw an FA Cup semi-final played there. The obvious appeal of the game, not to mention the revenue it generated, persuaded him to suggest to the other members of the groud committee that another football club could be founded. The owners of Bramall Lane formed a football team (Sheffield United) and advertised for players, many of whom came from Scotland.

In origin, then, United fans were men who were not dyed-in-the-wool Wednesday fans, drawn either from other, declining, clubs in the city or from the population around the Bramall Lane ground. Some may have simply wished to be part of a new ground and new team, representatives perhaps of the city's nouveau riche. Wednesday was the older, more traditional club which, as a gathering of shopkeepers, might be said to loosely represent the local male petit bourgeoisie. However, the differences in the social origins of the two clubs were not great enough to leave a lasting mark. Both were identified first and foremost with the city's major industry. The term 'Blades' was originally a journalistic cliché attached to any team from Sheffield, akin to speaking of the men from 'Steel City'. As such neither club can claim to have originated the term. In fact, it was Wednesday who were originally nicknamed the Blades. It was only in the early years of the century, after Wednesday moved to their new ground at Owlerton, that they lost the nickname Blades and were reborn as the 'Owls'. United then became known as the Blades. The term Blades has a usage beyond football. In 1882 during the Sheffield Riots, a Salvation Army Temperance Rally was attacked by a gang of muscular pugilists hired by the owners of drinking dens—the hired muscle was called the 'Sheffield Blades'.

Since the mid 1960s, both sets of supporters have referred to their rivals by the term 'pigs'. Used at times in a light-hearted manner, at other times it is meant to insult. The response of the receiver can thus vary from a wry smile to a punch. Context is everything. Wednesday fans believe they pioneered the insult, as a derivative of their ridiculing United's red and white striped kit which they considered akin to rashers of bacon. United fans claim their ownership is a consequence of Wednesday adopting the nickname of Owls—the pig was the lowest form of animal and therefore more suitable as a nickname for their rivals.

Family ties mainly determine an individual's football allegiance. Some have a father, and or brother, who supports the city rivals, but this should not be seen as the outward manifestation of some underlying family quarrel; contrariness can play a part, and in thousands of cases allegiance has been something accidental. Any change of allegiance, once given, is out of the question. Divisions based on football loyalty in the city do not have their origins in undeniable correlates of class, race or geography. There is no marked difference in localities from which the supporters come. Unsurprisingly there is a certain clustering of support in the districts surrounding the grounds of each club, Wednesday to the north, United to the city centre and south-east. Both clubs, however, draw support from every part of Sheffield and the surrounding villages and districts. There is no correlation here between football support and religious or political identity.

There were various forms of hostile but non-violent opposition around the notion of football loyalties that centred on identification with various colours, fan numbers and football chants. Thousands of United fans (and Wednesday fans) took part in some or all of these oppositions. The association of club colours has always been taken seriously. Almost from their beginnings, United have worn a kit of red and white stripes, with Wednesday in a similar one of blue and white. Match days see colour demarcated crowd division, but colour rivalry also exists outside of match day. Some United fans could never wear blue sweaters or jackets or paint their homes blue.

Wednesday's status as the oldest established professional club in the city was enhanced when both clubs were admitted to the Football League in 1892. The League had begun in 1888, clubs were required to fulfil a fixed programme of matches and guarantee gate takings to sustain the wages of professional players. The original 12 clubs agreed to share gate receipts (guaranteeing visitors a minimum £15). In 1892 the first division was enlarged from 14 clubs to 16, and a new second division of 12 clubs created. In a ballot, Wednesday were admitted to the first division, United to the second. Partly as a result of this, Wednesday have since been seen by many an observer as the city's premier club, giving the United fans something of a complex in respect of their more famous neighbours. One way this feeling has been expressed is in the building of the two clubs' grounds. At Wednesday's Hillsborough stadium, a magnificent cantilever stand was built in 1961, which helped to make it an obvious choice to host matches in the 1966 World Cup. It was only a matter of time before United, whose Bramall Lane ground was still shared with cricket and had only three sides, had a similar stand. Completed in 1975, it crippled United financially for the next 20 years. For most of their history Wednesday have been the biggest drawing club in the region, though not without some embarrassing exceptions. In 1978–79, when they were in the third division, Wednesday's average of 10,860 left them adrift of fourth division Barnsley (11,048) as well as United. And in 1971–72, with United newly promoted to the first division, their 33,189 average was almost twice as high as second division Wednesday's average. In 1991–92 Wednesday were the fourth and United the eleventh best supported teams in the country.

Everything seemed set fair for South Yorkshire over 100 years ago. United won the League in 1898 and the Cup in 1899 and 1902. Wednesday were champions in 1903 and 1904 and Doncaster reached the dizzy heights of seventh in the second division in 1902, their highest ever position. Since then it's all been a bit of a struggle. The First World War interrupted a promising spell—the two Sheffield clubs were sixth and seventh in 1915, United won the Cup and Barnsley were third in the second division. It wasn't until 1951–52 that all five clubs in the region were in the second division or higher. The two Sheffield clubs had a brief bright spell in the early 60s (fifth and sixth in 1962) and an even briefer one in the early 90s, but it never got much better than their FA Cup semi-final in 1993, when Wednesday stood 7th and United 14th in the Premiership. The 70s were a nightmare. The three smaller South Yorkshire clubs, Rotherham, Barnsley and Doncaster were all in the fourth division by 1973 (all in the bottom half in 1973–74) and the two Sheffield clubs sank in the second part of the decade. For one season, 1979–80, not a single South Yorkshire club was in the top two divisions, though Wednesday won promotion after a derby-packed year in the old third division.

The end of the twentieth century saw people consider the unthinkable in a Sheffield footballing context. In 1999 the United and Wednesday chairmen, Mike McDonald and Dave Richards, discussed a merger. As United played at Wolverhampton, McDonald met the Wednesday chairman as a guest at an Owls' game. Richards, a Sheffield-born businessman, would, one would have thought, known about the strength of local football feelings. McDonald, however, was born in Lancashire and a self-proclaimed fan of Manchester City. His idea was for a super-club representing Sheffield, playing in a kit of red and blue stripes in a new stadium built on the site of a former open-cast mine adjacent to the city's airport and close to the motorway. Both sets of fans were totally opposed. The local evening paper produced a poll showing that 98 per cent were against the idea. In truth, most fans did not take the plan seriously. Objectively and economically it had some credentials. The Owls were some £12 million in debt, the coffers were similarly empty at Bramall Lane, but over a century of footballing tradition cannot be bought and repackaged. Precisely because success has been so hard to come by, each club hangs on to its own identity all the more grimly.

The Founding Fathers

In the centre is Michael Ellison, without whom Bramall Lane and Sheffield United FC would not exist

Made in Sheffield

Football in Sheffield grew as a consequence of the Industrial Revolution. The coal deposits, iron-ore, timber (for charcoal) millstone grit (for grinding) and water power from the surrounding hillsides were ideal for steel production, which became the city's economic base. With the arrival of heavy manufacturing industry and the conferring of city status in 1893 came a civic pride noted decades later by George Orwell who, visiting Sheffield in the 1930s, wrote:

> *Sheffield, I suppose, could justifiably claim to be called the ugliest town in the world; its inhabitants who want it to be pre-eminent in everything are very likely to make that claim for it.*

It was a tough place that produced tough people who refused to be downtrodden. Seventeenth-century riots over religion, food shortages and epidemics continued into the next century against price-rises, unpopular legislation and arbitrary justice. Methodist preacher John Wesley found Sheffield people lively and affectionate in 1781, but King George III in 1800 considered the city a 'damned, bad place'.

During the period 1790–1820 the industrial base of Sheffield changed from a 'dependent artisanry' to factory based collective productivity. With this came a consciousness of exploitation resulting in a variety of uprisings. It also brought abject poverty. Local historian Sylvia Pybus states that in 1764 Sheffield people were regarded as 'moderate and temperate' thanks to well paid industrial production. Later, appalling use was made of child labour in mines and factories. Following the French Revolution, Sheffield became known for 'ignorance and disloyalty' and hosting a population which worked for three days on large wages and then drank and rioted for the rest of the week. Periodic riots occurred over food prices in the late 1830s because of a downturn in the demand for manufactured goods. In January 1840 there occurred the Sheffield Rising, which was reported to be an attempt by Chartists to 'Moscow' the city, their plans however were ruined by informers. Following this in the 1890s came the rise of anarchism. At the same time the city was a hotbed of Methodism, which attracted all strands of society.

The emerging industrial society of the late 19th century was to see the population of the city treble in 50 years. The city was noisy with the sound of industrial production and the atmosphere acrid with a combination of coal, sulphur and yeast from the dozens of breweries. Elections in Sheffield in the late 19th century were amongst the most savage and disorderly of Victorian times—Prime Minister Joseph Chamberlain was hit by a fish whilst campaigning. Nineteenth-century trade unionism brought murder and bombings to the city. What became known as the Trade Union Outrages were the product of feuds within the steel grinders union which lasted from 1829 to the 1880s. Gunpowder was used to blow up the grinding wheels of unpopular men and non-union grinders were shot dead. The government of the day established a Royal Commission on Trade Unions in 1867 to inquire into the Outrages. This found that 12 of the 60 Trades Societies in Sheffield were involved to some degree in the events. The Outrages ceased after the inquiry; the guilty men were never prosecuted. In 1861 one observer was moved to observe that the city was 'as devoid of the decencies of civilisation as it was in the Dark Ages'.

Sheffield has a continuous politically radical history. The steel-producing artisans and the factory/mining proletariat admired the skilled and strong man. In leisure time, such men played as hard as they worked. The former were self employed on piece work. Paid for what they made, they chose their own hours of work in their small workshops. They worked when demand required it, and when the water was not

An early photograph of the River Don flowing towards its junction with the River Sheaf c. 1880

frozen over and when they were not suffering the effects of over-imbibing. The regular absences due to the latter went by the euphemism 'St Monday'. The other aforementioned occupational cultures held similar reputations for beer drinking founded in the realisation that in such dangerous working environments, the next day could be their last. Sheffield is thus one of Europe's most blue-collar cities, and contains a population described by one sociologist as 'historically stubborn, and both sceptical and occasionally hostile to the interventions of national government'. Such an attitude produced a suspicion of those who set themselves up to be something they were not.

Bank Holidays and Rational Recreation

The early 19th century saw the Bank of England observing more than 30 Saints days and religious festivals. The Industrial Revolution, however, required of its workers a greater adherence to regulation. Eventually Sir John Lubbock introduced the 1871 Bank Holiday Act. The banker MP and Old Etonian held a Victorian sense of the common good. Persuading Parliament to vary the law about bills of exchange, he managed to negotiate four days annually wherein a bill due for payment would be deemed to mature the following day. The bank could thus have a day off. Lubbock sought a celebration of shared experiences for his bank employees primarily through inter-village cricket games. Lubbock's legislation laid down the present Bank Holiday system that was to be very influential in the football calendar for the next century.

The Factory Act of 1847 freed women and children from Saturday employment. Years later, men were to enjoy the same privilege. In this era, men of the landed gentry and their sons in the universities began to modify and regulate Folk football games of previous decades. Variations on what were to become the rules of Association Football remain the subject of scholarly debate. Sheffield had its own versions drawn up by members of Sheffield FC, which were accepted locally and then incorporated nationally with those drawn up in 1863 by the FA to create the first formalised rules of football.

What became known as Bramall Lane was an area of land owned by the Duke of Norfolk, which had for decades facilitated various sporting pastimes. In the mid-1800s a wall was built by the Duke of Norfolk enclosing the land, thus formalising the area as an official sporting venue. Such private enterprise for sport preceded the construction of municipal parks and recreation grounds. The area was originally named Whitehouse Lane and consisted of a cart track, which went the mile or so from Sheffield town centre to Heeley. The latter area seems to have grown because of the proximity of the river, which would provide the energy for the small cutlery-making workshops of the 'Little Mesters' of the time. The occupants of a nearby house were the Bramhall family who ran a sickle and scythe workshop. The Bramall Lane sporting arena opened in 1855 and was soon hosting a wide variety of sports. Athletics meetings proved extremely popular. Indeed, in 1860, club members of Bramall Lane were selling their membership tickets for ten times face value to spectators. Events held at Bramall Lane included athletics with slapstick comedy, including wheelbarrow races and donkey derbies—a sort of early 'It's a Knockout'. At the same time high quality athleticism was an integral part of the events and offered good prizes for elite-level performances.

By the middle of the century such races drew crowds of thousands and with it an attendant gambling. A system of handicapping was often used to throw in unpredictability and thereby make the gamble more exciting. What was known as the 'Sheffield system' (because of its semi-codified rules) produced many of the best races in Britain, these could be sprints or endurance running where men competed until they

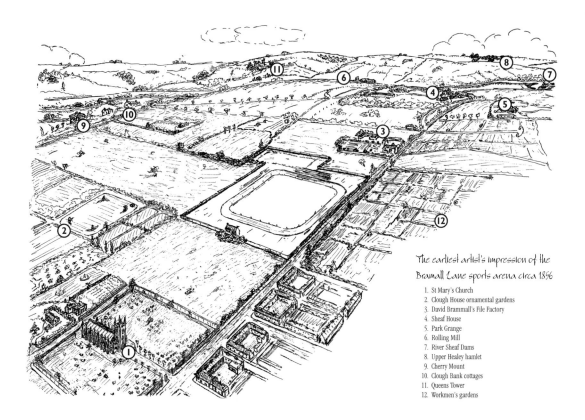

The earliest artist's impression of the
Bramall Lane sports arena circa 1856

1. St Mary's Church
2. Clough House ornamental gardens
3. David Brammall's File Factory
4. Sheaf House
5. Park Grange
6. Rolling Mill
7. River Sheaf Dams
8. Upper Healey hamlet
9. Cherry Mount
10. Clough Bank cottages
11. Queens Tower
12. Workmen's gardens

literally dropped. Such events were indicative of the people's needs for organised sport and saw the emergence of mass spectator sport as a phenomenon.

The reduction in the working day by virtue of the Factory Acts brought shorter working hours which saw a rise in leisure pursuits and pastimes, including sport. Developments in infrastructure also enabled people to move around Britain more easily. After train travel developed from the 1850s, people travelled to places in times never previously thought possible. At the same time, many in positions of power realised that sport could be commodified and that leisure as a product was a profitable arena. It was inevitable that the Bramall Lane arena would be approached by some of the emerging football clubs in the area.

Bramall Lane: The beginnings

As the city grew during the Industrial Revolution, city-centre land was becoming a premium; recreational space was losing out to the sprawl of factories and housing. In pursuit of a regular home for sport, some of the middle-class sportsmen (primarily cricketers) of the city approached Michael Ellison who, as well as a keen cricketer, was the son of the agent of the city's largest landowner the Duke of Norfolk. In 1854 the Duke dedicated 11.8 acres to sporting pursuits. For the Duke, donating land was good public relations—it also brought in rent. Mr Ellison specified that the arena be free from smoke; it was thus located towards the west of the city, thereby avoiding the industrial belching of the east end of Sheffield. The Duke negotiated a 99-year lease and charged £70 annual rent. He also stipulated that every cricket game be conducted in a respectable manner, and forbade the players to indulge in country pursuits, such as shooting pigeons or coursing rabbits. A Ground Committee ran the Bramall Lane sports enclosure that existed some 35 years before a football club was formed. Thus, from the mid-1850s, Bramall Lane provided for sport and at times charged spectators to enter.

Just outside the town centre, flat and well drained, the land at one time could host three cricket matches simultaneously. Six cricket clubs constituted Sheffield United Cricket Club Committee, the first time the

The view from the John Street side to the cricket pavilion in 1882

word 'United' was used for a sporting entity. As the name implies it was about unison, and the six agreed to pay an annual subscription of £70. As well as cricket, Bramall Lane staged athletics events and hosted crown green bowling, tennis, lacrosse and had an arena for cycling races and pedestrianism—an endurance walking contest around a specified track that could go on for more than 24 hours with betting on the outcome not unknown. Roller-skating was once contained within an elementary rink constructed behind what later became known as the Shoreham End Kop. In 1859 a pavilion was built with changing rooms, a social club and seats for spectators. As a consequence the Yorkshire Cricket Club was formed by the leading people at Bramall Lane and was the HQ of the YCC until 1899. Those given the task of managing the arena were probably chosen for their competence in administration rather than as representative of any particular sporting entity. No sporting club had any prior claim over any other to the Bramall Lane facilities—all had to hire a pitch to play.

The Straight Bats

The most popular team sport of the early and mid-19th century was cricket. The original Sheffield United Cricket Club founded in 1854 consisted of middle-class men. The other prominent cricket teams, Hallam and King Edward's, also drew their members from the middle-classes. By contrast the Heeley and Wednesday cricket clubs were of lower social origin in their selection. The United Cricket Club by-law number one stated that a proper 'costume' was required of all players. Each player received one set of kit which he was responsible for and should any damage accrue to such garments the players would be called up to face the committee and had to put their case for either the costs of restoration or replacement. By-law number three instructed that all reasonable instructions of the captain be promptly obeyed. Medical assistance and treatment required by the players was only paid for on the authorisation of the club secretary.

The Sheffield United Cricket Club was founded in the same Adelphi Hotel that saw the foundation of Yorkshire County Cricket Club and later on the Wednesday Football Club. The purpose of the United meeting at the Adelphi was to organise a Management Committee to run the Bramall Lane sports ground.

THE GREAT CRICKET MATCH AT BRAMALL LANE, SHEFFIELD.

PLAYERS OF ENGLAND v. AUSTRALIANS.
SCENE at the CLOSE of MONDAY'S PLAY.
SKETCHED FROM THE OFFICE WINDOW OF MR. BENJ. NICHOLSON, TOOL MANUFACTURER, BRAMALL LANE.

Test match cricket at Bramall Lane in 1884 England v Australia (Rotherham Independent)

The arrangement between Ellison and the Duke of Norfolk had arranged a lease and a fee, but the sports clubs of the city were not as forthcoming in their hiring of the facility as both had envisaged. The clubs in existence at this time were largely private affairs, maintained by the enthusiasm of members and friends. Those involved in games did not seem overly concerned about advertising their clubs in the local media. With the rent monies increasingly having to come out of Ellison's own pocket, new sporting commercial ventures were sought. Eventually the arena began to attract sportsmen and spectators such that by the 1860s, the Sheffield United Cricket Club was the wealthiest sporting body in the city. The growing awareness of the commercial value of sport saw the first turnstile introduced at Bramall Lane in 1872. Hosting a variety of sporting encounters, and able to donate money to both sport and charity, the committee did not initially see the potential wealth to be made from football.

Sheffield pre-rules

The origins of football will never fully be known. A variety of claims as to the first game exist globally. However, it is an undoubted fact that what became known as the Sheffield Rules were the basis for the formation of Association Football. Why and how these rules were made has proven contentious. Debate has raged in academe as to the role of social class in the popularising of the game. For some, Association Football is a product of middle-class 'missionaries' introducing the game to the urban and industrial working class in an attempt to provide a more reasoned and rational form of recreation in the late 19th century. Other research refutes this, stating that a variety of folk football existed for hundreds of years preceding the establishment of Association Football, and many of these games were not the anarchic, violent occasions many believe them to be.

A somewhat disorderly football fixture undoubtedly occurred in Sheffield's west side in 1793. An account of this event informs us that:

> There were selected six young men of Norton, dressed in green; and six young men of Sheffield, dressed in red. The play continued for three consecutive days. At the arch, which was erected at each end of the place selected, there was a hole in the goal, and those on the Sheffield side would prevent the ball from passing through the hole. Then those of the Norton side (not being so numerous as those of Sheffield) sent messengers to the Peak and other places in the county of Derby; in consequence thereof, a great number of men appeared on the ground from Derbyshire. Then those of Sheffield sent fife and drum through the streets of Sheffield to collect recruits and sufficient force against the Derbyshire men. The fashion then was for all respectable gentlemen, tradesmen, and artisans of Sheffield to wear long (pig) tails. Hence, at the conclusion of the third day, a general row or struggle took place between the contending parties, insomuch that the men of Derbyshire cut and pulled nearly all the tails from the heads of the gentlemen of Sheffield. I understand there were many slightly wounded, but none were killed; thus ended the celebrated football match, which aroused the bad passions of humanity for several years afterwards, insomuch that the inhabitants of Norton felt a dread of coming to Sheffield, even about their necessary business.

> (Bernard Bird, *The Perambulations of Barney the Irishman*, Sheffield, 1854.)

Other games followed between scratch teams throwing down challenges sometimes for money. One account exists of the development of the game in Sheffield in the mid-1850s.

> Football had never been played on any system at Abbeyside School till the Christmas half of 1856. Then, for the first time, a set of rules was issued. I remember with awe the majestic Rawlinson coming round the studies one evening before preparation, and doling out printed cards—one for each boy. On receiving my copy I timidly asked what it was for? 'Football rules', he said, 'and you have got to learn them by heart.'—It was said that we should be examined in the rules in a week hence, and that if we failed in a single clause we should be skinned alive. Poor wretches! How we quivered and quavered and tried to learn them, and how we found to our cost that there were worse things on earth than Greek verbs.

> (Rev. A.N. Malan, 'How Risden played for Abbeyside' in *Twenty-five Football Stories*, Newnes.)

No doubt seeking to address the sense of dread, some of the good men of the city tried to make the game a little more refined.

Sheffield Rules—OK?

In 1855 William Prest assembled friends, primarily former pupils of the Collegiate school in Sheffield, and founded a football club. However, it was not until October 1857 that the club's constitutions and regulations were printed. In the southwest suburb of Hallam another football club came into existence a few years later. But Sheffield FC is generally accepted as the pioneer of Association Football. Sheffield FC first met in a greenhouse about a mile from Bramall Lane. The committee consisted of the city's powerful; solicitors, merchants and steel manufacturers. One president was Frederick Ward, who was to become chairman of the Forge and Rolling Mills Company. One vice-president was related to the founders of Sheffield University. One committee-man became head of Vickers Steel Company. Others were prominent in the military and the legal professions. Both politically conservative and church-going, these capable men founded football as we know it today.

A guesthouse located on Queens Road was the home of Nathaniel Creswick. Creswick and Prest, aged 26 and 23 respectively, were part of a smart young set in Sheffield who were physically active and socially well connected. Nathaniel Creswick was a Sheffield-based solicitor, his co-founder a wine merchant. These two men had been privately educated, and on returning to Sheffield sought to find a sporting interest beyond the summer months when cricket had ended. The pair were named as treasurer and secretary of the world's first football club—Sheffield FC. Soon after this a friend donated a structure that acted as the club's headquarters, a greenhouse in the back garden of a house on East Bank Road. Playing on Saturdays, those who wished to play the new game were instructed to bring a red or blue cricket cap made from flannel. This was the first kit, the headwear providing a distinction that made a game of sorts possible. In a later meeting at the Adelphi Hotel, the rules of Association Football were laid down. The Sheffield Rules of 1858 were drawn up by committee. The eleven rules derived from a wider variety of rules, evident throughout the country stated:

The kick off from the middle must be a place kick.

Kick Out must not be from more than 25 yards out of goal.

Fair Catch is a catch from any player provided the ball has not touched the ground or has not been thrown from touch and is entitled to a free kick.

Charging is fair in case of a place kick (with the exception of a kick off as soon as the player offers to kick) but he may always draw back unless he has actually touched the ball with his foot.

Pushing with hands is allowed but no hacking or tripping up is fair under any circumstances whatever.

No player may be held or pulled over.

It is not lawful to take the ball off the ground (except in touch) for any purpose whatever.

The ball may be pushed on or hit with the hand, but holding the ball except in the case of a free kick is altogether disallowed.

A goal must be kicked but not from touch nor by a free kick from a catch.

A ball in touch is dead, consequently the side that touches it down must bring it to the edge of the touch and throw it straight out from touch.

Each player must provide himself with a red and dark blue flannel cap, one colour to be worn by each side.

Sheffield FC was formed, in their own words, 'to provide recreation for Sheffield's young gentlemen' and referred decades later to their opponents as 'gentlemen'. Their most influential founders, Prest and Creswick, were involved since 1859 in the formation of the Hallamshire Volunteers, the latter held the rank of Major. The Volunteer movement was begun in the belief that any invading French army had to be repelled, even as far inland as Sheffield! The inevitable drill and militaristic code that such a group required was supplemented by sport, no doubt in the belief that game-playing helped self-discipline which produced good soldiers. Football was to be part of this military enterprise, rules had to be established to ensure that participants, regardless of social background, could play.

All the football clubs in the area adopted the 'Sheffield Rules', producing what would have been the most significant uniformity of regulations in England at the time. The rules diverged from those of the FA in London published in 1863, notably on issues such as offside and awarding the free kick. Significantly Sheffield was the first to campaign for a neutral match official. By 1862 Sheffield was home to some 22 clubs, and to this day the oldest football rivalry in the world is that between Sheffield FC and Hallam FC. Matches between these two adversaries were sometimes played for charitable purposes, but matters were not always charitable on the pitch. On one noteworthy occasion, Nathaniel Creswick punched two rival Hallam players, who were impeding him against the rules of the game. There ensued a free-for-all, which required spectators to separate the brawlers.

Expansion and Accommodation

A crucial event in the nation-wide adoption of the 1863 FA rules was the Youdan Cup, named after the local entrepreneur and music hall proprietor Thomas Youdan. The tournament offered prize money and a silver cup, but the rules had to be agreed upon by all those taking part. The final, held in 1867, attracted 3,000 paying spectators. The rules proclaimed that the authority of the referee was paramount. The rules also allowed for the first side to score in extra time to win the game, therefore preceding the Golden Goal rule in world football by around 120 years.

A year earlier, representatives from Sheffield and London discussed playing a match on mutually agreed conditions. The ideas emanating from Sheffield influenced the FA, and a London v Sheffield match was played in 1867 under rules agreed upon by the two associations. A variation on the rules of the game was evident in Nottingham in the mid-1860s. Eventually, one Nottingham team hosted a Sheffield team, which meant that even further accommodation of sorts was being sought. Thirteen Sheffield clubs met at the Adelphi Hotel to discuss the creation of a Sheffield Association. This entity disagreed with the rules of the London-based FA on the issue of offside and penalties but in 1868, the Sheffield FA was constituted with 23 affiliated clubs.

Far from being a threat to its southern equivalent, the creation of Sheffield FA was considered a great support. Many believe the London entity may well have folded had the Sheffield body not begun. The good men of these committees were obviously prepared to continue their compromise. In December 1874, a Sheffield select played the Royal Engineers in a match that saw the Sheffield Rules adhered to in the first half and those of the London FA in the second. Three years later, showing characteristic pragmatism, Sheffield adopted much of the FA code. One consequence of this was a style of play based on an ability to pass rather than run and dribble. This also meant that defence and defensive players became a crucial part of the Sheffield style of play.

Sheffield can claim no end of football 'firsts'. In 1868 the Sheffield Football Association introduced the corner kick; four years later the Football Association in London did the same. In 1866, at the behest of the Sheffield football authorities (i.e. the secretary of Sheffield FC) the London Football Association

The Sheffield United cricket pavilion taken around 1885

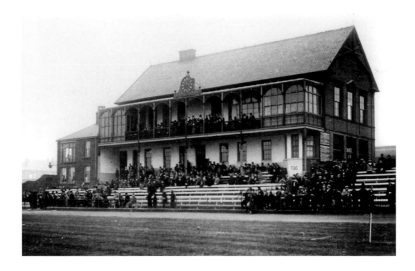

recognised the need for a tape between the goal posts thereby pioneering the idea of a crossbar. Such an addition only became obligatory following a football conference in 1882. A free kick for handball was first introduced in Sheffield, as was the wearing of shin pads and the first time a referee used a whistle to officiate occurred in a Sheffield Norfolk v Nottingham Forest fixture.

In praising pioneers we should not neglect those who inadvertently spread the gospel of football. Instrumental in formalising rules of the game was the Church of England. The latter half of the 19th century saw the expansion of Church schools; their existence consolidated by the 1870 Education Act, introduced universal, elementary education. Recreation was integral to the curriculum and an enthusiasm for this new game of football was evident in the pupils and encouraged by both their teachers and clergy.

England v Scotland at Bramall Lane in 1892

INTERNATIONAL FOOTBALL MATCH AT SHEFFIELD.

Seeing the Light

The first football match ever recorded at Bramall Lane was between Hallam FC and Sheffield FC in 1862. Significantly, the game was a fund-raiser for what was known as the Lancashire Distress Fund, set up to offer relief to the impoverished cotton workers of the Lancashire mill towns, who were losing their livelihoods as a consequence of the American Civil War which made the export of cotton impossible. The match ended in a brawl in what was described as a 'waistcoats off and fighting' scenario. Sheffield FC were to play games at Bramall Lane for the next 13 years, in what was a somewhat fractious relationship with the Sheffield United Ground Committee.

Meanwhile the game was establishing itself by games played beyond the city boundaries. The 1870s saw a Sheffield–London (1871) and Sheffield–Glasgow (1874) game. The former lapsed by the 1920s, but the latter became the second oldest fixture in international football after the England–Scotland international. The first game between these two football associations was played between Sheffield Club and the Queen's Park Club of Glasgow (founded in July 1867) and ended in a draw. The match was initially an attractive proposition and pulled decent crowds. In February 1878, Sheffield hosted a Glasgow team in front of a crowd of nearly 10,000. Later sides were selected from all Sheffield and Glasgow teams and when played in the time of professionalism would see a United and Wednesday select turn out against a team chosen from Celtic, Rangers, Queens Park, Patrick Thistle, Clyde and Third Lanark. Sheffield did not win a match until 1882 and then did not win again for nine years. Complaints about the expense of the exchange and lack of interest occurred in 1912, which may reflect the one-sided nature of the games; Sheffield were undefeated between 1906 to 1912 and did not then win a match from 1920 to 1925. This annual fixture between the two associations continued until 1950, the last game at Bramall Lane in 1949 attracted a crowd of over 22,000. Interestingly a game between Sheffield and Glasgow held at Bramall Lane in 1876 later saw Sheffield Wednesday officials seek out the star visitor, a player known as 'Reddie' Lang. He was to play for Wednesday whilst ostensibly employed in the cutlery firm of one of the Wednesday directors. Such a sinecure might be said to have made him the game's first professional.

Only a fool failed to recognise the popularity of football in the city, but the Sheffield United committee was burdened by its cumbersome structure, namely multiple sub-committees, and innovation was not easy. The fact that the first football match played at Bramall Lane ended in a major brawl did not endear football to the men on the various committees either. Meanwhile new sports were brought in to provide exhibition games and hopefully big crowds. In 1874 two American baseball games were played by teams from Boston and Philadelphia. Later in the year, a Sheffield–Glasgow lacrosse game took place. However it was technology rather than new forms of athleticism that initially packed the ground for football.

In October 1878 the Ground Committee organised an exhibition football game of local players with the Clegg brothers captaining the sides for the first ever game of football played under floodlights between the Reds and Blues. A crowd believed to be around 20,000 watched proceedings lit by four lamps hung some 30 feet high in the four corners of the pitch. Power came from two low wattage Siemens-made generators driving dynamos to the power of 8000 standard candles. Gate receipts were an impressive £300. The team captained by William Clegg won 3–0. The FA did not accept floodlights until the 1950s when, after successful experiments in the 1930s, they could draw upon the technology developed for searchlights used to seek German planes during the Second World War.

By the 1860s, the game of football was undoubtedly the most popular pastime in the city. By the late 1860s, any social boundaries that the game may well have erected in its origins in the city seem to have been broken down. Whilst the Sheffield United committee innovated by facilitating games of football it had not yet organised its own team.

An early Sheffield team.

The Formation of The Wednesday

The Sheffield Cricket Club was established in 1820. In 1867 the club (terming itself a gentleman's cricket society) changed its name to Sheffield Wednesday Cricket and Football Club, retaining the title until 1882 when the two sporting arms split. The cricket-loving pub landlord of the Adelphi Hotel in Sheffield city centre was crucial to the development of sport in Sheffield. Harry Sampson hosted a meeting in 1867 of the Wednesday Cricket Club, who were mulling over what could keep fellow enthusiasts together in winter. The answer was a football club which took the name Sheffield Wednesday. The first outing of The Wednesday football team was in late 1867. The following year saw them play home games in the Highfield area, close to Bramall Lane. Indeed, Wednesday were even to play games at Bramall Lane against other Sheffield clubs as part of knockout competitions for trophies provided by various patrons. However, the cost of hiring the ground forced them to seek an alternative pitch. The loss of income from their departure was to propel the United ground committee to form a rival team years later.

Meanwhile, Wednesday played at Olive Grove, leased to them by the Duke of Norfolk, and changed in the Earl of Arundel and Surrey pub. They remained here for 12 years leaving for Owlerton (some four miles away) in 1899 having had their application to join the Football League turned down. Wednesday joined the rival Football Alliance in 1890 and were beaten in the FA Cup Final in 1890. The following season Wednesday finished bottom of the Alliance. Crowd disorder at Olive Grove in 1892 led to the ground being closed for two months on the orders of the FA but in May of the same year Wednesday were admitted into the Football League.

Wednesday became openly professional in 1887—a process not without controversy. The success of the Sheffield factory side Lockwood Brothers, rumoured to be paying their players, instigated a group of Wednesday players to suggest an openly professional breakaway team to be known as Sheffield Rovers. The Wednesday Committee called a special meeting in response to this coming crisis and in April 1887 the decision to turn professional was made. Sheffield Rovers only ever played one game, but they were to change the face of football in Sheffield forever.

Some of the other clubs in the city at that time have interesting stories behind them. The cricket enclosure in Sandygate Road was the birthplace of Hallam FC, who can claim to own the world's oldest amateur football ground in constant use by one club. Referred to historically as Hallam and Stumperlowe FC, the club began as a cricket club and added a football section in 1860. Hallam first played Sheffield FC in 1862 in the first football match at Bramall Lane then, possibly because of the ensuing brawl, did not play their near neighbours again until 1905. Elsewhere Heeley FC was one of the biggest clubs in the city in the 1880s. Their ground, located off of Myrtle Road (around one mile from Bramall Lane), was enclosed and contained sheds for players to change in. They also attracted reasonable support; one game in the 1880s against the Wednesday drew a crowd of 9,000. Aware that the formation of a new football club at Bramall Lane would be detrimental to their interests, two of the Heeley FC officials implored Messrs Clegg and Wostinholm of the Sheffield United committee to take the name of Heeley FC and their club colours. The United directors did not wish to take over an existing club and refused the offer. Consequently Heeley FC objected to Sheffield United going both to the Midland League North and later Division Two of the Football League.

There were other footballing attractions albeit a few miles away. Based in the densely populated industrial heartland in the east of the city was Attercliffe FC which once had the distinction of playing in the FA Cup preliminaries in the late 19th century. Founded by workers in the steel industry and with John Nicholson as their secretary, the club played their games on the New Hall side of the river Don. The name Attercliffe reflects a pre-industrial existence wherein one corner of the river, known as Salmon Pastures, produced references to 'Otter's Cliff' which produced the later nomenclature Attercliffe.

One-Off Visitors

An FA Cup tie between the amateurs of Heeley FC and Lockwood Brothers FC took place at Bramall Lane in 1881. A poster advertising the match survives and is exhibited in the Hall of Fame. Whilst pre-dating the establishment of Sheffield United by eight years, the game illustrates that the Bramall Lane cricket clubs were making an income from renting out the pitch to football clubs. It also suggests that a football pitch was marked out years before Sheffield United FC began. Heeley FC actually had their own ground

The 1878 Wednesday team
Pictured after winning the Sheffield Challenge Cup, beating Attercliffe 2–0

33

around a mile from Bramall Lane. The fact that they moved the game against the Lockwood Brothers club suggests they anticipated a large crowd that only the Bramall Lane stadium could comfortably contain. The poster informs readers that the match would kick off at 3.00pm 'prompt'. The game was to be held on a Monday afternoon and advertised as the 'National Association Cup' probably as a consequence of the printer's artistic license. In origin the competition's full title was the Football Association Challenge Cup. This later became popularly known as the English Cup, then in the late 1920s became known as the Football Association (FA) Cup. Twelve names are listed for each team with readers informed that 'players will be selected from the following'. One player from each side would learn of his non-involvement probably shortly before kick off.

Some football matches at the time were simply bizarre. In 1880 spectators at Bramall Lane witnessed a game between Sheffield FC and the 'Sheffield Zulus', a name given to local players who blacked up their faces in an attempt to conceal their identities (and paid status) from any onlooking officials of the local FA. Such a game would see men playing for the Zulus under assumed names and receiving payment for their exhibition match. The Boer War of 1880–81 produced many British casualties, in what was a singu- larly brutal period of Imperial history. Britain lost over 20,000 soldiers and their widows and orphans needed caring for. Football matches were played and proceeds given to the war charities. Some of these games seem to have been given the nomenclature of the 'Zulu' as some form of recognition of the opponents in war in South Africa. However, success (and big crowds) saw these men start to line their own pockets with the proceeds. The FA considered this professionalism and called on the Zulus to stop playing. Indeed, the Sheffield FA suspended several players for their defiance of the request, which was lifted when those accused apologised.

A team originating in South Africa appeared on Bramall Lane soil in October 1899. This was a touring side selected from the Orange Free State who left their homeland in the summer of 1899 and arrived in Britain shortly after the outbreak of the second Boer War. The tour was probably more than coincidence. The Orange Free State was bordered to the north by the Transvaal and its Boer population, in the south was the British stronghold of the Cape. The Orange Free State was in the middle and was probably attempting to be neutral (or seeking friends) in the impending hostilities. The names of the touring side suggest that the team contained players of Afrikaner, British and indigenous black African origin.

The sending of a football team to Britain was probably an attempt by the politicians of the Orange Free State to express through football their support for the British. The nomenclature 'Kaffirs' was given to the tourists, albeit history does not tell us whether this term was adopted or imposed. The tour was not a success in terms of football. The visitors arrived late, and thereby had to cancel their first fixture against Aston Villa. Their first game at Newcastle attracted 6,000 fans but saw them heavily defeated and press reports ridicule 'the dusky sons of Africa' for their incompetence. The next day they played Sunderland who, no doubt aware of their visitors' abilities, sent out seven reserves. They were later to play Middlesbrough, Hibernians, Burton, and managed a 6–6 draw at Derby, attracting further match reports dismissing them as both a 'burlesque' and a 'pantomime'.

Two weeks after the Boer War was declared, the Kaffirs played against United at Bramall Lane. There was no pre-match publicity and no match programme, but 4,000 paid to watch a game which United won 7–2. The seriousness afforded the game was evident when United played goalkeeper William Foulke at centre forward (he scored twice) and at one time played without a goalkeeper. The crowd joined in the occasion and, press reports tell us, made repeated comments of 'Let 'em have a goal!' A subsequent report in the *Sheffield Star* described the visitors as a 'fine lot of fellows' who accepted the referee's decisions 'without demur'.

Financial considerations were hardly the reasons for the Kaffirs touring. The rearranged fixture with Aston Villa saw them refuse the gate monies because of their initial lateness. All funds raised from the turnstiles went to the Reservist Fund for the Boer War. The Kaffirs were never to tour again. Their presence is almost certainly one of the earliest forms of international diplomacy via football.

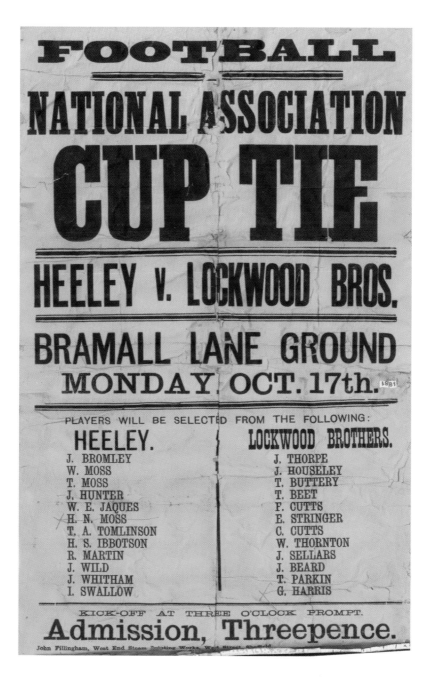

The first football poster for a match at Bramall Lane in October 1881

The Monday 3pm kick-off between Heeley and the Lockwood Brothers' works team was for the National Association Cup

The Formation of United

In 1875 the land which constituted Bramall Lane was extended and could now contain five cricket pitches. In 1889 The Wednesday had moved to Olive Grove having failed in their bid to rent the Bramall Lane stadium. The United Cricket Club Committee realised they had more to gain financially from owning their own team than agreeing a rented tenure with one already established. The committee whilst not impressed by having their turf churned up by football players recognised that this new game was capable of attracting huge crowds of paying spectators. The committee thus established their own football team named Sheffield United. Their motives were purely and simply commercial; the directors knew that if the product offered was good enough the local (primarily) working-class population would pay the admission fee to watch.

Two England International games hosted at Bramall Lane in the 1880s saw big crowds and the monies the committee earned invested in a new grandstand. Those trying to promote football were attempting to put on big games in the regions to increase awareness of the sport. The impetus for the formation of a football club came in 1889 when Bramall Lane hosted the semi-final of the FA Cup, the venue chosen probably because the ground had an enclosure. This saw an unprecedented (primarily locally drawn) crowd of 22,688 paying to watch Preston North End play West Bromwich Albion. More significantly, the game produced a £700 income for the cricket committee (the equivalent of around £1 million in today's money) and convinced them of both the need for and financial sense of forming a football team.

The view from the cricket pavilion to the John Street side
with St Mary's Church in the background

The Football League was begun in 1888 and consisted of twelve clubs. Fearing the antagonism of the Football Association, Sheffield Wednesday turned down the chance to become one of the first dozen. Instead they joined the Football Alliance, which came into being in 1889 and was promoted as a rival to the League. When the Football League created divisions one and two, United were accepted into the latter, whereas Wednesday were accepted into the former. The reasons for this probably lie in the Wednesday Club black-balling their city rivals in revenge for the refusal to allow them to play at Bramall Lane. Both Sheffield clubs made their pitch to join the top league in presentations by their committee members. Whilst Wednesday promised to turn 'dismal Olive Grove into a veritable paradise', United's David Hague spoke of 'the beauties of Bramall Lane'. In this instance age obviously preceded beauty and United found themselves a league below Wednesday. The newly formed United played for only one season in the second division. They won promotion by beating Accrington in a Test match at Trent Bridge, Nottingham, in an early version of the play-offs (which caused United no end of travails in the 1990s) and United remained in the old Division One until relegated in 1934.

ASSOCIATION FOOTBALL: THE FINAL CUP TIE AT THE CRYSTAL PALACE ON APRIL 15.

A Glorious First Decade

The 1860s to the 1920s was a time of great social change in Great Britain and the formation of Sheffield United needs to be put into the socio-political context of the late 19th century. Nationally, the decade from 1890 saw a rise in trade unionism and monumental industrial disputes. In the year United was formed, the gas workers had gone on strike for an 8-hour day and won their case. The impact of this led to a mass unionisation of northern-based workers. Union membership was a sign of rising confidence in the working class. In nearby Rotherham an industrial dispute in the coalfields forced Rotherham Town to organise charity matches for the strikers. Football attracted all social classes but the wealthy held power. Shareholders were invariably middle-class and, in Sheffield United's case, drawn primarily from manufacturing. By 1899 Sheffield United FC became a limited company, essentially a business with shareholders and subject to the fluctuations of market forces.

Football grew at a time of heightened debate around the rights of man. Political activism influenced by such ideas was evident in the city of Sheffield. The first record of a trade union in England comes from Sheffield in 1720. Later came trade such as the 1859 Association for Organised Traders, and the United Kingdom Alliance of Organised Traders, both of which were based in the city. Chartists were elected to the Town Council in the 1840s. The concept of citizenship replaced previous criteria that representation was dependent on property ownership and educational background. Incomes rose and in 1905 the Labour Party was born at the same time as trade unions gathered millions of members. An awareness of responsibility to all people saw the Liberal Government introduce the Old Age Pensions Act of 1908 to tackle poverty amongst the elderly. To qualify for the two to five shillings per week, applicants had to be over 70 and have earned less than £31 a year. This applied to over half a million people. In later years, two Liberal politicians, David Lloyd George and Winston Churchill, were instrumental in passing legislation in their capacity of Chancellor of the Exchequer and President of the Board of Trade, respectively, which sought to improve the conditions of the working class, but also provoked mass strikes. Artistic and intellectual endeavours blossomed nationally and locally producing innovations in music, drama, architecture and cinema.

The condition of the soul of man concerned many of this era. Preaching respect, politically conservative and prone to authoritarianism, the Methodism that was promoted and practised widely in Sheffield in this era provided for hard-working and uncompromising factory owners. Underpinning the football board-room was the same Methodist Chapel Sunday School philosophy which, before the 1870 Education Act made provision for universal education, had provided a basic education for all believers. Working on the principles of good works and charity, but with the belief that not everything could be left to God, the creed produced many a capable trade union activist and football pioneer. The distinguishing feature was an ingrained sense of responsibility for one's conduct.

Norfolk Row: The First Team (1889)
Six days after the Preston v West Bromwich FA Cup semi-final of 1889 the Sheffield United Ground Committee met at 10 Norfolk Row in the city centre offices owned by chartered accountant and estate agent Joseph Wostinholm, then secretary of Yorkshire Cricket Club. Hours later Sheffield United FC was born following deliberations by a variety of the local great and good. The club had no players, so adverts appeared in the Sheffield and Scottish newspapers. In the meantime, local tempers were raised.

Sheffield United FC in the 1891–92 season
Goalkeeper Charlie Howelett stands in the middle row hands in pockets, wearing his trademark spectacles

The United match programme in the 1934–35 season ran a series of articles that attempted a social history of the early days of the club. One such article, reflecting on United's origins, described how United began and tells of the anger of Wednesday officials and supporters:

> *Feelings arose well nigh to human hate and passion, which football is capable of rousing. It is scarcely an exaggeration to say that business bargains and relationships were influenced, private friendships shattered and even families divided owing to the claims of jealous football clubs…there was between the partisans of United and Wednesday, jealousy, rancour and uncharitableness.*

Perhaps to dilute this anger United sought players from outside of the city. The Scottish national side had not lost to England since 1879. Many football club directors based south of the border considered the Scots better at the game than anything available locally. The newly formed United club thus advertised in Glasgow newspapers for players. They knew that they would have to pay for the services of such players as the Rangers Football Athletic Club of Glasgow and their great rivals Celtic openly paid their performers. The Scottish game was free of the controversies over rules of payment that plagued the game in England, mainly due to differences in social class and a relative absence of public school attitudes. For this reason Scotland has claims to be the oldest professional footballing culture on earth—whilst conceding that the English formalised the rules. When professionalism was recognised in England in 1885, the Scots, realising the best players were all going to head south, abandoned the England–Scotland fixture in protest. Recruitment of Scottish players continued by English clubs for decades. Indeed, the United programme of October 24th 1925 tells of 40 club reps in Scotland that weekend.

The advertisement United placed north of the border produced a good response. The first United team included five Scots, alongside players drawn from within the city boundaries and others from Norwich, Staveley and Gainsborough. Some 50 per cent of the first United team were Scottish, with two each drawn from Dundee and Glasgow and one from Edinburgh. These players were attracted to the new club by the prospect of making money from jobs promised to them in the factories and work-places owned by the United directors in an early form of 'shamateurism'. United had looked on their doorstep as well as afar and signed Jack Hudson and Billy Mosforth from the Wednesday club. The diminutive left winger, Mosforth, was the first Sheffield-born footballer capped for England. Playing for a variety of local teams, usually the one who paid him best, Mosforth was to win nine England caps and was pioneering in as much as he was at one time the only non-University or public school-educated player in the national team. Later in the first season three players from Ecclesfield and two more from Scotland apparently with the names 'Jones' and 'Smith' arrived at Bramall Lane. United then attempted in the summer of 1890 to sign three players from Wednesday in what was probably a combination of eagerness and naivety. The United club discovered a week later that the signatures were on the wrong form. The documents were thus void and the transfers were off.

Before the Football League was formed, individuals would guest for a club. Some were later to sign professional when the League was established. The recruitment of players was thus a rather hit and miss affair. Prospective players often made a written application to the club secretary or were recruited through adverts posted by the club in the Sheffield and Glasgow newspapers. This method presumed that players had a degree of literacy. This was not always the case. Some ten years after the formation of

Sheffield United FC 1890–91
At this stage in the club's history the badge on the team's shirts was that of the Sheffield and Hallamshire FA

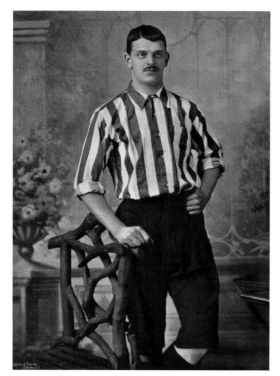

Mick Whitham in 1894, United's first ever international

the club, there remained a degree of bewilderment around United's recruiting policy. The match pro-gramme of September 9th, 1899 quotes from the *Athlete Muse*, which states, 'With Sheffield United you find men dropped in the team as if they had come from the clouds'. A few months later on October 21st one could read, 'There is not a Sheffield-born man in the United team, although it numbers a very large proportion of Englishmen, four being Teesiders'.

First Matches

The new club called Sheffield United began its football career with a degree of secrecy. The first ever game played in August 1889 was against Sheffield FC at the Sandygate Road pitch and was essentially a trial match played behind closed doors. The next game was played away at Nottingham Rangers. United lost 4–1 with a goal scored by the Dundee-born Robertson who in March 1890 was to become the first United player ever sent off in a game. He was to play 80 more games for United but no record exists of his career or even his first name. Further friendly matches followed, away to Lincoln and then Heeley, until on September 28th, 1889, the first Sheffield United team ran out in front of a home crowd of 3,000 paying supporters (and probably an equal number who did not pay) and lost 4–0 to Birmingham St Georges in a friendly. Another home friendly, played two days later saw United beat Grimsby 3–1 in front of 1,500.

Three days later, the United side beat a team drawn from the Kings Own Light Infantry 7–1 in front of a mere 300. Entering the FA Cup United had then to play qualifying games against Scarborough, Heeley, Sheffield FC and Rotherham before qualifying for the first round proper. This produced a 2–1 home victory over Burnley. Playing for United was a gentleman called 'Wilson' the true identity of whom has never been released. He was one of two United players playing under pseudonyms; neither were registered with United and therefore were in breach of FA regulations. The FA, however, were unaware of proceedings. The next round of the Cup saw another form of questionable practice when United were drawn at home against Bolton. The United committee ceded home advantage for a payment of £40 and watched as their team suffered its heaviest ever defeat of 13–0.

The white shirt worn by the original United team of 1889 reflected the state of shirt manufacturing at the time. White was an easily obtainable colour for a garment and was therefore cheap. There were few if any garment manufacturers of the time who dedicated their sales to sporting wear. Consequently the first United shirts were made and dyed by the Cole Brothers department store located on what was known colloquially as 'Coles Corner' which stood at the corner of the present day Fargate precinct opposite Sheffield Cathedral. In 1891 United introduced a thin red stripe into the white shirt. Quite why remains a mystery. One theory is that it was a subtle way of distinguishing their players from the opposition who might have also bought cheap all-white shirts. Another possibility is that, with Wednesday taking a blue strip, which had previously been the preserve of the Hallam FC, United adopted red, possibly inspired by Sheffield FC, whose kit consisted of red and black quarters. A more pronounced stripe was introduced onto the shirt in 1894. Curiously, ten years after its formation, the League Management Committee had still not issued rules that instructed clubs to declare a distinctive kit.

A Midland Beginning

Entering the Midland League in 1890–91, United played their first game away at Burton Wanderers and first home game against Rotherham Town in front of 5,500. After finishing fifth in the 12-team Midland League in 1891, United, having signed three players from Preston North End, applied to join Wednesday in the Football Alliance. The Midland League was not to the standard of the Alliance which was a rival to the Football League. United's application was refused amid allegations that the Wednesday representative had not supported their case, even lobbying against their application on the grounds that a 'one town, one club' system should exist. United instead joined the Northern League, which meant the nearest away fixture was Darlington, and finished third, thanks in no small part to the three Preston players. League games were however, only part of United's fixtures—they played over 70 matches that season.

In late 1891 Wednesday applied to join the Football League and publicised their plans to re-lay the pitch and improve their ground's facilities. United with 42 registered players responded by announcing their intention to apply to the League in mid-1892. In 1892–93 a second division of the Football League was formed comprising 12 teams. One of the newcomers was to be Sheffield United. Thus United joined the Football League in May 1892 on the same day as Wednesday. However, whilst the latter entered as part of the newly expanded 16-team Division One, United had to be content with Division Two. The five votes that United had polled on their application to join the top division were doubled by Wednesday. Smelling a rat, United asked to see the ballot papers, only to be told they had been destroyed. Thus the United directors started their League campaign with a legitimate grievance and no doubt a fierce determination to catch up with the Wednesday. Their first opponents were Lincoln, a crowd of 4,000 waited for the delayed kick-off on account of the visitors arriving late. The teams also left the pitch due to torrential rain. United won 4–2. Within a year they were to defeat Accrington in an end of season play-off and attained promotion and thereby joined Wednesday in the top division. Their first fixture in the first division occurred in 1893 and resulted in a 3–2 victory at Everton.

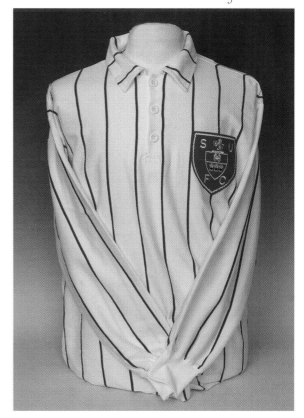

1891–1892 season shirt as worn by Ernest Needham

The new professionalism evidenced by United did not prevent them from participating in somewhat futile—but potentially lucrative—mid-season tours. Some form of income generation undoubtedly lay behind a tour of Scotland arranged over the New Year period 1894–95. This United team had nine inter-nationals and would be welcome at many grounds where football was emerging. The first game of the tour, however, took United to Bolton where they played Wanderers before setting off for Glasgow. Two days later they played Clyde and drew 2–2 in front of 1,000. The following day saw opponents from Leith Athletic of Edinburgh and a 2–1 victory in front of 900. On January 2nd United beat Dundee 2–0 in front of 4,500. The next day the tour ended with a 4–2 victory in Kirkaldy

An early image of the Bramall Lane ground c. 1885
The area around the perimeter of the pitch was a cycling track

over Raith Rovers. The tiring itinerary is even more remarkable, given that this was the middle of a League season. Indeed United played Wednesday at Bramall Lane on January 12th in front of 13,000. For reasons that remain unknown the club never went on such a mid-season tour again.

The Men who made The Blades

The men who founded United were the great and good of the city. Sheffield-born Joseph Beckett Wostinholm, already secretary of Yorkshire Cricket Club, became the first secretary of Sheffield United FC, having been secretary of the Sheffield United Ground Committee since 1862. A stockbroker, chartered accountant and renowned philanthropist, his philosophy was rooted in the Unitarian church. His offices were in Norfolk Row in the city centre of Sheffield and hosted the meeting that formally declared a football club by the name of Sheffield United. His task was to draw back the losses incurred by the cricket club, and then provide the funds to build a new pavilion. His legacy was the building of boundary walls and the Shoreham Street enclosure. He retired as secretary in 1902, died in 1909 and is buried in City Road Cemetery.

Alongside Wostinholm was Henry 'Harry' Stones, born in 1860 and who, having begun paid employment at the age of 13, worked his way up to become a partner in the Wostinholm and Stevenson chartered accountancy business. Turning out in his prime for both Sheffield Wednesday and Sheffield Albion, Stones was renowned for his ability to spot a good player and was the man who signed William Foulke for United. Archives tell us that Stones was the Assistant Secretary to Wostinholm at Bramall Lane in 1893, but his significance in football pre-dates this. Letters sent from Sheffield FC seeking to play at Bramall Lane in early 1889 are addressed to Harry Stones. This made sense; Wostinholm had little interest in football and made this fact quite evident in meetings. When the United club was formed the work doubled, Stones was thus made football club secretary, a position he held until retiring in 1898 when he was eventually replaced by John Nicholson. Stones contented himself as a director from 1899 of the Sheffield United Cricket Club. He died in 1922.

There was also Charles Stokes, a dental surgeon, who was a former player of both Christ Church FC of Heeley and Wednesday and a renowned runner in both the one mile and half mile events. Chairman of the Dental Board of the Royal Hospital and a prominent Freemason, Stokes became a member of Bramall Lane via the Bowling Green Club in 1869. Stokes joined the Sheffield United Ground Committee in 1875, and was later chairman of Sheffield United Football Club. A one-time Treasurer of Sheffield Football Association, Stokes was instrumental in helping to found Sheffield Wednesday. Despite this Stokes was the biggest enthusiast for the formation of a Sheffield United football club and went out of his way to see the entity progress. In February 1890 Stokes stayed in Southport's Victoria Hotel and in the billiard room overheard a rumour that the double-winning Preston North End team of the time were releasing players. Making his way to Preston next morning, Stokes signed three players who were to form the nucleus of the United side for the next five years.

The 1894–95 Sheffield United playing squad and backroom staff

Alongside Stokes sat William Beardshaw (known as 'Baltic' by virtue of his steel-producing factory of that name). Beardshaw had once played in a Sheffield FC v Glasgow game and for Sheffield United in a friendly match, and assisted in the formation of the amateur Corinthians FC. Founded in 1882, the Corinthians were a midweek team drawn from the ranks of the London-based aristocracy, who initially considered the nomenclature of 'The Wednesday'. Choosing later to play on a Saturday, and take the name Corinthians, they were to beat Blackburn Rovers in the 1884 Cup Final with a team that contained two Sheffield-born players. The Corinthians were versatile and in 1892 put a team together to play rugby against The Barbarians. History was made when the Corinthians played Sheffield United in the first Dewar Shield (the forerunner to the Charity Shield). Relations between the two clubs were very strong and a Corinthians side played at Bramall Lane in the early twentieth century in the benefit games of both Walter Bennett and Ernest Needham.

The Straight Road

The history of Sheffield football in its first 50 years is entwined with the lives of brothers John and William Clegg. Sons of William Clegg senior, three times Mayor of Sheffield, the pair became solicitors and were strict Methodists who gave their time freely to good causes. William was a Liberal councillor for 40 years and council leader for 24 years. His was a career and profile matched only by his brother, John (known by his second name Charles). Both Cleggs were capable athletes and played for local football teams and both were connected to the Wednesday team of the 1870s. Both played for Sheffield in the first game against London in 1871 and Charles played for England against Scotland the following year. They captained the two sides that played the first floodlit match at Bramall Lane in 1878 and became referees when they finished playing—Charles refereed the 1882 FA Cup Final and the England–Scotland fixture that same year. The first FA Cup semi-final at Bramall Lane in 1889 was refereed by him.

Charles Clegg held the status of the Official Receiver in Bankruptcy in Sheffield and when asked about his hobbies replied 'the furtherance of temperance and football'. Competing against the fastest professionals of the era in the 100-yard dash, he could run this distance in 10 seconds and was also capable of running the quarter mile in fifty and a half seconds. Charles was knighted by George V in 1927 in appreciation of his services as Chairman of the FA, thereby being the first person ever knighted for services to football.

A one-time President of the Sheffield FA, Charles became first Vice-President of the English FA, then Chairman in 1902. He was to keep this office and combine it with that of FA President from 1923 following the death of Lord Kinnaird. One commentator describing him in 1906 stated the following:

> *...a warm heart, a generous mind, a winning way and an unaffected courtesy... a solid, weighty, logical man... his principles are nailed to the mast... a long and wide experience in the frailties of human nature.*

Being the first boy in Sheffield to sign the Pledge (pledging never to drink intoxicating liquor in a procedure prompted by the National Temperance Movement assisted by the Methodist church) Charles Clegg is well remembered for his mantra 'No one got lost on a straight road'. His refusal to permit 'secret' payments to players or offer inducements to sign from opposing teams, whilst admirable in spirit, made him and United (and indeed Wednesday) somewhat different to many clubs of the era. In October 1899 the ethos of the club which had won a championship and an FA Cup in 1898 and 1899 respectively was expressed in the match programme: 'In our prosperity, let us not forget: in prosperity there's nothing so becomes the club as modest mildness and humility'.

Whilst Charles Clegg was a big fish locally he was to others a northerner from a place few would ever deign to visit. When chosen to represent England at a game in Scotland in 1872, Clegg was snubbed by his southern middle-class colleagues and never forgot such an attitude. Reluctant to permit professionalism in the game, he nevertheless acknowledged defeat on the issue and set about keeping the game on the straight and narrow. Locally he was to facilitate the amalgamation in 1887 of Sheffield FA and the Sheffield

League Champions 1898
The United directors and players with the Championship Trophy and the Dewar Shield (later renamed the Charity Shield)
United shared the Shield with Corinthians FC after the fixture ended in a draw

The Sheffield United board of directors, 1898

New Association, later known as the Hallamshire FA, the latter formed in 1877 when the former refused to accept any more teams into its jurisdiction.

In 1907 Clegg resigned his FA position when the mainly southern County Football Associations refused to accept membership from professional clubs. When the FA Council rescinded the agreed motion, Clegg was urged to reconsider and withdrew his resignation.

The African Missionary: Arthur Wharton

A degree of exoticism appeared in United's ranks a few years after their beginnings. Arriving from West Africa was a man who made footballing history in England. Coming from a conservative middle-class African Methodist background, Arthur Wharton became an athletic all-rounder, who held a British sprint record for 40 years. Initially turning out for Darlington by virtue of his attending a Methodist college nearby, he then played as an amateur for Preston in 1888 a few years after becoming the first man to run 100 yards in 10 seconds at a championship event at Stamford Bridge. A one-time outfield player, his athleticism saw him considered ideal for the position of goalkeeper. Wharton actually played one game for Sheffield Wednesday as a guest in a testimonial for the England international Billy Mosforth. He played at Bramall Lane for the Owls but was booed off for what was considered ineffective goalkeeping.

Wharton moved to Sheffield in 1888 to try to make a career as a professional runner. The attraction of Sheffield was due in no small part to Tom Bott—the fishmonger and general entrepreneur who invested in football, cricket and running and who was to become a director of Sheffield United in the 1890s. The idea was that Wharton would make money for himself and his sponsor from running whilst being trained by Billy Isaac, a black Sheffield-based runner. With races offering a first prize of £80, a lucrative existence was possible, however it was a precarious existence and Wharton decided to make a living as a waged sportsman, signing as a professional footballer with Rotherham Town. Whilst in Rotherham, Wharton became licensee of the Plough Inn. A year later he took a similar position in the Albert Tavern. Playing cricket for Greasborough, Wharton possibly enjoyed his time in Sheffield's neighbouring town a little too much, his death certificate recorded the cause of his demise as syphilis alongside a form of cancer.

West African-born Arthur Wharton England's first black footballer and United's goalkeeper for five games in 1895

It was whilst playing for Rotherham Town that Wharton came to the attention of United. A match between United and Rotherham in April 1890 ended in a brawl between rival fans and led to an FA inquiry into violence on the pitch. Years later, in 1894, Wharton signed for United. At Bramall Lane he rejoined four of his former Rotherham team-mates and had a friend and supporter in Tom Bott, by then the *de facto* team manager. He had the further incentive of managing a public house called the Sportsman and joining a club which had average home attendances of 6000 to 7000 which gave him the chance at last to make decent money in the game as he neared his 30th birthday.

In his time with the Blades, Wharton played just five first-team games; only one of which was a League fixture. This was a 2–0 defeat to Sunderland in February 1895. The other games were friendlies including one against Linfield of Belfast. Wharton returned to lower league football at Rotherham and after playing for Stalybridge, Ashton and

Stockport County, finished his football career in 1902. In his post football and sporting life, Wharton found himself hauling trucks down a coal mine. He died in Doncaster in December 1930 and was buried in a pauper's grave. A headstone was erected in his honour in May 1997, paid for from the funds of the Sheffield-based organisation 'Football Unites, Racism Divides' (FURD) and from a donation made by the Professional Footballers' Association.

New Formations

In May 1899 John Nicholson succeeded Harry Stones as the secretary of Sheffield United. Nicholson and the respective captains and the club's first ever 'trainer' George Waller, formed a triumvirate who chose the teams and the tactics and effectively ran the club. Formerly a lawyer's clerk, and secretary of the Sheffield and Hallamshire FA, Nicholson became United's first paid official. A former player with Attercliffe he was to prove to be the English game's longest serving secretary. His knowledge of league regulations was unsurpassable, and he produced the United match programme for 30 years. His most crucial relationship was with the team captain. In this context Nicholson was blessed by the leadership abilities of men such as Ernest Needham, Billy Gillespie and Albert Sturgess. Another crucial figure was Tom Bott who between 1898 and 1930 proved to be a hands-on director who, when not tending to footballing matters, was running his chain of fishmongers.

George Waller, the trainer (and meat carver at away game dinners) of the 1898 championship-winning side, was a former player of some repute. It would be fair to describe him as an all-round sportsman. Waller had played in a North v South international trial and appeared for Sheffield Wednesday in their 1890 FA Cup Final defeat by Blackburn Rovers. His leaving Wednesday for United should have occurred earlier, but incorrect paperwork frustrated the deal. A year later, in 1891, he was at Bramall Lane playing football in winter and cricket in summer—in the latter he represented Yorkshire. Moving to a position of trainer in 1893, Waller was a fixture at Bramall Lane until retiring in 1930. Brilliant with his hands, Waller was responsible for rectifying players' strains and aches; his skills were sought by cricketers and even famous actors of the era. He was to accompany the English national team on tours but his legacy for Sheffield United lies in the fact that he took four United sides to FA Cup Finals. Waller would have the United players meet early at Bramall Lane with their golf clubs, only to walk the 12 or so miles to Sickleholm Golf Course in Derbyshire, play a round of golf and then walk back again. Waller's leather cricket bag exhibited in the Hall of Fame, whilst in poor condition, is over 100 years old. Nothing else exists to commemorate Waller's life.

Professionalism

As early as the late 1870s, football in the South Yorkshire region was losing its purely recreational ethos. The game was being taken very seriously by many players and clubs and the revenue the game could generate was becoming very evident to officials and players. It was only a matter of time before players were to receive payments for their efforts. The 1880s was a decade of conflict as the more middle-class elements in football sought to prevent professionalism, initially restricting payments to legitimate expenses.

At national level, the era of the gentlemen amateurs, which saw football clubs dominated by middle-class young men playing for the love of football, did not last long after the FA was begun in 1888. The working-class teams from Lancashire were soon more than a match for the southern gentlemen amateur teams. Their success provoked (well-founded) accusations that they were paid to play.

An impending battle was inevitable between the northern clubs, collectively known as the British Football Association, and the Football Association. The former contained teams that were in many instances paying their players, albeit not too publicly. Following a Committee of Enquiry in 1885, the FA accepted waged footballers into the FA Cup competition but imposed restrictive conditions; that contract players would have to be born within six miles of the ground or club headquarters, or have lived in that area for the previous two years; would have to be registered with the FA, and would only be able to play for one club per season.

In this era of class consciousness and struggle the first suggestions of a players' union surfaced in 1893. Player selection was made by the directors who also bought and released players. The players were essentially waged labourers and, as such, sought to improve pay and conditions. By contrast, their employers wanted to keep costs down. Conflict was inevitable but, one may argue, was decided in favour of the owners with the introduction of a maximum wage in 1901. Many players felt, however, that they were worth more than the £4 maximum and it was this that eventually led to the establishment of the Players' Union.

The good men of the Sheffield FA were disapproving of professionalism, believing it would lead to gambling rackets. Despite this, Wednesday started paying players in 1887, at a rate of nine shillings for home games and two shillings more for away games. In the following decade, they paid bonuses in FA Cup ties. The opposition to professionalism manifest by Mr Beardshaw of Sheffield FC was forgotten when he assisted a few years later in the formation of a professional football club called Sheffield United.

The Sheffield United FC Championship winning side of 1898

The Sheffield United 1899 FA Cup winning team on their triumphant city centre return
Holding the trophy is Ernest Needham, captain of both United and England

A great deal of hypocrisy surrounded the issue of professionalism. Payments to good players were known to take place at nearly all clubs. Those towns that hosted industry had the perfect alibi in creating *de facto* professional players by pretending they worked in manufacturing and played for free. In 1885 there were 58 Scots classified as professionals in England many of whom had been promised a job, essentially a sinecure, which paid them whilst they played football. By the end of the decade half a dozen were in Sheffield.

The fears of professionalism might have been realised judging by accounts in the United match programme. On December 30th, 1899, the programme tells of a United director sitting at a game at Manchester City with a home director unaware of his neighbour's status. The City director informed the Sheffield man during the match that a linesman was in his pocket, the match official had been to his home earlier in the day where he was plied with champagne. Refereeing standards could also infuriate the mild-mannered men who ran Sheffield United. A match at Everton provoked the wrath of the United secretary, who was to write on October 12th, 1901:

> *Never had we had an official who has carried out his duties in a more one-sided manner…It is time his services were dispensed with and he be relegated to the position of spectator where he can show his partisanship*

The official was described as 'violently waiving [sic] his flag in jubilation', when Everton scored their second goal.

In their rush to pay wages to compete, many clubs costed above their income. The United match programme of January 20th, 1900 spoke of declining attendances and professional clubs in a perilous financial position; the majority of clubs in the League, the writer announced, were in debt and sustained only by 'enthusiastic optimism and generous support of a private nature'. The piece further argued that the game was being run on too expensive a scale and that the stress of competition had produced wage rises for players. This 'disease' was difficult to trace and diagnose, and the author suggested it might provoke the Football League and Football Association to step in and impose a salary limit on players.

The game attracted investments, primarily from businessmen. Local prestige was no doubt a huge factor in their willingness to invest their money and sit on the board. A limit of 5% on dividends to shareholders was what the football authorities had laid down. The board of directors took no remuneration from the game but realised monies were available via contracts that could be awarded to their building firms and other businesses be it in refurbishment of the stadium or supplying goods. The industrialists, merchants, solicitors, and brewers were crucial to the development of the game, albeit the latter were not influential in the Sheffield clubs of the 19th century, due no doubt to the influence of Methodism. That said the ethos was not one that promoted only receiving. Doing good works for those less fortunate was a duty.

Football and Social Good

Exhibited in the Hall of Fame is a medal belonging to Harry Stones which came from a tournament called the Hull Hospital Cup. This pre-season competition involved teams from the Yorkshire region, and saw a knockout competition that attracted large numbers of paying crowds, the proceeds of which went towards local hospitals. In this pre-welfare state era, hospitals existed on philanthropy and charity and football and footballers played their part in contributions to the greater good. In this tournament players were not paid for their services, but the winners received a gold medal. United twice won the tournament, which ended in the late 1930s.

Individuals who held status by inheritance of public office recognised the power of football. The Sheffield FA began a Cup tournament in 1879 for a trophy donated by local landowner the Earl of Wharncliffe with a percentage of gate receipts being given to local charities. In November 1899 Bramall Lane hosted a game between Sheffield Boys and London. Ten shillings of the gate receipts went to the Lord Mayor's fund, which was to be passed on to the wives and children of 'those gallant lads', doing duty for Queen and Country in the Boer War. In 1903 United played Wednesday and gave the gate receipts towards the building of Sheffield University. The fixture was the idea of Charles Clegg, who considered that the charitable efforts of the city's two big football clubs were paltry when compared to teams of comparable and even lesser status. The following year the same fixture saw the proceeds given to four hospitals in the city. The Firth Building Cup of 1913, provided by the steel baron and philanthropist, Mark Firth, was the product of a match played between United and Wednesday once again to raise funds for the building of the University in Sheffield.

The game also sought to look after its own. As early as 1867, those involved in the game realised the frailty of a footballing career. A Players' Accident Fund was suggested based on the idea that all players in the region donate to a central savings pot, the idea being to pay eight shillings a week to those in the fund who had been prevented from working by a football-related injury. The idea was never realised.

The First Fans

Putting money over the turnstile to watch a match was in this era not a luxury that needed saving for. For this reason the game was available for all social classes. The early spectators watching United were those classed as artisans (skilled workers not labourers) then, by the 1890s, it would seem that others of a slightly higher social class were also watching the game. As a consequence, the design of football stadiums became an issue as such people sought comfort, a degree of exclusion and an uninterrupted view of the match.

The game, when played well, offered excitement enough to sell itself to the curious. There was nothing to compare it with locally—rugby never took off in South Yorkshire. Match-going was a cheap form of outdoor entertainment which was extremely sociable and permitted a degree of partisan entertainment. The match programme in September 1899 tells of a United v Wednesday Reserve fixture, attracting a crowd of 4,000. On the same day, the Sheffield Wednesday first team, in their new ground at Owlerton, pulled a crowd of 12,000. The marketing policy to attract more spectators was not particularly sophisticated, thus the match programme on November 4th, 1899 could be blatant urging readers: 'Can we persuade you to bring your sister, cousin and aunts. We would like the novelty of taking the money to the bank'.

The football fan was a commercial opportunity for more than football clubs. Transport companies realised there was money to be made in football. Thomas Cook and Son advertised transport for United away games beginning in 1903, even advertising in the United programme for special trains to watch Sheffield Wednesday. Distinctions in transport style are seemingly as old as away support. A Mr F. Street of Woodbank Crescent informed readers of the match programme (January 17th, 1903) that he was 'getting up a saloon party' on the train to Arsenal and 'anyone desirous of joining' should make their applications to him. The journey was somewhat arduous. The Thomas Cook excursion travelled overnight, arriving at St Pancras at 6.40am, returning after midnight. The return fare was nine shillings. For home games special 'cars' (horse drawn carriages) ran from the Tinsley district and Blonk Street in the city centre to Bramall Lane before and after first team games in 1904–05. For a population used to working collectively in steel and coal manufacture, travelling to the match was an expression of the communitarianism that was their very existence. Collective emotion however could bring its own problem when the perceived injustice of one might provoke dozens to right the wrong.

Who's First?

As mentioned earlier, the formation of United did not please the Wednesday club or its supporters. Vindictiveness and hostilities were undoubtedly evident in the early 1890s when United arranged friendly games against top-class opponents on the same day Wednesday were at home in the League. The decision by the newly formed United to undercut Wednesday's admission prices by 50% at the gate and 33% for a season ticket did not help matters either. However, the clubs buried hostilities enough to hold the first United v Wednesday derby in mid-December 1890 at Olive Grove. Some 10,000 packed the ground, many sporting either red or blue colours in the band of their hats to display their allegiance. A 2–1 victory for Wednesday was the outcome. The return a month later at Bramall Lane attracted 14,000 and saw a 3–2 United victory.

In 1891 a Sheffield derby could be said to have provoked a new professionalism in the Wednesday club and to have provided for a macabre form of local rivalry. A 5–0 United victory at Bramall Lane stunned Wednesday, who ordered their players to henceforth attend regular training sessions. The following season the clubs met twice and supporters of both sides produced funeral cards announcing the death of their rivals. After United had won 5–0 at Bramall Lane, cards were produced which read:

> *In loving remembrance of the Sheffield Wednesday football team… who were safely put to rest… at Bramall Lane.*

A month later United lost 4–1 to Wednesday—a new card was on sale:

> *In pitiful remembrance of our idol, the Sheffield United football team, who departed their football life, struggling to the end.*

In an 1892 derby game, players from both Sheffield teams leapt into the crowd to fight spectators before 40 police restored order. Such a number of police suggests the altercation involved hundreds of participants.

The games were obviously prone to disorder because a few years later before a United v Wednesday fixture in December, 1903, the match programme read:

> *…we ask the spectators to refrain from showing their displeasure by booing, or making remarks at something, which, perhaps, a certain society might not agree with.*

Even the United players were not averse to sorting matters out themselves. One such hard-nut was Mick Whitham, who was around Sheffield United from virtually its beginning. He made his debut on March 24th 1890 in a friendly fixture against a side by the name of Halliwell in a 1–1 draw. Whitham was born in Ecclesfield just outside Sheffield in 1867 and initially plied his trade with Thorpe Hesley FC, Ecclesfield,

Sheffield United FC 1899 in front of the John Street Stand
The anathema of the United directors to alcohol consumption did not extend to their refusing
money for advertising the devil's juice at their stadium

Lockwood Brothers and even made one appearance in the colours of Sheffield Wednesday. Sheffield United signed him from Rotherham Swifts. A rugged player with a speciality shoulder charge, Whitham was part of the first Sheffield United side when they took to the field against Lincoln in September 1892. He would later jointly hold the honour of becoming the first international in United's history by being capped for England against Ireland on the same day that team-mate Harry Lilley won his cap against Wales. This was extraordinary but true; there were two England games in progress on the same day, both classed as full fixtures in completely different locations and with completely different sides.

Despite being an international Whitham responded to insults in the time-honoured fashion his background demanded. A game at Middlesbrough had seen Whitham play his normal robust way and his treatment of the 'Boro forward line had attracted derision from the home supporters. Between the ground and public house where the teams changed was a duck pond. It was here that several irate home fans decided to wait for him in order to 'sort it out'. On being accosted, Whitham obliged his potential assailants by stripping off his red and white shirt and left more than one of the unfortunate mob in the water. Persistent injuries ended his playing career in 1897. Whitham became a coach, firstly with Rotherham Town before moving on to Gainsborough Trinity (then a Football League club) from 1911–12. He then had a two-year coaching spell with the up and coming Huddersfield Town between 1913–14, before heading south to Southern League Brentford. Despite being involved with football for a long and fairly successful period the Whitham family had little to show for it. Furthermore Whitham did not enjoy the best of health—and he liked a drink. He died in 1924 after a 'short illness', leaving his wife to cope with two young boys. Shortly after she too passed away leaving the children aged eight and twelve alone in London. Out of the blue came relatives from Sheffield who they had never met, or knew existed, to take them up north and look after them. Despite the obvious family hardships, the England Cap worn by Whitham is still in the family's possession.

Football Footage: Jasper Redfern

Since the origins of the game, fans have enjoyed celebrating their own existence as much as the players who are the most visible symbols of a football club. There was thus a market for the fans who wished to see replays of both that witnessed earlier on the pitch (or missed due to distance or other circumstances) and to see their fellow supporters. The 1899 Cup Final between United and Derby County was the first Cup Final to be caught by cinematography. That this occurred is down to the entrepreneurial spirit of Sheffielder Jasper Redfern, who was the official photographer of Sheffield United. A pioneer of the art of photography, he had worked in circuses and saw the value of recorded images of people. Travelling with the club to games Redfern would both photograph events and take film footage. He would then advertise via posters and in the match programme where the footage would be shown—invariably a city-centre cinema. Redfern would always film the United following, which was a great marketing tool because hundreds turned up to see themselves on film. Following the crowd footage, the audience would generally be treated to ten minute highlights of each half.

Redfern became a well known figure in footballing circles, so much so that the 1901 Cup Final had a delayed kick off because Redfern was still busy in the centre circle taking photographs. Glass plates of Redfern's work survive today depicting United between 1898 and 1902. Some of the images are from the 1899 Final against Derby, others are team photos originating from 1897. By 1902 Redfern was advertising his Animated Picture Show in the Montgomery Hall nightly at 7pm, describing the event as 'high-class vaudeville entertainment'. The following year his show played at Sheffield's Albert Hall and provided a variety of footage: *'Sheffield up-to-date'*, *'America's Cup Yacht Racing'* and *'Holbein Swimming the Channel'*. Local images included the laying of the foundation stone at Sheffield University as well as fishing matches, *'Homing Pigeons'*, the *'Yorkshire Agriculture show at Hillsborough'* and a visit to Sheffield by Prime Minister A.J. Balfour. Other entertainment came via 'football footage', the Duke of Norfolk's wedding and footage he had somehow obtained of the Russo-Japanese War. As a side show Redfern would take and sell to the curious X-rays of their bodies. This latter sideline may well have hastened his departure from this life, dying as he did from radiation poisoning.

The First Match Programme: 1897–98

Football clubs were soon to realise the value of print media; for pre-match entertainment, promoting the club (and its forthcoming fixtures) and for establishing the culture of the football-related 'collectable'. Match programmes were initially single page editions containing the team line-up and forthcoming fixtures. These expanded when businesses saw the benefits of advertisements. Within a year of its beginning the United programme was 12 pages long. Collected by enthusiasts since their origin, programmes can produce huge profits for those who possess them. A 1915 United v Chelsea Cup Final programme (folded and slightly damaged) sold in 1998 for £11,500. A similar one sold for £15,000 in 2001, and in the same year a Spurs v Sheffield United 1901 FA Cup Final programme sold for £14,000.

A full programme collection exists in the Hall of Fame for the year 1897–98, which as well as being the first year of match programmes at Bramall Lane, coincided with United winning the League Championship. Costing one penny, the programme reveals the state of advertising in the city, the circumstances that were to produce a championship-winning club and the habits of the early supporters. As the season progresses, the programme features change slightly, and a more triumphant attitude enters on account of the club's footballing successes. Published by Northend Printers, located in Norfolk Row, Sheffield, the ornate front cover of the 1897 pioneer programme soon leant itself to advertisements,

A Christmas match programme cover from the first season of such publications in 1897–98

initially from Wilson, Peck & Co., makers and retailers of pianos and organs. The willingness of such an upmarket establishment to sponsor this relatively new game of football is notable. Inside pages see adverts for items and products which would have a natural home with football and its followers, one of which is embrocation lotion, in bottles and jars, with an endorsement by the Brooklyn 'Athlete' Club of New York and Forfar Athletic no less. For those recovering from the excitement of the day, Barry's Pure Cocoa might help them sleep and feel refreshed enough for a spell of lawn renovation, courtesy of Meggitts, who we learn supplied bone and horn dust for the Bramall Lane wicket.

1898 League championship medal awarded to J.H. Johnson
(Courtesy of Alan Johnson)

The perilous state of employment due to the local practice of piece work (i.e. payment by the number of items made) is perhaps evident in an advert which informs readers that William Turner, the pawnbroker, lends money for amongst other things, 'pianos, furniture, watches, jewellery…'. Local food production is advertised by Millers, who promote their sausages, pork pies and polonies. By contrast, the Cole Brothers department store state that as well as being 'general outfitters and practical shirt makers' they were also 'sole makers to the Sheffield United Club'. For the man about town, Samuels 'the noted tailor', advertise their clothing, whilst Wreghitts, hats, ties and guinea waterproofs, are on sale for 'Ye footballers and ye spectators' who want to be up to date.

With the autumn upon them, the good citizens of Sheffield may well have sought relief from the dark nights. Escapism was available in both bottle and verse. The former was available from Duncan Gilmour, 'purveyors of wines and spirits', and Windsor Ales 'sold in all the booths' in the Bramall Lane ground. The fine wines were available to sample and 'quotations' (prices) were given. For those wanting entertainment, the 'where to go tonight' section provided three possibilities. At the Theatre Royal was *The Gondoliers* comic opera. The Alexandra provided *The Sledge Hammer*; alternatively, one could enter the Empire and in between entertainment from the Variety Company watch footage of the Greco-Turkish War, and with it the advertised promise:

> …*War is brought near home to one by such pictures as these. You see all the horror of it. But you see the other side as well, as when in the awful scream of carnage, with shells bursting all around, a nurse comes into the picture to the relief of the wounded and dying.*

(October 4th.)

The following months saw new adverts enter the programmes, promoting coal merchants and Yorkshire Curd Cheese Cake. No doubt best eaten after watching *Robinson Crusoe* at the Lyceum or *Dick Whittington* at the Alexandra Theatre.

Technology was assisting fan culture as innovation permitted results elsewhere to be known. Fans are informed in the first programme of the club's plans to chronicle the progress of United and other teams every 15 minutes. This was to be done via a score sheet with the names of teams corresponding to the figures on a board erected in Bramall Lane. Modern technology, a reader learns now, permits knowledge of football results elsewhere. As the editor explains:

> *Before long we hope to have telephone communications in all the First Division grounds; but some of the secretaries are too full of other things to bother.*

(September 26th.)

For those interested, the height and weight of the 11 United players who started the season was given, and in addition to the team selection is a depiction of the formation.

The subheadings 'Club Gossip' and 'What the Papers Say' attempt to collate accounts of information relevant to the club and its fans. Comment is often brutally honest about the club's 'second-string forwards'. As an illustration both of the way the players were considered by the secretary and the intrigue that was evident in Sheffield football, we can cite the following:

> *Ernest Needham and Robert Howell were a wee bit off colour. They have to make up their minds to remedy this defeat today… Mr Brüster signed a league form for us the other day. He was interviewed by one of our alleged supporters the same day and promised an introduction to the Wednesday Committee… but the promise came too late! Mr Brüster is a man of his word and our 'friend' departed discomfited.*

(September 25th 1897.)

The club was aware that its players were attracting the attention of other teams. But even in victory were reluctant to praise them. Having won 5–2 the previous week, the programme notes:

> *We have a lot of fine players—every one of them wanting sugar plums every time they play. Men of that stamp are no good to us.*

(October 9th 1897.)

Some elementary form of questionnaire is evident by September, when an article titled 'Per Pigeon Post' informs readers that football is booming in Bristol and that United may go down there soon. Under the heading 'What the Crowd Says', one curious individual asks a question of female fans while another suggests others look at the ladies who gather in a specific area of the ground.

For those wishing to be part of this championship-winning season, the programme listed the prices for season tickets.

> *10/6 Self to Terrace. 21/- Self and lady to portion of John Street Stand or self to reserved seat on John Street Stand, obtained by an application to Secretary or Assistant.*

(September 25th, 1897.)

For those wishing to see the Blades away from home, a football special train is advertised to Nottingham Forest, departing two hours before kick off and costing two shillings. The following to Nottingham aroused some socio-political interest in the editor of the subsequent programme, who was to state: 'There were masters and men, lads and ladies.' The picture of this game is further enhanced with the sketches of an artist sent by the *Sport* to cover the game.

A sketch of a new stand to be built on Shoreham Street, was there for all to see in October. Meanwhile, Blades followers were given advice before a derby against Wednesday that attracted a crowd of 24,000.

The only full cap awarded to William 'Fatty' Foulke
1897 England v Wales played at Bramall Lane

Let the keynote of your trumpeting on Saturday next at Olive Grove be Play Up, United! Display your colours prominently and do not strike them whether Fortune smiles or frowns.

An away trip to Everton a few weeks later was enjoyed by the fans—if not United's goalkeeper. A reader learned of the day out in 'Toffee Town':

The trippers shouted, sang, told the porters tales when the train stopped, whistled all the tunes of the universe, and when they reached the Heeley Station, made the antient [sic] welkins ring afresh by a hullabaloo that might have been heard at Duffum!

However, the piece adds a line of admonishment for the home fans,

…it was cowardly of the spectators to throw stones at Foulke.

(December 6th 1897.)

A couple of days before the old year finished, a benefit for United player Bob Cain held at the pavilion at Bramall Lane saw acts ranging from a comic duet to a harp soloist to readings and recitals. A crucial game in the New Year saw 1,500 Blades travel to Aston Villa. The United team meanwhile made pre-match stopovers at Matlock Spa to prepare for games. In late February, with their first championship within reach, the programme tells a reader of how the club's success was down to 'our own selections' and those players who arrived at the club via 'agents' have been 'our worst failures'.

The victorious Sheffield United FA Cup winning team of 1899. United beat Derby County 4–1 at the Crystal Palace

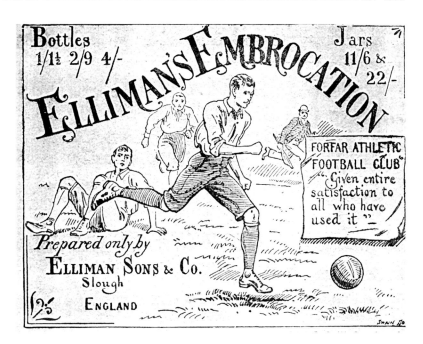

Elliman's Embrocation
An advertisement in the match programme informing aspiring footballers of the benefits of embrocation. A ringing endorsement comes from Forfar Athletic

In late February a programme reader learns that the directors of Aston Villa had introduced a library for the benefit of their players. United, meanwhile, announced in April their plan to secure the freehold of Bramall Lane and build covered courts for tennis and racquets, facilities for swimming, shooting, cycling, running and a social club. The football fever perplexed one onlooker who wrote of his experience in the April 2nd edition and describes his presence in the Bramall Lane pavilion for a United reserve game, after which he was guest of the United committee. He chronicles how two dozen gentlemen gathered around the open fire, awaiting the ring of the telephone which one of their number answered and then broadcast to the silent rest: 'United won four-none'. What followed was described by the onlooker as men 'fighting like mad bulls to get out of the small doorway' to relay the score to a crowd gathered outside the pavilion. Seeking an explanation from various jubilants, he fails to get an answer and calling on the services of a police constable he describes being unceremoniously pushed out of the building to walk home a sadder, if not wiser, man.

Champions 1898

Admitted into the newly-formed second division in 1892, United were promoted after their first season following the aforementioned Test match against Accrington. The first three seasons in Division One were ones of consolidation, finishing tenth, sixth and twelfth respectively. In 1897 United finished runners-up to Aston Villa and posted a profit of £1,066, which they invested in a covered area on Shoreham Street, which cost £1,390. This banked area behind the goal some time in the first decade of the twentieth century took on the title of the 'Shoreham Kop'. The word Kop was a product of the Boer war and commemorated the Royal Lancashire Regiment, which occupied the *Spion* (lookout) *Kopje* (hillock) outside of current-day Ladysmith, Natal. In the ensuing battle, the regiment lost 322 men. The occasion was not forgotten in Lancashire and when Liverpool FC upgraded their ground in 1906 with an elevated banking, supporters called for it to be named the Spion Kop in honour of the dead. A month later similar banking at St Andrew's Birmingham was given the same name. The first football ground with a Spion Kop

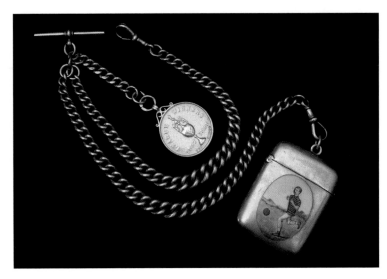

William Foulke's 1898 League Championship medal with chain and vesta case

was actually at the Woolwich Arsenal ground in South London whose cinder embankment had been called in honour of the war dead by the men of the munitions factory from which Arsenal took their name.

Finishing runners-up to Aston Villa in 1897 having won 13 of their 30 games, United's first programme of the 1897–98 season, stated the aim of the club as being 'to gain the championship of the League'. This was plausible. The club had great players in Ernest Needham, Walter Bennett, Tommy Morren, Rab Howell and Bill Foulke. An indifferent start to the season saw United undefeated but produced too many draws for aspiring champions. United though were crowd-pullers.

A crowd of 2,500 turned out in the rain for United's first home game of the 1897–98 season, which ended in a 2–1 victory over Derby County. A month later 10,000 watched a 4–3 victory over Stoke. A Sheffield derby at Olive Grove pulled in 24,000 and receipts of £620 and a 1–0 victory for the visitors. A following of a thousand Blades saw United win 4–1 at Everton but a dip in form in December saw United draw a home fixture with Wednesday in front of 37,289 fans paying a total of £962. Regaining form in the new year, United were competing with Aston Villa for top spot and beat Villa away in front of 43,000 spectators. A monumental game ended with a female Blade sitting in the directors' box flinging the contents of her box of chocolates over local dignitaries.

Football fever was hitting Sheffield. A game against Sunderland at Roker Park saw a reported crowd of 23,500, but was probably far more as the roof of a wooden shed used as the United players' changing room collapsed because of the weight of spectators standing on it, craning for a view. United director Tom Bott rescued the players by holding up a prop. United lost 3–1 in a game best remembered for two own-goals scored by Rab Howell from innocuous crosses. Playing only once more for United, Howell was transferred to Liverpool as rumours spread of his treachery in the face of financial inducements from Sunderland. United's next home game, a friendly, saw a 1–0 victory over Scottish champions Celtic. The English champions had beaten their Scottish equivalents—United were thus the best team in the world. The United players received medals, a bonus of £3 and a reception in their honour at Sheffield's Cutlers Hall.

United were to win 17 of their 30 league games and took the 1898 Championship ahead of Sunderland. Sunderland were a footballing power, but created ill-feeling amongst many Blades fans. Thought to be willing to pay cash to opponents to assist their own players, they also defied the spirit of the game in other ways. One such occasion occurred in April 1898 when they visited Bramall Lane again seeking a victory that would put them top of the table with two games remaining. The fixture clashed with the Home Nations international fixture. United released Ernest Needham for England, but Sunderland refused Ned Doig and Hugh Wilson permission to play for Scotland. Whilst the refusal was within their rights the act was considered unsporting. Two of the Corinthians players, C.B. Fry and G.O. Smith even offered to play for United in protest at this absence of sportsmanship. The request was turned down. The actions of Sunderland were however futile as United won the fixture 1–0. Beating Bolton the week after 1–0, as Sunderland lost by a similar score at Bury, United won the championship for the first time, thereby breaking the Sunderland-Aston Villa title stranglehold held since Everton's victory in 1891. Five years after joining Division One, United were League Champions, winning the title by five points.

Gentlemen and Players

The championship had one controversy accompanying it. This concerned the conduct of one United player who almost won the trophy for Sunderland. His name was Rab Howell, who holds the full name of Rabbi according to his birth certificate. Howell holds two distinctions; one is that he is the only England international to be christened Rabbi, the other is that he was England's first ever Gypsy-born international. Whilst playing for United Howell, one of seven siblings, lived in a caravan in Sheffield's Wincobank area. His father was a horse-trader and tinker. Notable for playing the game without socks, Howell was a tigerish mid-fielder who stood only five feet five inches tall and weighed in at eight and a half stones. His abilities saw him win two England caps in 1895 and 1899. He was to arrive at Bramall Lane in 1890 from Rotherham Swifts, making 240 appearances before joining Liverpool for a fee of £150. Moving club was in legend believed to be far from traumatic for Howell who simply hitched his caravan to a horse and journeyed over the Pennines.

Sheriff's Charity Football Shield winners medal awarded to J.H. Johnson

Sheffield United were the first winners of the competition, sharing it with the amateur side Corinthians following a 1–1 draw at Crystal Palace (Courtesy of Alan Johnson)

1899 Cup Winners medal awarded to Walter 'Cocky' Bennett

This medal was lost under a stand at Huddersfield Town for over 40 years before it was found and returned to the family after renovation work (Courtesy of S. MacCagnan)

OUR NEW STAND:

SHOREHAM STREET END.

THE NEW COVERED STAND AT BRAMALL LANE

The two own-goals he scored against Sunderland finished his United career. Howell was transferred three weeks later. Observers were kind towards him, describing the event as one of dreadful bad luck rather than an act of treachery carried out for financial gain. The United directors knew Howell walked a fine line. In 1897 he had faced the United committee on a charge of 'misconduct' only to walk away having received two pounds by way of compensation! Six months later he faced the same men, this time promising to mend his ways. The *Sheffield Telegraph* mentioned, without revealing more, that 'conduct such as his cannot be condoned'. Howell moved to Preston from Liverpool and his career ended with a broken leg in 1903. Preston asked United to play a benefit match for Howell. United responded stating they could not 'accede their way to the request'. Howell died at the age of 70.

The 1899 Cup Final Ball

The 1898–99 season saw United finish in sixteenth place. Between September 1st and January 1st, United went 22 league games undefeated. A fine team contained no fewer than nine internationals, eight of whom were to play for England and one for Ireland. In 1900 United finished second, two points behind Aston Villa. In 1901 United were beaten finalists to Tottenham Hotspurs, but redeemed themselves in 1902 by beating Southampton in the final. By 1904 the United side consisted of 11 internationals (ten English, one Irish) and for the next 30 years were a Division One side. This turn of the century team was probably the best in the world, but the club has never won the League Championship since. They did however find time to win the FA Cup in 1899.

A crowd of 73,833 packed the Crystal Palace stadium to see United defeat Derby County 4–1 in the club's first FA Cup Final. Losing 1–0 at half time, the Blades stormed back in the second half with goals from Billy Beer, Jack Almond, Fred Priest and George Hedley to take the silverware back to Bramall Lane. The route to the final was elaborate; victories over Burnley and Preston required replays before Nottingham Forest were defeated at first attempt. The semi-final tie against Liverpool went to no fewer than four games in what was probably the most strenuous the competition has ever known. The first, played at the City Ground, Nottingham, produced a draw amid chaotic scenes of Sheffielders arriving in dray carts and steam trains. The replay at Burnden Park, Bolton, was less eventful, but produced a similar result. The third replay was staged at Fallowfield in Manchester, which saw a large crowd encroach on the field of play and the match eventually abandoned because of poor light minutes after the gate receipts had left the area in safe custody! The final replay played at the Baseball Ground of Derby County saw a United victory.

Sat at the front of a picture of the 1899 Cup winning team held by the club is the match ball presented to Tom Bott by Sheffield United in appreciation of all the work he had done for them. This city fishmonger worked many long unpaid hours for United, and was given the nomenclature of Director of Football. The 1899 match ball remained in Bott's possession for many years and was given to a loyal employee many years later as a thank you. A United historian knew of the ball's whereabouts and after much persuasion United were allowed in 1965 to borrow it. Unfortunately, a member of United's coaching staff, believed to be the late Harry Latham, suggested placing a new bladder in the ball so that it could be inflated and look better for photos. On inflation it promptly burst into four pieces of decaying leather. The remnants spent the best part of the next 40 years in a bag under the stairs of a home in the Woodseats area of Sheffield. A sum of £1,500 saw the ball became the property of Sheffield United's Hall of Fame project.

The club were delighted to be given the opportunity to purchase the ball, but had little idea what to do with it until the National Centre for Leather Conservation came forward to offer advice. The Victorian tanning process had meant that the ball was suffering from 'red rot'. A treatment and restoration programme was undertaken at a cost of £3,500 to stabilise the condition. A plastic sphere was constructed just a little smaller than the original ball. The pieces of leather were then treated and carefully secured to the new template. The silver plaque added by the club bearing the name of the team was lacquered and not polished as the inscription was only legible as a result of dirt caught in the engraving. Located in the centre of the Hall of Fame, the ball is a permanent tribute to the team that lifted one of the game's most sought after trophies.

As well as providing a story, the 1899 Cup Final ball is integral to the development of Sheffield United. At the time, a mere decade into their existence, United owned a huge ground, but were virtually broke. The money that came into the club by virtue of the FA Cup victory, went towards the development of Bramall Lane, which in turn made onlookers see that club had ambitions and a future. Soon crowds increased and players far and wide wanted to play for what was seen as a great club.

Three 1899 Cup winners' medals are held by the Hall of Fame, all are 18 carat gold and made by Vaughtons of Birmingham. One belongs to goalkeeper, William Foulke, another to Walter Bennett and the third to George Hedley, who joined United in 1898 from South Bank, an amateur team from the North East. In 155 appearances for United, Hedley scored 39 goals and won one full England Cap in 1901. His career produced three FA Cup winners' medals, two with United in 1899 and 1902 and one with

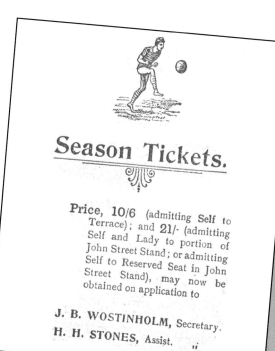

Season Tickets.

Price, 10/6 (admitting Self to Terrace); and 21/- (admitting Self and Lady to portion of John Street Stand; or admitting Self to Reserved Seat in John Street Stand), may now be obtained on application to

J. B. WOSTINHOLM, Secretary.
H. H. STONES, Assist.

The 1899 FA Cup Final ball

Wolves whom he joined in 1906 having left Bramall Lane in 1903 for Southampton. He later managed Bristol City. One interesting detail on the medal is the engraving that described the victory as the 'English Cup'. In 1999 the 1899 Cup Final winners' medal George Hedley was offered for sale at Christie's auction house in London. United chairman Derek Dooley agreed to buy the medal with a reserve set at between four and six thousand pounds. The auctioneer opened the bidding on the medal by stating that they already had bids submitted of £6000! The crunch bid came at £9,500. The medal was United's and made its way back from London into the hands of Sheffield United by way of rail for the second time in a century.

The Tin God

In early 2005 an important piece of football history came up for auction. This was the second FA Cup Trophy (won by Sheffield United in 1899 and 1902) known as the 'Little Tin God', which had replaced the original cup, stolen whilst in the possession of Aston Villa in 1896. One might ask how such a theft occurred. The answer is that it was customary in those days for local tradesmen to approach the cup winners to secure the trophy for display purposes in their shop windows to draw in the public. Villa had loaned the trophy to a local shoe shop from where it was stolen, never to be seen again. The replacement trophy won by United in 1899 was displayed in the window of a butcher's shop on the Moor in Sheffield city centre, in return all the players and directors involved in the victory received a leg of lamb. In the possession of other players' families is a commemorative medal for the 1899 Cup Final issued to them by a local Sheffield jeweller. It is reasonable to think that they had loaned the cup to his business and in return had received the gong by way of a thank you. The Tin God trophy was 'retired' in 1910, when Newcastle United beat Barnsley in the final and was awarded to Lord Kinnaird as a mark of appreciation for all the work he had done for the competition and for the game of football generally. The trophy stayed in the possession of his family until its auction a few years ago, when it raised the extraordinary sum of just short of half a million pounds by the generosity of David Gold, chairman of Birmingham City.

For many years, the boardroom at Bramall Lane contained a large, grand looking trophy cabinet, which featured many trophies and artefacts brought back from foreign tours. It also included memorabilia such as cuff links presented to former directors and even pictures of HMS Sheffield. For years nobody had paid close attention to the contents. In the midst of all this paraphernalia was one small, old, worn silver cup, somewhat over-shadowed by younger contenders. On careful inspection it turned out to be a one-third-sized replica of the famous FA Cup. It had been presented to Sheffield United to commemorate their first

Cup Final victory in 1899. In turn, the club had given it to United's director of football Tom Bott as a token of appreciation for all of his hard work. The trophy remained in his family until the 1950s when his daughter donated it to the football club complete with faded red and white ribbons that had adorned its full size cousin when it was handed over to United's Ernest Needham over half a century before. Some years later an over-enthusiastic cleaner decided that the dusty old ribbons made it look untidy, and promptly binned them.

Initiative and Innovation

The new professionalism that pervaded Sheffield United contained within it a good dose of pragmatism. In the 1890s United recruited many players from the north east, the first was George Waller one of the other earliest was Tommy Morren who signed for United on his way to Reading. Morren had won the Amateur Cup in 1895 with Middlesbrough Ironopolis and transferred to United in 1895 when United captured his signature in Sheffield railway station. Hearing that he was to leave the Boro and sign for Reading the United trainer, George Waller, walked to Sheffield railway station and, finding Morren on the train, took his travelling bag, forced him off the train and signed him there and then. Another north-eastern recruiting ground was South Bank, Middlesbrough, which produced Fred Priest, Ralph Gaudie and J.W. Richardson. Two others arrived from Darlington. Morren played in the Cup Finals of 1901 and 1902 and won a League champions medal. A combative and committed player he was to make 190 United appearances. His benefit match in 1902 was an 11am kick off on New Years Day against Wednesday. Following his football career he remained in Sheffield, running a newsagents and tobacconists business in the Ecclesall Road area.

Replica of 'The Little Tin God'

Taking Stock

At the end of the century, the Sheffield and Hallamshire FA (founded in 1886) had 40 affiliated clubs and 5,000 players, in a game virtually unrecognisable from just 20 years previously. Up until 1874, games were controlled by captains. It was not until 1881 that the participants saw the necessity of umpires, later called referees. As recently as 1870, the participants were still debating the numbers that each team should contain. In 1877, the 90 minute duration was implemented. In the same year, the FA Cup Final went into extra time (FA Cup replays were begun in 1884).

In the decade 1889–1899 Sheffield United FC had gone from an idea to a championship winning team with average attendances just below 10,000. In this decade, United could claim to have pioneered a style of play which they adopted for over 30 years. The United teams played with fast wingers who were encouraged to cross the ball at every opportunity. Another characteristic was a propensity for cross-field passes which could switch play in an instant. In Billy Hendry, Ernest Needham, George Utley and later Billy Gillespie, United had players with the intelligence to do this.

PROGRAMME OF
SMOKING CONCERT
To be held in the PAVILION at
BRAMALL LANE in aid of

R. Cain's Benefit, Dec. 29th,

COMMENCING AT 8 O'CLOCK,
*When the following Gentlemen have kindly
given their services.*

J B. WOSTINHOLM, Esq., in the Chair.

Mr. H. ELSE, Comic Song.
Mr. H. HELLIWELL, Baritone, " Wedding
    Morn."
Mr. J. HARRISON, Clarionet Solo.
Mr. F. PICKARD, { " Dahn ahʾr Yard."
    Comic.   { " Gussie."
           { " O'er Sky and Sea."
Mr. A. BAYLES, { " Come into the Garden,
   Tenor.   {   Maud."
Mr. E. QUANTOCK, { " The Raft."
    Baritone.   { " Jack's the Boy."
Mr. H. HAYES, " Where there is a will there
    is a way."
Mr. R. JOHNSON, Piccolo Solo, accompanied
    by Miss EDITH REDFEARN.
Mr. G. KERRIGAN { " Queen of the Earth."
              { " The Dessert."
Mr. W. J. COWAN, Comic, " I aint agoin to
    tell."
J. ROBERTSHAW, Esq., J P., Reading.
Mr. J. LINSTEAD, Baritone.
Mr. W. PARTON, Recitation.
Mr. DALE BUTLER, { " The Electrical
    Comic,   Battery Man."
             { " I wasn't sure."
Mr. J. W. FRANCE, Tenor, " Tell her I love
    her so."
Messrs. A. HILL and FANFIELD, Banjo and
    Mandoline Soloists and Duettists.
Mr. NORMAN HOPE, { " English as she is
    Comic.   spoke."
           { Humorous Sketch.
Mr. T. HANLEY, " Ahr Smøokin Consart."
Mr. J. ROBERTSON, { " The Wolf."
    Baritone.   { " Friar of Orders Gray."
Mr. G. E. HARDCASTLE, an Original Musical
    Sketch : " A Village Concert."
Mr. W. A. STUTTARD, Tenor, " Mona."
Mr. ELLIOTT, Auto-Harp Solo.
Mr. A. SHAW, { " On the Ramparts."
    Baritone. { " Asthora."
Messrs. HAYES and CONAN, Comic Duet :
    " The Bunk-a-doodle Corps."
Mr. DICK ARMITAGE, Comic.
Mr. J. SWIFT, Tenor.

Pianist - Mr. H. Ward.

ADMISSION, 6D. EACH.

Bob Cain's benefit night in 1898
The itinerary reveals some of the best entertainment on offer
in Sheffield in the late nineteenth century

By 1899, the club had bought the freehold to Bramall Lane (for £10,300) from the Duke of Norfolk on condition that it was not to be sold or used for any other purpose than that of recreation for at least 21 years. In this same decade, the ground had moved on from a simple stand on John Street to covered areas on both Bramall Lane and John Street, eventually leading to a 2,000 seater stand on the latter street. This was complemented in 1897 by the construction of a heaped end on Shoreham Street, which was partly covered. The century ended with work beginning on a cricket pavilion which would cost £6,000. The Bramall Lane enclosure could thus hold up to 60,000 people.

United's facilities were superior to most clubs. Public baths on the corner of John Street and Bramall Lane facilitated the clean up after muddy games and the location obviously impressed the FA, who chose it for England internationals in 1883, 1887 and 1897. The board of directors, in approving the building of the John Street Stand in 1902, were gambling a sum of £12,000 on developing that which they operated and owned.

In 1899 United became a limited liability company and in the ensuing share offer became owned by 422 shareholders. The change from a club run by committee to that of a limited company took away personal liability in case of debt. The shares were in part bought by existing committee people, but others in the city bought them as well. Interestingly no-one had a block of shares, nor in fact did anyone have more than one. Even in the 1970s, those holding two shares did so mainly by virtue of inheritance. For some 80 plus years Sheffield United were owned equally by around 400 people.

Football was bound up in drinking and gambling. A fan base had developed in this first decade which had its drink-related idiosyncrasies. Blades of this era borrowed a drinking song written in 1891 for the music hall male impersonator Millie Hylton and made it their own. Referred to as the 'Rowdy Dowdy Boys' the chorus went:

Then I say boys, who's for a jolly spree, Rum tum, tiddly um, who'll have a drink with me?
Fond of a glass or two, fond of a row or a noise, hi hi clear the way for the Rowdy Dowdy Boys.

There was money as well as noise to be made in football. Nationally the football phenomenon saw John Baines of Bradford begin producing football cards in 1897 which depicted players in action or player portraits accompanied by exclamations of 'Play Up!' or 'Saved, Sir!'. From its origin until 1920, some 13 million cards were sold. There was also illicit money to be earned (or lost). Gambling had been outlawed in England under the 1853 Betting Act. Victorian moralists were fearful of gambling and the professionalisation of football was considered by them as making the game prone to corruption. The game was never innocent. The very first Cup Final of 1872 had witnessed betting, and by the 1880s, betting was done in and around grounds. In its early days, the game had no tradition to guard itself against, but as early as 1892 the FA banned betting by players and officials of clubs under its jurisdiction and made clubs responsible for preventing betting in their grounds. Bills were posted at grounds stating the illegality of gambling. The national Anti Gambling League of 1890 kept a close eye on events around football. They may well have looked at the situation in Sheffield. In 1892, a Blackburn Rovers official made allegations at an FA Council meeting that Sheffield was a place where 'open and noisy betting on the field was practiced'. In 1900 Edwin Richmond, a Sheffield Magistrate, inspired a Council edict that the Chief Librarian of the city delete all betting news in newspapers kept by the city libraries.

Football developed in conjunction with beer drinking—in 1865 11 out of 13 football clubs listed in a Sheffield directory had public house addresses. Alcohol consumption was massive in Sheffield wherein beer was believed to be fortifying for steel foundry men and was used for cleansing the dusty throats of steel grinders and coal miners. A pub was located adjacent to nearly every factory gate from which apprentices fetched beer for their working elders. With 1,400 licensed premises in Sheffield by the late 19th century and 30 breweries, the Temperance Movement had a job on its hands.

The original share issue
The Sheffield United board raised 422 Original shares in 1899

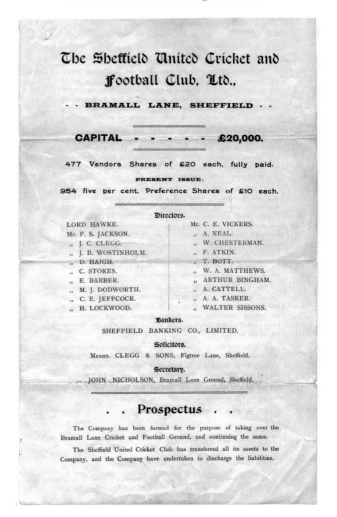

The Sheffield United Cricket and Football Club, Ltd.,
- - BRAMALL LANE, SHEFFIELD - -

CAPITAL - - - - - £20,000.

477 Vendors Shares of £20 each, fully paid.

PRESENT ISSUE:

954 five per cent. Preference Shares of £10 each.

Directors.

LORD HAWKE.	Mr. C. E. VICKERS.
Mr. F. S. JACKSON.	„ A. NEAL.
„ J. C. CLEGG.	„ W. CHESTERMAN.
„ J. B. WOSTINHOLM.	„ F. ATKIN.
„ D. HAIGH.	„ T. BOTT.
„ C. STOKES.	„ W. A. MATTHEWS.
„ E. BARBER.	„ ARTHUR BINGHAM.
„ M. J. DODWORTH.	„ A. CATTELL.
„ C. E. JEFFCOCK.	„ A. A. TASKER.
„ H. LOCKWOOD.	„ WALTER SISSONS.

Bankers.
SHEFFIELD BANKING CO., LIMITED.

Solicitors.
Messrs. CLEGG & SONS, Figtree Lane, Sheffield.

Secretary.
JOHN NICHOLSON, Bramall Lane Ground, Sheffield.

. . Prospectus . .

The Company has been formed for the purpose of taking over the Bramall Lane Cricket and Football Ground, and continuing the same.

The Sheffield United Cricket Club has transferred all its assets to the Company, and the Company have undertaken to discharge the liabilities.

The city was, though, more than beer and football. Its populace was interested in a variety of cultures, religions and philosophies. That it could combine the more cerebral with passionate football support should only surprise those who dismiss the game as a futile distraction for the frivolous. The game has always provided for a variety of meanings and, in their victories, the football clubs make thousands of their followers very happy.

Early product endorsement

The Sheffield United League winning team of 1898 endorsing a product first manufactured in 1841

RAB HOWELL INTERVIEWED.

It is quite customary to interview the captain and sub-captain of a team, but some of the lesser lights are never interviewed except they happen to strike "'ile."

Now, I chanced to drop promiscuously on the man who, I think, merits a little bit all to himself, if only for the way in which he shadows Spikesley. "Freddy does not like me," is Rab's oft-repeated expression, "an' I dunno why, for I always play fair," and no man can gainsay it ; he evens sticks closer than a brother, and brother footballers do stick close!

"Now, Rab," I said, "to begin, how old are you ? " "Well, I am no chicken, although I look like a lad; but I shall play a lot longer than most of them. You see, I never drink." "Well, how old are you ? Come, be sharp."

"Well, let me see. Mick's just thirteen months older nor I am, and he is——."

"Never mind Mick ; how old are you ? "

"I think I am thirty next." Thank goodness he had at last discovered his age !

"I think you were born in Wincobank."

"Aye, in Wincobank Wood."

"Were you at that time a tent-dweller or did you live like ordinary folks ? "

"My feythur had a caravan at that time, and——." "He was a hawker ? " "Nay, he was a horse-dealer." "You mean an ostler ! " "Nay, he used to buy and sell horses—and pots."

"Oh, then, he was a pot-hawker ? " "Nay, he was a potter ! "

"The report is that one day you were watching Ecclesfield play a practice match and they asked you to play. After that practice they put you into the first team. Is that so ? " "Yes."

"Then you went to play for Rotherham Swifts, and after that you came to us ? "

"Yes; me, Mick, and Arthur came together."

"You have played once, I understand, International for England against Ireland."

"I see you know it better than me, so please put it down that I ought to play against Scotland for England. It is time they gave it me ; and don't think I should be the worst man in the field, for I shouldna'."

"What an awful blow you are, Rab," I exclaimed *sotto voce.*

"Have you any other accomplishment ? "

"Yes ; I am open to box the best man about this place ; carn't I, Nudge ? " and he appealed to Needham to substantiate his prowess as a pugilist of the first water.

"I have heard it said you were a Volunteer." "Yes, I belonged to the Hallamshire Rifles, but I was too tall for them ! "

"Then you are a winner of prizes for pigeon-flying ? " "Nay, I used to sit on the top step and watch them fly to someone else's cotes. They was more than I could manage. You see, I like my money on t' floor. I've got two big pigs, an' I shall kill them this Christmas ; but all this hes nowt to do wi' football ! Just come and watch me play Freddy."

And away he went, the happiest-go-lucky individual it has ever been my lot to rub shoulders against.

The Villa, says a Birmingham paper, look like having to depend on the reserve forces, a little more this season. Howard Spencer, the popular back, has paid another visit to Mr. Whitehead, and the Manchester specialist advises him to give his knee a rest for another month and then see him again. The right back had another try with the ball previous to going to Cottonopolis, and finds he cannot twist about yet on his injured leg. The cartilage is in position, but rest is required to get back the normal power in the joint, and the doctor says it will be as strong as ever.

What is of a good deal of interest to us is whether Spencer will be fit enough to appear against us when our two games take place with the Villa. We want to beat Villa's best team !

We have been asked several times to give, for the benefit of our readers the difference in the doings of the United and Wednesday in the League since United were admitted in 1893-4.

In the last five seasons, up to the 27th of December, 1897, the records are as follows :

	Play'd	W.	L.	D.	For	Agst.
United	136	58	46	32	220	215
Wednesday	138	52	55	31	217	222

In other words United have scored 148 points to Wednesday's 135.

SOUVENIR
English Cup Final

CRYSTAL PALACE,
April 19th, 1902.

FOULKE.

Southampton

versus

Sheffield United.

Chapter 3

The World at Their Feet?

The death of Queen Victoria in January 1901 heralded the reign of Edward VII and a huge change in the social and cultural life of Britain. The Edwardian era saw a population with more leisure time and money than their predecessors. Football benefited from this. The 1901 FA Cup Final at the Crystal Palace saw over 110,000 in attendance, which confirmed that football was not just a pastime, but a business and for its players a livelihood. In short, it was to be taken seriously. The realities of professionalism began to change the game, and the paying spectators' money was now considered an essential part of the existence and success of the clubs. In the late 19th and early 20th centuries, the name of many a city was synonymous with sporting and industrial excellence and much of this sporting success was built on the back of local-born talent. Some may think it a romantic notion to believe that every young boy in the industrial North kicked a ball around in grimy smoke-blackened streets, dreaming of playing professional football, but there was a degree of truth in this. In the Sheffield context this culture of manual labour produced hard men who faced a life of harsh employment in coal mines or steel works; football was a temporary way out of this existence. Generally, however, if they made a name in the professional game they were only staving off the inevitability of having to get dirty in dangerous conditions.

The National Insurance Act of 1908 established that vulnerable members of society were the responsibility of the state. The creation of the Labour Party in 1905, arising out of the struggles of the collective industries of mining, steel, textile and dockworks brought a new spirit to sections of the population that were now more confident in challenging the established social order. Intellectual and scientific advances questioned the prevailing religious-bound authority. The new humanist and secular theorists made heroes out of footballers. The game was even considered crucial in maintaining the social mores of the time. As one patrician figure wrote:

> …The poorer classes in this country have not got the tastes which superior people or a Royal Commission would choose for them. Were cricket and football abolished, it would bring upon them nothing but misery, depression, sloth, indiscipline and disorder.
>
> F.E. Smith (cited in Mason 1980).

Football boomed in this decade. United's average crowd in 1903–04 was 17,000. The wages of skilled workers had increased over the previous two decades at the same time as they had enjoyed a five and a half day week. By 1914 12,000 football clubs existed, mostly at amateur level, and 750,000 players were registered nationally. The game was even included in the 1906 elementary school curriculum. By 1911, only four towns in England with a population of more than 10,000 did not have a professional club and whilst the income of professional teams was mainly from the turnstiles, others were subsidised by directors. The board was invariably local and drawn from the established or aspiring middle classes and their pursuit was prestige rather than profit. For the players, the maximum wage of £4 per week, established in 1901, brought a respectable income. Signing on fees when joining a new club brought a further income, albeit limited to £10. By 1905, the first £1,000 transfer had taken place, and attempts to limit the size of transfer fees failed. English clubs began to tour the globe and professional footballers, via cigarette cards, became national celebrities.

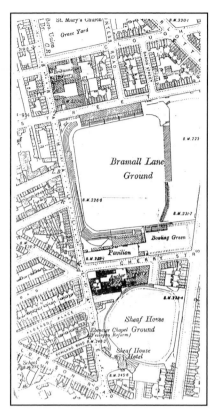

An aerial plan of Bramall Lane c. 1900

Money could bring footballing glory but buying success was considered poor form. In 1909, the United programme criticised a London team by the name of Chelsea for inflating the transfer market and buying success. Attendances at Bramall Lane in the final season of this decade saw 249,026 watch 19 home league games (an average of 13,107). Included in these were certain ladies who provoked a letter to the club programme in January 1910 advising them for the benefit of the rest of the spectators, not to wear hats. 1910 saw the first FA Tour beyond Europe, on which 16 players travelled to South Africa. The squad contained three Sheffield United players.

Grounds for Change

At the beginning of the 20th century, Bramall Lane was as good a ground as any in Britain. Furthermore, the football team it hosted had, in its thirteen years of existence, won one League Championship, two FA Cups and had been beaten finalists on one occasion. This young club had built the John Street Stand in 1895, but such was the success associated with Sheffield United, that they were able to rebuild it a few years later. A new cricket pavilion as well as terracing on other sides of the ground was also built.

The swift rise of the football club during the 1890s meant that the men who managed it had an obligation to deliver top quality facilities for the supporters. The John Street side of the stadium had seen many changes since the grounds 1855 opening, but when a fire destroyed the existing structure in November 1900 salvation came from one of football stadia's architectural pioneers. United had long been visitors north of the border and during a 1900 visit to the brand new Ibrox Park, Glasgow, the United delegation witnessed a building project completed by engineer Archibald Leitch. Soon after, Leitch contacted the United board offering to design a grandstand for Bramall Lane. The first example of a Leitch football stand constructed in England was at Bramall Lane, opened in 1902 at a cost of approximately £5000. Holding 3,800 seats, with standing terrace accommodation for a further 6000, the stand was the most luxurious yet constructed in the English game. For decades John Street was the nerve-centre of football operations; players changed and entered the pitch from here and up to 60 members of the press stared out from their roof-top office.

Leitch's creation gave sterling service to generations of Unitedites. The structure that replaced it also featured an updated, but less regal, gable in its roof. Today every fan walking through a turnstile in the South Stand of Bramall Lane, walks through a piece of Leitch handiwork as the turnstiles are the ones installed in John Street in 1902, serviced and put back to work. In 1908 Leitch built the North Stand at Hillsborough and later amongst others the stands of Sunderland, Newcastle, Tottenham and Fulham. Leitch's legacy can be found still in various corners of the Football League, although many of his masterpieces have been lost to the bulldozers and ambitions of football chairmen. The Leitch hallmark of criss-cross ironwork facades across the stands is still evident at places such as Goodison Park and Ibrox Park.

Taking a Gamble

Football provided for off-pitch entertainment as well. As early as 1908, the FA passed a resolution which described gambling on football matches as 'evil'. The FA bulletin of 1908 opined that the 'once untainted contests' were at risk of becoming 'merely the money struggles of sporting hooligans'. The FA President between 1890–1923, Lord Kinnaird, was also Vice President of the National Anti-Gambling League. The 1906 Street Betting Act prohibited betting transactions in public and forbade premises to be used for gambling. In response to the banning of public gambling, the football pools were begun. Newspapers started to offer fixed odds on predicting football results. Bookmakers produced coupons and gambling moved away from the football grounds. Fixed odd betting coupons saw 250,000 players a week by 1907. The National Anti-Gambling League however prosecuted two newspapers that published coupons. In response, the pools companies moved their operations to Holland (and later Switzerland) and collected monies by post. In 1909, legislation forbade loitering for the purpose of distributing handbills advertising football coupons. Earlier, the FA had extended the ban on betting from players and officials to everyone attending a match under their jurisdiction. Consternation about this situation saw United's chairman, Charles Clegg, threaten the permanent suspension of any player or manager discovered to be involved in coupon betting. The coupon business acquired legitimacy in 1913 with the Ready Money Football Betting Bill. A decade later the Football Pools Coupons began and are still in existence today.

Image and Substance

Some football-related entertainment brought no financial return to the mass of enthusiasts. Promoted as 'Local films for local people', the films of Sagar Mitchell and James Kenyon would pack church halls and local theatres in the early years of the 1900s. Based in Blackburn, the pair would tour Britain, recording the banalities of everyday life and then charge the very people they had filmed to watch themselves. The discovery of hours of these tapes in 2000 provided a priceless archive of Britain in Edwardian times. Part of the collection discovered was footage of a Bury verses Sheffield United game in 1902.

Preceding such footage were pen and ink sketches provided by cartoonists which became prolific throughout football newspapers and match programmes before the development of action photography. Usually seeking to portray a variety of incidents, via caricatures and sequences, the creators would provide a short sentence commentary, which attempted to depict the game as reported by the man on the spot.

Judging by the goods advertised in the match programmes, life in the new century seemed to be becoming ever more comfortable. In 1899 the programme advertised shops selling hats and gloves. Others could boast weekly sales of 6 tons of polony. The 1901–02 season had adverts for theatre productions and wedding rings adorning the front cover. Advice on the prevention of dog, cat and poultry disease was available in 1902, as was piano removal courtesy of a large man with a horse and cart. Alternatively, a reader could be impressed with a tailors that could boast '35,000 yards of cashmere

The John Street stand c. 1902. Designed by Archibald Leitch

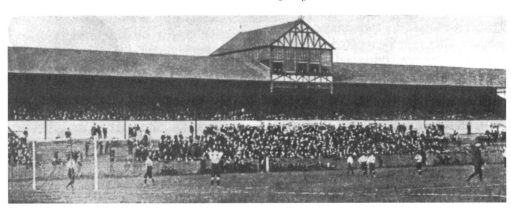

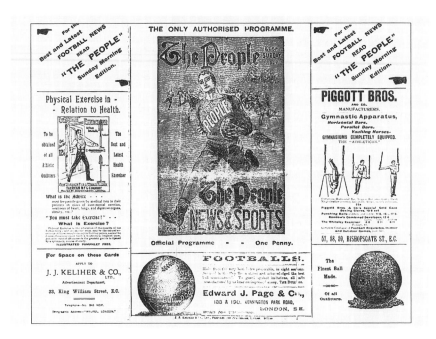

The 1901 Cup Final programme
This single sheet production was given to visiting dignitaries

trouserings'. Sensible items for a winter game, such as silk mufflers, hats and cardigans were available from Wreghitts store. Those seeking a coffee and cake after the game would, from 1903, enjoy the luxury of Davy's Coffee House on the corner of Castle Street in Haymarket. After a February 1902 game fans might want to watch 'Ronsbys Electrolytes'—an 'electrical review fan tableaux'—or listen to the 'Coloured Meisters' in the Empire Palace. Later in the year one could watch 'Chung Ling 500—The Marvellous Chinese Conjuror'. The same April programme, however, revealed an epidemic and advised:

> There is no need for Sheffielders to be very much afraid of the 'small pox scourge' as it is called in town just now. It is not as bad as it was in Sheffield some years ago, and the danger is almost infinitesimal.

Dangers to life still lurked from other sources. To some outsiders, the city's populace was considered beyond the pale. R.E. Leader in *Reminiscences of Old Sheffield* described the locals in 1902 as:

> If not viciously criminal beyond the average... the Sheffielders...were yet a turbulent race, very apt, whether with or without reason, to express their feelings by riot.

Behave Yourself

The decade saw disorder and hostilities continue at football matches. How much this was caused by events on the field of play or possibly by the gambling that the game attracted is impossible to know. But the events caused consternation enough for the United match programme to voice its disgust at both

The 1901 FA Cup final team relaxing at the Sea View hotel, Skegness

certain club's officials and advise their own fans on appropriate behaviour. In 1900 commenting on rough play at the hands of opponents weeks previously, the Secretary stated with moral certainty that:

> The man who goes in for the knocking out process at football in an English Cup tie with his eyes open deserves himself to be knocked out. We are perfectly aware that such a doctrine is opposed to all the cannons of Christianity, but at the same time it is one which in this particular instance commends itself.
>
> (February 24th.)

Some five years later in the Christmas day match programme an article titled 'Hints to Spectators' advised supporters on their conduct in regard to footballers:

> If by chance the visitors should win, remember the best side often loses. Also bear in mind the visitors appreciate playing before an intelligent crowd. Never 'Chip' the poor person in goal. Remember if he made a mistake he would like to change place with you, who, being infallible, would do so much better. Instead of shouting your instructions to the players, give them in writing your suggestions beforehand, and possibly the players will endeavour to fulfil some. Before complaining audibly, think a lot, and after thinking say nothing.

Two years later the programme carried a full page article giving advice to United fans as to their more general behaviour entitled 'Don't for Spectators' the readers were informed:

The England caps of W.H. (Harry) Johnson awarded between 1900 and 1903

Don't think because you are on the Stand you have a right to shout instructions to players. They know what to do without any assistance from you.

Don't boo at the referee because he gives a decision, which you think wrong. He has his opinion as to what happened, and his opinion is surely worth as much as yours.

Don't commence shouting 'send him off' if one of the opposing team happens to commit a foul on one of your pet players. Would you shout the same thing if the positions were reversed, and one of your own side had committed the offence?

Don't make yourself a nuisance to those around you by continually bellowing at the top of your voice, it gets on people's nerves and takes away a lot of the enjoyment of the game, besides making yourself look ridiculous.

Don't snap your neighbours nose off because he thinks differently to you. You have come to see your side win, and he has perhaps come to see the others.

Don't get excited and bad-tempered when you argue about this player and that. It does no good in the end, and only breeds bad feeling, and spoils your enjoyment of the game.

(October 19th, 1907.)

England shirt badge awarded to Harry Johnson c. 1901

By 1908 the programme told the reader of how one miscreant, who had twice kicked a referee at a game in the Midlands, was sent to jail for a month. People had to lead by example or risked being made an example of. The latter principle saw the above-mentioned miscreant face a jail sentence. The former principle saw United search for a team captain who would lead men to footballing glory. They found just the man in 1891.

The Captain: Ernest Needham

Making his debut for United at the age of 19 in 1891 was the Chesterfield-born Ernest Needham who historians have claimed was United's greatest ever captain. The captain of the United side Needham joined, the Scottish-born Billy Hendry, was targeted by the United Board to provide an on-field drive that many felt the club lacked. Hendry was signed in 1891 from the famous 'Invincibles' of Preston North End and his character and strong leadership laid the foundations for United's ensuing success. In Needham the United board saw similar leadership qualities. In only his second season as captain (1896–97), United finished second in Division One, missing the championship by the narrowest of margins. The 554 games Needham played for United included two FA Cup Final victories and a League Championship. A game against Wales in 1902 saw Needham captain his country for the first time. This was a major landmark in that he became the second player of professional status to do so and the only United player ever to achieve the distinction.

Needham was spotted by United scouts plying his trade for Staveley FC, nicknamed the 'Old Foot and Mouth', a description derived from the way their football was played. The players were renowned for their competitive edge and 'getting a foot in', while the crowd, although small in number, were known for their partisan support. This small north-east Derbyshire village club hosted giants of the era, such as Aston Villa, Derby County and Nottingham Forest but two factors contributed to their demise as a potential League club. One was the small crowds, the village was a fraction the size of Staveley today, built as it was around the sprawling iron works. The second was the decision of the football club to sell part of its land to the railways, which wanted to build the Great Central Railway line to London.

Upon signing for United, Needham was given a handbook of rules and regulations to abide by. This footballer's bible gives a fascinating insight into the life and times of the late 19th century professional footballer. The rules specify:

> The Captain shall return the ball to the Storekeeper immediately on the conclusion of the match.
> Players will be provided with an outfit, and they will be held responsible for any loss or damage sustained to it through neglect on their part. Every player shall look after the football costume and shall keep it clean and in good repair at his own expense.
> In the event of a player requiring a new outfit, or any part of it, he must report to the Trainer, who will note it in his weekly statement to the committee.

The United secretary John Nicholson could be blunt in his appraisal of Needham's performance. The match programme of February 17th, 1900 states: 'Did you ever see Needham so completely at sea as last Saturday?'. However, Needham was soon to win admiration from opponents of international calibre which reflected the fact that he was captain of a side that had won everything the English game had to offer and was an automatic choice for England for eight years winning 16 caps. In 1902 the great C.B. Fry, the Oxonian, Corinthian, Southampton and England player, described Needham in a column he wrote for the London-based *Strand* magazine:

Ernest Needham
The United and England captain

Action from the 1901 FA Cup Final replay
United and Tottenham Hotspur at
Burnden Park, Bolton

*The prince of English halfbacks… an amazing example of genius and science in a game… He is
short and stockily built: and in his ordinary clothes or even in football gear, which hangs rather
wide on him, he has rather an air of solidity. Stripped, however, he is a picture of square thighs, but
small in the ankle and very small in the foot. His head is set low upon rather high shoulders, giving
a finishing air of compactness. He is a concentrated figure, full stored with energy. He wears an,
almost careworn expression…He travels smoothly yet with renewed force from cheek to cheek as a
spinning top cannons from the pins on a bagetelle board… Then he does what he likes with the ball
for the use of his side, always striking without pause exactly the most opportune and negotiable
opening… Valiant and sedulous in defence: ever the busiest man on the field. He seems at times of
stress to multiply himself into several men… He may not have—few Southrons have—the peculiar
hard-hidden, angular obstructiveness of the best Scotch hards; but he has what is equally effective,
an inspired blend of unblinking watchfulness and masterful cunning.*

(February 15th.)

Nicknamed 'Nudger' because of his ability to withstand close contact and win the ball against bigger
men, Needham was considered a master of close control and incisive passing. Standing at only five feet
five inches tall Needham was part of what was remembered as the 'midget half-back line' alongside Rab
Howell and Tommy Morren none of whom were taller than five feet six inches.

Needham played for United for 21 years until he was 39. Two benefit matches were awarded to him, one
against Corinthians in 1898 the other against Stoke in 1907. A fund-raising evening in the cricket pavilion
saw a lecture on the *Pilgrims tour of USA* by Mr Fred Milnes, illustrated with 150 'lantern slides'. Entrance
was sixpence. The relevance of this event to Needham is tenuous, but it was a curiosity that brought in
money. Retiring from the game in 1910, Needham coached United's reserves and scouted for the club, for
how long we are not sure.

Needham led the United team that featured 11 full internationals, ten English, one Irish. Needham also appeared for the Football League team, a selection of the best English players drawn from the Football League. International duty still manifest a pecking order based on social class and reflecting the amateur professional schism. The former category included C.B. Fry and G.O. Smith, who would dine at after match banquets on separate tables from the professionals like Needham.

Needham died from pneumonia in 1936. The whole of Staveley turned out to watch the passing of the local legend and pictures of his funeral made both local and national press. Buried in Staveley Cemetery the inscription on a marble crucifix set atop marble edgings reads:

> *Ernest Needham, Died March 16th 1936, A Beautiful Memory.*

Paying the Slouchers

In 1898, a game against Wednesday produced gate receipts for the United committee of £25. This information was imparted in the match programme. The listing of gate receipts in the programme was regularly done suggesting that the committee had little to hide from the fans. Fans could thus assume the little financial outlay they made went towards paying the players and the upkeep of the ground. The cost of match-going was not prohibitive, by 1907 a 'tiered' season ticket cost between 12 and 15 shillings. For 21 shillings the match goer could have a reserved and numbered seat 'for self and lady'. Those attending could watch a United side chosen from their 30 professional players who no doubt sought ever-better financial rewards for their efforts. The prohibition of the win bonus caused the United directors to ponder the causes of their poor League run in October 1901. The match programme stated:

> *We have still sufficient belief in the integrity of our men to believe that there is some other reason which we have not yet fathomed, and we refuse to believe that a mere loss of money is at the bottom of the trouble.*

Weeks later in the October 12th match programme the suggestion that had been raised elsewhere of a maximum wage for footballers was described as 'a sad mistake', because '…it puts the inferior man on a level with the staff. This is contrary to all business principles, as a man ought to be paid what he is worth'. Furthermore 'If the association do take the matter up, they will make a grievous mistake and practically kill first-class football'.

Suspicions of corruption in the game arising out of arguments between club and players saw United's Charles Clegg sitting in an Emergency Committee Meeting of the FA in March 1904. He voiced his concern that some clubs were ignoring the prohibited bonus payments opining that, 'If such gentlemen fail in their duties how can we expect the game to be kept pure and clean?'. Perhaps realising the futility of the wage imposition he asked the FA at the same meeting to 'rescind the resolution'. In 1905 the FA's Rules Revision Committee proposed a maximum wage of £4 per week for the first year of employment, rising to £6 after two years' service. Possibly to ensure that ambition did not exceed income, the number of players a club retained was to be limited, as were transfer fees. By 1906 a maximum transfer fee of £350 was implemented, described somewhat curiously as a 'salutary rule'. That same year United's match programme told of how 75% of gross earnings at Bramall Lane were spent on players' wages.

The bonus issue remained a controversial topic. In September 1908, at a time when clubs were talking of breaking away from the FA and its restraints and forming a new league, the FA proposed an amnesty to all clubs who had broken the rules of payment. A meeting of clubs in October favoured the introduction of the win bonus, which some argued would raise the standards of the game. The same meeting heard a proposal that the rules of football finance be changed to allow clubs to make their own financial arrangements with their players.

Players could achieve national status, but did not see much in the way of financial benefit. An FA Edict in 1906 stated that FA Cup victories should only be rewarded with medals and that the 'giving' of pianos, jewellery and watches should not be done as a way of supplementing the £200 per annum maximum wage. The players realised that to improve their lot collective action was needed and in 1908 held the first national meeting of the Players' Union. In a closed room, 60 club representatives met, but only eight claimed they had ever received bonuses. Players of this era could upset the more traditionally minded with their sartorial excesses. The United match programme quoted a W.I. Bennett, who had written in the recently published *Book of Football* that:

> *I do not like to see footballers getting £4 a week slouching about in mufflers and dispensing with collars. It brings the game into contempt with the very class we want to draw to our matches.*

(January 6th, 1908.)

Prejudice remained an issue. Charles Clegg resigned as Chair of the FA in 1907 over their threat to refuse membership to professional clubs. Considering the matter as one embedded in the class prejudices of the FA's Southern Amateur representatives, Clegg argued with knowing hints that:

> *The present prosperous financial position of the Association is not due to any exertions of the amateurs, but wholly to the professional element. But these amateur representatives are not above dipping into the funds earned by the professionals…*

A 1907 game between Corinthians and Newcastle to contest the London Shield saw the teams eat a post-match meal on separate tables. Clegg described this scenario as the product of the Corinthian's 'snobbery and priggishness'. The editorial of the United programme stated that if the teams were good enough to play together, they were good enough to dine together. But social class was only part of the story. The men who played the game and those that administered it were often at loggerheads. Sheffield United were no exception.

Labour Relations

The Players' Union challenged FA regulations over their members' rights to go to law over contractual disputes. The issue concerned the end of the maximum wage, the right to free transfer, unlimited bonuses and compulsory benefit games. The primary issue—the right of their members to seek redress in a court of law—was possible according to the FA, but only with their permission. The FA were dismissive of the Players' Union, considering it a one-man show and actually suspended some players who refused to resign their membership. The Federated Trades Union supported both the players' cause and players when suspended by the FA. In 1909 the Players' Union fought a case in law at Croydon Country Court to get professional footballers classified as manual labourers and thus be entitled to benefits under the Workmen's Compensation Act.

The United club secretary used the club programme to plead poverty arguing, 'if these were granted, how many clubs would be able to survive one season, with the debts which are hanging over the majority of the football grounds?' On the eve of the new season a meeting between the FA and players resulted in a truce. Players suspended for industrial action were reinstated. In the early summer of 1909 a County Court judgement decreed that footballers were 'workmen' under the Workmen's Compensation Act. As a consequence, clubs had to insure and protect their employees against injury and under the law had to pay monies when injured. They were also free to place a player on 'compensation allowance' of £1 per week instead of the £4 weekly wage of the footballer.

Men and sheds

United players leaving the temporary changing room at Bramall Lane in 1902

SHEFFIELD TURN OUT PUNCTUALLY WEARING THEIR COLOURS

AND QUICKLY NET A GOAL

COMMON HAS A LITTLE DIFFERENCE WITH ONE OF THE CROWD

WHICH IS AMICABLY SETTLED AT HALF-TIME

NEEDHAM, WHEN SHEFFIELD SCORED THEIR SECOND GOAL

SOUTHAMPTON'S GOAL

FRANK GILLETT

Illustrations from the 1902 United v Southampton FA Cup final

The amicable end to Alf Common's altercation depicted herein was not quite the story as told by others at the game

By 1912, however, the secretary of the union argued that players should not be considered manual labourers to avoid having to make contributions under the provisions of the Insurance Act. This would cost the players 4 pence a week but could provide them with £208 per annum relief if sick. The clubs declined to both pay a player under the Workmen's Compensation Act and allow him in addition to receive the state contributions via the latter Act. Clubs were prepared to pay £3 10s weekly to injured players, 'even if brought on buy his own misconduct or neglect'. The players wanted the extra 10s from the club and the state.

The FA called a special general meeting with clubs in December 1909 to discuss wages. The issue was decided by secret ballot of all players. The United secretary tried to put the issue in context and stated in the match programme, 'the vast majority of professional clubs cannot afford a penny to allocate to dividends for the benefit of shareholders...' adding, 'for every sovereign received by the poor unfortunate shareholders, the players took £133'. United made a loss of £1,292 on the 1908–09 season but had, what they called, a paid-up capital of £18,670. The proposed 1909 meeting never took place. Instead, the Management Committee of the Football League called their own meeting in January 1910 in which they insisted that clubs were to have the right to retain players if they offered them £208 a year.

Amidst all this debate and rancour football was played and United did very well. They won an FA Cup and lost in the final of another. The one they lost was memorable.

Beaten Finalists 1901: Pie Saturday

Some of the names who had built Sheffield United in its early years were at the peak of their careers at the turn of the century. The side during 1904–1913, whilst never really threatening to win anything, were seldom haunted by the ghost of relegation. Finishing 14th in the League in 1900–01, United had some consolation in being beaten FA Cup Finalists. A poor run of just two wins in 15 League games produced questions over the ability of the team. Even so, Walter Bennett and George Hedley were chosen for England and Peter Boyle for Ireland. When the team lined up at Crystal Palace against Tottenham in the 1901 Cup Final the game was significant in that it attracted the largest crowd yet recorded for a football match in England at 110,802.

Many fans left the stadium after 15 minutes due to the discomfort experienced by the packed swaying crowds. The attendance was reviewed months later and the crowd stated in the *Crystal Palace* magazine was 121,815. The 2–2 result thwarted the awarding of the trophy to the victors by General Sir Redvers Bullers, Commander of the British Army in the Boer War. The replay a week later at Burnden Park, Bolton, saw Spurs win 3–1 watched by a mere 20,470 on a day that is part of Bolton folklore.

The shopkeepers and entrepreneurs of Bolton, expecting a massive crowd, had produced huge quantities of pies for the expected hordes. The meagre crowd that turned out meant that the tens of thousands of pies which could not be sold had to be given away—a day remembered in legend and jest in the history of the Lancashire town as 'Pie Saturday'. The choice of venue for the replay was, in hindsight, ridiculous. With no cut-price Football Special rail fares at the time, the journey from London was expensive and arduous. Few travelled the 200 miles. United had few complaints about the result. That said, United director Tom Bott did point out that the players' accommodation the night before the game was next to a factory producing manure and a 'frightful odour'.

United's match scheduling pre and post the final are worth noting. The route to the final saw victories over Sunderland, Everton and Wolves. United were then drawn against Aston Villa in the semi-final. The first semi-final ended 2–2, the replay five days later produced a 3-0 victory. Nine days later United played the final having played a league match at Newcastle in between. The 2–2 drawn final required a replay, played only six days after a league defeat to Liverpool. Two days after the replay United went down 4–0 to Wednesday in front of a crowd of only 11,000 and next day beat West Brom at Bramall Lane in front of a sparse crowd of 1,050.

The final made history on three levels. Firstly this was the first time that a Football League team had lost to a non-Football League club. The Spurs side were members of the Southern League and were to become the first London club to turn professional (whilst still in the Southern League). Secondly this was the first time the FA Cup Final was filmed. A circus poster in Manchester advertised the broadcasting of the game to be shown in cinemas on the evening of the match. Finally, as mentioned earlier, the first game broke all previous FA Cup Final attendance records.

Each of the four runners-up medals displayed in the Hall of Fame tells a story. The one awarded to William Foulke is blank. Like many of his team-mates Foulke did not honour the medal with any personal engravings. Disappointed with not winning the Cup, Foulke was known to have put the medal in a box and placed it in a drawer where it remained for decades. The polar opposite in character to Foulke was

The 1902 FA Cup Final team presented on the Bramall Lane bowling green

team-mate Walter Bennett; his runners-up medal contained the rather curt engraved message, 'From Walter to Lillian Bennett'. The soldering on of a now-removed pin suggesting that the medal was used as a fashion brooch. The engraving chosen by Harry Thickett is minimalist. Only his name is inscribed—a reader would have no idea which club he played for. Peter Boyle's medal reads, 'P. Boyle Sheffield FC' omitting to mention 'United'. Similar to Thickett's, it bears the marks of being converted into a brooch. The disdain shown towards the medals was not repeated the following year. United were taken to a replay once again but this time came home jubilant.

Cup Winners 1902

Whilst United's League form proved inconsistent, they had the consolation of travelling to Crystal Palace again in 1902 for another FA Cup Final, and returning to Sheffield as 2–1 victors (following a replay) over Southampton. In the first game Alf Common scored a goal for United and punched a spectator, who he believed had kicked him. Urged by FA secretary Frederick Wall to apologise to the spectator, Common attempted to do so in the half-time interval. The spectator refused the apology. The Southampton equaliser three minutes from time was believed to be offside. The referee claimed that the ball had struck a United player and so played the opponent on-side. Charles Burgess Fry, known in posterity as C.B. Fry, captained Southampton and was a brilliant sporting all-rounder who played for England in football and cricket. His long jump record stood for 21 years. Less active pursuits produced prolific writings, often on sport; he also stood as a Liberal Party Parliamentary candidate. As a delegate to the League of Nations, Fry was offered the opportunity to become King of Albania as part of the Treaty of Versailles. For some reason he refused the honour.

Whilst footballing success could put a smile on the face of players and fans it did not provide a secure career. In most cases even a trophy winning career did not set a man up for a post-football existence. Moments of philanthropy and generosity are evident in this era from the United directors in the darkest of tragedies, but such monies did not last a life-time. Inevitably, knowing every game could be their last, players became entrepreneurial and some worked the system to their advantage. The pursuit of a good living brought entertainers who knew their worth and played the crowd accordingly.

The Final Shift: Walter Bennett

Walter 'Cocky' Bennett was born in the mining village of Denaby near Doncaster in 1874. The family produced three outstanding footballers. His brother Mick played for Sheffield Wednesday, appearing in the 1890 Cup Final. Another brother, 'Tip' was a professional with Barnsley, while Walter was to become a Sheffield United and England legend. United tried to gain his signature from Mexborough Town on several occasions, but both he and in particular his father held out for the best deal. He finally became a United player in 1896. A right winger described initially as slow and carrying too much weight, Bennett could later be described as having superb dribbling skills coupled with a fine shot. He made his debut in February 1896 at the Hawthorns home of West Bromwich and made eight further appearances that season. Bennett became the mainstay of the United side that won the championship in 1898 and the 1899 FA Cup. Furthermore, Bennett had the distinction in 1901 of playing twice for his country against Scotland and Wales.

Injured during the first 1902 Cup Final game Bennett received a winners' medal after the United board contacted the Football Association to request they award him a medal in recognition of his appearance in the original game. Their blessing made this the first instance of such largesse from the FA. Transfer listed in 1903 Bennett fought his way back into the team but eventually left for Bristol City for a £50 fee to join his old friend and team mate Harry Thickett who was manager. He won a second division championship medal with Bristol but found it difficult to settle in the area and, in 1907, gave up football, returned to Denaby and took a job working down the local pit. One April morning in 1908, having finished his shift and making his way back from the coalface, a huge rock fall occurred. Bennett, aged 34, lay dead with a broken neck under the debris leaving a widow and four young children. (In the year of Bennett's death, a staggering 1,306 men died in pit accidents nationally.)

The Sheffield United squad of 1903–04
Eleven players were of international status,
however, there was not one instance when all eleven played in the United team together

Bennett had received a benefit game in recognition of his service to United in December 1904, the Blades lost 2–1 to Corinthians. Because of poor weather conditions only 3,213 people turned out, thus Bennett did not get the chance to put aside too big a nest egg from the proceeds. After his untimely death, United directors to their credit donated the monies from a match between United and Mexborough Town to his widow. Bennett's remaining family, even in later decades, were not in a secure financial position. The England caps, his England shirt and medals were however kept safe and handed down through the generations. Soon after Bennett's death a nephew received his 1899 Cup winners' medal, which he proudly wore on his watch chain. He was a Barnsley fan, who followed them to a game at Leeds Road, Huddersfield Town. Leaving the crowded ground by jumping over a boundary wall, the leap unknown to him at the time detached the medal from the chain. The medal was lost to the family. Amazingly, decades later, when building work was underway at the Huddersfield ground, workmen discovered the medal. It had been hidden under shale and mud for the best part of half a century. Huddersfield Town placed an advertisement in the regional press announcing the discovery. Through an unbelievable chain of events, the family were reunited with the medal.

The Bennett story continues with later generations. Born into the same mining background, George Maidin spent his entire working life down the same pit that claimed his grandfather's life. Contacted by the Hall of Fame via a fortuitous lead, John Garrett met the elderly man in 2000 at his pensioners' bungalow. Following polite conversation explaining the reason for the visit, Maidin entered the room holding a large battered plastic carrier bag and uttered the immortal: 'There isn't much, but have a look and see what you think!' The items contained were: an 1898 League Championship medal, an 1899 FA Cup winners' medal, a 1901 England v Scotland cap, a 1901 England v Wales cap, a 1901 England international shirt, an 1896–97 Sheffield and Hallamshire cap, a 1904–05 reserve team championship medal, and a 1906 Division Two championship medal from Bristol City. The host was not wealthy, yet, out of sight under a bed in his home, was a treasure trove of football memorabilia worth a five-figure sum. Bennett's untimely death close to a century earlier must have plunged a widow and her children into financial despair. Those who inherited them later must have repeatedly faced the possibility of selling these treasures to pay the rent or place food on the table. That they remained in the family speaks volumes about the respect Bennett engendered. The collection was initially loaned to the Hall of Fame by Maidin (who died two years later) and was then bought for the club by a benefactor.

The 1898 League Championship medal in the Bennett collection celebrates the club's one and only title triumph. The medal, however, tells a story. Upon achieving this most desirable of awards, the United board were mortified to discover that the Football League did not actually award medals at the time—the club had to purchase them for the players. Awarded months after the Championship, arguments raged as to who, amongst the playing staff, deserved one (George Hedley had played four games, but this was not considered enough to merit a medal.). How many medals were made is not known, but they were manufactured by Vaughton's of Birmingham, and the design was based on a template for all clubs who received such an accolade. The medal contains the football club's coat of arms and has the player's name engraved on its edge.

The England shirt worn by Walter Bennett against Wales in 1901 was one of his two full international appearances. The condition of the exhibit is not what it could be; this is because the shirt has never been washed from the day it was worn. The picture, which depicts him in 1904 as one of the 11 internationals in the United team, shows him wearing the shirt along with the cap.

The Daily Mirror 1906 illustrating the cricket crowd at Bramall Lane

The Final Shot: Bill Barnes

A player can change the course of a club's history without ever being aware of doing so. Bill Barnes was born in West Ham, East London in 1877 and joined United from Leyton in 1899, making his United debut against the 'Kaffirs' at Bramall Lane. Over the next few years, Barnes, though an excellent player spent much of his time in the reserves because he played in the same position as Walter Bennett. Barnes patiently waited his chance, watching United win the FA Cup in 1899 and then taking a runners-up medal in 1901.

At that time, the wage most players could earn at a club would be more or less the same throughout the League, so the financial benefit of leaving one club to join another would be limited. There would always be exceptions, but one can imagine that this situation would have led to a generally happy and stable ship. When United reached the Cup Final in 1902, Barnes had played and scored in three out of the four previous games, but only watched United play their biggest game of the season. In the replay United ran out 2–1 winners, Walter Bennett was injured, and the returning Barnes scored the winner.

The traditional Cup Final team picture of the winners with the trophy was never taken. The one that was published is of the side that met Southampton in the first game and so included Bennett. Therein lies a story. After the replay victory, Bill Barnes requested a transfer back to London for 'family reasons'. The request was granted and four days after the final Barnes signed for the fledgling West Ham United in the

1902 FA Cup winners medal

Awarded to Bill Barnes who scored the winning goal against Southampton

1901 FA Cup runners-up medal

Annoyed that United did not win, United's William Foulke left the medal without any engraving in a drawer

91

Bill Barnes, scorer of the
1902 Cup Final replay winning goal

borough of his birth. He had left the United squad before a photograph was taken. United thus became the only club in the history of the FA Cup not to be photographed with the trophy. Barnes' return to London was genuine in as much as he was to join the family silversmith business in East London. He then had a long career with London and southern clubs, playing for Luton, QPR and Southend. Shortly before the First World War he moved to Spain and coached Athletic Bilbao. The First World War began a month later. Barnes enlisted for active service and returned to Spain after the war in 1918 and coached the Basques for three years. He died in 1962.

Barnes had been given the 1902 match ball as a token of appreciation for scoring the winning goal. He used it when teaching his young son how to kick a ball on the flagstone paving in the family yard. Ripped and battered the ball was eventually considered worthless and binned. His 1902 medal is the only one from that final featured in the Hall of Fame. Acquired in 2000, the medal was purchased privately and in good faith. The club were however stunned to discover that it had been missing from the family's possession after a burglary at Barnes' son's home several years previously. Conversations between United and the family took place with South Yorkshire Police acting as liaison. It materialised that Barnes' son was still alive and his 90th birthday was looming. A deal was struck between all concerned and an invitation was accepted to attend a party in his honour in Arundel, Sussex. The family decided that the medal should remain with Sheffield United on the condition that the son could have it in his possession again for a time. The family journeyed to Sheffield the following year to return the medal shortly after the death of Barnes junior.

Fatty: William Foulke

William Foulke was born in the Shropshire mining village of Dawley in April 1874. Within 18 months he was living in Blackwell, a mining village in Derbyshire in which young men like Foulke would finish formal education in their early teens and enter the pit with their fellow villagers. The village had an excellent football club, which won everything locally, and attracted many a spectator. One match in April 1894 was refereed by a man who was friendly with one of United's directors. Impressed by Blackwell's goalkeeper, the referee impressed upon the director the need to sign this player immediately. The player was Foulke. Blackwell Colliery received a £20 transfer fee as Foulke signed for Sheffield United in April 1894 after playing a match at Matlock.

The big man walked more or less into the first team, replacing Charlie Howlett, the United keeper fabled for wearing spectacles. Foulke moved to Sheffield and married at Trinity church on Nursery Street subsequently lodging with the family of his new bride. From the area of his birth, the working-class spelling of his surname was Foulke. Landed gentry with the same name, for whatever reason, added an 's' to the end. His birth certificate states the former spelling. At his marriage, the future Mrs Foulke decided it would suggest more status if the 's' was added. That said, Sheffield United's records maintain the surname as Foulke. The man himself could seemingly not make a preference. His 1899 FA Cup winners' medal uses the spelling without an 's', whereas his 1898 League Championship gong uses it. Non-conformity would always be a byword with Foulke.

Until 1892 goalkeepers could be legally challenged by the opponents. Forwards charged Foulke at their peril. One who did whilst playing for Everton in 1899 needed medical help as a consequence. The United match programme of the following weekend explains the circumstances:

>   ...Lawrence Bell appeared to take a special delight in charging at the burly form of the United Keeper. Whether Bell had any serious intention of succeeding in overturning Foulke we can't say, but on one occasion when the ball was slowly dropping in the United goal, Bell rushed full tilt at the goalkeeper, who calmly sent the ball flying up towards midfield. Foulke then collided very vigourously with Bell, who bounced off the 19 stone of solid matter, and the next item of importance was lifting the too-energetic Lawrence from the ground by the jersey collar with one hand, and afterwards, handing the aforesaid Lawrence over to the Everton trainer for repairs...

In such circumstances, the presence in the goal area of a six foot two man weighing 19 stones who could catch the ball with one hand was a definite advantage. Foulke proved an instant hit with the supporters, and indeed, was selected for England to play against Wales. A degree of eccentricity was evident in Foulke at an early age. Willing to run out of the penalty area to kick the ball clear, he was famed for swinging on the crossbar when play was at the other end. Considered remarkably agile for a man of his size, he would, despite his age, shout at his experienced outfield colleagues.

Two categories of people seemed to annoy him. One was opposition centre forwards, the other was Wednesday fans. One of the former had once threatened, in a pre-match discussion, to take him out of the game. In the course

William 'Fatty' Foulke in FA Cup Final action v Southampton at the Crystal Palace, 1902

THE SHEFFIELD GOALKEEPER TAKES A HUGE KICK

of the match, the same fellow had the audacity to attempt a foul on Foulke, who promptly picked him up by his ankles and dangled him until he pleaded to be put down. In October 1897, United met Wednesday at the Olive Grove ground. During the second half, Foulke received abuse from the Wednesday fans and some individuals overstepped the mark. Consequently Foulke, during the course of play, stepped behind the goal entered their enclosure and 'accosted' several of the abusers.

Sheffield United records during the 1897–98 championship-winning season reveal that Foulke was on a weekly wage of £4. During the summer months, where no football was being played, Foulke took home £3. This was not far behind club captain Ernest Needham who was on £5 per week throughout the year but unlike his team mates, had a £20 bonus written into his contract should the club win the FA Cup. As the club became successful Foulke increased his earnings. He owned his own home close to the ground at a time a house on Shoreham Street cost around £50. As time grew, so did Foulke. His wife fed him well. When the Blades lifted the FA Cup in 1899, Foulke's weight was given at eighteen and a half stones. By the 1901 Final, the figure was in excess of twenty stones and, by the time of the 1902 Cup victory he tipped the scales at a colossal 23 stones.

In 1899, before the FA Cup Final, Foulke was interviewed by the *Sheffield Independent* newspaper and was critical of Balfour, then Tory Prime Minister. This indicates both a political awareness and a willingness to be controversial, neither of which were particularly evident in football circles then or now. He was also renowned for what people at the time called 'foolery', be it with his own team-mates in training or with fellow passengers and railway staff on away journeys. Tales are told of him using coal dust to black up his face and pretend to be a singing minstrel. Other tales recall him arriving at the dining room before his team-mates at away games and eating all 11 breakfasts. On the pitch, meanwhile, his performances were generally excellent. Able to marshall his defenders, he was fearless in confrontations and must have enjoyed both excellent concentration and self-discipline when facing provocation from rival players and fans. That said he was not a man to be riled. The 1902 Cup Final against Southampton at Crystal Palace

THE ASSOCIATION FOOTBA

William Foulke in action as seen by a cartoonist. United wore white shirts and crimson shorts for the Cup Final

saw United denied victory by a goal which, even the goal scorer admitted, was offside. At the end of the game Foulke, in his anger, had tried to wreck the cupboard door in the changing rooms. Stripped of his kit, he had whilst naked gone looking for the referee who hid. Winning the replay saw the Cup returned to Sheffield; however, the maximum wage had recently begun in football and with it the stipulation that no win bonuses be awarded. It also forbade rewards of any type being bestowed on the players. The victorious squad appeared in Sheffield with a crate of champagne obtained by Foulke. So as not to break the rules of the game, Foulke arranged for a bottle to be consumed at each of the players' houses.

Foulke was also a skilled cricketer and played in the inaugural Footballers Only cricket match against Wednesday in 1895. He was thus subsequently to play first-class cricket at County level for Derbyshire where his appearances increased the crowd numbers. Foulke remains on record as both the heaviest ever first-class cricketer and the heaviest ever professional footballer.

A benefit match for Foulke was arranged against Glasgow Celtic. Played on a Monday afternoon, the attendance was a mere 2,500 but the takings were supplemented with a social evening at the Bramall Lane pavilion, which saw 300 diners enjoy entertainment from singers, comedians, female impersonators, a hand-bell ringer and a ventriloquist. Foulke invested the money that football had given him in a general store and a beer house. A daughter was born in 1903 to add to his three-year-old son and as his business boomed so did football. Innovations in the game saw the replacement of the kidney-shaped 12-yard line by the 18 yard box in 1902. The direct free kick and the playing of advantage when it suited the forward

TIE   AT   THE   CRYSTAL   PALACE.

PH CLEAVER.

FOULKE – THE SHEFFIELD GOAL KEEPER

TAKING A KICK

line followed in 1904. Speed was becoming a virtue, Foulke was proving to be an anachronism. Following a bad run of form he was replaced by the 19-year-old Joe Lievesley.

In 1905 Foulke was transferred to a newly-formed club in London by the name of Chelsea. The fee was £50. Six thousand flocked to Chelsea's first home game with Foulke in the line-up. Aware of his crowd-pulling attraction, Chelsea employed men to stand outside railway stations in the vicinity bearing sandwich boards exhorting readers to come and see the 24-stone goalkeeper. The transfer provoked one newspaper to call him 'one of the curiosities of football'. His alleged response on learning this was to state 'I don't mind what they call me, as long as it doesn't interfere with lunch.' Foulke was to continue his crowd-winning antics in London, at one time carrying a couple of small boys under each arm to the delight of the crowd. However, his stay in the capital lasted only a year and returning to Sheffield he signed for Bradford City, but was permitted to train at Bramall Lane. This arrangement lasted a month, possibly because his humour and antics were no longer in keeping with the new professional ethos that was entering the game at the top level. The deterioration in his fitness saw Foulke retire from professional football in November of 1907. Devoting himself to his Sheffield-based business, Foulke was now a spectator at Bramall Lane. His sporting interests were now horse racing and gambling at the pitch and toss meetings at a site overlooking Sheffield City centre. These pastimes and legitimate business interests brought him domestic servants, silk scarves and gold watches.

Foulke was an irreverent character who treated people in a similar manner regardless of their class and status. Team-mate and Irish international Peter Boyle often fell foul of Foulke's attentions on the training pitch. Foulke was known to run up to coach George Waller with his protesting colleague draped across his shoulders to inform him that, 'due to a painful Boyle on my neck, I will not be able to train today'. It was a regular sight to see Foulke jogging around the Bramall Lane pitch with Harry Johnson under one arm and the unfortunate Boyle clutched tightly under the other. A team-mate and close friend, Walter Bennett once had his wages removed from his shoes during a training session. Bennett was distraught to discover his loss with no one seemingly knowing what had become of his money. Several days later the cash was returned with profit by a hysterical Foulke—he had 'borrowed' Bennett's wages to bet on a dead cert at the races, which had romped home. The minutes of Sheffield United board meetings record a request that the coach reprimand Foulke and ask him to desist from gesticulating towards members of the committee sitting in the stand if United were losing. It is also known that Foulke was fond of the occasional pint or two.

Which one's Fatty Foulke?
William Foulke in the Chelsea net with one colleague reluctant to join the team in a co-ordinated arms-crossed pose

William Foulke's Sheffield store and beer shop in his post-football days
The venue was well-known to gamblers, and as a consequence, police officers

William 'Fatty' Foulke
The heaviest professional footballer in the
history of the English game

His beer house, the Kings Head, was a large place with stables. Foulke was an animal lover and any stray found in the area was taken to him for safekeeping. When walking in the town, he was normally accompanied by a large pack of dogs. One night in the Foulke household movement was heard in the stables. Mrs Foulke despatched her husband—possibly the best deterrent to burglaries in existence in Sheffield at that time. Foulke found an invalid with a speech impediment, claiming he was seeking shelter from the weather and meant no harm. The stranger explained that he had lost his job and had been made homeless. Foulke returned to the kitchen to inform his wife that they would have a guest for supper. The following day Mrs Foulke took their new guest to Thomas Wards steelworks where a relative, who was a gate man at the factory, set him up in a job. The man became practically a member of the family, staying with them until his death. The Foulke family paid for his burial.

Foulke's generosity was not appreciated by all in the city. His pub was a venue for illegal betting and he faced police raids. Others, aware of his wealth, burgled his house and stole two of his football medals, one of which was the 1898 League Championship medal which has since been recovered and is now in the Hall of Fame.

It has been written that Foulke died in penury after contracting pneumonia saving penalties for pennies in a Blackpool sideshow. Nothing could be further from the truth. Mrs Foulke had built up a good business and looked after her husband's interests. A pub and shop in prime areas of Sheffield town centre were the cornerstones of the empire; indeed both remained family businesses long after the big man's passing. His granddaughter Selina tells how when the brood were on holiday at Blackpool he came across a sideshow wherein children were invited to take shots at a stall-holder in a goal in the street. Ever the showman, Foulke took off his jacket, rolled up his sleeves and gave the participants a chance to beat the great 'Fatty'. Aged 42, he died in a nursing home in Sheffield in 1916 and legend has it that the doors of the home had to be removed to allow the undertaker to remove the body.

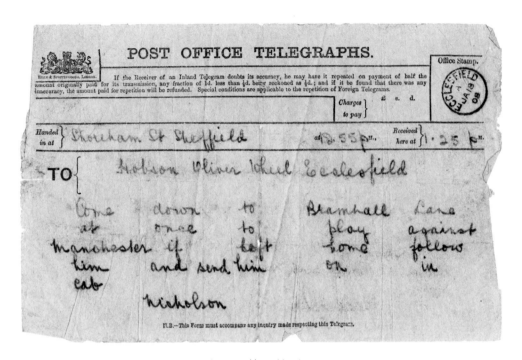

Telegram sent to Judd Hobson
He had 90 minutes to prepare for a match against Manchester United in 1908

Foulke was buried in Burngreave Cemetery in 1916. The streets were lined with people wanting to pay their last respects. The marble headstone reads:

> In Loving Memory of William Henry Foulke, late Goalkeeper of the Sheffield United Football Club.
> Died March 16th 1916.

When his wife died, 're-united' was added to the gravestone. Jimmy Simmons, who scored for United in the 1915 FA Cup Final, was a nephew of Foulke. His great grandson, Richard, played in goal for United's juniors 60 years later.

The Johnsons: The Blades Royal Family

The district of Ecclesfield in the north of Sheffield, once a village in its own right, was once of some renown for the footballers that came from within its boundaries. A once powerful family in that area, the Kirke-Smiths, provided many rectors over the generations for the parish and one of them, Andrew Kirke-Smith, was also an excellent footballer. Several years ago the oldest England international football shirt known to exist, which was worn in the first England international game, was sold for £18,000 at auction. The shirt had been worn by Kirke-Smith. One of the other natives of Ecclesfield, Mick Whitham, became United's first England international.

The Ecclesfield churchyard is the final resting-place of one of the most influential names in the first 50 years of Sheffield United—W.H. Johnson, better known as 'Harry'. Born in the village in 1876 Harry signed for United in 1895 and over the next couple of years forced his way into a young team that was

The Blades royal family c. 1928
Left to right: Tom Johnson, 'Old' Harry Johnson and 'Young' Harry Johnson

fast becoming one of the powers in the English game. Hard working, scrupulously fair, intelligent and having a cheery personality, Johnson played at right half and was famed for his never-say-die attitude. An accomplished player, Johnson was to play 275 games for United and was to win six international caps, notably representing England against Scotland at Bramall Lane in 1903. He also won the League Championship with United in 1898, two Cup winners' medals and a Cup runners-up medal.

Never moving from his roots—his descendants still live in the same house he built on land he acquired over a century ago. Johnson was very much a part of the village life, his caps, medals and trophies were regularly displayed at the church youth club. Johnson's career was finished by an injury sustained at Sunderland in 1906, although he made fleeting appearances in the first team as late as 1909. The end of Johnson as a player signalled the end of the United side which had been so feared and admired. Other players had been transferred or ceased to be the power that they once were. After playing, Johnson became a member of the coaching staff at Bramall Lane, effectively right hand man to trainer George Waller—who happened to be Johnson's next door neighbour—helping United lift the FA Cup in 1915 and 1925. His two sons, Harry and Tom, would also become prolific United servants and would represent the Blades in Cup Finals. The only final appearance not to feature a Johnson in the line-up was the 1915 victory over Chelsea, however Harry was by then United's first team coach.

Johnson's son young Harry made his debut for the Blades in March 1916 as a centre forward. The change in the offside rule in 1926, which ended the careers of many of the 'old school' defenders, saw young Harry prosper. He made 395 first team appearances as a centre forward, scoring 252 League and Cup goals. Leading scorer for ten of his twelve seasons at Bramall Lane, young Harry scored 20 hat tricks and once scored five in a game. He was also the first man to score a hat trick in a Sheffield derby, which he accomplished in an FA Cup tie in 1928. In the 1927–28 season, he scored 43 League and Cup goals including five in one game against West Ham. Two weeks later, he hit four against Arsenal. He missed more chances than he scored, an accusation he always cheerfully admitted to, yet he could score goals that were described as unbelievable. He could also lay claim to being the first United pin up and received fan mail from admiring females. In pictures he is always immaculately dressed, usually in the fashionable plus fours baggy golfing-style trousers, a tobacco pipe clutched between teeth completed the look. Full international honours eluded him, although he did make one appearance for the Football League XI. He also equalled his father's feat of lifting the FA Cup after the 1925 final. Throughout all this young Harry was never a full-time player. A Barnsley Grammar School boy, he qualified as a metallurgist and worked in Hadfield's steel factory. By the end of the 1920s young Harry's career at United was over, his final appearance being against Sunderland in 1931. He joined Mansfield Town, where the goals still flowed, but finally retired as a player in 1936. He maintained the family loyalty to United, taking to the terraces as a supporter in his post-football life.

Another Johnson then appeared. The United policy of bringing forward its own talent paid off with Tom Johnson, born eleven years after young Harry in 1911. Big and sturdy, Tom was completely different in build to his elder brother. Tom joined United in 1928, but first-team appearances were thin on the ground, in fact, at the end of the 1933–34 season Tom's application to become a full-time pro was rejected. A good game on Boxing Day 1935 proved to be the turning point of his career and he became part of the team that powered its way to the 1936 Cup Final. On the morning after one of the biggest personal days of his life, he met his team-mates at Sheffield Victoria Station at 9am to travel to London to play in the biggest game of his footballing career. Tom took his wedding vows on the day before he was to appear in the showpiece game of the season at Wembley. Mixed with the then customary telegrams of wedding well-wishers were telegrams of good luck for the Cup Final. Interestingly the new Mrs Johnson, complete with in-laws, travelled down with the players. United were unlucky to run out 1–0 losers to Arsenal. Johnson played a superb game in the heart of the Blades' defence. In subsequent seasons, Johnson took the mantle of captain and proudly led the club back to Division One in 1939. He remained registered as a United player until 1946. He joined Lincoln City for a brief spell, tempted there by the manager, friend and ex-Blade, Bill Anderson, where he won a Division Three championship medal. In retirement Johnson was employed at the Chapletown-based steel company, Newton Chambers. He died in August 1983.

The family line did not end there. Tom Johnson's grandson, Steve Myles, became a Sheffield United youth team coach in the 1990s, working and bringing along players including Curtis Woodhouse, Lee Morris and Wayne Quinn. One of the greatest encyclopaedias on football and family history was his grandmother, Gwen Johnson. Gwen remembered her father-in-law Harry and the stories passed down from his grandparents of 'footballing' games which took place over a period of days between the villages of Ecclesfield and Pitsmoor, involving anything up to 100 players on each side.

The Game Goes On: Harry Thickett

Certain players' names conjure up images of bygone days. One is Harry Thickett, born in 1873 in a district of Doncaster known as Hexthorpe. Thickett appeared for the first time in a Blades shirt against Grimsby Town in a friendly in January 1891. At the time he was a player with Rotherham Town (a forerunner of the current Rotherham United) but, in these pre-professional days, it was possible to turn out in friendly fixtures for any club. Thickett made several other appearances for Sheffield United that season, the last being against his own side Rotherham Town. He returned to Bramall Lane in 1893 for a sum of £30, this time as a fully fledged Blades player. He walked straight into the United side, a team that had won promotion to the old Division One the previous season. He made his debut in a 3–0 home drubbing by Everton and quickly became a lynch pin of the legendary Sheffield United 'midget' defence. The same defence once weighed in at 50 stones, with Foulke contributing 21 of them, and Thickett and Boyle each carrying 15 stones apiece—it was a heavy but very effective stopping system.

Thickett became one of the mainstays of Sheffield United for the next decade. International honours came in 1899 with a solitary cap gained against the Welsh, along with appearances for Football League representative sides. Thickett won every major honour in English football whilst at United and was widely recognised as one of the best full backs of the era. In 1895, Thickett was struck down by the typhoid epidemic sweeping the country. This caused him to miss the whole season. Thickett, however, fought his way back and was soon representing the Football League XI. Whilst recovering, Thickett attended a United board meeting where he offered to take a cut in wages as he did not feel he had justified the full amount the club paid him due to his lack of availability.

Thickett was known to play when physically not really able to. As United prepared to meet Derby County in the 1899 FA Cup Final, a rumour was put around by a doctor working at the Footballers' Hospital in Manchester, that Thickett had been playing games wrapped in 40 feet of bandaging, numbing the pain with whisky. The doctor soon after retracted the story. What effect this had on the medic's business we will never know but it fuelled the legend of Thickett. He played in the 1902 Cup Final with four broken ribs and, carrying the same injury, played for England against Scotland a week later.

In 1901, 5,103 people attended a benefit a game for Thickett in which United beat Aston Villa 6–2. The editor of the special issue programme described Thickett as a 'grand player with pluck and superior judgement' who intends to 'finish his playing career with United, others need not apply'! The various contributors told the reader of his severe illness in 1895 believed in hindsight to be rheumatic fever. The dedication tells of his willingness to play when not fully fit and how he was the best full back the club had ever had.

Whilst at Skegness with the team in training before the 1901 Cup Final, Thickett learned that his wife had been taken seriously ill. He returned to be at her side as she died, leaving him a widower with four children. Within days, Thickett arrived back at the team's base declaring himself ready to play in the final. His wife was buried in Doncaster General Cemetery days before United lost the replay to Spurs. The club

Sheffield United FC 1903
On the front row, extreme left, is Herbert Chapman, who went on to manage Huddersfield Town and Arsenal to Championship victories

SHEFFIELD UNITED F.C. TEAM OF 1903.

A "Star" reader sends us this photo of the Sheffield United football team, taken at Lowestoft during training for an early round of the Cup in 1903.
Front row: — Herbert Chapman (inside-right), Tom Morren (centre-half), " X," Mr. T. Bott (chairman) "Cocky" Bennett (outside-right), H. Johnson (right half). Second row:—F. Priest (inside-left), George Hedley (centre). Third row:—G. Waller (trainer), Bert Lipsham (outside-left)) Mr. C. Carter, Harry Thickett (full back), E. Needham (half-back), Jack Housley (asst. trainer). Back row:—Bill Foulkes, Peter Boyle (full back), L. Lewis.

had to act in these unprecedented circumstances and it was voted by the board of directors that a sum of £5 be awarded to Thickett.

Thickett played his final game for the Blades in 1904. He signed for Bristol City as a player-coach, but it was not long before he stepped up to manager. With little money to spend Thickett brought several players from Bramall Lane, most notably his long-time team-mate, Walter Bennett and squad player Archie Annan. All the records that still stand today in the history of Bristol City were set under his leadership. They won the second division championship in 1905–06 and in 1909 appeared in their first (and so far only) FA Cup Final. During this golden age, City set a benchmark for success. Their percentage of games won (70%) has been bettered by only one other club since. Their run of 14 consecutive League victories has been matched only by Manchester United (1904–05) and Preston North End (1950–51). In 1906–07 City missed winning the League title by three points. Results in 1910–11 tailed off and an FA Cup defeat at home by non-League Crewe cost Thickett his job. Surprisingly, the fall from favour with the board at City followed his being awarded a testimonial in recognition of his services.

In 1910 Thickett bought a pub in Trowbridge, Wiltshire. A National Service medical exemption certificate, dated June 1918, shows that Thickett had been a member of the Army Reserve of the First World War, but was at this point considered permanently unfit for any further form of military service. Thickett's weight, given by the Army doctor, was an amazing 24 stones 7 pounds, showing perhaps that the post-football life of a licensed victualler was very agreeable. Thickett's life ended at the young age of 48 in November 1920, he was buried in Trowbridge Cemetery.

Dynasty and Tragedy: Joe Lievesley

The north-east Derbyshire mining village of Staveley was, in the early days of English football, a great provider of footballing talent. United's Harry and Thomas Lilley came from Staveley which was also the home of Joe Lievesley.

Signed in 1899 on a free transfer at the recommendation of Ernest Needham, Lievesley went on to become an England international. He joined United as an understudy to William Foulke and the athletic, tall, and calm Lievesley learned from his mentor. When Foulke was sold to Chelsea in 1905, Livesley took his chance and went on to represent the Sheffield and Hallamshire select, the Football League, and England, and was part of the 1911 Football Association tour of South Africa. The tour was ground-breaking in being the first time the Football Association had taken a representative team beyond Europe. On this prestigious excursion were no fewer than three United players; Albert Sturgess, Bob Benson, and Joe Lievesley. (Lievesley's tour cap today hangs on the wall of Champs Bar around a mile from Bramall Lane.) Following their return, Benson joined Arsenal, followed soon after by Lievesley who played his last game for United in October 1912. In what is probably the first team photo of Arsenal at their new Highbury ground, one can see the beginnings of the London-based club attracting established international players. However, things turned sour for Lievesley as a much longed-for child died in infancy. Staveley, family and friends were a long way away and he returned soon after the tragedy.

Lievesley won Cup medals in his career and is remembered as an outstanding goalkeeper in a moderate United team. He was the first goalkeeper at the club to wear a different jersey from his team-mates in response to a 1911 directive from the FA that instructed clubs to differentiate the goalkeeper from the outfield players. Lievesley chose a green jersey, a choice that endured for most of the century in British football. During the First World War Lievesley turned out as a guest player for Chesterfield Town. Also in the team was a brother of Ernest Needham. The pair were caught receiving illegal boot money payments for their services. The club was closed down as a consequence.

The Lievesley's proved to be a famous footballing dynasty but suffered great tragedies. Two of Lievesley's brothers were professional footballers and one son, Leslie, played for Manchester United, Crystal Palace, and Torquay before going on to manage Turin of Italy. Leslie died in the tragic plane crash on the Superga

The 1909 Sheffield United FC line up in front of the John Street terracing

mountain in 1949 which took the lives of 31 people including 18 players who formed the bulk of the Italian national side. Another son died in his youth of tuberculosis. Desperate to save him, Lievesley attempted mouth to mouth resuscitation but to no avail. From this life-saving attempt he too contracted the disease and died shortly after in 1941. Five footballers from the Lievesley family are buried together in the cemetery of Rossington Church, Doncaster.

The Can-Do Man: Billy Beer
Signed by United in May 1897, William (Billy) Beer has the unusual distinction of being the only player in the club's history to write a cantata—a short oratorio for four voices. Confusion surrounds his place of birth—for some it is Saltburn in the North East, for others it is Poolsbrook in north-east Derbyshire. Indisputably he came from mining stock and probably originated in the former and moved to the latter. His name is also a bone of contention. His football league registration spells his name 'Beir' whereas the club consider the correct spelling to be 'Beer'.

Tall and lean with a good shot, he was a forward who moved later in his career to be an out and out wing half. He was actually to play many positions for United after signing professional in April 1898. Making his United debut in November 1897 in a trial versus the Corinthians, Beer was to become a regular and played in the 1899 FA Cup Final scoring the second goal in United's 4–1 victory. In 1901 he began to miss games and despite scoring the winning goal in the fourth semi-final fixture against Liverpool did not make it to the team that ran out in the 1901 Cup Final. Beer was transferred with team-mate Charlie Field to Small Heath (later Birmingham City) and on his debut returned to Bramall Lane in a team that beat United 4–1. Retiring from football in 1910 Beer emigrated to Australia and spent ten years as a sheep farmer. Returning to Britain, he was to manage Birmingham City between 1923 and 1927. Following this he became a licensee. Legend records that as a serious musician and composer, Beer's leisure time was occupied as a church organist. His move to Birmingham was apparently predicated upon the offer of a position as organist in a Methodist chapel. The specific cantata cannot be traced to this former Blade. Whether it was ever performed to an audience beyond regular church-goers has not been possible to ascertain.

The Common Man: Alf Common

Whilst playing for United in 1904, Alf Common was subject to a £400 bid from Middlesbrough which was rejected. An improved offer from Sunderland of £525 saw him make his way to the North East. Within four months, however, Common had signed for Middlesbrough for the first £1,000 fee in British football. The transfer infuriated the directors of Sheffield United who had been very accommodating when told by Common that if he could not sign for Sunderland he would give up the game. Under this emotional pressure, the directors let him go and even wrote a letter explaining their decision to the League Management Committee.

Alf Common
The first £1,000 transfer

Upon returning to Bramall Lane with Middlesbrough in February 1905, Common scored the winning goal. The following month the United match programme of March 11th, reflecting on Common's actions, referred to him as 'the wandering Jew of football' but he remained at Ayresome Park for five years—1905–10. He fell out with Boro over a fee of £250, which had been promised as part of the benefit game. He was stripped of the captaincy when directors learned of his acts of drunken violence. Eventually, aged 30, he moved to Arsenal and later Preston. Upon retiring from football, he bought a pub in Darlington, and lived there until he died in 1946.

Time proved a healer and United seemed to have forgiven Common, describing him in the match programme of September 11th 1915 as 'the famous old Borough war horse had a heart of gold'. A reader learns furthermore of Common distributing fresh eggs and rabbits to the poor and infirm. In February 1918 the match programme tells of Lance-Corporal Common now living in Kent and acting as chairman of the local football committee adding 'he is doing a great deal, not only to keep up interest in the Army, but to uphold the game in its best sense'.

Common could be said to have instigated the transfer deadline system. When he joined United, Middlesbrough were fighting relegation and had not won away from home for two years. They signed four players to avoid the drop. The expense of this ploy worked but many clubs considered this bad form. The FA soon after imposed a transfer fee limit of £350 and inquired into Middlesbrough's finances. Evidence of irregular payments was discovered and Middlesbrough were fined £250. Facing relegation 12 months later, Boro' bought the Derby forward Steve Bloomer and avoided the drop once again.

Brown's Envelope?: Arthur Brown

Born in Gainsborough, Lincolnshire and signed in 1902 aged 17 from his home town club, Arthur Brown was for decades England's youngest debutant. Playing centre forward, this youngster entered a great but fading United team, which between 1904 and 1915 went through a transition, but still finished in mid-table most seasons. In 1908 Brown refused to re-sign for United and demanded a transfer, claiming he wanted to return to Gainsborough for family and business reasons. The family had a builders' merchants and masonry shop which Brown claimed he wanted to join. But money talked and he was then sold to Sunderland in 1908 for a then world-record fee of £1,600.

Brown had a great shot on him and was an opportunist goal-poacher. He was without doubt an excellent player. He was also the youngest player in United's history to receive a benefit match, which produced a sum of £232, at the tender age of 23. After his transfer United and Gainsborough faced questions from the Football League. The latter were found not guilty of trying to poach the player. Clearly another club had tapped Brown up. United invited the FA to inquire into the matter. After the hearing, United had to pay the cost of the FA commission when the latter decided Brown's evidence was 'contradictory and unsatisfactory'. Years later it was discovered that a brown envelope that he had received at Darlington railway station, allegedly courtesy of Sunderland, was enough to buy him a row of terraced houses in his native Gainsborough. The money he earned allowed him to leave the game at the age of 27 to work in the family business.

From Co-op to Pauper: John Lang

Whilst the game brought wealth for some, it did not reward all who pulled on a football shirt. The Glaswegian, John Lang was born in 1881 and by the mid-1890s was turning out for the Glasgow Co-operative Society FC before heading south and signing for Barnsley. Recognised, at what today would be called youth international level by Scotland. United signed him at a time when they seemed unable to win a game. This fast and tricky inside forward scored 13 League goals in 103 League appearances before being transferred to Leicester Fosse in 1908. A benefit match the following year saw him £200 better off. He later returned to South Yorkshire to play amateur football with Denaby United and work down the coal mine. Not much else is known about him, bar the fact that he died in 1934 in poverty and was buried in an unmarked grave in Dinnington Cemetery.

Temperatures Rising: Peter Boyle

Other players negotiated deals to the detriment of dressing-room camaraderie. Peter Boyle arrived at Bramall Lane in 1898 from Sunderland for a fee of £175. The tough tackling full-back of Ireland (and the club's first Irish international), was described in the match programme as a player who:

> *If things are going badly with his side, he tucks up the left leg of his knickers rushes into the fray as if dear life rested on the result.*

No doubt his recklessness wanted reward. He won five caps and an 1899 and 1902 FA Cup Winners' medal with United as well as a 1901 Cup runners up medal. He would have won more caps had he not refused to travel to Ireland preferring to play for United. He scored one goal in his 187 appearances. Boyle's departure from Bramall Lane in 1904 to join Motherwell came in the same year he was twice suspended by United for misconduct. Relations were soured by what Boyle considered a failed promise from the club to reward him with a benefit match. His departure led to acrimony between the player and club being played out in the press. One accusation from the United programme described as 'Mr Mackie's football revelations' suggested that Boyle had received a £60 signing-on fee from United. The accuser was the former manager of Sunderland and Middlesbrough, who may well have been attempting to get his own back on United for their accusations against him when managing the aforementioned clubs. The United Board refuted the allegation as 'absolutely false' (December 26th, 1908). Boyle's son Tommy was in the United Cup winning team of 1925.

Staying Put?: Walter Hardinge

It was not just money that motivated players, some were hard to fathom. The Maidstone-born Walter Hardinge had a reputation with a cricket bat, and eventually played cricket for Kent and England. He also played football for Tonbridge and Maidstone before joining Newcastle United. After ten appearances for the latter he signed for Sheffield United for £350 in December 1907. The claim that he never saw a Football League game until he played for Newcastle is believable because the south was dominated by the Southern League. Undoubtedly a gifted all-round sportsman, Hardinge was also a very bright fellow who opened a business in Sheffield in May 1912, albeit the business might not have met with the approval of the board because he was transfer listed a year later. Playing at inside forward, he was a clever if somewhat inconsistent player. Periodically dropped, he remained an enigma but was good enough to represent England in 1910 and also play for England against Australia in a cricket Test match in 1921. Possibly Hardinge's problem was not knowing what career to pursue. In December 1910, United agreed a £600 fee with Arsenal but Hardinge refused to go south. The transfer circumstances were fascinating. United had initially asked for £700 but the Board's minute book states that they would accept £600. Hardinge had held out for 25% of the fee in excess of the £350 he had cost United. The debate was academic because he refused the transfer. He also declined a transfer to Bolton two years later and when Spurs came in, in the same month, the United directors agreed a £700 fee and promised Hardinge £250 in lieu of a benefit. Hardinge once again refused to go.

Hardinge was eventually transferred to Arsenal in 1913 for an agreed fee of £1,000 which was lowered to half of that in a deal that needed the intervention of an FA commission because of his refusal to sign. We can only speculate that Hardinge could not make up his mind who he wanted to play for. At the same time he was quite precocious in seeking the best possible deal. Perhaps it was no coincidence that during the wartime years he was a Chief Petty Officer in the Royal Naval Air Service and in 1918 was Chair of a meeting that formed the Football Players and Trainers Union. When his playing days were over, Hardinge coached the reserves at Tottenham Hotspurs and later become a director of the company which produced the Wisden Cricketers' Almanac.

Union Dues: Bert Lipsham

United's first ever Players' Union representative was the Chester-born, grammar school-educated Bert Lipsham who was employed in the offices of the Official Receiver when he turned his attentions to football and joined Crewe Alexandra. He joined United in 1901. A fast outside left, he helped United to win the 1902 FA Cup and won three England Caps. When chosen for England in 1902 he took the club's England international quota to nine. Lipsham later qualified as an accountant. An unassuming, well-mannered gentleman, he was renowned for his hard crosses. Astute and business-like, he combined his football abilities with running a tobacconist's shop on Shoreham Street and took out paid advertisements for his cigars in the match programme. He made 102 consecutive appearances in a United career which totalled 259 League and Cup appearances, scoring 34 goals. Lipsham was to become a key player in the emerging Players' Union. He knew his rights but the pursuit of fairness hastened his departure from the Lane. In 1907 he refused to play for United reserves upon returning from injury arguing that this re-introduction was not the procedure for other players. Suspended for a week by United he was soon on his way to Fulham. He was to manage Millwall before emigrating to Canada, seeking the opportunities the New World afforded the enterprising. Settling in Toronto, he helped to spread the gospel of football and was instrumental in establishing the Canadian Football Federation. An eventful life in Canada saw Lipsham survive a rail crash only to lose an arm in a saw mill accident. A tour of Canada in 1962 by the United team was facilitated by Lipsham's family.

The second decade of Sheffield United FC began as well as anyone with affections for the club could have hoped for. The team were Cup Winners, the stadium was improving all the time and crowds were growing. In this new century, football was a national leisure-time fascination without parallel. Only a calamity could change this state of affairs.

The Sheffield United FC line up of the 1908–09 season. A free gift to supporters

Come on my lads and lend a hand. We can do our football when we have done our war

Football Front Lines

The second decade of the twentieth century was a troubled time both locally and globally. In the early years industrial unrest and economic hardship hit the South Yorkshire region badly. By 1915 however employment was available to all men by virtue of a world war. Football had a role to play in both arenas of conflict. The game was encouraged by industrialists in times of social worry and was later to become a recruiting ground for soldiers.

In 1912 pit-managers in the South Yorkshire region organised teams and competitions for striking miners, reportedly to keep the men from trade-union activity. Whether this attempt to deflect men from social activism worked is not known. Similarly, the city's largest employer, steel magnate Sir Robert Hadfield, promoted the game with the intention of combating industrial unrest and, no doubt, increasing the fitness of his employees and implicitly their productivity.

The First World War was declared in August 1914, shortly after the beginning of the football season. The football programme began, but critical questions were raised in Parliament as to this state of affairs. In the *Daily News*, the scout leader, Baden-Powell, spoke out to footballers, reasoning:

> War is the real man's game, full of honour and adventure for those with guts in them. Come on my lads, and lend a hand. We can do our football when we have done our war.

The conflict was to take the lives of a generation of young men.

The decade saw unprecedented standards of living for the vast majority and both football and other entertainment were the beneficiaries. The changing nature of leisure in Sheffield and its associated moralities is evidenced in 1911–12. The Alexandra Theatre advertised in the match programme a twice-nightly production of *The Girl who Knew a Bit*. The same young lady might possibly have got to know a bit about football as well. In 1910, a season ticket at Bramall Lane cost 12 shillings and sixpence and gave admission to 19 first team games. For 21 shillings, one received a reserved and numbered seat that might have admitted the aforementioned as a 'lady companion'. There was a fair bit to watch and commercial considerations convinced the men who ran Bramall Lane to host the Australian rugby team's tour fixture game against a Yorkshire side in September 1911. Those seeking to know a bit had fewer goals to cheer but more technicalities to appreciate. Football was becoming more 'professional'. In the 1889–90 season the average goal per match ratio was 4.67. In 1909–10, the ratio was 2.96 due to better defences and tactics. Despite the absence of goals there was still plenty to read about.

Virtue and Rewards

Crowds were flocking to football and many footballers were assumed to be living a life of luxury. Their hours of work made them relatively idle compared to the long hours others worked in industrial production. Their minimum wage made them the envy of millions. The football clubs had to deal with changing economic circumstances and the rise of player power. But the established football order still had control and showed it when the Football League's Management Committee, somewhat bizarrely, refused to allow a fund-raising game to be played between English and Scottish branches of the Players Union in 1912. The wealth the game was attracting troubled the game's guardians. This was to such an extent that, in March 1914, no transfers were permitted between clubs if the Management Committee

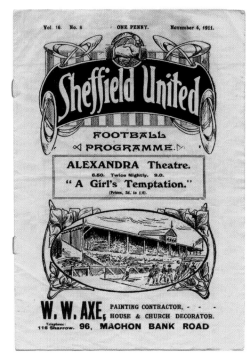

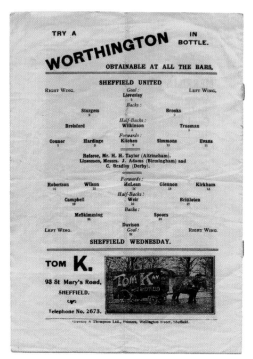

A 1911 match programme v Sheffield Wednesday
Davison, in the Wednesday line up, was later to manage United

considered a transfer was sought for the purpose of obtaining an unfair advantage or was considered contrary to the spirit of league competition.

A better spirit was pursued by the Sheffield United chairman who, in November 1910, spoke of his distress at the habit of some United fans of jeering injured visiting players. An appreciation of the same Charles Clegg in the *Athletic News* of February 1911, spoke of him as a 'wise and sound legislator, a man of few mistakes… straight as an arrow'. This admired and straight-talking man presided over a team with modest lifestyles and habits. A photograph from the club programme of January 1911 shows the United squad enjoying a day trip to Hathersage in Derbyshire.

Players pay and conditions slowly improved in the early part of the decade. In 1910 the FA proposed financial rewards for finishing in the top five of the League and for progressing in the FA Cup. The aim was to improve standards of play, particularly at the end of the season when clubs secure from relegation had few incentives. The money was to be distributed amongst the players. Football and conspicuous consumption were seeking each other out. Perhaps it was no coincidence that September 1910 saw the first advertisement for automobiles in the match programme from a company based in Porter Street, Sheffield.

Football provided an income for others, some of this caused consternation, though for many it was deserved. A 1913 Parliamentary inquiry into gambling concluded that the practice remained a menace to football. The Football Association and Football League lobbied Parliament to legislate against betting on football. In 1920, Sir Henry Norris, MP and Arsenal chairman, drafted the Ready Money Football Act that sought to prevent clubs being associated with coupon betting. At the same time good causes still benefited from the game. The annual charity match between United and Wednesday in 1911 provided £1400 for local projects. But the reality of the players' existence was brought home in the match programme of September 1911. This showed images of former players receiving medical assistance courtesy of J. and N. Blackburn, 'Sheffield's bone-setting specialists', who from their Ecclesall Road surgery claimed to cure 'lameness, footballers' knee, sprains and fractured bones'. Players did not make enough from the game to provide them with a secure post-career existence. Their freedom and pay had still to be fought for.

Building by Numbers

As the team of the Victorian and early Edwardian era began to fade, United struggled to emulate the success of their early years. They became somewhat staid, never actually threatened with relegation but never offering a realistic challenge for honours. The free-flowing and gentlemanly manner in which the Victorians and Edwardians had played gave way to a more competitive ethic. Between 1906 and 1913 United only once got beyond the first round of the FA Cup. This was in 1906 when having beaten Manchester City they were then knocked out by Blackpool conceding home advantage (for a £250 inducement). For seven years in succession United were knocked out in the first round. Between 1908 and 1915 the Club won nothing. Some of the old guard remained, Ernest Needham played an active part until around 1908. Harry Johnson retired to take the role of coach after persistent injury ended his playing days. Other quality players were sourced and became a part of the set up, but things just did not gel. However, in the lead up to the First World War, a team of strength, character and determination emerged. Names appeared that would have a profound effect on the club over the coming years. The end of Ernest Needham's career would rob the club of its leader. Others were to wear the armband, but, in an era when the captain would have a say in many decisions, the special figure to replace Needham was still being sought.

The situation was obviously affecting supporters. The 1912–13 season saw the United secretary lament in the match programme that despite being unbeaten for a two-month period some two years previously,

Season tickets for Bramall Lane 1914–15 and 1915–16

A muscular 1914 Sheffield United line-up with shirts displaying wider red stripes than hitherto evidenced

the six home games in that run produced only one payday for the club of over £500. He surmised that had such success occurred elsewhere, the gates would have been double those at Bramall Lane adding with some pique: 'This proves that Sheffielders are not as keenly interested in class football as in other parts of the country'. The judgement was harsh. In the 1913–14 season total league attendances numbered 378,410 (well up on the 314,051 of previous years). Considering there were 19 home games this produced an average crowd of 19,916. The spectators who did attend faced instruction from those who ran the club. In the match programme under the title 'Do' were listed twenty-five positives for players and fans to seek. Those pertinent to fans read:

> ...conduct yourselves as sportsmen when watching the game. Your conduct to a large extent, is responsible for the conduct of the players...Do not ironically cheer your own side. Football players have feelings, they are as mad as you when they make mistakes or play bad...refrain from making yourself a nuisance to everybody near you by shouting out the names of players and telling them what to do...keep quiet when one of your own players is fouled, it doesn't make things better by advising him to get his own back.

This was not the first such instruction—neither would it be the last. However there was behaviour more consequential afoot which threatened the very existence of the game and the lives of its players.

The Great Sacrifice

Entering the war in 1914, Britain was the only participant without compulsory military service. The Football League continued despite calls to suspend the game to permit all young men to volunteer. The FA in response allowed the War Office to recruit in football grounds during the half-time interval. Military bands marched on the pitch and potential recruits were asked to enter the field of play and march behind the musicians to the nearest recruiting station. The Bramall Lane pitch was used both to recruit and, during the war, to teach drill to battalions before being sent on active service. But the numbers joining at football grounds were not as large as the War Office hoped.

Blank pages appear in the United match programme in the 1915–16 season. On such pages were the words 'To Let'. The First World War was a reality and was affecting football. In 1915, the football league programme was suspended and was not to resume until 1919. Regionalised football saw United as one of 14 clubs in the Midland League. There were some 5,000 professional footballers existing in Britain at the time and many were to join their contemporaries on the battlefields of north-east France. Many never returned.

Football could be played, but no player was to receive payment for playing. Somewhat remarkably, Aston Villa, Birmingham and Wolves, as well as Blackburn, Sunderland and Newcastle did not operate teams during the war-time period. No matches could be played that necessitated long journeys and clubs and local authorities could refuse games if they considered it would disturb the production of munitions. There was to be no League Championship Trophy or medals, league football was to exist only on a regional basis. Players were allowed to play for clubs in areas they might have moved to as part of military service. A percentage of the gate money from matches was handed over to the Football League to be distributed to war charities—the Midland League gave five percent. By the end of the 1914–15 football season, only seven clubs from England and Scotland had a balance to the good. Some of this loss of earnings may well have been a consequence of the largesse of the clubs towards injured players. The United match programme of September 16th, 1916, informed readers that the club guaranteed £3 a week to its players, irrespective of average earnings. Furthermore that when a United player was injured, the club would pay, subject to the consent of the FA, the full amount he would have lost whilst off work, the commendable spirit was explained in the match programme:

> *The players give their services, and it is only reasonable that they should not be the losers if they are prevented from working caused by injury whilst playing for the club.*

The war was not going well, and by December, 1916, all unskilled males under the age of 31 were pronounced eligible to join the army. The United secretary stated that this ruling would have implications for football clubs but did not expand his presumed doom-mongering. Still permitting the game to continue, the Government permitted footballers to attest their willingness to serve their country and thereby avoid conscription. Throughout the country attendances at football fell by about half and the Football League drew up a wage-cut scheme for players: those on the maximum £5 a week had their income reduced by 15%, those on £4 and £3 took a 5% cut. The monies were put into a fund for clubs in difficulty.

Sheffield United made a significant contribution to the war effort and during the course of it had no fewer than 15 players on active service. The war provoked pathos. A letter appears in the United match programme of October 21st 1916 from a soldier appealing to the club to send a match ball to the front line. Some of those who could kick a ball on the front line were never to return. Jack Nuttall, a former United reserve, was one of the first to join the Footballers Battalion. (At the end of 1914, Sir George McCrae, Chairman of the Local Government Board of Edinburgh, called for footballers to volunteer and fight together. The outcome was the 18th Battalion of the Royal Scots.) Nuttall was to contact United to inform them of the death in action of Jimmy McCormick, a former United player who had attained the rank of sergeant. United's secretary wrote in the match programme: 'He paid the Great Sacrifice'. In April 1917 the United winger Jimmy Revill, a Lance-Corporal, was killed in action having left United after five years' service. For such men, and the millions of others who died alongside them, a war charity match was held at Bramall Lane on New Year's Day 1916 and another on Easter Monday 1917. The latter was between Hadfield's and the National Projectile Factory, with money going to local war charities. A further charity match at Bramall Lane aimed to raise money to buy an ambulance and saw 5,000 cigarettes distributed to the wounded soldiers in attendance. The widow and family of Jimmy Revill received £130 following a benefit match in January 1918.

1915 FA Cup winners medal
Awarded to Bill Cook who also
achieved a similar honour in 1925
(Courtesy of Dora Winter)

1912 Cup winners medal awarded to George Utley
(Courtesy of Martin Utley)

Towards the end of the 1916–17 season, United had to ask the management committee of the Midland
League for financial assistance to the sum of £50 to allow them to carry out their fixtures. In the same
month, the recruiting age limit was raised to 41. When the season resumed in the summer of 1917,
soldiers on leave were commanded by army order not to travel any distances to play matches. Some got
round this by playing under a *nom-de-plume*. The war years saw games between Leeds and Sheffield
United become famed for their brutality, but it was cash rather than kicks that caused most consternation.
Clubs throughout the country were pleading poverty and pondering the possibility of corruption. The
absence of money in the game provoked the possibility that players were accepting bribes to throw
matches. A report published in February 1918 raised this issue in Scottish football despite the Scottish FA
permitting a payment of £1 per player per match for all players. In late October 1917, some of the English
clubs complained about the measly 20% of gate receipts they received at away games. Asking for 25%, the
request was refused by the Football League. United claimed that they gave visiting clubs over and above
what they received when they were visitors. At Bramall Lane the 1916–17 seasons' deficit was £210, the
early part of the 1917–18 season had already produced a deficit of £90.

At a time of war and the deaths of millions one could argue there were far greater beneficiaries of the
limited money in society than football clubs. Football however played a role in recompensing the families
of the fallen. The Football National War Fund begun in 1917 provided assistance for dependants of
footballers killed or injured in war. The FA donated £5,000 to it and the Football League gave an unspecified
sum. Benefit matches for the fund were permitted in May and August. At the same time, the stipulation
that wartime football was to be played without cups, medals and trophies was withdrawn. Many felt that
the FA Cup should also be placed in mothballs over the duration. Others in higher places saw it as a
valuable morale booster during these dark times. The competition over the 1914–15 season took place as
usual.

The Khaki Cup Final

The 1915 FA Cup Final between Sheffield United and Chelsea at Old Trafford was played whilst the world was at war. The Cup Final programme of this historic fixture is one of the most sought after for collectors. The programmes were bought in their thousands by soldiers who attended the game whilst on leave. Tragically, many were retrieved from the bodies of the thousands who died on the battlefields of the Somme and Ypres weeks later. The programme was the standard format for league matches at Manchester United, but contained a three-page insert relevant to the final. Ambivalence around the fixture was manifest in the local media. The *Sheffield Morning Telegraph* stated that United's participation brought shame on themselves and the city. By contrast, the *Sheffield Independent* stated that the game manifested the best of 'British Gold'. Part of the crowd included members of the Sheffield Pals Battalion (one of the many hundreds of Pals Battalions consisting of life-long friends) that was to lose 513 of its number a year later in active service.

The Blades arrived in the final having beaten Blackpool, Liverpool, Bradford Park Avenue, Oldham and Bolton Wanderers in the semi-final held at Ewood Park, Blackburn. The final, held on a late April Saturday, attracted 49,557 to Old Trafford, the usual venue of Crystal Palace having been requisitioned as a troop camp. It was the first and only time that Old Trafford hosted a Cup Final (although it hosted Cup Final replays in 1911 and 1970). Torrential rain and fog did not deter the crowd, many of whom wore their

A Final Glance: Military personnel in attendance at the 1915 FA 'Khaki' Cup final

The 1915 FA Cup Final programme
The team details were inserted into the cover of the existing
Manchester United programme

military uniforms. The preponderance of such attire
described by one witness as a 'sea of khaki' saw the
game commemorated as the Khaki Cup Final.

United's opponents were only a decade old and
playing their first ever final. Struggling in the League,
they were no match for the Blades who won 3–0 with
goals from Simmons, Fazackerley and Kitchen. The
United captain, George Utley, received the Cup from
Lord Derby whose speech alluded to the War effort
and urged everyone to 'go out and play a sterner
game for their country'. A low-key celebration in a
Manchester hotel ended the day. Many commentators
at the time argued that had the war not intervened to
disrupt football, United could well have dominated
English football for the next five years.

Many would argue even today that the game should
not have been played. The most vociferous opposition
came from the religious lobby and the Labour Left.
Aware of this sentiment, the victorious United team
returned to Sheffield relatively anonymously,
alighting the train without a reception committee
and went home somewhat surreptitiously in a fleet
of taxis awaiting them by the Wicker Arches. There
was no celebratory dinner. The FA Cup was taken to
Bramall Lane and remained in the John Street Stand
for the next five years, because the Cup competition
was suspended shortly after and did not resume until
1919–20. The sombre photograph of the victorious
United team reveals a reality that saw celebration not
in tune with the world's situation. Told not to smile,
the United team, whilst obviously proud of their
efforts, had to be seen to be at one with the national
mood. When the war ended the United team and
Directors held a celebration dinner in the Bramall
Lane cricket pavilion—five years after the day.

The Khaki Cup Final match programme exhibited in
the Hall of Fame is one of just seven known to have
survived. The publishers of the programme presented
the day as a competition between the 'Cutlers' and
the 'Pensioners'. The United team contained nine of
the men who reached the semi-final in the previous
season. The line-ups for both teams is interesting in
that for Chelsea the tallest player stood at 5'11' while
for United the tallest is described as nearly 6'. The
population were smaller then compared to today and
football teams reflected this. Advertisements in the
programme allude to the war and depict two smiling
soldiers enjoying 'super leather dry soles' on their
boots. Elsewhere, an advert propounds the virtues of

sterilised Milk Stout which, a reader learns, contains more nutrients than a glass of milk and, being sterilised, is free from the dangers that accompanied milk drinking at the time.

Labour Relations

Sitting behind a prominent former Labour MP, professional Yorkshireman and Wednesdayite at a football conference in London in 2000, one could not help but overhear some interesting views he was putting across about the roots of the two Sheffield football clubs. The crux of his opinion was that the early fan base of Sheffield United was drawn strongly from the Catholic Irish immigrant population, focused around the old Scotland Street area of the city. The basis of his argument was that, because of the number of Irish players drafted into Sheffield United, in particular Billy Gillespie and later Jimmy Dunne, the Irish swore allegiance to the Blades. By contrast Wednesday were the team of the indigenous.

Two facts stand out; undoubtedly Gillespie and Dunne are two of the greatest players to pull on the red and white stripes, but Gillespie did not become a Blades player until 1911, 22 years after the birth of the club. This would mean that the fan base of the club would have been more than decided on its own criteria. It would, however, be fair to say that the Irish internationals who have played for the club have left their mark for various reasons. Probably none more so than Billy Gillespie, who played for United in 448 league games, scored 127 goals and played in the Ireland teams of 1913 and 1914 that beat England.

Whilst Gillespie's migrant status is interesting he is just one of many players of this decade that not only handled themselves well on the football field but could also negotiate a good deal from football club owners. A variety of individuals are hereby presented whose strong-minded individualism in some instances got them great rewards from the game yet at other times saw them effectively have their career ruined by falling foul of the club and its moralities. Some stretched the boundaries of the criteria for international representation. Yet others fell foul of local 'hard-men' and the football disciplinary system. Amongst these public lives a native of the South Yorkshire region was putting what he had learned while a player at Bramall Lane to good effect elsewhere. The actions of some of the lives that follow changed aspects of the English game forever.

Billy Gillespie

Irish Eyes: Billy Gillespie

Billy Gillespie was born in Kerrykeel, County Donegal in 1891, the son of a policeman. Playing football with Derry Institute, he was poised to sign professional forms for Linfield when the now defunct Leeds City made their move. Gillespie's father was dead set against his son becoming a footballer, wanting him to get a proper job or trade. But the lure of a wage that, even in those days, would have been far greater than his father's won the argument. Gillespie signed for Leeds in 1910. His signing for the Blades came about via the man he was eventually to replace. The great Ernest Needham had not given up his United playing career lightly, and was still appearing for United's reserves into his forties. A 1910 game pitted Gillespie against 'Nudger', and Gillespie, playing in his role as a striker, tore the old stager inside out. Needham informed the United management that they must make every effort to sign the player. A fee of £500 was agreed. The transfer nearly collapsed when the wily Gillespie refused the terms of £4 per week offered by United's secretary John Nicholson, Gillespie insisting on £5.

Two International caps awarded to Billy Gillespie

Legend has it that the young man shook Nicholson's hand, thanked him for his interest and began to leave the room. It was at this point that Nicholson found the extra pound. It was to be money well spent.

Gillespie was a bedrock of United teams between 1912 and 1930, initially as an inside forward and later as a midfield general. He was a magnificent captain who inspired many a United team to Cup heroics. He made his Blades debut on Boxing Day 1911 away at St James' Park, Newcastle. The Blades drew 2–2 and Gillespie scored. He was to score 14 goals in his first 27 games. Two years later Gillespie won his first full Irish cap when he scored both goals in Ireland's 2–1 first ever victory over England. The following season saw Ireland win the Home International Championship for the first time and the Irish defeat England 3–0 at Ayresome Park, Middlesbrough. The final cap of his 25 was awarded when he was 40. He scored 13 times for Ireland. For United he proved to be one of the final pieces in a jigsaw that George Waller and John Nicholson had been building. Gillespie would have added a 1915 FA Cup Winners' medal to his haul of trophies but for a broken leg sustained in the first match of the 1914–15 season against Sunderland that kept him out of the game for a year.

War service robbed many players of their best years. Gillespie enlisted with the Irish Horse Artillery, and made fleeting appearances for United when on leave. He returned post-war to a Sheffield United team that would have to rebuild. The man that returned was instantly recognisable to football fans and sports cartoonists for years. The man who had gone off to war had a full head of hair, the one who returned did not. The bald head and stern appearance that seemed to radiate a calm authority began a new chapter in United's history.

Gillespie made a comeback with United in 1919 when the League resumed and was a central figure in the United side that avoided relegation in 1920 and 1921. Whilst he remained the kernel of the team, the arrival of new players transformed United. Old and experienced heads such as Bill Cook and Harold Gough were joined by locally produced young and exciting talent such as Harry Johnson. Fred Tunstall and David Mercer arrived from Scunthorpe and Hull respectively and their wing play saw them both capped by England. Tunstall played 491 games in the red and white, whilst Mercer turned out 250 times.

George Green joined a midfield combination that became formidable in the English game. Green, a ball winner, played alongside Gillespie and Tunstall, the latter was exceptionally fast, Gillespie had brilliant distribution.

In 1923 Gillespie accepted the captain's armband from Albert Sturgess who left Bramall Lane for Norwich after 15 years service. The broken leg sustained in 1914, coupled with the years lost to the war, changed Gillespie from being a nippy out and out striker into a clever inside forward. He was one of the first of a new breed of footballer; deep thinkers who would study the opposition closely, seeking the best way of inflicting damage. His passing was legendary, and he used the long ball to switch defence into attack instantly. Gillespie's first English manager, Herbert Chapman at Leeds, is often credited, especially with his great Arsenal side of the 1930s, for revolutionising training methods and tactics. However the effect that the thinking employed by Waller and Needham had on the game, and in particular on the young Chapman in his time as a United player should not be forgotten.

In his first season as captain Gillespie led the Blades to the semi-final of the 1923 FA Cup, meeting Bolton Wanderers in a game played at Old Trafford. The gates at the ground were forced, the official attendance was 72,500, but the true crowd was believed to be well over the 100,000 mark, a record at the time of any game staged outside the capital. United lost to a David Jack goal, one that cost the Blades a chance of meeting West Ham United at the first-ever final played at the newly-built Wembley Stadium. It would only be two years before Gillespie led United to victory over Cardiff City in the 1925 final. Along the way the team disposed of legendary amateur side Corinthians, then Everton, West Bromwich Albion and Wednesday. United held the advantage of being drawn at home in every round. The semi final against Southampton took place at Stamford Bridge. United ran out comfortable 2–0 victors.

Team selection in this era was a task conducted by the Directors, George Waller and probably the captain. In the Wembley dressing room before the FA Cup Final, some twenty minutes before kick off a decision was made to replace Tommy Sampy with Tommy Boyle, son of the former United Irish international and Cup-winner, Peter. Years later, Sampy, a great Blades servant would give differing accounts of how the selection affected him. In some interviews he reasoned that in the same circumstances, he would have made the same changes, given that Boyle had been in better form. Other stories suggest that the late change left a bitter taste. Sampy would later be quoted as saying that his whole football career was a complete waste of time, whereas in other interviews he stated that would not change a thing. Although we have no proof, it has been said that the club wanted Boyle to have the chance of mirroring the success of his father. The Irish connection might also have played a part in Gillespie's reasoning. Boyle's team mate on the day, Harry Johnson, was the son of former United cup winner and England International Harry Johnson senior. Thus two sons of two previous United finalists wore the United shirt that day.

Gillespie was to carry on his leadership of the Blades on the field until the 1931–32 season when he handed the armband over to George Green. He had taken United to another titanic semi-final battle in 1928 against Huddersfield Town, which covered three ties played at Old Trafford, Goodison Park and Maine Road watched by a then record number of spectators.

18ct gold pocket watch presented to Billy Gillespie by the Irish FA in recognition of their winning the Home International Championship 1913

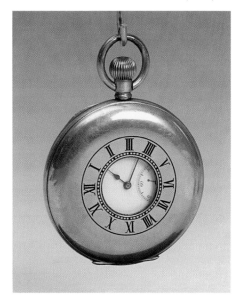

He left United in 1932 to manage Derry City in Northern Ireland. To this day the club plays in the red and white of Sheffield United in appreciation of the set of shirts that Gillespie took with him as part of the deal.

Bizarrely, as war broke out in Europe in 1939, Gillespie returned to his beloved Sheffield, living in the Abbey Lane area and did his bit for the war effort in the steel factories and munitions plants. His house received a direct hit. Remarkably the trophies of his illustrious career survived unscathed. His wife died tragically young in the late 1940s and was laid to rest in Abbey Lane cemetery, just a short walk away from the family home. The surviving family lived for a time in Germany finally settling in Bexley, Kent from where Gillespie became a United scout. Reporting on players and meticulously working out his expenses, Gillespie worked for the Blades in this capacity until his 80th birthday. Shortly before reaching the age of 90, Bob Wilson and *Football Focus* interviewed Gillespie as the oldest surviving captain of a Cup Final team. The interview was conducted in the calm of his own living room and provided three hours of the most intact account a viewer could ever hope for.

One evening shortly after the interview, Gillespie bade the family good night. As always, his Cup Winners' medal was hung on his fob-watch chain in his pocket. The following morning the family found he had died in his sleep. His funeral took place in Sheffield—the city he felt was his own. His surviving family loaned the Cup Winners' medal, an Irish international shirt, his Home International winners' watch, his Sheffield United pocket watch, and a selection of Ireland caps insisting that, if there was to be a museum at Bramall Lane, Gillespie would be a part of it.

Benefit and Doubt: George Utley

The missing piece of the jigsaw for United in this decade was George Utley who was to captain the club to national honours. Utley was born in the village of Elsecar near Barnsley in 1887. Local football brought young Utley to the attention of Barnsley FC; he was to make his professional debut for them in 1906. Utley was to become part of a golden era for the Oakwell club. Gaining a reputation in football as tough as the mining town from which they heralded, Barnsley were to play in both the 1910 and 1912 FA Cup Finals, running out losers in the former, against Newcastle at the Crystal Palace, and as winners in the latter against West Bromwich Albion. The first game against the Baggies was drawn and it was decided that the replay would be held at Bramall Lane. A crowd of just under 40,000 turned up to see the Tykes run out as winners. The ever-impressive Utley stood out to the watching United directors and he was soonto become United's midfield general and captain.

Utley is the only Barnsley player to win a full England cap. In recognition of such ability United paid £2,000 for his signature in November 1913. His skill initially attracted the attention of United's Billy Gillespie, who wrote a letter to United secretary John Nicholson recommending the club buy him. The fee paid equalled the record transfer fee of the day and such was the club's desire to have him that Utley was given an unprecedented five-year contract and promised a benefit game at the end of it.

With a characteristic hard shot, long throw and physicality Utley was to play in midfield for England eight times. He remained a Lane regular until 1922 when he departed for Manchester City before eventually joining Fulham as player-coach. Later Utley managed Bristol City before becoming a games teacher at a public school. Utley continued his involvement in football by scouting for his old friend and former Bolton Wanderers legend Joe Smith at Blackpool and was responsible for the transfer of post-war United favourite Eddie Shimwell to the Tangerines, along with Blades and Owls' favourite Walter Rickett.

The achievements Utley attained in the game were to find their way into the Hall of Fame via a degree of controversy. The 1915 Cup Final medal was given to a family member in Bolton. In 2000 a call to the club from a John Utley living in West Yorkshire revealed that he had been left the Sheffield United medal by his father—the brother of Utley—who had been a police officer and one of the infamous 'flying squad' gang busters in 1920's Sheffield. Legend in their side of the family has it that Uncle George once got into difficulties whilst swimming. Rescued by John, the grateful George promised him the United medal. Other items now in the care of the Hall of Fame provoked family anger. In the early 1960s Barnsley FC held an exhibition of memorabilia in a town-centre hotel. Loaned to this collection were the Barnsley Cup Final shirt, England shirt and caps and other memorabilia. However everything was stolen. The shirt on display was discovered behind a bar in a pub in Hoyland. The Utley family never forgave Barnsley for their negligence and years later were happy to give what remained to the care of Sheffield United.

Utley died in Blackpool in 1966. Astute in financial dealings, he married a wealthy woman following the death of his first wife. There were no children from either marriage and when the second wife died he gave her money to her family, arguing that he had enough and they could distribute it as they pleased. Utley's palatial home was attended to by two housekeepers. In his will it was stated that regardless of who inherited or bought the land the two were to remain in a house on the estate for the rest of their days on a peppercorn rent.

Utley's legacy to the game was primarily off the pitch. He could be said to have changed the face of benefit and testimonial games in British football, even to this day. The procedure at the time Utley signed was for players to negotiate wages and benefits. The usual practise for a long-serving player was for them to take the gate receipts from one match that was not a derby game or against a big club. This was challenged by Utley, then aged 32 in early 1920, who not only chose the then mighty Sunderland as the opposition but was granted a benefit after only four seasons and not the usual ten. He was by virtue of the big gate to receive around £1,000, a phenomenal sum for the time. That the United board were prepared to move

Sports science 1914
The United squad training in the ballroom of the Norbreck Hydro Hotel, Blackpool, before the 1914 FA Cup semi-final
The trainer-coach George Waller stands besuited rear left

Frolics in Lytham. The United squad relaxing in 1914

the boundaries for him suggests that his presence at the club was considered crucial. Considerable dressing-room unrest was however created by this event.

In late February 1920, Sheffield United directors received a letter hand-written by the team captain, Billy Gillespie. Sent to the club secretary, but addressed to the 'Sirs' that constituted the board, the subject was Utley's benefit. It pointed out that not only had Utley been at the club less than five seasons but also his choice of opponents broke with a tradition that prevented players choosing 'big' games or derbies for their benefit. The letter begged to seek the reason for what the signatories considered preferential treatment 'seeing that in regard to service he is less entitled to a benefit than some of the undersigned'. A total of nine players, professing to be 'your obedient servants' signed the letter. Curiously the first page turned over onto page three then continued on what is page two. The letter is also signed at the bottom of page two. Four days after the letter was written, United beat Sunderland 3–1 in front of 36,000 at Bramall Lane. For reasons we do not know Utley did not play, Billy Gillespie did—and scored a hat trick.

Utley had his promising career somewhat ruined by the war. Being a key player the club were anxious to keep him. It would seem they were prepared to bend benefit procedures to give him a good payday to prevent him leaving. Via a source at Bramall Lane the Football League found out about the players' unrest. As a consequence of this letter, the benefit system changed forever. Since that day clubs have had a signed benefit payment arrangement after an agreed (and written) duration of stay. Alternatively a club may award a benefit, which has not been written into a contract as recompense for unexpected termination of employment—for example a career finishing injury. George Utley was obviously satisfied with his payday. He remained at Bramall Lane for another two years.

24.2.20

To :- The Directors of Sheffield
United Football Club.

Sirs,
Having noticed
in this morning's paper
that Saturday's match,
versus Sunderland, is to
be set apart for Utley's
benefit, we, the undersigned
beg to ask the reason of

this exceptional proceeding
We had been given
to understand that no
player was to have a
definite match set apart
for his benefit; but that
a fixed sum, as has been
given in the case of other
players, was to be guaranteed.
This has naturally
caused some dissatisfaction
among the players in
general, for why should

Utley have preferential
treatment, seeing that,
in regard to service, he
is less entitled to a
benefit, than some of
the undersigned,
We remain, Sirs,
Your obedient servants
W. Gillespie
W Cook
J E. Kitchen
A. Sturgess   H H Pantling
S. Fazackerly   WH Brelsford
                 J Simmons
                 H. Gough

Fortitude: Albert Sturgess

Sturgess was a tough player who knew how to fight his corner. In the first of his 15 professional seasons whilst at Bramall Lane he earned 7s/6d a week but had no summer pay and claimed he could not afford to marry. He thus threatened United with enlisting in the Army. This threat got him a £10 on the spot payment, a further £5 later and a marriage at the end of the same week. The 1915 Cup Winner was renowned for playing despite injuries and had his own remedy for strains: 'strap a hot brick, wrapped in a thin cloth around the muscle'. Sturgess signed for United in 1908 from Stoke. He stayed until 1923 when he joined Norwich. In this year, aged 40, he had become United's oldest League player and at Norwich became one of English football's oldest ever debutants. A first class professional who gave 100% every game, Sturgess was a reliable and consistent player. He played in every position for United and played twice for England in 1911 and 1914 at right and left half reflecting his ability with both feet. He also toured South Africa with the England squad in 1910. He returned to Sheffield after Norwich and ran a bone-china shop on Ecclesall Road. He died in the city in 1957.

Border Crossings: Bob Evans

The caps of Bob Evans on display in the Hall of Fame belong to a man who had the rare distinction of representing two countries at international level. Born in Chester to Welsh parents, Evans was originally capped by Wales when playing for Aston Villa. Bought by United in 1908 from Villa for an unspecified fee, his abilities on the left wing brought him to the attention of the England selectors. The United club secretary, John Nicholson, argued that as Chester was in England, Evans qualified to play for England. Records for international selection were not what they are today and as a consequence Evans later turned out for England. Sheffield United records give no explanation as to why he decided to change nationality, or the reaction from his team mates. His last game for Wales was against England at the Racecourse Ground, Wrexham. His first appearance for England was against the Welsh at the same venue. He won four England caps in total but all reports state Evans always regarded himself as a Welshman.

Evans also had the distinction of being a key part of the 1915 FA Cup winning team and made a total of 220 appearances, scoring 39 goals for United. Curiously, records show that Evans played for Sheffield United away at Bolton in April 1915 and did not appear again for the club until a game against Wednesday in December 1918. This may have been down to him playing his part in the war effort or injuries or a combination of both. He made his last Sheffield United appearance in a 3–0 victory over Sheffield

Wednesday on Boxing Day 1919 at Bramall Lane. His FA Cup Winners' medal and a Wales and England Cap were bought by the club from Christie's auction house in 2000.

Forging A New Career: Jack English

Jack English joined United in 1913 from Watford. Born in the North East he was first spotted by Preston and then joined Watford. After less than a year in the south, United bought English for £500. He eventually left United on a free transfer in May 1923. A hard-tackling full back with a fine footballing brain, English's cerebral abilities were matched by terrific pace and precision passing. His full-back partnership with Bill Cook was respected throughout the game. When he finished playing, English went into football management, firstly with Nelson then with Exeter and Northampton. At the latter he is remembered as one of the most successful managers in the club's history. His son, also called Jack, holds the all-time goal scoring record at Northampton for his feats in the 1950s.

English played an international trial game but never gained a full cap. He did, however, represent the Football League and played in a wartime charity England-Scotland international. A neat player and a heavy smoker, he insisted on a two-year contract on joining United. He was also unusual in playing his final game for United in 1916 but not leaving Bramall Lane until 1923. Herein lies a story.

During the First World War English returned to Durham and worked in the shipyards and played in a factory team called Darlington Forge. Problems arose, however, when neighbours Darlington FC went out of business and Forge took over the ground, the colours and the name (dropping 'Forge'). English was the player-manager of both the old and new Darlington clubs and wanted to stay on in the North East. This would have been fine if his club had remained under the nomenclature of Forge. However, once accepted into the Football League (Northern Section) English was in breach of Football League regulations because he was still registered as a United player. United would not grant him a free transfer and in the meanwhile tried to sell him to Sunderland. In 1919 Sunderland offered £1,000 but United refused. They then offered £1,250 but English demanded 50% of the £250 increase. The FA were informed—presumably by United. In this impasse United kept his registration until May 1923. English could then play for Darlington, where he remained for the next five years, even taking them up to the second division.

Whose Round?: Harold Gough

Chesterfield-born Harold Gough started his football career with Bradford Park Avenue and after just three games in 1911 joined Castleford. In April 1913 United paid £40 for him and put him straight into the first team due to an injury to United's regular keeper Ted Hufton. His last game for United was a County Cup fixture against Wednesday that took place in May 1924.

Frequenting public houses has been the ruin of many a fine footballer. But for Gough his managing a pub was to signal the end of his United days. Gough was innocent of any drunken excesses, but guilty in the eyes of an intransigent football chairman. The tee-total Methodist Charles Clegg forbade any player from living or lodging in licensed premises. His views on the temptations offered by the demon drink saw him consider such places too enticing for young footballers. Instructed to find alternative accommodation, Gough refused. Gough was not an easy player to replace. He had played for a North v England side in 1921 (but let in five goals) and played for England and went on the FA tour of South Africa in 1920. But he had, in the eyes of the United directors, done the unforgivable and resided in a business place 'which directors might deem unsuitable.' A combination of licensed premises and Sheffield United directors could ruin a career.

In August 1924 Gough appeared before the Football Committee of United who informed him he had broken his contract. In September he was to admit in a letter to the board that he had 'acted in ignorance' and to help the situation was prepared to repay his summer wages. This cut no ice as in September Gough was suspended from the game by the FA. The following month his FA registration was cancelled. In August of the next year Gough learned that United were demanding a transfer fee of £2,400 for him.

In the same month he applied to the Football League to have the fee reduced but had his application rejected. The FA further stipulated he could not revert to being an amateur and so play for other clubs perhaps for surreptitious payment.

Gough was suspended from the English game until January 1925. The procedures hint at the collaboration of football's governing bodies with football clubs hierarchies. Gough considered the fee United were seeking prohibitive to interested clubs. The lack of enquiries from other clubs was in all probability because he was blacklisted from the game. The United Board's minute book of November 1925 details a request from United to the Football League to reduce the fee to £1,500. Even when the suspension was lifted no League clubs came in for Gough (or if they did the player was not informed) and he was thus found playing in 1925 for non-league Castleford and later Harrogate Town. Eventually in February 1927, aged 37, United sold Gough to football league side Oldham Athletic for just £500. He later played four games for Bolton Wanderers and over 50 for Torquay before retiring in 1930 reflecting no doubt that keeping a pub cost him 30 months of his footballing career and a Cup Final medal.

Ungentlemanly Conduct: Billy 'Beau' Brelsford

The strength of the 1915 team lay in a formidable defence consisting of Billy ('Beau') Brelsford, full backs Bill Cook and Jack English with Harold Gough in goal. Up front was Jimmy Simmons, Bob Evans, Wally Masterman, Albert Sturgess and Stan Fazackerley. Such men carry fascinating biographies and one that concerns us here is that of Beau Brelsford.

Born as one of six boys in 1885 in the Darnall district of Sheffield, Beau Brelsford began his footballing career in 1902 with Attercliffe moving two years later to Tinsley Park Colliery before representing Lodge

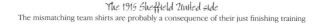

The 1915 Sheffield United side
The mismatching team shirts are probably a consequence of their just finishing training

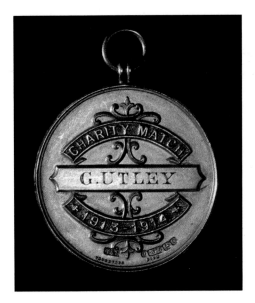

1914 Charity match medal
United v Wednesday, the match was
played to raise funds for the Firth
Building at Sheffield University
United won 2–0

Inn in the Licensed Victuallers league, and later Rawmarsh Albion. In 1907 Brelsford joined Doncaster Rovers; two years later he joined United who generously donated £20 to his former amateur club. He made his debut a few months later and was a regular in the United side until given a free transfer in 1924 to Taunton. He returned only a year later in the capacity of assistant trainer his experience taking United to the 1925 and 1936 Cup Finals. Brelsford remained at Bramall Lane until 1939. He died in Sheffield in 1954, aged 69.

Brelsford was a tough character on and off the pitch. His physical abilities made him one of the first players to be sent off for violent conduct. Games against Wednesday saw him and his opponent Teddy Glennon conduct mutual recriminations throughout the 90 minutes. In 1916 during wartime football, a fight between Brelsford and Glennon saw the pair disciplined. Glennon was banned from the game for four weeks; Brelsford received a six-week ban, thereby attaining the longest ever disciplinary ban given to a Sheffield United player.

His unwillingness to back down from confrontation resulted in Brelsford having a party piece unique to football—both then and now. He was able to stand a coin upright in a dent in his skull. The compression came courtesy of the notorious Mooney gang who plagued Sheffield in the late 1920s and early 1930s. The gang attempted their extortion tactics on the Darnall Greyhound track then managed by the Brelsford family. A huge street fight between the Mooneys and the extended family of Brelsford resulted in a head wound inflicted by a cast-iron cellar grate wielded by one of the Mooney gang.

The 1915 Cup Winners' medal won by Brelsford is inscribed with the FA coat of arms. The footballers depicted emphasise the essentially amateur mentality that prevailed in football. This design can be traced back to 1896 and seems to have survived until 1948 when a new trophy was made and new medals produced.

The 'W-M' Man: Herbert Chapman

Herbert Chapman, one of the greatest club managers in the English game and the man considered the inventor of the W-M formation, was once a Sheffield United player. Born in the pit village of Kiveton Park, six miles beyond the Sheffield boundary, Chapman signed for United from Northampton in May 1902, whilst at Sheffield Wednesday's Owlerton Stadium watching his brother Harry play for the Owls. He made his debut a couple of weeks later, against Sheffield Wednesday, and made a total of 21 League appearances for United, scoring two goals. A decent but slow player, Chapman's pedestrian style may have been a consequence of his absence from regular fitness training on account of a somewhat itinerant lifestyle. As a qualified mining engineer, Chapman travelled the country in his employment. That said, he always seemed to find a team to play for; his footballing roll-call includes Kiveton, Ashton-Under-Lyne, Stalybridge, Leeds, Rochdale, Swindon, Spurs, Notts County and Northampton. It was as a manager that he found fame with both Huddersfield Town and later Arsenal.

His managerial life began in 1907 at Northampton, then in the Southern League. He joined Leeds City in the second division in 1912 and managed to survive the closure of the club. During the war years whilst

The 1915 FA Cup winning side
The victors were instructed not to smile due to the solemnity of the time and the huge casualties sustained in the Great War

managing Leeds, Chapman implemented a system whereby all officials and players donated 5% of their wages to the National Relief Fund. He also attested his willingness to serve in the armed forces if called upon and took a munitions factory job to help the war effort. In the meantime, he was replaced as manager by George Cripps. Remaining heavily involved in the club, Chapman became secretary but resigned at the end of 1918. One week later Cripps resigned and controversy ensued. The club's accounts were never made public and in response a League Commission demanded to see the books. This request was refused and as a consequence the club was expelled from the League, all the players were sold and Chapman and five others banned from any future involvement in the game. In 1920 a new entity called Leeds United was founded, having played one season non-league, Leeds was successful in its application to join Division Two. Once the League decided that Chapman was innocent of all allegations, he was permitted to become manager of Huddersfield Town. He was to leave shortly before they won their third consecutive championship joining Arsenal and achieving a hat trick of championships at Highbury. Arsenal won all domestic honours including five championships in this era with a team full of internationals. Unfortunately Chapman did not see the full fruit of his work. Catching a chill in training, he died in 1934 of bronchial pneumonia.

Chapman changed forever the English game's approach to tactics. He held weekly team meetings to discuss positioning using a magnetic model pitch for the benefit of his players. He encouraged the same players to make their own suggestions and is credited with the now taken for granted notion of planning set pieces. With Huddersfield Town he stressed the importance of defence as much as that of attack and in 1925 the Terriers did not concede more than two goals in any game in a championship-winning season. Chapman can also be credited with beginning the use of the centre half as a 'stopper' position in response to changes in the off-side law in 1925. In Chapman's era all teams had a goalkeeper, two full backs, three half backs, and five forwards. Chapman innovated by pulling the centre-half further back to stop forwards surging through the middle. He also altered team formation. What had been previously five players in a line saw him relocate them into a 'W' formation, with an 'M' formation at the back to complement in what was the beginning of man marking and zonal defending. This also allowed the full backs to pivot. Chapman also introduced the concept of counter-attacking and concentrating on goals that began in defence as a consequence of winning possession there. In the 1930–31 season his Arsenal team scored 127 goals. The great Alex James was left to roam in what would nowadays be considered a *libero* role, which was revolutionary at the time. Equally innovative was his changing of the Arsenal socks from red and white to blue and white, a strategy he reasoned would aid team mates to recognise each others legs in tight situations.

Such was his status at Arsenal that a bronze bust of Chapman met all who entered the so-called 'marble' hall of the Arsenal ground from shortly after his death until the closure of Highbury in May 2006. A couple of years ago, the Arsenal manager Arsene Wenger, speaking of Chapman said that he was, in his thinking, some 20 years ahead of his time and created more off the pitch, philosophically, for Arsenal than the trophies he won.

Reading the Game

The war ended in November 1918. The following year the football programme resumed, the Football League extended divisions one and two to 22 clubs. Football attempted to resume where it had left off. The 20% of the home gate remained the stipulated payment to the visitors. The players' wages, based on their income in 1915, rose by 50%. A suggestion to increase the bonus to £2 for a win and £1 for a draw was deferred to the Football League AGM in June. If this was implemented the players' wages would have raised United's wage bill by £2,000 per annum. Alarmed by the possible wage rise the club used the match programme to tell of the 200% rise in the cost of sporting apparel over the war years with rail fares also rising by 50%. The minimum admission charge to football whilst raised to one shilling also caused a moan. United declared that the clubs were only 50% better off because Entertainment Tax took 25% of the gross gate. The Players' Union rubbed salt in the wound in February 1920 suggesting a 100% rise for players from the 1915 wage, their logic being that the public was paying 100% more to enter the ground than in pre-war days.

Football was changing and many aspects of the game were bewildering those involved over the previous decades. A United programme of April 5th, 1920, informed its readers that Aston Villa had adopted blackboard lessons in instructing their players:

They make it one of the first subjects in their curriculum, and having learned the theory the players are taken onto the field and have to put theory into practice

Theory and practice had met every Saturday for Blades fans since 1890. By 1891 Sheffield had four Saturday evening sports specials. Assisted by advances in printing methods, publishers were able to turn out the thousands of copies the public sought between 4.50 and 5.30 every football season Saturday. Inseparable from the game of football in Sheffield was, and remains, the Saturday evening *Green 'Un* sports paper first published in 1907. Printed on green paper by the Sheffield *Telegraph and Star* the newspaper contained the football results from around the country and match reports specific to the South Yorkshire clubs. Other pages contained a weekly analysis of the state of affairs in the region's six professional clubs, as well as brief reports on the clubs in the higher echelons of the amateur game. Amateur leagues and Saturday and Sunday leagues were also catered for, and the letters page was one of the earliest avenues for fans' opinions to be aired. The first edition came out at 5.30pm and was sold by vendors at strategic parts of the city centre, usually close to transport terminals. A later edition, with greater clarity and more detailed away match reports, appeared at 6.15pm. Other sellers would travel around the city's pubs and clubs throughout Saturday evening

The *Green 'Un* existed for over 95 years on formulaic reports. Its missing late results were part of football culture until the mid-1980s and it was the accompaniment to many a Saturday night out. By the late 20th century, many such newspapers in other cities were obsolete. Satellite TV gave the fullest picture of Saturday's events and up to the minute score lines. Mini LCDs providing goal replays killed the need for late print editions. That said, nothing can cover grass-roots football, be it the under-10s or over-35s like the *Green 'Un*.

A mere thirty years after its beginnings the game was firmly entrenched in the national psyche to the extent that royalty were acknowledged before Cup Finals. A source of succour during the war years, the naysayers who pronounced against football could only watch on as the game grew in popularity and helped to sustain the home front. That said, the termination of world conflict did not produce what the politicians promised. The land fit for heroes did not materialise in the 1920s, and the struggle for pay and conditions was to become integral to the game. In the industrial troubles of the following decade, Sheffield was particularly hard hit.

FINAL TIE

Of the Football Association
English Cup Competition

APRIL 25th, 1925

STADIUM

British Empire Exhibition
Wembley

Official Programme - 6^{d.}

Printed and Published by
Fleetway Press Ltd 3-9, Dane Street High Holborn, London, W.C.1

The 1925 FA Cup Final programme commemorating the occasion of United's last major trophy

Chapter 5

United We Stand

Football boomed at the beginning of the new decade. In recognition of the boom a new national stadium was designed. Wembley Stadium was built in just 300 days. Able to hold 100,000 spectators the stadium took centre stage in the 1924 British Empire Exhibition promoted as symbolising the 'one soul and mind' of the Empire and became known globally as the spiritual home of English football. The game came into the domestic home via *'Newfootie'*, a board game played on blankets or rugs with cardboard footballer figurines. However not all proceedings in this decade were monumental or playful. A national miners' strike erupted in 1921 and lasted three months following the refusal of mine owners to match the salaries paid between 1917–21 when the government took control of coal production. In the course of this dispute schools, aware that food in the most hard-hit places was at a premium, took on the role of providing breakfast for pupils. A miners' strike leading to a general strike followed in 1926. The mine owners asked the miners to accept a pay cut and work an extra hour per day. The miners refused and the government intervened to subsidise the mine owners' losses. A Royal Commission concluded that a reorganisation of the industry was needed and wage-cuts were inevitable. The cuts were refused by the Miners' Federation; in response the miners were locked out of their places of work. The Trades Union Congress called a general strike that lasted a week. Other unions returned to work after this, the TUC having agreed terms with the government. The miners stood alone for the following eight months.

The desperate economic situation that was a consequence of this strike affected football locally with thousands unable to pay the Bramall Lane admission cost of one shilling for adults and four pence for boys. Following this industrial strife, the 1927–28 season is remembered as one of the most exciting ever in the history of the first division. All bar the top four were in danger of relegation until the final month of the season. The two eventually relegated, Spurs and Middlesbrough, were strangely enough, two of the better teams. Spurs were in mid-table two weeks before being relegated and in the previous season Middlesbrough had scored 122 goals in winning the Division Two championship. The decade was one in which all top-flight clubs were more or less equal and transfer fees high in relation to other costs of living. The United following of this era, earning an average wage of £2 a week, were generally modest in their expenditure, simple in their demands and polite in their disappointment. A home victory would see the team cheered off the pitch; defeat brought mutterings but no collective booing. Shouts of 'Up the Blades' filled the Bramall Lane air and, in the last years of the decade, cries of 'Tunny Dunnit' honoured United's prolific goalscorer Jimmy Dunne and his provider Fred Tunstall. Pre-match entertainment was provided by local brass bands. Match-time sustenance was available at the bottom of the Kop with trestle tables covered in linoleum from which cups of Bovril and meat pies were sold.

Bills, Beer and Bibles
Despite impending industrial conflict, many football clubs early in the decade had decent incomes and made modest profits. Only Blackburn and Wednesday in the first division failed to make a profit on the 1919–20 season. Both had invested heavily in transfers in their attempts to avoid relegation. This worked for Blackburn but not for Wednesday. United's profit for this season was £3,521 on gate receipts of £30,376 and after an Entertainment Tax bill of £7,020. At the beginning of the 1920–21 season a United player received £5 weekly in his first full season rising to £9 weekly after four full seasons of service. An international cap would bring him a further one-off payment of £6. Five years service would bring a benefit game and entitlement to a free transfer, albeit, the programme informed fans: 'he could not, under existing laws, take his benefit and say "Goodbye, I'm off" '. Social mores accepted there were days on which a player

Young workers while away their time during a period of unemployment in the 1920s
Many youngsters were often laid off as soon as they completed their apprenticeships in the period just after World War One

might not wish to ply his trade. FA rule number 25 stated that a player could not be compelled to play any match on Good Friday or Christmas Day. Furthermore, Sunday amateur football games were not recognised by the FA. When the latter subject was raised in December 1924, Charles Clegg, in his capacity as President of the FA, squashed the idea, stating matter-of-factly: 'Better for the country and better for the game that we should not have it'.

Both football and the wider society were evolving. A change to the offside rule in 1920 meant a player was not offside from a throw or a corner. The ladies cloakroom at Bramall Lane, which had been routinely opened for county cricket, was from January 1921 to be opened for the first-team football games. In November 1920 the Tolputt Company on London Road began advertising its range of cars in the match programmes intimating a more sophisticated form of consumerism entering Sheffield society. More adverts for city centre restaurants saw readers enticed by the finest ales, cigarettes and steak teas available from a variety of premises. Other leisure pursuits in the cinema and theatre saw the programme cover of November 1923 advertise '*Prisoner of Zenda*! World's wonder film'. Excursions became available to London and East coast seaside resorts. For those in search of outdoor pursuits, adverts appear for overcoats, 'sports suitings' and even fur coats. The wares of a gift shop regularly appear as do the services offered by a plumber, no doubt reflecting developments in household sanitation.

At the same time public drunkenness and brawling remained a regular feature of weekend nights. The Salvation Army had no fewer than five branches in Sheffield, all of them in tough working-class districts.

For many working-class men of the city, the bars that lined Attercliffe Common were the centre of their world. Outside the Adelphi Cinema in this district, open-air meetings of the Salvation Army would see a 40-strong band playing hymns with 100-plus listening. It was not unknown for their meetings to be attacked by toughs funded by the brewers, who stood to lose a fortune if Temperance spread. The Salvation Army played on the Bramall Lane pitch once a year, usually at Christmas. The rest of the time match-day music came courtesy of the tram drivers in the Sheffield Transport Band, or from those who had joined the Sheffield Imperial Band.

Cups and Cots

In 1921 the good men of the Sheffield and Hallamshire FA launched a new football competition. Named the County Cup, the tournament involved both Sheffield clubs and the three other professional teams in South Yorkshire—Barnsley, Rotherham United and Doncaster Rovers. The latter three were initially considered minnows in relation to the Sheffield clubs, and relished the chance to play their bigger neighbours on an annual basis. This sentiment was not reciprocated by either the Blades or the Owls. Financial possibilities were, no doubt, a huge consideration for the local FA because the derbies the tournament generated provided them with much welcome income.

From its very beginnings, the Sheffield clubs did not select full strength sides for the County Cup. The fixtures became occasions for combining core and fringe players. The tournament was essentially meaningless, but did provide for local bragging rights for the fans. In its 61 years of existence, only seven of the 110 ties attracted a crowd of over 20,000. One notable attendance was two dozen short of 50,000 at Hillsborough in 1949, when United beat Wednesday in a semi-final. The fixtures for the tournament were often haphazard and finals were often played months after the preliminaries. At times the competition never took place. In 1971, despite United beating Rotherham 4–0 in the semis, no final was ever played. When it was played, the final could be twelve months late—United's 1974–75 final took place in the 1975–76 season. In the 1970s the Blades–Owls fixture became the occasion for mass fights between rival fans who had no league fixture between 1971–79 to trade threats and punches. The competition came to an end in 1982 when United were in Division Four, and Barnsley and Rotherham two divisions higher. Even Doncaster was one league above United at that time. In May of 1980, only 826 people watched United's 6–1 win over Doncaster. United won the trophy on 21 occasions and were beaten finalists 13 times and won 25 out of 27 County Cup matches played between 1951 and 1966.

Charles Clegg
Sober and walking the straight road

Whilst the income from the tournament went towards developing the game locally, there were others more helpless to consider. Around the same time as the County Cup was begun, a hospital cot fund committee was inaugurated by the very same Sheffield and Hallamshire Football Association. All clubs in the area were notified of the fund and advised as to how they could be associated with it. They were expected to donate and did so albeit often without publicity or fanfare.

Gamesmanship

The United chairman and chair of the FA, Charles Clegg, whilst pro-charity, was somewhat antagonistic to change and in November 1925 voiced his opposition to new tactics appearing on the football field, in particular, what he called the 'W-arrangement' and the 'spearhead thrust' (effectively, the counter attack). In his opinion, tactics should remain as they were:

> ...there is no necessity for wing men and the centre forward being thrust out in advanced positions. Keep the line, and let the forwards maintain their places.

Leather case ball c. 1920

Clegg also considered the new throw-in provision to be under-utilised, arguing:

> *...all they do is stand behind the touch line whereas they could get a swinging motion and propelling power and still keep some portion of each foot on the ground with the aid of body balance.*

Some United players at this time stood where they should not really be, and in doing so forever changed the markings on the football pitch The arc on the edge of the penalty area which is such an integral part of the football pitch can be traced back to a Burnley v Sheffield United fixture at Turf Moor in 1923. The home side were awarded a penalty. In response, United's captain Billy Gillespie lined his team up in a row just outside the penalty box, thereby hindering the penalty kicker's customary long run up. The penalty taker, Bob Kelly, insisted to the referee that the United players were not ten yards from the penalty spot but the United players refused to move. Despite this, Kelly scored. A debate ensued arising from United's actions and the tactic was copied throughout the country. Intervening in the controversy, a Sheffield-based referee sketched a plan of an arc to be added to the penalty area. The idea was published in the Sheffield *Green 'Un* and caught the attention both of the local and national Football Associations. Some 14 years later, in 1937, the idea of the arc was adopted and has been an integral feature of football pitches the world over ever since.

Profits and the People

Despite financial hardship crowds flocked on occasion to Bramall Lane in the first half of the1920s. A Christmas Day morning game at Bramall Lane in 1923 against Cardiff drew a crowd of more than 50,000. In 1925 an FA Cup fourth-round replay against Sunderland saw 62,000 pack Bramall Lane and bring the club receipts of £3,981. Despite this, players' wages at Bramall Lane were cut in 1922 from the £8 per week average that most clubs were paying. The Cup-tie bonus was reduced to £2 from £5 in all qualifying rounds, and Cup Winners could now expect to pick up just £20, not the previous £50. The maximum available from a benefit match was restricted to £650. Yet United had made a profit, albeit modest, of £490 in the 1921–22 season. Later again in April 1923 the club proposed to reduce players' wages even further amidst fears that United might join the ranks of the many clubs finishing the season in debt.

A thank-you from United's Directors:
An 18ct gold hunter watch presented to United's
captain Billy Gillespie after the 1925 Cup Final victory

Suggestions were even voiced that the playing staff might be cut by up to 30%. Things did not seem to improve over the next year. By September 1924, the subject of bonuses was again debated by the United board; certain players were suspected of turning out for the club not fully fit in pursuit of their income.

And so it continued. In September 1926, United's secretary wrote in the programme of how only four clubs had made a profit every year since the war and how by mid-1926 six Division One teams had posted up losses on the previous season. That said, the combined profits of the rest was just short of £80,000. What was peculiar about the six others was not specified. Despite this doom and gloom, monies went out of the game to good causes. Football in its various forms donated some £90,000 to war charities between 1919 and 1925. The United secretary saw a variety of benefits that the game had brought to the morality and comportment of many, but still sought improvement. He was to argue that:

…football has provided the people of this country with good, healthy enjoyment in the open air and has been a potent force in the direction of temperance and improved personal appearance… but one often doubts whether it has improved the fairmindedness of the general public; far too many of those who look on are fanatical supporters… who would infinitely prefer to see their favourites victorious in a poor game than see them narrowly defeated in a glorious fight for supremacy.

The glorious fight saw the people victorious in other local arenas. In 1926 the Labour Party took control of Sheffield Council under the slogan 'the will of the people must prevail'. Its three-seat victory over the Liberals meant that the Socialists made Sheffield their first-ever major city of control. However the national economic crisis and an unpopular national Labour government when added to 20% unemployment in the city saw Labour lose power in 1931 at the expense of the Progressives representing the national government of Ramsay MacDonald. Labour returned to power a year later with a majority of four. But 1926 was momentous for the most militant action ever taken by British trade unionists. In early May, on the instructions of the Trades Union Congress, two million men and women employed on the railways, in public transport, printing, dock work and iron and steel stopped work. This was in support of a million miners who had been locked out by pit owners seeking to cut pay and lengthen working hours. The strike affected every inhabitant of Britain and in response the government mobilised soldiers. The strike was called off on TUC orders after five days, on a promise that the outcome of a

Fred Tunstall's Football League Tour of Canada cap 1926

Drama in Fitzalan Square during the General Strike of 1926
Strikers are confronted by mounted policemen

Royal Commission investigating the coal mining industry be implemented. The miners continued their strike alone until December; some were literally starved back to work. Many were to lose their jobs as a consequence of their union activities. The relationship between owners and workers was high on many agendas. Football was no different.

Playing a New Game

Footballers were in the public eye more than their predecessors, but subject to debate as to what were appropriate leisure pastimes. In October 1926, United's Billy Gillespie and Fred Tunstall appeared in what was described in the match programme as a film called '*Football*', shown at the Albert Hall, Sheffield. Footage of this film has never been found. In December of the same year, the Manchester City and Welsh international winger Billy Meredith featured in a football drama called '*The Ball of Fortune*', also screened at the Albert Hall. This saw Meredith become the first British player to star in a full-length film playing the role of a football trainer in an 87-minute adaptation of a novel written by Sidney Horler. This film is similarly lost to posterity.

Meredith had a long if somewhat controversial footballing career. Playing club football with Manchester United and later Manchester City, he was to win 48 Welsh caps. He won his final cap aged 45 and made his final League appearance shortly before his 50th birthday. He was chair of the first meeting of the Association Football Players' Union in 1907. Two years previously he had been suspended from the game for a year having been found guilty of offering the captain of a rival team £10 to throw the game. In his defence, Meredith claimed he was acting on instructions from his manager.

The issue of the clubs' jurisdiction over their players when not playing or training was troubling club officials in1926. Some clubs instructed players not to ride motorcycles either as driver or pillion. The issue of command and compulsion was debated in the United programme, a writer asked whether clubs had the power to specify such prohibition, concluding, 'anything which savours of undue risk might be construed into a breach of agreement'. In September of the following year, the discussion centred on cigarette smoking, concluding that in moderation it did the player no harm, but ideally the player would refrain from smoking the day before a game and on match day. When not smoking, some players had learned to drive. In October 1927 the programme stated with a degree of consternation, albeit possibly over wealth-related pique rather than health-related concerns, 'At…one club we have in mind more than one player drives his own car, and drives to the ground each morning to do his training'. By December 1927, United's secretary speculated on the possibility of the first £10,000 transfer.

One could say he had little to worry about, even if such a transfer fee was realised. That year had seen a crowd over 60,000 for the visit of Wednesday and, with half the 1927–28 season gone, United's average attendance was 24,555 but still the clubs pleaded poverty. In 1928, only one third of Football League clubs claimed to be in credit, others according to the United secretary, were existing by transfer fees, overdrafts and the largesse of creditors. The cause of the problem, in his analysis, was unusually wet weather that had reduced attendances and provoked clubs to seek alternative funds. Methods used to raise money included bazaars, prize draws, whist-drives and even disposing of their grounds to greyhound racing promoters to capture the late 1920s wave of public interest around betting on the dogs. A somewhat remarkable statement, in the February 22nd, 1928 United programme, seemed to suggest the emergence of football-related socialism, informing readers that, '…the opinion that the rich clubs should be taxed to help the poorer ones is gaining adherence every day'. Amongst whom he did not specify. Somehow this idea never caught on.

The Numbers Game

The stay-away fans the Secretary was moaning about were missing a goal treat. Further changes in the offside law in 1925 made scoring goals easier when it reduced the number of out-field players needed to stay on-side between attacker and goalkeeper from two to one. The goal ratios tell the tale. Between 1920 and 1925, first division games were averaging between 2.47–2.88 goals per game. Between 1925 and 1930, the ratio had risen to 3.61–3.80. Middlesbrough was the first club to score 100 goals in the 1926–27 season, a feat achieved by March. The 1925–26 season saw five clubs score 100-plus goals, including Sheffield United, who became the first top division club to score 100 goals since the end of the war. On New Years Day 1926, United beat Cardiff 11–2 at Bramall Lane. Played in a quagmire, the Cardiff team had seven internationals but also had a Scottish goalkeeper named Farquarhson who was widely believed to have played the game still recovering from the previous night's Hogmanay revelries. The visitors scored the game's first goal and had the consolation of scoring the last. Curiously the Cardiff defence and United forward line were identical to the ones that had met in the previous year's Cup Final at Wembley. Then in November of the same year, United suffered their greatest ever home defeat when trounced 7–1 by Huddersfield.

Not everybody was impressed by the proliferation of goals. The club programme of September 1927 stated that the change in rules had quickened the pace but not added to the skill of the game and as a consequence football today 'is nothing like as scientific as it used to be'. A somewhat censorious message to so-called 'would be reformers' informed readers of plans to introduce into the game a 'painted' match ball, numbers for each of the players' shirts, and an end to Good Friday, Christmas Day and mid-week games if they were considered to be interfering with industrial production. A different coloured ball eventually appeared in the mid 1950s and numbers on the back of players' shirts first appeared in 1928, introduced by former Blade Herbert Chapman when managing Arsenal. However, it was not until 1939 that numbering became part of the FA regulations and was directly related to positions on the field. Further innovations saw the 1929–30 season begin with new regulations on players' footwear and on penalty kicks. The most significant change in the long run was that which introduced the right of players to defend themselves when charged with offences on the field.

The Attacking Game

Some citizens of Sheffield needed defending—others were justifiably punished. Letters from 'ratepayers' to the Sheffield press in the 1920s and 1930s complained about the noise, swearing, rowdiness and betting, which was caused by football, disturbing Saturday afternoons. Because of this, the provision of football pitches for local young men was not a priority of the Socialist City Council, which in the inter-war years had even banned collections for junior football club funds. Sheffield Magistrates discovered they had been sending youths to prison for playing football in the streets in 1928. Unknown to them, the exact nature of the crime had been changed in the prosecution evidence to a charge of 'disorderly behaviour'.

The most serious disorderly behaviour in the city was pub-related violence, the product of a gang vendetta over the control of the 'pitch and toss' gambling rings. The 'Gang Wars' as they became known, are still remembered in the oral history of Sheffield and achieved national notoriety, earning Sheffield the title 'Little Chicago'. Violence began in 1923 and continued for five years resulting in one murder, hangings and several serious injuries. Some lived in fear of attack by razors and 'life preservers' and even cellar grates. The *modus operandi* of the 'Cellar Grate Gang' (a sub-section of one of the criminal fraternities) was to strike opponents with these readily available objects and return them when the job was accomplished so that no weapon was apparent if apprehended by police. Captain Percy Sillitoe, who took over as Chief Constable of the city during the anti-gang operation, is credited with gang-busting. In his autobiography, he told how the Mooney Gang:

> Had virtually complete control of the poorer districts… these districts were without any doubt as rough and lawless as any to be found in England. The publicans and shopkeepers lived in daily terror… Frequently victims were taken to the infirmary terribly injured. But the gangsters had spread such terror that the injured victim would rarely be persuaded to come voluntarily to court and testify.

Emulating their elders, junior gangs were formed in late 1927 with members in their late teens and early twenties. Frequenting the city centre in daytime they would hassle pedestrians and pickpocket and at night demand free drinks and cigarettes from publicans and customers. They also fought one another with weapons. Participants were slashed—one was murdered. The police responded in kind and a 'Flying Squad' of six plain-clothes policemen was established to smash the groups. These hand-picked officers spoke a language that local men understood when they met force with force. After various acts of violence and murder, two brothers, by the name of Fowler, were sentenced to death by hanging. Local football pre-occupied them even in their darkest hour. The final letter, written by one to his mother, stated his hope that Sheffield Wednesday would have a good season in his absence.

The early years of the decade had little to commend themselves to local people. However, the middle of the decade eventually provided the last ever FA Cup victory for United. Surviving documents from the day tell us much about both the game and the city of Sheffield. Another source of such information came courtesy of one man who left Bramall Lane with a limp in 1932.

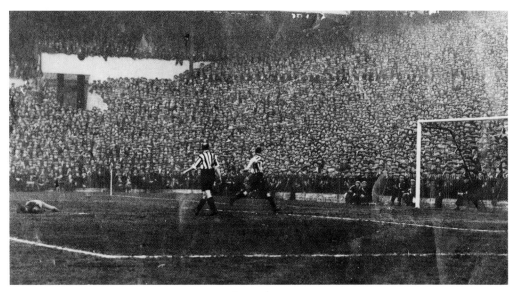

Caps and cups
A packed Shoreham End watch United's Harry Johnson under the eyes of Billy Gillespie in January 1923
The prostrate Nottingham Forest goalkeeper joins the 39,000 spectators at this cup-tie

Failing Strikers: Fred Johnson

Fred Johnson, aged 92 in 2006, was taken to his first game at Bramall Lane at the age of ten in 1923. He was accompanied by his father who was one of just 45 survivors out of 1,000 British soldiers during one days' fighting at the Battle of the Somme in the First World War. Beginning on July 1st 1916 the battle that ended some 20 weeks later saw 60,000 British wounded and 95,000 fatalities. Football enthusiasm assisted this armed combat. A football kicked into the no-mans-land between the German and Allied forces by one of the British commanding officers was the signal for British troops to chase after it on the way to engage the enemy. Few were to return to play the game in peacetime Britain. Being one of the lucky ones, Johnson senior's reward in peacetime was working down a mine at Tankersley a few miles from the family's High Green home.

With his father withdrawing his labour in the course of the 1926 General Strike, no wages came the way of the Johnson family. Survival was due to donations from the unions, who also ensured their members each received a pair of boots. The less fortunate children in Sheffield city centre were remembered for walking barefoot. Digging in the local woodlands seeking coal for both warmth and cooking became a daily duty for a 12-year-old boy. Some sustenance was provided by a daily government allowance of a loaf of bread; meat came from catching rabbits. Local schools had no sporting provision, the village had no boy's football team and nobody had a football kit. The nearby village of Chapeltown played in the Sheffield Junior League and gave Johnson his footballing start at the age of 16. Junior football usually saw pitches adjacent to public houses. This made commercial sense for the publicans who contributed to the team kit in the expectation that the players and their supporters would drink their beer after the game. Facilities were minimal, the after-match wash down came from buckets of cold water drawn from wells. Away games saw the team climb into the back of a supporter's open-backed truck with a tarpaulin offering some protection from the weather.

The 1925 FA Cup team in 'civilian' clothing

Leaving school at 14, the job opportunities for Johnson were the nearby Newton Chambers Fabrications factory or the pit. Johnson found himself down Silkstone Colliery as a pit-pony driver, working ten-hour shifts, six days a week for 17 shillings a week. Watching Billy Gillespie and Fred Tunstall in United's colours was the best entertainment on offer for a teenager who dreamed of joining the Blades. A letter to Bramall Lane, written by his father, tipped the club off about his son's potential. A scout was sent to watch him joining others from Leeds and Mansfield. Signing for United aged 18 meant Johnson could still live at home and the amateur status he enjoyed saw him train every Tuesday at Bramall Lane. Impressing Teddy Davison at a trial match, Johnson remembers walking off the pitch with Davison's arm around his shoulders. However, his United career ended soon after with a bad ankle injury. Strapping his leg up for training, the limb would give way at the ankle joint when the strapping was loosened and Johnson would fall over. Some of the United coaching staff thought he was drunk. The United director, Blacow Yates, was also a surgeon. Aware of the severity of the injury, he told Johnson his United playing days were over. Another surgeon, Professor Finch, demanded he hang up his boots. Aged 19, Johnson took his advice, left Bramall Lane and never played top-class football. He was however to play a few seasons at Halifax Town given a lift to training and games by former United legend Fred Tunstall who was seeing out his playing days with the Shay Men.

Aged ten, Johnson remembered United losing an FA Cup semi-final to Bolton at Old Trafford in front of 72,000. Two years later his father considered him too young to attend the 1925 Wembley Cup Final, but heard about the United victory third-hand. He was not to witness the return of the victorious team to the city. Thousands of Blades, however, travelled to both London and the city centre. They were the last Blades to ever see United players holding the trophy. The 1925 team is considered by football historians as one of the greatest ever United sides. The club had last won the Cup ten years previously. The re-building process in the intervening decade had produced a team of excellent players, many of whom had fascinating biographies.

Bringing It Back Home: The 1925 FA Cup Final

Prior to the big day at Wembley the United squad trained at Scarborough cricket ground, travelling to London on Friday afternoon. For long-serving United coach George Waller the occasion was familiar. This was the sixth Cup Final in which he had taken part. It was, however, the first time the club had played at the newly-built Wembley. A crowd of 91,763 saw United beat Cardiff 1–0 by a goal scored late in the first half by Fred Tunstall. Before the kick off United captain Billy Gillespie, then one of the most respected and easily recognised faces in football, entered the Cardiff City dressing room, wearing his full kit. In his hand he clutched an autograph book. This book went with him to every ground United played at, and each home team was invited to sign it. Cardiff had not been a League club for long and, although they featured many great players of the time such as Jimmy Blair and Fred Keenor, the final was a landmark in their history. As opponents signed the book Gillespie wished each of them good luck.

Reports of the time suggest that Gillespie believed that Cardiff would concentrate on United's main threat, Fred Tunstall. Consequently, Gillespie starved Tunstall of the ball, thereby we might conjecture, lulling the Cardiff defence. At the optimum moment, however, Gillespie fed the ball to the right wing to Harold Pantling, who passed to Tunstall who scored the goal that won the Blades the Cup for the fourth time in their history. Gillespie led the team up the 39 steps to the Royal Box to receive the Cup from the Duke of York, who later became King George VI, and his winners' medal from a young lady who was to become better known as the Queen Mother. This time, the Cup returned to Sheffield with the full pomp and circumstance that had been denied in 1915. Perhaps the most fortunate player on the pitch was United's goalkeeper Charles Sutcliffe. The Bradford born Sutcliffe joined United in 1924 and played only 53 games for the Blades. Saving a penalty in the semi-final he kept a clean sheet in the final and remained at Bramall Lane for only one more season. The loss of his Cup winners medal from his watch chain whilst bagging sand to assist the Second World War home defences was no doubt a personal trauma. However the loss may well be placed in context when a reader learns that a bad bout of flu prevented Sutcliffe from taking his place on the maiden voyage of the *Titanic* in 1912.

The Cup Final programme informed the reader of the fine traditions of Sheffield United. The curious learned that all the team were English-born with the exception of Irishman Gillespie. That said, the United team did not contain any player born within the city boundary albeit a few were born a few miles outside. The Blades line-up contained four internationals; Gillespie had played for Ireland 18 times while Harold Pantling, David Mercer and Fred Tunstall had ten England caps between them. The Cardiff team contained seven inter-nationals; four for Wales, two for Scotland, and one for Ireland who had earned a combined total of 47 caps.

A 1925 FA Cup Final ticket
The admission price in today's money would be ten pence

The heights and weights of the players are itemised in the programme; the Blades did not contain a single player over 5'11", nor anyone weighing over 12 stones.

Cinematography, military-led melodies and innovations in technology were features of the day. The final was unique in being the first ever filmed by International Cine Corporation Limited. Long shots were taken from an aeroplane above Wembley and copies of the footage were carried by plane to Sheffield and Cardiff to be broadcast in local cinemas on the night of the game. The militarism associated with sporting fixtures is evident at the back of the programme, which itemises the music to be played by the bands of the Irish Guards and the Royal Air Force. The tunes the musicians played drew upon timeless classics, but also paid due respect to the Welsh and Yorkshire theme of the occasion. Thus the *Savoy Welsh Melody* gives way to the *Two Yorkshire Dances*. Later on, *Steel for Steel* and *Yorkshire Folk Songs* lead on to a selection of Welsh melodies. The following page advertises the forthcoming three weeks of searchlight displays at the stadium titled *London Defended*, and further promotes a military pageant to be held a few miles away at Olympia.

The return of the team to Sheffield saw a huge public welcome for the train-travelling victors. On the outskirts of the city, jubilant supporters bordered the railway for miles. Upon the train's arrival at Victoria Station, the waiting Imperial Prize Band began a rendition of the tune *The Conquering Hero*. Nearby, vendors sold balloons, rosettes, replicas of the FA Cup and portraits of the players. Such was the enthusiasm of the crowd outside the station that the police were unable to hold them back when the train arrived. Awaiting the team and officials were three open-top charabancs which would, respectively, host the players and their wives, the officials of the club and an accompanying brass band. Crowds of over 10,000 gathered outside the Town Hall; nine mounted police attempted to control them. The team was covered in confetti and in the High Street the *Sheffield Telegraph* had arranged for fireworks to be let off from the roof of their offices. A poignant moment occurred when an old footballer by the name of Bob Hancock, who was an invalid as a result of a spinal injury, was allowed to hold the Cup aloft to the cheers of the crowd. Around half an hour later, the procession made its way to waiting crowds at Bramall Lane. From here, the three vehicles were driven to the Royal Victoria Hotel for a 7pm dinner.

Cardboard cut-out

United's greatest goal scorer Harry Johnson with his watch and cigarette case c. 1925

The FA Cup stood at the head of the dinner table. All the dinner guests wore red and white rosettes. The great and good of the city were present, as were the directors of Barnsley and Sheffield Wednesday. The toast was given by the Lord Mayor, who praised the presence of the Wednesday director Arthur Dickinson and, aware of the impending industrial disputes, expressed his wish for similar unity in the city between capital and labour. The Lord Mayor was the first to drink the champagne poured into the Cup, which was then passed around the table. The United captain Billy Gillespie made a speech following the response to

A football rattle from the 1920s

the Lord Mayor from John Nicholson. In his speech Gillespie made special reference to team-mate Tommy Sampy, who had travelled to London but did not make the team. Gillespie also praised George Waller, whom he described as 'a good old sort' who, whilst strict at times, allowed the players freedoms that they did not abuse. In response, Waller pointed out that this was the fourth dinner he had attended in celebration of United winning the Cup. He also acknowledged the presence of two ex-players that he had trained decades previously for Cup Finals and their two sons also present in the room who he had similarly trained to win this Cup Final.

Alderman Cattell toasted the Football Association and its wise government and, aware of his company, praised the FA President Charles Clegg who, in response, claimed that no game was better controlled or organised. Clegg then introduced a degree of controversy stating:

A 1924 Benefit match medal awarded to Bill Cook
United drew 2–2 with Wednesday

Directors cut
To celebrate the 1925 FA Cup success the United board awarded themselves their own medal based on the one received by the players

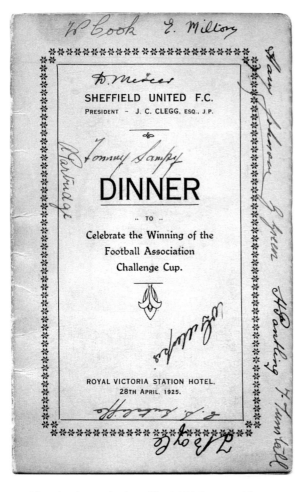

The order of service brochure at the 1925 FA Cup winners' dinner, signed by the United team

One thing, however, I am not prepared for. That is that our game should come under the control of Government in the form of a Ministry of Sport. That matter has been started recently and I think that the sooner it is understood that those who are carrying on sport in a voluntary way are not prepared to submit themselves to any Government control the better.

The final speech was made by Sir William Clegg on behalf of what he called 'a very large number who are real Wednesdayites'. He added that, on Saturday when news came through of United scoring at Wembley, a huge cheer in appreciation had been raised at the Wednesday v Hull City fixture.

The 18-carat gold Cup winners medals were produced by Vaughtons of Birmingham. The design was standard for the occasion, embossed with the FA coat of arms and awarded to the 'English Cup Winners'. Enclosed in a box made of leather and wood, the players were expected to engrave it as they wished. Some would have their names and the date inscribed, others would favour their name and the two teams. Such medals were not generally kept in cabinets behind lock and key, instead they were worn alongside the watch that all men about town of the era wore on their Albert chain attached to the waistcoat. A commemorative medal to mark the Cup victory was made for the board of directors. Also made by Vaughtons, the medal is similarly 18-carat gold. It differs from the players medal inasmuch as it had a design derived from the Sheffield City coat of arms but has replaced the two figures from Greek mythology with two footballers.

Each of the 1925 Cup winning players was awarded a commemorative pocket watch. Made by Thomas Russell and son of Liverpool, the timepieces were designed by and presented by the United board of directors as a thank-you present. Many team photos of this time include the players holding a stuffed toy. This was owned by United's Bill Cook, it was based on the 1920's cartoon character Felix the Cat, infamous in the silent movies of Paramount Pictures. The stuffed toy was considered a lucky mascot which went everywhere with the team—even Wembley.

One week after the final the club took all the players and their families to the Yorkshire seaside resort of Scarborough. Travelling with them on the train was the FA Cup. The group gathered on the beach outside

The 1925 FA Cup winning team
Note the superimposed FA Cup trophy and lucky mascot Felix the Cat

the swish Grand Hotel and placed the trophy, adorned with red and white ribbons, on a sandcastle. Attracting considerable attention from other seaside revellers, the United team challenged eleven local lads to a full-scale beach match—and promptly lost.

> **The United Cup winning team contained England internationals, and one individual who won two FA Cup winners' medals in the space of a decade with United. One player who was the product of the emerging youth system at Bramall Lane made his reserve team debut in Sheffield on the day of the final, and came from a family of eight professional footballers. Relatives of all these men were tracked down as part of the Hall of Fame project and their medals and other memorabilia were donated to the display. These are their stories.**

Daddy of the Club: George Green

George Green was born in Leamington Spa in 1901 and came to the attention of the Blades during 1923 whilst turning out for Nuneaton Borough. The £400 fee that saw him move to United proved to be one of the best bits of business the club were involved in at that time. The player took the step from the Birmingham League to the first division easily and was an ever-present in the United line up for the following two seasons. Green would form part of the very effective left-sided triumvirate, along with Billy Gillespie and Fred Tunstall.

Winning eight England caps over eight seasons, Green became the second most capped England international in the club's history. Green also played for the Football League XI on many occasions.

Referred to as either 'Daddy' because of his paternalistic nature or sometimes 'Fiddler' because of his abilities on the violin, he was remembered by his team-mates at Sheffield Midland Station sat on a luggage barrow with his fiddle case preparing for the 1925 Wembley journey. In his later years at Bramall Lane, Green took over the captaincy from Tommy Sampy. United was Green's only professional club, and his United career ended with him holding the unwanted distinction of being the captain of the first United team to be relegated.

On leaving United, Green became player-manager of non-league Leamington United. When this ended he took a pub and kept his international caps in a case behind the bar. His Cup Final medal was kept in a drawer. The England shirts had been cut up to make bandages and dusters; childhood fevers in his house were doctored by strips of the flannelette shirt. Green met his wife in unique circumstances. He saved the lives of four people who had fallen into the Birmingham Ship Canal. One of those saved he was to marry. The marriage produced three daughters. On his death the daughters had each been given what they and Green considered equal amounts of caps and memorabilia. The FA Cup winner's medal, it was agreed, would spend four months a year in the three daughter's households to avoid disputes. When contacted by the Hall of Fame the daughters were faced with a dilemma. Not wishing to part with the medals or caps of their beloved father, they were equally convinced that no history of United would be complete without items that commemorated him. As a compromise they donated his 1925 Cup Final shirt. This had spent years at the bottom of a linen chest. Occasionally it was to line the bottom of a shopping trolley when the same daughter left the home fearful that if left alone it would disappear. The shirt in the Hall of Fame has never been washed since the day it appeared at Wembley.

Dignified Force: Harold Pantling

The enforcer: Harold Pantling

Another 1925 Cup Final shirt donated to the Hall of Fame was worn by Harold Pantling, United's hard-working, tough-tackling right half. Harold 'Harry' Pantling was born in Leighton Buzzard in 1891 and was signed (along with Thomas Ashbridge) from Watford in 1914 for £850, making his debut for United at Bradford City in February 1915. His other appearances that season were made in defensive positions, standing in for Albert Sturgess, Jack English and Bill Cook. Pantling managed half a dozen first team games in his first season, but did not make the final eleven for the 1915 Cup Final. In the intervening decade he proved a forceful and capable leader on the pitch in contrast to a quiet business-minded person off it. Forceful might be too kind a word for Pantling. He was considered the hard man of the team and would execute retribution on rivals who upset his team-mates.

Few could remember him having a bad game, a fact that was recognised by the England selectors who awarded him a cap against Northern Ireland in 1923 at the age of 32. Not called upon to perform military service in the First World War he was thus able to play football in the restricted regionalised Divisions that existed between 1916 and 1920. As the wartime league got under way players were not always available, consequently Pantling began to feature more and more in the starting eleven. Building his reputation he set a Blades' record when he became the first player to be sent off twice in the 1917–18 season, once against Huddersfield Town and once against Leeds City.

His footballing career at Bramall Lane was ended in an FA Cup fifth-round tie against Sunderland in 1926 when in front of a crowd of 62,000 he sustained a serious leg injury. He recovered sufficiently to play for Rotherham, but after only two seasons bought the Burgoyne Arms pub in Sheffield. When his career ended he left the game completely and never again set foot in Bramall Lane. Proud of his time at United he displayed a variety of memorabilia on the walls of the taproom. However not all his clientele wanted to reminisce over his Blade days. In the 1920s members of the Mooney Gang began causing trouble on his premises but the police were never called, Pantling was a hard man and looked after matters himself. He also proved astute in business. He was driving an Austin Princess by the early 1930s and was always well dressed. Pantling died in 1952 of lung cancer despite never smoking. Phlegmatic and dignified to the end he left the family home and admitted himself to hospital where he died days later.

The FA Cup shirt worn by Pantling became the property of a grandson who wore it whilst gardening and creosoting fences. In this era Cup Final players had just the one shirt which they wore for the duration of the match. The shirt had no number on the back, nor a badge on the breast. The garment was made by Bukta, a company briefly owned by United director Stephen Hinchliffe in the mid-1990s before his business empire collapsed. Made of heavy cotton, the shirt has three neck buttons and buttons on the cuffs. The cut is longer at the back than the front and it could thus serve, when its football days were over, as a nightshirt. Held to the light, one can see evidence of stitching that would have held a cloth badge. The badge was detached from the shirt and displayed on the wall of Pantling's pub, alongside his medals and caps. The Cup Final team did not have numbered shirts. That one exists on this one is down to a grandson, who added the number 11 whilst playing in it in the 1970s.

Assistance Given: Fred Tunstall

Fred Tunstall was one of United's finest pre-war players. Born in Staffordshire, he joined United from Scunthorpe in 1920 for a then Midland League record transfer fee of £1,000. In modern football parlance Tunstall would be credited with many 'assists' to the scoring exploits of his team-mates, particularly those of Jimmy Dunne. Standing at 5' 7", Tunstall came from a South Yorkshire coal mining family but did not play football seriously until aged 18. De-mobbed in 1919 after four and a half years with the Royal Horse Artillery, he joined a couple of local amateur teams in the Barnsley area where his talent was recognised by the town's professional club. However, they would not pay the requested signing-on fee of £10. Consequently, aged 23, Tunstall signed for Scunthorpe, and after just 19 appearances, joined Sheffield United making his debut days later against Spurs at White Hart Lane. The low key transfer had evidently caught the Spurs manager Peter MacWilliam unawares. Absenting himself from his team's fixture, he was watching Scunthorpe—in the hope of signing Tunstall.

A cigarette card featuring Fred Tunstall who scored the winning goal for United in the 1925 Cup Final

A one-time coal miner, Tunstall was very strong and had a long raking stride which was deceptively fast. He could strike a dead ball with a ferocity not seen in the United side for the previous 30 years. His crosses for Dunne and Harry Johnson were so hard that the latter admitted having second thoughts as to whether to connect with his head. Tunstall became an essential part of a triangle of talent, playing on the left wing alongside George Green at left half and Billy Gillespie at inside left. Offers for Tunstall came in from Manchester City, Huddersfield Town and Nottingham Forest. By 1928 he had missed just 13 games in eight seasons, and was not dropped until November 1930.

His debut saw United lose 4–1. From this inauspicious beginning Tunstall went on to play 437 League games and score 129 goals. A further five goals were scored in 35 FA Cup ties, one of which was the 1925 FA Cup winner. He also won seven England caps in an era of few international fixtures and represented the Football League XI. Loyal and proud, Tunstall would frequently play whilst carrying injuries. He stayed with United for almost 12 years before being sold to Halifax Town in 1932. Leaving Halifax to manage non-league Boston United, the meagre resources there saw him acting as physio, groundsman, scout and even painter. The post-war United legend Joe Shaw visited the club on a scouting mission in the late 1960s. He found Tunstall working as the groundsman warming himself by a brazier. On his watch chain hung his FA Cup Winners' medal and the Cup Final commemorative watch.

Tunstall died aged 71 in 1970. Contacted by his solicitor in the early 1980s, Sheffield United bought his collection of footballing honours for a very reasonable price. Tunstall specified that upon the death of both him and his wife, United be offered first option on his collection. The medals were the first items placed in the Hall of Fame.

The Contortionist: Bill Cook

Few players who have worn the stripes of the Blades can claim to have won an FA Cup winner's medal. Bill Cook was fortunate enough to have won two and these over a decade apart. Cook joined United in 1912 and became part of the team as it made the transition into the modern game. Cook was born into mining stock in the North East village of Unsworth in 1890. He came to the attention of Sheffield United as a 22-year-old plying his trade with local side Hebburn Argyle and was signed to take the right back shirt worn for many years by Bob Benson. On Cook's arrival, Benson switched sides and took over as captain. Being double-jointed Cook would amuse team-mates in training by wrapping his legs around the back of his neck. If not a footballer, he could have been a music-hall contortionist.

Cook became an integral part of the team that became such a force in the lead up to the outbreak of the First World War, eventually claiming a Cup Winner's medal in 1915. His chances of being capped by his country were snatched away by the war years during which he served his country but turned out for United when the chance arose. Following the resumption of the Football League—and unlike many of his contemporaries—Cook settled back into the side. Carrying on from where he had left off, he played in the 1923 FA Cup semi-final against Bolton Wanderers and gained his second FA Cup triumph in 1925, where he was vice-captain to Billy Gillespie.

Cook's last appearance for United's first team came in January 1927. During all the years he played for Sheffield United, his family remained in the North East and he was one of the few players on United's books who received a railway pass. Cook travelled to Sheffield to train on designated days and lodged in a house on Kearsley Road near to Bramall Lane. Bizarrely, when his United career ended he decided to buy a shop in Sheffield and move the family down.

Cook later ran a pub in the Sharrow district of Sheffield before settling down to a life in the steelworks. He never owned a car and

Bill Cook

was famous for walking great distances and advocated clean living and physical exercise. One mid-evening he answered a knock on the door to find a police constable from Woodseats Police Station standing before him. The officer enquired as to whether Cook had been out walking that afternoon and whether he had lost anything. Replying 'yes' and 'no' respectively Cook looked puzzled. The officer then asked with a straight face: 'So you didn't play in the 1915 Cup Final for United then?' before handing him the Cup Winners medal which Cook had dropped and which a finder had handed in to the police.

A Final Glance: Ernest Milton

The 1925 Cup Winners' medal of Ernest Milton is the only one of its type still contained in the original box. Milton kept his medal under lock and key and resisted the fashion of wearing it on a watch chain. One of eight brothers, three of whom became professional footballers, Milton was born at the end of the nineteenth century in Kimberworth, Rotherham and signed for United from Parkgate in 1916. Working in the war years in the coal mine he signed professional forms when hostilities ceased. His brother, who had won the League Championship with Sunderland, was killed on active service in France in 1917.

Ernest Milton

A degree of confusion and even controversy appears in Milton's early times with United. In 1918 he was to claim that he signed amateur forms as a result of misrepresentation. A year later he apologised in a letter to the United board and offered his footballing services hoping there was no ill-feeling. No other document exists to cast light on this issue. Probably both parties were keen to draw a veil over proceedings. Playing as a left back Milton made 271 appearances in United's colours and scored four goals. An able athlete, he was also a very good crown green bowls player. The green at Bramall Lane adjacent to the cricket pavilion allowed him to practise after football training—at his peak he represented Yorkshire. At one time in the early 1960s the Millhouses bowling team in the south west of Sheffield had no fewer than three FA Cup winners from the Blades playing for them—Milton, Bill Cook and Billy Gillespie.

Milton's playing days ended soon after the 1925 Cup Final. The change to the offside law did not suit his game. His life post-football was modest. After being out of work for 18 months he eventually became a partner in a coal delivery business. Burgled later in life, all the medals he won in football were stolen, bar one. The FA Cup Winner's medal was fortunately in safekeeping with a grandson in the Midlands. The medal on display in the Hall of Fame appeared at Wembley in the FA Cup semi-final in 1993 around the neck of his United fan daughter. When Milton died in 1984, he was still living in the terraced house near Bramall Lane that he bought on joining United.

On the day he was buried the hearse containing his body was driven around United's Bramall Lane stadium. The vehicle was under instructions from his wife to pause momentarily in the South Stand car park. It was her belief that before he left this world he would wish to have a final look at his beloved Bramall Lane.

The Office Boy: Jack Pickering

In 1925, at the tender age of 15, Jack Pickering signed for Sheffield United from Mortemly St Saviours Boys Club. Football clubs did not have the apprentice system for mid-teen talent at the time and were not allowed to sign players as young as 15. To get around this Pickering was signed under the title of 'Office Boy' and some elementary office work was found for him to add to the deceit. Pickering was a grammar school boy from Barnsley and was good with numbers. Unfortunately the job he took up in 1929 to supplement his part-time football income was in a bookmaker's which caused apoplexy for the Methodists on the United board of directors. They soon found him a position they considered more suitable and he eventually qualified as a chartered accountant.

Pickering scored in his trial match against Burnley reserves on the day of the 1925 Cup Final. He was just 16. He made his first-team debut in February 1927, aged 17, and proved a very capable ball player who could execute the cross-field long-distance passing that characterised United teams for decades. A well-groomed individual, he seemingly never broke sweat and preferred method over ostentation. He saw his job as passing with minimal effort and

A 1932 photo of United's Jack Pickering wearing his England shirt

considered he had done something wrong if circumstances forced him to beat an opponent. He did the job that was required on the pitch and, throughout his time at United, remained a part-time player. Pipe smoking and a slow dresser, he was always the last to leave the dressing room.

He remained at Bramall Lane for 23 years and in 550 League games scored 200 goals. He was subject to transfer enquiries from Arsenal, Liverpool and Everton, played for the Football League, and made one England appearance against Scotland in 1933. Once dropped by United he scored six goals in his first match for the reserves. He played his final game in January 1948 and left United in May. Moving to the south coast he became an hotelier and briefly coached Poole Town. He died in Bournemouth in 1976.

> **Three individuals who were part of the Bramall Lane set-up in the latter part of this decade left legacies of both fame and infamy. One was to become one of the club's greatest ever goalscorers, having quite probably learned his trade whilst detained for his political sympathies. Another, whilst taking on the role of Union (and implicitly political) activist, was to have his career finished having bit the hand that fed him. Another individual played only one game for the club but was to make a name for himself at both club and international level in various parts of Europe. His footballing knowledge was not however particularly appreciated by those who ran the game in his native land.**

Republican Movements: Jimmy Dunne

Born in Dublin in 1905, Jimmy Dunne holds the club's scoring record for his feats in the 1930–31 season when he scored 41 League goals plus five more in the FA Cup. His football ability is remarkable when his personal history is taken into consideration. Dunne probably learned his football courtesy of an internment camp in Ireland whilst imprisoned under suspicion of Irish Republican Army membership. In the turmoil that was Ireland between 1916 and the early 1920s, many a young man lost his life or liberty for his beliefs. Dunne survived the era to play football at the highest level but at one time was detained without trial in the Currough Barracks of County Kildare in the company of hundreds of fellow republicans. Brought up playing Gaelic games with their associated anti-British ethos, we can only surmise that the seven-a-side Association Football permitted in the camp fulfilled some role in his later sporting, and even political, development. The techniques required for a centre forward became second nature to Dunne and, in him, United had one of the greatest players of his era. He played at Bramall Lane for 8 seasons before moving to Arsenal in 1933.

Jimmy Dunne

Playing Association Football with Shamrock Rovers at the age of 18 Dunne moved to England two years later to join the now defunct New Brighton. Only four months later he signed for United for a £500 fee. A slow start saw him considered something of an enigma. Impressive in the reserves, his form was not replicated when chosen for the first team. He played only one full game in the 1926–27 season and only eight in the season that followed. The final game of 1928–29 saw him score two, the following season he scored 36 goals in 39 League games and bettered this by scoring 41 in 41 games in 1930–31 plus a further five in FA cup ties. In 1931–32 he scored 32 in 37 games and 26 in 40 games the season after.

Renowned for his brilliant aerial ability and powerful heading, Dunne was nicknamed 'Snowy' by virtue of his blond hair. Fast with great control and capable of using both feet, Dunne was difficult for any defender and to cap it all was particularly dangerous in dead-ball situations. He was by any definition a dashing player who had a footballing brain. He twice scored four goals (three with his head) and four times scored a hat trick. Capped for Ireland in 1928 whilst a United reserve, he played many times for his country with appearances complicated by two issues. One was the seasickness he suffered; colleagues remembered his reluctance to cross the Irish Sea in winter. The other was the complexity of recognition in Irish football. The Belfast based FA was recognised by their English counterparts, but the South did not have FIFA recognition.

Dunne's goal-scoring abilities attracted the attentions of other teams. United turned down bids from Birmingham in 1928 and Huddersfield the year after. In 1932 Arsenal offered £10,000, which was close to a record fee for the time. They eventually got their man the year after for £8,000. A move to London was

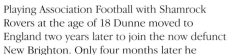

Harry Johnson showing the attacking prowess that made him the greatest goalscorer in the history of Sheffield United

not a success. In fact, United tried to re-sign Dunne in 1935, only for a cartilage injury to scupper the plan. In 1936 Dunne moved to Southampton for £1,000. A year later, he was captain and coach of Shamrock Rovers. Five years later, he was coach of Bohemians of Dublin. He died in 1949 and is buried in Deansgrange cemetery in north Dublin. His gravestone holds a photograph of him in his beloved United shirt.

A Failed Gamble: Albert Chandler

Making his final appearance for United, appropriately on April 1st, 1929, was the Carlisle-born full back Albert Chandler. Arriving at Bramall Lane from Newcastle in 1926 for a fee of £2,600, Chandler proved to be a solid player, particularly effective in slide tackles and made 80 League and Cup appearances. Off the pitch he was the club's Players' Union representative. He also enjoyed a gamble. Unfortunately the Union subscriptions he took from his team-mates went towards his pursuit of doubling his money and in 1928 Chandler was unable to pass on the subscriptions. When this came to light, the United directors decided to deduct the subs owed to the Union from his wages. He was also placed on the transfer list at the same price United had paid for him three years earlier.

He requested on three occasions that the club reduce his fee, which they did by a few hundred pounds each time. The player was under the illusion that only the transfer fee was holding back interested clubs. In truth, a statement written by the United board that accompanied the transfer list, stated that the player's registration was 'to be refused due to special circumstances'. Other clubs knew that this apparently innocuous statement hid a host of detail. Chandler was due to join Mansfield Town, then applying to join the Football League, but was never to play for them, probably because they realised their pursuit of League status would not be helped by being associated with such a character. In November 1929 Chandler was playing for Northfleet United in Kent, a year later for Manchester Central and later again for Holmhead in the Carlisle and District League. He was still a United player in 1932 in that the club still held his registration. By then his fee had been reduced to £250, but still no professional club came for him. Chandler's League career was effectively finished by the United board, appalled at his behaviour.

Prophet or Traitor?: George Raynor

The Hoyland-born outside right George Raynor played only one first-team game for Sheffield United, but went on to become the manager of the Swedish national side and Juventus of Italy. Turning out for junior club sides, Elsecar Bible Class, Mexborough Athletic, and Wombwell Town, Raynor signed for United in April 1930, aged 23. His one appearance came in October 1931 in a County Cup fixture against Wednesday. Placed on the transfer list six months later, he was released on a free to Mansfield Town and in later years turned out for Rotherham United, Bury, and Aldershot. Very fast and tricky on the ball, Raynor's undistinguished lower-league career produced just over 160 appearances. Turning his hand to coaching, however, he rose to remarkable heights.

Raynor became coach of AIK of Stockholm before being appointed coach to the Swedish national team. In the 1948 Olympics his Sweden side defeated England. Returning to England that same year, he managed the Great Britain Amateurs, only to return to Sweden the following year to manage the national side whom he took to the final stages of the 1950 World Cup in Brazil. Eight years later he led them to the final on home soil in which they were beaten by Brazil. In 1953 his Sweden side drew 2–2 with Hungary in Budapest. Officials from the English FA watched the game in advance of the impending visit of Hungary to Wembley. Raynor advised his English visitors how to play against the mighty Magyars. Ignoring his advice, England lost 6–3 at Wembley and the following year 7–1 in Budapest. When asked about this, Raynor opined that the English were too proud to learn from a small country like Sweden —a fault, he claimed, of 'British rigidity'.

An autobiography written in 1964 titled, *Prophet or Traitor*, set out his ideas on how to improve the English game. These included an 18-team top division, a winter break and a system which made youngsters study the game. His coaching success with Sweden attracted the attentions of wealthy Italian clubs, and in the early 1950s Raynor coached Juventus and Lazio. Saving Lazio from relegation, Raynor resigned after becoming convinced that his players had thrown a match. In the early 1950s, Raynor returned to England as manager of Coventry City. The directors of the club were seeking instant success, but Raynor's preferred method was to build on youth, reserving transfer funds for experienced players to hold key positions. When a general manager was appointed to oversee his position as team manager, Raynor resigned.

Unable to find another professional club, Raynor was, by late 1956, coaching football and teaching English to Hungarian refugees living in emergency accommodation provided by the Derbyshire Miner's Welfare in Lincolnshire coastal resorts. He was saved from this position by returning to Sweden where, two years later, he managed the losing finalists of the World Cup. In recognition of his achievements, the King of Sweden made Raynor a Knight. In 1960, the Sweden team under Raynor became only the second foreign nation to defeat England at home. Returning to England, he was still unable to find a league club and the only offer came from Skegness Town in the Midland League. Remaining here for two years, he went back to Sweden for the last time and then returned to England, finally getting a managerial position in the mid-60s with Doncaster Rovers. He died in Buxton, Derbyshire in 1985 and was buried in his 1960 Swedish national team tracksuit.

> **The decade ended with the game integral to the national psyche. The broadcasting media helped by technological advances, realised the attractions of the game. Throughout the country people were to gather in millions around the wireless to listen to live match reports. Others gathered in their thousands, and with the aid of printed media, were to sing songs which soon found their way into the communal football crowd gatherings.**

Back to Square One: Radio Broadcast 1927

The first live football radio commentary by the BBC was an Arsenal–Sheffield United fixture, played at Highbury in January 1927. A live sports broadcast had been trialled the previous week at a Rugby Union international between England and Wales at Twickenham. Considered a success, the BBC decided to do the same thing for Association Football. Because of its proximity to the BBC's London headquarters, Highbury was chosen and the 1–1 draw was listened to by millions. Two commentators sat in the Avenall Road grandstand at Highbury amongst a crowd of just under 17,000 and whilst one described the play, the other spoke over him with just the words *1–2–3–4–5–6–7–8*. The logic of this was evident to listeners who had bought copies of the *Radio Times*, which carried a diagram of the Highbury stadium and numbered the pitch in eight sections (four in each half). Thus *1–2–3–4* would inform the listener where the ball was when United were defending. When they broke out beyond the halfway line

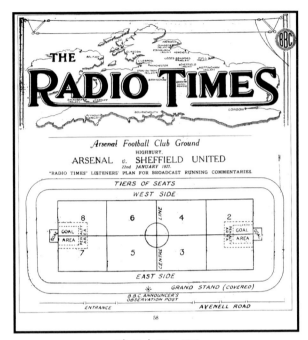

The Radio Times 1927

Advertising the first radio football commentary involving Arsenal and Sheffield United

5–6–7–8 warned the listener of their proximity to the opponents' goal. Many believe that the much-used adage 'back to square one' was derived from such broadcasting.

The Football League debated whether broadcasting would affect gate receipts. The northern clubs were badly hit by unemployment and were critical of what radio coverage might do to attendance figures. However, their fears were overcome and by 1931 the BBC was broadcasting over 100 games a season and even broadcast the FA Cup draw in 1935. The results service provided by the BBC proved to be particularly significant to the punters playing the pools. When the BBC's *Sports Report* began in 1949 the game and the broadcasting service became synonymous in the nation's consciousness.

Abiding Memories: Community singing

Emerging in the mid-1920s was a national movement that promoted community singing. Collective renditions of popular songs and hymns were performed by hundreds and, at football matches, tens of thousands of enthusiasts. Sponsored by the *Daily Express*, such singing swept the nation in a phenomenon that had its roots in a combination of the Victorian music hall and the communal singing manifested by the Allied troops in the First World War. The 1927 FA Cup Final was the first to witness pre-match community singing. The *Daily Express* enclosed song sheets in that day's edition. The singing spread to football grounds around the country. Locally, singing was supported by the words to songs inserted in editions of the *Yorkshire Telegraph*. Football magazines similarly published words to songs in anticipation of their readers' enthusiasm. The songs chosen were those considered suitable for the moment and varied from *What shall we do with the drunken sailor?* to *Charlie is my darling*. Some were naval shanties, others such as *It's a long way to Tipperary* and *Keep the home fires burning* were legacies of the troop songs of the First World War.

Explaining this short-lived phenomenon is difficult but the answer possibly lies in communal singing being promoted as an antidote to the social tensions evident in Britain after the General Strike of 1926. Via song people were, albeit temporarily, united in a shared enthusiasm. The enduring legacy for football gatherings was the hymn *Abide with Me* written in 1897 by a Devon-based vicar as he faced terminal illness. The words commemorate loss, with tints of end-of-life regret. The composition struck a chord with King George V who reputedly requested the hymn to be sung at the 1927 final. Since that time its singing has been a Cup Final tradition. The song, and the context, was functional. No lesser a person than the king of the realm, surrounded by the middle class, was momentarily, but very publicly, united in song with around 100,000 members of the lower orders. It was a unity possibly more imagined than actual, but the melody and words were sentimental enough to suit the sacred occasion, both then and even today.

There was plenty to sing about as the decade ended. The city had come through dreadful industrial disputes and United had survived both the economic complications of the time and won the FA Cup. About to enter their third decade at the top level of the English game, the Blades were a worthy and, depending on what one believed, relatively wealthy entity that could attract some of the game's best players. The United club secretary could state on September 14th, 1929, as the decade drew to a close that, 'it is becoming increasingly plain that in these days of highly commercialised sport there can be less and less room for sentiment'. Little over a decade later the singing stopped as a World War began and bombs fell on the city. In late October 1929 the New York Stock Exchange crashed. The era known as the Great Depression ensued throughout the next decade. Industrialised countries were the worst affected. As a city based on heavy industry, Sheffield suffered more than most. However, a policy of re-armament begun in 1936 saw the demand for steel and coal rise. Sheffield thus saw a booming economy and a United side return to the top flight in 1939.

Early memorabilia—
1920's 'Bertie Blade' statuette
and United mug

Sheffield United as depicted by cartoonist Harry Heap in 1931

Goodbye to all That

The game was rapidly going global. The first World Cup tournament held in Uruguay in 1930 was notable for the absence of England and the other Home Nations teams all of whom had withdrawn from FIFA in 1928. In response after the tournament the FA invited world champions Uruguay to test their abilities against English clubs. The South Americans did not accept. Players from around the world started to appear in the English game. In 1933, South African born players turned out for Liverpool and Frank Soo, born in Buxton the son of a Chinese laundry man, played for Stoke. In October 1930, Bramall Lane hosted an England v Ireland international, the fifth such accolade in United's history, albeit 27 years since the last one. In December 1934, United hosted the players and officials of FK Austria, who were to watch a United game days before playing an exhibition match against Sheffield Wednesday. In 1933, United eventually crossed water to play exhibition games in Belfast, Derry and Dublin, the latter two matches arranged by virtue of the transfers of Billy Gillespie and Jimmy Dunne. The game in Dublin saw the establishment of the Duggan Cup, which was played annually in the mid-thirties between Shamrock Rovers and Sheffield United and then fizzled out. New influences of both ideas and players were to enter the English game. Football became a chance to gaze upon people and admire their ways or have stereotypes confirmed.

United began the decade with Charles Clegg as President, leading a 15-man board of directors. Two years later, however, the match programme for April 1932 was printed with a black border in commemoration of the death of Club Secretary, John Nicholson, killed in a road accident outside Sheffield's Midland station on his way to join the squad for a match against Aston Villa in Birmingham. With Nicholson died over 30 years of dedicated service to United. The match programme contained a dedication, which stated:

> ...a white soul has gone to the choir invisible... a straight, true man... if he could not speak good of a man, he never spoke ill... every future cup final day will be like a revolving tombstone to the memory.

New Trainers?
Modern football emerged out of the 1930s. The decade was one of the most significant in the development of the game in England, producing innovation both on and off pitch. That which we now take for granted in terms of tactics, club organisation and media coverage developed as the game became ever more ingrained in the national consciousness. At national level, a former referee and secretary of the FA, Stanley Rous, was appointed secretary to the FA in 1934 and sought to implement a coaching scheme from schoolboy level to national team. Newspapers which hitherto provided factual match reports became more questioning, seeking that considered news-worthy and celebrity-led. The letters pages of local newspapers became the forum for fans' debate. Radio and later television embellished both the aural and visual enchantment that was and remains the core of the game.

The decade started well for United. Their profit on the 1930–31 season was £1,868. The club programme hinted of two clubs elsewhere 'living on the bank' to the sum of £10,000. The majority of United players were paid between £5 and £6 per week; first teamers earned between £7 and £10. The match programme in August 1932 explained their failure to pay the full going rate for a first-class player was due to the world economic depression.

A year later, United sold their leading goal scorer Jimmy Dunne to Arsenal. Responding to the supporters' fury, United chorused in time-honoured fashion that the club had to sell because they needed the money. They also claimed income through the gate was inadequate after a succession of poor seasons. Whilst blaming a lack of support was par for the course, the club did seek improvements elsewhere. United were part of a Football League representation urging, unsuccessfully, the Chancellor of the Exchequer to abolish Entertainment Tax because of the financial burden it was placing on football clubs.

By 1937 United had 33 players on their books, none of them over the age of 30. A player's wages were usually far better than those of the workmen who paid to watch him. The club secretaries, who basically did the bidding of the board and ensured the clubs ran smoothly, fell by the wayside as tactics and, indeed, the game generally became more sophisticated. The footballer's image was becoming ever more available in the *Topical Times* football magazine and later in TV newsreels. In 1938, the FA Cup Final was broadcast live for the first time. A Player's orders now mainly came from a man with a title of 'secretary-manager'. Such men had negotiated new powers for themselves, which impinged on players' pay and conditions. They became the public face of the clubs in the eyes of the fans and the media. Typical of these was the South Yorkshire-born Herbert Chapman, who would not sign players for Arsenal if they smoked or were renowned for drinking, seeking instead players who favoured abstinence and domestic comfort. Such a tactic was obviously considered commendable as Chapman earned the phenomenal wage for a manager at that time of £2000 a year and had a five-year contract.

In 1934, two years after appointing their first secretary-manager Teddy Davison, United finished bottom of the League table. The choice of Gateshead born Davison as manager was somewhat unusual in that he was a former Sheffield Wednesday player with no fewer than 424 League and Cup appearances in the Owl's colours. He also had one England cap. He later became player-manager at Mansfield Town before joining Chesterfield with whom he won the division three (North) championship. Intelligent, shrewd and incorruptible, Davison remained at United for 20 years and left a side that had great potential.

The close season of 1932 saw an unprecedented number of trainers appointed or dismissed in the English game. At Bramall Lane, George Waller had retired in 1930 and had been succeeded in the position of trainer by Tom Radcliffe. Radcliffe had played for Arsenal, Brentford and Notts County, before acting as masseur both to the England cricket team, and national football team as well as elite level boxers, athletes and university teams. His stay was brief, just two years, before being replaced by David Steele. The latter, a former Huddersfield Town and Scottish international, joined United after winning the Danish Championship with Bold Klubben. He too stayed for just two years, before leaving to manage Bradford City in the summer of 1936. In turn, he was replaced by Dugald (Duggie) Livingstone, a former Celtic, Aberdeen and Everton player, who left United in 1948 to manage Newcastle and later the Belgian national side.

Going Down: Life in Division Two

Relegation was a new reality for Sheffield United at the end of the 1933–34 season. Promotion eluded United until 1939. In the meantime, the club sought to sustain the crowds that a club of their status considered was their right. This caused a degree of resentment when, by April 1935, an Easter Monday home fixture against Fulham attracted just over 12,000 fans (in the same April, only 4,014 turned up to watch United play Notts Forest) and with it the condemnation in the following week's match programme:

> *A first class club cannot be maintained adequately on such poor support… Sheffield's poor support of its clubs is the talk of the whole country…*

Economic depression kept many from spending their money at Bramall Lane but playing ability was, no doubt, a contributing factor. Fortunately for the club and its coffers, things improved on the pitch in 1936. Indeed, between mid-December 1935 and up to and including their reaching the FA Cup Final in April 1936, United were defeated only three times in 29 matches. The 1937–38 season was heartbreaking in that United lost out on promotion on goal average. The following season saw a very strong United team formed around a backbone of goalkeeper Jack Smith and a solid defence of Harry Hooper, Albert

1930's Boots and shin pads

Cox, Ernest Jackson and Tommy Johnson. The forward line saw the prolific Ephraim 'Jock' Dodds frightening defences on his way to becoming the club's leading scorer for five consecutive seasons.

The early part of the 1938–39 season was typified by inconsistencies—with United winning only four of their first 14 games. Good victories were soon followed by bad defeats. To address this, United bought Jimmy Hagan from Derby County in November 1938 for a fee of £2,925. This outlay was soon justified when the club began a period of consistency that put them in second place by January 1939. In the same month a Cup tie at home to Manchester City attracted a crowd just short of 50,000 and victory that brought a home fixture against Grimsby Town. For this fixture the attendance was over 62,000. The tie was drawn and the Blades lost the replay. Towards the end of the 1938–39 season with United's promotion hopes on tenterhooks, leading scorer Jock Dodds left for Blackpool. His transfer request was accepted and, of the many clubs who sought his signature, he chose Blackpool—a sum of £10,000 was agreed. The England international Ted Sandford was bought from West Bromwich for his calm experience and George Henson from Bradford replaced Dodds as the league table saw Wednesday neck and neck with United.

The last game of the season saw Tottenham visit Bramall Lane with United needing a win to go up. Spending the evening before the game in a Derbyshire hotel was a form of psychology, or maybe kidology, by Secretary-Manager Teddy Davison. Realising that United's home form was poor (lost three, drawn nine) but their away form was excellent (only two points off a record for the division), Davison made the home game an 'away' game with the overnight stay. The strategy seemed to work—United took the lead after ten seconds. The game ended in a 6–1 victory and United were promoted behind Blackburn Rovers and above Wednesday by one point. After only three Division One fixtures, however, the league was suspended in 1939 following the declaration of war.

Ownership and Control

The men who controlled United in this decade remained guided by the teachings of Methodism. They led by example and epitomised the belief that virtue was its own reward and lived the unblemished life personified by hard work and sobriety. Their financial commitment to the club was primarily one of guaranteeing loans, usually with low interest. Their return was the glory by association of any footballing triumph and the hope that on leaving the board their money would be returned. One director at the time Mr George Lawrence, known to all as 'Bladesman', might be considered more generous than his colleagues. Modelling himself on Charles Clegg, Lawrence loathed gambling and was a well-known philanthropist. He funded the open-air swimming pool in his home village of Hathersage in Derbyshire and offered cash for transfers but the board said no. This former newspaper seller was a self-made man and former referee who not only funded an annual, pre-season day out and dinner in Hathersage for the United squad, but also, out of his own pocket, paid for a roof to be built over the Kop in 1936–37. He also bought Jock Dodds, United's top goalscorer in the 1935–36 season, an Armstrong-Siddley car as a show of appreciation. But God works in strange ways and Lawrence was killed during the Luftwaffe bombing of Sheffield, whilst driving to his razor blade factory (hence the nickname). Many similar men to Lawrence, by virtue of owning businesses, had the power of employment and so could provide footballers with the promise of jobs, at times to supplement their footballing income or as a guarantee should a football career not work out. If this were not possible, they could usually have a word in an ear to ensure favourable conditions for their players, aspiring or departed, in a variety of circumstances.

Others, not troubled by biblical foreboding about money-lending and speculation, sought profit rather than status from football. They were to attract the wrath of the football administration of the time. In 1931, the Football League Management Committee sought to close down the pools companies. As a consequence, a dispute remembered as the 'pools war' began. With the approval of 64 of the 85 League clubs, the fixture list was withheld long enough in the course of the week to prevent pools coupons from being printed and distributed for the weekend. Unfortunately, ignorance about who was playing who and where, was reflected in match attendances. This situation was eventually challenged by the chairman of Leeds United. The lists were published as normal weeks later—a tacit acceptance that football and gambling were inseparable. Then the law courts decided that the pools was an issue of skill rather than chance, and therefore did not fall under the Gambling Act of 1853. By 1939 10 million people in Britain played the pools.

Footballers might still have the job their peers wished they had, but their union was weak and the discipline imposed on them on occasion at their place of work would not have been tolerated in many other professions. A form of player power was evidently emerging early in this decade. In January 1931, United's secretary in the match programme lamented 'players who know it all' and spoke of the prevalence of players who resented interference from directors and colleagues. No more was written, but the words hinted at a growing articulacy and even militancy amongst the club's employees. The board still ran the show and would not be slow to remind players who called the shots. The maximum wage, fixed in 1922 at £8 a week during the season and £6 during the summer, remained the same in the 1930s. That said, Sheffield United paid the maximum wage to just four of their 21 professionals in the 1934–35 season and awarded none of their players a benefit match between 1931 and 1936.

Footballers' Lives

It should come as no surprise that when opportunities arose for extra income players grabbed it. Thus Harry Hooper, the United captain in the 1936 Cup Final endorsed Cherry Blossom shoe polish for a fee of less than £20. In the contest for better pay, by the outbreak of war in 1939 the Players' Union had enrolled 2,000 players and was seeking to gain compensation payments for players injured out of the game during the decade. The Football League, however, was seeking at the same time to stop the emergence of amateur Sunday football and to prevent stadiums being used for sporting activities other than football.

With a lot of free time compared to other men of their age, footballers faced the temptations offered by this decade. The social life of Sheffield was far more limiting than in later decades, but alcohol was freely available; money, however, was not. Many a player who had moved to the city to play football saw their lives consist of a small house above a shop near Bramall Lane. Here the matriarchal figure of Mrs Mavis Cocker looked after four professional footballers. Known colloquially as 'Cockers Lodgers', she provided bed and board for United's footballers in her Kearsley Road home in Sheffield's Sharrow district.

Off the pitch the players' pleasures were primarily sedentary. The cinema was more often than not the place of choice after training. Some cinema managers provided free tickets for footballers. Those seeking more excitement could walk to the Hyde Park dog tracks. The 30's footballer like his counterpart decades later still made statements by sartorial cuts of cloth. The more fashionable of the time would wear Plus Fours appropriated from the golf course to the city centre hang-out. Suits tailored by Barney Goodman on The Moor would be worn to the dances held at the Cutlers' Hall and the City Hall, which opened in 1934. Those seeking a less hectic sustenance were to be found in the Milk Bar opposite the Town Hall or

Birds and footballers

Tommy Johnson shows his shooting
accuracy courtesy of the Earl of
Wharncliffe's estate, 1936

Davy's Corner House or Burts Café sat in the company of those who paid to watch them. Those preferring beer to tea and buns frequented the city centre licensed premises of Nell's Bar or The Nelson, The Grapes and The Angel.

The players were under strict instructions from the club not to be seen out socialising on a Friday night. Alcohol consumption remained anathema to Charles Clegg. Living where beer was served continued to cause players to leave the club. The aforementioned Mrs Cocker became landlady of The Chantry at Woodseats and took in United star Alex Forbes as a lodger. This caused boardroom consternation as this was clearly in breach of club, and contractual, regulations. The matter was resolved when Forbes moved soon afterwards to Arsenal. The Red Lion at Heeley, a favourite watering hole of Blades' players for decades, could have caused boardroom consternation when the United goalkeeper Jack Smith began dating Emma Thompson, whose parents ran the pub. A 'secret room', located at the back of the pub and concealed from public view by a thick curtain, was reserved for United players. As a consequence, the prying eyes of manager and Methodist teetotaller Teddy Davison, were unable to find any miscreants when he occasionally came searching for his wayward players.

A New Ball Game

A new managerial sophistication was entering the game. By December 1934, Arsenal were paying £100 per month towards a scouting network consisting of ex-players and managers. The former Spurs' manager Peter MacWilliam headed this organisation with a roving commission to find the best players in the land. It was also Arsenal that innovated with a covered pitch-side dug-out. Sheffield United's contribution to modernity was more modest, beginning in 1935 the match programme cover page was produced in colour. Two years previously, the programme advertised electric lamps. More primal human requirements were evidenced in 1936 when the headline 'Wake up your liver bile' advertised liver pills, apparently to 'relieve tiredness'.

In November 1930, Sheffield Wednesday's innovative training methods included the rotation of players. The stated logic from Wednesday was that colleagues could learn more about the game from putting themselves in their team-mates' positions. The following year a debate took place at the FA on the possible banning of the slide tackle. This was not implemented, but one ban that was brought in during October 1930 was on stadium clocks. The FA was fearful of possible discrepancies between the time displayed and the time as dictated by match officials. The ban came out of a fear of disorder that may have ensued in disputed scenarios.

Same game, new ball: the T-ball model as it appeared in the 1930s

More advanced technology was similarly unwelcome. In December 1932 London clubs met to discuss floodlights. Their willingness to embrace the technology was not shared by provincial clubs, probably fearful of the cost of installation and electricity bills. There was still, however, confusion over long standing socio-religious issues. In December 1931 the English FA refused to allow players to represent Ireland when selected to play a match against Spain under the jurisdiction of the Free State FA because it would involve playing a game on a Sunday. Plans for a winter break were

Liver bile!
A graphic lesson in bodily functions in the September 1938 match programme

discussed in January 1932, hard pitches and semi-darkness had caused player injuries; the cold was discomforting for spectators and had resulted in poor crowds. The mid-term break idea was dropped on realisation that the season would extend to May and could impinge on cricket.

The concept of the substitute was pioneered at an FA trial match in Huddersfield in April 1932 when a player was allowed to replace one taken off injured. The FA subsequently decided that substitutes could be introduced 'by arrangements made before the commencement of the match' but not in any game played under the rules of a competitive match. The emphasis in coaching was still on strength and stamina, albeit spa-baths and trips to coastal resorts became more common before crucial matches. The aim was to impress more than ever the paying crowds. Problems arose however when the crowds stopped attending through no fault of the players.

Moving targets

Bramall Lane hosted the 1938 FA Cup semi-final, which no doubt offered some relief to the club's perilous financial situation. But football was not prohibitive in its prices. A season ticket to Bramall Lane at the beginning of the decade cost a 'Gentleman' seeking to sit in the centre stand 48 shillings. An 'accompanying lady' would pay 24 shillings. In the event of the lady being unable to attend, her ticket could be transferred to a gentleman who, on production of the ticket, would have to pay a further two shillings and sixpence. Season tickets for the terrace cost 30 shillings. A regular could, for this outlay, watch up to 25 games a season.

Regardless of social pretensions, which may have accompanied a supporter's location in Bramall Lane, Sheffield suffered terrible unemployment in the early and mid-1930s on account of the world economic slump arising out of the Wall Street Crash. The subsequent Great Depression brought unemployment, poverty and, no doubt, considerable anger. To assist social harmony in both 1932 and 1934, Sheffield United attempted to reduce admission for the unemployed following a similar policy begun by the Rugby League, but the Football League Management Committee refused them permission. Also in 1934, in response to rumours that the unemployed would storm the gates at the next home game, hundreds of police surrounded Bramall Lane. The club seemed to be quite paternalistic towards the unemployed in its midst, even allowing a physical training display by the unemployed under the aegis of the Yorkshire Unemployed Advisory Council before the final home game of the 1938–39 season. Unemployed leagues were organised mid-decade by the local FA with the support of the local press and city council and hand-in-hand with property owners. Private pitches were made available—a paternalism by those with power and money to those with neither.

Even in times of hardship mutual fandom did not mean all would pull in the same direction. In 1936 C.E. Sutcliffe, the President of the Football League, called for fans to be more fair and in their spectatorship not barrack rival players. The same year, Sheffield police played their Glasgow and Ulster counterparts at Bramall Lane, curiously allowing half price entry for the unemployed. Most intriguing, however, was a match programme advert on February 15th, 1936, informing readers of a mock trial titled *The Case of the City Hall Liar* to be held in Sheffield police court in aid of the Sheffield Discharged Prisoners Aid Society.

In the 1938–39 season, the club publicly recognised the loss of thousands of local fans who, by virtue of new housing developments (i.e. large council estates), had moved from the slums of central Sheffield to their new outlying dwellings. Their relocation meant that going to the match now had to include transport costs. The economic situation of the decade destroyed some League clubs. Merthyr Tydfil were voted out of the Football League in 1930 following protests from English clubs who left games against the Welshmen with less than £1 as their part of the gate takings. The Depression Years saw 75% unemployment in the Welsh town and only a few hundred could ever afford the ninepence admission. In times of recession, the South Yorkshire region's coal miners were guaranteed three shifts a week. Each shift paid ten shillings. When not working, many were found in the market area of the city centre, where they would assemble to seek labouring work for the day. By 1938 with war approaching, the city saw near full employment as its population was called upon to provide coal and steel needed for armament production. It was difficult to speculate with such boom and bust economies. Football clubs would sensibly be cautious in contracts and wages.

The Libero Position?

Some physical recreation cost nothing. The social cost of pursuing it, however, proved very high for certain enthusiasts. The match programme of August 29th 1931 contains an advert headed 'Don't forget Longshaw'. Underneath is a photo of four young women walking on a path in the countryside. The seeming simplicity of the image and message hides a radical political movement. Readers are implored in these three words to join a day on the moors for health and enjoyment. No other context is provided. The photograph is an anomaly and stands out to a reader. Nothing similar had preceded it, and nothing comparable was to follow. So what was it about? The Longshaw estate is adjacent to the Fox House pub in Derbyshire where generations of Sheffield-based ramblers have met to begin their countryside walks. Originating as a shooting lodge (and today a National Trust property) the call to meet in this location would be a product of a primarily middle-class humanist-socialist movement tinged with elements of William Morris inspired Utopia that was seeking to open the land restricted to the masses by aristocratic landowners. These bourgeois socialists were different from the industrial proletariat but similarly sought a better world. In part this was to be located outside the city with all its capitalist and nihilistic ways.

The better world included good food ethically grown, communal living, and the right to roam on land, which in their philosophy had been taken from the people by an invidious system of privilege. The practice of hiking provided women with their first opportunity to enjoy physical exercise alongside men. The overt political involvement came via the communist-backed British Workers Sports Federation. As the popularity of walking in the countryside grew, the landowners restricted access. A political fight was inevitable. The protagonists were to organise a mass trespass on the Duke of Devonshire's land which included Kinder Scout in the Peak District. The movement claimed the location was common land and therefore they had the right to roam. Some 400 activists marched on the land in 1932. Five of the roamers were arrested and convicted on a charge of riotous assembly and jailed for between two and six months. The right of access to open spaces became a serious part of the political agenda.

How such an advert made its way past the men who ran the club and into the United match programme is open to speculation. A month before the adverts appeared Longshaw House had been purchased by the National Trust. The same page in the match programme had been vacant in previous weeks. The advert was an 'in-fill' and could either be considered a form of early advertising by the National Trust or maybe the Duke of Devonshire was trying to head off the impending antagonism by inviting walkers to roam in a limited area of his estate. We will never know.

8   Sheffield United Football Programme.

DON'T FORGET
LONGSHAW

A DAY ON
THE MOORS

Photo: Sheffield Telegraph

THURSDAY NEXT,
SEPTEMBER 3rd.

Health and Enjoyment.

(Bus Service to Fox House).

The August 1931 advert inviting readers to walk on the Derbyshire moors
A row of cars in the background suggests a wealthy walking fraternity—possibly a Sheepogs Trials Day, even if those doing the walking are here presented as exclusively female. The proposed walk on a September Thursday afternoon is sold to the reader as something to benefit 'health and enjoyment'. There is no obvious political inference in the image

Some of United's finest
Messing around in boats before a match at Torquay ten days before the Cup Final against Arsenal

The First Fan Club

Social activism was manifest around the football club when the United supporters organised themselves into a fan club. In November 1930 the emerging Sheffield United Supporters Club began to advertise its existence in the match programme. The adverts informed readers of their social events, which ranged from an Armistice dance to a fancy dress party in the Bramall Lane cricket pavilion. The autumn of 1930 further announced whist drives, golf tournaments and the founders' ambition to achieve a 500-person membership by Christmas. An annual outing to Liverpool was announced. A year later, special trains advertised travel to watch United play at Leicester where the fans walked from the railway station to place a wreath at a memorial for the Leicester war dead. Interestingly the day out did not depart for Sheffield until 12.30am. The supporters club 1930–31 board and committee saw a local councillor as chairman and club director, J.T. Stokes, acting as vice-chair. The committee contained six women—of the three named, only one surname corresponds to one of the men's names listed. The Honorary secretary of the club was the landlord of the Old Crown on London Road where the supporters club first met. Joining cost one shilling and for another shilling a member could wear the supporters club badge that depicted two crossed knives and the club name.

The literature of the time states that the purpose of the supporters' club as being 'to move in a body and support the club vocally; to let players know that we are backing them up whether they win or lose'. The promise of first refusal when tickets were allocated for Cup Finals was a privilege that membership bought. The supporters club were allowed their own page in the match-day programme by 1933. One article saw them opine about how economic hardship was causing thousands to stay away from Bramall Lane. Shortly after, a benefit match against Sheffield Wednesday saw United let the unemployed in for half price, no fewer than 2,122 out of a crowd of 8,000 entered in such circumstances as a consequence.

Lapping and laughing in pre-season training 1936-37

The supporters club existed beyond United games. It ran excursions to England v Scotland fixtures in Glasgow. As a consequence of the new willingness to travel, the match programme from 1935 saw adverts for Beauchief Coaches. By 1935 the supporters club was controlled by five trustees and could advertise the Blackpool Illuminations as an added extra after watching United play the home team. Some 3,000 Blades fans travelled to Blackpool and the emerging identity of the supporters saw them institute Friday night socials in the cricket pavilion. By the mid-30s the supporters' club vice-chair was the Reverend Tyler Lane whose parish was nearby.

The previously mentioned Blackpool trip was notable for the sale of copies of United's 'Bing Boys' signature tune song sheets, the profits of which went to a children's seaside holiday fund. The Blades' fans enjoyed the evening in the Blackpool Tower music hall, dancing to the resident band which played for them a rendition of *Play Up, United*. By Christmas 1938, the supporters club membership had reached 2,000. Two months later a junior version was begun. In the same month fans met for a church service in Tyler Lane's chapel in the company of directors and players. An angling section was formed in 1939, whilst others preferred the day trips the club organised to Skegness. Sheffield United now existed beyond match day and the most recognisable form of shared enthusiasm was to know the words to Blades' songs.

The 'Bing Boys'

A sub-section of the supporters club was a 15-strong gathering who took the nomenclature of the 'Bing Boys'. The origin of the 'Bing Boys' title probably lies in a series of 'Bing' music reviews held at London's Alhambra Theatre. One in 1916 titled *The Bing Boys Are Here*, starred George Robey and Violet Lorraine who performed the famous *If you were the only girl in the world*. Written by Joseph Green, the 'Bing Boys' song, specific to United, was copyrighted and a music score exists to honour the tune and words.

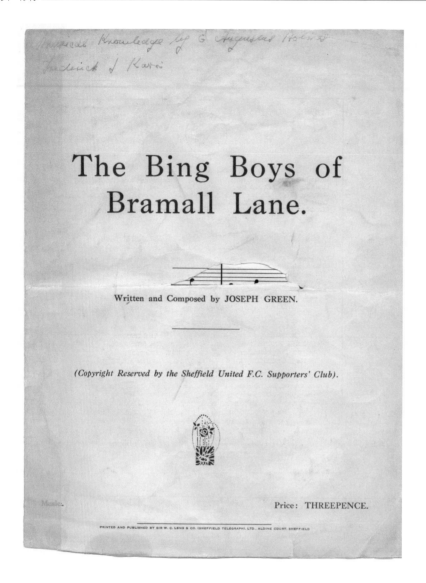

The lyrics were:

Come along, come along. Can you hear the Bing Boys calling, come along?
Can you hear the glad refrain? Should Auld acquaintance be forgot?
Shall our voices rise in vain? No!
No need to get excited when supporters of United are the Bing Boys of 'The Lane'

Alternate verses went:

> *Never let your spirits wane*
> *We're here to cheer you through, mi lads,*
> *And we'll strive with might and main*
> *Ho! To back up old United*
> *And to join you're invited*
> *By the Bing Boys of the Lane*
>
> *Let us see you up again*
> *We're staunch supporters one and all*
> *And misfortune shall never prove our bane*
> *So if today we're thwarted of a win*
> *We're not downhearted*
> *We're the Bing Boys of the Lane*

The music sheet informs a reader that the song was the winner of a competition to find the best United song. Profits from the sale of the song-sheet were to go to the Poor Children's Holiday Fund of the *Sheffield Telegraph*, which printed the threepenny sheet for free.

The era also saw Blades' fans sing a song that was associated with the club until the early 1990s. *Ilkla Moor B'aht 'At* was set to Thomas Clark's 1805 tune *Cranbrook* some time in the late 19th century. The despondent eight verses celebrating death and cannibalism became synonymous with Sheffield United as far back as the 1930s. The 1927 *Daily Express Songbook* contains a version with many Calder Valley references. A member of a Halifax choir outing probably composed the song, which became the unofficial Yorkshireman's 'National Anthem' by the 1920s. The anthem toured the country with the United following. As a result of its 'success' at away games—primarily in annoying the hosts—the singing of its verses became part of home game's pre-match routine.

> **The songs that football fandom provoked went some way to relieving the misery that the economic situation had brought to hundreds of thousands of Sheffielders. With little to cheer about and United stuck in the Second Division, the chance to cheer the Blades at Wembley arose in March 1936. The day was momentous and the team's return celebrated. The only thing missing was the trophy.**

No Substituting Quality: The 1936 FA Cup Final

In December 1935 the draw for the FA Cup was made live on the radio for the first time. Broadcast by the BBC, the Secretary of the FA, Sir Stanley Rous, provided the necessary atmosphere for the listening millions by repeatedly shaking the numbered pot balls in the velvet bag. The draw was traditionally held on a Monday lunchtime following the previous weekend's games. It was only with TV broadcasting in the 1980s that the draw was moved to Saturday evening, occasionally Sunday evenings, and even late on Monday. Five months after the 1935 draw United faced Arsenal at Wembley in the FA Cup Final.

United made their way to Wembley as other Northerners were seeking similarly to win something in the Capital. The Blade's visit to the 1936 Wembley FA Cup Final occurred in April. This coincided with a time of great social upheaval, both in Britain and in Europe. On the domestic front, 200 men from Jarrow County Durham marched to London in the autumn of 1936 to lobby Parliament in protest at the 68% male unemployment in their town. Their aim was to confront the National Government led by Stanley Baldwin. The journey took 25 days and included stop-overs in Barnsley and Sheffield. On their arrival at the House of Commons, Baldwin refused to meet the men or their representative, stating 'civil strife leads to civil war'. Similarly avoiding them was Ellen Wilkinson, the Labour MP for Middlesbrough East, who had waived them off only a month earlier. The welcoming rally held in Hyde Park was organised

The Sheffield United v Arsenal 1936 Cup Final match programme

instead by the Communists. In Europe, meanwhile, the Berlin Olympics was Hitler's opportunity to show-case the Nazi society he was creating and the assumed supremacy of the Aryan athlete. Comfortingly United's route to Wembley contained neither debate around political systems nor claims about the eugenics of its athletes.

United beat Burnley at home and drew with Preston away before despatching them in the replay at Bramall Lane to play Leeds in the fifth round. A huge 68,287 crowd—the biggest ever recorded at Bramall Lane for a football match—saw a 3–1 victory to United. The commemorative oil painting by John Warburton, finished in 2000, shows this famous day which suggests self-restraint by thousands who had assembled along the touchline on the former cricket pitch. It also suggests considerable artistic licence as the day was famous for its thick fog. The semi-final against Fulham was played at Molyneux, Wolverhampton. The Cup however was not to be United's. A Ted Drake goal scored at Wembley in the second half was enough for Arsenal to win. The defeat was no disgrace; the magnificent Arsenal team were to win five championships and two Cup Finals this decade.

The final, held in late April, attracted a crowd of 93,384. The United squad trained days previously in Torquay and travelled from the West Country on the morning of the game. Their 9.26am train would arrive at Wembley just two hours before kick-off. After the match the players were instructed to make their *own* way to the Hotel Grand Central in Marylebone, Central London for a dinner dance. The following day the squad were to travel to Maidenhead in Berkshire to join a Thames boat cruise to a hotel in Windsor before returning for a late afternoon appointment at Madame Tussauds Wax Works. The evening saw them at the cinema watching a recording of the FA Cup Final. The team left London on the Monday at midday.

The Cup Final match programme cost sixpence. Introducing a reader to the 'Empire Stadium, Wembley' the adverts contained within it promote ice hockey, played at the adjacent Empire Pool, and a forth-coming boxing evening. A portrait of King George V who had died in January takes full-page pride of place. A variety of drinks popular at the time are advertised: egg-flip, 'Seager's gin', 'Lanson Champagne', 'Watneys beers' and 'Bovril' with its ditty 'A player may miss a kick, but he musn't Mrs Bovril'.

The pre-match programme of music illustrates the significance accorded to the military on such occasions, and the emerging influence of cinema alongside pre-established opera classics and communal favourites. Those in the stadium at 12.45 could listen to the Royal Naval band playing *Ship Ahoy, Why was I born?*,

1936 FA Cup Final tickets

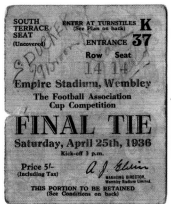

United's goalkeeper Jack Smith collects the ball in the 1936 FA Cup Final

and *I love you, Gypsy*. The band of the Irish Guards then took over playing *Colonel Bogey* and 'gems' from the operas of Gilbert and Sullivan, followed by film score excerpts and waltz medleys. One hour before kick-off came a marching display by the Services Band followed by around half an hour of communal singing accompanied by the band of the Welsh Guards culminating in a rendition of *God Save the King* minutes before kick-off.

The post-match dinner menu was exotic for men of a Sheffield upbringing. Few would have tasted Russian caviar, turtle soup, Scotch salmon or braised sweetbreads (sheep's testicles). The post-meal relaxants included cigars and vintage wine. The latter was, no doubt, useful to endure the elaborate post-match toasts. They began with one for the King, next came a 'Sheffield United FC' toast made by the Lord Mayor of Sheffield, which was to provoke a response from the United chairman, Alderman Platt. Then came one to the FA followed by another to 'The Team', which required United captain Harry Hooper to respond to honour his manager Teddy Davison. Even 'The Press' earned a toast and were in turn expected to respond. Last but not least before an evening of dancing to the Jules DeVillez orchestra, came a toast to the president of Sheffield United, Charles Clegg. In reply Clegg spoke of how the English FA was stronger then ever, and made a pointed reference to those spectators: 'who seem to know more about the game than those who have had to manage it on the field and off the field'. His speech was interrupted by applause when he commended United for 'playing the game' and not trying to 'rough it'.

No royalty was present for this 1936 final, and some of the fans quoted in subsequent press reports claimed that the community singing was not as vociferous as in previous years. What was memorable for this day was the presence of a number of aeroplanes and autogyros, chartered by film companies seeking newsreel of the game in defiance of the Wembley Stadium authorities, who had refused filming inside the ground. Copy of unofficial film taken of the final reached Sheffield at 8pm on the same evening and was screened in local cinemas an hour later.

The 1936 FA Cup Final team lined-up in front of the cricket pavilion at Bramall Lane

The United team turned down the offer of a civic reception at Sheffield Town Hall. They stuck by their mantra 'No cup, no reception'. Football analysts stated that United's wingers had not performed and that the United's left-hand side was deficient. One unusual excuse came from United's Tommy Johnson, who complained about the air-borne distractions over the stadium stating:

> *The aeroplanes did not actually put us off our game, but at the same time they made an awful din and at times interfered with our concentration as we were apt to look up at them and take our eyes off the play*

He also added that if the goal frames at Wembley had been oval instead of square (like the majority of goal frames in League football), the header from Jock Dodds that struck the woodwork would have gone in. The 1936 final was unforgettable for Johnson. The day before he had married Gwen Dawson and telegrams of good luck were sent to him before the game, some addressed 'c/o Sheffield United, Wembley'.

One of the most unusual of football memorabilia in the Hall of Fame was a product of the 1930's LNER (London & North Eastern Railway) network which saw locomotives named after football clubs en route. The *Sheffield United* ran along the LNER and later between Norwich and Sheffield until 1958. All the clubs were offered a name-plate when the locomotives were retired. Until the mid-1970s the name-plate was placed above the players tunnel in the John Street Stand. To a collector the plate is worth around £25,000.

1936 FA Cup Final Rosette
Worn by Tom Johnson's wife Gwen

The 1936 FA Cup Final
post-match celebration
dinner menu

SHEFFIELD UNITED
FOOTBALL CLUB

FOOTBALL ASSOCIATION
CUP FINAL

CELEBRATION
DINNER

HELD IN THE
WHARNCLIFFE ROOMS,
HOTEL GREAT CENTRAL, LONDON N.W. 1.

SATURDAY,
25th APRIL, 1936.

The nameplate from the steam engine 'Sheffield United' decommissioned in 1958

The Hall of Fame project managed to track down a number of objects surrounding the 1936 Cup Final. The lives behind the medals and shirts are all very different. A variety of tales thus follow.

Blood and Sweat: Ernest Jackson

On display in the Hall of Fame is the 1936 Cup Final shirt worn by United's 22-year-old defender Ernest Jackson. The shirt produced by Bukta was, as the collar tag explains, made specially for the Jack Archer Sports outfitter shop located on Bramall Lane. This outlet existed from the early part of the 20th century to the mid-70s and always had a connection with United. Owned at one time by George Waller, it was then taken over by George Utley in 1915, who in turn sold it to local entrepreneur Jack Archer. The latter broke with tradition in that he supplied both United and Wednesday with kit. The 1936 shirt differed to that worn in the 1925 final by virtue of having a much higher collar. The three neck buttons of the former have also been replaced by a string-drawn ribbon effect. The badge is a derivative of the City Coat of Arms, but more sophisticated in its design and stitching than that of the 1925 shirt. Having been worn at Wembley the shirt was never washed by those who owned it over the decades. The garment returned to Wembley in 1993, when worn by a grandchild of Jackson supporting United in the FA Cup semi-final against Wednesday. At the bottom of the front of the shirt are bloodstains, a souvenir from the final, courtesy of Arsenal's Alex James.

Born in 1914 in Sheffield and raised a Unitedite, Ernest Jackson played 400 games for the Blades scoring 19 goals. Jackson was signed by United in 1932 from the Sheffield works team Atlas and Norfolk, and might have achieved England honours had not the Second World War ruined his chances. Exceptionally strong, fast, and classy; Jackson captained United for a spell in 1946. His reliability and honesty were recognised by the club following a year as player-coach of Boston United when Jackson returned to become part of the Bramall Lane coaching staff in 1950. Jackson walked out of Bramall Lane five years later following a bust-up with the then manager Joe Mercer. Having left football Jackson worked in a steel

ERNEST JACKSON.
Sheffield United Right Half-back. Season 1938-39.

Ernest Jackson in 1938
The fashionable footballer of the era wore his collar up whilst resplendent
in huge shorts and hooped socks.

factory until his retirement and spent his leisure time pigeon-fancying.

Jackson's conditions of service offered four days before the 1936 final and the concomitant details of employment titled 'Agreement for Hire of a Player' are worthy of highlighting. The first stipulates that the player:

...hereby agrees to play in an efficient manner and to the best of his ability.

Point number three states that the player will:

...do everything necessary to get and keep himself in the best possible condition so as to render the most efficient service to the club.

Point five specifies that the player:

...shall not engage in any business or live in any place which the Directors [or Committee] of the club may deem unsuitable.

Point six was far-reaching in its demands, stating:

If the player shall prove palpably inefficient, or shall be guilty of serious misconduct or breach of the Rules of the Club, the club may, on giving 14 days notice to the said player, or the Club may, on giving 28 days notice to the said player, on any reasonable grounds, terminate this Agreement and dispense with the services of the player.

For agreeing to all this, the player received a one-year contract worth £6 per week with £2 per week extra if selected for the first team. The contract is fascinating for its vagueness, which gave the employers considerable opportunity to work the agreement to their advantage. It is impossible to qualify what constitutes 'efficient' and 'best of his ability'. The requirement that a player keep himself in the best of condition might be considered easier to evaluate; if overweight or unfit by virtue of consumption of an inappropriate diet the players would have little to complain about. But unexpected illness or conditions arising out of the polluted environment that was Sheffield left considerable scope for controversy. The latitude point five gave the board could and did cause controversy for decades. Licensed premises were, as we have seen, considered by the United Board unsuitable premises for United players to reside in. If the parties were in conflict and the board felt that they had a case a United career could be ended with 14 days' notice. That constituting 'serious misconduct' or meriting the description of 'palpably inefficient' was always going to provoke contention. These were very subjective criteria for both on and off field behaviour.

The Twelfth Man: Albert Cox
Sitting next to coach David Steele for the duration of the Cup Final was the 18-year-old Albert Cox, who travelled in the days before substitutes as 'twelfth man'. Interviewed in 2002, Cox reminisced on the match and his career. Born a miner's son in the Rotherham pit village of Treeton, Cox was the only boy of four

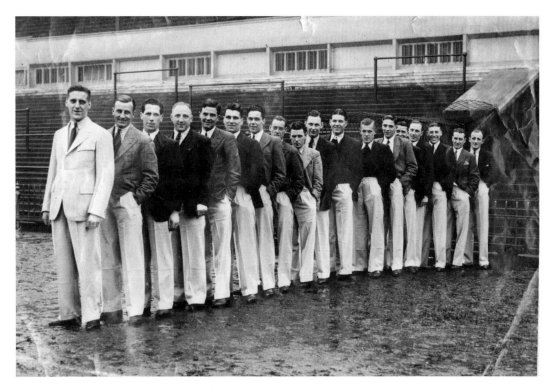

Keeping their shape. The United squad's reward of trousers from a local tailor for reaching the 1936 FA Cup Final

siblings, and left school at 14 to become an engine-wright at the local colliery. The area produced tough boys who, out of economic necessity, were very fit. Aged 13, Cox was a part-time butcher's boy delivering meat on a bicycle over a wide area. His school team were local champions, and Cox attracted the attention of the well-connected men's teams in the area. Eventually Wolverhampton Wanderers offered him a contract but, preferring to stay at home and with a United fan as a father, Cox took a drop in earnings and joined United. Living two doors away was Jessie Pye, who played a season with United before joining Notts County and later Wolves, and going on to win England international honours. For over two years Cox combined his colliery work with part-time status at Bramall Lane until, in 1935, he signed as a professional at £3 a week with a £2 bonus when making the first eleven. One year later, Cox found himself at Wembley Stadium in front of a crowd of over 93,000.

To attend training and matches at Bramall Lane, Cox travelled on the bus with Blade supporters from his village. Football and its demands were easy compared to what the coal mining industry demanded of its employees in the late 1920s and early 1930s. On a good day a coalface worker would earn seven shillings but, in times of recession, work was reduced to a three-day week. The ever-present dangers of pit work visited the Cox family most cruelly when a cage carrying miners down the shaft fell and badly injured his father. Unable to work any further, the compensation offered was in Cox's words 'just a few coppers'. Fortunately for the family, Cox had just begun his football career and was able to fund his own living and that of his parents and siblings.

After reporting to Bramall Lane at 10am each day, the first hour was invariably taken up with lapping (running around the pitch), which was then followed by ball practice. Occasionally the squad were asked to return in the afternoon for an hour of passing and shooting, or a game of five-a-side. Speaking highly

WEEKLY
ILLUSTRATED
2ᴰ
Saturday, April 25, 1936
No. 43.   VOL. II

SHEFFIELD UNITED
(Back Row) WILLIAMS, STACEY, WILKINSON, SMITH, JOHNSON, McPHERSON, BOOT, STEELE (Trainer)
(Front Row) BANTOR, BARCLAY, DODDS, HOOPER (Captain), COX, BIRD. (Inset), PICKERING

SPECIAL CUP FINAL NUMBER

Eyes right! The back cover of the 1936 Weekly Illustrated

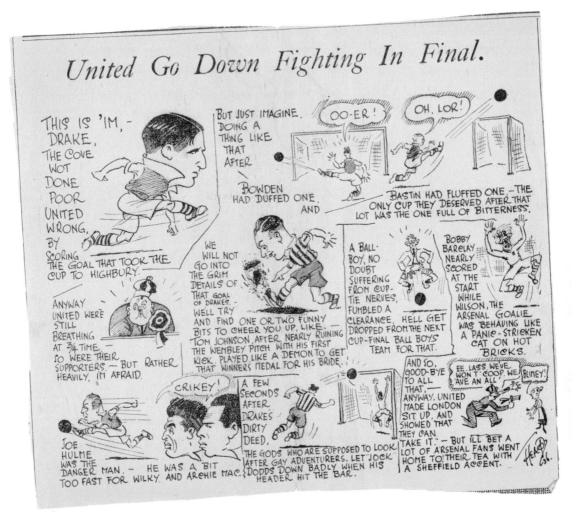

The 1936 Cup Final as seen by cartoonist Harry Heap

of manager Teddy Davison, Cox considered that he had the confidence and loyalty of his players. Davison's trainer Duggie Livingstone, who succeded David Steele after the final, was, in Cox's opinion, a good trainer who would demonstrate everything he asked the players to do. The captain was Harry Hooper, who would shout instructions to team-mates throughout the game. Thus Cox claims he was not overawed at 18 when playing an FA Cup semi-final against Fulham. Whilst disappointed at not being in the first team for the final, he considered that youth was on his side and his chance would come again. On the day of the final, his duties were reserved for the dressing room helping to strap up the limbs of team-mates and giving out sustenance in the form of cups of tea.

Fast and fit, Cox played the whole of his career as a full-back willing to go forward. Reliable and unspectacular he was a steady regular for years; he also had a good shot and could use both feet. Playing in the war years for the Wanderers Services football team that toured to entertain allied troops, Cox also played for

United when on leave. Resuming his United career in 1946, Cox partnered Fred Furniss at full-back until the early 1950s. His United career lasted 333 first team games until 1952 when he transferred to Halifax, then in division three, for a fee of £200. His departure, however, was slightly controversial in that the issue of public houses and United's Methodism again raised its head. Aware that his career would not last forever, Cox decided to move into business, and chose to become a licensee of The Brunswick in Sheffield's Woodhouse district. This enterprise would constitute a breach of contract in the eyes of the directors. Possibly to avoid impending controversy, Teddy Davison transferred Cox to Halifax. Choosing to live in his pub and travel daily, the move did not work out because the distance was too long and the journey too arduous in winter. After years as a publican, Cox took a shop in Treeton and scouted for John Harris in the early 1970s. Cox died in 2003 aged 85.

Smiler: Jack Smith

United's goalkeeper in the 1936 final could well have become a national sporting hero on another continent in another sport had his parents not been so rootless. Born in Stocksbridge, north of Sheffield, Smith moved with his family to the USA aged ten in 1921 and, whilst living in Philedelphia, excelled at baseball and was offered a sports scholarship. However, he returned to Penistone with his family after five years and, while playing outfield for Bolsterstone FC, was forced to play in goal when a team-mate was injured. The reflexes that baseball had taught him saw him turn in a brilliant performance. Remaining in goal for the rest of the season Smith soon attracted the attention of both Sheffield clubs. Whilst his family were United fans, he trained with Wednesday, who loaned him to Worksop. United seized the opportunity to sign him in 1930 because his status at Wednesday was that of an amateur.

The 21-year-old Smith was soon considered to be of first-team quality and had a great first season. He lost his place the following season, but his loss of form was explainable when after months of pain, an X-ray revealed a hairline fracture of the wrist. An operation mended the break and Smith never looked back, he became United's first-choice goal-keeper for the next 17 years until 1949. In his early years Smith was a steady rather than outstanding keeper but he developed and his best years were between 1934 and 1939. During the war years Smith became a PTI and rarely missed a match, making 203 consecutive appearances between December 1935 and October 1947. Good on angles, technically superb and brave, the international honours many tipped him for never came for some reason.

Mine!
Jack Smith punches the ball under pressure from Arsenal's Cliff Bastin

New formations
Sheffield United team for season 1936–37

Remembered by all in the game at the time as a superb goalkeeper, Smith had a happy disposition—hence the nickname 'Smiler'. He was always found wearing a cap when playing into the sun, which after 17 seasons was a somewhat sad garment. By contrast, off the pitch, Smith was an immaculate dresser. He played his last game against Skegness Town in 1950 and joined the United training staff in 1952 coaching the B team. 18 months later, Smith was forced out of retirement during an injury crisis and at nearly 40 years of age played eight games until the first-choice goalkeeper was fit. Smith died in Sheffield in 1986, one of only two players in the English game to play in all 42 league games of 1938–39 and 1946–47.

Team Colours: Bobby Barclay

Playing inside right for United at Wembley was a Newcastle-born England International called Bobby Barclay, who joined United aged 24 in 1931 for £3,500 from Derby County. Six years later he left for Huddersfield Town for a £7,500 fee, which also took Eddy Boot alongside him. Barclay made 264 United appearances between 1931 and 1936 scoring 77 goals. He scored three goals for England in his three full internationals, and was selected for the final international even though United were by then a Division Two side. With an ability to deliver pinpoint passes and having a great first touch, Barclay was a great provider for Dodds and Dunne. He would return to Bramall Lane to make eight wartime guest appearances for United.

After finishing his playing days, Barclay joined the coaching staff at Huddersfield Town, regularly returning to Sheffield to watch United. A one-time publican, he kept his United memorabilia in a trunk in the attic of the pub. His two daughters inherited his memorabilia and agreed to sell much of what they inherited at an auction, keeping one shirt and one cap in their possession.

Sheffield and Hallamshire representative shirt
Worn by Bobby Barclay 1931–32 and manufactured by
Suggs of Sheffield

The cream shirt of the Sheffield and Hallamshire Football Association was worn by leading local players of the five league teams in South Yorkshire selected to represent the local FA in challenge matches. Barclay's shirt was worn in a 1932 for a game against the Glasgow FA at Ibrox Park. These annual games did not end with the now ritualised exchange of shirts, but were for the players to keep as a memento. The off-white colour was probably chosen because of its neutrality in local football. The badge displaying the Sheffield Coat of Arms is embroidered and functions as a breast pocket.

Boot and Hoops

Harry Hooper, the captain of the 1936 FA Cup team did not always lead by example. As a chain smoker who enjoyed a few pints or more and wore plus fours he was, by anyone's measure, a character. Yet his achievements in football are exemplary. A fast and fierce-tackling hard man, he was also an excellent striker of a dead ball and had a great record of penalty taking. Originating from Nelson, Lancashire, Hooper first played for Nelson before joining United in 1930. In his 18-year association with United he made 307 appearances before leaving to join Hartlepool. Coaching spells at Huddersfield and West Ham followed as did the job of manager at Halifax Town. His son, Harry junior, played for West Ham, Sunderland, Wolves and Birmingham City in the late 1950s and early 60s.

The man who travelled to Wembley in 1936 as a spectator is responsible for the only artefact of blue and white colouring in the Hall of Fame display. Originating from Laughton Common, South Yorkshire, Eddie Boot signed for United in 1935. Boot had travelled with the squad to the final but did not make the team, and the following season, after making 41 appearances as a left-half, he, along with team-mate Bobby Barclay, was jointly transferred to Huddersfield Town for £7,500. His new club made it to the FA Cup Final against Preston in 1938 in what was to be the first ever final decided by a penalty. The shirt exhibited in the Hall of Fame was worn in that final, and Boot's association with Huddersfield lasted some 26 years and ended with him as club manager. Throughout his time in football Boot remained a Blade. He returned to Sheffield, post-football, and ran a mechanical engineering firm in Attercliffe. The shirt he wore in the 1938 Cup Final was donated to United by Boot's son.

> Whilst the local culture produced players who were generally deferential towards their employers there were always going to be exceptions. Some by virtue of their ability or character could and would not be told what to do. As the wider society they lived in struggled for rights of employment and improved pay, it was inevitable that such attitudes would permeate football's dressing rooms. Collective action however, whilst the core of the culture of football when performed on the pitch, was not manifest in off-field oppositions. Many a player realised that in getting the best deal for himself he had to go it alone and negotiate with whoever seemed to hold the best opportunities. To this end United's 1936 finalist centre-forward Jock Dodds might be considered the man who facilitated an incident in the English game that changed labour relations between clubs and players forever.

Goal Bandit: Jock Dodds

Born in Grangemouth, Scotland, in 1915 and christened Ephraim, the boy known as 'Jock' throughout his adult life, played close to 500 games of top-class football, scoring over 450 goals. In his 203 League and Cup games for United Dodds scored a remarkable 128 goals. Aged 21, Dodds was the youngest member of the United side in the 1936 Cup Final. He very nearly scored the equaliser. About to head the ball from just inside the 18-yard box, a punch to his head from Arsenal's Wilf Copping, knocked him off balance. The ball hit the crossbar instead the back of the net.

Dodds' remarkable goal-scoring abilities are matched by a somewhat remarkable life. His father died two years after his birth. Soon after his mother moved to Durham and remarried. In a region devastated by recession, Dodds was reduced to stealing vegetables from farmers' fields for the benefit of himself and his parents. Avoiding detection, Dodds would always be noticed in other areas. At school a teacher took a great interest in his football abilities and Dodds was soon playing in the local club teams, Shell-Mex and Medomsley Juniors. He then attracted the attention of Huddersfield Town, for whom he signed on a 'ground staff' contract in the early 1930s. Two seasons in the reserves saw Huddersfield release him. There was little money in the game as yet and, to save money on bus fares, Dodds would walk the four-mile journey to and from the ground every day—a new club would get a very fit centre forward with a few bob saved. At the time, United had sold centre forward Bill Boyd to Manchester United and seeking to replace him had made a failed attempt to bring back Jimmy Dunne from Arsenal. On the recommendation of the assistant manger of Huddersfield, Dodds signed for Sheffield United. After six months in the reserves, Dodds was promoted to the first team at inside left. He did not score in his first three games, but in his fourth scored four against Southampton. In the 1935–36 season Dodds was the second division's top scorer with 36 goals.

Not the enemy—
The 1938 FA Cup Final shirt worn by former Blade Eddie Boot of Huddersfield Town

Over the next three seasons, Dodds was to be United's leading goalscorer. He was to impress many other clubs and impressed a few non-football people in Sheffield's fashionable circles. In March 1939 he moved to Blackpool for £10,000. What apparently impressed the Blackpool directors was a challenge Dodds had executed on the Blackpool goalkeeper, Jock Wallace, in a previous season. The imposing frame of Wallace ended up prostrate with a broken shoulder. The Blackpool board were so impressed they signed Dodds, with the player collecting £600 of the transfer fee. Dodds justified the move stating that the foul industrial air of Sheffield was playing havoc with the asthma that debilitated his mother who had moved to the city to be near her son. The air at Blackpool was far more agreeable. He remembers, however, that £50 of the transfer fee due to him was retained by Sheffield United, who argued that it was theirs because he had not completed the full season.

He left Sheffield something of a legend on and off the pitch. In United's colours he was one of the Football League's most fearsome centre forwards who could disturb experienced international-standard opponents. Immensely strong and prepared to go in where it hurt, Dodds was a battering ram of a forward. Off the pitch he was famed for frequenting the dance halls where he would keep the company of many of Sheffield's loveliest. He was to escort the great entertainer of the era, Gracie Fields who apparently

Sewing the shirt
United's Tommy Johnson on the right with two unknown gentlemen learns how a needle and thread works
The obliging lady attaches numbers for the first time onto Sheffield United shirts in August 1939

sought his company when playing one of the music halls in the city. Another place he frequented was the greyhound racing-track. He was to take up training of the beasts, which proved consequential for Dodds and his team-mates. One dog Dodds entered in a race had been dyed a different colour to that which it was famed for. Dodds was attempting a betting coup and was entering the good runner as a 'ringer', seeking to make a good return by placing a large sum on this presumed outsider. Pouring rain ruined the scam. The dye ran faster than the dog did and its true colours were revealed—Dodds was banned from the track. Ever pursuing income from such tracks, Dodds cared well for his dogs. So much so that his team-mates would sometimes find themselves waiting for treatment from the club's masseur whilst a four-legged hopeful lay on the treatment bench as Dodds politely demanded his trainer care for his dog before the evening race.

Dodds arrival at Blackpool saw them lead the table after three games. However, the war interrupted what might have been a brilliant team. That said, his 161 games for the Seasiders produced 223 goals, including eight on one occasion, seven on another, five twice, and three no fewer than 20 times. On the day he scored eight (against Stockport County in 1941) Dodds even missed a penalty as Blackpool won 9–2. The seven he scored against Tranmere in 1943 produced the then fastest-ever hat trick in world football, which took around 3 minutes. (The record fell in 2004, in a Division Two game between Bournemouth and Wrexham, the Bournemouth centre forward James Hayter scored a hat trick in two minutes 20 seconds.) Assisted by the Blackpool legend, Stanley Matthews, Dodds had no better provider in English football.

RAF war service saw Dodds acting as a physical training instructor. He played for the RAF in representative games, and nine times for Scotland in war-time internationals. His Scottish appearances produced nine goals, including one in a 5–4 victory over England at Hampton Park in front of an estimated 140,000 spectators. Afterwards Dodds travelled back in a third class compartment courtesy of the Scottish FA, who also billed him for the tea and buns his mother had enjoyed pre-match in the player's hotel. War-time football saw Dodds playing as a guest for Fulham and West Ham. In the 1941–42 season Dodds scored 66 goals. Returning to Blackpool when the war ended, Dodds married and began various business ventures.

He also enjoyed six lucrative months playing in the Republic of Ireland for Shamrock Rovers. Not subject to FIFA rules, the money the Irish could pay was double the minimum wage in England. Following his stint in Ireland, Dodds resumed his Blackpool career but was also offered the possibility of signing for Sheffield Wednesday or Arsenal but eventually chose Everton, who paid £7,000 for him. In 55 games for Everton he scored 36 goals. Moving to Lincoln City in late 1948, he scored 38 goals in 60 games, and then retired from the game.

His retirement was somewhat early and was no doubt influenced by pressure from the Football Association, who considered he had brought the game into disrepute. His crime in their eyes was in recruiting players from England and Scotland to play for clubs in Bogota, Colombia which at the time was not affiliated to FIFA and was therefore outside the jurisdiction of any football association. The six players who made money from this venture are known in posterity as the 'Bogota Bandits' and included two England internationals of the time. Dodds was instrumental in Neil Franklin, George Mountford, Charlie Mitten, Bobby Flavell and George Higgins playing games in Bogota. Two others, Roy Paul and Jack Headley, arrived in Colombia but did not play any matches. The precise role of Dodds in this affair has never been fully revealed. As Dodds recalls, out of the blue he received a phone call from a stranger asking him to consider playing in Bogota. The money was excellent, but the realisation that he was aged over 30 saw those who made contact later suggest the high altitudes of Colombia would not suit a man of his age. As a consequence they asked him to be the mediator and recruit players on their behalf. In the book

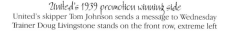

United's 1939 promotion winning side
United's skipper Tom Johnson sends a message to Wednesday
Trainer Doug Livingstone stands on the front row, extreme left

Bogota Bandit, author Charlie Mitten describes how Lady Bridgett Poulett had opened the Middleton Towers holiday camp in Morecambe a decade earlier and married a Colombian by the name of Lewis Robledo. The fact that Dodds was in the seaside entertainment business of Blackpool, some 20 miles away and no doubt well known to socialite Poulett, strongly suggests that the middleman was Mr Robledo.

The FA was furious with the players who travelled and imposed a ban on any further such ventures. Those who sought a new life in Colombia were soon to return, dissatisfied with conditions and not always paid what was promised. Some were banned from football by the FA, although the bans were eventually lifted. What was significant about the whole affair was how the minimum wage in English football was leaving players open to offers from abroad, which some were quick to accept. Aware of the attraction and the consequence to the English game of future potential movement, wages in England improved. The stage had been set for a contest between the player and his employer by a handful of professionals and Dodds was instrumental in the whole thing. Labour relations would not be the same again.

Offered the manager's position at both Port Vale and Stoke City, Dodds turned them down to concentrate on his hotel and leisure interests in Blackpool. His properties in the resort included a nightclub regularly visited by both Matt Busby's Manchester United team and Bill Shankly's Liverpool team in the late 1960s and 70s respectively. Dodds was a famous host to various figures from showbiz as well. Aged 88 in 2004 Dodds was a non-smoking vegetarian who would take a sauna three times a week, and was still involved in a variety of business ventures. Dodds will go down in history as one of the few men to play for Sheffield United, be capped by his country and serve time in a British prison. In 1963 he pleaded guilty to the re-labelling of a huge stock of condemned condensed milk and for this crime was given a six-month custodial sentence at the Old Bailey.

United in Europe for the first time
The tour itinerary of the May 1936 six-match tour of Denmark

MATCHES.

THUR. 28th MAY at AARHUS.

SUN. 31st MAY at AALBORG.

WED. 3rd JUNE at COPENHAGEN

FRI. 5th JUNE at COPENHAGEN

SUN. 7th JUNE at NYKJÖBING

MON. 8th JUNE at ESBJERG

Playing Away:
The First European Tour

The first World Cup tournament hosted by Uruguay in 1930 saw the self-omission of the Home Nations. British football was, out of arrogance, limiting itself to innovations in the game. Foreign players and coaches in Continental Europe were producing new styles of play that saw Italy win the World Cup in 1934 and again 1938. English Football clubs in response, became ever more curious about their near neighbours and with improved transport facilities began to venture abroad in a spirit of curiosity and fraternity. It took a while but United eventually joined them.

In 1936 a United side travelled into mainland Europe for the first time. Between 1900 and 1924 United received many invitations to play exhibition games in what was then the Austrian-Hungarian Empire. United turned down all offers. The only good reason for United's refusal to travel lies probably in Methodism—Charles Clegg would not have his club playing on a Sunday, which was a possibility in foreign lands. Confusion reigns, however, because Clegg was also president of Sheffield Wednesday, who toured Denmark in 1911. United had crossed the water to Ireland in the 1930s to play games but would not go further.

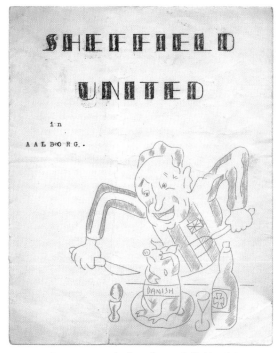

Programme cover for the Aalborg v Sheffield United friendly in Denmark, 1936

The Danes for some curious reason depict the visiting Blade man as about to finish off the Danish pig. Inside a poem is complimentary to the visitors, proclaiming as it does, "You can win, because you eat our bacon…Aalborg is a funny town"

The fact that United accepted the offer to play in Denmark in 1936 could be attributable to two factors. One was undoubtedly due to the profile the club had gained in the 1930s. The other was that Clegg was old and infirm. He could probably be ignored by other more 'progressive' directors. The invitation from Denmark came in February 1936—two months before the Cup Final. The six-game 14-day tour saw the squad travel to Harwich to board a ferry to Esbjerg and begin their itinerary. The success of the fortnight changed United's thinking. The following year the club toured Sweden. United were in later decades to become one of the most 'global' of English teams by virtue of their post and pre-season tours.

Crossing the Divide

In April 1939 a 6–1 victory over Spurs saw United promoted to Division One by a one-point margin over Sheffield Wednesday. Only a few weeks later in May, the directors, officials and players of both clubs dined together at the Grand Hotel after the two had competed in the County Cup Final. A toast by the Lord Mayor celebrated both Sheffield clubs and the Wednesday directors expressed their pleasure in witnessing United's success. Interestingly, a Mr W.G. Turner stated that this was his 33rd year as a Wednesday Director, adding that United had been formed 'because of discontent between the leaders of Wednesday'. Describing matches between the two clubs in the early days as 'dog fights', he told his audience that the two clubs were now on the friendliest of terms. Photographs published in the *Sheffield Telegraph* show supporters of both United and Wednesday marching behind a brass band to celebrate United's promotion. Whilst willing to provide words and images for appropriate occasions, exchanges of players between the two Sheffield clubs was, however, a very rare occurrence.

As the decade ended and Sheffield United could celebrate 50 years of existence, an outsider to the city might find curiosity in the relative absence of players, who crossed the United–Wednesday divide. What an observer makes of this depends on the historical starting point. United began their life with two former Wednesday players—Jack Hudson and Billy Mosforth. Soon after Mick Whitham arrived having played the odd game for Wednesday and George Waller arrived having made 32 League and Cup appearances for Wednesday including an FA Cup Final match in 1890. In 1892, after two years at Middlesbrough Ironopolis, Waller joined United.

None of the above could be said to have joined United *directly* from Wednesday, or vice versa. The first to do so was Billy Mellor, who was a fringe player with United in 1892–93, but left to join Wednesday in the latter year. Over a decade later in 1905, Frank Rollinson joined Wednesday after a season as a United reserve. The Sheffield-born Oliver Tummon joined Wednesday as a professional in 1903 and made 48 appearances in the blue and white. Leaving in 1910 for Gainsborough Trinity and two years later joining Oldham, Tummon returned to Sheffield during the war years and, playing for United in 1915, signed as a professional when the war ended. He remained at Bramall Lane until 1920 when leaving for Barnsley.

The first major signing across the divide was Whitwell-born Bernard Oxley, who had joined United from Chesterfield in 1928 and left Bramall lane for Wednesday in 1934 for a fee of £1000 following United's relegation from Division One. After three seasons with the Owls, Oxley signed for Stockport. Robert Barnshaw joined Wednesday in 1910, but an injury saw him return to his native North-East where, three years later, United signed him from Hebburn Argylle on a free. In the following decade Charles Taylor signed for United when released by Wednesday. Another player of this era, John Shenton, cost United £50 when he joined them without telling United he was actually still registered with Wednesday. In the late 1930s George Cole, a Wednesday reserve, joined United and played just one first team game. When Joe Cockcroft signed for United in 1948 from West Ham, they were not only signing a former Owl, but also signing their oldest ever debutant. The 37-year-old was slow and missed a couple of penalties before being released. Why so few players signed for their neighbours is hard to fathom. Relations between the two clubs were generally good, hence the presence of Owls officials at United banquets. One might read too much into the absence of direct exchange. A similar situation could be found between Manchester United and City, and Liverpool and Everton.

War Footings

The game was still inherently conservative, but was changing. The regal Charles Clegg had died in the summer of 1937. Some 18 months previous, the King had died and a reserve game at Bramall Lane saw a two minutes' silence and a singing of both *Abide with Me* and the national anthem in his honour. Ominously in October 1938 an advert in the programme appealed for Air Raid Precaution (ARP) volunteers, describing it as 'a real man's job, in which fitness and courage play a vital part'. All that was needed was 'good sense and good health'. Significantly, in March 1939 a new Royal Artillery Regiment was being raised in Sheffield. In the same month, a full-page advert stated how the city needed 12,000 ARP men and warned ominously: 'Sheffield is NOT ready'.

A 1–0 victory at Elland Road, Leeds in September 1939 was completed a day before Britain declared war on Nazi Germany. The United team was unbeaten that season. Upon the declaration of war, a sub-committee of the Home Office considered closing down all forms of popular entertainment. Meanwhile, a circular to clubs from the FA encouraged them to get players to join the Territorial Army. Players at some clubs signed up *en bloc* for local regiments. The FA meanwhile forbade Armed Forces personnel from registering as professional footballers. The Government banned the assembly of crowds. Within a week the Football League instructed all clubs to release players from their contracts; players were effectively unemployed, although some hope was available when the Government lifted its ban on sporting activities outside of densely populated areas. The areas where matches could take place were then extended, provided the police did not object, and eventually games could take place anywhere providing attendances were no higher than 15,000 and took place between clubs that could travel 'there and back in a day'.

The League was to be reorganised initially into eight divisions. Players could be paid 30 shillings a match and could 'guest' for clubs local to their military or war service place of work. The offices of the Football League were requisitioned by the Office of Works, but the Government had decided that sport would have a beneficial effect on the morale of the nation. The first war-time matches began in October 1939.

The games were useful for raising funds for war causes. The implementation of the League, however, was hampered by poor weather conditions and fixture changes, which saw in 1940–41 a new formation of Regional North and South and with a placing system based on goals scored not points awarded. Cup ties avoided replays by using extra-time then a 'sudden death' format until a winning goal was scored. A War Cup competition was introduced, which was integrated into the second half of the season. However, the war in the Malaysian Peninsula affected the world's rubber supply and controls were imposed on the manufacture of football bladders. The same balls were used throughout the season.

Bramall Lane was badly damaged by enemy bombing in December 1940. Targeting the steel-making of the city, the Luftwaffe blitzed Sheffield and ten bombs fell on the ground destroying the changing rooms, John Street Stand, the roof of the Shoreham Street Kop and the pitch. United played five games at Sheffield Wednesday's Hillsborough stadium, one at Millmoor and one at Scunthorpe before returning to Bramall Lane. Ever enterprising, the club made £35 from the sale of reclaimed timber from the bombed stands.

Devastation
The view from John Street in December 1940 following a
direct hit on the corner with the Shoreham End

Combined Services
(Germany)
v
Sheffield United FC

War and Peace

Attendances at football matches were very poor at the beginning of the war. In December 1939 just 5,000 watched a Sheffield derby. Things slowly improved though, and by Christmas Day 1940, 15,000 turned out for the same fixture. It could have been higher, but that was the maximum figure allowed at football stadiums by the government's War Commissioner. Fearing an air raid during a match, this number was reckoned to be the maximum able to exit quickly. The Commissioner had even suggested both Sheffield clubs play at the open fields of Abbeydale Park to avoid this exit scenario altogether. Whilst an income was available from football throughout the war years, the war reminded many players how precarious their profession was. When the League was disbanded as war began, the professional footballer was effectively unemployed, but the club retained players' registrations and could command their return. The Football League format was regionalised but the pre-war wages were not paid to the players because of the reduced ground capacities. The best a player could hope for was 30 shillings a game. As a consequence, a variety of scams emerged in football whereby players more or less established themselves as free agents and played under a variety of names. The footballer became a war time itinerant worker. The guest player system produced some memorable line-ups for hitherto poor and small teams. Proximity of army barracks meant that said clubs could on occasion turn out a team consisting of six internationals. Others used the system to their advantage by 'guesting' for cash and often playing under the pseudonym of 'A. Newman' or 'A.N. Other'. The United team at one time included Jackie Milburn of Newcastle, and later England, and Laurie Scott of Arsenal and England. United and Wednesday even shared first-team players in these years. Hillsborough favourites Walter Millership and Hugh Swift played once each for United. One game at Bramall Lane was against a team from the Polish Air Force. One consequence of this was an ersatz style of play which, whilst still providing entertainment, was not the real thing, a situation exacerbated by the absence of promotion and relegation.

As the war progressed crowds picked up, people became used to war conditions and, after 1942, the chances of a daytime raid on the city were so slim that people felt safe. On Christmas Day 1942 a crowd of 34,500 saw a Sheffield derby at Bramall Lane; the 15,000 attendance limit was disregarded at the clubs' and authorities' convenience. By 1944 a match at Bramall Lane pulled in 48,000. On VE Day in May 1945 United played Wednesday in a match in celebration of the Allied victory. When the League resumed as normal in 1946, the fixture list was a replica of the 1939–40 season. In the opening game against Liverpool 28,000 were at Bramall Lane to watch a team that played together in the war years and had promised much. However, the bombs had taken away one third of the seating capacity of Bramall Lane and with it a huge potential income. Whilst the crowds flocked to see football in peacetime, the club was unable to compete financially with others. Success was to be elusive and good players would have to be sold.

Digging and Rolling

The first two years of the decade were fateful for football. When the air raid sirens sounded, the public transport system stopped. The bombs did not always follow, but when they did the population sought refuge in basements and air raid shelters. The Sheffield Blitz came in December 1940 and killed hundreds. The uncertainty brought about by possible air raids, and the actual bombings, affected football training sessions. Aspiring and established players could not always get to where they were expected to be to practise or play matches. If Blades fans can thank the Germans for one thing though it was for sorting out the Bramall Lane pitch. Before a large bomb landed on it, there was regularly six inches of sludge in front of the kop. The bomb churned the area up and gave United the opportunity to install drainage—all the players helped with the digging.

Because of war-rationing, the best refreshment the Bramall Lane match-goer could hope for was a cup of Bovril. Should they wish to read all about the game, all that was available was a football supplement in late Saturday editions of the *Sheffield Star*. Depending on the time of year, kick-off was 2.15 or 3.00. The crowd always contained a fair sprinkling of military caps as the troops came home on leave. There were a few chants to join in with; *2–4–6–8, who do we appreciate?... U–ni–ted*. More elaborate renditions were drawn from a 1935 Anti-Mussolini war song; the words were slightly changed:

> *Roll along Sheff United, roll along*
> *Put the ball in the net where it belongs*
> *If Rickett gets the ball*
> *It's sure to be a goal*
> *Roll along Sheff United, roll along.*

The rationing of the war years meant not only that the bread baked was off-white but that football boots and playing kit were in short supply and difficult to obtain. One thing not in short supply in Sheffield was fit young men. The presence of many young men in the city by virtue of holding war-time 'reserved occupations' meant that when the war ended, United had a squad which had played together regularly. Manager Teddy Davison had the foresight to realise that normality would, one day, return. For this reason, he nurtured many young players. It paid dividends; United won the war-time Northern League in 1945–46 with a team consisting of nine Sheffielders, the majority of whom had received a signing-on fee of only £10.

The football played on the resumption of the League in 1946–47 was hampered by mud and rain; the situation exacerbated by the worst winter in recorded history. Public transport was halted by snow storms, water pipes froze for weeks, fuel shortages closed factories and schools, streets were blacked out because lighting was not working. The cold made people weep. The football programme was severely disrupted and was not completed until June. The late forties saw rationing still a reality and the mantra of 'work or want' pervade. There was little time for sentiment in re-building. The nation had seen many industries nationalised, but power cuts, low wages and housing shortages remained. Recovering from the war was not as quick as people had expected. Austerity was the ethos of the day. The food was plain and to make matters worse a better world was visible via the Hollywood movies available in Sheffield cinemas. Football did not change; facilities were not developed and tactics remained static. United finished sixth in Division One in 1946–47 and made the quarter-final of the Cup. However, the 1948–49 season was a disaster and after a run of 14 games without a win, United were relegated.

War-Time Football

The 1940 war-time Cup Final had a crowd limit of 50,000 and kicked off at Wembley at 6.00pm. But football seemed a particularly futile pursuit at a time when thousands were losing their lives at Dunkirk. Significantly for Sheffield United, the first footballer turned serviceman killed in the war was Joe Carr, who died during the Dunkirk evacuation. Carr had played in all three of United's 1939 first-division games, before the division was abandoned with United in second place. Whilst he returned from having joined the army to play a Sheffield derby in March 1940, he died three months later on active service. Carr was one of 75 footballers who died while serving in the British forces. Harry Hampson, the first United player to enlist in 1939, died from septicaemia in 1942. Hundreds of others by virtue of working in essential industries or remaining in Britain teaching physical training were to continue their playing careers in what remained of the Football League, supplemented by a proliferation of exhibition games which were considered good for public morale for the duration of the war.

At the end of the war a threatened players' strike forced clubs to raise the minimum wage to £1 a week above the 1939 minimum. In 1946 clubs were given partial relief from the 1917 Entertainment Tax and

The John Street Stand and terrace after the Luftwaffe bombing in December 1940

the maximum wage was raised to £10 in winter and £7 in summer. By the 1948–49 season over 41 million people paid to watch League games in England.

Post War Realities

The 1945 war-time Cup Final was attended by most of the royal family in recognition of the role the game had played in sustaining civilian morale over the previous five years. Whilst the traditions of the monarchy were thus sustained the political spectrum was changing. The election victory in 1945 for the Labour Party was seen as a signal from the electorate to start anew. The Welfare State was born three years later in a nation existing in a state-planned austerity manifest most obviously by rationing of items such as fat, cheese, sugar, bread, potatoes and petrol. Vegetables and fruit were sometimes hard to find, as was soap. Women spent hours a day queuing for essential household items. Chocolate and bananas were so hard to come by as to be considered luxury items. Pubs were even known to run out of beer. Rationing did not end until 1954. The domestic arena provided entertainment via the wireless programmes *Housewives Choice* and *Workers' Playtime*. Homogenous, obsessed with decency and with narrow horizons, football was some relief from the monotony and mundanity of Britain in this decade. The first day of the 1946–47 season saw over 944,000 spectators watch 43 League games. A post-war record crowd of 61,000 packed Bramall Lane for an FA Cup fixture against Stoke City in January 1946. The huge numbers forced the officials to close the gates and refuse further admission 30 minutes before kick off. The thousands outside forced the gates and entered for free. Those who witnessed the day considered the attendance was greater than the pre-war 68,000, which remains United's official record attendance.

The players of the time were usually fed one meal a day by the club. Throughout England, supporters sacrificed their ration coupons so as to provide their players with decent food and even kit. For the United players, post-war recreational luxury was provided by visits to Droitwich Spa for baths considered good for the body and soul. For United's home games, the footballers' lot saw an 11.30am rendezvous at Davy's Cafe on the Haymarket. A choice of fish or chicken, followed by rice pudding, led to a game of snooker in a billiard hall on Cambridge Street and a saunter to Bramall Lane. The kit and boots were laid out by the 'odd job man' and the tidying up was done by two char ladies. After the match the players might spend their earnings at the City Hall, listening to the band sounds of Carl Gibson, Harry Roy and Joe Loss. More private dates saw young couples listening to Sheffield's 'Mr Organ' Reginald Dixon playing his theme tunes before the film began at The Gaumont cinema. The club's annual Tour Dance at the Cutlers' Hall saw supporters buy raffle tickets for a top prize of a trip on a Sheffield United Tours excursion. The top of the bill on one such evening was a 20-year-old London-born entertainer called Max Bygraves.

During the 1930s and 40s United, amongst other clubs, got around the rule on not signing anyone under the age of 17 by introducing nursery teams. A variety of teams took on this role—Woodbourn, Norton Woodseats, Fulwood and Shiregreen-based Oaksfold. In the early forties one of the most important of these was St George's. Young hopefuls for United were managed by a Reverend who was good friends with United trainer Reg Wright. Whilst the vicar was Church of England and Reg Wright a Methodist, the former was able to move heaven and earth to get his youngsters to play on the Bramall Lane pitch and find sports goods when none were believed to be available in the city. Born in Dronfield in 1901, Wright

Bramall Lane December 1940
The pitch was ruined by the bombs

had played for Wednesday in 1920 and appeared in a war-time game for United aged 39 when the team was short of players. He was coach to the 'A' team which had begun in the mid-1930s as a deliberate policy of seeking local-born youngsters. The team played in the mid-week league that gave aspirants and trialists the chance to impress for the Saturday reserves or first team. This paid off, because by the late 1940s United had good local-born players coming through the ranks.

A Land Fit For Heroes?

The end of the war saw industrial unrest by doctors, miners and transport workers. The same era also saw the emergence of a newly confident player power. What followed was a two-year dispute between the Players' Union and the Football League. The players sought improved pay and conditions, which led to the threat of a strike and eventually to an increase in wages. The post-war Labour government, whilst radical in its social reforms, did not support major changes in football. In their defence, the government could argue they had enough problems dealing with housing shortages, food rationing, a proliferation of strikes by crucial occupations and the rise of the black market economy. At the same time football was a very cheap form of entertainment and the Chancellor even reduced admission costs in what was no doubt a populist move to provide some form of bread and circuses for the masses. But the same people who ran the game before the war resumed control and governed the clubs in what proved to be a time of phenomenal attendances. It was only natural that with huge crowds the players could ask where the money was going. It certainly was not to them; the maximum wage in 1946 was £20 per week. Footballers, like many men returning to a post-war world, were seeking security but like millions were greatly disappointed as to what the nation could offer. Their occupation was hampered by a shortage of football boots and even footballs. The best a player could hope for was a benefit game as a reward for loyalty to a club. Five years service usually produced a reward of £130, but benefits were at the power and discretion of the club and many a player did not receive what he thought he deserved. In this situation, allegations of players receiving under the counter payments were rife.

Two years after the war ended, the Labour government decided to nationalise the coal mines. To reduce the balance of payments austerity measures were introduced. At the same time, negotiations between players and their employers made little progress. The threatened footballers' strike was prevented by the use of the Emergency Powers Act which stated that any industrial action had to give notice to the government and those seeking strike action had to submit themselves to arbitration. This delaying tactic assisted the government and gave football clubs time to get their acts together. In the ensuing negotiations the League came out on top. The footballer of the era suffered as much as the people who paid to watch him play. They too had inadequate housing; they too had to search hard for good food. The situation in Britain in 1947 was such that a touring Swedish team, Norrkopping, brought their own food with them. Like the people who watched them, footballers had no security of employment and their wages were not vastly different from what many skilled men on the terraces were earning. One example might suffice here. One United player, Eddie Shimwell, was demobbed on a Friday and returned to the family home on the early hours of Saturday. Some 12 hours later he was a trialist at Sheffield United and within a month was an England reserve. Whilst good enough to be a squad member for the national team, Shimwell was forced to leave United when he resided with his fiance in her mother's public house in defiance of a contractual agreement which stated a player could not live in licensed premises whilst in the employ of Sheffield United. He joined Blackpool for a fee of £8,000. Football, however, was still seen by many as a way out of misery and poverty. Thousands of young men sought to make it whilst over ten million played the football pools, hoping the correct predictions would bring them untold riches.

Bramall Lane urgently needed rebuilding in the 1940s. The money invested in the ground was, therefore, lost from the pot towards potential transfers and even wages. The club had no local sugar daddy; the directors were local businessmen and city dignitaries. Mr Senior Atkin was a silversmith, Mr Frank Copestake ran the wholesale fruit market, Mr Dick Wragg was a builders merchant. Both Mr George Marlow and Mr Ernest Graham had held the office of the Lord Mayor of Sheffield—but this did not imply they had fabulous wealth. In the company of such gentlemen on match days were often the good men of the Sheffield Chamber of Trade and Cutlers' Company but the city was not awash with money. The hotels United stayed in during this decade were not always the best, but the players received, on top of their wage, a daily meal after training and could look quite dapper when on their way to games in regulation blazer with high-waisted pleated trousers, complete with turn-ups. Football still beat waking early to clock on for a minimum eight-hour day in dirty conditions. The game also offered the chance for foreign travel and meeting those who had travelled far.

Foreign Legions

In 1945 the United team travelled to Berlin to play an exhibition game against a Combined-Services XI. United thus became one of the first teams from an allied nation to visit post-war Germany. The three-day trip saw the squad board a Dakota plane at RAF Cranwell and fly to Berlin for the game held at the Olympic Stadium. The opposition, drawn from the three Services, included Leslie Compton of Arsenal and England and his Highbury colleague, Eddie Lewis. United lost to the Services team 1–5 in front of 15,000. A visit to the Berlin Chancellory meant the United squad encountered impoverished Berliners seeking cigarettes in exchange for fur coats. On guard in the district in which the squad stayed were soldiers from the Soviet Republic and Mongolian borders, whose unsmiling faces disturbed the players. One of the squad, Walter Rickett, swapped cigarettes with locals for what he considered well-produced vests and underpants. The United goalkeeper, Fred White, brought back a fragment of the bombed out statue of Count Maximillion Von Spee the German Naval Commander who died in 1914.

Post-war attempts at producing a pan-European friendship saw Sheffield twinned with the Dutch city of Eindhoven. Matches between Select XIs representing their respective cities were annual events in this decade. When the Sheffield and Hallamshire FA sent a team it was fairly representative of the city, drawn from United, Wednesday and Sheffield FC. The post-war return to normality also saw the first foreign team playing United at Bramall Lane. This occurred in November 1946 on a Monday afternoon in front of 16,000 fans, and saw the Swedish club Norrköping trounce United 5–2. The match programme informed readers of how '… the pupil has become virtually on a par with the master'. A somewhat patronising attitude that assumed Johnny Foreigner could not play the game as well as the British. Norrköping were champions of Sweden and contained players who soon after were to sign for big Italian clubs, most notably Nils Liedholm. United were without Jimmy Hagan but otherwise had a full team. The Sheffield public watched the Swedes take a 3–0 lead within half an hour. Pulling two goals back, United then conceded another two in the final five minutes. The Swedes left the field to great applause. The media blamed United for lowering themselves to the Swedes' standards by trying to imitate their short passing game. The Swedes reported how, on scoring their fifth goal, a United director burst into tears. In their defence, the Blades hit the woodwork three times and only two days before had played a tough game at Arsenal.

> **The players who wore the shirt of Sheffield United in the war years and post-war were to a man born out of hard times and, whilst stoical by comparison with today, were highly professional. Following footballing careers at times distinguished, at other times modest, such men had little to show for their efforts besides aching limbs. Thankful for what football gave them in times of scarcity and danger, they asked for little and received little in return. They epitomised both a masculine and generational ethos. Their memories some 60 years later are matter of fact and reveal little in the way of bitterness or pity-seeking.**

The United squad about to board an RAF Dakota for Berlin at RAF Cranwell in 1945

The Home Front: Fred Furniss

Fred Furniss made his United debut in 1941 at the age of 18, in a game played against a backdrop of air-raid sirens, at Goodison Park Everton, in front of just 2,100 spectators providing gate receipts of £94. Born in 1922 in Sheffield's Darnall district, Furniss knew the hardship and struggle that grew out of the industrial disputes of the 1920s and the Great Depression of the early 1930s. As the oldest of seven children, Furniss scavenged coal with his collier father from local slag heaps to cook, and stay warm when the mines were on a three-day week. Contented and loving his football, Furniss at the age of 14, was picked to represent Sheffield Boys. Weeks later he left school and enjoyed a few weeks holiday which was then the transition from boy to man. Out of the blue a man called at the family door, a 'gaffer' at the nearby Hampton's factory. He came offering an apprenticeship on condition that Furniss play football for the works' team. Charlie Hampton, the factory owner, was a good friend of one of the directors at Bramall Lane.

A former Hampton player tipped off Fulwood Amateurs—then United's nursery team—about the ability of Furniss. United sent a postcard inviting him to play. He accepted the offer and, a few months later, received another postcard—this time from United manager Teddy Davison, asking him to report for training. However, the exhaustion of 12-hour shifts and disillusionment with perceived lack of progress at United began to tell:

> *I got browned off… Nobody was interested in me. We got 7/6 a week expenses which weren't bad…but I left.*

Persuaded to return, soon after came another postcard; the manager wanted Furniss to report to Bramall Lane to play at Everton. The war was in its second year.

During the early war years Furniss became a Bevin Boy. Named after Ernest Bevin, the Minister for Manufacture and Industry, the term described those young men aged between 18 and 25 who were called-up to mine coal. They were considered to be on active service but wore no uniforms and were

The team sheet of the Combined Services XI v Sheffield United, played in the Olympic Stadium, Berlin in 1945

classified as civilians. Around the country thousands of young men went down the mines. Others worked in in reserved occupations such as shipping, transport and steel-production. Not all were local lads, some were middle-class and a lot of miners resented the latter. But, being a local lad, fit and a footballer, Furniss was liked. He spent 18 months working shifts in Orgreave Colliery until, one day, a runaway coal tub nearly killed him. Seeing it coming, Furniss crouched in a two-foot wide gap but lost the skin off both knees and refused to go down below again. His offer to do any job on the surface was considered insubordinate and he was sacked. Two months later, he got a letter telling him to report for Army training at Lincoln. Fortunately, the war in Europe had ended. Whilst he did not see active service, Furniss saw action via sport representing the army at running, boxing and football. He played for the Army against an FA XI and, when he could, he played for United. Signing amateur forms in 1941 Furniss had made the right-back position his own by 1943. He signed professional in January 1943 and was a core member of the League North championship side of 1945–46. A core player in the side that won promotion to Division One in 1953, Furniss played his final game for United in February 1955.

By his reckoning his appearances for United should read 485 first team games. He was a regular in a defence that included Ted Burgin and Albert Cox; for years they were automatic choices. Furniss was never dropped and the maximum injury absence he suffered was seven weeks. Very strong and very fast, he was years ahead of his time in being an over-lapping defender. His competitive edge extended to penalty taking and he missed only two out of twenty. Contemporaries talk of him as the best uncapped full-back of the time.

Until marrying at the age of 29, Furniss lived at home with his parents. Away matches saw players permitted to take a male guest with them. Furniss took his father. The pair endured eight-hour journeys to matches in London, which brought the chance to see Tommy Trinder at The Palladium. Furniss played three times for a Sheffield and Hallamshire FA select on a tour of Holland and played in the Isle of Man versus Sheffield Wednesday exhibition match. He played in the first floodlit match at Bramall Lane in 1954, and the second, against Hibernians of Edinburgh.

Furniss signed a contract annually until one day in May 1955 the letter came telling him he was being released. Prospective buyers were told he would cost £1,000 which he thought a bit steep, but there was more to it than that:

> They'd decided on that 'cos I was due a second loyalty bonus. What they reckoned on was if someone paid that I'd get me £750 and the Club would get a nice £250 windfall. Well, I went to the Players' Union and they had words and United had to pay me the money and let me go free.

Furniss left earning £16 a week with a £2 bonus when the average skilled worker in the city was on about £5. He considers his United wage good money for a man his age and his first home was in the desirable district of Ecclesall Road. Others in the team got more. Furniss was aware of 'bungs' to star players. It was the great unspoken and whilst such monies provoked dressing-room resentment nobody raised the matter publicly.

Joining Chesterfield in August 1955 where Teddy Davison was now manager, Furniss was given the job of coaching the juniors. After three years, he left to play a season at Worksop. Running a haberdashery business then a fruit and vegetable shop Furniss played local football until he was 55 and exhibition games until his mid-sixties. He then took up refereeing. At one time he was in the top ten snooker players in the city—a product of free afternoons as a footballer. He also once made the last eight of the national Flat Green Bowls Championships. A life of moderation ensures that even in his 80s he can swim daily and dance in the evenings.

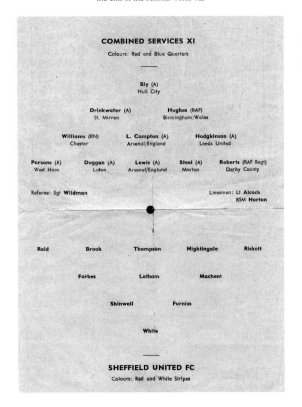

Going into Europe
Sheffield United become the first English side to play in occupied Germany at the end of the Second World War

COMBINED SERVICES XI

Colours: Red and Blue Quarters

Bly (A)
Hull City

Drinkwater (A)   Hughes (RAF)
St. Mirren   Birmingham/Wales

Williams (RN)   L. Compton (A)   Hodgkinson (A)
Chester   Arsenal/England   Leeds United

Parsons (A)   Duggan (A)   Lewis (A)   Steel (A)   Roberts (RAF Regt)
West Ham   Luton   Arsenal/England   Morton   Derby County

Referee: Sgt Wildman   Linesmen: Lt Alcock
                                                 RSM Horton

Reid   Brook   Thompson   Nightingale   Rickett

        Forbes   Latham   Machent

        Shinwell   Furniss

            White

SHEFFIELD UNITED FC

Colours: Red and White Stripes

Safe Custody: Fred White

Teaching a teenage goalkeeper how to kick straight has never been an easy task. In the early 1930s, the 17-year-old Fred White learned a degree of accuracy when his coach put two house bricks either side of the case ball. If the co-ordination of brain and limb was somewhat out, the consequences were painful beyond belief. One might argue the method brought results—White had played for Wolverhampton Schools in the English Schools Final in 1931 and joined the local professional team on the ground staff aged 16. Between 1927 and 1944, the club was managed by the famous Major Frank Buckley. A former commanding officer of the First World War Footballer's Battalion, he was known as the 'Iron Major' who ruled the club with a strictness that would not be tolerated in the contemporary game. At the same time Buckley was innovative, issuing all players with a 'do's and don'ts' rule book and introducing the rowing machine as a training tool. He also introduced the controversial 'monkey gland' injections, in which players were injected with what were believed to be performance-enhancing substances. Whilst keen on the applications of science, he opposed the introduction of a white match ball. Tremendously successful at generating funds from transfers, Buckley considered South Yorkshire a hotspot for football talent and the Rotherham team Wath Wanderers was Wolves' nursery. The club liked what they saw in South Yorkshire and even asked United's Teddy Davison to replace Buckley in 1944.

Buckley was not an instant success. It took a decade of management before Wolves won trophies at the highest level. Fred White, however, was not to be part of Wolves' success. Unable to break into the first team after thirty months, he signed for Everton in early 1935. Eighteen months later, in May 1937, he arrived at Bramall Lane, signed as reserve keeper to Jack Smith. White spent years in the reserves by virtue of Smith never missing a match. White did not make a single first-team appearance before the war. It was only when Smith joined the RAF and was relocated that White took over the goalkeeping jersey. Avoiding being conscripted by working in the reserved occupation of specialist building, White made his debut for United in December 1939 and in pursuit of a game would travel overnight to and from Sheffield from his Wolverhampton base. In war-time he guested for Nottingham Forest, Mansfield, Rotherham, Wrexham and even Sheffield Wednesday. In a game for the latter he fractured his skull in a collision. Interestingly, he was once treated in the Royal Infirmary having collided in a match with his United colleague Alf Settle. Two of the latter's teeth were embedded in White's knee. An infection was setting in. White was treated by Blacow Yates, a United director and surgeon, who used a relatively new derivative of penicillin, thereby making White one of the first people in the city to receive antibiotics. White's huge hands were useful in both the building trade and goalkeeping, but injuries were a constant problem caused by a combination of great physical courage and, observers of the time argued, poor positioning.

White's thirteen years at Bramall Lane produced 133 war-time appearances but only 44 Football League appearances. He left United in 1950 for Lincoln for whom he turned out 42 times. When he retired as a player he worked for Dick Wragg—who became United's chairman in 1974—as a foreman agent and traveller rep. He was also a part-time trainer and scout for United under Joe Mercer, and from 1956 to 1971 was trainer for United reserves. His final job in football saw him compiling scouting reports for Queens Park Rangers' Sheffield-born manager, Jim Smith, in the 1980s.

By anyone's standards a decent and friendly man, White had married the daughter of one of United's benefactors. The two were confident, sociable and well liked. They were not phased by the new, which was good news for a man forcibly brought to the city. A German national by the name of Carl Witt spent three years in the early 1940s as a prisoner in the Lodge Moor POW Camp on the outskirts of Sheffield. A German army paratrooper, he had twice fought on the Russian Front and when wounded in the Netherlands was taken prisoner by the Allied Forces and eventually found himself in Lodge Moor via the Isle of Wight. The Lodge Moor camp contained many fit young men who were capable footballers. They trained hard out of boredom and once challenged United to a game. This took place, albeit the fixture was not publicised. Before the prisoners were repatriated at the end of the war, Witt asked United for a trial and began training twice a week at Bramall Lane. Recognised by team-mates as both a good player and decent individual, he was a popular figure and White regularly took him home for dinner.

The United board, whilst recognising Witt's talent, considered that signing a German was too politically contentious. United's loss was the gain for both Stuttgart and Bayern Munich, for whom Witt played on returning to Germany. For the next 55 years Fred White and Carl Witt visited each other's homes annually.

Feigning the Issues: Albert Nightingale

Born in the pit village of Thrybergh, Rotherham, in 1923, Albert Nightingale came from a coal mining family and was the youngest of four boys, all of whom played professional football. His father was killed down the pit, his mother brought up the family of eight children. Of his three elder brothers, two played for Rotherham United and one turned out for Doncaster. The oldest, who played regularly for Rotherham, was, like his father, killed in a pit fall.

Turning out for Yorkshire Boys at the age 14, Nightingale signed for United aged 17 and weeks later was in the first team. Leaving school at 14, the only realistic career option was coal mining. In his late teens in 1941 he was working in Thurcroft Colliery, whilst training for United. His dual status made life as a miner a little bit easier:

> *Mostly we trained instead of going down the pit because many people in the pit were United fans but, employed as a coal face worker, we had to show our faces now and then...*

Sheffield United line up at the Valley, Charlton, in September 1946
The second away game following the end of the Second World War. Holding the ball is captain Jimmy Hagan

The Football League v Ireland, 1946.

Jimmy Hagan is second from the right in the front row. Middlesbrough's Wilf Mannion is extreme left, front row. Arsenal's Joe Mercer, who was later to manage United, stands behind Hagan. Next to Mercer on the right of the back row is Dennis Compton, who represented Arsenal and England at football and England at cricket. He was known in his era as the 'Brylcreem' boy for his endorsement of the hair gel. The goalkeeper Frank Swift in the middle of the back row was killed in the Munich air disaster of 1958

Nightingale could earn 30 shillings for a first-team appearance, which was more than coal miners were earning for a week's graft. The job of a footballer had the benefit of free food and massages from Lol Livingstone (Duggie's brother), employed at Bramall Lane specifically for assisting muscular relief. The good work of the masseur was somewhat compromised when the United dressing room regularly saw Nightingale standing by the open window having a cigarette. He put this habit down to pre-match nerves, but revealed that half the team smoked 20 a day.

Playing at inside forward and occasionally at centre forward, Nightingale was a regular in the Championship-winning United side of 1946, finishing as top scorer with 23 goals. A difficult opponent to mark, Nightingale had good close control and was hard to knock off the ball. Making his debut in 1941 at Hillsborough he was to average a goal every other game. He was a player whom opponents and opposition fans did not always appreciate famed as he was for his ability to dive and win penalties. Forty years after his playing career had ended he admitted that he 'could fall over on the half way line and get a penalty'. The penalties he won made a significant contribution to United's championship win. His background and occupation made him a hard man on the pitch. One opponent by the name of Jimmy Scoular took a particular dislike to Nightingale's antics and would threaten him throughout the match. Nightingale would reply that the threats were useless because his opponent was too slow to catch him. Frightened of nobody, Nightingale played in a United side which was the toughest in its history. Besides Nightingale and the hardest of the lot, Walter Rickett, were Harry Latham, Albert Cox and Colin Collindridge, local boys from mining backgrounds who could and did frighten most of their fellow professionals.

Nightingale stayed at United for close to seven years and earned a maximum of £10 a week. He was grateful to the club and the Sheffield medical profession who contrived a story so that he avoided

National Service. Realising his value to the club, a doctor friendly to United wrote a report stating that Nightingale was on the verge of a nervous breakdown and so should avoid the call-up. He was thus able to play for United and earn decent money. A transfer request in 1948 saw Newcastle offer a signing-on fee and a promise to find his wife a job. Nightingale turned them down reasoning, 'I didn't know a soul up there, there was no need to go'. Eventually after 225 appearances and 88 goals, he left United for Huddersfield for £10,000 as part of a deal that saw the arrival of two players from the opposite direction. He stayed there for three years, before moving to join Blackburn Rovers for £12,000 in 1951. After three years at Blackburn he signed for Leeds in October 1952, then managed by Raich Carter. After only a handful of games at Leeds, Nightingale suffered a ligament injury and never fully recovered. Nightingale was well respected by the Leeds fans and when released was the recipient of a £5,000 cheque, courtesy of fund raising events by the supporters club.

When his playing days ceased Nightingale lived in the same house in Huddersfield for over 50 years and took a variety of jobs from school caretaker to golf course green-keeper and ambulance driver. Nightingale died in early 2006.

> **Players arrived at United from other parts of the UK. One arrival exemplified great personal ambition and one man moved to Sheffield with just the clothes he wore on his back. The transfer deal he was later part of saw him make the big time. The same deal manifested a reluctance to relocate to Sheffield's grimy environs from a more established player. The story of the two lives reveals some of the happenings emerging in the English game of this decade.**

Scottish Journeys: Alex Forbes and Paddy Sloan

Born in Dundee in 1925, Alex Forbes became a Scottish international in 1947 three years after joining United. A sporting all-rounder, Forbes was a powerful swimmer and capable snooker player who also represented Scottish teams at ice hockey against visiting Canadian and American sides. A chance meeting in a Dundee street with a mate saw Forbes asked to make up a football team that became known as Dundee North End. Playing centre forward, he came to the attention of Sheffield United via a letter sent by a Dundee resident recommending a local-born goalkeeper to Teddy Davison. Davison's response was that United had enough people in that position, but were short of a centre forward. A week later, Forbes arrived at Bramall Lane, carrying only his football boots in a brown paper bag. Following a trial United signed him, found him a job and Forbes made his debut in September 1944. The club also moved him to left half, despite him being naturally right footed. He made 124 appearances for United and scored 17 goals.

Playing for United in 1946 Forbes entered the Everton dressing room to meet his hero the England captain Joe Mercer. Later when captain of Arsenal, Mercer in all likelihood remembered Forbes when Arsenal wanted a midfield terrier to break up opponents' play and give the ball to more talented midfield players. Forbes held this position at United. He was to sign for Arsenal in 1948 for £16,000, the rumour was he was 'tapped-up'. A ferocious tackler and good distributor Forbes did well at Highbury, winning an FA Cup-winners medal in 1950 and a championship medal three years later. He played 217 games scoring 20 times for the Gunners. He was transfer listed at Highbury at his own request. United were asked by Arsenal if they would like to have Forbes back. The answer for some reason was no but then the request to consider taking him back was surrounded by mystery and the subject of rumour. Forbes left Arsenal for Leyton Orient and eventually finished his professional playing days at Fulham in 1958. Moving to Sligo in the Republic of Ireland, Forbes then emigrated to South Africa where he lives today.

Paddy Sloan joined United from Arsenal as part of the deal that saw Alex Forbes move south. Sloan's subsequent move from United to AC Milan made history and had a degree of intrigue that resulted in United paying probably their first agent's fee. Joshua 'Paddy' Sloan was born in Northern Ireland in 1920

How we laughed
Left to right: Albert Nightingale, Bobby Reid, Jack Smith, Alex Forbes and Eddie Shimwell
share a joke during training in 1946 with trainer-coach Duggie Livingstone

and as a teenager made a name with Glenavon. Aged 15, he was signed as an amateur with Arsenal but his mother refused him permission to leave for London. Two years later he joined Manchester United but was released to Tranmere in 1939. For much of the war Sloan was in Canada—there being no conscription in Northern Ireland during the Second World War. By 1945, however, he was wearing the shirt of Ireland in games against England and Wales. A year later Sloan turned down a move to Everton and joined Arsenal. He then signed for United for £6,000 in May 1948, the month after Alex Forbes left United to join Arsenal.

A class player used to the splendours of Highbury and the attractions of the capital city, Sloan did not want to join United. Throughout his brief stay with the Blades he continued to live in London. He lasted only three months at Bramall Lane and played just 13 games—the final one an exhibition match against Sheffield Wednesday on the Isle of Man. His departure from United created history. In joining AC Milan Sloan became the first professional British player to sign for an Italian club. United got their money back and more—Milan paid £7,000 for him. In United's minute book a sum of £100 was given to Arsenal's manager Tom Whittaker 'in appreciation' for his role in securing the transfer. Possibly Whittaker realised that having got Forbes from United by possibly questionable means, the least he could do was help out the club he had taken him from. Sloan lasted just one season at Milan and later played for Brescia. Years later he was to be a player-coach in Malta with Rabat. Sloan emigrated to Australia where he died in 1993.

A club could control a player's future by virtue of holding his registration. The best a player could do was to hold out for a better deal when the annual contract renewal arose. If a player had a long-term injury or had mediocre ability, his bargaining power was virtually non-existent. Good players by contrast could hold out and get the best possible deal. In what follows, the lives of two players are presented who, whilst very different characters, were both considered vital to the post-war Sheffield United team. One was a legend by virtue of his football ability, the other had more limited ability but could talk a good game. One was to hold out and get what he wanted, the other despite a politically radical family tradition, could not see that footballers militancy was a worthwhile cause to fight for. The latter was to eventually leave United having negotiated his own deal in what could be considered a supreme act of individualism; the former got what he wanted from the club by obstinacy. Precisely what monies this individual earned, antiquity cannot tell us because no records of payment exist in the club's archives next to this man's name.

Some footballer's lives deserve a book to themselves. One whose life would be graced by such a text was the man considered by all Blades of a certain age as the greatest player in the club's history. His years at Bramall Lane saw him test the boundaries of the permissible and at times drive his trainers and directors to distraction—but his performances on the pitch were unsurpassable. He was to leave Bramall Lane to achieve much wider recognition as a coach.

Mr Wonderful: Jimmy Hagan

Born in Washington, Tyne and Wear in 1918, Jimmy Hagan was the second oldest of eleven children, only seven of whom lived to their fifth birthday. His Whitehaven-born mother had been orphaned and lived with an aunt in Waterloo, County Durham, whilst his father was a coal miner and former professional footballer with Newcastle, Cardiff and Tranmere. Earning £4 a week down the mine, Hagan senior rented the three up, three down family home where a French organ dominated what constituted the living room. Childhood for Hagan involved cricket in the street, milk bought from the local farmer and, occasionally, free vegetables from an adjacent farm. The family ate well, despite their obvious poverty.

Tragedy and misery were an integral part of Hagan's upbringing. His sister, Alfreda, died aged four having choked on a pea; his brother Alfred died of a twisted bowel at the age of two. Attending the local Catholic school, Hagan was taken out by his father, infuriated at the school's obsession with catechism. He was subsequently brought up in the teachings of a Church of England school. Remembered by siblings as a bright, helpful boy, Hagan was devoted to his mother. However, his painting of her which he completed in his teens, was deliberately burned by his father. Hagan

The 16-year-old Jimmy Hagan shortly after signing for Derby County in 1936

Jimmy Hagan leading out a Combined Services XI in Servette, Switzerland

senior was a man of intense rage and jealousy. Hagan's father was a drinker and that may well have been the reason why Hagan never touched alcohol throughout his life. Eager to please as a boy and in his youth, Hagan is remembered by those who knew him well as a man who rarely had a bad word to say about anyone, even his father.

His footballing ability saw him selected for Durham County and later England schoolboys. Whilst playing for his country he was accompanied by a school teacher. His mother could not afford to travel, his father refused to. His father did, however, negotiate on his son's behalf when, at the age of 14, Derby County and Liverpool sought his signature. He joined Liverpool on the ground staff. The Football League however said 14 was too young and forced him to return home. Soon after, negotiations were again conducted in the Hagan front room and Derby County became his next destination where his age did not seem to perturb the same men at the League. Lodging in Derby with a Mrs Thomas, for whom he became a surrogate son, Hagan would send £1 of his £3 weekly wage home to his mother. After becoming a professional, he paid the fees for his sister to attend the Northern Commercial College. In Derby he met Iris, who worked in the Rolls-Royce factory. They married in her hometown. The international forward line at Derby however meant Hagan's first team opportunities were limited.

Hagan joined United as an inside-forward in 1938 at the age of 21 for £2,923. His task at Bramall Lane was to help United complete what for many years had been promised but not realised. Having been relegated in 1934, United found it hard in the succeeding years to gain promotion and whilst they got to the FA Cup Final in 1936, they finished third in the League thereby missing promotion. The following season, United finished seventh. The sale of Bobby Barclay and Eddy Boot in 1937 to Huddersfield did not go down well with the fans. Bringing in Teddy Ashton from Barnsley to play alongside Jock Dodds promised a lot, but

United finished third, yet again narrowly missing promotion. In the 1938–39 season, Hagan, aged 20, made his debut and went on to score 11 goals as United finished second and finally got promoted. Their progress ended in September when war was declared and the League was suspended.

During the war, Hagan was a Physical Training Instructor in the Army in Aldershot for whom he played 100 games. He was also to see front-line war service and play for England in war-time internationals. England internationals in this era were not recognised with a full cap. Hagan played 16 times in such circumstances and captained the United team that won the 1946 Football League North championship. When England beat Scotland 8–0 in 1943 the England forward line read; Stanley Matthews, Raich Carter, Tommy Lawton, Dennis Compton and Jimmy Hagan. The football world in the late 1940s was astounded that Hagan only ever earned one full England cap—in 1948 against Denmark in Copenhagen. Why his selection was overlooked subsequently is open to conjecture. One prevalent view was that Hagan was too independent a mind to be tolerated by the committee that selected the national team.

In 1946–47 as the League returned to its pre-war format, Hagan considered leaving the game and taking up accountancy. Reluctant to re-sign for United, Hagan was permitted to remain on amateur forms, whilst the United committee tried to convince him to re-sign as a professional. His intention to quit the game needs to be put in the context of the money available at Sheffield United. The AGM of 1946 showed that the club had made £4,500 profit, had put £5,000 into a reserve fund and had a further £9,150 in hand. The same AGM learned that Hagan turned down the club's offer of the maximum wage. Hagan eventually got what he wanted even though no records exist at Sheffield United of his wages. It was widely believed that this so-called militancy had cost him his place in the England team.

Hagan wanted security after football and realised he needed to learn a skill, which meant learning another job whilst playing for the club. Hagan was United's star player—the board could not realistically move him on. He was, borrowing from a BBC programme of the time, a one man 'Brains Trust'. Hagan even considered becoming a driving instructor but eventually qualified as a surveyor. He worked for a company owned by a United fan and was permitted to train in the evenings and when it suited him.

The One Man Brainstrust? Jimmy Hagan, thinking ahead

Hagan could be a stubborn man and some considered him bloody-minded. Critics said he was not a team player. The United board once remonstrated with the manager Reg Freeman that Hagan was not playing for the team. Freeman's response was that no matter what he advised him in training, Hagan did what he wanted once out on the pitch. Without a doubt he was single-minded, but he also kept very strict regimes which included being teetotal and a non-smoker. He was also renowned for doing extra training. One of his idiosyncrasies was that at the end of training he enjoyed precision shooting, which required that players shoot and hit the crossbar. On the pitch he was not a shouter or a motivator but he held the captaincy, only relinquishing it in 1949 when United were relegated.

Jimmy Hagan with Wolverhampton Wanderers' Billy Wright
before a 1949 Cup tie
The blazered Ken Aston was the referee who pioneered the
red card system of contemporary football

Many in the game believe Hagan should have been voted Footballer of the Year in 1953, when aged 35. The glossy football magazine *Charles Buchan's Football Monthly*, raved over him. Fan power probably got him selected for the FA tour of Canada in 1950 and of Australia the following year, which saw him as one of three United representatives alongside Ted Burgin and Joe Shaw. His main task was as a provider. This saw him take corners and throw-ins, as well as executing lobs, typified by subtlety and a deftness of touch. Never fast he was seconds ahead by virtue of football intellect. He used a full array of skills—the back heel, the body swerve, the shimmy and the feint. He had a great first touch, great control and a good shot. If one sought a weakness it was in his occasional ambling. Often subject to unwanted attention from opponents Hagan could give it back; one tackle broke the leg of Huddersfield's Conway Smith. The one sending off in his career occurred after he hurt an opponent in a game against Swansea. For many not used to him, he was rather blunt in conversation.

He was the greatest Sheffield United player ever, yet his off-pitch persona was rarely seen by the fans. He loved to party in the company of people he knew well. Living in a club house in the Norton area of Sheffield, he had a circle of friends drawn from his team mates, Harold Brook, Alf Ringstead, and Graham Shaw. Away from Bramall Lane he was a friend of the contemporary football royalty of Stanley Matthews, Len Shackleton, Joe Mercer, and Jock Dodds. He particularly enjoyed a card game known as 'The Clock Has Struck'. Eschewing the bright lights and the trappings of celebrity Hagan would delegate written requests for his autograph to his wife and her good mate Molly. The pair would contrive his signature on the letter of reply. He enjoyed comedy programmes and opera and at his funeral had requested the playing of the Chorus of the Hebrew Slaves from Verdi's opera *Nabucco*. He was good at bowling, golf, played tennis and enjoyed cricket. He also invented a game he called 'golf-foot', which required players to kick a ball around the golf course.

In February 1951 Hagan, then aged 32, was offered the chance to join Sheffield Wednesday. The fee was believed to be over £32,000, which would have been a record transfer in British football. The United directors left the decision to Hagan; he turned the move down. He considered it incredible that anyone would want to pay that amount of money for a man of his age. He also loved United and realised that going to Wednesday would be considered a betrayal by Blades' fans. He was also looking forward to an FA Select tour of Australia. At the Sydney Cricket Ground, the visitors beat Australia 17–0 in two inches of mud. Hagan scored four goals and in a game against Tasmania, the visitors won by a similar scoreline with Hagan scoring eight.

Hagan played regularly for United until September 1957. His appearances became sporadic when his former England colleague Joe Mercer took the manager's chair at United for the last two years of his career. Mercer tried to break up the core of the United team that Hagan thought highly of and considered his football family. Hagan realised his time was up. His testimonial at Bramall Lane in 1958 produced a 30,000 attendance and saw United play an All Star XI team which included Stanley Matthews, Tom Finney, Brian

Clough and Bert Trautman. In a business venture with Harold Brook, Hagan co-owned a sports shop on London Road but the business did not last long.

Upon retirement Hagan's United record read 442 first team games and 151 goals. At the end of his career, Hagan lived in a rented semi-detached home and owned a modest car. His wife had a low opinion of his former employers, a dispute over the proceeds of his testimonial muddied the water. To Hagan though, Bramall Lane was a place of good memories to which he returned and where he felt humbled when invited onto the pitch before games in the 1960s and 1970s. His legacy is both aural and emblematic. Blades of a certain age will remember singing his praises by slightly altering the words of sing-a-long tune, *Wonderful, Wonderful Copenhagen* from the 1952 film *Hans Christian Anderson,* to 'Wonderful, Wonderful Jimmy Hagan'. The badge that adorns the team shirt and all Sheffield United paraphernalia is a product of Hagan's artistry. The badge, whilst evidently taken from the insignia of the Gurkha Regiment, was first seen adorning team blazers when United played a European Tour in the early 50s. The design lay dormant until the late 1970s when it was found in the bowels of Bramall Lane. Slightly altered, it appeared on the team shirt and has become synonymous with Sheffield United ever since.

Jimmy Hagan striking a contemplative pose complete with England cap in 1949

Hagan was never asked to be United's manager, Dick Wragg did not believe he could communicate his ideas. His first managerial position was at Peterborough, a club in the Midland League until 1951. Hagan was 40 when he took the manager's chair, but he won the Division Four title in 1961. The team scored 134 goals in 46 games (a record that still stands) in front of an average attendance of 15,000, and exceptional crowds of up to 22,000. Two years later, whilst the club were second in Division Three, Hagan was sacked. Soon after he took the manager's job at West Bromwich. His time as manager there saw them reach two League Cup Finals. He walked out on the Baggies after arguing with the board. This bad blood came as a result of what could only be described as a players' revolt, combined with a dispute over transfers. The revolt arose over the wearing of tracksuit bottoms. On a cold winter's morning, many of the players, led by no less a figure than Don Howe (a key figure in the management teams at England and Arsenal in his post playing days), refused to train without the warmth of a tracksuit. Howe even threatened to take the players out on strike if their demands for tracksuit bottoms were not met. The strike did not happen, but Hagan knew the players' actions were the beginning of the end. Years later, at a dinner in London, Howe apologised to Hagan. By this time Howe himself was a manager and, shaking Hagan's hand, reputedly said, 'You were right and I was wrong'.

Hagan's time at Albion was not without off-pitch drama. In 1964, whilst at the club's training ground, Hagan inadvertently reversed his car down a grass bank. He was unaware of the 150-metre-long incline with a canal at the bottom. His Vauxhall Cresta somersaulted four times before landing in the water. Hagan was rescued by his players and escaped with superficial cuts. As he entered the ambulance, Hagan gave instructions to his assistant as to the line-up for the match the next day. He also enquired after his briefcase, which had remained in the now-submerged car, from which Hagan had crawled through an open window. His time with West Bromwich lasted from 1963 to 1967 and produced a decent income that could purchase a four-bedroom detached house and a car.

The bronze statue of Jimmy Hagan in the Hall of Fame

In 1969, whilst scouting for Manchester City, jointly managed by Joe Mercer and Malcolm Allison, Hagan started a driving school. Shortly afterwards he was approached by a football club based in the Iranian capital Tehran but, having visited the city, turned down the job, considering the political situation too risky to move his family to. A short time later, he was approached by the Greek side, Panathinaikos, and, by contrast, Southend United. However, it was the Portuguese giants Benfica he finally opted for, with the former Bogota bandit Charlie Mitten acting as middleman. Visiting the Stadium of Light, Hagan met the great Eusebio, whom he considered the most brilliant footballer in the world. His mind made up, he accepted a one-year deal, and won the championship in his first season. The two-year deal that followed saw him win the 1971 championship without losing a match. In the same season Benfica made it to the European Cup semi-finals, losing narrowly over two legs to Ajax.

Hagan managed a club that regularly attracted crowds of 80,000. The fans loved him and many speak of him as the best manager the club has ever had. Hagan received the best tables in restaurants and meals on the house, and he and Eusebio became great friends. However, he was infuriated by bureaucracy and by the allegations of corruption that pervaded the Portuguese game and he had little time for the club's directors who forever sought to interfere with his team selection.

Hagan left Benfica in September 1973 in what was a bitter departure, which resulted in a court case that was never satisfactorily resolved. His split with the club came on the day of a testimonial match for Eusebio. During the day the squad trained as normal although three players decided not to train hard, considering the evening game an irrelevance. They ignored Hagan's repeated warnings about the consequences of not improving their work rate and that evening were left out of the team. The president of Benfica, Dr Borge Coutinho, on reading the team sheet, entered the dressing room and insisted that Hagan select the three. Hagan's response was that he picked the team and reminded the president that his contract said as much. The president insisted that all three play to which Hagan replied that if they did he would walk out. Under instructions from the president, the three got changed and played. True to his word, Hagan walked out and never returned. That night Hagan's wife was entertaining the wife of England World Cup-winning captain Bobby Moore. Two hours later, on the doorstep of the Hagan household stood the Benfica president with another director and Eusebio. All pleaded with Hagan to change his mind and return, but Hagan refused and took his wife and guests to the Estoril Casino and enjoyed a dinner. Shortly after, Hagan began legal proceedings against Benfica for breach of contract.

The laborious legal system of Portugal eventually ruled in favour of Hagan in 1978, agreeing with him that his contract specified that he chose the team and no one else. Benfica appealed and, for reasons that remain a mystery, Hagan was not invited to attend the subsequent court hearings, which went on for a further eight years and were eventually won by Benfica. As a consequence, Hagan did not receive a penny from the club, a great injustice considering that shortly before leaving he had signed a three-year contract worth in the region of £50,000 a year. The one witness who was prepared to offer evidence in support of Hagan was killed in a car crash the day before he was due to testify.

Shortly after leaving Benfica, Hagan took over as manager of the small suburban club, Estoril. The club's directors owned many of the areas restaurants, who paid Hagan partly in kind with free food. In April 1974 an attempted coup began the Portuguese revolution and in this dangerous climate Hagan took his family to a new job in Kuwait. The Kuwaiti job with the Al-Arab Club lasted for two years and was brokered by Graham Williams who had played under Hagan at West Bromwich Albion. In the summer of 1976 Hagan returned to Portugal to manage Sporting Lisbon. The two-year contract was seen out without any trophies being won. Soon after he took charge of Belenenses before brief spells with Beira Mare, Vitoria Setubal and eventually Boavista. This latter invariably mid-table, small club were to win the Portuguese Cup under Hagan, beating Sporting in the semi-final. However, due to alleged irregularities, the game had to be replayed; Boavista won again. Yet more irregularities were uncovered but, in the third replay, Boavista were once again the victors. Boavista achieved more in the 1978–79 season than in their entire previous history. However, living in Estoril and travelling to the city of Oporto was tiring, Hagan left the job shortly after his team won the cup. He retired from management shortly after. He returned to England and became an adjudicator on the Pools Panel, alongside the Marquis of Bath who became a great friend.

In 1960 Hagan began a novel based on football, provisionally called *The Boot*. He stopped writing on taking the Benfica job. Its contents are undeniably autobiographical. In 1993 Hagan was diagnosed with Alzeheimers, he stayed in the West Midlands for three years before moving to Sheffield to be close to his sister. He died in a Sheffield nursing home in 1998. Pride of place in the Hall of Fame goes to a statue of Hagan. After his death a memorial lunch was held at Bramall Lane. The event sold 300 tickets and with the money raised the directors of Sheffield United commissioned a statue at a cost of £14,000. What would constitute a suitable launch for the statue was discussed by the curator of the Hall of Fame and Hagan's only son, David. The result was a commemorative dinner for 450 with the guest of honour being Eusebio. On the night Eusebio spoke in honour of his former manager and unveiled the statue.

England v Ireland
Football League medal
Awarded to Jimmy Hagan in 1947
(Courtesy of David Hagan/Jackie Stewart)

Still smiling, United's Jack Smith chaired off the pitch by team-mates following his final game

In what follows the man offering kind words about Hagan was also a significant footballer of his era. From a political background the man was willing to confront those in positions of authority in the game but could not see the need for radical behaviour in pursuing pay and conditions. Human nature and its frailties combined with a realisation that, compared to the men he had grown up with, the occupation of footballer was infinitely better rewarded, toned the opinion of a potential Union fire-brand.

Union Dues: Colin Collindridge

An extended family in the mining village of Brough Green, Barnsley, provided Colin Collindridge and his sister with a close-knit home. Leaving school in 1934, aged 14, Collindridge was apprenticed to a printer. Local league football occupied his free time and at the age of 15 Collindridge played against men twice his age. On the touchline were two aunts who, when their beloved nephew got kicked in the air, would enter the field and assault the protagonist. An opinionated persona can be traced to an uncle who was the Labour MP for Barnsley in the 1930s and a father who was Labour Councillor (and Mayor) for Wombwell, as well as Leader of the Yorkshire Miners.

Playing for Wombwell Main in 1936 Collindridge impressed a watching Wolves scout. The following year aged 16 he signed for Wolves ground staff on 50 shillings a week with a promise from Major Buckley, the Wolves' Manager, that he would offer him professional terms on his seventeenth birthday. Six weeks later Collindridge was dismissed from the club. He never found out the reason why.

Not wanting to return to the printing trade Collindridge defied the words of his father and took a colliery job. He was soon to know the perils of the pit face; a thumb end was taken away by an accident. On Saturdays Collindridge played for Shipcraft United in the Barnsley League. Paid one pound a game boot money by a shady pair of brothers who ran the team, he was to attract the attention of Reg Freeman, then managing Rotherham. Training twice a week at Millmoor Collindridge emerged as a quality forward playing reserve team football at the age of 16. Aged 17 Nottingham Forest offered part-time status with a guaranteed job at a nearby cigarette factory. He turned it down; he wanted only professional status.

Moving to Skegness to work as a photographer's assistant Collindridge was soon after to arrive at Bramall Lane via a family connection:

> My second cousin married Alf Settle, who was a United player. He came into the Institute one morning and told me to come to Bramall Lane for a trial. He advised me to 'get stuck in'. Well, that was a stock phrase for our village. At the Tuesday morning practise I went straight through Dick Young…

The tough tackling impressed United Manager, Teddy Davison, who in January 1939 signed Collindridge as a professional, only days after his eighteenth birthday. He could earn £2 for a first team appearance and half that for a reserve game with a further pound to be gained for winning. Advice as to how to make it in the game came from the United trainer, Duggie Livingstone:

> …he said to me, 'Forget the good manners your mother taught you if you're gonna make it in football'.

Training consisted of a series of 80 yard sprints interspersed with 20 laps of the pitch and a game of football. Teddy Davison, the team manager, was in Collindridge's opinion less significant to the squad than Livingstone.

> …at times in training he would take the squad to the centre circle and tell us that this was the time to grumble to him—away from the ears of the manager and directors. He would then take issues to Davison.

The ten-week summer-time close season saw the basic wage paid, and permitted Collindridge to live and learn the photography trade in Skegness. The club sent his wages direct to his mother. Things developed both in the darkroom and in the world of football when he reported back for training in 1939. War was declared on September 3rd, just 20 days before his first team debut. For the next five years professional football was put on hold and consequently what might have been the best footballing years of Collindridge's life were spent elsewhere. In 1941 Collindridge joined the Air Force. He was stationed in Nottinghamshire as an armourer, loading and unloading bomber planes. This arduous and very dangerous work kept him match fit. A chap from Notts County then offered him a fiver a game. He played regularly for them between 1942 and 1945 and saved the match money which was an excellent earning considering his pre-war wage at Bramall Lane.

At the end of the war football began again as a professional entity. Returning to Bramall Lane, Collindridge trained Tuesday, Wednesday and Thursday with rest days on Friday and Monday. A free lunch in the clubhouse after training was a perk of the job, as was the allocation of two tickets per man for each home game. Crowds flocked to Bramall Lane after the war and the United team duly entertained them. A home game against Stoke saw over 50,000 paying spectators and Collindridge score a hat-trick despite being marked by the England centre-half, Neil Franklin. Favoured to win the double United lost a sixth round tie to Newcastle on appalling ice and snow. The severe winter brought a fixture pile-up that probably cost United the title. The following season United sold players they should not have. Inevitably their fortunes declined.

United had a fine player in Collindridge. Very fast, very strong and with a hard shot and fine heading ability, Collindridge was both hard working and brave. At slightly under six feet tall and weighing eleven stones he scored goals and frightened defenders. Opinionated, forceful and raised in the occasionally brutal politics of a Yorkshire mining village, it was only natural that Collindridge would become the Professional Footballers Association's representative at Bramall Lane. His two years as the PFA rep (1950–51) came about by informed consensus:

> People took turns for 12 months. One day Jonah [George Jones] came in and said 'My time's up'.
> I asked who was next and he said 'You!'. Everyone laughed. That's how I became rep.

The task was to listen to what his team-mates wanted and advise them as to the realistic chances of getting what they wanted. This done, he was then tasked with taking matters to Teddy Davison 'in a nice manner'. Was the game exploitative of its casual labourers (i.e. footballers)?

> Look at the reality… I'd got flash suits, clean fingernails and women around me thanks to my job as
> a footballer. Our wages were far better than the working man. I'd little to complain about…

When he did complain the United board listened. One remarkable incident nearly brought about a players' strike. The principle of the dispute was won by the players, although the monies paid were not all the players hoped for, and was paid out with a veiled threat:

> When I joined United in 1939 I got a £10 signing-on fee. After, when we signed again, [in 1946] only
> Jimmy Hagan and Alex Forbes got money for singing on. I asked Teddy Davison why can't they pay
> all of us? He said he'd take it to the Committee. The Committee sent word that they weren't paying.
> So I told Davison to tell them that 16 professionals were in the Players' Union and if 11 of them went
> on strike you'd be struggling. Returning from the Committee Davison brought news that a five pound
> signing on fee was agreed—but it would be taxed and any further talk of strike action would see
> players as reserves to the reserves.

A pervasive belief in the United dressing room was that Jimmy Hagan received more wages than team-mates. Such a belief, which would refute all notions of collective bargaining and equality, did not worry Collindridge:

> …Hagan was the brains. You could have paid him ten times more than what they paid me and
> I wouldn't have minded.

Collindridge knew Hagan better than most by virtue of rooming with him on tours and away games. He knew his likes and knew why the England selectors disliked him:

> He didn't say much out of place. Loved dark chocolate, favourite song was Bing Crosby's 'Cool
> Water'; didn't suffer fools though…Spoke up if it needed saying. He got picked for England and in
> the hotel in Copenhagen the trainer—also the trainer at 'Boro—told the squad to be in bed at ten.
> Jimmy told him he only ever slept after midnight and took himself for a walk around Copenhagen.
> It got him into the England selectors' black books… never got picked again.

The United trainer Duggie Livingstone and Hagan didn't get on. This tension split the dressing room. Livingstone was sacked when he told the directors that the squad he had would only take the club into division three. Collindridge's friendship with Hagan provoked cross words with the trainer when Hagan was relieved of the position of team captain.

It was Thursday morning. I was having treatment when Livingstone walked past and said 'You're captain Saturday'. When he told me Jimmy was dropped I let rip with obscenities and told him to shove his bleedin' captaincy.

Stories flow from Collindridge describing the intrigue that was the United dressing room in the late 1940s. There was dissent over which player received a car courtesy of the club and which did not. Another player was believed to be selected by virtue of him being the secret love-child of one of the Board of Directors.

Sheffield United v Manchester United
Colin Collindridge in the uncharacteristic position of punching the ball from his own area
Deputising for United regular keeper Jack Smith who had left the pitch with an injury

The Players' Union meetings held in Manchester were led by Jimmy Guthrie of Charlton as Chairman, and Frankie Broome of Aston Villa as Vice-Chair. Voted onto the Players' Committee, the problem as Collindridge saw it was his fellow members:

> *There were two shysters who hated each other more than the Football League. I pulled out citing 'business reasons' but in truth whilst Guthrie was trying I couldn't see any end to that union as such…*

Had United players genuine axes to grind?

> *Jimmy Hutchinson came to me with a problem. He'd scored three at 'Boro and the following week he's not on the team. He was a nice cultured fellow and he asked me what should he do? On the grapevine I'd heard that Albert Nightingale, a rough lad who'd worked down Silverwood Colliery, had let it be known that if he weren't selected he was on the transfer list. I said to Jimmy that Albert was seven years younger than him which weren't actually true—he'd sold the club a false birthdate but they didn't know this and anyway the club would keep the younger of the two. Sure enough Jimmy left within a year…*

By the time Collindridge left United one leg was an inch shorter than the other, but his bank balance was quite healthy. A bad knee ligament injury sustained against a cynically dirty Wolves side meant he could never again turn on a ball as in his prime. His final appearance in a United shirt occurred in April 1950 at Brentford. He was to leave in August after 142 league appearances and 52 goals. Preston North End came in, seeing him as the ideal partner to Tom Finney. But jobs with guns and bombs were sparse in that area, plus in Collindridge's words, 'I just didn't fancy it—the pubs weren't as good'. Instead he went to Notts County remembering a promise one of the club's directors made to him should United ever release him. Mr Colley, the hosiery millionaire, was however away in France when he called in to Meadow Lane. A degree of free enterprise followed:

> *…I walked out of the ground and over to Nottingham Forest ground to have a look and bumped into the trainer, Tommy Graham, who I knew from RAF days. I asked him whether he wanted a left winger. The regular left winger had broken his leg a week before. Minutes later I'm in the manager's office and they sorted it out…*

Was this a breach of contract? Possibly, but no-one cared. The transfer fee was around £12,000 which was good business and Collindridge was happy with the move. He was also disillusioned with team-mates for what he considered too much moaning about Jimmy Hagan. Collindridge remained at Trent Bridge for four years playing 151 games and scoring 45 goals. His first return to Bramall Lane saw him help Forest defeat his old club 4–1.

Six months after his departure Teddy Davison travelled down to Nottingham and gave Collindridge £150 for, in Collindridge's words, 'being a good servant, polite and never bothered him or the Club for extra free tickets'. It was added to the bonus he got for five years service to United, which amounted to £650 less £250 tax. Following Nottingham Forest, two seasons with Coventry City (1954–56) produced 34 Division Three appearances. His final football pay day came at Bath City. Now living in a Nottinghamshire village, Collindridge is one of the most remarkable characters in United's history.

The 1940s was a time of recovery for both society and football but things had changed forever in many respects. Not all of it was obvious—the social mores of the time still saw cinema audiences stand to respect renditions of God Save the King. Sheffield United was still dominated by a parochial concern and were held back by a relative shortage of stadium seating, which meant lower gate-takings. In this era Sheffield Wednesday, with Eric Taylor emerging as secretary-manager, became more influential in national football circles. Publicity-conscious Taylor was to purchase the best floodlights the game could offer at the time and rebuild the Hillsborough stadium.

Things were, however, slowly changing at Bramall Lane as the new decade dawned. Joe Mercer became the first man in the managerial chair who was not out of the Methodist-teetotal mode. Appointed primarily on the say-so of club chairman Senior Atkin, his arrival was not to the approval of all the board. This did not perturb Atkin who celebrated his bluntness in conversation, but nevertheless hated addressing AGM audiences. With wealth founded on the cutlery and silversmith industry, Atkin was quintessentially traditional but rather unusual in refusing to use the then recent invention of Sellotape, arguing that with string such a product was not necessary. New ideas ran up against established and eccentric attitudes. The new decade was to see the club seek a new direction and then return to what it knew best.

FURNISS, F.   COX, A.   BURGIN, E.   HITCHEN, H.   LATHAM, H.   SHAW, J.

THOMPSON, D.   BROOK, H.   SMITH, F.   HAGAN, J.   COLLINDRIDGE, C.   JONES, G.

SHEFFIELD UNITED F.C. 1949-1950

Familiar faces—the 1949–50 Sheffield United side

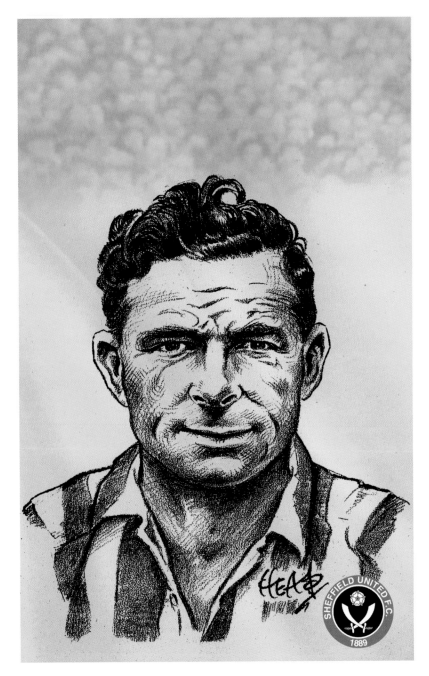

Jimmy Hagan as seen by cartoonist Harry Heap in 1950

Never Had It So Good

The 1950s was an era of dull conformity. The Festival of Britain did not cheer many people up outside of London and the Queen's Coronation of 1953 was not particularly memorable albeit for most people, it was their first sight of television. Whilst there was high employment, wages were low and savings were small. Great footballers such as Stanley Matthews, Tom Finney and Nat Lofthouse were emerging, but English football had been too insular and in this decade received its comeuppance. England finally entered the World Cup, hosted in Brazil, in 1950 and having beaten Chile then lost 1–0 to a USA team consisting of part-timers. Four years later England lost to Uruguay in the World Cup quarter-finals. However, it was a 6–3 home defeat to Hungary in 1953 that caused the most consternation. The trouncing was the first defeat of the national team on home soil by continental opponents. The blame lay with the men in blazers. The England team of the 1950s was selected by the first national team manager and director of coaching, Walter Winterbottom. His chosen men, however, still had to be ratified by the National Selection Committee. These well-meaning amateurs denied the manager autonomy and authority. The selection foibles saw men of genius status, such as Stanley Matthews, periodically dropped. The England set-up was however attempting to become more sophisticated. A youth team had begun in 1947; an under-23 side started in 1954. Despite this, the English national side never got beyond the World Cup quarter-finals between 1950 and 1962. In a return fixture against the Hungarians in 1954 in Budapest the hosts won 7–1. The defeat by Hungary had many consequences; tactics, training methods and style of kit were all changed. The FA selectors even accepted they had to heed the opinions of professionals—but they still picked the team. With European competitions beginning, English clubs were virtually forbidden to compete in them by the Football League. Manchester United challenged the insular attitude of football's governors in 1957 and reached the semi-finals of the European Cup.

As Sheffield United sat at the bottom of Division One at the end of the 1955–56 season they could reflect on what they were losing out on. The Inter-City Industrial Fairs Cup had begun in 1956, which saw Birmingham become the first English club side in European competition. The Games coincided with industrial fairs and could thus take three years to complete. The competition was to evolve into the current day UEFA Cup. Modernity and technology became integral to the domestic game in the shape of floodlights. A February 1956 Portsmouth v Newcastle fixture was the first league game played under illuminations. The screw-in stud made its appearance this decade thereby revolutionising football footwear forever. England beat Brazil 4–2 at Wembley; the Brazilians left the pitch briefly in a protest over a disputed penalty. The decade was to end with the world focusing its collective sympathy on the young but recently dead. The Busby Babes of Manchester United, with an average age of 23 were destroyed by the 1958 Munich air disaster as the plane crashed on the runway after refuelling in Munich on its return from a European tie in Yugoslavia.

The Houses of Football

The post-war shortage of housing affected Sheffield United's recruitment of players. The bombs that fell on the city had destroyed hundreds of homes. Other residences were full due to hasty marriages as a consequence of the war. The demobbed man had often married in haste whilst in uniform and thus returned to find himself searching for a job to pay for a marital home. In an attempt to make the club more attractive to good players, United bought properties and rented them to players. This began in the early 1950s and saw four houses bought on Hollythorpe Rise. These two bedroom semi-detached homes were luxurious in comparison to the prospect of living in one room in the home of in-laws until deposits

A 1951 team photo before a game at Ewood Park, Blackburn
Left to right. Back row: Furniss, Latham, Burgin, Cox, J. Shaw, Hitchen
Front row: Ringstead, Brook, F.E. Smith, Hagan, Hawksworth. United won 5-1

could be saved or council housing became available. A more basic provision came via the landlords and landladies who took in players as lodgers. In 1955, the average wage for United players was £8. By 1958, players could earn £20 a week and a £4 win bonus, but the board minutes reveal that the United directors squabbled for three meetings over whether to pay £3 towards a gas cooker for a player in a property owned by the club. Things could only get better.

Team formations at Bramall Lane were still akin to pre-war football—two wingers, a centre forward and two inside forwards. This proved partly effective and in 1951–52, United were pushing for promotion and beat Wednesday 7–3. However, poor form after Christmas saw them finish eleventh. In the summer of 1952, manager Teddy Davison resigned to be replaced by Reg Freeman who in the traditions of the club was a devout church-goer. Whilst thoughtful, knowledgeable and dignified, Freeman was not going to change the face of football at Bramall Lane. His philosophy on football until he died in the job, in August 1955, was to score as many goals as possible and concede one less.

A draw at Fulham in 1953 saw United promoted to the first division as champions. Integral to the team was Irish international Alf Ringstead, signed for £2,500 in 1950 from Northwich Victoria. Ringstead finished top scorer with 22 goals; Harold Brook and Len Browning were second equal with 17 each.

Tragically Browning was forced to retire only weeks later at the age of 25 having contracted tuberculosis. Playing wide on the left was Derek Hawksworth, bought from Bradford City in the same season for £12,500. He scored 103 goals in 286 games. United remained in the top flight until 1956. This relegation saw the club recognise the need for better training conditions. In the late 1950s United took over a training area called the Ball Inn ground. This area of land, leased by the Duke of Norfolk, was formerly the home of football played under the auspices of the Sheffield Licensed Victuallers League and later the Sheffield Schools Athletic Association. United took over a controlling interest in the pitches and pavilion. One beneficiary was the Bramall Lane pitch, now spared the daily training sessions of its players.

The Enlightenment

The match day programme throughout much of the 1950s depicted the enclosed arena that was Bramall Lane. In keeping with tradition Wardonia razor blades remained a dominant advertising space within. Other adverts indicate a rise in consumer power—Kenning's Car Wash appeared in 1953, as did excursions to Blackpool Illuminations. In the same year an advert appeared for the first time depicting a woman enjoying the benefits of Jubilee stout. In the ground, however, the only advertising display was one on the top of the John Street Stand advertising United's director Arnold Laver's woodyard, which lay adjacent to Bramall Lane.

The Bramall Lane ground changes reflected technological innovations. Floodlight pylons appeared in the early 1950s and United played a number of friendly games as a way of popularising the new technology whilst waiting for the Football League to permit floodlit matches. Thus visiting Bramall Lane in 1954 and 1955 were Hibernian, Clyde, Dundee and St Mirren from Scotland. From further afield came Esbjerg of Denmark, and the Graz Sports Klub of Austria. In 1956 the visitors were Radnicki Nis of Yugoslavia, and in 1959 Lucerne of Switzerland. The most exotic visitors of this decade, however, arrived in October 1958 when Bella Vista of Brazil played a game to demonstrate the capabilities of the floodlights. The Shoreham Street kop was extended in 1953 to produce what was known for the next 40 years as the 'white wall', an annexe which offered an excellent view to the few who could get there early enough on match day. In 1954 the John Street stand was extended so that by 1958 the club could host 35,000 spectators under cover, a fact broadcast on the programme cover throughout most of the 1959–60 season. A United–Wednesday FA Cup quarter final in 1958 saw a temporary stand holding 3,200 erected on the cricket pitch and the crowd limited to 60,000.

Football still collected for charity and was becoming more generous with players. The abolition of Entertainment Tax in 1957 saw a rise in players' wages and the sanctioning of bigger cheques for benefit matches. In December 1959 Blacow Yates, the United director, presented United's Tommy Hoyland with a £1,000 cheque for his ten years service—the first four-figure cheque for a player's benefit in the club's history. Christmas match-day collections in 1953 were for the Westminster Abbey restoration fund. Cash was king; the commercial practicalities around football saw United

Wardonia razor blades
A brand name of razor blade produced by the Thomas Ward steel factory in Sheffield
Ward's advertised their wares for decades with Sheffield United

FLOODLIT MATCH Kick-off 7.30 p.m.

versus

HIBERNIAN F.C.

TUESDAY, 23RD MARCH, 1954

Match programme cover, March 1954
Advertising that United now had floodlights and were playing friendlies at Bramall Lane to celebrate the fact

supporters advised in a January 1953 match programme that when seeking tickets for a forthcoming cup fixture 'personal and telephonic applications will not be entertained'. During the decade Billy Russell, studying at Loughborough, played for United's first team in the status of amateur player. The legacy of the gentleman amateur was further personified when, in October 1957, Sheffield FC played Queen's Park of Glasgow at Bramall Lane in celebration of the 100th anniversary of the former. The special guest at the match played on a Thursday at 2.45 was the Duke of Edinburgh. However, a disappointing crowd of just 5,000 saw a 2–2 draw, indicating probably the lack of interest in the amateur game.

Sheffield United Blazer Badge c.1953
Fabled to have been designed by Jimmy Hagan

Noughts and Crosses

The United supporters club was getting more active by the year. Membership was two shillings and sixpence and their specifically designed badge or brooch cost one shilling and threepence. A juvenile supporters section was started in 1954. Weekly evening meetings invited supporters both to talks on football and the chance to play games. Supporters dances were held and Sheffield United Tours motor-coaches, in existence since the late 1930s, began advertising away travel in the match programme. The supporters club donated the goal nets to United in the summer of 1957 and gifted the club a cheque of £1,000 a year later. After United were relegated in April 1956, what the programme called a 'ginger group' of shareholder critics voiced their opposition to the board of directors at the Annual General Meeting. The protest was to no avail. The directors were all re-elected by large majorities but the very mention of criticism of the board was something new to United publications. In September 1954 during a home defeat, the crowd had even begun to slow handclap the team, this provoked the following comment in the programme for the next home game:

> We think that our countrymen demean themselves when they follow continental crowds like sheep and indulge in slow handclapping.

United still sought bigger crowds and in 1957 the programme commented that 'attendances of 25,000 are needed at Bramall Lane to keep the finances in order'. A critic of this reasoning might ask where the money in football was going because the 1950s saw an agreement reached between the Football League and the Pools companies over the use of fixture lists. In exchange for allowing the companies to use the copyright, the Football League received £3million in the course of the decade. Other monies were also coming into sport by virtue of the £5million promised by the Tories towards sport and leisure in Britain. Finances went into the game but the monies did not produce trophies at Bramall Lane.

Foreign Movements

Despite the processes of modernity that were affecting football the United directors were rather parochial characters. In an unprecedented move, the 1956–57 match programmes featured profiles of United's 11-man board of directors and paid officials. The language used to detail their lives and personal qualities is remarkably blunt. Two things are striking. One is the level of their involvement in local matters beyond football. The other is the longevity of their association with the club. This extends to paid officials with two boasting an association of over forty years.

A team of Hagans
A photograph sent by a reader to the *Sheffield Star* suggesting the ideal United line up before a match at Preston in 1950

Such men were not the most forward thinking of their era. A match programme reader could learn the opinions of Senior Atkin, the chairman of the football club committee and managing director of a silvers-miths business. In December 1955 Atkin had written to BBC commentator Kenneth Wolstenholme accusing him of bias in favour of foreign teams when commentating on matches between English and continental sides. The programme informs a reader that:

> Atkin disagreed with Mr Wolstenholme that these foreigners were the last word in football and pointed out also that the type of football they play 'is not football, as the Englishman knows it'.

He opined further that, if competing in the English first division, none of these foreign clubs would finish beyond mid-table. The letter was shown by Wolstenholme to a 'leading continental club manager'. The response, passed to Mr Atkin, stated amongst other things that they would not wish to play within a league where winning points was all that mattered at the expense of experimenting with style. Adding for good measure, 'so your football has become static and it moves like a wartime convoy—at the speed of the slowest'. Style of play was concentrating the minds of more than one United official. As early as November 1953 the programme notes informed a reader that:

> ...to achieve success there's no need to be ultra artistic. In the Football League's intense competition, there's no stage available for ball trickery suitable for a music hall turn.

England had recently lost 6–3 at Wembley by the trickery and artistry of the Hungarians. The United squad had travelled to Wembley to watch the match. Some people could not see the light. Others from outside Sheffield were to leave United frustrated at the limited ambitions the club provided.

Trainer Reg Wright explains what to do with the ball at a 1952 training session
Left to right: Hitchen, Cox, Shaw, Smith, Browning, Hawksworth, Hutchinson, Furniss, Ringstead, Hagan

Service with a Smile: Joe Mercer

The arrival at Bramall Lane of Joe Mercer saw United choose a manager who was unlike any of the others who had previously held the managerial position at the club. From George Waller to Reg Freeman, the United trainer-managers had been of similar disposition. In choosing Mercer, United were perhaps admitting that such men were now a rarity or an anachronism. Mercer's appointment reflected two forces in the game at the time. One was the rising power of the chairman, who was in some clubs now *primus inter pares* over his board of directors. The other was an acknowledgement that the national media could play a role in managerial selection. Mercer had finished a quite brilliant footballing career, but when approached by United was gainfully employed in his greengrocery shop. The move for Mercer was a gamble, probably arising out of chairman Senior Atkin's friendship with a high-profile football writer. The writer was the mediator between the club and Mercer. The outcome was a new United manager who broke the mould.

As a player with Everton and Arsenal, Mercer won every honour available in domestic football. He is remembered by many as the most successful player of his era, winning the 1950 Footballer of the Year award aged 35 as well as three League championships, and an FA Cup Winner's medal. He was also captain of England as well as turning out 247 times for Arsenal. Mercer was to cut his managerial teeth at Bramall Lane before going on to Aston Villa, Manchester City, Coventry and, eventually, England as caretaker manager. Awarded an OBE for his services to the game, Mercer was an avuncular figure. His biography was fittingly titled *'Football With A Smile'*. He died, aged 76, in 1990.

Born in Ellesmere Port, Cheshire, Mercer's father was a former professional footballer, and Mercer learned the game in informal all-age games played in the streets. He left his job, working for the nearby Shell oil refinery, to sign for Everton in 1932. Establishing himself as a left-half, he was both skilful and intelligent and an integral part of the Everton team that won the League in 1939. In the same season, he received his first England call-up. A bad injury sustained in an England–Scotland fixture affected his mobility and form. Whilst recuperating, he was transferred to Arsenal for £7,000, but remained living in Liverpool so as to run his grocery store.

Footballer's wives, 1950's style
The United players' better halves at one of the many parties thrown by Jimmy and Irene Hagan

The demands of the game on a key player were hard. A League fixture against Manchester United saw a crowd of 80,000 watch an Arsenal side containing Mercer, unaware he was carrying seven penicillin injections to combat flu. The Gunners were to win the title conceding a then record low of just 32 goals. In 1950 Mercer lifted the FA Cup as Arsenal triumphed over Liverpool. Three years later he decided to retire shortly after winning the League, again with Arsenal. Aged 40 his career was ended when he broke his leg playing against Liverpool. A Highbury crowd of 33,000 cheered him off as he lay on the stretcher, all realising he had played his last game. He remained in hospital for six weeks.

Mercer's coaching career began with the Pegasus amateur side, which was made up of graduates of Oxford and Cambridge Universities. In the late 1940s he had regularly flown to Ireland to coach the Bohemians, who played on Sundays. In the mid-1950s he volunteered his services for Tranmere. In 1955, however, he took up a full-time position at Bramall Lane, succeeding Reg Freeman who had died at his desk. In Mercer, United had what might be considered their first 'showbiz' manager. An England inter-national and captain of Arsenal, he was also a man willing to speak his mind and one who always had, in public life at least, a smile. Quick to inform any critics that he was the boss, Mercer's arrival came as a shock to many on the board of directors.

Mercer's time at United was not his happiest in football. Accustomed to the standards of Arsenal and England, Mercer found facilities and attitudes at Bramall Lane inadequate and perplexing. His appointment was not done with diplomacy. After the interview, Mercer was told to wait in a room along the corridor and when called by chairman Senior Atkin entered the boardroom to hear Atkin introduce him as manager to his fellow directors. Few of them appreciated this surreptitious appointment. Aged 41, Mercer received a five-year contract due to run until 1960. He wanted to be one of the new breed of hands-on managers, actively involved in coaching sessions. Within a month however, Ernest Jackson, the long-time player turned first-team trainer, resigned after disagreements with the new manager. In response Mercer promoted assistant trainer, Harry Latham. Despite a decent Cup run, United were relegated at the end of the season and Mercer was fully aware that the disgruntled board were not united behind him. Regardless, Mercer continued his task and finished seventh and sixth in the next two seasons. The absence of a promotion did not stop Mercer's name being linked with bigger clubs. In 1956 the Arsenal manager Jack Crayston resigned and the Gunners offered Mercer the job. After careful deliberation, Mercer decided to remain at Bramall Lane.

Blades fans were slow to appreciate Mercer. When relegated, he sold key players to bring in money; Jim Iley went to Spurs for £20,000 in a move that provoked massive hostility from fans who believed Mercer had forced him out. Some 18 months later, he sold Colin Grainger to Sunderland for £17,000, once again to the fury of the fans. The absence of money to spend (crowds averaged 18,000) combined with injury problems, frustrated Mercer to the extent that in December 1958 he applied for and got the manager's job at Aston Villa. His last match in charge of the Blades was the last time they were to play on Christmas Day, winning 2–1 at Grimsby. Mercer left United making references to the club's lack of ambition. He was convinced they would never win a trophy.

The new job saw him in familiar circumstances at the end of the season—Villa were relegated. An anonymous telegram sent to him from Sheffield read 'Congratulations, Joe. You have done it again'. Winning the second division championship the following season, Mercer was able to attract very good young players and was soon considered a future England manager. Given the task of coaching the England under-23 side, Mercer pulled out due to ill health, a condition no doubt linked to Villa's poor form. He was to leave Villa Park in July 1964 by 'mutual consent'. In 1965 he joined Manchester City the forgotten team of English football, and became part of a coaching partnership with Malcolm Allison, who had recently been sacked by Plymouth. The partnership proved a phenomenal success as City went on to win the League Championship (1968), FA Cup (1969), and the Cup Winner's Cup and League Cup (1970). Between 1965 and 1970 City won five trophies in five seasons. In later years Mercer was to become caretaker manager of England.

> Mercer's opinion that United lacked ambition might have some truth in it. The directors were not forward thinking and they were fractious. Little monies were available for transfers because little money was being generated. Bramall Lane was a three-sided football ground and the club was too set in its desire to fill the ranks with local-born players who cost next to nothing. One director challenged this inertia. One player epitomised what the club would tolerate from its playing staff.

The Committee Man: Dick Wragg

Joining the Board in 1953 was Dick Wragg who was later in life to become the first President of Sheffield United. Born in Attercliffe in 1910, Wragg once played for the United A Team and later Sheffield FC and Macclesfield. Wragg made his money from a builders' merchants and having joined the board seemed to have kept out of the row generated by the appointment of Joe Mercer. Elected to the Sheffield United Football Committee in 1955, Wragg became club chairman in August 1968. He joined the FA committee in 1963 and as an FA Councillor obtained a position of power in the English game further strengthened when he joined the FA's International Committee in 1968. He eventually became chair of this committee and had a large say in the appointment of England managers. His ambitions even saw him become a member of UEFA.

Wragg sat in on many controversies at the club. On the retirement of Jimmy Hagan, Wragg had opined to board members that he did not believe Hagan could impart football knowledge to others. Hagan's success with Benfica proved this opinion wrong. Ten years later, Wragg was chairman when Mick Jones and Alan Birchenall were sold for £100,000 each against the wishes of the manager. However he was responsible for changing United's thinking and finances forever. Wragg played a significant role in removing cricket from Bramall Lane and the subsequent planning of the South Stand. In August 1968 he was instrumental in ending the system of six separate committees at Bramall Lane, implementing one committee instead. At national level he was part of the crisis in the England national side when, in 1977, Don Revie left the England job for the more lucrative offer of the managers job in Kuwait.

United 1956
Players training despite the snow on the Bramall Lane terraces
Left to right: Hagan, Hoyland, Howitt, Ringstead, Wragg, Coldwell, Burgin, Waldock

Pipe smoking, amiable and usually smiling, Wragg was an avuncular figure who preferred to be addressed as 'Mister Wragg'. In the 1960s, he was genuinely trying to push United forward in the game and was very influential in the change of policy after 1967 that recognised the limitations of relying on local born players progressing through the ranks. He encouraged manager John Harris to spend money and look around the lower divisions and Scottish leagues, albeit it was in Wales that Harris acquired Len Allchurch and Gil Reece. The signing of Tony Currie from Watford may well have been attributable to Wragg. Earlier in the year, United had knocked Watford out of the FA Cup and Wragg was believed to have an agreement with the Watford chairman to sign Currie when Watford's Cup run was over. Wragg retired as chairman in 1974, but remained in the honorary position of President until his death in 1992 at the age of 82.

Special Reserve: Roy Ridge
Between 1950 and 1964 Roy Ridge spent the whole of his 14-year United career, bar three months, in the reserves. The epitome of the footballing nearly man, Ridge played over 400 reserve-team games. Born in 1934 in the village of Ecclesfield, then north of the city boundary, Ridge was the younger of two boys of a father who worked in the steel industry. In 1949 when playing for the top local under-16 side, Oaks Fold, he impressed a watching United scout. He was asked to start training twice a week at Bramall Lane.

Signing as a part-time professional in November 1951, Ridge soon after played for the reserves and made the first team at 19. The side was always chosen at Thursday evening board meetings. Ridge took his usual place on the 10–6 night shift at a steel works. A local reporter then phoned the factory to tell him he would be playing at Old Trafford in 36 hours. A kindly foreman, seeing the conflict of interests, let him go home early, and later moved him onto permanent day shifts to help his football career. Following the Manchester United match, Ridge played the next ten first-team games and, aged 20, signed professional forms and left the factory. As a part-time pro, along with the factory wage, he was on £10 a week. A full-time footballer received £12 a week. First-teamers earned £14. Attaining the status of professional and first-teamer was arduous. Quite a few young men in those days thought they were special—until they went training at Bramall Lane. They then found they were just one of 50 others turning up each Tuesday and Thursday.

Ridge's next first team match was a County Cup fixture in April, but he was obviously thought of as one for the future because he was part of the squad that toured Germany in the close season. However, the next season Ridge made only one first team appearance and, incredibly, did not play another first-team game for the next six years. Then, after one first-team game, he was never picked again. Thus after 11 outings in his first three months at Bramall Lane, Ridge received only two call-ups in the next 11 years.

Most of the problem was that for seven years United's defence virtually picked itself. The two full-backs, Cecil Coldwell and Graham Shaw, were contstant fixtures. When they were unavailable there was competition from Jeff Smith and Cliff Mason. If it were of any consolation, similar to the first team, the reserves also had a core that remained constant for seven years—Ridge, Dennis Shields, Harry Orr and Dennis Finnegan. Reserve team matches were always competitive, there was the financial incentive of the £2 win bonus and the chance of impressing the first team manager who occasionally turned up to see who was pushing or promising. There were also punters to entertain. Games at Manchester United and

Just good friends
Eight of the 1951 Sheffield United team in the communal bath at Bramall Lane. On the right of the picture is Len Browning, who was forced to retire from the game soon after having contracted tuberculosis

Everton could attract crowds of 10,000. Bramall Lane saw a regular 2–3,000 and more when the opponents were Wednesday.

National Service interrupted Ridge's early career. Allowed to delay joining-up because of his work in the steel industry, Ridge had to serve his country when he was 21. During these two years the man who signed him for United died and was succeeded by Joe Mercer. Stationed in Kent, Ridge would return whenever he could to get a reserve team run-out. But he was not to be one of Mercer's men, in fact the manager offered him to Bournemouth but Ridge turned the move down. The only other club that showed interest was Brentford in 1960. This deal fell through when United's next manager, John Harris, refused their request to take Ridge on loan before making the deal permanent.

There was little incentive to seek a move elsewhere. By this time, the first team were on £20 a week and Ridge and his reserves took home £17. His departure aged 30 in 1964 was a pleasant occasion. Over a lunch he signed for fourth division Rochdale with the stipulation that he did not have to move from his Sheffield home. The pinnacle of his limited career was finishing third in the Central League in 1960.

Longevity should not always be equated with mediocrity. In this decade United had four players who between them made some 2,300 League and Cup appearances. Three were good enough to receive international recognition (if not always international caps) and all were born in the vicinity of Sheffield. Moving club was not part of their footballing aspirations. They served the club that found them as teenagers and did so without histrionics or resentment. Their departures were not happy occasions for the most part. For all the service they gave the club, the monies they thought were rightfully theirs seemed compromised by circumstances the club did not always explain in advance or compensate for. Perhaps there is no happy ending in the game which has no room for people beyond a certain age and ability. Maybe a naivety pervaded footballers who never believed their final game would arrive and had not made plans for their post-football days. In this era the one certainty a footballer faced was decades of working in another occupation after he had left the world of football.

The Longest Ever: Joe Shaw

A statue standing ten inches high can be found placed discreetly in a living room sideboard. The inscription reads, 'Twenty years service as a loyal player'. Above the words is a cast of a boy in his teens in an old football shirt, long football shorts and old-fashioned boots kicking a ball. Commissioned by the Football League, only six such statues were produced and Joe Shaw of Sheffield United was one of the recipients.

Born in Murton, County Durham into a coal-mining family, Shaw followed Sunderland and his boyhood hero was Raich Carter. An uncle employed as a gateman allowed him into to Roker Park free. When Shaw was ten years old the family moved to Upton in South Yorkshire. His father remained working down the mines, whilst Shaw proved a good school pupil. His association with the local colliery began at 15 when chosen for the pit's football team. Against his father's wishes, Shaw took a job at the pit, but after five days decided it was not for him. Soon after, he was employed on the railway, working on the footplate of steam engines.

Following a game between Upton Colliery and United reserves, United's manager Teddy Davison invited Shaw for a trial. Shaw impressed and was signed up and went on to make a record 714 appearances for the Blades. He made his first team debut aged 16 in 1945 in a war-time game against Huddersfield Town and then spent three seasons with the reserves. He made his full League debut in August 1948. Initially playing as an inside forward, Shaw moved to wing-half which suited his tackling ability.From 1954 was to be found at centre-half despite standing just 5' 8" tall. In August 1962 Shaw made his 500th League appearance and in August 1965 his 600th league appearance, aged 37, against West Ham. At the time of this latter game, the United side contained players with incredible longevity; Alan Hodgkinson had 350

appearances, Cecil Coldwell 399, Graham Shaw 400 and
Brian Richardson 250. The team produced great friendships
and, at away games, Shaw was known as one of the four
voices which sang harmony at the back of the team coach.
His final appearance for United came in February 1966.
Eighteen months later he took the manager's position at
York City.

One of the Greatest: Joe Shaw

The accolades he received from some of the great figures of
football suggest that United had in Shaw one of the English
game's all-time greats. Nat Lofthouse stated, 'I never looked
forward to playing against him; I always came off second
best'. Bill Shankly commented, 'One of the greatest players
since the war…one of the best defensive brains in the world'.
Johnny Carey, ex-Manchester United and later manager of
Nottingham Forest called him, 'An aristocrat amongst
footballers'. Tom Finney said he was, 'the unluckiest
uncapped player in post-war years'. And Derek Dooley
regarded him as, 'The best centre-half in the land'. His own
manager, John Harris referred to him in 1965 as the finest
uncapped player in England, and in his testimonial in the
same year Shaw received tributes from no less a person than
Stanley Rous, then president of FIFA. Stanley Matthews also
described him as the best uncapped player of his day and
Matt Busby described him as both a manager's dream player and the greatest uncapped player he had
ever seen. In his 21 years with United, Shaw was never booked and was spoken of with a variety of words:
modest, loyal, great ambassador, gentleman, model professional—all of them testimony to his integrity.

As a player Shaw was renowned for his unflappable style and for a technique that saw him steal the ball
from an opponent's boot. He marked some of the great names in the history of English football—Tommy
Lawton, Nat Lofthouse, Brian Clough, Alex Young, and Bobby Smith. The mystery as to why he did not
achieve full international honours has never been fully explained. One obvious reason was the presence
of Wolves' Billy Wright, who won 105 Caps playing in the position that Shaw could have occupied.
Another reason, which many have suggested, is that Shaw spent his career with an unfashionable
northern club i.e. Sheffield United. He nearly made it in 1955 when was chosen as 12th man in an
England v Scotland match. He also represented the
Football League XI when it was managed by Joe Mercer.
In 1951 he was part of an Australia tour organised by the
FA, which also included United's Ted Burgin and Jimmy
Hagan. Over a decade later in 1962 Shaw toured Canada
and the USA with an England Select.

England tour of Australia cap
Awarded to Joe Shaw in 1951

A new footballing world was opening up and United
were part of it. In Shaw's time United played exhibition
games in the USA and Canada and beat a Ukranian
national side who happened to be there at the time. A
game played against the Ontario All Stars was memorable
for kicking off at the unearthly hour of 8.15am. For all
the showbiz the game was pursuing, Shaw remained a
quiet and unassuming man. Aged 19, he met his wife to
be, Hettie. His marriage produced two daughters and
much happiness. Any photos of Shaw in his football

The 1953 second division champions with the shield
Front row left is manager Reg Freeman. Front row right is trainer Ernest Jackson

career see him in the company of his family. He opened the first bowling alley in Sheffield, in Frecheville in the 1950s, and presented trophies to supporters' clubs at the Embassy Ballroom. For 17 years his home, a modest semi-detached, was rented from United and his first car was a Mini. Playing on a one-year rolling contract, a draw produced a £2 bonus and a win £3.

Shaw never received a loyalty bonus from United albeit he was awarded two testimonial matches. The first was organised by Major Strutt, a chap from United's newly emerging commercial affairs office. The second saw an opposition team including Jimmy Greaves, Stanley Matthews, Ronnie Clayton, George Eastham and Tom Finney. The latter game was watched by a crowd of 30,000 and Shaw received a cheque of £480 after tax on a £750 gate. He left Sheffield United in 1966 and combined football management at York City, then in Division Four, with running a small drapery business in Sheffield. After two seasons he gave up the managerial job. Soon after the business failed. For a time he became groundsman at the playing fields of the De La Salle School at Beauchief Hall. He tried his hand again at management at Chesterfield between 1973 and 1976, but this venture was brief when he realised the club had no money.

His time with United was both historical and relatively uncontroversial. It is remarkable to realise that in the early part of his career he was playing with Jack Pickering who had played in the 1936 FA Cup Final. His one controversy at Bramall Lane came in 1956, when he put in a transfer request, following what he considered an 'unsettling period'. The 1956 dispute with Joe Mercer was the only time Shaw

The 1952–53 second division championship-winning team
in the John Street dressing room with trainer Ernest Jackson in the centre

considered leaving Bramall Lane. If any club came in for him, he was never to know about it. He sat out 13 games. Other than this dispute, his time at the Lane and his teachers therein provide good memories. Coach Archie Clark is remembered as a good character, who made match day interesting with a pre-match pick-me-up of whisked eggs and sherry. Obviously keen on mixing things, the same man threw salt in the players' bath water. Training regimes were unsophisticated—lapping and jumping, with little ball work in the early years. Shaw's playing career ended when he was 38. The circumstances were discreet if upsetting then and when recollected in 2003 at the age of 74:

> *John Harris had a word on the coach coming back from a game; 'Have you ever thought of packing it in' he said. 'Finish at the top'. What can you say when your manager suggests it?... I emptied my locker at the end of the season... I told everyone 'I'm packin' in'... it's not very nice... it's hard work...*

With that he chokes back words. Some 36 years had passed since the day of departure. Hettie smiles at the pair of us and states for both our benefits: 'Don't start him off... he'll be crying in a minute'. Hettie elaborated in Shaw's absence, explaining even now 'he lives for football'. But the game did not want him and after playing he had little to offer. He scouted for United, loved the task, but cannot name a player he brought in who made it. His training of the United youngsters was a time he loved. But they did not win anything under him. He applied for the job of groundsman at the Ball Inn ground, but did not get it. In the early 2000s he was present every home game in the Bramall Lane Platinum Suite, reading out the team sheet to the assembled pre-match diners and corporate guests. In return he received a meal and two tickets in the South Stand.

The last pair of boots worn by the legendary Joe Shaw in 1966

A Benefit night held in the Bramall Lane Platinum Suite in 2002 saw 400 diners pay £40 for both dinner and speeches in praise of Shaw. The evening made £7,000 for Joe and Hettie. Living a modest existence in a Sheffield suburb Shaw offered diners some unprovoked advice stating:

You only get out of the game what you are prepared to put into it. I would recommend any player to stick to one club; loyalty is usually repaid.

Graham Shaw

Local Hero: Graham Shaw

Born in the Pitsmoor district of Sheffield, Graham Shaw was on United's books at the age of 14 whilst learning to be a sign-writer in a firm owned by a United Director. A sporting all-rounder Shaw represented Yorkshire schools at cricket and was a national boxing finalist. Choosing football above the other sports and United above Wednesday he was to make his United first team debut aged 17 in 1952 after only six Central League games. Arriving by bus expecting to play his seventh against Wednesday reserves at Bramall Lane he was instead driven to Hillsborough at 1.30pm because of a late injury in the first team squad. Ninety minutes later Shaw walked out onto the pitch in front of a record post-war Sheffield football attendance of 65,000.

So began a long journey that ended 17 years later in 1967 after 478 League and Cup appearances. No Sheffield-born player will ever better this for United. The defence he was part of played together for almost seven years; Alan Hodgkinson, Cecil Coldwell, Joe Shaw, Brian Richardson and Gerry Summers. In the middle Richardson clogged and clattered, Joe Shaw anticipated and stole the ball. Amongst such company Shaw was the classy right-footed left back, the one comfortable on the ball and a good short-ball distributor. Whilst not an attacking full-back he scored a fair number of goals. Tasked with taking free kicks around the half-way line his orders were to punt it between the posts towards the back. Sometimes both forwards and keepers missed it. Other goals came via penalties; his 75% success rate was the result of a consistent method—low, hard and aim for the stanchion.

The 1952–53 United team
Lined up before a packed Bramall Lane for the first home match having returned to Division One

Such consistency and overall ability was recognised at international level. Shaw represented England at under-23 level three times in 1955–56 (selected the day he began National Service) and England 'B' three times. Five times between 1958 and 1964 he made the full England team and was never on the losing side. In and out of the England side and a regular in a United team that yo-yo'd between Divisions One and Two, Shaw never sought a transfer. However, one of his four United Managers, Joe Mercer, tried to sell him after only seven months in charge and just days after Shaw had captained the England Under-23s. The move to Stoke City offered no financial gain and Shaw turned it down not wanting to play for anyone else. Mercer later apologised for his remarks that Shaw lacked the killer instinct to make it at the highest level. He was an automatic choice for the next seven years for Mercer and his successor John Harris. After 11 seasons as an automatic choice Shaw faced two seasons in and out of the reserves. Wearing his first team shirt was his brother Bernard, ten years his younger. His final United game occurred in 1967 when aged 33. A Testimonial the same year against Wednesday attracted 18,000. It all ended at Bramall Lane by post in May 1967 A letter thanked him for his services and wished him well for the future.

A season with Division Four Doncaster, was followed by a year as player-manager at Scarborough in the Northern Premier League. Disenchanted with the game, Shaw then sought alternative employment and bought a cafe with money from the Testimonial. After 15 years he sold his by now two cafes and became landlord of The Sportsman, 200 metres from Bramall Lane, packed on match days and home every night of the week to United's largest Supporters Club. Remaining a devoted United follower, Shaw was Chairman of the Future Players Fund for five years in the early 1980s. This club-sanctioned entity sought to identify and fund the purchase of players. The Committee of 10 men organised various functions but never raised large sums of money. Eventually it folded. Shaw continued to serve in his pub until February 1998. Feeling unwell, he took a few days off, before visiting the doctor, who diagnosed advanced stages of cancer. He died ten weeks later. The funeral was attended by dozens of ex-players and the congregation of mourners was so vast that traffic had to be diverted by police.

Mister Sheffield United: Cecil Coldwell

Departing from Bramall Lane in 1983, Cecil Coldwell holds the distinction of having served Sheffield United for 32 years. At the time of his departure he had been at United for over one third of its existence. As if having played 478 first-team games, being captain for nine seasons and then being coach for 15 years was not service enough, Coldwell was also twice called upon to be caretaker-manager. Often spoken of as 'Mr Sheffield United' and as the best manager United never appointed, Coldwell celebrated goals with the long-forgotten manner of a smile and handshake and ran out as team captain to the strains of *Ilkley Moor*.

Born in 1929, Coldwell's father was a steamroller driver, his mother had a full-time job bringing up five kids. The teenage Coldwell would leave the house in the Stannington district and watch United and Wednesday on alternate Saturdays. A happy childhood and an untroubled school career saw Coldwell become a brick-maker in Marshall Refractories aged 15. Bradford City expressed an interest in the 17-year-old factory player but two years of National Service put paid to that. Returning from the Army, Coldwell played in the Yorkshire League for Norton Woodseats, the City's best amateur team of the time. Scouts from professional clubs regularly watched their games. One from United saw something he liked and in 1951 United gave the club £50 for Coldwell's signature with a promise of a further £50 if he made the first team. After a year on part-time status, Teddy Davison signed Coldwell on professional terms and at the age of 21 gave him his first team debut.

His appearance in the first team would have come quicker and would have been more regular but for the capable Fred Furniss holding the full-back position. When he did break into the first team Coldwell remained there for ten years becoming part of the defensive line-up alongside Joe Shaw, Graham Shaw, Gerry Summers and Alan Hodgkinson. Alternating as a youth between centre-half and full-back, Coldwell decided on the latter as his ideal role and became, in the memory of those who watched him, an intelligent, reliable and steady player, capable in the tackle and cool under pressure. Not particularly physically imposing or naturally fast, his game by his own admission was based on anticipation rather than speed. The late Jimmy Hagan, a one-time team-mate, once commented that no player worked harder than Coldwell to make himself a class player.

Never booked or sent off Coldwell was considered by all as sporting, helpful and an essentially decent man on and off the pitch. Whilst he was reading the game others were watching with interest, albeit too late in the day:

> *I was told by one of the directors of the FA when I was 34 that I was the best full-back in England but that they couldn't select me because of my age. It was nice to know that however.*

Cecil Coldwell

Various managers recognised a quality in Coldwell. It was Davison's successor, Reg Freeman, who picked him regularly for the first team. Joe Mercer made him team and club captain—a role he performed between 1959 and 1968. Despite his elevated status and being an ever-present in the first team, Coldwell never saw anything greater as a player than a one-year contract. Renewed annually following a chat in the manager's office, the financial rewards were a win bonus of £4— a draw saw £2 added to the basic wage.

Off the pitch the captain had duties to fans and managers. The former role required him to attend youth clubs and supporters club presentation nights. The latter saw him as the link between player and manager to whom he would occasionally convey what he calls:

> *Team matters . . . if they thought they were being trained too hard or they were getting the wrong type of training.*

First-team appearances began to fizzle out in late 1966. A few games followed when first-teamers were injured, but Coldwell occupied himself as player-coach of the reserves and in 1966 the team won the Central League championship. The same year saw a testimonial game for his benefit against an All-Star XI and crowd of 10,525. It was a much appreciated payday, but 'not enough to buy a small business' because admission costs were reduced for such games.

SOUVENIR **6**D. PROGRAMME

CEC COLDWELL
TESTIMONIAL MATCH

SHEFFIELD UNITED
VERSUS
ALL STAR XI

ON MONDAY, 31st OCTOBER, 1966. KICK-OFF 7.30 p.m.

In 1968 Coldwell accepted the offer of a job as first-team coach from manager John Harris. As the game was becoming more professional and demanding, Coldwell realised that badges and certificates would be needed and so qualified as an FA coach. A few years later he was coach of a United side storming Division One. As a model professional himself he could not countenance laziness. His dedication and long hours paid off and eight managers retained him as either a player or a coach. The club directors recognised something as well and twice made him caretaker-manager. One stretch in 1976 between the departure of Ken Furphy and arrival of Jimmy Sirrel saw Coldwell hold the fort for a month. Then in 1978, when Sirrel left, Coldwell took charge for 13 games losing only a few before Harry Haslam took over. Similar to Haslam and his assistant Danny Bergara, Coldwell was given a five-year contract.

The financial security this contract offered was some recompense from a chairman who behaved strangely towards Coldwell. Presumably annoyed by the public support Coldwell had in 1978 for the vacant manager's job, which occasionally manifested itself in the local press, the chairman told Coldwell he was not to talk to journalists and to forget about the job—he would never be manager. Aware that some of his fellow directors were impressed by Coldwell's achievements, the chairman then banned Coldwell from entering the boardroom after games, thereby preventing the admirers from chatting with him. Surviving that chairman, who departed in 1981, Coldwell had another battle on his hands later that same year when Ian Porterfield took over as manager and brought in his own coaches. Coldwell, however, still had three years left of his contract and was not going anywhere.

Not part of the new man's plans Coldwell suffered what he calls 'terrible times' under the new regime, who phased him out of their training sessions and placed him away from them at the dining table. The inevitable departure in April 1983 was a relief albeit a sad occasion and one which required some self-evaluation. Without any grand farewell Coldwell left with no idea of what to do next day. He returned soon after for a second testimonial game. Played against Sheffield Wednesday in May 1983 the game drew a crowd of 9,500:

> *I think it happened because certain people felt bad about what they'd done and what I read into it was that by having a match and giving me some of the income, they saved themselves a pay-off which would be calculated on years of service. It wasn't so much a gesture of good will as a way of reducing what they would have to pay. They also had to take out costs of policing the match.*

After a few months reflection, Coldwell bought a newsagent's shop on a large council estate in Sheffield which required 12-hour shifts. A similar venture in one of the more upmarket parts of Cheshire between 1987 and 1995 ended in retirement. A busy retirement involves Coldwell in crown-green bowling and voluntary work with the disabled via the local church.

Alan Hodgkinson

Safe Keeping: Alan Hodgkinson

That a man born in 1936 in a South Yorkshire pit village should spend his life working with his hands would not surprise anyone. Such working-class communities passed manual work through the generations like a cultural legacy. Few, however, would spend over 50 years catching or teaching others how to catch a football. A one-club career produced an appearance record bettered by only one man in the history of Sheffield United. As a consequence, Alan Hodgkinson is Sheffield United's most famous living goalkeeper.

Had his father had his way, however, his hands would have been put to use as a concert pianist. Shot-stopping is incompatible with playing Schubert's sonatas, but at one time it was a close call. On leaving their piano lesson, the man known to all as 'Hodgy' and his elder brother would go to the local recreation ground to play football. Duetting on the ivories, the brothers played to audiences of 400 at Butlin's talent shows. Their father could play as well as sing and encouraged their participation in the Sunday school choir, but it all ended when he realised that football had taken a greater hold on his son than the keyboard. An uncle had taken Hodgkinson to his first United match and, whilst playing truant from school at the age of 13, Hodgkinson saw a childhood hero in Bert Williams, the Wolves and England goalkeeper. Playing for his school brought his selection for the best local eleven of Rother Valley Boys. This led to Worksop Town where he contented himself in the Yorkshire and Midland League playing against ex-professionals. Soon he was in the company of current professionals when a scout invited him to train twice a week with United. By the age of 17 Hodgkinson was playing for the United team in the Yorkshire League and the same year signed professional forms. With no apprentice professional status at the time, the signing was recognition of a precocious talent. Signing professional Hodgkinson received a £50 fee and a £7 weekly wage, reduced to £5 in summer months. Worksop received £250 from United. Aged 18 he made his debut in United's reserves. By the time he retired Hodgkinson had made 675 first-team appearances.

His professional status was hard-earned. For the previous two years he had worked six days a week on the butcher's counter of the local Co-op store. An understanding manager allowed him to work a 5am–midday Saturday shift so he could play for United in the afternoon. Solitary training on an area of Bramall Lane known as the Bowling Green, adjacent to the old cricket pavilion, would see Hodgkinson repeatedly throwing balls at the cricket pitch roller. The unpredictable return flight assisted his catching and reflexes. At 5' 9" Hodgkinson was not big for a goalkeeper. He trained hard to develop upper body strength and agility. There were no special training regimes for the goalkeeper. Ahead of him in the first team was Ted Burgin, who played for the England B team and made the 1954 World Cup squad. Spectacular in his saves and popular with the crowd, Burgin was going to be a hard act to follow. Aged 17 Hodgkinson accompanied the first team on a tour of Germany whilst Burgin was on England duty. Two consecutive defeats early in the 1954–55 season saw ten goals conceded and bottom of the table United were set to face top of the league Newcastle the next Saturday. Told the day before that he was playing, a worried Hodgkinson travelled with the team on Friday and endured a night out at the Newcastle Empire watching American crooner Guy Mitchell. Against all logic, the visitors pulled off a victory next day.

After only 13 full League appearances Hodgkinson made his England under-23 debut but National Service slowed the phenomenal rise. Between 1955 and 1957 his duty to Queen and Country saw him progress from wireless operator to regimental police. Playing with the British Army team, which included Duncan Edwards and Jimmy Armfield, Hodgkinson lined up against a Football Association Select XI. United's new

England shirt badges awarded to Alan Hodgkinson

manager Joe Mercer watched the match and afterwards told him that he was in the first team as soon as duty allowed. Hodgkinson left the Army in February 1957 and a few months later was playing for England against Scotland at Wembley after only 28 first-team appearances. Whilst winning only five full caps (and never finishing on the losing side) Hodgkinson was on the bench as part of the England squad some 40 times. He went with the England squad to Chile for the 1962 World Cup and four years earlier was a member of the 'Shadow Squad' for the World Cup in Sweden.

For 14 years Hodgkinson was a Lane favourite in his trademark green shirt and black shorts. Quick to the ball, agile and good at anticipating the intention of forwards, he was considered a safe pair of hands. He developed what he calls telepathy with centre half Joe Shaw. Strong shoulders and arms produced a very brave keeper who had remarkably few injuries and missed only a dozen games in all that time, half of them due to bouts of flu. Always conceding fewer goals than number of games played in a season was his yardstick of success.

Joe Mercer was remembered by Hodgkinson as the first training-pitch manager at Bramall Lane. He would stand in the middle of practice matches. Willing to bawl out his players after poor games, Mercer would then forget everything by Monday morning. His successor John Harris provided Hodgkinson with his most unusual fitness test. Before a match at Fulham Hodgkinson informed the manager that he was not

A 1958 team photo taken in front of the John Street terracing
Left to right. Back: Mercer, Hodgkinson, Thompson, Latham
Middle: G. Shaw, J. Shaw, Richardson, Mason, Summers, Ridge, Gratton
Front: Ringstead, Russell, Pace, Coldwell, Simpson, Lewis, Hoyland

fit because of a strained back. Taking him into an empty room, Harris found somebody's briefcase. Seizing it he repeatedly threw it at Hodgkinson over a green baize table with the instruction that he was to dive and catch it. Still unfit to play, United lost 5–2 and Harris did not speak to Hodgkinson for a month.

Hodgkinson never had more than a two-year contract, and the close season saw the arrival of the dreaded telegram informing players whether they had been retained. There were win bonuses and 'crowd money' when gates were above a threshold. After promotion to Division One in 1961 Hodgkinson was given £30 a week basic. In 1966 on reaching the semi-final of the FA Cup, the United players were handsomely rewarded by the directors with inscribed barometers and £5 raincoats. When Hodgkinson ceased to be a United first-team player in 1972 he was part of a Division One team attracting big crowds, but was paid £45 a week.

His 1968 testimonial match was played against Wednesday in front of over 15,000. He received £4,000 but was informed that all the cash from the fans paying to enter the kop had gone missing. He was thus deprived of close to £10,000. Four years later, after his final match he never played in goal again even for a charity game. Offered the chance of a comeback by John Harris when John Hope, the man bought to replace him, hit a bad time, Hodgkinson refused. United offered him the chance to run the reserves which he accepted for three seasons. A 22-year involvement with United ended in November 1975. Having studied an FA management course Hodgkinson joined former United team-mate Gerry Summers as assistant manager at Gillingham.

The six years at the Kent club saw Hodgkinson's career develop to coaching the England under-18 goalkeepers. He was later goalkeeping coach to Graham Taylor's England set-up and goalkeeping consultant to Coventry City, Manchester United, Everton, and Sheffield Wednesday. In the early 1990s the United manager Dave Bassett offered him work, but he was too busy to accept. A coaching job at Glasgow Rangers led to Hodgkinson becoming part of the Scottish national side coaching team; he was in the dug-out with the Scotland manager at the World Cup in France '98. He became guru to Arsenal and England's David Seaman and spotted a talented keeper whom he recommended to Alex Ferguson by the name of Peter Schmeichel. In 2006 Hodgkinson was still coaching, this time with Oxford United where he was assistant to the Sheffield-born Jim Smith who, as an apprentice at United in the late 1950s, was tasked with cleaning Hodgkinson's boots. Some 50 years after Hodgkinson's England debut he was still teaching others.

> **Whilst the game attracted big crowds and wages were better than ever, even the best players of the time could not plan their futures. Their contracts were short and footballers wages, whilst above the national average, would not look after them too long beyond their playing days. A letter could arrive anytime and the home they lived in could be re-possessed at only days' notice. Players turned out in the Blades colours in this era who, many felt, had they played with other more glamorous teams would have attained international honours. Some excited the Bramall Lane crowds and went on to live modest lives albeit, occasionally, resenting their lack of recognition until their dying day.**

Learning Late: Harold Brook

Born in Sheffield in October 1921, Harold Brook excelled in Sheffield schools cricket and football leagues. Brook came to the attention of United during the early years of the war plying his trade in the local leagues. He made his first-team debut at left back at Lincoln in September 1941 in a 9–2 defeat. Brook could only play periodically due to military service but would become a permanent fixture in the starting line-ups of the 1945–46 season when the Blades were crowned champions of the Football League North. Many people were very surprised that Brook failed to gain international honours. By way of compensation he would eventually captain the United side that would become champions of Division

Two in 1952–53. Brook played at the time when there was a defined wage limit and a playing contract of generally just one season. The players waited in anticipation for the summer letter informing them whether or not they would be retained. The summer of 1954 was no different and, even though injury had marred his season, Brook had no reason to suspect that he would be released. His wife Irene was expecting twins and they were comfortable in a house owned by the club. A letter then arrived informing him that his services would not be required by United. He was effectively rendered homeless after 111 goals and 289 appearances.

The opinion of the United club doctor was the reason for the decision to let him go. The medic feared Brook's leg injury would not withstand another season. Fortunately on the Saturday that Mrs Brook delivered twins, manager Raich Carter at Leeds United signed Brook for a fee of £600. The Leeds doctor held a different opinion as to the capability of the leg. Over the following three seasons Brook teamed up in an attacking formation of John Charles, Don Revie and former Blade Albert Nightingale. His partnership with Charles produced 30 goals a season and promotion for Leeds to the top flight. The passing years made Brook a better player. He learned a great deal playing alongside greats like Hagan and Charles and once famously stated that, 'you only learn how to play the game when you're too old'. Retiring from football, Brook began a successful career in Sheffield as a newsagent. An earlier business venture saw him involved in a sports shop partnership with colleague and friend Jimmy Hagan. Brook died in 1998 in Sheffield.

Not Forgetting: Alf Ringstead

In the mid to late 1950s United fans watched Harold Brook and Jimmy Hagan disappear down the tunnel for the last time. The fans also lost a player that many remember as one of the most exciting wingers they ever had the privilege to watch, his name was Alf Ringstead. Between 1950 and 1958 Ringstead played regularly in United's colours, and scored 109 goals. In the 1952–53 season, when United were promoted to Division One, Ringstead was United's top scorer with 23 goals.

Born in Dublin in 1927, Ringstead grew up in Ellesmere Port and began plying his trade with non-League Northwich Victoria. He was signed by Teddy Davison for £2,500 and made his debut, aged 23, in December

Republic of Ireland cap awarded to Alf Ringstead

Republic of Ireland v Austria
The hat trick ball awarded to Alf Ringstead in 1953

1950 against Coventry City at Bramall Lane. In front of 28,000, he scored in a 2–0 victory. He scored in the next two games as well. Fast and two-footed, he could finish with both his head and feet and lose markers with ease. Republic of Ireland honours soon followed. Ringstead won 20 Caps and scored seven international goals, which placed him high up the ranks of most capped players in United's history. The second division championship medal in 1953 was his only domestic honour. After four managers in nine years Ringstead played his final game of 271 League and Cup games against Cardiff City at Bramall Lane in April 1959. He left soon after for Mansfield Town.

Retiring from football in the early sixties, Ringstead remained in Sheffield balancing his job as a rep with an impressive golfing handicap. He and many of his former colleagues (and their wives) played off excellent handicaps. Like many of his contemporaries, however, Ringstead succumbed to Alzheimers. In his final few months and seemingly unable to comprehend much around him whilst sat in a care home, two ladies sat with another resident recognised the famous player in their midst and said; *'Have you seen who that is? That's Alf Ringstead ..., you know, the one who used to play for Sheffield United'.* Despite not having uttered a word for days, Ringstead reached across and tapped her on the arm saying; *'And the Republic of Ireland'* before lapsing back into his own silent world.

The Deadly Doc: Derek Pace

How do we know how good a player was when we were not around to see him? Maybe statistics can provide an answer. A player with a career total of 302 appearances and 175 goals should impress any football enthusiast. This was the ratio set by Derek 'Doc' Pace who was born in the Midlands district of Bloxwich in 1932 and picked up his nickname following a spell in the Medical Corps during his National Service. He came to the attention of United manager Joe Mercer when playing for Aston Villa and signed for United for a fee of £12,000 in 1957. It took Pace just eight minutes to score his first goal. Pace would prove to be a great signing on Mercer's part, but one he would live to regret. When Mercer quit United in April 1959 to take over as Villa manager, he looked constantly for a goalscorer of the calibre of Pace.

Fearless, clever, good with both feet and extremely fast, Pace blossomed under the guidance of Mercer's successor John Harris and became an integral part of the United team that gained promotion to Division One at the end of the 1960–61 season. This was the season that also saw the monumental FA Cup semi-finals against Leicester City, which ran to three meetings before United lost 2–0 at St Andrew's. A popular figure in the dressing-room, Pace was one of the game's characters and one remembered warmly by colleagues and fans alike.

The 1964–65 season saw Pace's appearances interrupted after just a few games by illness—a game against Burnley would prove to be his last for United. Harris was keen to promote his exciting young players and blooded Alan Birchenall alongside Mick Jones. Soon after Pace found himself playing for Notts County. In 253 appearances for United, Pace scored 140 goals and was United's top scorer for five seasons between 1958 and 1964. Settling in the Midlands after finishing in football, Pace became active in the Boy Scout movement. He died of a heart attack, aged 57, in 1989.

Some footballers in the latter part of this decade manifested a degree of independence which their predecessors had largely avoided. Gifted to the point of receiving international accolades, such men knew that there was more to life than the regimes of a football club. Their challenging of the status quo was done in very different ways. Such figures are significant; the deferential society was slowly changing by the late 1950s and footballers were to become beneficiaries of the wider societal shift in power.

Bracing!
The United squad in pre-season training at Skegness complete with woolly jumpers and plimsolls
Left to right: Bailey, Hitchen, Furniss, Cox

The Singing Footballer: Colin Grainger

The ability to entertain was always a reliable route out of poverty and manual work. Some people were born double lucky in being good footballers and good singers. One such individual was Colin Grainger, who epitomised the late 50s in cashing in on the melodies that came via the radio waves from the USA. Able to emulate Hollywood and Broadway's finest, Grainger was also much emulated himself by aspiring young footballers. The cousin of Edward Holiday, who had played for England, Grainger was also the brother of Jack, who played for the England under-23s. Born in the village of Havercroft, Grainger started his football career as a regular in the Barnsley and District Junior leagues.

At the age of 17, Grainger joined Wrexham by virtue of his cousin Dennis playing there. However National Service in the South of England meant he had few opportunities to play for them. In mid-1953, after only five first-team appearances for Wrexham he was brought to Bramall Lane by Reg Freeman for £2,000.

After a slow start, Grainger began to establish himself as a United regular in 1954–55. The man who bought him then died in the summer of 1955; the following year United were relegated. Despite this,

Grainger and his team-mate Jim Iley were chosen for the Football League XI against their Irish equivalents. Grainger was then selected to play for England. He made seven international appearances and scored three goals. Six of the appearances came when he was a United player, the most famous of which was England's 4–2 defeat of Brazil at Wembley in May 1956, when he scored two goals. Extremely fast with a powerful shot and an ability to cross a ball from all angles, Grainger was a thrilling player. He was also closely marked by defenders and as a consequence sustained many injuries. He was to receive brutal treatment from second division opponents but it was a yard short pass from England colleague Johnny Haynes in an England v Wales fixture that allowed a Welsh full back to tear right through Grainger, inflicting a serious injury.

Grainger's short career at Bramall Lane (98 appearances and 23 goals) ended in February 1957 when he moved to Sunderland for £17,000. The United match programme explained the reasons for his departure and blamed the fans, 'his transfer was dictated by force of circumstances created by the inadequate support we have received at Bramall Lane all season'. Sunderland, however, were soon relegated and, although Grainger made 120 appearances, he scored only 14 goals. Transferred to Leeds in 1960, Grainger lasted only a year before joining Port Vale and later Doncaster Rovers.

In 1956, whilst in Finland with the England squad, Grainger got up after the team dinner and sang for the table. His talent was recognised and people began asking him to sing at weddings and cabarets. Singing was, in fact, his summer job away from football and for ten years Grainger combined daytime professional football with night-time night-club crooning. The ultimate accolade was appearing on TV in a Hughie Green talent show. Dubbed 'the fastest man in football' in his prime, Grainger was at other times sharing the stage with Jerry Lee Lewis. In 1957 his stint at the Sunderland Empire saw him break box-office records. The £20 a week he earned in football was small beer compared to the £100 a night he could get from showbiz. He played at the London Palladium and at his peak received 50 fan letters a week. Supporting the Beatles in a gig at Manchester, he recalled the dressing room scene of Ringo Starr on his knees playing with a yellow Dinky toy. In 2002 Grainger released a CD, *The Singing Footballer*, with a selection of tracks drawing on inspirations which varied from Al Johnson to Julio Inglesias. Singing might have been his first love, but in the 1970s he left both sport and showbiz behind because his main income before retiring came from working in the wine industry. Scouting reports for United manager Neil Warnock occupy his retirement in West Yorkshire.

The Cat: Ted Burgin

The very consistent goalkeeping talents of United's Jack Smith were a hard act to follow, but somebody had to do it. The task fell to Stannington-born Ted Burgin who, whilst in the RAF in 1949, wrote to United asking for a trial but forgot to state his playing position. A trial was granted and Burgin soon signed professional forms and made his debut weeks later against Swansea Town. Standing only 5'7", Burgin was small for a goalkeeper, but Teddy Davison was a former England goalkeeper also on the small side, and no doubt did not see this as a problem. What Burgin lacked in judgement made was made up for in bravery. As a consequence, he broke his wrist, arm and shoulder in various pile-ups.

A credit to his profession on the pitch, Burgin caused problems off it. Burgin was christened the 'cat' by his fellow players in tribute to his agility and was one of the fittest men in the squad. He ran three miles over and above his daily training duties. He was to be an ever-present in United's 1952–53 second division championship-winning team. Burgin's abilities received national acclaim and saw his selection for the 1951 FA touring party to Australia. He was selected as a reserve for the full England side against Austria. He twice represented the England B team and was chosen for the England tour of South Africa in 1956.

Whilst incredibly athletic, he had some memorably awful games, most notably a 4–1 home defeat to Rotherham on New Years Day 1953 and a 7–2 home defeat again to Rotherham in mid-December 1957. Such performances brought questions as to his commitment to the Blades' cause over the holiday period. He was eventually replaced by Alan Hodgkinson, who looked at the damage evidenced by Burgin's hands and assured him he would never be a goalkeeper in his mould.

Ted 'The Cat' Burgin
Punching the ball clear at Loftus Road,
home of Queen's Park Rangers.
Watching Burgin's efforts are colleagues
Furniss, Cox and Shaw

Burgin presented the more respectable of football administrators with problems. In the United minute book of 1952–53 the directors are recorded as asking for better behaviour from Burgin. He had refused to wear a tie when on England duty in Yugoslavia, and thus brought embarrassment to the club. Burgin was also prone to being slightly uncouth. On a United tour of Germany he threw the dinner table bread rolls in the direction of the directors. His presence provided a dilemma. On his day he was a brilliant player; United's officials had thus to occasionally accommodate his character for the benefit of team performances. This may well not have been tolerated in earlier days, but the mid-50s saw the pursuit of results in some instances come first and the desire for gentlemanly conduct finish second.

Burgin knew his worth and would not tolerate being told what to do. In 1956, Burgin requested a transfer and did so again the following year. Inquiries came from Sheffield Wednesday and Hull City. United wanted £12,000, which would have been a record fee for a goalkeeper, £1,000 more than that paid to Queens Park Rangers by Manchester United for Reg Allen in June 1950. Whilst looking elsewhere, Burgin was offered a job in South Africa and a position as a PT instructor as well as part-time football. Aged 28 at the time of his second request, Burgin considered that United was asking too big a fee for him. For a goalkeeper of his ability the fee was not particularly prohibitive. Perhaps his reputation preceded him because, despite his international status, he left United for a much smaller club.

In December 1957 after 281 United appearances Burgin moved to Doncaster Rovers. Succeeding the Irish international keeper, Harry Gregg, Burgin broke his collarbone after just five games. He then moved to

Leeds United, broke his collarbone on his debut and never got to live in the club house he was promised on signing. After two years he joined Rochdale in January 1961 and made 207 appearances in five years. He then went on to semi-professional football, becoming player-manager of Glossop in July 1966 and played for both Oswestry Town and Buxton. He worked for Rochdale council before moving to Fylde to retire in 1965.

At the end of the decade, the Conservative Prime Minister Harold Macmillan was to tell the electorate what they already knew: 'Let's be frank about it...most of our people have never had it so good'. His years in power (1957–63) brought unprecedented standards of living for the majority of people. The Empire was diminishing but teenagers were richer than ever. Youth as a concept had begun and became synonymous with trouble. Some of the consternation was a product of envy. The early 1960s was the time when in the immortal words of Poet Laureat, Philip Larkin, sexual intercourse began. The text of D.H. Lawrence's Lady Chatterley caused judges apoplexy but the swinging sixties were upon us, and footballers soon found out, in many respects, they had never had it so good.

Blades' fans official organ
A 1954 supporters' club circular

The great defence of the 1960s
Left to right. Back row: Coldwell, Hodgkinson, G. Shaw
Front row: Richardson, J. Shaw, Summers

Chapter 9

From Slave to Suburbia

Tommy Trinder was best known for his comedic music-hall quips. In his capacity of Chairman of Fulham, he once stated that if the maximum wage for footballers were abolished he would pay his star player Johnny Haynes £100 per week. Trinder was true to his word when in January 1961, the maximum footballer's wage of £20 a week was abolished in the face of a potential players' strike and the agitation of the Professional Footballers Association. In response, the men who ran the clubs colluded and, arguing for the benefits of equality in a team game, paid similar wages give or take a few pounds. The players themselves agreed that it was wrong for individual contracts to be negotiated. Thus while the maximum wage disappeared, it was not replaced by a financial free for all. Good money was available to players by virtue of the bonus system, be it for a win, appearance money, top six positioning or making it to the Cup semi-finals. But little changed in the wider occupational culture for the first few years of the decade. The Sheffield United locker room was certainly never going to be a hotbed of player radicalism with seasoned professional and captain Joe Shaw and a Union representative in the figure of Cecil Coldwell.

Money was entering the game like never before. In 1964, the BBC programme Match of the Day began at a cost to the broadcasters of £5,000, which saw all 92 clubs initially receive £50 each. First broadcast as 45 minutes of highlights on BBC 2, the first show attracted an audience of 75,000. It was soon to move to BBC 1. Football also became more read about than ever; by the mid-sixties, Manchester United's George Best was known to everyone in the country. With his good looks and bachelor lifestyle, Best appealed to a generation in mutiny to both their parents and the nation. Best epitomised the new working-class male; aspiring, hedonistic, and socially mobile. With celebrity status and ever-increasing wages, good footballers were now able to move away forever from what they born into. Others less gifted with their feet sought riches another way. An estimated 12 million people were playing the football Pools in 1962. The industry became the seventh largest in Britain by the early seventies with £800 million gambled each year. Monies were needed both by fans and players. There were more matches to play and players to pay. The League Cup began for United in October 1960 and in September 1965 Tony Wagstaffe became United's first ever substitute, replacing Alan Birchenall at Fulham. To bring in more money United built the Bramall Lane stand in 1966 at a cost of £100,000, which seated 3,000 and thereby increased Bramall Lane's seating capacity by 50%. To fill it and other space, the club sent out a mobile ticket office to the town of the following week's visitors. Meanwhile, young fans began to indulge in behaviour previously unknown at football grounds. In January 1968, 350 Blades returning on a special train from a Cup tie at Watford destroyed lighting fixtures, toilets and fire extinguishers. On the Shoreham End hundreds of youths and young men sang together of their desire to fly above Sheffield Wednesday's Hillsborough stadium and defecate over that below. Football hooliganism had arrived in its earliest manifestations courtesy of the Shoreham Boot Boys.

Moving Times

Adopting the slogan 'City on the Move' at the end of the decade, Sheffield council sought to sell itself and the city as a modern, go-ahead urban entity. Integral to this marketing ploy was the promotion of sport. The 1966 World Cup Finals had put Sheffield on the map by virtue of Hillsborough hosting some of the games. Wednesday had built both a magnificent cantilever stand and a new west stand. Their ground could comfortably hold 50,000. Investment in the Bramall Lane ground was needed. United could only look on and realise that their footballing ambitions would always be thwarted by having a three-sided

The Bramall Lane stand under construction before its 1966 opening

ground. In 1967, the club's AGM voted 37–26 to get rid of cricket. There was subsequent talk of dividing the Bramall Lane land to have both a football and a cricket stadium. This was thwarted when the Yorkshire County Cricket representative demanded no less than a 20,000 seating capacity. The United Board minutes reveal the club discussing with the city council the possibility of selling Bramall Lane in return for land on the southern boundary of the city. The talks fizzled out. The site identified was soon to house the Batemoor council estate.

Unitedites might take the moral high ground and argue that in their shabbiness there was integrity. This was not always the case at Hillsborough where an infamous press story in 1964 revealed a betting ring in the Wednesday dressing room. The subsequent FA inquiry and criminal court case saw custodial sentences for three Wednesday players. The three had each won £100 by backing their team to lose a First Division game in 1962. Further investigations found other games at other clubs were rigged. More bans followed.

The expansion of the Universities was to produce a growing generation of revolting students. Some spoke of liberties; others denied freedom to footballers. In 1964 the United duo Joe Shaw and Graham Shaw were 'kidnapped' by the city's University students as part of their early autumn Rag Week celebrations of misrule. Taken away from their homes on the Friday evening before a home game by the seven-strong Rag Committee, the pair spent the night in the home of one of their kidnappers. The local press and United were informed that the return of the two players was dependent on a donation of £50 to the Rag Week charity. A *Sheffield Telegraph* reporter was taken to the residence blindfolded and the picture in the next day's paper showed the two footballers sitting in armchairs reading *Twickers*, the Rag Magazine, apparently unfazed. The United Manager, John Harris, failed to see the funny side of this and called the police declaring the men 'missing persons' and stating in the media that the event was 'beyond a joke'. The club paid the money; the players were released five hours before kick off to a livid Harris, who never mentioned the event again. Surely two fit men like Joe Shaw and Graham Shaw were not going to be taken by a few puny students? The former explained the circumstances to the author in 2003:

> Okay... they didn't use coshes or anything like that, but there was around seven of them and we had been persuaded by numbers...

Persuasion elsewhere in this decade saw British clubs make their mark in European competitions. Glasgow Rangers reached the finals of the 1961 European Cup Winners Cup; two years later Tottenham won it. Two years later, West Ham equalled this feat. The following year England won the World Cup at Wembley. The European Cup was won by Glasgow Celtic in 1967, and remained on British soil a year later when Manchester United defeated Benfica 4–1. Leeds United won the Inter-Cities Fairs Cup in the same month. Early in the decade Tottenham had become the first English team of the twentieth century to win the League and Cup double in the 1960–61 season.

Whilst all this was happening, United were promoted to Division One in 1961, but were playing catch up with Wednesday who had ended the season as Division One runners up. The following season, both Sheffield teams finished in the top six. United were sixth and also made it to the last eight of the FA and League Cups. The two Sheffield teams spent seven years in the same division until United's relegation in 1968— Wednesday followed them down two years later. For the Sheffield match-goer however the football

Joe Shaw enjoys promotion celebrations in 1961

United's captain Cecil Coldwell and Wednesday's captain Tony Kay
Cec offers best wishes to before a league match at Bramall Lane in October 1962. In 1964 Kay was jailed
for his part in a betting scandal alongside two other Wednesday colleagues (Peter Swan and David Layne)
Convicted on a charge of match fixing, Kay received a custodial sentence of four months

programme could still be slightly chaotic. The 1962–63 winter was one of the worst on record. Between Christmas and mid-February, United played only one game. In February, a home match against West Ham was postponed three times and when it did take place, was the first game in Sheffield for two months. In the catch up that followed, United played three FA Cup ties in 11 days.

The decade saw the last non-professional player in United's first team and the first £100,000 sale of another. The 22-year-old Manchester University chemistry graduate, Tom Fenoughty, was registered with United as an amateur until 1963. He then had part-time professional status when he made his United debut in 1964. Shortly after when aged 25 and when a first team regular, Fenoughty became a full-time professional. A few years later United's top scorer Mick Jones joined Leeds United thereby becoming United's first ever six figure sale.

Many considered the sale of Jones paid for the newly built Bramall Lane stand. Others considered the deal was done to further United chairman Dick Wragg's ambitions in football administration. It was alleged that Wragg needed a vote from the Leeds United chairman to get a place on FIFA's International Committee. To soften the blow of Jones' departure, United paid a club record fee of £40,000 for Willie Carlin from Carlisle United in 1967. The fee was equalled soon after when United landed Arsenal's Colin Addison. A day later, however, another fee of £100,000 saw Alan Birchenall leave United for Chelsea. Players were becoming more mobile and, for many, the game was to take them to places they had hitherto only dreamed of.

Sheffield United Tours

From the early 1960s to the late 70s, Sheffield United travelled globally playing more exhibition games than any other English club. Initially these tours, which began in the 1950s, saw United travel no further than Holland and West Germany. Indeed, between 1953 and 1976, United played 15 times in the Netherlands. By the 1960s, however, the club was involved on occasions in six-week tours to Canada and the USA (1962) Australia and New Zealand (1965), Paraguay, Mexico and Chile (1966), Argentina and Bolivia (1967) and Peru, Ecuador, Mexico and Chile (1968). Such travel whilst broadening a player's horizons, brought them no extra pay beyond a £5 daily expenses allowance. In the latter tour, the United squad were accompanied by a doctor supplied by the Football Association. Mexico was to host the 1970 World Cup, and the England set up wanted to see how European players survived the heat and altitude of the region. The United players were, in effect, guinea pigs for the national team. One particular tournament, in the antipodes in 1965, was called the BOAC tour after the initials of the British Transcontinental airline seeking to promote, through football, its new long-haul flights. The airline flew the team free, paid for their accommodation and one of their officials presented the cup that United won. The team also earned the club a £1,000 victory prize for their four-week 11-game effort.

The following year (1966) United travelled to Chile in a tournament consisting of a Chilean national side alongside their Mexican equivalents. Spanish club side Sevilla and AC Milan of Italy made up the rest. Beating Sevilla 4–1, United lost 2–0 to Chile in front of 80,000 fans and drew 1–1 with Mexico. The final game was a formality; United thrashed AC Milan 4–0 and finished second behind Mexico. The necessity for such exhausting tours has never been explained. Nothing exists in United's record books articulating the logic for them, or the finances involved. Almost certainly United were given these tours by the English FA at the request of their foreign counterparts. Bigger clubs would have taken other less arduous destinations. United seemed gluttons for punishment. One plausible explanation is that United manager John Harris, having no personal life beyond football, could not stand the close season. The six-week tours occupied him as much as it did the team.

Gentlemen John: John Harris

The 25 games between the departure of Manager Joe Mercer and the arrival of his replacement, John Harris, saw United win 17 times under the charge of Archie Clark. In his role of caretaker-manager Clark had done wonders, but he did not get the job. Instead United appointed John Harris, the 41-year-old Glasgow-born player-manager of Chester. The new man had a good football pedigree; his father had played for Partick Thistle, Oldham Athletic and Newcastle before managing Swansea where he had signed his son as a 15-year-old. In later years, John Harris made guest appearances with Spurs and Wolves before joining Chelsea in 1943 where he remained for 12 years. In 1944, Harris received an FA War-Time Cup runners-up medal from General Eisenhower, later to become President of the United States. He was captain, aged 37, of Chelsea's 1955 championship winning side. A bachelor, Methodist and teetotaller, Harris was a man of integrity, who would never utter a swear word and who avoided the limelight. Living with his mother, who openly drank and smoked, his passion was football. Frugal and modest in his living, Harris was known to put cotton wool in his arm pits to avoid perspiration dampening his shirts.

Taking the manager's job in April 1959, United finished fourth in Division Two at the end of Harris's first season. The following season the club was promoted and made it to the semi-finals of the Cup with the Blades pair, Doc Pace and Billy Russell, getting 40 goals between them. Stability helped the campaign; the six men who constituted the defence missed only four games. At the same time, Harris and his assistant Archie Clark were developing a good youth policy. These youngsters; Len Badger, Reg Matthewson, Mick Jones, Bernard Shaw and Alan Woodward, were drawn from South Yorkshire and came of age in 1963–64. By 1966, the United side was the youngest in its history. Of the regulars, ten were local born and only one cost a fee—Welsh International Gil Reece. The captain, Len Badger, was 21 years old.

Harris's 10 seasons as manager at Bramall Lane produced two promotions to the top division and five top half finishes. Paying poor wages by the standard of the day, Harris assembled teams who, at times, played superb football. Reluctant to spend money, which no doubt pleased his board of directors, Harris made his first purchases when paying Swansea £12,500 for Len Allchurch and Rotherham £15,000 for Keith Kettleborough. The signings Harris made were usually astute and the £26,500 he paid for Tony Currie in 1968 was one of the greatest steals in the history of the English game. His policy on youth however was confusing. In the mid-1960s, he and his assistant Archie Clark could boast nearly a full first team drawn from the juniors. Then he seemed to favour buying in experience over youth, a tactic that was to prove costly when injuries struck. Whilst his predecessors had brought in many of the players that provided the backbone of his early teams, what Harris was able to do was bring out the best in them, without ever muttering a curse.

Willing to fine his players for indiscretions and sendings off, he was frugal in his personal life and believed that as a manager he should balance the books of the club. He did not permit his players latitude when on long distance foreign tours; he wanted them in their rooms early. When some broke curfews he would lecture them on responsibility. Finding communication with players difficult at times, and loath to express humour or warmth, Harris remained a father figure to some young players, albeit one who was very distant. Harris never joined in a training session, preferring to watch, often from the back row of the Bramall Lane stand. Using a 4–4–2 system he favoured the use of wingers and never promoted defensive play; even away from home he sought victory. After his team talks the players would discuss what they thought was ideal for the match, Harris would remain in the room silent and listening. Whilst he favoured players in his own mould, he gave ability a free reign and tolerated flamboyance when it produced results. Demanding 'proper trousers' and blazer and ties when on club duty, Harris enforced smartness and, initially, short hair. He was, however, lenient towards genius and allowed Tony Currie to keep his flowing blond locks and wear his shirt outside his shorts.

Harris was a man who liked routines. Home games invariably saw the United players meet at 11.30 at the Kenwood Hotel and eat a steak dinner. London games invariably saw the squad in the Bonnington Hotel. Because of his time at Chelsea, Harris had friends in high places and occasionally used a contact at Buckingham Palace who provided his squad with a pre-match tour of the building. Harris was occasionally generous, albeit not with his own money. Whenever he saw women outside Bramall Lane he would try to muster complementary tickets for their benefit and would advise the Secretary when compiling pay packets to add a few pounds into certain envelopes if he thought the player had done well the previous week.

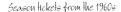
Season tickets from the 1960s

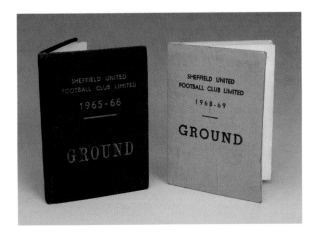

Twice moving 'upstairs' at United in 1968 and again in 1974, Harris was replaced, in the first instance, by the 42-year-old Arthur Rowley and then by the 41-year-old Ken Furphy. When elevated Harris was twice given the title Football Executive, but was really no more than a Chief Scout with a grander title. His move upstairs in 1974 came with a three and a half year contract which would have taken him to his 60th birthday. He lasted less than the term of the contract and, realising he was superfluous to requirements, left United in 1977, accepting the job of Chief Scout at Sheffield Wednesday under Len Ashurst. He remained at Hillsborough for four years. Harris died in 1988 in Sheffield after a debilitating illness.

International caps awarded to Graham Shaw 1959–1963

The First Sacking: Arthur Rowley

Arthur Rowley was appointed to the position of United team manager in July 1968 shortly after their relegation from Division One. Rowley was the son of a semi-professional goalkeeper and brother of Jack Rowley, who had played for Manchester United and England. Another brother was Albert, who played for Notts County and Wolves. Rowley himself had been a very good player. Five days after his 15th birthday Rowley guested for Manchester United in an unofficial war-time game. Signing amateur for Wolverhampton Wanderers in 1942, he moved to West Bromwich in 1944 and turned professional. Four years later, Rowley was transferred for £12,000 to Leicester City. In the 1956–57 season, he scored 44 goals in 42 appearances, including four hat tricks, as Leicester won the second division championship. Rowley made one appearance for the England B team in 1956 and scored in the 4–1 victory over Switzerland. Aged 33, he signed for the lowly Shrewsbury Town taking them to promotion from the fourth division scoring 38 goals in the process. Retiring from playing in 1965 at the age of 40, Rowley took the manager's job at Shrewsbury.

Rowley's move to Sheffield United came out of the blue. Whilst he had been a tremendous player, what he had achieved whilst managing Shrewsbury was not exactly earth shattering bar a couple of cup giant-killing feats. With a low budget, Rowley had produced a decent team, who on their day could match the big boys. Rowley played the W-M formation and allowed free range in movement. In the memory of one of the Shrewsbury players the team of Rowley actually played 'off the cuff'. Rowley had a very good eye for a player, and enjoyed balancing full-backs with wingers. The consequence of this was exciting games and often high score lines.

Rowley took the managerial position at Bramall Lane at a time when his and John Harris's duties had not been clearly defined and the people Rowley had to work with had all been appointed by Harris. This new

Arthur Rowley (centre), with John Harris (left) and Dick Wragg, after Rowley's appointment as United's manager in 1968

structure was meant to be a partnership between Rowley and Harris and produced a restructuring of the coaching staff. This saw Rowley ostensibly in control of team affairs assisted by John Short who was designated the role of accompanying Rowley to away games and attending injured players. Cecil Coldwell held a corresponding role with the reserves. Harry Latham was given charge of the United juniors. In his first season, Rowley's team finished in the top half of the second division. Whilst his stay was short and his departure shrouded in mystery, Rowley had an evident talent for recognising potential. He was responsible for bringing in some excellent defenders in Ted Hemsley, Dave Powell, John Flynn and Eddie Colquhoun. He also attempted to sign the Everton forward Alex Young. Disappointing results however saw Rowley become the first ever Sheffield United manager to be dismissed.

Almost a year to the day of his appointment, and on the day the club reported a loss on the year's workings of nearly £100,000, John Harris resumed his position as team manager. Rowley claimed to be completely unaware of his impending sacking. Rumours abounded as to the 'real' reason for his departure. Rowley's involvement with and ownership of racehorses had attracted the consternation of United chairman Dick Wragg only weeks after his appointment. Players remember Rowley occasionally not appearing in the dug-out until 10 minutes after kick-off when a big three o'clock race was broadcast. Players also recall uninspiring team talks that reflected a quietly spoken, and even introverted, individual. Just as significant to his departure was the fact that at the time some of the United players were in dispute with the club over a pay incentive. Such insubordination did not impress Dick Wragg who sacked Rowley on his return from a pre-season tour of Holland, probably for failing to quash the players 'revolt'. Upon leaving Rowley congratulated the agitators for obtaining a better deal.

In 1970 Rowley took over as manager of Southend United and brought them their first promotion two years later. Four years later, when the club was relegated, he was dismissed. Leaving football, he worked for the Vernon's Pools company before retiring in the Shrewsbury area. He died in December 2002 with the accolade of scoring 434 goals in 619 League football games, more than any player in the history of English football.

> **Rowley's first signing for United was a player he had signed as a youngster for Shrewsbury. The player was an all-round sportsman with an independent mind and a keen brain. His memories cast more light on both the Rowley era and the managerial crises that followed the second departure of John Harris. The late 1960's footballer was more prepared than his predecessor to question those who employed and coached him. The age-long contest between employer and employee was to be played out within new boundaries. Whilst players might win the occasional battle the outcome of the wider war was still balanced in favour of the board and those that reported to it.**

Hitting the Boundary: Ted Hemsley

The German bombing of the Potteries meant that Ted Hemsley grew up in South Shropshire in a fit and intelligent migrant family. A grandfather had been a professional footballer with Aston Villa, Hemsley's father had played in the RAF XI in a team containing 10 internationals. His younger brother became a professional footballer with Shrewsbury. His father was a self-taught chief surveyor; his grandfather, brought up poor, had taught himself maths. By the age of 14, Hemsley was a grammar school boy, attracting talent scouts from both professional football clubs and county cricket; he accepted schoolboy forms with Wolves. However, a dispute with Manchester United over player registration saw Wolves suspended from playing youth team games. Hemsley left and soon after met Arthur Rowley, then player-manager of Shrewsbury Town, who after watching him play for the school one morning, promised Hemsley that if he signed for Shrewsbury, he would soon play for the first team.

In 1962 at the age of 16, Hemsley signed as a full-time professional with Shrewsbury. He received news of his debut when the headmaster informed him during school assembly that a car was waiting to take him to join the team coach. He was to play in a Division Three fixture that same evening at Bradford. The 1–1 draw was made memorable because the Shrewsbury goal saw Rowley equal the British goal-scoring record of Dixie Dean. The 16-year-old, Hemsley, joined the squad drinking champagne in the communal bath. His teen years had seen him play centre forward then move to midfield. He was to finish as a full-back, and whilst naturally right-footed, took free kicks with his left. Hemsley was also a competent cricketer. In his mid-teens he was netting at Warwickshire, but eventually signed for Worcestershire who in the mid-1960s were a very powerful outfit. The presence of players such as Ron Hedley, Tom Graveney, Norman Gifford, and Basil D'Oliveira meant that Hemsley's first team appearances were limited to Test times. Breaking into the first team in cricket was slow compared to football, but Hemsley holds the distinction of being United's only first-class cricketer and footballer since the early 1920s.

In Hemsley's six years at Shrewsbury the club were rarely out of the top five of the then fourth division, and had gained a reputation as 'Cup giant killers'. When, in late 1968, Arthur Rowley accepted the manager's job at Bramall Lane, Hemsley was the first player he brought to Sheffield. The £30,000 fee produced a three-year contract, and a basic £35 a week plus £5 appearance money. Two months later Hemsley got married, and two months later again, moved into a bungalow in Dronfield, rented from the club. Rowley inherited a squad that was mainly local in origin and had known each other since their teens. Believing that complacency had set in, Rowley brought in outsiders like Hemsley and weeks later Dave Powell and Eddie Colquhoun to shake up the dressing room.

Ted Hemsley

Within a year of being appointed however Rowley was sacked. Hemsley believes an incident of player power, quickly sat upon by the United's Board of Directors, forced them to make Rowley the sacrificial lamb. On a tour of Holland, the United squad had a team meeting to discuss win bonuses. The realisation of many of the United players was that this team could gain promotion. The £5 a point bonus United were paying, however, was a pittance compared to the £20 a point being paid at the same time at Coventry and Aston Villa. The debate, involving in particular Hemsley, Len Badger, Colin Addison and Gil Reece, was not heated and there was no mutiny. Rowley sat in the meeting alongside United's two other coaches, and accepted that the players had an argument, which he would put to the Board. On his return he was sacked. In Hemsley's opinion it was the treachery of someone in the room in Holland, who had obviously phoned people in Sheffield to inform and warn them of proceedings.

The 1969–70 season saw Hemsley in United's Reserves, and as a result a realisation that he should either move on or work harder. He was to win a first team place via the latter route. The returned John Harris saw both a left-back and a sweeper in Hemsley. Promotion was to be United's. When Eddie Colquhoun was injured, Hemsley was called upon to be captain. The pre-match dressing room of this promotion-winning team was unusual. A bottle of 'medicinal' whiskey was always available. A dram was routinely taken by Eddie Colquhoun seconds before entering the pitch. Alan Woodward was a pre-match chain smoker. Trevor Hockey went into his own world as he kicked holes in the wall. Hemsley rationalises these events, explaining that the footballer's existence is essentially about frames of mind central to which was fear:

> *This was a small squad, not paid a great deal of money. Few people stepping out on that pitch did not have some kind of strapping on an ankle or a knee. Very few players would not be carrying some type of injury, and at any one time half the team would have received pre-match cortisone injections. The crowd who turn up think that by virtue of running out in a shirt you are 100% fit. We know we're not, and that affects concentration and provokes fear.*

Hemsley was once laid on the massage couch and received seven cortisone injections. Moments later he found himself unable to stand up. The medics, however, simply assisted Hemsley in stretching exercises before sending him out to play 20 minutes later.

A very capable player, Hemsley's name was mentioned as a potential international by no less a person than England's goalkeeping great at the time, Gordon Banks. A consistent player, Hemsley played under four United managers. In his final two years at Bramall Lane he was the club's PFA rep, thus he had cause at times to negotiate with his managers. This latter capability probably hastened his departure from Bramall Lane. As an articulate and intelligent senior professional, Hemsley was in many senses a manager's dream—with the potential to be a nightmare. The manager, who inherited him in 1969, was John Harris, who Hemsley remembers as knowledgeable and modest. Harris's advice was always very simple; win the first tackle. Harris gave his players plenty of freedom; their Monday night ritual beer drinking session in Sheffield's Penny Farthing club usually resulted in at least half of the squad vomiting in training next morning. The squad members were very close and would attend supporter's clubs social evenings together. Hemsley believes this built a rapport with fans, and kept critics off their backs when performances were poor. The squad was still close 30 years later.

Newly promoted to Division One in 1971, Hemsley was paid £60 a week; other clubs in the same division paid up to three times that amount. When he finished with United in 1977, Hemsley earned less than £100 per week. How good the promoted team really were was tested pre-season against a mid-ranking Dutch side called FC Twente. United lost the game 2–0, but Hemsley remembers the score line was flattering. Days later the Division One fixture list was published; Hemsley remembers sitting with colleagues speculating on where a point might be won. This publication and the 2–0 defeat frightened the squad and in a players' meeting all agreed they would have to run and train harder or they were going to look ridiculous. The training methods of this Division One outfit saw constant games between the first and second teams, but also saw a lot of practices between forwards versus defenders. Training sessions for Hemsley involved marking his mate, Alan Woodward. The pair had an agreement; Hemsley would allow Woodward to run past him and cross, but next time Woodward had to allow Hemsley to dispossess him. This was done to impress John Harris, who would spend training sessions sitting alone on the back row of the Bramall Lane Stand. This lofty position earned him the nickname amongst his players of 'God'.

Away games saw a regular card school of up to eight players. One of them was Hemsley. On only one occasion—when one player lost £100—did Hemsley consider his intervention was needed. Sensing that the loss (a considerable sum in those days) might take away the focus that the player needed hours later, Hemsley called the game off, and negotiated an agreement with the players that in future a different card game would be played with less financial consequences. The only slight dressing-room disagreement of his time occurred in the days when United were top of Division One. As a consequence of this status the players were of media interest, Hemsley sought agreement that all media fees obtained by any one of them be pooled and distributed equally. Only one player refused to join this arrangement.

In 1974 Harris was replaced by Ken Furphy who considered that ranting and raving at Hemsley would improve his game. One memorable five-a-side training session saw Hemsley on the receiving end of a tongue-lashing. A furious Hemsley volleyed the ball into the groin of his manager, who upon recovering his composure abandoned training. In a subsequent chat the air was cleared and Furphy changed tack. The team that had been together for the previous three years was beginning to crack. The players Furphy brought in, usually mates from his previous clubs, were no better than those already in the dressing room. Playing poorly but getting results saw United miss out on a place in Europe by one point. Hemsley received a late season injury and was replaced by the young David Bradford in the final six games. At the beginning of the next season, the new defensive formation was retained. Hemsley told Furphy that if the team played without an established back four, they would be relegated. By the autumn United were as good as down and Furphy was sacked.

The very name of United's next manager, Jimmy Sirrel, produces a mixture of mirth and anger in Hemsley. The writing was on the wall when Sirrel's first signing was a young left back by the name of Paul Garner. When fit Hemsley was in the Reserves. Practice matches invariably saw the first eleven play the second eleven—invariably the seconds won. The team contained Hemsley, Jimmy Johnstone and two very capable youngsters in the shape of Simon Stainrod and Keith Edwards. This team was top of the Central

WITH THE COMPLIMENTS OF **Ty·Phoo** LTD., BIRMINGHAM 5
TEA

The 1964 United line-up in conjunction with Ty-phoo Tea

The tea company produced small cards found inside packets of tea and larger cards that could be sent for when coupons had been collected

League; the first team was struggling in Division Two. One memorable game played on Friday morning at the Ball Inn saw a game last for over 100 minutes, and resulted in a 11–2 victory for the second eleven. When the squad met the manager at Bramall Lane at 2.00 that afternoon, Sirrel came into the dressing room, and as Hemsley remembers it (imitating Sirrel placing his index finger on his front tooth): 'I went up the hill with my team…I came back down with a headache'. The manager then gave an incomprehensible lecture; Jimmy Johnstone burst into giggles. Considering this scenario ludicrous, Hemsley declared he could no longer listen and, informing Sirrel that the first team had no confidence in him and would be beaten tomorrow, walked out. United lost the next day.

Hemsley's concern for the reserve team and the young players in it saw a massive fallout between him and Sirrel. This resulted in Hemsley leaving United. Weeks after the team talk walk-out by Hemsley, Sirrel accompanied the reserves to Old Trafford. The home side contained eight Internationals; the Blades' goalkeeper was a youngster, whose biggest match to date was playing for Sheffield schools. Sirrel's pre-match talk was simple, but hardly inspiring: 'Waste of time going out there tonight… Good Luck'. A furious Hemsley took control, and told his players regardless of the eight Internationals and the 8,000-plus crowd, that everybody had to enjoy what was to follow and put their fears behind them. United won 5–1. The reserve team contained some decent players; Johnny Giles took two to West Brom, but at a PFA dinner Hemsley was to meet managers who quizzed him as to why no second team players at United were available for loans or fees. Ian St John, in charge of Portsmouth, had even inquired after Hemsley. On returning to Bramall Lane, Hemsley accused Sirrel of ruining the career prospects of players including his own. The affronted Sirrel responded by repeating his claim that the phone had never rung.

The exchange ended in an impasse but ended Hemsley's United career. His representation on behalf of what he believed were wronged players, cost him a Testimonial. He remains the only senior professional of nine years longevity at Bramall Lane, who did not receive a Benefit game. He thereby missed out on a potential payday of £15,000. Up to the day of the argument, Sirrel had been prepared to support Hemsley's case. Their final words in the aforementioned argument saw Hemsley question whether the argument affected his Testimonial. Sirrel's response was that Hemsley had 'no —— chance'.

Taking time away from the game, Hemsley then signed for Doncaster Rovers and played for two seasons under Stan Anderson and his successor Billy Bremner. Meanwhile Hemsley played first class cricket for Worcester and ended a twenty-year association with the bat and willow in 1982. Remaining in Sheffield, Hemsley took over a bookmakers' business for a decade and today combines general entrepreneurship with income from a position as a horse racing ring inspector, a job description which causes his former team-mates no end of mirth.

Hemsley's full-back partnership with a local-born Blades hero lasted for close to a decade. Len Badger was the first person Hemsley met on arriving at Bramall Lane. Informed by the player than he was in charge of team discipline Hemsley reflects with irony that 99% of both off and on-field trouble that he got into was a result of Badger's doing. The life and footballing times of Badger illuminates the ultimate in rags to riches. The local boy made good lived the life of the quintessential 1960s footballer and then in time-honoured fashion took a pub when his playing days were over.

Stamped Out: Len Badger

Being born shortly before the end of the Second World War meant a childhood of post-war austerity for Len Badger. This situation was made more difficult by the death of his father ten years later. An upbringing amongst the factory grime and noise of Sheffield's industrial area of Tinsley Park produced a happy family of a brother and sister and a remarkable mother who worked from dawn until late afternoon cooking for students at Sheffield's Collegiate College. The road to Bramall Lane began for Badger on the three pitches belonging to the colliery near the Badger household. Badger taught himself the game by watching United and practising behind the schoolyard and on the local cobbled streets.

In his mid-teens, Badger's teacher recommended him for a trial with Sheffield Boys. Not selected for the next trial, he turned up anyway and when a full-back failed to appear volunteered to stand in. He had a good game and was picked to represent the city. The team did well and lost an FA schoolboy cup semi-final to Manchester in front of 15,000 at Bramall Lane. The same year Badger represented Yorkshire Boys and then England Boys. Aged 14 Badger could have signed for any number of professional clubs but chose the team he supported—Sheffield United. He was signed as one of the ground staff in 1960 on a weekly wage of £6. The training offered was not very sophisticated, but it was changing. Endless lapping of the pitch perimeter was slowly being replaced by an emphasis on technique. The early 1960s saw the emergence of the qualified coach and the desirability of FA coaching badges. In the summer months of his first year Badger found himself learning other techniques of income, namely working as a barrow boy in Sheffield's Parkway market and laying kerb stones for the United chairman's building company. He had no need to do such tasks when, in 1962, he signed full-time professional. The wage was now £35 a week and his 17th birthday was spent in Toronto as part of an 18-man United squad on a close season tour. Days later he was sitting in a Times Square hotel in New York City watching a colour TV that had 15 channels. It was a long way from Tinsley.

His first-team debut came in a League cup-tie at Bury in October 1962. His League debut six months later was at home to Orient. Meanwhile, both Badger and his United team-mate Bernard Shaw played for England at Wembley in the Junior European Nations Cup Final in front of 45,000. The right-back position at Bramall lane was Badger's for the next 13 years. He made 539 first team appearances, scored eight goals and played under four United managers. He was an attacking player, fast, accurate in the pass, capable of a terrifically effective slide tackle, and could throw a ball a long distance. Between 1964 and 1968 Badger played for the England under-23 team 13 times under the managerial eye of Alf Ramsay and later Joe Mercer. Three appearances for the Football League XI came his way in 1967. Whilst never making the full England team, Badger was part of the squad of 40 selected before the 1966 World Cub, but missed the selection for 1970.

The exciting era that was the late 1960s and early 1970s, saw Badger hanging out in the Nether Edge Jazz Club and the Penny Farthing night club. Photographs of the era show Badger at the cutting edge of fashion. The long hair, cut away to reveal thick side-burns and the wide shirt collar worn outside the sports jacket. The Oxford bags fall nicely over platform soles. The smile is more a grin about to turn into a smirk. He had the talk and the looks. The virtue of Sheffield's womanhood was a lot safer when Badger, at the age of 22, married a local girl.

In appreciation of Len Badger 1973

Renting his marital home from the club, he experienced for the first time an inside toilet and bath with running water. By 1970, and on good money by local standards, Badger did what many footballers of this era did and moved to a new housing estate in the village of Dronfield. Whilst living comfortably the existence was somewhat precarious. Only ever on a two-year contract the renewal in the close season was the green light to try to negotiate a wage deal. The best basic wage he received from United was £80 per week in the mid-1970s. With a £30 bonus for points won Badger never earned more than £8,000 per annum. The biggest cheques that came his way were two five-year loyalty bonuses of £500, and £12,000 from his 1973 testimonial match against Wednesday. Such monies were invested in business ventures. The retired footballer of this era became synonymous with the ethos of business entrepreneurship.

In the 1960s, players' wages at Bramall Lane came every Thursday in a brown envelope. Two days

The first-ever pop music performance at Bramall Lane
Danny Harman and the Wildcatz in front of the John Street stand in late 1963

later, some of this money was lost in a four-man card school, consisting of Badger, Alan Woodward, Tony Currie and Ted Hemsley. Their game was 13-card brag and this foursome played together for eight years.

Some places were not so welcoming to Badger. One nation caused an incident that made Badger the front page of national tabloids. On a United tour in 1972, Badger, alongside Tony Currie, was refused entry to Kuwait by virtue of having an Israeli stamp on his passport. United were due to play an exhibition game in the Middle East en route to New Zealand. The hosts refused entry to all people with Israeli stamps. The apologetic Kuwaiti authorities put the pair on a plane to Bombay. Whilst their team-mates sweated in temperatures close to 100 degrees Badger and Currie relaxed in a six-star hotel. The era was not always as glamorous as the hotels the team now stayed in. An earlier tour to Argentina had been more dramatic. Badger remembers pulling a team-mate off a bedroom balcony of the Hotel Intercontinental. The depressed colleague had decided to end it all—instead he got the hand of Badger round his neck and hours of talking to.

Following United's relegation to Division Two in 1968 John Harris returned as first team manager. Three years later United were back in the top flight following a ten-game unbeaten run to end their Division Two campaign. Then followed a club record 12-match unbeaten run in Division One. Badger played in all these matches in a team that attacked mainly down the right-hand side using the astonishing talents of Badger, Currie and Woodward. An automatic first-teamer under Ken Furphy's managerial regime, Badger

Joe Shaw

The reward for 600-plus games
Joe and Hettie Shaw receive a drinks cabinet from United Chairman
Dick Wragg before a home game in February 1965

fell out with Furphy's successor Jimmy Sirrel. The established players in the United dressing-room ridiculed Sirrel. He in turn was contemptuous of their abilities. Sirrel considered Badger too short to be a full-back. Badger's response, that at the age of 32 he was unlikely to grow much more, was lost to his critic who sold him to Chesterfield, then managed by former team-mate and United captain Joe Shaw. Playing for the first time in Division Three with his new club proved a struggle. It was a different world, one which did not particularly value a cultured right-back. However when Joe Shaw was sacked his successor Arthur Cox gave Badger a renewed appetite for the game and made him team captain and fitter than he had ever been in his career. A few months later Badger broke his leg again. After 46 appearances for the Spireites he hung up his boots.

A business partnership begun years earlier meant Badger was part-owner of a paper producing factory. Disaster struck when the company went into liquidation. Aged 37 Badger had to sign on the dole. He was soon working again selling advertising space for the *Sheffield Star*. Badger's attempts at football management went no further than Norton Woodseats in the Yorkshire League. But paid work put paid to football when in 1982 Badger teamed up with a former school teacher and bought a pub and wine bar in the—by now—Sheffield suburb of Dronfield. This venture then saw him move to another pub in 1991, which he runs to this day. A fanatical Blade, Badger attends Bramall Lane for home games and still has time for his many well-wishers.

The six figure transfer fee arrived this decade. Sheffield United did well out of this escalation in payments, selling two players for £100,000 in a matter of months. Whilst the fans were furious at this perceived lack of footballing ambition the club was grateful for the monies which paid for both players wages and ground developments. The two players subject to such a fee came from average working-class backgrounds and both went on to have diverse but very good careers. One epitomised the confidence of the aspiring working-class male of the time. The other lived well but remained modest. One travelled Europe with his team and sang in the newly obligatory football-team pop song. The other entertained without a script. Their return to Bramall Lane provoked very different responses from the United faithful.

How Much?: Mick Jones

Mick Jones joined United in 1962 and was sold to Leeds United in 1967 for £100,000 by chairman Dick Wragg. A furious John Harris offered his managerial resignation over the sale. He had good reason to be angry; in his five years at Bramall Lane, Jones had finished as top scorer in three seasons and made his England debut at both Under-23 and full level. It was small recompense to manager and fans that Jones was the first United player to be sold for a six-figure sum. Whilst at Leeds Jones continued to appear at international level, but did not make it to the final 22 for the 1970 World Cup squad.

Born in 1945 to a Unitedite father in the village of Rhodesia near Worksop, Jones was recognised in his early teens as a potential footballing talent. Spraying bicycles for a living after leaving school, his appearances for Dinnington Miners Welfare brought him to the attention of United, who in 1961 invited him to train twice a week. After the first game he was signed as an apprentice earning four times the wages he was used to. Thrown in a skip and covered in boot polish, he recovered from his Bramall Lane initiation at the hands of his team-mates to begin his tasks, which included cleaning kit and stoking the boiler. Within 18 months these menial duties were left behind when Jones signed professional forms.

A commitment to youth policy by the United management saw Jones make his debut at Old Trafford in April 1963 at the age of 17. A few days later on his eighteenth birthday he scored twice in a 3–1 victory at Manchester City. His home debut produced a goal and a standing ovation and, by late 1963, the centre forward position was his in a team that combined youth in the shape of Len Badger, Bernard Shaw and Tony Wagstaffe with the experience of Joe Shaw and Graham Shaw. The 1964–65 season saw Jones paired up with another youngster by the name of Alan Birchenall. The latter scored eight goals in his first nine appearances and the fair-haired United duet referred to as the 'blond bombers' had scouts from bigger clubs flocking to watch them. Meanwhile, Jones was selected in November 1964 for the England under-23s alongside team-mate Len Badger and scored the opening goal in a 5–0 defeat of Romania. A call-up to the full England squad came in mid-1965: Jones went on a tour of Yugoslavia, West Germany and Sweden and became the youngest centre forward in the history of the English national team.

By the end of the 1965–66 season Jones had made 100 first-team appearances and had scored his 50th league goal. He also had a week's wages docked by John Harris for breaking a curfew and going out drinking. A few days later he turned out for an England under-23s against Turkey when, for the first and only time, three Sheffield United players represented a national side in the shape of Len Badger, Alan Birchenall and Jones. Finishing the season as the club's leading goal scorer, Jones was part of a United squad that toured South America for six weeks. Requiring an oxygen mask after a game in Mexico City, Jones was confined to bed for days after.

The final home game of the 1966–67 season brought rumours of interest in Jones from Matt Busby at Manchester United. The close season saw Jones teamed up for the first time with Allan Clarke of Fulham in the England under-23 team. Within two years they were together at Leeds and formed the deadliest attacking duo in the English game. United officials informed the footballing world at the beginning of the

Mick Jones unsettling the Aston Villa goalkeeper in August 1965

1967–68 season that Jones was not available, at any price. However, with United bottom of the table and unable to progress due to a three-sided ground, the board succumbed to a £100,000 offer for Jones from Leeds. Manager Harris's resignation offer was politely refused. Jones was the third £100,000 footballer in Britain. Soon after Alan Birchenall left for a similar sum to go to Chelsea. The local media was full of indignant letters criticising United's lack of ambition and selling policy in what was to become a familiar refrain over the next three decades.

Joining the world of Don Revie's Leeds introduced Jones to a world of carpet bowls, bingo on the team coach and a level of professionalism hitherto unknown to him. He played in European competitions within weeks of joining. The squad even travelled to long distance domestic games by air. Leeds were League champions in 1969 and Jones was the top scorer. Nicknamed the 'Leeds Machine' Don Revie's team was one of the best in the world in the late 1960s. It was also a team loathed by rivals, but Jones is not one of the Leeds players remembered with disdain. The following season saw the Jones and Clarke pairing play classic games against Chelsea in the 1970 FA Cup Final and Celtic in the European Cup semi-final in front of 136,000 at Hampden Park. The 1971–72 season was memorable for both football and Jones. In the middle of the campaign Leeds performed a pre-kick-off synchronised warm-up routine hitherto never witnessed before in an English game. They also sported apparel ahead of its time with each player having a named tracksuit and numbered tabs on their socks.

Brave and good in the air, Jones attracted the attention of England manager Alf Ramsey, either side of the 1966 World Cup. Having the dubious distinction of being the lead vocalist on the Leeds' 1972 pop-song single *Marching on Together,* Jones's most visible moment in the memory of many football enthusiasts came minutes after the end of the 1972 FA Cup Final. He was to climb the steps of the Royal Box to receive his winner's medal from the Queen with a dislocated elbow sustained late in the game. Upon reaching Her Majesty, Jones was made aware that his captain Billy Bremner had picked the medal up on his behalf minutes earlier. He was a spectator two days later when a draw with Wolves cost Leeds the championship and the double.

Leeds were champions in 1974 and, on his first return to Bramall Lane, Jones was made captain. The visitors won 2–0 and Jones received a great ovation from the Blades fans. He finished the season as Leeds' top scorer and supporters' Player of the Year. It was also the beginning of the end for the ageing team. They lost their mentor, Don Revie, who left to manage England. His replacement for just 44 days was Brian Clough. In the ensuing turmoil Jones discovered bone lesions in his kneecap. Struggling for a year with the injury, he retired in October 1975. Taking a job as a sales rep, Jones then owned a sports shop in Maltby, South Yorkshire. He was then to try his hand as a market trader. Aged 61 in 2006 Jones is a match-day fixture a Bramall Lane in his role of Platinum Suite corporate host.

A Footballing Bombshell: Alan Birchenall

The next £100,000 departure from Bramall Lane involved a footballer who epitomised the emergence of the footballer as rival to the pop star and general 'lad-about-town'. Known to some fans as the 'Blond Bombshell' by virtue of his one-time flowing locks, and sometimes as 'The Claw' because of his ungainly left leg movement, the man known throughout football as 'Birch' was Alan Birchenall, born in 1945 in London's east end. Birchenall's family moved to Nottingham when he was four. He thus grew up supporting Notts County and played for Notts Boys in a team which included Mick Jones. Birchenall turned down the offer of a schoolboy trial with Nottingham Forest out of his supporter loyalty to County. He thus began his working life aged 16 earning £3 per week on a factory assembly line. Six months later, having changed jobs, Birchenall was cycling to work and shovelling coal into a factory boiler. Scouring brake drums of buses in his next job provided Birchinall with strength, stamina and a work ethic which was attracting the attention of scouts in amateur level football.

The 55-hour working week was supplemented by two nights' training with the juniors of Notts County, who had eventually come to notice him. Saturday home games saw him finish at midday before turning out for his team. Away games were problematic because he could not always arrive on time for the team coach. Consequently, it was whilst playing for a leading amateur Saturday afternoon team that Birchenall, then aged 17, was watched by United's assistant manager Archie Clark who invited him to a trial at Bramall Lane. United liked what they saw and weeks later Birchenall was part of United's 1964 youth team that won the Groningen tournament in the Netherlands. Touring the red light district of Amsterdam with team-mates on the eve of the final, the youngsters pooled their money and drew lots to see who would enter the cubicle of one of the alluring women. Birchenall 'lost' but was turned away by the lady of the night as she considered him too young for business. Physical activities of another kind were made available to him courtesy of the men in suits at Bramall Lane. One unusual summer saw the teenage Birchenall work a fortnight alongside three United team mates on a Wiltshire farm belonging to the United director Arnold Laver. Their labour was used to reap the harvest in a training process recommended by John Harris to toughen up his young players.

Lodging in Nether Edge, Birchenall eventually moved in with Len Badger and his mum. Happy with this domestic arrangement Birchenall set a goal scoring record in the Northern Intermediate League—he scored 65. He was part of a team that attracted a crowd of 5,000 to Bramall Lane to watch them win the Northern Intermediate Cup. In between goal scoring feats, Birchenall did his best to ruin Len Badger's courtship but, on signing professional in 1964, could then afford to go out on the town on his own by virtue of his £15 a week wage. Before that, however, a degree of pain came Birchenall's way when United's older professionals shaved his pubic region and rubbed liniment in the area to remind him of

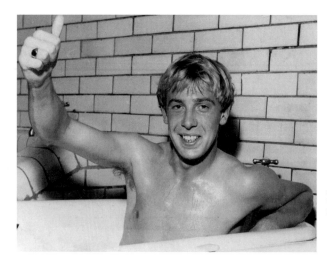

Alan Birchenall
United's blond bombshell, smartening
himself up for a night on the town

his position in the club. Always one for the wind-up and a good time, Birchenall was to be the unofficial social secretary at a variety of clubs he joined. He was also in charge of curfew breaking.

Making his professional debut at Stoke in September 1964, Birchenall enjoyed his first pre-match steak and then ate the remains of Graham Shaw's meal and several rounds of toast. Two chocolate bars and sherbet dabs were taken for dessert, which caused some regret when he learnt one hour before kick off that he had been chosen to play, not just to travel. Days later he was playing for United against Wednesday at Hillsborough and scored both goals in a 2–0 victory. Playing alongside Mick Jones, the two shared 16 goals in 10 matches. The innocence of youth, combined with a degree of arrogance, saw him threatened with a broken leg by elder journeymen if he made them look silly. Birchenall was also innocent in his applying liniment to his face before a match, which required the club doctor to pour water over him to stop the burning. Following the victory over the Owls, Birchenall was promoted to a standard contract of £35 per week, with £5 appearance money and a £4 win bonus. In his first week he took home £53, which was five times the average national wage. Months later he bought a soft-top Triumph Spitfire for £600 cash. His buddy, Len Badger, did likewise and the pair tossed a coin for who would drive off with the red one.

The United team hung out together, and Birchenall was inevitably in the thick of things. Late drinking was enjoyed in the Rickshaw Chinese restaurant and Birchenall would regularly join Sheffield-born singer Joe Cocker on stage at the Penny Farthing nightclub. Their rendition of the rhythm and blues classic 'Walking the Dog' would see the United players in the room shout the refrain and spray beer over Birchenall. The Wednesday players in attendance, preferring soft drinks, would watch in stunned silence. Alongside adventurous team-mates, Birchenall would be one of five who would squeeze into a borrowed Mini seeking the delights of a night out in Nottingham.

Birchenall played various parts in a variety of foreign tours. An end-of-season BOAC sponsored tour in 1965 involved United and Blackpool on a six-week tour of New Zealand and Australia. The two clubs were to play 12 exhibition games. Realising this would be exhausting, the players had agreed to fix the game so that each won the same amount. This was done without the knowledge of the club managers, but was to ensure that no-one in either camp came home disgraced. Even the score was agreed upon in advance; the first match was to end 3–3. Seconds before the final whistle of this opener Blackpool scored, thereby ruining the arrangement. For the remaining games, all bets were off and the teams kicked lumps out of each other and even fought at a post-match party when the respective players competed for the attentions of local nurses. A year later United toured Mexico, Chile and Paraguay. The following year saw a tour that produced exhibition games in Chile, Peru, Ecuador and Mexico. A two-game trip to Norway preceeded a three-match tournament three days later in Mexico, which saw the players requiring oxygen masks before a holiday in the beautiful resort of Acapulco. Equally breathtaking for some was the sight of Birchenall and team-mate Bernard Shaw gyrating in the suspended cages of an Acapulco disco—they having replaced the scantily clad young women. This did not impress the local police who drew their revolvers to hasten the departure of the United squad.

In 1968 Birchenall was transferred to Chelsea for £100,000. Weeks later he got married. He was to learn well from his notorious Chelsea playboy colleagues the ins and outs of west London high life. Birchenall claims to be responsible for saving the life of the wife of a Chelsea chairman on a post-season tour. As she lay unconscious in the sea, following a fall whilst water-skiing, Birchenall jumped in and saved her. A few months later he was sold to Crystal Palace by the same chairman. His career produced over 500 League games and nearly 300 goals in 18 years as a professional. On his return to Bramall Lane in a Chelsea shirt, Birchenall ran to the Shoreham End Kop and expecting the acclaim he was used to was surprised to hear refrains of 'Birchenall's a puff'. His response was a two-fingered salute. Today Birchenall conducts pre-match on-pitch entertainment at Leicester City.

Two United wingers of this era started life in similar social conditions—but hundreds of miles apart. One was local, the other became an adopted local by virtue of his popularity amongst team-mates. One lasted the reign of two United managers, the other saw four men in that position. The latter sought a new life in the New World, the other died too young.

24 Years in Tulsa: Alan Woodward

A humble Barnsley upbringing was typical in producing Sheffield United footballers in this era. Alan Woodward came from such a background and is remembered by every Blade watching United in the 1960s and 1970s. Woodward's father worked down the pit and decorated houses in his spare time; his mother worked in a bakery. Having no footballing talent or ambition did not prevent Woodward senior taking his two sons to watch the local team and occasionally to Sheffield Wednesday. The elder brother to Alan managed a couple of seasons with Barnsley but never made it. It was left to Woodward junior to go on to higher things. Playing centre forward for Barnsley Schoolboys he replaced an injured outside-right one match and so impressed the trainer that he remained in that position the following week and indeed most of his professional footballing career. The excellent Barnsley under-15 side also included Jimmy Greenhoff who later played for Manchester United. The team won the South Yorkshire Schoolboys and the English Schoolboys Trophy. Inevitably professional clubs looked closely at this team and approaches were made to Woodward from Barnsley, Leeds and Sheffield Wednesday.

Beer talked in a number of ways in the football negotiations around Woodward. The youngster and his father were invited to meet the Wednesday manager, Vic Buckingham. The latter was to make the wrong impression on the pair. The young Woodward did not like the way he talked; the elder was astute enough to notice the words were a product of alcohol. Days later the pair met with Leeds United manager Don Revie, who offered Woodward's parents a pub in Leeds in return for their son's signature. Then in stepped Sheffield United in a two-pronged attack that had obviously been thought through. Woodward remembers the technique:

There was John Harris and Archie Clark. Now Archie liked a drink so he took me Dad to the pub. John Harris stayed on the sofa talking to me Mum. They invited us to a match at Bramall Lane and picked us up in a car and I met the players after.

The Sheffield United squad in pre-season line-up 1968
Left to right. Back row: Wagstaff, Barlow, Hodgkinson, Gordine, Cliff, Munks
Middle row: Hill, Currie, Fenoughty, Mallender, B. Shaw
Front row: Woodward, Carlin, Addison, Badger, Buckley, Reece

In March 1962 Woodward signed for United as an apprentice on £7 a week. Coached by Harry Latham, the youngsters at times trained with the first team and daily cleaned up after them. Some 18 months later Woodward signed professional forms and, aged 16, made his Central League debut at Maine Road. He made his first team debut aged 17 at Anfield. Manager John Harris worked on the principle that if a player was good enough he was old enough, and instructed Woodward to take on the full back and cross to Mick Jones. Throughout his time under Harris, match day advice was not particularly technical. In Woodward's memory the United changing room invariably resounded to Harris crying, 'Get stuck in'.

Ignoring the manager's mantra Woodward played his own game. He was fast, could cross a ball with few equals in the game, and had a terrific shot. He avoided tackling and by his own admission headed the ball less than half a dozen times in his career. His thing was scoring goals; 'If I didn't score I was upset even if we'd won'. His most memorable goals were two in the 3–2 defeat at Derby in December 1975 and a 35-yarder in a 3–2 defeat of York City in the League Cup. His most memorable game was a 1–0 defeat of Leeds at Bramall Lane when a broken finger sustained by Alan Hodgkinson after eight minutes saw Woodward selected to be stand-in keeper for the remainder of the game. Throughout his playing days he smoked 20 cigarettes a day. Two other United players smoked as much as him, seemingly without troubling their fitness.

> We had a day at some college where they did tests for blood and body fat. The top three in fitness were me, Keith Eddy and Eddie Colquhoun...we were the heaviest smokers.

Unsettled in the mid-70s Woodward considered leaving United. Newcastle and West Ham tried to buy him before United manager, Jimmy Sirrel, gave Woodward a £10 a week pay rise—which was all Woodward wanted but in hindsight was a pittance for a player of international standard. The best deal he ever got at Bramall Lane was £110 a week basic. All contracts were for two years with a two-year option added on.

Woodward's mentor John Harris once stated that Woodward's one fault was that he did not realise just how much talent he had. His penalty taking was legendary; his corner kicks amazing; these alone produced a dozen goals in his United career. The Leeds United and Scotland captain, Billy Bremner, once described Woodward's ability as 'terrifying'. At international level, Don Revie and Alf Ramsey admired Woodward's technical ability, but questioned his heart for the game. His head would go down if he failed to trap a ball. It usually took a great through ball from Badger or Currie to liven him up.

As a schoolboy Woodward had represented England. As a senior professional he was twice chosen for Football League XIs, both against Ireland, and late in his career was offered England B honours when selected by Ron Greenwood to tour Malaysia and New Zealand. What could have been the pinnacle of a playing career was refused:

Alan Woodward

> I knew that my playing days at United were up...I'd already talked to Tulsa Roughnecks and I didn't want a two-month trip following a nine-month season.

He was a great entertainer, but not a leader of men. Dropped in 1972 after a spell of bad form, the first team lost whilst Woodward scored four for the reserves. He was selected for the first team a week later. Off the pitch Woodward's pursuits were sedentary—namely fly-fishing. The glamorous side of the game, which was fast emerging, he hated:

> One time we all got a jacket with 'SUFC' embroidered on the pocket. One day I was wearing it in Sheffield when shopping. I didn't like the attention the badge brought. I remember going into a store and cutting the pocket off.

It would take more than a missing top pocket to fail to notice Woodward. With grey hair from the age of 14, thick sideburns and a helmet-like hairstyle, Woodward was recognisable from half a mile away to any Blade. Unease with publicity was responsible for his leaving United for the USA. An off-pitch love tryst troubled Woodward. Having left his wife for the United manager's secretary, Woodward was news value. He could not cope with the press intrusion, he was followed whilst out shopping and photographers hid in bushes outside his home. The USA offered refuge. He played his last game for a United team led by Harry Haslam at Fulham in September 1978 wearing the number 6 shirt. Including League, Cup and friendly games, Woodward made 639 appearances for United scoring 193 goals. In October 1978 he joined Tulsa Roughnecks jointly managed by the former Derby County players Alan Hinton and Terry Hennessey. A two-year contract gave him double what he earned at Bramall Lane and a free car. Playing against Johan Cruyff, Franz Beckenbauer and Carlos Alberto in the newly re-launched American Soccer League, was a great end to his career.

Woodward had wisely taken his coaching badge whilst at United—on a course at Hillsborough run by Howard Wilkinson. But it was to be Gridiron football that made use of his talent. A season with Oakland Thunderers as 'kicker' saw Woodward turn down offers from the prestigious New England Patriots, 'I could have made a fortune. But I was tired of living in hotels and airports'.

His 1974 Testimonial against Sheffield Wednesday brought him a good pay-day. Today he wants for little. Living in Tulsa, Woodward now is in charge of maintenance of the American Airlines fleet at the local airport. His involvement in football is limited to coaching teenagers and selling kit in his sports shop. Now with wife number four, his Barnsley accent is enhanced with a Midwest drawl. Returning to South Yorkshire every few years, Woodward keeps in touch with his ex-team mates of the early 1970s. His friendship with the United commercial manager, Andy Daykin, saw United tour the Midwest in 1989 with Woodward's assistance throughout.

Wing and a Prayer: Gil Reece
Making his United 1st team debut in August 1965, Gil Reece was to be a part of the Bramall Lane first team for the next six seasons, and was to win international recognition from his native Wales. Born one of five brothers in Cardiff, Reece was released by his home town club in his mid-teens and trained as a plumber whilst playing amateur football. Rescued from obscurity by then fourth division Newport County, Reece played 32 games for this modest outfit and began attracting attention from many clubs. He chose United above the rest and arrived at Bramall Lane in April 1965 for a fee of £10,000. A month after his United debut, Reece made his debut for Wales.

Whilst at Bramall Lane Reece won 16 caps out of a career total of 29. A broken leg in November 1966 interrupted his career, but he returned in 1967 and was to score many a long-range goal. He also proved useful in the air for a man standing just 5' 7". Reece finished the 1967–68 season as the club's top scorer. The 1969–70 season saw United attempting once again to get out of Division Two. Reece was part of a forward line of huge potential alongside Alan Woodward, Colin Addison and John Tudor. Poor away form, however, saw United finish sixth. Sustaining his goal-scoring and supplying ability, Reece was a huge part of the 1970–71 United team that won promotion to Division One. He scored a number of vital goals. In the penultimate home game of 1970–71 he scored one of United's five as they beat challengers Cardiff City 5–1 in front of 43,000 at Bramall Lane. He was to play just one season in Division One, then moved to Cardiff in September 1972 and had a final League season at Swansea in 1976. In his seven years at Bramall Lane, Reece scored 67 goals in 225 appearances.

An understated 'hardness' by virtue of a boxing family background saw Reece brave in the tackle. He was also a fun-loving character off the pitch with a strong silent streak. A training ground argument with his centre-forward team-mate Colin Addison once escalated into a centre circle punch-up. Addison insisted on the ball to his feet, Reece equally insisted on playing it in front for him to run on to. Neither would back down over what they believed was right. At other times when perceived incompetence came his way, Reece's silence spoke volumes. Before an international match in East Germany, Reece was left off the flight so as to accommodate a Welsh FA official and had to make his own way to Leipzig. He would not talk about this incident with United team-mates. In 1970 when not selected to play against England, he left the team hotel in South Wales and stayed nearby with his mother. No United colleague was to learn any further details. Despite this Reece was still selected for national honours in later years and played his final international in 1975.

A post-football plumbing business was supplemented by running a hotel in Cardiff. However, cysts in his right leg began to cause severe problems and an amputation of the limb was required in April 2000. The circumstances of the operation provoked Ted Hemsley to contact the PFA. In an ongoing court case, the PFA explored the possibilities of medical negligence. Alongside Len Badger and Geoff Salmons, Hemsley visited Reece in late 2003 and the four spent six hours reminiscing on old times. In December of the same year Reece died at the age of 61. Seven of United's promotion-winning team attended his funeral, as did most of the Cardiff City line-up who played in the great 5–1 United victory at Bramall Lane in 1971.

Welsh international Gil Reece going for a high ball in United's match at Fulham in September 1966

Alan Hodgkinson tipping one over the bar at White Hart Lane in 1967

Player of the year trophy
Awarded to Alan Hodgkinson 1966–67

FIFA medal awarded to Alan
Hodgkinson in 1989 for his work
with the Scotland Under 16s Team

Alan Hodgkinson gathers safely
against the backdrop of the
cricket pavilion in 1969

Precious Flowers and Acid Tongues

The late 1960s saw football-related competition no longer confined to the football pitch. The gangs of youths who now populated the 'Ends' brought a new form of fandom that shocked their parent's generation. As violence manifested itself in youth protest around the world, thousands of working class teenagers in Britain indulged themselves in a competition around the match day that contained its own manifestations of winning and losing. Any male between 14 and 20 could join in, the participants however had to be prepared to punch or be punched in defence of the reputation of, variously, Sheffield United, the Shoreham End and the City of Sheffield. This also meant competing with city rivals Sheffield Wednesday.

The hooligans' activities sounded at times innocuous, at other times faintly ridiculous and occasionally malicious. In February 1967, the *Sheffield Star* reported that on the evening before the United–Wednesday derby, Wednesday fans had painted slogans on the walls of Bramall Lane. The article considered this, 'one of the worst incidents of pre-derby match hysteria the Bramall Lane ground had ever known'. Far worse was to come over a year later. Headlines in September 1968 informed readers that the club would ban for life those responsible for throwing acid during disturbances on the Shoreham End between rival fans attending a United v Wednesday benefit game. Two men needed hospital treatment, another three received medical treatment at the ground. A week later the teenage culprit, who had carried and thrown the acid, received the amazingly lenient sentence of a three-year probation order.

Fortunately not all football-related disorder was of such magnitude. In the same month, the *Star* reported the unlikely scenario of 200 Blades 'hands linked' running through a city centre subway trampling flowerbeds and knocking two pedestrians over after a match. The following month a small and unsensational article reported 40 windows broken near the Bramall Lane ground. The damage was blamed on United fans, but no indication of the circumstances was given. In April 1969, the *Star* reported that gangs of youths had once again trampled flowerbeds outside the Town Hall after a United match. Then in September, a youth was arrested for leading a large group of United fans along a shopping precinct singing, waving a bottle and looking for Wednesday fans. The following month told of trouble caused by 500 youths after a Wednesday–United match at Hillsborough.

Football hooliganism had arrived and provoked a political response. What followed was government reports and dismissive attitudes. The chairman of United, Dick Wragg, speaking in 1968 about the recently published Harrington Report (a government-sponsored inquiry into football hooliganism), called it, '…so much nonsense' adding:

> …we don't need a bunch of professors to tell us what to do about the problem of hooliganism in soccer. In fact I think the problem has been exaggerated, we don't get a lot of trouble in Sheffield.

Others in powerful positions would disagree. The first mention in Sheffield policing circles about football hooligans came in 1968 when the Chief Constable made the observation that:

> The year has brought another disconcerting trend to the area, that of open public disorder with hooliganism at and around football.

The following year, the Chief Constable noticed an improvement:

> A pleasing aspect to the year has been the reduction of incidents involving hooliganism at both football grounds in Sheffield. The provision of extra police personnel in the vicinity of grounds and in the city centre following matches brought about a considerable improvement in behaviour and resulted in the prevention of wilful damage and nuisance.

The 'improvement' continued over the next few years:

It is pleasing to report the improved behaviour of football supporters throughout 1971…there were no offences of wilful damage and nuisance on the scale of those experienced two years ago.

The extent of the disorder two years previously had evidently been down-played. The 1970s, however, was to see massive disorder at Bramall Lane, and the involvement of police, politicians and club officials in seeking to curb the excesses of young Blades and their counterparts from throughout England.

The 1960s brought unprecedented changes in the composition and behaviour of the football crowd and, indeed by the end of the decade, the behaviour of players. Social values were being challenged outside of both the game and the football ground. The rise of the concept of 'youth' saw greater freedom for adolescents, freed earlier in the decade from the requirements of National Service. Football became a battleground, literally on the terraces as young fans gathered to fight and ideologically, with the old structures and strictures ceasing to be relevant to a profession that epitomised the new consumerism. Big money transfers were to become the norm. At one level all seemed well; English clubs were to dominate in Europe over the next decade. The national side, however, sat out two World Cups. The fighting spirit of the English was to be associated more with fans than with the players. For Sheffield United, however, the decade that had started so promisingly, ended in a place they had never been before.

The United squad pose before the 1969–70 season
Obviously impressed by the photographer's new stepladder

Tony Currie
At the Ball Inn training ground in 1973 presenting his better side to the photographer

Stand Up—Fall Down

United began the decade in the top flight. By 1979 they were in Division Three for the first time in their history. In between, they had missed out on a place in Europe by one point and had built a four-sided ground. Promotion to Division One in May 1971 saw crowds of over 40,000 flock to Bramall Lane. The high stakes of getting into the top division influenced a key game between United and Hull City three weeks before the end of the 1970–71 season. Some 41,000 saw a United defeat in a game infamous by virtue of the referee calling all 22 players together in the centre circle after 20 minutes to warn them of the consequences of their mutual brutality. United's one home loss of the season did not prove conse-quential and weeks later 43,000 packed Bramall Lane to see a 5–1 victory over Cardiff which made promotion virtually certain. Getting into the top flight required a special mix. The two previous seasons had seen mid-table finishes before manager John Harris signed Trevor Hockey from Birmingham. Hockey's mid-field task was to win the ball and give it to the 20-year-old Tony Currie, whose skills were becoming the talk of the league. The subsequent first division United side is remembered as one of the best to ever wear the red and white stripes. Five of this team represented their countries; Gil Reece was capped 29 times for Wales, his compatriot Dave Powell gained 11 caps. Nine Scottish caps were won by Eddie Colquhoun. Alan Hodgkinson won five England caps, and Tony Currie 17. On top of this, Alan Woodward had England youth credentials and Len Badger had played for the England under-23 team.

A stunning start to the 1971–72 season saw United top of the first division in September. The team played great football and Tony Currie was the kind of player never before seen by Blades fans—long blond hair, shirt covering his backside and blowing kisses to the crowd as he beat opponents. He won his first England cap at the end of this season. Eventually, the team finished in mid-table, hampered by an absence of cover and a shortage of younger players pushing for a place. The close season and first few weeks of the 1972–73 season saw a flurry of transfers. At the same time, cricket at Bramall Lane ended and work began on the building of a new stand where the cricket pitch had been. Opened in the summer of 1975, the 8,000 seater South Stand was completed at a cost of around £1m. United spent the second half of the decade financially stricken, never capable of reaching the average 31,000 gate needed to pay for its cost and the interest payments of the loan taken to build it.

Money Talks

Sheffield had 1% unemployment in the late 1970s and the impregnable Labour vote saw municipal socialism subsidise public transport, making the city the cheapest place in Europe in which to travel. The wider population of Britain were, like football clubs, looking for greater income, consequently the early seventies saw United playing games on midweek afternoons and kick offs moved earlier in the day to beat the dusk. Industrial disputes had produced the three-day week, which brought power cuts and electricity shortages. Prime Ministers went to the electorate asking 'who ruled the country—the government or the unions?' Whilst pondering the question, United fans could enter the newly built Bramall Lane Restaurant for a pre-match three course meal.

As credit became acceptable in the wider economic system, a loan system for clubs to obtain players had begun in the 1969–70 season. This was not utilised by United until February 1975 when Gary Jones arrived from Bolton. Footballers' wages continued to rise, their income assisted by television money. In 1979 the BBC and ITV signed a joint £2.3 million deal to broadcast football for the next four years. This was renewed in 1983 for £5.2 million over two years. Commercial considerations saw the introduction of new tournaments.

In 1970, the Watney brewery introduced a pre-season cup tournament open to the previous season's two top-scoring teams from all four divisions. Innovative in being the first English competition to decide drawn ties with penalty shoot-outs, it was also one of the first trophies to carry the name of the sponsor. Representing Division Two in 1970 were Hull City and United. Having beaten Aldershot 6–0, United lost to Derby County 1–0. Two years later United were representing Division One alongside Manchester United. Defeats of Notts County and Peterborough brought a final against Bristol Rovers at their Eastville ground. A goalless draw meant a penalty shoot-out which United lost 7–6.

The Global Brand

United entered countries that English football barely knew in this decade. In 1972, a three-week tour of Zambia saw United play the national team five times. One game attracted a crowd of 80,000 and was watched by President Kenneth Kaunda. Against a township elect on this tour, United took an early 3–0 lead and the crowd turned ugly. The referee whispered to the United defence that he would give their opponents a goal if they would provide the home team with an opportunity. This was duly arranged and the crowd were somewhat placated. In the mid-70s, United played games in Algeria and Tunisia and were also to be found in Gibraltar (1972), France (1972, 1975, 1976), Cyprus (1974), Poland (1974) and New Caledonia (1975). The latter trip was memorable for crossing two international datelines on June 8th, thereby permitting United's Len Badger to enjoy two birthdays. One game saw United play an Israeli XI in February 1972 and produced a memorable match programme cover the week after which showed Trevor Hockey shaking hands with the former chief of staff of the Israeli Defence Force and later Minister of Defence, Moshe Dayan. This match was part of a mid-winter break played days after a 5–0 defeat to Arsenal. The Israeli XI drew 0–0 with United in front of a crowd of 17,000. On the Tuesday following the Israel match United hosted the Ukrainian team Dynamo Kiev, to whom they lost 2–1 in front of a crowd of over 18,000. Why the Ukraines visited Sheffield for this game has never been explained.

Summer 1973
Bramall Lane hosts its final
game of county cricket

Young cricket enthusiasts remove the
permitted souvenirs of one square foot
of Bramall Lane turf

SHEFFIELD HOPES ARE PINNED ON THESE MEN

No pressure there, then?
The 1971 promotion team, about to begin their first division campaign
Left to right. Back row: Salmons, Barlow, Powell, Currie, Hemsley, Badger, Woodward
Front row: Hope, Reece, Ford, Colquhoun, Hockey, Deardon, Hodgkinson

Tournaments hosted by Cyprus and Gibraltar in the mid-1970s saw United play English and foreign teams. One, held in 1974, with the grand title of the Cyprus International Tournament saw United in action against two local cubs and Levski Spartak of Bulgaria.

Average Developments

The realisation that football clubs had to look beyond the turnstile for income was dawning. United's average crowd in season 1971–72 was 33,000. Later in the decade a Boxing Day fixture between United and Wednesday at Hillsborough in 1979 attracted a crowd of 49,309, a record for a Division Three game that will never be beaten. There was no pleasing some though. In January 1975, halfway through the club's most successful season since the war, United chairman John Hassall used the match programme to berate his fans, both for their lack of vocality and low numbers. With average crowds at 21,000 Hassall opined the age-long lament from the United Boardroom that only an average of 30,000 would enable the club to compete in the transfer market. Meanwhile, to boost income United's first souvenir shop was opened in 1971 in a terraced house adjacent to the ground, selling T-shirts, football boots, scarves, shirts, teddy bears, autograph sheets and pennants.

Money-raising lotteries became part of match-going. One played at Bramall Lane was titled Golden Goal. Fans bought a ticket, which revealed a time between 1–90 minutes. If the time of the first goal corres-

A victorious United squad celebrates
The champagne flows following the 3–0 victory over Watford that guaranteed them a return to Division One in 1971

ponded to the number, a cash prize was won. This was actually started in 1960 by the club's 'development fund' renamed 'development association' in 1969. As clubs began to look elsewhere for income, companies, public organisations and interested individuals could, from 1970, become match-ball 'donors' and have their names in the programme and announced over the Tannoy. This same year saw United appoint a 'Commercial Consultant' renamed six weeks later 'Commercial Manager'. By 1973 the Commercial Manager had an assistant. Then came a semantic process—the former was titled Marketing Executive in 1980, then later that same year Commercial Manager again. The post-holder then found himself holding the title of Commercial Director in 1982.

Other commercial schemes were started in 1974–75, one being match sponsors who were given advertising space in the match programme and pitch-side hoardings and complimentary tickets for a few dozen employees in return for parting with several hundred pounds. In the 1976–77 season the United team was sponsored at £6 a point by a trucking company. The same year saw pages of the match programme sponsored. Sartorial style came second to the pursuit of income. United's team shirt changed at the whims of the manufacturer. At one time in this decade, a thin black stripe appeared between the broad red and white stripes. The following season saw the white collar replaced with a round neck. The stripe was eventually broadened to accommodate the name of a furniture store, as United sold the shirt to commercial sponsors.

Hard Enough?: The Shoreham Boys

Others connected to United wore their colours with pride and promoted messages on their football-related apparel. Most popular of the football souvenirs of this era were sew-on patches. Usually a few inches in size, the patches were circular, football boot shaped or in the 'V' for victory hand. The wearers were invariably young men, denim-clad and often sporting long hair. Many would admit to being part of the Shoreham Boot Boys 'hooligan' following. They were to fight their equivalents, home and away. They fought in their opinion for the reputation of both the football club and the city.

This was the era of gangs of rival fans invading each other's 'End' before the match in pursuit of 'taking Kops'. The procedure was well known to all participating. Rivals were expected to enter the home end

On the pitch
Blades fans seeking to take negotiations a little further with opposition fans and police at Hull City in 1981

and seek, through violence and intimidation, to move the home gathering. Might was right, and reputations for 'hardness' won and lost. Most of the drama took place an hour before kick off. In response, the club made various efforts to entertain fans before games ranging from brass bands to police dog displays. Periodically throughout the decades, schoolboy penalty competitions took place and occasional games of football were played by attractive women to the amusement of the predominantly male crowd. The best intentions in the world were having little impression on contemporary youth. The 'Young Blades' Club, founded in December 1965, had 600 members and organised film shows, trips to away games and football coaching sessions. However, the club closed in January 1967 after youngsters set off a fire extinguisher and broke windows at a meeting. The troublemakers were reported in the *Sheffield Star* as being two 12-year-olds. In 1972 the *Green 'Un* carried an appeal from the chairman of United for better behaviour from Blades followers and less profanities to be heard in their chanting. The appeal had little effect. Fourteen years later similar appeals to responsibility were printed after a match between United and Wednesday when the *Green 'Un* spoke of the 'foul mouthed yobs' after they had sung 'tatty and sad' chants which had supposedly made 'fellow fans, players and management wince'.

Football-related disorder occurred on a large scale in the 1970s. In April 1972 fights in and around Bramall Lane between United and Newcastle fans resulted in 54 arrests. Days later, 30 arrests were made during, before, and after a match against Manchester United. In both instances, missiles had been thrown between rivals on the Kop; local shops and homes had windows smashed. For the moment, such incidents were only back page news. Amazingly, following a day of disorder the same fans were even praised by police for their good behaviour. The first week of the 1972–73 season illustrated the scale of disorder. The *Sheffield Star* headline '18 Sheffield Soccer Rowdies fined £990' detailed how, at a match two days previously between United and Newcastle, a total of 83 fans were arrested. Weeks later, the visit of Chelsea produced 41 arrests. Then, two weeks later, front-page headlines reported 68 arrested in an account of fights between Blades and Manchester United fans. In the 1972–73 season a total of 276 arrests were made inside Bramall Lane. As a result, United finished top of the 1973 *Daily Mirror* 'Soccer Hell

Raisers Table of Shame'. Wednesday were two places behind with 258 arrests. Sheffield thus achieved national notoriety as a centre for football hooliganism.

The club obviously tried to discourage such behaviour. In October 1975 a photograph and small article in the *Star* showed a hundred Blades on the Bramall Lane End waving at the photographer. When rivals did not, or were prevented by the police, from entering the Shoreham End, Blades would take the fight to the newly-declared 'Visitor's End'. The police and club officials could not grasp what was going on and so produced an appeal. Under the caption 'Are you a problem fan?' the article explained how watching the match from this area created 'crowd problems'. The following year the Club Secretary appealed to Blades fans not to stand there 'in the interests of ground safety' explaining that 'the tendency upsets policing arrangements'. The following year the club, no doubt under police pressure, made a public announcement which no longer talked around the issue. The Club Secretary told the *Star* prior to a match against opposition who were expected to bring a crowd of 5,000:

> *We have decided on a strong line. Any Sheffield United fan going into the Bramall Lane end tomorrow will be assumed to have gone there looking for trouble. The Authorities have been instructed to put people outside the ground at the first sign of trouble. Any serious offence will be prosecuted.*

That was the punitive response. The club also attempted to appeal to people's better nature.

Schemes and Opinions
One pioneering scheme attempting to appeal to a wider family audience was begun at Bramall Lane in the mid-70s. United Manager, Ken Furphy, believed the drop in attendance at the time was due to fearful parents not allowing their children to attend matches because of hooliganism. Furphy thus invited parents with children aged under 15 to attend Bramall Lane one Sunday morning to discuss plans for a

Young Blades in jubilant mood on the Shoreham End c.1970

A 1970's Sheffield United duffle bag
The cause of many a schoolyard scuffle with Owls fans

young supporters club. In April 1974, Furphy also instigated an open-day at Bramall Lane; thousands of predominantly male under-fifteens, queued in the pouring rain for the privilege of viewing the dressing rooms and watching the players train. No such insight into the club had ever been afforded young Blades.

Soon after a supporters' club for young (under 16s) United fans who were 'educated, dedicated supporters' (EDS) was established with a forum consisting of parents, police and a local referee. An 'EDS pen' was set aside on the Shoreham End with railings around it. Entry to the pen was only possible by showing an EDS pass, which also saw a reduction in admission. Parents volunteered to act as stewards, both at home games and aboard their dedicated coaches to away games. Their intentions were good; the EDS pen had a regular attendance of between 100 and 200 (99% of them boys). Some, who wanted no part in this adult-controlled affair joined, mainly because it allowed cheap admission to home games and then, having climbed over the fence, would stand at the back of the Kop with the hooligans. The local police were enthusiastic, regarding it an unprecedented success and a cure for hooliganism. At the time Chief Inspector Mosely was head of the force's Juvenile Bureau and Community Relations Department. He saw the EDS as providing young supporters with both a carrot and a stick.

The 'carrots' were cheap travel, and the chance to meet United players. The 'stick' was the termination of membership for misbehaviour. After two years, the EDS membership was 4,000, none of whom had apparently committed an offence. The idea folded following the departure of Ken Furphy in the autumn of 1977. By the late 1970s the EDS pen became the disabled enclosure financed by the Football Trust. The same area was later renamed after a private health care company.

Still the hooligans fought. Local public opinion manifested itself in 1977 in neighbourhood activism. A symbiotic relationship between local fears and the media need for a story saw the *Star* articulate the circumstances, fears and demands of these residents. In March, front page headlines 'Streets besieged in Fan's Battle of Bramall Lane' described after-match fights between Blades and visiting Nottingham Forest fans. Two policemen needed hospital treatment, one was hit by a brick, and a Blade sustained a broken jaw. Nine arrests were made and windows of nearby houses were broken. A local vicar organised a residents' petition presented to local councillors, who in turn signed it and presented it to the Council and the Club. Signed by 700, the petition demanded a month long closure of the Bramall Lane ground after every major act of hooliganism, more police protection, and compensation from the club for damaged property. National politicians were brought into this local issue. The then Minister of Defence and Sheffield Labour MP, Fred Mulley, told a resident in a letter he made public that he would visit the next match at Bramall Lane and discuss matters with Ministerial colleagues. The Minister could still watch a fight by 1977, which some might argue was recompense for the generally awful football on offer by this time. Had he taken his seat two years previously, matters on the pitch would have distracted him from events on the terraces.

5

Managing well: Ken Furphy

Despite two very good subsequent seasons since gaining promotion in 1971, John Harris, at the age of 56, was asked by the United Board in late 1973 to step aside and accept the position of 'football executive'. Another change saw the longstanding chairman Dick Wragg stand down in 1974 to concentrate on his role in the FA's International Committee. He was replaced by local building entrepreneur John Hassall, a director since 1963, and who, whilst wealthy, was not rolling in money. This was a pity because at the end of the 1973–74 season United reported losses of £170,000. They were thus forced to sell good players. Money was proving to be a rock around the club's neck. New incomes were needed. In 1974, Derek Dooley, the former Wednesday team manager, joined United in the club's emerging commercial department. The most significant incomer, however, was a man heralded as the new face of football. A young 'track suit manager' with good public relations skills.

The 41-year-old Ken Furphy was articulate and image-conscious. Born in 1931 in Stockton-on-Tees to strict Methodist parents, Furphy's childhood ambition to be a professional footballer was thwarted temporarily when he was accepted into the local grammar school where only rugby was played. Living for the weekends, he found a game with an Under-15 junior football club. Apprenticed at the age of 16 as an electrical fitter, the tedium of the job saw him walk out. An uncle who ran an auto electrical garage took him on and, whilst learning about wires, Furphy became a regular for Stockton Boys and later Northern League Evenwood Town.

An Everton scout liked what he saw and Furphy went to Goodison Park for a week's trial and was asked to sign on. A wise father refused to let him go full-time, insisting that he sign part-time and that the club provide a job in the city's Ford car assembly factory. Whilst Furphy attained his City and Guilds, his relative isolation from the full-timers saw him play just six reserve-team games. But watching the great Brazil team on television and studying tactics made him aware that the 'push and run' style promoted at Everton was not for him. When given a roasting by the manager for running with the ball he knew that a separation was inevitable. The nearby non-league Runcorn gave him a one-year contract and £3.50 a week, which, on top of the £5.00 a week he earned from the car industry, meant a good income. When National Service called, the RAF decided that he could be a Physical Training Instructor.

Given the job of cleaning windows whilst recovering from an Achilles tendon injury, the RAF squadron leader told Furphy to pick a place—anywhere—and he would send him there. Choosing the nearest airbase to Stockton so as to be with his wife, Furphy picked up both his marriage and footballing career. Writing to all North-East clubs for a trial only Darlington replied. They wanted a full-back; despite never having played in that position, Furphy said he was one. Playing 12 reserve-team games at full-back he then made the first team as right-half. He played 380 League and Cup games over the next nine years in the Third Division North. Leeds nearly signed him and Chelsea offered £15,000 after a Cup tie which saw him mark their star forward Jimmy Greaves out of the game.

Ken Furphy
At other times a tracksuit manager

Asked to teach school kids by the Darlington player-coach, Furphy found he liked it and, judging by the increase in numbers, the kids liked him. In 1958 he attended Lilleshall and gained his full coaching badge under the tutorage of Walter Winterbottom and Stanley Rous, both of whom thought highly of him. In 1960, at the request of Stanley Rous he visited Nyasaland in Africa. Accompanied by an interpreter, driver, Land Rover and 100 footballs, he coached hundreds of kids and covered hundreds of miles for three months. He eventually coached the national youth team and was probably the first British professional to coach in Africa in a missionary ideal which Furphy explained as, '…something to do with the last chance to stop independence.'

Returning from this safari, Furphy was offered the job of player-coach at Darlington. After 45 games he was told at the age of 32 that he was surplus to requirements. Still living in a council home, Furphy was now out of the game and the auto electrical business was wobbling. Making a decision to make a go of it in football he applied and was accepted for the manager's job at Workington, then in Division Four. Within two years crowds were up five-fold, a reserve team and youth team were established, the club was promoted and topped Division Three. Aware that such a sleepy town could be the graveyard of ambition, Furphy applied for the manager's job at Watford.

Watford were ambitious and offered £4,000 a year, a club house and a club car. A 5–1 defeat in his first game convinced Furphy that, even at 34, he could do a better job than his two full-backs. He played for the next four years taking great pride in being, even at 38, the second fastest player in the squad. Gaining promotion to Division Two and having a series of good FA Cup runs brought Furphy to the attention of the football world. A precocious 18-year-old impressed Furphy when, in a five-a-side trial match in the Watford club car park, no one could get the ball off him. He was signed immediately. It was Furphy who discovered Tony Currie.

A young Tony Currie causing discomfort to an Aston Villa defender

The departure of Currie from Watford to Sheffield United in 1968 caused arguments between the Watford manager and chairman. The latter having paid £30,000 to have more seating installed at the ground wanted his money back. The angry Furphy demanded money to buy three new players; the chairman refused. By now coaching for the FA in European seminars and on courses at Lilleshall, Furphy decided that the inevitability of relegation would reflect badly on him and resigned. Fortunately, third division Blackburn Rovers approached him; Furphy made nine new signings in two weeks and achieved a 19-game undefeated run. When top of the table John Harris asked him if he fancied his job at United. Furphy accepted in early 1974 on a £10,000 salary. A firm believer that looking good made you play good, one of Furphy's first acts was to kit the squad out with snazzy new tracksuits. He then briefly made Tony Currie captain. Then he found the true state of the club's finances.

Aware of ground developments, upon accepting the United job Furphy sought assurance from the Board that he was not being employed to build a grandstand:

The 1974–75 United squad
Left to right. Back row: Goulding, Hemsley, Faulkner, Conroy, Brown, MacAlister, Badger, Garbutt, Franks, Ogden
Front row: Woodward, Bradford, Field, Eddy, Currie, Colquhoun, Deardon, Nicholl, Speight, France

They told me they'd got £250,000 in their account, a £500,000 deal with a supermarket behind one goal and a £250,000 deal with a petrol filling station on one corner... the stand would pay for itself.

Six weeks after he joined United, the City Council refused planning permission and the development plan was in ruins. On the pitch, Furphy saved the club from relegation and the following season produced a team that finished sixth and beat every team above them. The team lost only two of the final 18 games. Finishing one point outside of a place in European competition the season's average home crowd was 22,500. In response, United gave Furphy a new two-year contract and a salary of £13,000, making him the highest-paid manager in the country. Months later at a match at Birmingham, photographers gathered around the visitors' dug-out and the Sunday tabloids begin to speculate on Furphy's successor. Six months after being told he was doing a great job, Furphy was out of one.

The newly built South Stand meant United had big debts. Furphy was instructed by the board to search for players aged between 23 and 26 with a re-sale value. Forced to sell a top-class player in the shape of Geoff Salmons, Furphy brought in a few players he had known from Watford and Blackburn with mixed success. Realising he needed a centre-forward to replace the injured Bill Dearden, Furphy agreed a deal in the summer of 1975 to buy Manchester City and England forward Francis Lee for £100,000. The board refused the deal arguing that such money was not available. A few weeks later a relatively unknown third division forward by the name of Chris Guthrie was signed for roughly the same fee; the signing was a disaster. Furphy explains the circumstances:

> *Guthrie had scored a lot of goals for Southend. He was a tough bugger and a Geordie—I could always handle them. I bid £40,000, they said forget it. So I did. Then United's chairman, John Hassall, phones me asking me 'did I get permission from the board to approach a player?' The Southend chairman had been onto him. He wants to interfere, but I'm having to explain the nature of the game and how you always offer less than you're prepared to pay. He then tells me to come with him to meet the Southend chairman on the motorway. Anyway in some motel I said £50,000 plus Terry Nicholl. Southend said 'No way'. They wanted £90,000. I said to the chairman 'Let's go, he's not worth it'. He then says 'Okay, we'll give you £90,000'. I looked at him and said 'Are you sure?' He says to me 'You want him don't you?' I said 'I do, but not at that price'. The chairman bought him in effect, not me…*

In his first season, Guthrie scored 12 goals in 40 games and in his second scored six goals in 23 games before leaving for Swindon for £25,000.

The relationship between chair and manager went downhill as the team hit bottom of the league. Maybe the chairman was as perplexed as the fans as to how a team on the verge of qualifying for Europe could be relegation fodder only months later:

> *We got off to a bad start and never recovered. It was all down to a pre-season tour of Tunisia. John Hassall was invited to send the team to play a match to open a new stadium. It was worth about £10,000 to the club, but I said no way, we needed a month's training to gradually get harder or we'd be getting injuries. A board meeting decided in his favour and in Tunisia three players got injured. In the first few games of the new season we had three reserves in. That was the start of it…*

Only three months into the 1975–76 season, Furphy was sacked. The season ended in relegation as United went 19 games without a win. Yet whilst managing United, Furphy was also the England under-23 team manager and tipped in some circles for the position of England manager.

Eight weeks after leaving United, Furphy accepted a manager's job with New York Cosmos, the biggest team in the newly established North American Soccer League. Accepting the job on the morning of his departure Furphy spoke to United director Albert Jackson who passed on the word from his chairman that the club would pay Furphy £10,000 compensation for his dismissal on condition he never divulged this fact to anyone. The club then back-dated the fee, which meant Furphy paid 80% tax. The cheque he finally received was for the sum of £2,400. The 'EDS' supporters club for young fans that Furphy had established was ended in what Furphy believes was an act to erase any legacy of him.

Teetotal all his footballing life and reluctant to swear in front of women, Furphy was always well groomed, relaxed in a collar and tie, and had a philosophy founded in hard-work. A social reformist zeal saw him attempt to install CCTV cameras in the Bramall Lane ground in 1975 both to film the match for training purposes and to record the hooligan miscreants for the benefit of police. The board ruled against the idea.

Furphy spent seven years in America managing a side that included Pelé. He then coached for the FA in Bermuda, and managed the US national team in a bi-centennial tournament against Italy, Brazil and England. His success rate of wins and draws made him, when a survey was compiled in 2000, the fourth most successful post-war manager in English football. In 34 years in football, 21 of them as a manager, Furphy was recognised by the best of his peers. Bobby Robson employed him as a scout and Graham Taylor, when England manager, used him as a European scout. After failing to get the vacant manager's job at Exeter in 1984, Furphy decided to get by with a couple of sports shops in Devon, which gave a decent income, but introduced him to ten-hour working days. Selling up, he retired in the mid-1990s occupying his time with radio commentary for the local BBC radio. A brief attempt at management at Exeter ended acrimoniously in 2000 after a public falling-out with the man he had been brought in to advise.

When injuries and suspensions of key players were combined, the frailties of the United team Furphy had assembled became evident. The United Chairman, John Hassall, lost patience, the pair fell out and Hassall sacked Furphy. The same chairman took the club into Division Four six years later after three more managers proved to be not up to the job required. Hassall was to leave United in 1981, similarly unable to do the task his position conferred upon him. One might argue that the departure of the long-time chairman, Dick Wragg in 1974 thrust the young Hassall into an intolerable position. Whilst a successful builder Hassall's football knowledge was not that thorough. The rest of the board were equally lacking in experience as to how to run a football club. The full details of Hassall's chairmanship of Sheffield United remains one of the great omissions of this text. The request for an interview was not granted.

Aye...: Jimmy Sirrel

The man replacing Ken Furphy might have had the word 'eccentric' invented for him. A strange looking man, with a strong Glaswegian accent, Jimmy Sirrel was prone to pontificating and riddle-making. Few people would ever claim to know the man well. In the opinion of the man himself, few people were as good as he at football coaching. Beginning life in the dreadful conditions of tenement Glasgow in the 1920s, Sirrel began his working life as an apprentice coppersmith. At the age of 16, he cycled daily across Glasgow to the Govan shipyard for twelve shillings and sixpence a week. Under the clocking-in system, being 15 minutes late meant dismissal. Dock work was an essential industry and Sirrel could have avoided active war-time service. However he joined the Navy and, following a month's training, boarded a ship with the rank of Petty Officer. Fearing he might not return, Sirrel married his Glaswegian girlfriend Cathy. A week later he sailed to West Africa just as the war ended and did not see Britain or his bride for six months.

Stars in stripes: Sheffield United FC 1976
Left to right. Back row: Sirrel, Colquhoun, Brown Faulkner, Franks, Guthrie, Coldwell
Front row: McGeady, Garner, Ludlam, Currie, Bradford, Woodward, Flynn

When ashore Sirrel turned out for the depot select team and at the end of National Service was offered contracts by no less a trio than Celtic, Rangers and Arsenal. Sirrel chose Celtic, whose manager Jimmy McGrory paid his outside right a £60 signing-on fee in 1946, and a basic £4 a week plus £2 win bonus. Whilst Sirrel made the first team, he did not make a career at Celtic. Bradford Park Avenue signed him a year later on a free. Remaining there for two years, Sirrel realised that whilst he would never be a top-level player, he had at least moved from a room with a kitchen to a bungalow with hot water and a bath.

After Bradford PA came three years at Brighton (1951–54); Aldershot then gave him a semi-detached home to live in as part of the deal. On the departure of the Shots manager, Sirrel accepted the job of trainer. Meanwhile, he bought second-hand anatomy and physiology books. He saw it as his job to be able to discuss player injuries with medics. Sirrel also took his FA preliminary coaching badge, and by 1958 had gained his full coaching badge at Lilleshall under Stanley Rous. A year later he was employed as an FA staff coach, a position he retained for the next 30 years. Mightily impressed by lectures given by Dutch football guru Wile Coerver, Sirrel was to lecture on the imperatives of control and possession.

After nine years at Brentford as trainer and acting manager he became the manager of Notts County in 1969. Their success was phenomenal as County went from Division Four to One with the opprobrium of 'Land of the Giants' given to them by critical opponents. A team of tall players out-muscled and out-jumped the opposition as the team played to its strengths. The side did, however, contain the brilliant midfield skills of Scottish International Don Masson.

In 1975 Notts County were giving performances that impressed the United Board. John Hassall approached Jack Dunnett, his opposite number at Notts County about the possibility of taking Sirrel. A deal was struck, and the new manager took up his position at Bramall lane in October 1975. Sirrel lasted less than two years. Sirrel's ability to work with little money no doubt impressed the United directors. His arrival saw him dismantle the team that nearly made it into Europe. His replacement youth policy produced some very good footballers. But things were not right on the playing field, or in the dressing-room or boardroom.

Sheffield United shirt c. 1974
The club badge is the City of Sheffield coat of arms

Daily confusion with the manager's instructions amongst players on the training pitch combined with hostilities between manager and directors to produce dire results. It was four months into his reign before United achieved their first victory. In January 1976 United went six games without scoring a single goal. Relegated by March, United then won their only two away games of the season, then strangely lost only once in their final six games. The statistics said it all—scored 22, conceded 82. A few weeks later Tony Currie left for Leeds for a fee of around £250,000. The new season held out promise, but the results were erratic. United finished eleventh attracting crowds just above the 10,000 mark. Further poor performances culminated in a dreadful run of defeats and the departure of Sirrel as United stood second from bottom.

The club was in what seemed to be terminal decline. Money was tight, the players were in cliques and some of the coaching staff were the objects of their ridicule. Sirrel had a communication

View from the Lane End: Eddie Colquhoun takes the acclaim in 1975

problem and his speaking in riddles confused the most eager of professionals. Sirrel's manner could be abrupt, which alienated both the senior players and the directors. His behaviour was, to say the least, eccentric and his pre-training session penalties, taken into an empty net after a blast of a whistle he held around his neck, would result in the manager taking the acclaim of the empty Shoreham End Kop when the ball went in. Sirrel claimed an unquestionable pedigree as a respected coach who had done wonders at Notts County. He blamed the United Boardroom for the situation. For Sirrel the most memorable example of the chaos at Bramall Lane was realising, on his arrival, that the club had signed as a full-time professional an Irish-born player who was registered disabled in his home country.

What United got was a man for whom the word 'dour' was invented. Scottish, Protestant, soberly dressed and with a face dominated by a large tooth, he was enigmatic if not photogenic. Money, the perennial problem of Sheffield United, was the main issue. The situation in his eyes was so hopeless that within weeks of arriving at Bramall Lane, Sirrel had offered his resignation. The Chairman did not help matters. In Sirrel's memory, John Hassall would greet him each day by entering his room asking, 'Who've we sold today?' Faced with this reality the solution had to be youth development. To this end Sirrel persuaded the club to buy a Victorian property in Sheffield's Nether Edge district, which he named Moncrieff House. This became a hostel for youth team players; at its peak some 12 players lived there. Under Sirrel, Simon Stainrod, Tony Kenworthy and Keith Edwards made their debuts, all aged 17. Another home-produced talent Gary Hamson went to Leeds in July 1979 for £140,000 after 123 first team games. Some decent service was also received from John McGeady, Steve Ludlam and Steve Conroy.

Sirrel claims he never had a backroom staff, which is his way of criticising the contributions of Cecil Coldwell and Alan Hodgkinson. He was unable to win the respect of senior players and the methods employed at Notts County did not work at Bramall Lane. He could not explain why the United players hated the monotony of constant five-a-side games. When the first team played the reserves, constant references to Notts County did not endear him to the United players and stopping Tony Currie in training to inform him, in front of everyone, what Don Masson would have done in similar circumstances was not a winning move. Those involved in the club at the time insist that Sirrel was sacked in late 1977. Sirrel claimed he walked out after resigning. He resumed his old position at Notts County a few months after leaving Bramall Lane, and continued to lecture at Lilleshall. He received an honourable mention in the autobiography of Sir Alex Ferguson. Asked in 2003 if he regretted his time at Sheffield, Sirrel responded:

> No… I couldn't do what I wanted to do. The Board held me back. The players weren't up to the job. I don't see it as my fault, I was the best trainer coach of my era…

Happy Harry: Harry Haslam

Succeeding Jimmy Sirrel as United manager in 1978 was Manchester-born Harry Haslam. Strictly speaking, he was successor to Cecil Coldwell, who had taken the managerial job on a temporary basis, but successive defeats in January of 1978 forced the board to look for a man with more managerial experience. An undistinguished footballing career saw Haslam play only two League games for Oldham and seven for Leyton Orient. The one-time Manchester United apprentice might reflect on what could have been had the war not hindered his playing career. Living up to his nickname, the cheerful character arrived at Bramall Lane from Luton Town, where he had, at one time, been employed in the commercial office before moving on to scouting, before being appointed assistant manager. When Luton manager Alec Stock left in 1972, Haslam was appointed manager and built a reputation for both bringing young players through, and being very astute in the transfer market. Such qualities obviously appealed to a club with no money.

Whilst Haslam had led Luton to Division One six years previously, his start at Bramall Lane was not very impressive. United won only six of the season's remaining 16 games. Things were not right with the playing staff, consequently the summer of 1978 saw a massive turnover; nine players left and twelve arrived. Those leaving, however, included the most promising youngsters in Keith Edwards, Simon Stainrod, Imrie Varadi and Ian Benjamin. Their departure, in some instances, brought in very good transfer income. Their replacements, whilst experienced, were not able to last the pace.

Haslam brought in talent from distant shores and is remembered for allegedly attempting to sign a relatively unknown 17-year-old by the name of Diego Maradona. Haslam instead returned from his 1978 Argentine scouting mission with fringe international Alex Sabella. Two players joined United from the recently-formed US Soccer league. Barry Butlin and Jeff Bourne had vast experience in English football but had sought out the riches of the States and were now seeking a final pay day. Three other players came from abroad—Len de Goey from Sparta Rotterdam for £130,000 and Pedro Verde from Spanish club Hercules Alicante. The main purpose of Verde seemed to be one of keeping his fellow Argentinian Alex Sabella company. Playing only six games in his time at Bramall Lane, Verde is remembered only for taking home the Sheffield and Hallamshire County Cup—one of the few games in which he played and scored. The disappearance of the trophy provoked a police inquiry as to its whereabouts. Some 20 years later, Verde was revealed as the uncle of Manchester United's Juan Sebastian Veron. Haslam also brought in Martin Peters, the 1966 England World Cup winner. Perhaps Haslam's enduring legacy to the English game should be for bringing with him to Bramall Lane South American assistants. The Uruguayan, Danny Bergara, became his senior coach and the Argentinean, Oscar Arce, taught the youth team and scouted for Haslam.

As part of the £160,000 United paid for Sabella in the summer of 1978, his Argentine club, River Plate, played United in a friendly at Bramall Lane in late summer 1978. A crowd of 22,000 turned out to see a 2–1 victory for the visitors who included five of the World Cup-winning squad. Sabella certainly brought the crowds in; 19,000 attended for his first game against Orient; 36,000 watched a League Cup tie against Liverpool weeks later. Whilst the Argentinean had sublime skill, he was too often two passes ahead of his

United's first black footballer
of the twentieth century
Ian Benjamin, being chaired by
team-mates Dougie Brown and
John Flood on hearing of his
call-up to the England under-18
team in 1979

mediocre team-mates. Results were disappointing—United did not win once in seven games in late autumn and crowds fell to below 12,000. Away form was awful—just two victories all season, United were relegated to Division Three for the first time in their history in May 1979.

Having lost the opening game of the 1979–80 season, United went on a winning run to the top of the table before facing Wednesday at Hillsborough on Boxing Day. Despite the 11am kick off, the game was watched by a crowd of 49,300. United lost 4–0 in an occasion still celebrated by Owls fans as the Boxing Day Massacre United found it hard to win for the next four months. The following season proved equally dissapointing and by January 1981 successive defeats and Cup knock-outs provoked chants of 'Haslam Out'. In response, citing ill health, Haslam offered his resignation and was replaced by Martin Peters. On the final day of the 1980–81 season, United needed a point at home to Walsall to avoid relegation. After conceding a penalty in the 88th minute and staring at Division Four, United were themselves awarded a penalty in injury time. With the regular penalty takers unwilling to take responsibility for such a momentous kick, it was left to Don Givens, who placed the ball slowly in the keeper's arms. United were relegated. Interestingly, their two-goal positive goal difference is the only time a team has been relegated with a goal surplus. Furthermore, United only sank into the bottom four of the table that season on the final whistle. Haslam died five years after his departure from Bramall Lane.

Three careers are presented. The three players epitomise football in this decade, representing as they do the glamorous maverick, the emergence of the black football player in the English game, and the opening up of the English game to global football talent. One such individual spent eight years at Bramall Lane and played for England. Another lasted only months before leaving on a trajectory that was never fully realised, but did bring international recognition at youth level. The final character nearly made a World Cup winners squad, but found himself in the English Division Three less than two years later. He was to attain more international caps upon leaving United and became assistant manager to two national teams.

The Mercurial: Tony Currie

Brilliant footballers bring problems for Sheffield United fans and managers. From the 1960s those with proven or promised abilities have left Bramall lane for glory and greater riches elsewhere. Tony Currie, a footballer forever associated with Sheffield United, was a football genius who left Bramall lane in 1976 seeking trophies and footballing glory, only to return a decade later in a new life.

The story begins in Cricklewood, North London. The formative men in Currie's early life were a younger brother and three uncles. His father walked out on the family when Currie was just four years of age. Consequently, Currie lived with his mother in an extended family household of 12, three of them were bachelors who doted on their nephew and watched every game of his career.

His footballing ability was evident from an early age; QPR signed Currie on schoolboy forms, but released him at the age of 15. Days later, he began work with a small building firm. The youth team coach at Watford then offered a six-week contract—extended to six months and, soon after, professional terms. One year later, in 1968, United signed the 18-year-old Currie for the strange price of £26,500. Arriving in Sheffield at night and in the rain, Currie's lodgings provided some welcome in the shape of team-mate Paddy Buckley. On Friday nights the pair went greyhound racing and ten-pin bowling. On the pitch, Currie's dream debut saw him score and show maturity beyond his years. To assist this precocious talent, manager John Harris bought a midfield ball-winner called Trevor Hockey who received simple instructions—win the ball and give it to Tony Currie, who then delivered 60-yard passes and scored 40-yard goals.

Tony Currie

No one like Currie had ever worn a United shirt. To the crowd's delight Currie would perform the 'Currie Shuffle'. He would flick his right-foot and feint to the right then move the ball past the bewildered defender with the other foot. The motion was learned by Currie in 1961 from Hendon's Jewish left-winger, Miles Spector. Currie epitomised the changing notion of masculinity in this era. The side-partings that dominated the team photos of the 1960s were confined to history. Players no longer looked like their fathers. With long blond hair and a tight shirt worn over his shorts like a mini-skirt, Currie looked, at times, like a muscular young woman. Occasionally, after dribbling around rival players, he would wave to the Bramall lane crowd or blow kisses to roars of appreciation. In April 1975, in a home game against Leicester, a goalmouth scramble left Currie on the floor in close proximity to former Lane favourite Alan Birchenall. The two smiled, and kissed on the lips, a moment captured by a photographer from a Sunday tabloid. The image became one of the enduring photos in football for that era—two good looking players with long blond hair rubbing noses and lips. The kiss raised questions in the House of Commons; it also produced an offer to both players from a

That's enough!
A colleague attempts to pull Tony Currie away from
the evident charms of former Blade Alan Birchenall
during a match between United and Leicester City in
April 1975

German gay magazine. Neo-Nazis sent death threats to both players and the picture won the European Sports Photograph of the Year.

Currie was good-looking and men, as well as women, knew it. He was strong; there was no hint of effeminacy. Furthermore, he could ridicule those who in appearance and temperament were more traditionally 'masculine'. He once took the ball into attack only to stop, put his foot on it, and gesture in bewilderment for supporting colleagues; the implication was they had to keep up with him. But his most renowned exploit in a United shirt occurred in 1975. A certain Alan Ball, a 1966 World Cup winner then of Arsenal, had made disparaging comments about United days before a match in 1972. He endured mass Blade chants questioning his parentage whenever he appeared at the Lane. During a 1973 fixture and with Arsenal 5–0 up, Ball interrupted play and sat on the ball in a show of contempt for United. In the same fixture some 19 months later, United were 4–0 up in 17 minutes. Prompted by United goalkeeper John Hope, Currie made amends for 27,000 Blades and team-mates past and present and sat on the ball and invited Alan Ball to come towards him and take it off him. At the same time Currie remained enigmatic; few fans knew him off the pitch. He was ill at ease at public events. He kept a low public profile; his social life was spent with his team-mates. He also had a lot on his plate; between 1974 and 1979 his wife had severe depression.

He and a few others in this era changed the nature of players' relationships with fans. Like Stan Bowles, Rodney Marsh and Frank Worthington, Currie was flamboyant, rakish, and precocious. He, like the others, made the game look so easy. As a consequence, Currie received adoration unknown towards footballers in Sheffield. Fans wanted locks of hair, he was the mystery star in the BBC quiz show *A Question of Sport*, poster portraits of him adorned the United souvenir shop. The Shoreham End sang that he walked on water and that his eyes shined like diamonds and that he was the king of the land. Currie had a Ford Popular with a personalised registration plate of 777 PPP. He was occasionally petulant and when substituted trudged off, making his displeasure obvious to all in the ground. His team-mates, however, brought him down to earth. They called him 'Beefy'. The name had nothing to do with physique, it was a nickname coined by Mick Heaton and Len Badger whose idea of a joke was 'Beef Currie'.

He won his first of 17 England caps in 1972 and captained the under-23 side. Ken Furphy gave him the captain's armband in 1974 and again periodically in 1975–76 when Keith Eddy was not playing. His managers did their best to deflate him at times. Ken Furphy criticised him publicly for not training hard and lacking motivation. Jimmy Sirrel described him as 'brilliant in training, not too brilliant in games…'. Currie insisted he loved both training and games:

Tony Currie in Messiah pose
United beat Watford 3–0 in May 1971 to win promotion to Division One

I wanted to be the best every day and every match. What people don't realise is that the other team want to stop that. At times there were two men marking me and kicking me and sometimes that tactic worked. If I did not perform, it wasn't a question of not wanting to know—people don't realise how bloody difficult it was sometimes...

Interviewed in 1993, Currie declared that not once in his United career did he start a match in 100% mint condition. At times the injuries he carried were caused by opponents' boots, at other times by his own recklessness. In 1971 whilst boiling an egg he tipped the pan of scalding water over his right foot. It ballooned and blistered and he limped to the phone box (superstar footballers did not have phones in their homes in this era) to inform John Harris of his disability. Less than 24 hours later and with four pain-killing injections, Currie was hammering balls around in United's 2–0 defeat of Arsenal.

United were relegated to Division Two in 1976. Two years previously, Currie had signed a six-year contract, which would have kept him at Bramall Lane until he was 30. A year later he turned down a move to Manchester United, mainly because the chairman, Dick Wragg, promised to build the United team around him. However, Wragg did promise that if United were relegated they would let him go. Weeks after being relegated, whilst on a team holiday in Gibraltar, manager Jimmy Sirrel told Currie to report to John Harris on returning. The latter put Currie in the car, drove him up the M1 to Leeds and told him of his fate. The fee was a pathetic £265,000. Two years later Currie returned to Bramall Lane wearing a Leeds shirt. The visitors beat United 4–1—Currie scored one of the goals. When he took to the pitch, Blades cheered him and chanted his name. But, when Leeds went 2–0 up, abusive chants about his physique were heard. Approaching the Shoreham End, Currie lifted his shirt to display a torso that was the lightest of his playing career.

The Leeds manager, Jimmy Armfield, bought Currie to replace the brilliant Johnny Giles. Currie became captain of Leeds, played 11 of his 17 England games whilst there, and was in a team full of internationals. But after finishing sixth, Armfield was sacked. After 124 games in three years at Elland Road, Currie asked for a transfer; his wife had to return South. He cost Tommy Docherty at QPR £400,000 and captained the Rangers at Wembley in the 1982 FA Cup Final. In his four years at Loftus Road, he was coached by Terry Venables, who went on to manage England. After 80 games at Loftus Road, a recurring knee problem restricted his appearances—the Astroturf experiment at QPR did not help matters.

Good pay-days were promised to good players in their twilight years. The downside was travelling thousands of miles. A £40,000 fee took Currie to the Canadian Toronto Nationals. Unfortunately, the five-month contract promising £11,000 collapsed after eight weeks. Currie limped home with just two weeks' pay. Aged 33, Currie made his debut in the Vauxhall-Opel League for Chesham United, a small Buckinghamshire outfit his brother was captain of. The appearance of Currie doubled the normal gate. Meanwhile, at Bramall Lane, chairman Reg Brealey had obviously been told wondrous stories about Currie, and offered him a three-month contract. The United manager, Ian Porterfield, was not keen on the idea and nothing came of it. There was no end to the Currie farce; Southend signed him on a three-month trial, but on his debut he ran out of the tunnel and, stepping over the touchline, sustained an injury. Sidelined for six weeks, he managed two reserve games before being released.

Next stop was Torquay in Division Four, where his old QPR colleague David Webb was manager. Whilst still a cut above anyone else on the pitch, a lack of pace meant flying tackles sometimes connected. After 15 games the knee played up again, and Currie returned to London to deal with two types of pain—the physical one of throbbing ligaments and the mental one of divorce. Unable to play for a year, he had time to reflect on the future; it was not looking good. Wiped out financially following the divorce, Currie returned to the family home. A job in a video shop did not last and his attempt at cab driving ended when the car blew up. Drinking too much, out of work and broke, Currie bought a one-day bus pass and toured London taking photos of historic sights.

The decade that fashion forgot
Relaxing on Lindrick golf course are Ted Hemsley, Tony Currie, Cecil Coldwell and Alan Hodgkinson

While attending Tony Kenworthy's testimonial in Sheffield in 1986, Currie met and later married a local girl. His presence brought the realisation among many Blades that their hero could do with a hand. A benefit game was organised and on a Sunday afternoon in 1986, 26,000 people turned out for him at Bramall Lane. Some great players gave their time that day—Geoff Hurst, Alan Hudson, Billy Bremner, George Best, and Frank Worthington. A year later when the Football in the Community scheme began at Bramall Lane, a high-profile name was sought. Currie has had the job for 20 years now and Blades, young and old, male and female, still ask for his autograph.

A cap awarded to Tony Currie
England v Sweden 1978

A New Look: Ian Benjamin

Making his United League debut in April 1978 in a 4–0 defeat at Cardiff was a 17-year-old who has two claims to posterity for Sheffield United. One is that he was the first black player to play for the first team in the twentieth century. The other was that he was the first player in the club's history to have Tracey as a forename. Ian Tracey Benjamin came on as a sub at Ninian Park and took up a central midfield position next to the former captain of Scotland, Bruce Rioch. History was made.

Born into a family of 11 children on the Caribbean island of St Kitts, Benjamin came to England when his parents migrated to work for Nottingham transport. A strong Methodist household produced two professional footballers—his brother Tristram played for Notts County and Chesterfield. Turning down the offer of schoolboy forms with Nottingham Forest because he supported Notts County, Benjamin came to the attention of United whilst playing schools football in Nottingham. After negotiation with United's scout, Neville Briggs, Benjamin signed schoolboy forms at Bramall Lane, aged 15. He arrived in Sheffield with just a change of clothes and no football boots. A week later he turned out for the 'A' team whilst lodging in United's newly-established hostel at Moncrieff House. A shopping expedition courtesy of Sheffield United saw him with both boots on his feet and clothes on his back.

Aged 15 Benjamin played twice for the reserves and at 17 made his first appearance for the United first team in a friendly match against the Argentines of River Plate. He did okay with his first touch, and spent the remainder of his 20 minutes supplying Alan Woodward. His next home game was in the final match of the 1978–79 season in which United need to win by a seven-goal margin to avoid relegation. Benjamin scored two penalty goals in a 2–2 draw with Leicester. This was no mean feat. The mid-season departure of Jimmy Sirrel brought in Harry Haslam. For this big relegation fixture responsibilities were somewhat confused. United's regular penalty-taker, John Matthews, was injured; thus when penalties were awarded a volunteer was required. Benjamin took the responsibility, and scored his first goal within five minutes of the game starting. The second came in the final few minutes.

Benjamin loved his time at United. His team mates at the hostel looked after him well. United's first team likely lads, Tony Kenworthy and Mike Speight, introduced him to beer at the age of 16, however Benjamin left United in late summer of 1979 at the age of 17. He held for a while the accolade of the most expensive teenager in British football—a record overtaken a few weeks later when Malcolm Allison signed Steve McKenzie for Manchester City from Crystal Palace. Benjamin's transfer was a consequence of the break down of United team-mate Alex Sabella's proposed move to Sunderland. Benjamin left a club for whom he had played just 12 first team games and found himself in the company of internationals and with 5% of the signing-on fee in his bank account. Then a top six first division side, West Brom were famed for their three African-Caribbean players. Benjamin was, he believed, joining a club that positively sought out black players. Life was looking good. What could possibly go wrong?

The answer lies in a number of circumstances, only some of which were in Benjamin's hands. Appearances in the England youth side came to an end by virtue of what Benjamin admits was his own immaturity. Too distracted when in Yugoslavia with local girls and acting big time meant he was never again selected. The move to West Brom produced just one full appearance in two and a half years. Falling out with Atkinson's successor, Ronnie Allen, Benjamin asked six times to be released. He wanted to return to Bramall Lane. The absence of recognition was a mystery, but his arrival at West Brom suggested a degree of intrigue. Having played a couple of United first team games in August 1979, Benjamin travelled to the Hawthornes to play for a Black XI v West Brom in a Testimonial game for the Baggies Ally Brown. The emergence of the African-Caribbean-born players into the Football League meant a full team of black players could be assembled to play exhibition games. Lining up with George Berry, Bob Hazell and West Brom's 'Three Degrees' of Brendan Batson, Laurie Cunningham and Cyrille Regis, Benjamin took the eye of Ron Atkinson then manager of West Brom. The same man specifically watched Benjamin in a West Brom–Sheffield United reserve team fixture. Things got confusing when Benjamin was called back by United when on his way to join the England Youth team. He was then taken by Neville Briggs to

Chelsea visit Bramall Lane in September 1971
A 1–0 United victory was watched by 40,651 hundreds of whom watch from across the cricket pitch

West Brom where he signed professional forms in the West Brom car park. Asked what he wanted in wages, his response of £30 a week was immediately accepted. Holding the status of professional footballer he then played a match against West Brom who signed him days later for £140,000.

The move was a disaster and Benjamin's contract was eventually paid up. Seeking another club, Benjamin trained with Jimmy Sirrel's Notts County. He was then approached by Ron Atkinson, now in charge of Manchester United, who asked him to attend United's training ground. Benjamin duly arrived but in his recollection was ignored and kept waiting for half an hour whilst Big Ron watched a video. Affronted by what he perceived as Atkinson's ignorance, Benjamin refused the three-year contract that Atkinson offered when the video had finished. In Benjamin's evaluation in 2006, the issue was very simple:

> ...he'd kept me waiting. I would never do that to another player or person. If he'd have turned the TV off, I'd have signed 10 minutes later...

Leaving Old Trafford, Benjamin played that night in a trial game for Notts County reserves. Big Ron rang him the next day and repeated the offer—Benjamin again refused. A two-year deal at Peterborough rescued Benjamin from oblivion.

Playing professional football until his mid-30s, Benjamin was the epitome of the journeyman. The list of league clubs reads: Northampton, Cambridge, Chester, Exeter, Southend, Luton, Brentford and Wigan. His non-league line-up reads: Kettering, Chelmsford and Corby. He then became player-manager of Southern league Raundes, and then took a similar position at Worboys Town and later Wisbech Town in the Jewson League. Benjamin scored 149 goals in just over 550 League appearances. He had a fine career in football, and to this day reminisces with affection about Sheffield United for the opportunity they gave him and the way he was treated. Now working in the tool hire business, he combines his day job with the part-time manager's job at Soham Town FC.

> **Until 1978, players from overseas were to all intents barred from the English game. In February 1978, a meeting of the European Community declared that all football associations under its auspices were to allow freedom of movement of players from the Continent. This was ratified by the English FA, who stipulated that they would limit foreign imports to two per team. The Professional Footballers Association admitted foreign imports after the Football League had accepted freedom of contract. Whilst the English game had previously had the occasional foreigner, the trickle became a flood from 1978. Whilst the city of Sheffield had some of the lowest levels of immigrants of any similar sized place in Britain, Sheffield United FC were at the forefront of the arrival of overseas footballers.**

The Alternative Maradona: Alex Sabella

Argentina assembled a wonderful team for the 1978 World Cup which they hosted and won. The startling playing talent evident in the team saw two English club managers arrive in the capital Buenos Aries shortly after the finals. One was Harry Haslam of Sheffield Untied. The 20-hour flight was to a destination considered very insecure. Argentina at the time was in economic turmoil and controlled by a military Junta in a regime known, retrospectively, as 'The Time of the Generals'. Some 30,000 Argentineans died at the hands of the regime. The dead are commemorated collectively today as 'The Disappeared'. When not torturing or murdering, a couple of the Generals held important positions in football clubs; the regime was *de facto* in control of the Argentine Football Association. Nothing moved in or out of the game without their knowledge. The military were to grant the national team coach Cesar Luis Menotti three months of daily preparation with the national squad. As a consequence of such preparation, Argentina beat Holland 3–1 in the final. Three players in the World Cup winning squad—Alberto Tarantini, Ricardo Villa, and Osvaldo Ardiles, left Argentina soon after the final to join English clubs. The latter two joined Tottenham; Tarantini joined Birmingham. A fourth Argentinean joined Sheffield United. His name was Alex Sabella.

Posterity claims that the delegation from Sheffield United was offered a 17-year-old footballing boy wonder by the name of Diego Maradona. Then playing with Argentinos Juniors, Maradona had missed the final 22 of the Argentine World Cup squad but was recognised as a future football genius. The story circulating for over 25 years claims that Sheffield United could have taken Maradona for somewhere around £500,000, but declined. One suggested reason was that the United Board considered the price too high for an untried youngster. Another more contentious reason was that the Generals would only permit Maradona to leave upon receiving a substantial financial kick-back which United would not pay on moral grounds. Context is everything here. United were broke and would never have paid such a sum for a player who was just a boy.

One thing that United did know and did pay for was local knowledge. In the Argentine political milieu a respected middle-man was essential for business. United obtained this in the shape of Antonio Rattin, who had achieved infamy in English footballing history in 1966 when as captain of Argentina he had refused to leave the Wembley pitch having been sent off on a World Cup quarter-final against England. Rattin was, in fact, the first professional footballer ever sent off at Wembley. After a nasty game, the normally taciturn England manager Alf Ramsey refused to allow the England players to swap shirts with the South Americans and even called the Argentines 'animals'. The Argentine nation never forgot this insult. The notoriety Rattin achieved in England was matched only by the adulation with which he was held in Argentina. A one-club career at the mighty Boca Juniors of Buenos Aries meant Rattin was already the stuff of legend. His contempt for the English at Wembley brought him further adulation. The United chairman John Hassall paid for Rattin to visit Sheffield in 1978 and have his photograph taken against a

The Blades' Argentinian star Alex
Sabella celebrated in badge form 1978

Bramall Lane backdrop. The photograph was a precursor to a financial deal, which saw Rattin employed as an Argentine talent scout for United.

How this situation came about begins with the Uruguayan, Danny Bergara, who arrived at Bramall Lane in 1978 as a coaching assistant to Harry Haslam. Bergara was one of five brothers and two sisters born in 8,000 square miles of arable farmland in the middle of the Roucha Province in Uruguay. When his father died in 1949, his mother found the upkeep of the estate too much and moved the family to the capital city of Montevideo. Bergara proved to be a good footballer and was to play for Racing Club at the age of 16, and the Under-18 national side. He was top scorer in the South American Champions League in 1959–60. This ability attracted the attention of European teams and in 1962 Bergara travelled to Spain to sign for Real Majorca where he remained for five years and where he was top scorer for four consecutive seasons. He later played for Seville and Tenerife, before a bad injury ended his career.

Marriage changed Bergara's destiny. He met his English-born wife in Palma, Majorca while she was working for a travel company owned by Doug Ellis, the chairman of Aston Villa. The pair decided to seek out a new life in England and in 1972 moved to St Albans. Bergara then began searching for a job in football. A relative of his wife's knew Harry Haslam, then manager of Luton. Bergara contacted him and took coaching sessions for the Luton youth team on a voluntary basis. Impressing Haslam, Bergara acquired a work permit courtesy of the Luton Town chairman, who told the Home Office he was loading lorries for his haulage firm. Whilst Bergara had studied coaching in Spain, he had never actually coached a team before, but as he explained in 2003:

> I could kick a ball better than most, so when I told them to do something, I could usually demonstrate it for their benefit.

Bergara enrolled on the FA coaching programme at Lilleshall led by the FA Technical Director, Charles Hughes. Hughes had only played for England at amateur level. He was a proponent of the long-ball game. Bergara considered the teaching awful, but managed to restrain his criticism to become the first ever foreigner to qualify under the English coaching system. By 1980 Bergara was coach of the England youth team. In the same year, whilst compiling an intelligence report on Nottingham Forest for Nacional of Uruguay before the two sides met in the Intercontinental Cup in Japan, Bergara met Brian Clough and asked in mock innocence asked what system he played. The response was enlightening:

We don't play in our own half, we play in the opposition's, so we get it into their half as quick as we can.

Bergara took this advice during his time as reserve team coach at Bramall Lane, where he started in 1978. The team did not waste time with passes from goalkeeper to full back and was, for a time, top of the table. When Haslam left Bergara remained put to assist Martin Peters and his successor Ian Porterfield at youth and reserve team level. Leaving Bramall Lane in 1988 Bergara managed Rochdale, thereby becoming the first foreign-born manager in the history of the English game. In later years he took charge of Stockport County, leading them to Wembley four times in three years. Later again, he managed Rotherham and Doncaster, and in 2005, aged 63, was scouting for Sunderland. Whilst Bergara did not set the English footballing world alight, his presence was historic. Claiming no knowledge of the Sabella-Maradona saga, Bergara was significant for paving the way for later foreign-born coaches. He also brought another South American to Bramall Lane who was to make the initial contact with Antonio Rattin.

The character of Oscar Arce is crucial to the Argentine story. Whilst playing in South Africa, Arce met and later married an Englishwoman. Living in England in the late 1970s Arce became youth team coach at Milwall and got to know Bergara by virtue of attending coaching courses at Lilleshall. When Haslam asked Bergara who he might appoint to coach at youth level at United Bergara recommended Arce. Arce was thus to contribute to United's playing personnel in two ways. The obvious one was his tutorage of the young. But in this instance he was pivotal in negotiating with Rattin to recruit Argentine talent for United. He was also crucial in bringing Pedro Verde to United from the Spanish club Heracles. Somewhat appropriately Arce was to leave United shortly after Verde disappeared with the County Cup trophy.

Alex Sabella 1978
The stripes disappear to accommodate sponsors

Arce was a footballing journeyman. He had played for Estudiantes in 1962 before joining Medellin in Colombia the following year. He then had a brief spell with Spanish side Real Oviedo before signing for Aston Villa in 1968. He reputedly told Villa he was an international, this was not strictly true and once found out was quickly released by Villa manager Tommy Cummings. This marked the end of Arce's playing career. His career as a coach then progressed, but for short-lived periods: Estudiantes 1972–73, Norwegian side Sogndal 1973–74, Millwall Youth 1974–77, Sheffield United Youth 1977–81, Swiss side Sion 1981–82, and then Ivorian side Mimosas (1982–83). After a ten-year break from football Arce resumed coaching Mimosas and is now coaching in Morocco. This global football figure would travel wherever a position needed filling. With a wealth of experience and speaking English and Spanish he was to contact Rattin and arrange the deal on behalf of Sheffield United.

Stepping on the plane to Buenos Aires in July 1978 was Harry Haslam. Haslam had also invited the managers of Spurs and Arsenal, Keith Burkinshaw and Terry Neill respectively, to travel with him. The former did, the latter

Alex Sabella in the River Plate stadium April 2006

had second thoughts. The Arsenal board thought the political situation too risky to travel. At the last minute Neill's place on the plane was taken by the *Sheffield Star* journalist Tony Pritchett at the invitation of Haslam. Interviewed 25 years later, Burkinshaw explained that whilst not a personal friend of Haslam the pair were familiar by virtue of having discussed what to do with a problem player that Newcastle (where Burkinshaw was assistant manager) had bought from Harry Haslam when at Luton. A surprise call from Haslam to Burkinshaw in 1978 saw him being offered a World Cup winner in the figure of Osvaldo Ardiles. This player apparently could have been United's but the United board could not afford the fee asked and could not pay the wages a World Cup winner would command. Meanwhile, Haslam told Burkinshaw he was going to Argentina to 'see a lad play' and if he liked him, would bring him back. There was no mention in Haslam's conversation of the name Maradona.

The trip proved fruitful for Tottenham. Liking Ardiles from what he had seen from the televised World Cup, Burkinshaw phoned his chairman 24 hours after having landed in Argentina and secured authorisation to pay the £320,000 transfer fee. Upon signing Ardiles brought a mate with him, and suggested Burkinshaw sign him as well. This was Ricky Villa, who whilst only playing twice in the 1978 World Cup finals, had similarly caught the eye of Burkinshaw. Offered at the same price as Ardiles, Burkinshaw signed him five minutes later. The two Argentineans were not paid any more or less than their top paid British-born colleagues. The pair proved brilliant signings and won Tottneham the FA Cup in 1981. That no more players from the Argentine arrived at Tottenham was a consequence of what Burkinshaw refers to as 'problems' with agents and Argentine club presidents. Whilst the agents were doing nothing illegal, monies of such volume were being taken by them and the Argentine club president as to cause consternation in the Spurs boardroom. Such payments also went against the grain for the honest Barnsley mining-village born Burkinshaw who was to walk away from Spurs bitter at the commercial ethos that in his opinion ruined the club.

Haslam and Pritchett were met in Argentina by Arce and Rattin. The Argentine press got wind of the contingent and published stories that they had come to buy the young football genius known colloquially as 'the boy'. Maradona's reputation in Argentina, even at the age of 17, was huge, but he was largely unknown in Europe. Or was he? Haslam, according to Jimmy Burns' book *Hand of God*, met Maradona and learned that, in a country led by the military and facing economic meltdown, the presence of US dollars in the right hands could be fruitful in negotiating the transfer of football talent. Maradona mentions in his autobiography that he had learned that he was interesting English clubs in 1978 but does not specify if any of the interest came from Sheffield United. According to Burns the £500,000 starting price for the youngster was way beyond what United could afford. This is perfectly plausible.

Shortly before his death in 2001 Tony Pritchett was asked about the circumstances of the Sabella transfer. The response was succinct but adds to the mystery. According to Pritchett, United were seen with the right people but did not make the right decision:

> *In Argentina to be seen with Rattin was like walking with Christ. He was the 'link man'.*
> *Harry Haslam took Oscar Arce with him, but neither seemed aware of Maradona. Anyhow 24 hours later in Buenos Aires their press said we'd come to steal 'the boy'. I honestly don't think Haslam was after him. Anyway Arce went missing for a couple of days so we were left with no-one who could translate. Spurs took Ardiles and Villa. Then Maradona was offered to United by Boca Juniors—at £600,000 plus well-greased palms to certain people to get him out of the country. The greasing was for the Generals, some politicians and some FA figures. They also made it known that there would be an uproar if Maradona left. United didn't have that money. The money man at Bramall Lane was Albert Bramhall and he died soon after. I rang the 'Sunday Express' and told them about Spurs and made myself a few quid for the story… United ended up with Alex Sabella for £160,000. Haslam thought he'd got a world beater, but he became a liability—he didn't want to train on match-day and had different methods of preparation to the rest of the team…*

Visiting Argentina in 2006, I discovered that there were different versions again of the Maradona story. Undisputably, the middle man was Rattin, who explained that he had been contacted in early 1978 by Oscar Arce (whom he had not previously known personally) and had been flown to Sheffield at the club's expense to meet Haslam and had been given the accolade of United's South American scout. For this he was paid US $400 a month for ten months. He had no ambitions to scout and no knowledge of the English language. With the hindsight of 26 years, Rattin realises that a command of English and a better business brain could have made him millions as a South American player agent. According to Rattin, United's target was a 30-year-old Boca Juniors midfielder by the name of Mario Zanavria. However, watching a Boca v River Plate game, Haslam was impressed by Sabella which was fortuitous because the 30-year-old Zanavria was not interested in United's offer. To facilitate matters, Rattin introduced Haslam to the president of River Plate and a deal was struck to take the 22-year-old Sabella. Sabella knew nothing of Sheffield United so Haslam, in Rattin's memory, used English football history to impress upon Sabella the opportunity the move offered for him to lead United out at Wembley. The fee according to both press reports and United's records was £160,000. Rattin, however, insists that the fee was US$60,000 (£40,000 sterling), a small difference of around £120,000. The financial discrepancy was never explained.

Sabella had two years legal training before becoming a professional footballer. He replied to questions in a considered manner. His transfer fee was thus a matter between the respective club presidents. His wage at Bramall Lane was better than at River Plate but the same as his team-mates. He received a signing-on fee but it was not notable. Sabella's arrival in Sheffield saw the terracing open on a Saturday morning to permit 3,000 fans to greet his first training session. His United debut in August 1978 produced a 2–1 defeat by Orient in front of 19,000, and hundreds of torn-up newspapers as fans attempted to re-create the Argentine World Cup ticker tape welcome. Whilst mercurial in touch and in his ability to go around opponents in comparison to his team mates, Sabella objected to any form of training, however light, on match days and found training harder than he was used to. At away games Sabella had his own room—his team-mates had to share. The River Plate side Sabella had arrived from contained seven of the national side and won games easily. In England he was part of a team

Antonio Rattin
United's Argentine agent and former captain of
Argentina and Boca Juniors

that had to fight for victory. The English game was frenetic and technically inferior to that to which Sabella was accustomed. Brilliant in short passing and industrious, Sabella was technically untouchable in the division. Consequently Sabella attracted the attentions of Terry Venables at Crystal Palace and Ken Knighton at Sunderland. The offer of £600,000 from the latter was turned down in the belief a bigger club might take him. The visit of Mrs Sabella to Sunderland on a winter's afternoon may also have influenced the choice. Sabella lived for a few months in a Sheffield hotel with Steve Finnieston, then bought a house in the Waterthorpe suburb; Oscar Arce lived 50 metres away. A regular visitor was Danny Bergara and when Oscar Arce moved house the new arrival was fellow Argentine, Pedro Verde. Sabella was thus never short of Spanish speaking company which, in hindsight, he believes held his footballing progress back.

Sabella left United after 88 games and 10 goals. At the end of the 1978–79 season, Jimmy Adamson took him to Leeds for £400,000. Sabella played against Manchester United and Liverpool in his first year, but made only 22 appearances for Leeds in two seasons. The main reason was a change of manager. Adamson's replacement, Allan Clarke, wanted one-touch training—every day. This was anathema to Sabella, who left Leeds returning to Argentina to join Estudiantes, now managed by Carlos Bilardo. This player-manager combination saw Estudiantes win the championship in 1982 and 1983. Sabella also played eight times for the national team upon his return.

Retiring as a player in 1989, Sabella linked up with his former River Plate team-mate (and the youngest ever World Cup winning captain) Daniel Passarella. The latter took charge of River Plate for five seasons with Sabella as his assistant. The duo then managed the Argentine national side from 1994 to 1998 and held a similar position with the Uruguayan national side between 1999 and 2001. Leaving for Palma in the Italian Serie A, their European adventure lasted just 40 days. They then led Monterey to the Mexican championship before managing Corinthians of Sao Paolo in 2004. In January 2006 the pair returned to where it all began—River Plate, where Sheffield United nearly bought the world's greatest footballer— or didn't, depending on who you believe.

> By the late 1970s local and national media had established the 'newsworthy' status for football-related disorder and violence in Sheffield. In 1977, the first significant political response to football hooliganism in the city resulted in the delivery of a petition by local councillors to national government, demanding some form of action. Meanwhile, Blades fans in 1979 invaded the pitch as their team drew 2–2 with Leicester City and were thus relegated. Some fans attacked visiting players. Amazingly the club (and fans) escaped punishment from the FA. Bramall Lane was, at times, a tricky place for visiting fans. That said, between 1952 and 1979 on only one occasion did home attendances dip below the five-figure mark—in 1969, 9,645 watched a game against Blackburn Rovers. In seeking to make fans comfortable United overstretched themselves. The building of the South stand on the former cricket pitch ruined United this decade. Its funding and construction was dependent on average crowds of 31,000, which United had attained in only three seasons since 1946. The pursuit of a modern stadium was, however, a seductive idea amongst both supporters and the local media. The seduction of the foreign born, however, proved short-lived, it was 13 years after the departure of Sabella that United next signed a foreign player. Players were no longer the first individuals that Blades fans discussed over the next decade. Their significance diminished in conversations about the club, overshadowed by the activities of chairmen and managers.

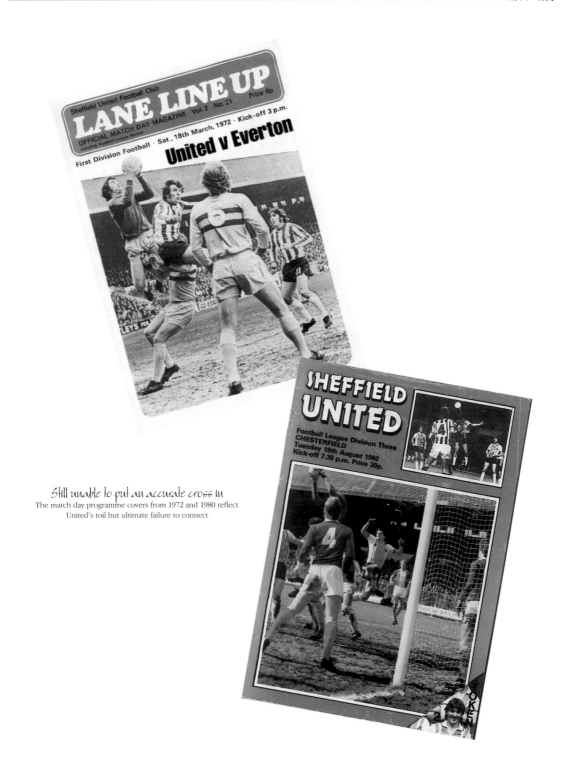

Still unable to put an accurate cross in
The match day programme covers from 1972 and 1980 reflect
United's toil but ultimate failure to connect

Part of the 10,000 United following on the pitch at Feethams,
Darlington, as United win the fourth division championship in May 1982

Chapter 11

Changing Places

A crowd of 16,000 saw United relegated to Division Four on the final whistle of the home match against Walsall in May 1981. United lost 1–0 and dropped into the bottom four of the table for the first time in the season, becoming the first club in Football League history to be relegated having scored more goals than they had conceded. A year later, United were Division Four champions with 96 points and only four defeats. United then moved from Division Four to Division One in eight years. This decade produced probably the most unusual gathering of Blades fans ever when, in May 1984, 400 travelled to Burnley to see the home side lose 2–0 to Hull City. The latter needed to win by three goals to leap-frog United and win promotion. The ninety-four minutes of football was one of the most tortuous in the history of United, but resulted in celebrations in Burnley and on the streets of Sheffield.

Football had a bad press in the 1980s with its associated violence and the deaths at Heysel, Bradford, Birmingham and Hillsborough. The same decade also saw a massive rise in monies pouring into the game via sponsorship and TV revenues. Despite this, the majority of football clubs went through the decade without any form of coherent business plan whilst directors started to pay themselves for running their clubs. Changes were imposed on the game from local and national governments and from the football authorities. In this milieu, the Sheffield United chairman Reg Brealey stressed the romance of local identity and promoted the rhetoric of both 'community' and 'family' in relation to the football club. His vision of wider society saw him instruct United's players to visit prisons, schools and hospitals. At the same time he sought a maximum return for his football investment via a stock market flotation. This decade was dominated by chairman Brealey, his three team managers and three players who produced enough entertainment and controversy to entertain and bewilder Blades fans, often at the same time.

The Workers United?
The industrial base of the city and region changed forever in the 1980s. The change was imposed and provoked resistance which resulted in occasions of mass public disorder. The 13 weeks of the national steelworkers' strike of 1980 resulted in 160 arrests in Sheffield. At one time 1,200 police officers were dedicated to dealing with keeping the peace. The miners' strike of 1984 lasted the best part of a year and was centred around the South Yorkshire coalfields in what was probably the most bitter industrial dispute in twentieth-century Britain. The strikers and those supporting them received a multitude of injuries at the hands of riot police. Some 1,700 strikers were arrested in the region and the policing costs for South Yorkshire were close to £40 million for the year. The dispute spilled over to football. Matches at Bramall Lane saw disorder between fans and police and rallying cries in support of the Yorkshire miners and their leader, Arthur Scargill. 'Coal, not dole!' stickers adorned United fans attire, both blazer and designer hooligan wear. By the end of the decade, the manufacturing base of the city remained but with less than a third of its previous workforce. Some figures might suffice here; in 1920 steel production in the area employed 120,000 people, by the late nineties, it was less than 10,000. The 56,000 employed in coal mining in 1971 were less than a thousand in just three pits by the late 1990s. Lost with this was the long held belief that the city's football fortunes could affect industrial production.

The streets of Sheffield were spared the rioting by the disaffected young that characterised all major cities in England in the summer of 1981. The despair and rage notable in urban areas elsewhere was largely absent in Sheffield. Whilst sections of Sheffield youth were dominating the UK pop music charts, men steeped in masculine traditions and strength walked the city streets by virtue of the National Union of

Blades acclaim United as Division Four champions after the final match of the 1981–82 season

Mineworkers moving its headquarters from London to Sheffield in 1982, thereby locating itself in its heartland of membership and support. The city council was idiosyncratic, radical and provocative. Sheffield became nationally renowned in the 1980s as the 'Socialist Republic of South Yorkshire'. Flying the red flag of international socialism on the roof of the Town Hall on the wedding day of Prince Charles and Lady Diana Spencer was not the most diplomatic of gestures. Neither was the 5,000 strong Thatcher Unwelcoming Committee that greeted the Prime Minister's visit to Sheffield in 1987. There was no escaping the city's non-conformist legacy. The city-born former school teacher turned manager of Sheffield Wednesday, Howard Wilkinson, stated in 1984 that Sheffield was 'an area that produces footballers and people that understand football. There's only one gaffer for every 2,000 people'. Some in the status of 'gaffer' however were not up to the task required.

Ghosting Out: Martin Peters
In May 1981, United entered what many considered the purgatory of English football. The season in Football League Division Four was, instead, a chance for United to rebuild and go on to greater things. How United came to be champions of Division Four needs explaining.

Part of the blame for the decline lies with a man who had achieved the pinnacle of football achievement. Martin Peters won the 1966 World Cup with England, but could not transfer his playing abilities to those less talented when employed in a managerial capacity. One of only two English footballers to have scored a goal in a World Cup Final, Peters was famously described by England manager Alf Ramsey in 1966 as 'ten years ahead of his time'. Quiet and easy going, his laid back style concealed a determined character who could give as good as he got from defenders. Born in Plaistow, east London, to a father who worked on the Thames as a lighterman, Peters was a schoolboy centre-half who moved to full-back and played for England as inside-right. Representing England at schoolboy, youth and under-23 level, Peters had played at Wembley at the age of 15 in front of 95,000 people. He captained the England under-23 team and made his debut for the full team only one month before the 1966 World Cup began. He won the World Cup aged 22 and was part of the legendary trio from West Ham alongside Geoff Hurst and Bobby Moore. Versatile and enigmatic throughout his career, Peters had begun his footballing life at West Ham. Signing for Ron Greenwood in 1959, Peters made his first team debut in 1962 and in the three games that he played that week, turned out at right-half, left-back, and replacement goalkeeper. Aged 26 in 1970, Peters moved to Tottenham Hotspur for a then record British transfer fee of £200,000. Despite making 722 League appearances, Peters never made a fortune out of football and was frugal to the point of re-using a teabag when on a pre-season tour of the USA. The financial reward for winning the World Cup was a share of a £22,000 pot which, after tax, brought Peters around £700.

In 1974, Peters won the last of his 67 England caps. A year later he was sold by Spurs to the then second division Norwich for £50,000 where he spent six seasons, five of them in Division One. Peters occasionally captained the side, played until aged 36, and was voted the finest player in the club's history a few years ago. Released in the summer of 1980, Peters joined Sheffield United as player-coach and was promised the managerial position on Harry Haslam's departure. The third division football then on offer at Bramall Lane did not suit Peters, who preferred guile and experience to the knock-about of the lower divisions. Peters was to claim that few of his United team-mates were on the same wavelength. But colleagues also found Peters on a different frequency. On away game stop-overs, Peters would not appear among the

Leader of the pack

Gary Glitter, back row, third from right, before a benefit match at Bramall Lane in 1982
On the right of Glitter stands a character from TV sitcom *Mind Your Language*, four to the left of Glitter is comedian and
TV presenter Charlie Williams who died mid-2006. A Frank Spencer character front right makes up the chosen company

squad until midday and would then eat a lunch of prime steak, allegedly written into his contract. Those around him tucked into scrambled eggs on toast by virtue both of economy and new dietary thinking for high-performance athletes. The smell of sizzling steak did not lead to squad harmony amongst those eating dry toast.

After Harry Haslam was briefly moved upstairs to General Manager in January 1981, Peters presided over a United team that won only three of the season's remaining 16 games. United were relegated on the final day of the season. Peters' one signing, Don Givens, missed the last-minute penalty, which would have ensured third division survival. Peters evident silence when United's regular penalty taker, John Matthews, refused to take the penalty spoke volumes of his leadership. In hindsight, Peters admits he had not the knowledge for the manager's job and his attempts to bring in an assistant failed—the club claimed such money was not available. He was also perturbed by the intense football rivalry in the city. The playground taunts his three children received, coupled with comments from Owls fans made to him when out shopping, was a world Peters was not accustomed to. One year into his three-year contract, Peters met the then new chairman Reg Brealey who arranged a 'mutual agreement' package which saw Peters depart and the club buy his house.

After Sheffield United, Peters quit football and worked in the warranty business with his former West Ham and England team-mate, Geoff Hurst. Today, Peters can be found on the after-dinner speaking circuit. In 2006 he published his autobiography. The text was not particularly revealing about his time at United. Interviews in 2006 revealed that Peters was under medication for bouts of depression.

The Outsider: Reg Brealey

Reg Brealey was a man who produced demarcations in Blades supporters whilst keeping them better informed about the club than they had ever been before. In pursuit of the latter, in the early and mid-1980s, Brealey published a free newspaper available to all supporters titled *Blades News*. He also made himself available to fans, particularly at away games where he would regularly be found standing with the visiting Blades. Aware that the English game was changing, Brealey provided office space for the expanding Promotions and Commercial Departments, realising that football could no longer rely on turnstile revenue for its future. To this end Brealey produced gradations of fandom based on wealth and age. The more discerning could buy comfort and exclusion by joining the Executive Club with its fenced off seating area and luxury away travel (they even flew in a chartered aeroplane for a Southend game in 1984). The Junior Blades appealed to the young fans and the Senior Blades to the elders. Brealey had his finger on the pulse of Thatcherite Britain. A contributor to the Tory Party and part of the General Synod of the Church of England, Brealey was quintessentially an establishment figure. However, the local political establishment did not welcome him as keenly as Blades fans did.

Chairman Reg Brealey amongst the Junior Blades c.1983

Born and bred in Lincolnshire, Brealey made his fortune in property and joined the board of Lincoln City in the 1970s. Brealey was introduced to the chairman of Sheffield United, John Hassall, by Dick Chester who had left Lincoln City to become club secretary at

Bramall Lane. With the club in all sorts of financial problems, Chester suggested to his chairman that he talk with Brealey who had a reputation for corporate problem solving. Following discussions in June 1980, Brealey was invited to become United's finance director. Weeks after being asked, Brealey produced a financial assessment for Hassall which called for the removal of the management of Haslam and Peters and an end to the policy of selling off of the best of the young talent the club nurtured. Not long after United were relegated—to Division Four. Hassall walked out on a club £1m in debt and with an annual trading loss of £725,000. Asked by other directors to be acting-chair, Brealey became full-time on the death of fellow director Albert Bramhall. Aiming to emulate what he did at Lincoln, Brealey attempted to re-capitalise the club and to this end launched a share issue. He underwrote the launch and was left owning 90% of shares at a personal cost of around £1 million. Brealey claims he never wanted to be chairman of United, the job came to him by accident and he remained in it because he was the majority shareholder. Ownership of hotels in the USA and Lincolnshire, restaurants in the Mediterranean and London, a construction company, and, reputedly, two piston aeroplanes and a helicopter made Brealey rich in anyone's language.

Brealey set out producing, promoting and marketing United as 'The Family Club'. What followed over the years was a concerted publicity effort, via merchandising brochures that promoted United as both 'The Caring Club' and 'The Friendly Club'. There was more to Brealey's scheme than profit; in 1982 he outlined his intentions in the *Sheffield Star* explaining that:

> *There is the recession, unemployment and the associated social problems. We see football as a great safety valve, and making our club the Family Club is, I feel, a contribution we can make.*

Brealey had a vision to build the Bramall Centre. In March 1981, Brealey sought planning permission from Sheffield council to demolish the Shoreham end kop and utilise the land behind it to build an 11,000 seat stand with private boxes. Behind this was to be a shopping complex, a 150-bedroom hotel, restaurant and

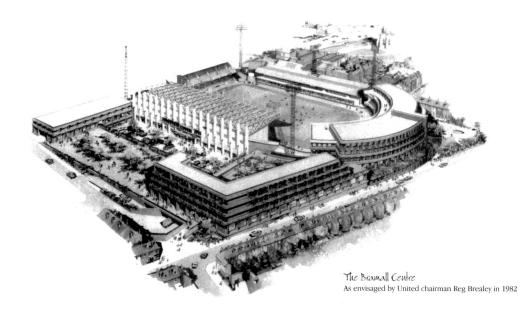

The Bramall Centre
As envisaged by United chairman Reg Brealey in 1982

The Blades 'Hooligan Element' in action at Huddersfield 1989
By the late 1980s the conflict between rival fans was enacted outside of the football stadium

wine bar, sports complex, conference centre and car park. The scheme, costing £5 million, would be financed by a London-based development company called Land Assets and would provide 600 new jobs. In September 1981 Sheffield city councillors declared the plans unacceptable. A stumbling block was the proposed shopping centre; councillors feared it would impact on town-centre trade. Furthermore, the locale was designated a 'Housing Action Area' by the council and the scheme conflicted with their plans. The councillors also wanted an alternative way of financing the project. The following July a new Brealey scheme, this time costing £20m, was submitted. The plan again proposed an all-seat kop, hotel, restaurant, and sports centre, running track and, in addition, proposed a trade warehouse, residential accommodation and, ironically, a plan to bring back cricket to Bramall Lane. The proposal was again rejected by the council and finally dropped when an appeal to the Department of the Environment failed. The refusal by the council was considered political by United supporters. The Tory capitalist was not being allowed to develop facilities for which the renowned Socialist council had their own plans.

Following a Tottenham Hotspur initiative Brealey planned to make United a publicly quoted company. The shares were on sale for two years but no buyer appeared. His personal financial dealings, however, were the subject of unwelcome publicity. Despite winning 'Share of the Year' in 1978 on the stock exchange and being a candidate again two years later, Brealey was investigated by the stock exchange in 1989 and arrested by Fraud Squad officers on suspicion of insider dealing of shares in an Indian-based company he owned. Brealey was acquitted in Crown Court in 1990 of charges under the Company Securities Act 1985. A month later Brealey was arrested in India and questioned on allegations of breaching currency exchange regulations. The issue concerned his chairmanship of the world's largest Jute producing factory, which employed 18,000 people. Accused of stealing £2.5 million from pension funds and not paying wages for six weeks, Brealey claimed in response that the charge was a vendetta against him by a former employee whom he had sacked. He faced further criminal charges in 1991 but the prosecution against him was dropped. The Crown Court judge dismissed the case after only two days and awarded Brealey costs. The company shares, however, were worthless. By March 1993 the company had a trading loss of £4.2 million. Faced with accusations of failing to match employer pension contributions in the mills, an arrest warrant was issued against Brealey by an Indian court, but no extradition order presented. In April 1994 disturbances at the Jute mills saw mobs rampaging and managers beaten and the temporary closure of the mills. The problems were, in Brealey's opinion, due to the inconsistency of suppliers.

Impartiality and the BBC
Brealey's plans to fill the ground were hit by the behaviour of certain sections of United's following. Whilst wanting their behaviour curbed he did not want to pay a bill over which he had no say. This brought another collision with the local political powers. In late 1983 Brealey challenged South Yorkshire Police Authority's legal right to charge for policing at football matches, arguing that since the club had not requested policing, no contract existed between them. Besides, he argued, the issue was a public order matter and therefore policing should be free. Brealey also claimed he could quote figures to show that the costs were higher in South Yorkshire than anywhere else in the country. In response, the police threatened to close Bramall Lane if they considered it to be inadequately policed. A game scheduled for January 30th, 1984, was under threat of having to be played behind closed doors. An impasse followed and by June 1985, United were in debt to the police to the tune of some £122,000. The matter went to the High Court in February 1986, with Brealey telling how he proposed employing a lone police spotter to watch for trouble. This officer would alert others on standby outside the ground and the club would only pay for police called into the enclosure. After a hearing lasting a week, Brealey lost the case and the club was ordered to pay the police for their presence at the ground. The judge stated that police duty at the match constituted 'special police services' within the meaning of the 1964 Police Act, and added, 'if the police attend in order to enable the match to take place, then I consider a request to be implied'. Brealey decided against an appeal to the House of Lords and was left with a debt of £400,000 to the council and legal fees.

In 1981 the Chief Constable of South Yorkshire reported not only on the violence of football fans but the logistical problems they created:

> I doubt if the Football League's programme would be sustainable without the commitment of large units of police manpower to certain matches. That commitment is not only to prevent disorder in the football stadiums, but to patrol nearby areas to ensure that local residents and business people can live or ply their trade without being molested by chanting and often drunken 'invading' supporters. The police service is not organised to hold large numbers of officers as a permanent reserve to deal with public disorder. The reserve which is created must come from the man on the beat. The more frequently we are called upon to deal with incidents such as the city centre problems, and unruly spectators en-route to football matches, the less time officers will spend patrolling the residential estates.

A report from the city council in the early 1980s recommended that the council target those communities which produced the hooligans. The question as to what the targeting would involve was not answered in the report nor did it specify where in Sheffield the hooligans lived. The truth was that the authors had no idea.

The day that produced the biggest disorder in the decade around Bramall Lane was a Saturday in February 1985. On this day, 400 Blades met in pubs in the city centre in expectation of the arrival of their Leeds equivalent hours before the 3 pm kick off. The deployment of some 280 police prevented the factions meeting before the game, but trouble occurred in the ground when United took a 1–0 lead. In response, the visiting fans began breaking seats and throwing them onto the pitch. One group of Blades replied in kind and also released a nautical distress flare in the direction of the visiting fans. Hundreds of Leeds fans then attempted to pull down perimeter fencing, which provoked 50 police to draw truncheons and charge at them aiming blows at their fingers. After the match around 300 rivals clashed in a two-minute running fight a quarter of a mile from the ground. The day resulted in 34 arrests but no reported injuries. Three hours after the match Blades fans fought with Owls fans in a city centre pub that they both inadvertently

United Chairman Reg Brearley 1984
The grandiose claim hung from the South Stand
was for an impending rally by American Evangelist
preacher Billy Graham

found themselves in. The disorder of the day did not impress the city fathers. A meeting between senior police chiefs and council officers resulted in council funding being allocated to the police to prevent any repetition of the disorder. The meeting also discussed the possibility of installing closed circuit television surveillance in Bramall Lane. Despite the words of the politicians and the establishment of specialist offices via the police, those labelled hooligans continued their activities and even celebrated their notoriety.

Whilst the club at boardroom level was seeking both a re-brand and indeed a new brand identity so were some sections of United's following. The core hooligan element from the mid-eighties called themselves the Blades Business Crew, abbreviated to 'BBC'. The term BBC first appeared on a 1985 leaflet produced by one of the gathering. Consisting of an inner clique of 12 mates who attended the same school, the BBC encompassed another 60 who regularly met on Friday evenings to socialise in the pubs on London Road, around half a mile from Bramall Lane. The gathering fought on two fronts, literally. Weekend evenings saw many a confrontation with their equivalents drawn from fans of Sheffield Wednesday in Sheffield city centre. Hostilities between the two groups were based on ideas of trespass and transgression, embedded within personal issues and mutual allegations of bullying. At other times the BBC were involved in confrontations with their equivalents on match days. Regardless of the opponents, those who constituted the gathering preceded conflict with the chant 'B–B–C'.

Following the adoption of the title, metal lapel badges were produced by a Blade. The design borrowed from the club motif but substituted the white rose and scimitars for the skull and crossbones beloved of pirates. Contrary to both police beliefs and popular wisdom, the BBC did not have a quasi-military organisation nor did joining the gathering require any *rite de passage*. The gathering was exclusively male spanning an age range from late teens to mid thirties. A willingness to spend time with fellow Blades and, if need be, assault or be assaulted in the cause were the two most essential requirements. A degree of sartorial nous was expected and thus designer labels proliferated as this Blade gathering emulated hooligan groups throughout the country in becoming part of the 'casual' sub culture of the 1980s.

The gathering borrowed from the most unlikely contexts. A chant premiered in Doncaster bus station on the way home from a match in Hull in 1986 borrowed the tune from Aaron Copeland's *Appalachian Spring* and amended the words to the Shaker folk song popularly known as *Lord of the Dance*. The Blades boast thus declared:

> *Fight, fight, wherever you may be*
> *We are the boys fron the Steel City*
> *And we'll fight you all, whoever you may be*
> *Cause we are the famous BBC*

The police took a dim view of such gatherings and the position of the Police Football Liaison Officer was established in Sheffield in 1980. The officer's primary duty was to liaise with counterparts in other forces to discuss their respective supporters. This position was superseded in the mid 1980s by the position of Football *Intelligence* Officer.

The Blades' hooligan element brought the club a national noteriety. The arrest of Brealey and the consequent press interest brought ever greater unwelcome publicity to Sheffield United. As police and council officials sought to destroy hooligan gatherings Brealey's dreams for the club were destroyed by the council's intransigence and the failure of the appeal to the Department of the Environment. As a consequence Brealey decided to sell his shares and leave United. This proved hard to do. One possible buyer provoked national ridicule for United. The man tasked by Brealey to steady the ship was, fortunately for the club, a national treasure.

The Big Man: Derek Dooley

For over 35 years, a big man was a daily presence at Bramall Lane. Born into a family with footballing ability in the Pitsmoor district of Sheffield in 1929, Derek Dooley was the younger of two brothers whose father was a file cutter at the vast Firth-Vickers factory. Invited for trials at Bradford City, Mr Dooley senior dismissed the approach upon realising that employment in the steel works paid better. Celebrating his 11th birthday in an Anderson air-raid shelter avoiding the Sheffield blitz, Derek Dooley's schooling was conducted in houses via a system known as Home Service Schooling. When the coast was clear, Dooley went to watch his Sheffield Wednesday favourites. Leaving school at 14, he continued to play whilst he earned money. Dooley attracted the attention of those in the know and, aged 15, received a telegram from Lincoln City asking him to report to the Denaby United ground in Rotherham to play for the visitors. He scored the consolation goal, and Lincoln signed him. In three games in the Third Division North, Dooley scored three goals and was chosen for a Sheffield and Hallamshire Under-18 select and promptly scored four in his first game. The trainer of Wednesday asked him afterwards if he was interested in meeting Eric Taylor, Wednesday's General Manager, and the man who picked the team. Dooley signed days later as a part-time professional for the Owls.

Derek Dooley
Striking a typical pose in his Sheffield Wednesday days

People started talking about Dooley as the next big thing in English football—aged 17 he stood 6' 2" and weighed in at 13stones 10pounds. Capable of powerful shooting and a Yorkshire sprinting champion, he had the indefinable asset of attitude—he feared no-one and he could not be intimidated. Turning out for Wednesday teams in the Hatchard and Yorkshire League produced bags of goals—he scored eight in one game. The inevitable first-team debut occurred in 1949. In his first-team career there were only five games in which he did not score and when forced to retire Dooley had scored 64 goals in 63 games for Lincoln and Wednesday. At one time the first division's second highest goal-scorer, Dooley was close to being called up for England duty. Then disaster struck.

A February Saturday at Deepdale, Preston, in 1953 witnessed a tragedy forever etched in the footballing memory of the Sheffield public. An icy pitch was protected by a layer of straw and fertiliser. In the first half Dooley sustained a cut leg, in the second half the same leg was broken in a collision with the Preston goalkeeper. Gas gangrene from the fertiliser entered the cut and, with no antibiotics, Dooley's footballing career was over. On the Saturday night he was in traction in hospital, but 24 hours later he noticed an absence of sensation in his toes. The following day his leg was amputated to his upper thigh. For the next nine weeks Dooley was prostrate in hospital. Married eight months previously and still living with his parents, Dooley now had no home, no job, no trade and a 20-year-old wife. Football tried to help. The Professional Footballers' Association donated £200 and a Testimonial match at Hillsborough saw a Sheffield XI play an International XI in front of a staggering 58,000 in what was the first game played there under floodlights. He received £7,000 from the gate receipts and sacks of mail. Strangers sent money. The total proceeds of all these donations helped Dooley to buy a house for cash. He lives in the property to this day.

The first job offered came from the *Daily Mirror*. The task was simple enough—watch a match and phone the reports in for Sunday morning. In return they paid Dooley what he was getting at Wednesday when his career ended—£14 a week. He did this for two years and got his life together. Then once again he went to see Eric Taylor when his sense of morality was conflicting with the demands of journalism. A Wednesday director at that time, a Mr Gunstone, owned a bakery and gave Dooley a job. Employed as a telephonist-receptionist on £8 a week, Dooley remained at the firm for eight years rising to the position of Assistant Sales Manager. At the same time he was employed as part-time coach to Wednesday's juniors.

With growing commercialisation and revenue sought beyond the turnstiles, clubs in the early 1960s were experimenting with something called Development Funds. Initially Taylor asked Dooley to sell tickets to the Gunstone's work force—he sold dozens and offered to run the scheme. Appointed Wednesday's Pools Manager in 1962 on £20 a week, Dooley no longer coached the juniors as Saturday was his busiest day. Nine years later Dooley was manager of a different sort at Hillsborough—first team manager—in what must be the only example in football of the pools manager converting to team manager. Assuming control when the team were lying eighteenth in the second division, Wednesday were in virtually the same position when he was sacked nearly two years later. His first season saw the club finish fourteenth. A decent start to the second campaign ended with a month of bad results due, in Dooley's opinion, to a mystery virus that infected the entire first team. Just when performances were improving and players were recovering, he was sacked.

His final day in charge was memorable. Believing that people would be too busy with festivities to notice, the Wednesday chairman, Matt Shepherd, sacked Dooley on the morning of Christmas Eve. The staff of the *Sheffield Star* were all in the pub and printers had to rush back to get the special edition out. After 20 years of service Dooley left Hillsborough in tears. Wednesday honoured his contract until the end of the season. But the promise of life-long employment made by the previous chairman was not quite what Dooley expected. Returning to the ground a month after his dismissal he asked about the promise and was offered a job selling match tickets. Disgusted, he walked out and did not return until 20 years later in his role as a director of Sheffield United.

This capable and industrious man was never short of work. Weeks after leaving Hillsborough he became a sales rep for Stylo Matchmaker football boots but gave it up in 1974 to become commercial director for the rivals of his beloved Wednesday. Over the next 30 years Dooley held just about every job there was at boardroom level at Bramall Lane. That he should consider taking a job with United was down to the kindness of John Hassall, the United chairman, who invited him to Bramall Lane to watch a game and offered him a job in the burgeoning commercial department. Dooley turned the pools system around and only Liverpool beat United in being the first English club to carry an advert on the team shirt. The match programme was revamped and Dooley instigated match-day sponsorship. His path from commercial director to club chairman was tied up with the appointment of Reg Brealey as United Chairman. Wanting his football experience on the board Brealey made Dooley an associate director. For the first time clubs were permitted to have one paid director—Dooley became United's in 1985 and got a vote on the board with it. Three years later he became managing director with a hand in everything from mediating between manager and chairman to sorting out ground improvements.

Dave Bassett signing on as
United Manager 1988 in the
company of Managing
Director Derek Dooley

An integral part of the eight-year managerial reign of Dave Bassett, Dooley was a much-respected public figure. Capable of minimising the occasional excesses of Brealey, he became a mediator in the fractious relationship between chairman and manager that characterised the early 1990s. Whilst a natural diplomat, even Dooley could not avoid the controversy of the 1990s. As a consequence he was relieved of his position at Bramall Lane in the early 1990s and for nine months was out of the game. Then, after Chairman Paul Woolhouse's disappearing act, the remaining board members recalled Dooley to become chairman. In doing so he also became the first former professional footballer to become a club chairman. Leaving the board by choice in 1996, Dooley was given the honorary title of Vice-President of the club. The title did not convey his formidable influence in the club's corridors of power. Whilst Dooley's ostensible task was to mix with the directors of visiting clubs and run a few committees, he was consulted on nearly all matters of policy and personnel. He was crucial when hiring and firing team managers throughout the 1990s.

In 1993, Dooley was made a Freeman of the City—the only sportsman in the city's history to receive the accolade. In 2003 he was deservedly recognised in the New Year's honours list with an MBE. This unassuming and dignified man refers to past events as 'pitfalls'—most of us would call them calamities. Fortunately he was never alone, for in Sylvia his wife of 50 years, Dooley had a remarkable woman whose hospitality towards the strangers who found themselves in the United boardroom was legendary.

> One stranger appeared at Bramall Lane courtesy of his friendship with Reg Brealey. The man came from the East bearing untold riches. Seeking to change the profile of Sheffield United the man was, instead, to change his own profile dramatically. In reality he brought no money to the club but flushed out prospective buyers. Which boardroom toilet he would flush provided the good men who ran the club with a scenario they had never had to consider before.

(Photos courtesy Sheffield Newspapers Ltd.)

LUCKY ANDY

Andy Daykin our Commercial Manager was one of the lucky ones. As the man responsible for the arrangements for the concerts from United's point of view, he had the privilege of meeting Bruce Springsteen back-stage and of presenting him with a traditional Sheffield gift.

The Boss (Bruce Springsteen) plays Bramall Lane, 1988
The 25,000 crowd generated so much urine the playing surface suffered damage

Sam the Man?: Sam Hashimi

In March 1990 Blades fans at an evening game at Barnsley sang 'We're so rich it's unbelievable'. What provoked this sentiment hitherto never heard from the mouth of a Blades' fan, was the revelation that chairman Reg Brealey had found a buyer for his shares and, ultimately, the club. The prospective owner was an Iraqi-born London-based hotel owner with a degree in engineering. Initially revealing to fellow directors that potential buyers from the Middle East were interested in the club, Brealey brought the man into the public eye days later. Married with two children and softly spoken, Sam Hashimi was revealed to the media as a buyer who had made an offer for the shares and was willing to take on all outstanding loans and debts.

Brealey revealed Hashimi to the press on the afternoon of an FA Cup tie at Barnsley. With accented English, Hashimi declared his love for the city of Sheffield and United. Next day Blades learned that Hashimi had the financial backing in the shape of four Arab sheiks and an Arab prince. One backer was rumoured to be the Mayor of the Saudi Arabian capital city, Jeddah. The commercial possibilities of Middle East ownership were promoted by Brealey; potentially, he believed, millions of Blades fans were to be found there and United matches could be broadcast live on satellite TV. Brealey even proposed to take a group of fans to Saudi to help the marketing of the club. The Middle East plan did not work out.

The presence of Hashimi caused boardroom chaos, but it did provoke other interested parties to show their cards and attempt to buy Brealey's shares and thus the majority ownership of the club. This is examined in the next chapter.

In 1994, Hashimi decided that a permanent transfer of another sort was needed. His wife Trud had been allowing him to dress in women's clothing, but he insisted on going further and having a full sex change. During a bitter divorce battle, Hashimi suffered the indignity of jail after breaking a court injunction forbidding him to see his two children. After his release came surgery at the Gender Identity Clinic in London costing more than £40,000. When Hashimi returned to Bramall Lane in October 1998 it was as Samantha Kane, a glamorous 5'10' woman. Seeking employment as chief executive of the club, Samantha stated that she had half a million of her own money and several million from Middle East businessmen to invest. The plan was to build a leisure complex and begin an Arabic-speaking satellite channel dedicated to Sheffield United. Granted an audience by the Bramall Lane directors, Samantha stated her intention of making the club another Manchester United, adding 'football is becoming attractive to women, and I'm ideally placed to capitalise on this. I just don't think my sex is an issue'. Samantha was not appointed to the vacant position.

Four years later in July 2002 Samantha was national news when in an historic court case, she challenged the British government in the European Court of Human Rights to be legally recognised as a woman. Hitherto the law in England had failed to recognise an individual's new identity following gender reassignment surgery. Thus, one could argue, they were denied full rights under their new gender and daily life could be both embarrassing and confusing. Whilst the ruling did not overcome UK law, it forced the Judiciary to consider the ruling in future similar legal disputes in England and Wales.

An autobiography, *Samantha Kane—Two-Tiered Existence,* explained how, as a child, Hashimi had played football in Iraq and involved himself in masculine schoolboy pursuits. However, preferring to play with his sisters' dresses and toys, Hashimi believed from a young age that he was a woman in a man's body. Visiting Sheffield to launch her book, Samantha spoke of her plans to be involved in Sheffield United and claimed that becoming the first woman chairman of the football club would be for the good of United. She was also seeking a media career and proposed to launch a soccer magazine aimed at women. By 2004 this individual was neither Samantha nor Sam, but had changed name to Charles. A one-hour documentary, broadcast on BBC1, explored the life of the man, presenting him as both argumentative and tragic. Charles was about to take legal action against the psychiatrist, who had diagnosed 'gender dysphasia', which Charles now considered a mistake.

The Iraqi-born transexual Sam Hashimi/Samantha Cain
A prospective owner of SUFC in 1988 and years later a potential chief executive

Henderson's Relish
Sheffield's very own contribution
to world cuisine. Blades purchase
red and white labelled bottles in
preference to the blue and white

A Tam O'Shanter Blade accessory c. 1980–1982
Best worn with Lonsdale sweatshirt or donkey jacket

Solid artisans with unambiguous sexuality were still in evidence at Bramall Lane. Three arrived in the city to take the managerial reign under chairman Brealey. Two came from north of the border, the other was unequivocally London. All had very different personas and styles of management and all left Sheffield United with a degree of anger.

Take Good Care: Ian Porterfield

Remembered in English footballing history for his famous goal in the 1973 FA Cup Final that saw second division Sunderland beat Leeds, Ian Porterfield was a Scottish born, left-footed midfielder who had arrived at Sunderland in late 1967 from Raith Rovers. Following his 10 years at Roker Park, Porterfield was loaned to Reading and then signed for Jack Charlton, then managing Sheffield Wednesday, in 1977. A keen footballing brain was recognised by the senior figures at Hillsborough and many, including Porterfield, considered that the manager's job was his when Charlton moved on.

A manager's job finally came his way when, in 1980 at the age of 33, he took over from Emlyn Hughes at Rotherham United, then struggling in the third division. Within 18 months, Porterfield had won promotion. Articulate, committed and possessing a good tactical awareness, Porterfield built an entertaining Rotherham team on a shoestring—he was known to paint the stands in the absence of any money to pay someone to do the task. A few miles away, Sheffield United were now in Division Four. In debt to around £1m, the club had been unable to find a good manager. Six years previously, United had finished sixth in Division One, three managers later, they were in their lowest League position in their history.

United offered Porterfield the manager's job which he took without question. The reluctance of some Blades fans to welcome a former player for Wednesday was overlooked in Porterfield's early days. Releasing nine of his inherited squad, he brought in six players, three on nominal fees and three costing huge sums by Division Four standards. Thus, £90,000 brought in goalkeeper Keith Waugh and £100,000 secured winger Colin Morris. A steady beginning to the 1981–82 season ended with two consecutive defeats in September. Money was again spent and a £100,000 fee brought the 24-year-old Keith Edwards back to United from Hull City where he had scored prolifically since joining them from Bramall Lane as an 18-year-old. United lost only two further League games that season and Edwards terrorised fourth division defences, leading a forward line that scored close to 100 goals. United were promoted with 96 points as champions in front of an average home crowd of over 20,000.

The following season saw a mid-table finish with a team that was not a happy unit. The most outstanding memory of this season was United's signing of the hero of Hillsborough Terry Curran in the autumn of 1982 for £100,000. The signing was Reg Brealey's doing and was conducted without the approval of Porterfield. The signing upset both Wednesday and the United manager. The following season, United were promoted to Division Two and all was well again. Astute signings of Paul Stancliffe and Kevin Arnott produced performances that put United amongst the front runners. The late season signing of Glenn Cockerill saw United win five of their next seven games. An agonising last four matches saw United's destiny left in the hands of Burnley, who in their final game had to avoid being defeated by Hull City by three clear goals, thus allowing Hull to go up at the expense of United on goal difference. Hull won 2–0 and United were promoted to Division Two. After only three seasons in control, Porterfield had achieved two promotions.

The cash hitherto made available by Brealey to Porterfield dried up in the mid-eighties. Ordered to reduce the wage bill, the relationship between chairman and manager deteriorated. This affected team performances, the final home game of the 1984–85 season attracted less than 8,000. Winning only three away games all season, United conceded five goals on four occasions and rumours proliferated that the manager was willing to play weakened teams to demonstrate to his chairman the lack of depth in his squad. United finished the season 18th and cries of 'Porterfield out!' were becoming louder and more frequent. In response, Porterfield brought in players of vast experience. This was a short-term policy, which saw some excellent players such as Peter Withe and Ken McNaught being brought on board and also brought the stigma of the team being called 'Dad's Army'. The early part of the season saw United win six out of seven games only to then go five games without a win. Once again crowds dipped to barely 8,000 and in March 1986 a 5–2 drubbing by Norwich at Bramall Lane saw a car-park demonstration by thousands of disgruntled fans. After five years and two promotions and placing United seventh in the second division—their highest league position for a decade—Porterfield was sacked over the phone, having left Bramall Lane whilst the board deliberated his future.

Porterfield's departure might be considered a victory for fan power. Whilst this was the public face of protest, a more private one was a product of board member Paul Woolhouse, who allegedly fed stories to the local media of boardroom disquiet with the manager's style. Despite his reign coinciding with a steady rise up the league, the club finances were in disarray. The club lost money every one of his five years in charge, the largest annual deficit was £853,000, the smallest £129,000. The ten-year contract he was given by Brealey, unprecedented in English footballing history, produced £400,000 in compensation for Porterfield.

From Bramall Lane, Porterfield moved to Aberdeen to follow in the footsteps of Alex Ferguson, who was departing for what was to become a 20-year plus reign at Manchester United. After Aberdeen, Porterfield became assistant to Bobby Saxton at Chelsea in 1988. He then moved to a similar position at Bolton Wanderers. A year later, he was manager at Reading and 18 months later back at Stamford Bridge as manager. After this brief spell of 29 matches he departed and surfaced as manager of the Zambian national side in 1993–94. Late 1994 saw him manage Saudi Arabia and two years later he returned to Africa to coach Zimbabwe. Later again, he took the managerial position for Oman and then Trinidad and Tobago. Returning to Africa in 2001, he coached the Ghanaian side Ktosho Antlers before leaving a year later to coach the South Korean team Buscon Icons.

Seemingly bewildered
Ian Porterfield upon receiving his whisky for manager of the month award 1982

Few people in Sheffield would ever claim Porterfield as a friend. A dour and occasionally complex personality concealed a dedicated and committed football man. His mannerisms were perceived by many at Bramall Lane as arrogant and Porterfield's public utterances were, at times, ill-considered. To a journalist's questions about disgruntled fans, Porterfield replied that if fans did not like what they saw they should not come to the game. For many years he was tolerated, even protected, by his chairman, who was content to overlook his active social life in return for success on the pitch. Porterfield had generally brought in good players, the only exception being the then record purchase of centre forward Alan Young from Notts County for £165,000, who proved a failure, but attracted a similar fee from Brighton in 1984. In his six years,

Porterfield had spent less than £500,000 net. He had organised a team that was, in the mid-eighties, cautious and sought to score on the break. His style was functional rather than entertaining. When interviewed in 2001, Porterfield was convinced that he had done a good job at Bramall Lane and that given time and financial support he could have done better.

Youth Trials: Billy McEwan

The 21 months that saw Billy McEwan in charge at Bramall Lane did not provide much by way of good memories for Blades fans. Brought in by Ian Porterfield to coach the youth team, McEwan was to replace his fellow Scot in March 1986. Under his guidance, United's juniors had won the Northern Intermediate League in 1986 and, aged 34, McEwan was asked to stand in as caretaker-manager. The first nine games of the season saw him win three and lose twice. Financial difficulties exacerbated by regular home crowds of under 10,000, were no doubt primary considerations when the board offered McEwan the job on a permanent basis in the close season. Alongside him was Danny Bergara as chief coach and Derek Dooley in charge of contracts. Youth was given a chance, but none really made the grade. Moving on the older pros brought in by Porterfield made sense but the sale of top scorer Keith Edwards to Leeds United for £125,000 did not. However, the sale was inevitable because of the player's contempt for the manager. A poor team produced erratic results, and attendances remained low. One home game in March in

Billy McEwan
United's youngest ever manager aged 29 in 1986

1987 against Crystal Palace saw only 6,647 turn out. Fans sought entertainment, but any distraction would do and the memorable game at home to Portsmouth saw three visitors sent off as United struggled to a 1–0 victory, courtesy of an own goal.

The 1987–88 season saw more experienced players leave and the arrival of centre forward Richard Cadette for £130,000 from Brentford. Fast and enthusiastic, he was unable to do what centre forwards are paid to do—score goals. As a consequence, United won one game in 16 from October 1987 to January 1988. A 5–0 home defeat to Oldham in front of 9,500 fans saw an emergency board meeting convene at half-time and McEwan resign after the game. The young players McEwan bought in were not ready or not good enough. The dressing room was not happy and the club seemed in terminal decline. Unable to bring in players who might have made a difference, McEwan put in long hours for little return. He remained in the game for the next 20 years as manager of Rotherham and Darlington and as assistant manager at Derby County. In 2005 McEwan was to be found managing York City in the Conference League.

United's fortunes changed when McEwan's successor was revealed to be Dave 'Harry' Bassett. Bassett joined United in January 1988 when United were nearly bottom of the second division. When he left eight years later, the club were back in the same position as when he started. On his departure, Bassett was the fourth-longest serving manager in the Football League.

Let's keep it sweet
Bertie Bassett and 'Harry' Bassett getting to know each other at Bramall Lane January 1989

Harry's Games: Dave Bassett

The man who was to become famous throughout English football for his expletives and smile was born in Willesden, northwest London in 1944. The only child of a football mad bus conductor called Harry, Dave Bassett became known to all as 'Harry' for the rest of his life. Showing youthful footballing promise, Bassett represented the county before Fulham offered an apprenticeship, which he turned down in favour of a ground-staff position at Chelsea. A few youth team games did not produce a contract so Bassett turned his talents to other money-making avenues. Aged 16 he began work in an insurance company. Having learned the ins and outs of pensions and investments by experience and night-school, Bassett was running his own brokerage in his mid-20s.

When not trying to make the big time at Chelsea or on the stock market, Bassett turned out for Hayes Town in the Isthmian League and, for six months, Wycombe Wanderers. Aged 21, fame came knocking at the door when a scout from Watford offered a trial. Bassett signed on under a man who was later to become United's manager, Ken Furphy. A few reserve games, occasionally alongside a promising youngster called Tony Currie, impressed Watford's coaches, but Bassett turned down professional terms. They could not compete with a company car, favourable mortgage rate and steady job that came via the insurance company combined with what Hayes Town paid on Saturdays. Equally important was a realisation that he was not good enough for the top flight of English football. Any lingering doubts about his chosen path were soon shattered—literally. Playing with mates in a Sunday morning pub team, Bassett broke a leg and Watford lost interest. After 18 months, Bassett returned to football playing in a 'midfield general' role, and captained Walton and Hersham in a 1973 FA Cup humiliation of Brian Clough's Brighton. The same year, Bassett received the FA Trophy at Wembley and was selected to represent England's amateur side.

When Alan Batsford, the manager of Walton and Hersham, left for Wimbledon he took half the team including Bassett. Bassett played against Leeds in two FA Cup-ties in 1975 and was a regular in the team that won the League three years in succession. After promotion to the Football League in 1977, Bassett played 36 games in Division Four and was appointed assistant manager. When Batsford's successor Dario Gradi left to manage Crystal Palace in 1978 Bassett took the hot seat. Departing with Gradi was the Wimbledon chairman Ron Noades. To save Wimbledon FC from going out of business Bassett guaranteed £100,000 of his own money. One of the remaining directors, Sam Hamman, eventually bought Noades' shares and became the new chairman. For the next six years everything was sweet between the two, but then problems began. The end product was Bassett achieving two distinctions in football—the then record for the shortest reign of a Football League manager (three days), and managing two clubs both of which were relegated in the same season.

The first claim to fame occurred in 1984 when Noades, having sacked Alan Mullery, convinced Bassett to take the Crystal Palace job. He accepted because of Hamman's refusal to pay him what he asked after his success at Wimbledon. Three days after departing, Bassett returned. However things were still not right and shortly after Bassett left to join Watford. Their chairman, Elton John, sought him out as successor to Graham Taylor who had taken the Aston Villa job. The other Watford directors were annoyed with his appointment because the chairman had not consulted them. A local journalist then dug up stories from 20 years before of a notorious Sunday morning pub team in a local league. The 21-year-old player-manager was a certain Dave Bassett and the team had 'disciplinary problems'. Too many at Watford did not want a man with such tendencies so Bassett left after seven months, 'mutually'.

In late 1987, the Sheffield United chairman Reg Brealey contacted Ron Noades for advice when looking for a new manager and Brealey duly appointed Bassett on Noades' recommendation. His impact was immediate—four months after his appointment United were relegated to Division Three while Watford suffered relegation as well. Appointed with 15 games to go, United lost nine and won five, finishing third from the bottom. The team then lost the play-off with Bristol City and went down. Bassett's offer to resign was rejected by the United board. United then won just about every week for two seasons and the fans made a hero out of one of Bassett's signings—a man who until joining on a free could not get a game in Brentford's reserves and was about to start a window-cleaning round.

By 1990 United were in Division One after 14 years absence and Bassett was the greatest thing since sliced bread in the red half of Sheffield. In the second half of the 1989–90 season the club, and in particular Bassett, was subject to a six-part BBC2 documentary titled *United*. This gave the club a public profile never seen before or since. The fly-on-the-wall style provided a remarkable insight into the United players' view of their occupation and, indeed, what their wives thought of football. The transfer deliberations of a board meeting and the contests between directors were broadcast. Fandom was represented by a combination of devoted members of the Supporters' Club and by a couple of self-confessed hooligans. Central to the whole series was Bassett, who was revealed as a man unable to complete a sentence without an expletive, yet maintained a remarkable rapport with just about everyone employed at the club, regardless of their office.

In his pursuit of footballing success Bassett was pigeon-holed for most of his career by his association with Wimbledon's 'Crazy Gang' and the long-ball tactic. The 'Crazy Gang' nomenclature, taken from a 1950's music hall variety troupe, was applied to the Wimbledon squad, who were irreverent to the big clubs and star names they found themselves amongst. Indulging in initiation ceremonies for newcomers and existing as a hard-working unit who would out-muscle and intimidate any team, they were not to everyone's liking. The route one tactic was synonymous with Wimbledon. This no frills style was derived from a 1950s statistical analysis of how goals were scored by Wing Commander Charles Reep and developed further by FA Technical Director Charles Hughes. The concept had a mathematical justification; goals were usually scored from inside the opposing penalty area. It made sense to put the ball there as quickly as possible. It had worked for Arsenal in the 1980s and later Watford and Sheffield Wednesday under Graham Taylor and Jack Charlton respectively. In adopting the tactic at Wimbledon and Sheffield United, Bassett was travelling down a well-worn (and successful) route. This tactic got Wimbledon from non-league football into sixth place in Division One. Bassett undoubtedly offended football 'purists' but chose sides and tactics according to the standard of opposition.

In pursuit of winning, the clubs under Bassett acquired a poor disciplinary record. In his defence the players he had at United were more enthusiastic than cynical. Bassett was no angel as a player and he encouraged a sense of fun in his players wanting, in his words, 'neither robots nor goody two-shoes'. His attitude to his players was in marked contrast to most of his contemporaries. Never wanting to hold authority by aloofness, he would come down hard on those who transgressed the few things that annoyed him—in particular trust. He would sign players with a history of being troublesome because he had self-belief that he could sort them out. Reputations did not worry him because, in his memorable phrase on signing the notorious Vinnie Jones, 'When you're building a team you're looking for good players, not blokes to marry your daughter'.

Watching his defenders 'fanny-dangling' with the ball?

If Bassett had a football philosophy it was in wanting each man to play with pride and respect for both themselves and their employers. When looking at a player he would ask the following, 'Does he understand the game? Is he athletic? Is he brave? Is his character sound?' In his years at Bramall Lane dozens of players came and went, some in not totally amicable circumstances. Not every player wanted to give their all for the cause and some, as he saw it, pulled their foot and head out of challenges once too often. Bassett was notorious in football for paying low wages. Prone to being stubborn in some things, he would also admit his mistakes.

Bassett sought equal treatment for his teams and, instead of just moaning about referees, put together a video in 1992 of what he considered their inconsistencies against his players. Bassett was not always so calculated; consequently he could be relied upon when ruffled to say something memorable. Thus the three-sided ground at Bramall Lane between 1992–95 made for a 'poxy atmosphere', defenders who did not do as they were told were 'fanny-dangling with the ball'. The reluctance in one season of any referee to award United a penalty saw him suggest that the only way his club would be awarded one was if one of the team 'got gang-banged in the box'. His players were occasionally 'brainless', he had forwards who 'couldn't hit a cow's backside with a banjo', and he never liked his selections rolling about feigning injury like 'poufters'. During an after-dinner speech in Sheffield he joked about not wanting his two leading goal scorers, Tony Agana and Brian Deane, as next-door neighbours, prompting a walk-out by the leader of the Sheffield Council because Bassett's comments about the two players were 'racist'.

His recruitment policy inadvertently brought dressing-room divisions. In his early years at Bramall Lane Bassett brought in a dozen south-east born players. Training sessions saw North v South games with no holds barred. He sourced players from all places, bringing in Paul Rogers from non-League Sutton in what will probably be the last ever occasion at United of a player leaving a non-League team to join a Premiership club. In 1993, Bassett brought in two Norwegian internationals, paying £475,000 for Jostein Flo who scored 22 goals in 79 appearances and became the first United player to play in the World Cup Finals when representing Norway in 1994. Three months after Flo's arrival came fellow countryman Roger Nilsen, who cost £550,000 and played 177 games before ending his career in England with Tottenham Hotspur. A year later Bassett brought two Australians back from a pre-season tour. He also brought a strange chap to Bramall Lane for one afternoon. This 6' 7" teeth n' tan Californian, by the name of Tim Robbins, preached a quasi-evangelical ideology called 'constant and never-ending improvement' (CANI). He would get mass audiences shouting 'Bangstab' and 'Yowie' in pursuit of something called 'self-actualisation'. Having bought his book and video, followers made him tens of millions of dollars richer. The effect he had on United players was not quantifiable.

Ebullient by nature, well dressed and occasionally very funny, Bassett was destined to become a TV panellist. Not backward in self-promotion and favouring sections of the media Bassett would not have his players talking out of turn or giving away dressing room secrets. The early years of phoning up certain reporters to rant at them for what he considered unfair comments about him and his team ended when he mellowed and in a sense, subverted their copy by getting inside the corridors of power. When the subject of the United board of directors arose Bassett was, in public, diplomatic. At gatherings with friends he was less circumspect—the stories he told of players and chairmen were libellous, but probably true. Offered a place on the United board in 1992, Bassett turned it down because he could not see how the two jobs were compatible. If he had accepted he would have had the casting vote over the sale of centre-forward Brian Deane to Leeds in 1993. When Deane was sold only half the income generated by the sale was given to the manager. When Bassett went public saying that the club needed new players, Brealey replied by asking why the 39 on the club's books was insufficient. United were relegated, promotion proved elusive, crowds plummeted and mass protests against Brealey were evident during matches. Amidst all this, Bassett had to try to keep a team in good spirits and get results. But as he put it, 'we were at war and I hated it'. Bassett remained at Bramall Lane until 1995. His departure, detailed in the following chapter, saw him fighting against massive odds to keep a team and even a club afloat in an era of boardroom chaos.

Forwards and wingers, by virtue of scoring or supplying goals, receive greater accolades that their team-mates. Such men win games and a turn, feint or flick can see them remembered for decades. Burdened with the responsibility of scoring, such men are different in many instances to their team-mates. All eyes are on them and they shoulder the blame of misses as well as the adoration of scoring. Arrogance helps. Self-belief is crucial. In what follows, the lives of three forwards who wore the red and white stripes to varying degrees of success are analysed. Two left only to return and score again. The other, in the eyes of thousands of Blades fans, should never have played for the club. The former two are still revered in fans' memories, the latter is still spoken about with a degree of contempt. All three had varying degrees of self-belief born of their upbringing and early career. All three had the chance to play for Sheffield's other professional team. Only one did.

Golden Boots: Keith Edwards

The barmy days of the early 1980s, when both sets of Sheffield supporters had little to shout about but did so with a passion, usually when the worse for drink, is the era that invokes memories of one of United's greatest goal scorers. With boyish looks and a manner that never seemed perturbed by anything, Keith Edwards was, whilst on the pitch, both brilliant and arrogant. Many clubs bought him and many good managers tried to change him but Edwards never quite reached his full potential. He could and should have played at a higher level, that he did not probably lies in a character that was not easily understood and which did not suffer those he considered fools gladly.

Keith Edwards about to frighten defenders in 1982

Edwards was born the youngest of four boys in Middlesbrough in 1957 to London-born parents evacuated to the North East to avoid the blitz. His father, whilst a good player, did not make the grade but found contentment working as a clerk in a chemical factory, his mother was a cook. All four boys excelled in sport, but Keith made a name for himself at schoolboy football playing for Stockton Boys and Durham County as a centre-forward or in midfield. After scoring twice at an under-15 game at Ayresome Park, then the home of Middlesbrough, Edwards was invited to train with the club. He tried it but did not like it and left. What Middlesbrough did not pursue others did. Edwards accepted an invitation to a three-day trial at Wolves and then had a trial at Leeds. Watching him score that day were Jack Charlton and Billy Bremner. Neither team wanted him. Interestingly, Edwards' first league goal was against Wolves and in 1986, Leeds, managed by Billy Bremner, signed him for £125,000.

Leaving school at 15, Edwards took a job as a trainee salesman at a dairy. With money in his pocket and a company car at 17, Saturdays would find him playing for a youth club team. Ken Furphy, then manager of Sheffield United, noticed something in a trial. Furphy recalls that the scout who first brought Edwards to his attention warned him that this youngster might do nothing for most of the match, but would usually get a couple of goals. True to prediction Edwards did

The Adidas golden boot presented to Keith Edwards
Top scorer in the Football League 1981–82

nothing and, just as Furphy's patience was wearing thin, scored twice. United signed him in August 1975 and Edwards began his professional football life in the reserves under the eye of coach Alan Hodgkinson.

It was all so promising for Edwards at Bramall Lane in his late teens. The excellent team that finished sixth in Division One in 1975 was built around a core all aged over 30. Knowing their days were numbered, Furphy introduced promising youngsters such as Gary Hamson, Simon Stainrod and Tony Kenworthy before he was sacked. When a permanent replacement was found in the shape of Jimmy Sirrel, Edwards' appearances became more regular—not that he tried too hard to impress. As he saw it his job was to score goals or make them, others had tasks to do which he could not, 'I tried tackling people and it hurt…so I didn't try it again'. A debut in an FA Cup fixture at Leicester was followed by a League debut a month later. Over the next 30 months, Edwards made 64 first-team appearances and scored 29 goals. In September 1977 Sirrel was sacked and eventually replaced by Harry Haslam. In his short spell under the latter's eye, Edwards only remembers confusion:

> He tells me I'm the next Malcolm MacDonald and goes on about 'I always like an ace card up my sleeve'…That was no good to me sat on the bench trying to get a game.

Ten months after arriving Haslam sold him down a division to Hull City for £50,000 and replaced him with Steve Finnieston from Chelsea. Costing a club record of £90,000, Finnieston played 23 League games, scored five goals, and retired from the game with injuries less than two years later.

The start of the 1979–80 season found Edwards at Boothferry Park, the ground where he had scored his first away goal for United two seasons earlier. The three years here saw Edwards motivated by both anger and arrogance:

> I was disgusted with United for selling me. I looked at the ground and the players at Hull and would think 'I'll tear this place apart and leave for something better'. I did as well…

Unfortunately, Edwards always seemed to score against United. In a Division Three match in 1979 he scored twice in Hull's 3–1 victory and caused a spot of bother. The 5,000 following from Sheffield directed insulting songs at him. When his second went in he came over and replied with a few choice words and gestures. For the next 20 minutes police were pulling Blades out of the terracing. His last goal for Hull was against United in 1981 and days later he became the most expensive signing in the fourth division joining Ian Porterfield's new set up at Bramall Lane. Scoring 42 goals in his first season Edwards

Keith Edwards

Signing autographs for young admirers at a Sheffield United open day in 1981

won the Adidas Golden Boot for being the Football League's highest goal scorer. The ceremony was at the London Hilton and at his table were Kevin Keegan, Elton John and TV comedians Freddie Starr and Lennie Bennett. The £10,000 award that accompanied the trophy Edwards split amongst his team-mates in a magnanimous gesture. Strangely enough, he won another Golden Boot in 1983–84 and for some reason—he never found out why—was presented with the trophy by a man in the car park at Bramall Lane. There wasn't even a photographer. Four years later, when at Hull again he got another similar trophy. Then aged 31, he had scored 29 goals in one season.

Initially partnered at United by Colin Morris, Edwards seemed to score at will and United walked the fourth division. United gained promotion again two years later, but Porterfield was dismissed when the club were seventh in Division Two. One of the reasons he got the push was the United crowd chanting for Edwards as the team were losing 5–2. The relationship between Porterfield and Edwards started off so well, if not a little confusingly:

> It was all daft talk about 'horses for courses'… I didn't need all that crap. You end up seeking an explanation for what he was explaining…Then he starts putting me on the bench for the first 14 games of one season when I could guarantee him 20–25 goals a season.

He was the fastest player at Bramall Lane and very resilient to injuries. Able to find space, Edwards could play with both feet and had a wonderful ability to shoot on the turn. He could treat the less gifted with contempt; he once dummied a through ball fooling both his marker and the goalkeeper whom he ran round to stroke the ball into the net—but only after he had smiled at his admirers on the kop. His repertoire expanded when he was allowed to take set pieces; he was deadly with free kicks close to the box and could whip over a good corner.

Wherever Edwards played he had rows, usually with the managers and always with team-mates. Most of the 15 managers he played under got the sack whilst he remained. Every club he played for fined him for something, the maximum under Porterfield was two week's wages. Following Porterfield a new young manager wanting to be regarded as a disciplinarian took over at United. It wasn't long before Edwards fell out with Billy McEwan. Edwards left United in August 1986. Jack Charlton, then managing Sheffield Wednesday, made inquiries. Edwards nearly went to Seville in Spain when a friendly match saw him and Colin Morris run them ragged. United accepted their offer for the pair and the two players and their wives met to consider the logistics of living there when the Seville manager was dismissed and the deal was off. Edwards' last game in a United shirt was thus in Spain and after eight and a half years he left with the statistics of 261 League and cup appearances and 143 goals. McEwan, who fell out with Edwards in his first week as manager sold him to Leeds for £125,000.

Losing in the FA Cup semi-final and promotion play-offs could not distract from a good season at Leeds which produced 28 appearances and 10 goals for Edwards. However, a year after joining Leeds, Edwards rejoined his old boss Ian Porterfield, now in charge at Aberdeen. The £60,000 fee produced six games and two goals in six months and a stay in Scotland, memorable mainly for Edwards's only long-term injury. Hull City appeared again and gave Aberdeen what they paid for him. The manager who brought him back to Hull, Brian Horton, was sacked soon afterwards, as was his successor, Eddie Gray. In 55 appearances for Hull, Edwards bagged 29 goals, a brilliant achievement considering the club finished the season at the bottom of the second division. Significantly, he scored more goals that season than the England internationals Kerry Dixon and Ian Wright who played in the same division for successful clubs.

Edwards's journeys then become shorter but more frequent. In September 1989 the former United coach, Danny Bergara, paid a club record of £50,000 to take Edwards to Stockport County. He returned the investment with ten goals in 27 games but left six months later, on loan, for Huddersfield who later bought him. A hip injury, however, started causing problems—a year after retiring from the game he was forced to have a hip replacement—and the niggling injury made the manager Eoin Hand think Edwards was not interested. To make matters worse, Edwards was regularly late for training because of delays on British Rail, which he used after losing his licence. Released on a free transfer in September 1991 and after 305 goals, Edwards days in the Football League were over.

Blades away, trespassing on someone's pitch in the mid-80s

Teams still wanted him. A few months at non-league Stafford Rangers was followed by a stretch at lower division Alfreton Town, a signing made in unusual circumstances, 'I was playing golf every day. The manager was a roofer doing some work on the clubhouse and asked me if I wanted a game. So I signed for them'. It didn't last long. His attempts at roofing with the manager lasted just three days. His applications to manage and coach United did not produce an interview. Out of work, out of luck, and out of love, Edwards had to reappraise his life and sought a new career. On a physical level his health let him down—permanent discomfort was a product of football injuries. Out of work at one time for over four years, in 1996 Edwards became the match summariser on BBC Radio Sheffield. This ability has won him many admirers for his perception, his take on the game and his forthright opinions.

The Life of Brian: Brian Deane

The 6' 3" 14 stone man with a Leeds accent and a seeming reluctance to smile makes for a somewhat brooding and hounded presence. This is misleading because Brian Deane was one of the most courteous and polite footballers a fan could ever wish to meet. A product of migrants from the Caribbean island of Nevis, who moved to the Chapeltown district of Leeds, Deane was the youngest of six children. Hard working parents provided for a family that stayed together and prayed together daily, sustained by an Anglican faith that remains with him to this day. This secure home produced a diligent schoolboy who became a superb footballer, who was to represent his home city between the ages of 12 to 16 and eventually England in 1991.

Professional clubs noticed him; Bradford, Barnsley, Notts County and Leeds offered schoolboy trials but none offered a contract. Playing for non-league Yorkshire Amateurs in 1985, Deane wrote to Division Four club Doncaster Rovers for a trial. The chief scout there was from Leeds and remembered Deane from schoolboy days. He recommended him to the manager, Billy Bremner, who signed Deane on a part-time basis whilst he studied Physical Education at Doncaster College. Succeeding Bremner in 1987 was the former Sheffield Wednesday player Dave Cusack who made Deane a full-time professional for the reward of £60 per week. After doing well and scoring 12 goals in 66 games Deane asked Cusack to put a word in with any big clubs after a centre-forward. Whilst the manager was a big influence on Deane's career, he initially thought him too soft to be a professional target man. Furthermore, he was not impressed with his heading ability and once described him as 'like Bambi on ice.' The United manager Dave Bassett saw something he liked, and in July 1988, paid £30,000 with a further £10,000 promised should Deane make 30 first-team appearances. The rest is history—Deane stayed for five years at Bramall Lane and left the club for nearly 30 times what he cost.

Deane had remarkable ball control for a big man and developed a tremendous heading ability. Bassett publicly stated in his early days that Brian would improve when he ceased apologising to rival players after he had flattened them. A pre-season friendly at Skegness saw him for the first time in a United shirt, followed by a League debut at Reading. He scored in both games, the crowd took to him immediately and the chant of 'Deano' was heard at almost every game for the next five years. He could score from almost anywhere—flick on headers from low crosses and high crosses or lift it over the goalkeeper from 6 yards or 20-yard strikes. A partnership with Tony Agana produced three hat tricks for Deane and 60 goals between them in one season.

Fast, strong and level-headed, Deane was always willing to listen to advice. For this he thanks Bassett whom he credits for allowing him to 'extend' himself. International recognition came in 1991 when chosen to play for the England under-21 team which saw 200 Blades travel to the game at Walsall to chant his name (and boo a Wednesday player also in the team). In 1991 and 1993 England 'B' and full international honours came Deane's way. A total of three caps made him only the second post-war centre-forward from United to play for England. One thing that did not happen any more was getting overdrawn at the bank. When at Doncaster, he was permanently in this state. His first season at United saw him take home £250 a week. In 1992 Deane had signed a two-year contract with United with a gentlemen's agreement that he could leave after a year. He had ended the season as the club's top scorer with 20 goals but, with a year of the contract remaining, Deane was prepared to move on and submitted a written transfer request.

Deane's goal in the 2–1 victory over Manchester United in August 1992 was the first in the newly formed FA Premier League. The game was played at Bramall Lane and was watched by a crowd of just over 28,000, the highest in the country that day. The final game of the 1992–93 season saw his last goal for United; Deane departed two months later to Leeds. In 273 first team appearances he had scored 119 goals. In four of his five seasons he was almost an ever-present and he was sent-off only once. When he was sold the club was in boardroom turmoil. The chairman was technically Reg Brealey, who had resumed control after Paul Woolhouse had fled to avoid the police. Two clubs wanted Deane, Leeds offered £2.7 million then Sheffield Wednesday bid £3.2 million. Instructed by Bassett to talk to Wednesday manager Trevor Francis, Deane had as he saw it a 'no-win' situation. He chose to join the former Owls boss Howard Wilkinson and so, having signed a four-year contract, returned home to Leeds:

> *It would have been easy to go to Wednesday but Blades would have hated me...but if I'd stayed they'd hate me for asking for a transfer.....*

The transfer turned into a media circus and Deane became the pawn in a power struggle between chairman and manager. The latter presented the matter as one of selling his best player whilst he was on holiday. The former said there was no choice, given the financial state of the club. The following season United were relegated and Deane, in his Leeds colours, facing his previous club was booed by sections of the Blades' following based on the mistaken belief that the only reason he left United was for more money.

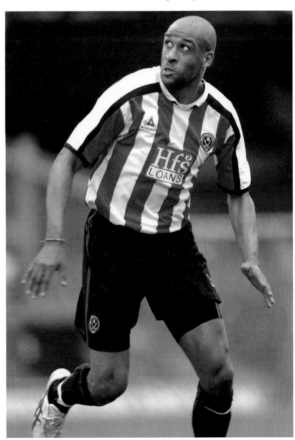

Brian Deane
United's last full England cap

His time at Leeds wore him down. Dressing-room cliques were not helping his game and he was being played out of position. After 110 games he decided not to sign a new contract and sought pastures new. A few clubs made offers, including Feyenoord and Strasbourg, but he ended up back at Bramall Lane in July 1997, convinced by Mike McDonald and Charles Green, that things were all sorted out and the club had ambition. The fans welcomed him with open arms and chanted his name in joy once again. In 28 first-team games he scored 13 goals and his trademark goal celebration of arms aloft with index fingers pointing down was a welcome sight to success-starved supporters. He left United six months later, in January 1998, for a fee of £1 million, this time without drama or protest. The status of the club chasing him silenced any criticism because all fans knew that if offered a chance to play for Benfica who was going to choose to remain with United in the first division? Also fans were by now so resigned to the club selling players to

The first Flashing Blade Fanzine
Seeking to take football out of the hands of property developers
and the fists of hooligans

the detriment of playing success and realised that protest was pretty useless. He thus joined Graham Souness in the Portuguese sunshine. Once again he left United behind the back of the manager, his sale being arranged by the chief executive. Leeds received half a million of the fee. Eighteen months after joining Benfica, Deane returned to England, joining Middlesbrough for £3 million. United had not negotiated a sell-on clause. Further contracts with Leicester, West Ham, Leeds and Sunderland saw him score regularly. In 2005 Deane moved to Australia signed by former Liverpool captain Steve McMahon at Perth Glory. He then returned to Bramall Lane in late 2005 on a six-month contract thereby becoming the first player in United's history to be signed three times. In that time his first-team appearances came as a sub and with his first touch of his first game back he hit the bar. After repeated chants of his name, Deane was brought on for the final five minutes of the final home game of the 2005–06 season as United celebrated their return to the top flight. In total, Deane played for United 273 times and scored 119 goals. One distinction he holds is being the most popular black player in the history of Sheffield United.

Deane never let anyone down. A genuine and modest character he was the ultimate professional. A career in coaching surely awaits a man who has invested wisely what football gave to him and lives an exemplary life.

Terry's Torment: Terry Curran

One of eight boys from a South Yorkshire mining family, Terry Curran went to a school that played only Rugby League. Ever contrary, he refused to play the game. As a consequence, he was not to play organised football until he was 16 when a local team was formed. In a pit village where gambling and greyhounds provided the main chance of a financial windfall, the school-leaving Curran worked as a labourer on building sites and later in a textile mill. Football abilities rescued him from this life. At the age of 16, playing for the village alongside his elder brother, Curran scored a consolation goal in a 17–1 defeat and impressed watching scouts from Aston Villa and Blackburn. Games against Halifax Town reserves and Doncaster Rovers reserves provoked offers of full professional terms from both watching managers. In the car on his way to sign for Halifax with his father and brother, Curran changed his mind and signed instead for fourth division Doncaster, managed by Maurice Setters. Being slightly built, the manager suggested he should spend the close season on a building site laying concrete.

After one season the 19-year-old Curran left Doncaster and joined second division Nottingham Forest under the managerial partnership of Brian Clough and Peter Taylor. The fee was £75,000 and his wages rose to £90 a week. Officially this was a huge wage increase, unofficially it was only a third more than he had received whilst at Doncaster:

> ...I was advised to ask for a transfer, which I did and refused to sign any new contract, which I did. In return I was promised that any money I was losing from an improved pay offer would be reimbursed on transfer and until my contract ran out and the transfer went through I met a bloke every week on the A1 who gave me £40 cash..

The talents of John Robertson and Tony Woodcock at Forest made it difficult for Curran to get a game. Eventually Tommy Docherty at Derby County took Curran for £75,000 but after only nine months, Curran moved to Southampton managed by Lawrie McMenemy. The short stays at clubs combined with on-pitch antics saw Curran develop a reputation:

> I'm calm off the pitch, but at five to three I changed. First to get it were the referees...first challenge and I'd be there shouting at him. I'd get booked and I'd be thinkin' later 'What did I say that for?' The answer is I don't know, it's something I've never been able to account for.

On his day he was as good a winger as anyone in Britain. He was a showman and fans' favourite who had natural talent, did not have to train hard and who livened up any dressing room. Fast and with an ability to make defenders look clumsy, he was also strong and had a tongue that gave defenders a lot of lip as part of the wind-up that fans rarely hear. He attracted attention from the highest levels of English football. Some excellent managers bought him and whilst at Bramall Lane both Manchester United and Arsenal made bids before he left for Everton for £100,000. He could have come to Bramall Lane in the late 1970s, Harry Haslam inquired about him and Curran promised Haslam that if he signed for him he would keep the team in Division Two. The deal did not come off and United were relegated, with Curran by then playing for Jack Charlton's Sheffield Wednesday.

A super-charged Division Three in 1979–80 saw United running away with the division until a derby at Hillsborough in front of 49,000 saw Wednesday win 4–0. Curran ran the match and United hardly won for the rest of the season. In the return fixture at Easter, 45,000 saw a 1–1 draw which included a goal scored by Curran when he received the ball at the corner flag, beat three defenders and curled it round the goalkeeper.

Terry Curran 1980, in his Hillsborough prime
Crossing the city proved more problematic than crossing the ball

Repeatedly shown on TV it became a contender for Goal of the Season. Wednesday were promoted. In Curran the Wednesday fans had a hero the like of which they have not had since. His personal fan club numbered 400 and he cut a record, *Singing the Blues,* which sold 3,000 copies. He was however called some strange names by the Wednesday manager, Jack Charlton, who insisted that every player had a responsibility to defend. Such insistence riled Curran and in one home game, when 5–0 ahead, upon receiving the ball in the opponents box he bewildered his team-mates as he dribbled the ball back to his own goalkeeper—having beaten three rival players. He then signalled to the manager that he was doing as he had been asked. Charlton was not impressed.

At the peak of his popularity in 1981 Curran did what few men have done in over 115 years of professional football in Sheffield—he crossed the city. For the Owls the move was an unforgivable betrayal, for Blades it was a great way to humiliate their city rivals, but how could they accept a man who had done so much that peeved them?

> *Reg Brealey had been tapping me for months to join United. I was the only person in Sheffield who thought I could do it without causing problems. I was in a contract dispute with Wednesday and United's offer was very good even if it meant dropping from Division One to Three.*

The three-year deal United offered included a £50,000 signing-on fee payable over the course of the contract. When he was close to signing, others jumped in. Newcastle and Everton made offers and Jack Charlton conceded their contract dispute and said Curran could have an £11,000 re-signing fee tax-free. But it was too late: a tribunal valued him at £100,000, Wednesday said he was worth five times as much, but the tribunal heard Curran ask if that was the case why, with crowds of 30,000, did they only pay him £300 per week? A furious Wednesday demanded cash immediately from United and Curran began his United career scoring in pre-season friendlies in Scotland.

The move to Bramall Lane lasted six months. Curran scored only three goals in 42 first-team appearances. United fans never took to him, he in turn only played well on a couple of occasions. When he was good he was brilliant, but unfortunately his best performance, in a cup match at Stoke, was his final one in a United shirt. The dressing room was not fully behind him. Whilst he and United captain Tony Kenworthy became good mates but he never hit it off with United's goal-scoring hero, Keith Edwards—the crosses that produced goals were not acknowledged by the latter. Off the pitch Curran ceased going to city-centre night clubs, 'I got it from both sets of fans…it got dangerous'. Realising he had made a mistake Curran asked for a move. Another factor played a part—he was signed by a chairman not a manager. He felt he was forced on a man who was not that bothered about picking him. Following the Stoke game he signed for Howard Kendall at Everton.

The fans loved him at Everton and he had three happy years there. He won a championship medal but missed a season with a bad injury. A free transfer to Huddersfield followed and he stayed a season before Lawrie McMenemy signed him again whilst managing the ailing Sunderland. Rows with the manager saw him leave soon after, effectively sacked on disciplinary grounds, and after a couple of games with Grimsby Curran packed the professional game in. The death of his father from cancer around the same time affected him profoundly. Losing interest in the game and much else, Curran tried a variety of jobs and found a niche in a pallet business. The persistence of a fan of non-league Goole Town paid off when, after a three-year absence from the game, Curran agreed to turn out for them. Within weeks he became the manager, crowds trebled, the team went on a nine-match unbeaten run. Then Curran discovered that he was managing for no wage whilst his players were getting what he paid them plus back-handers. He walked out and joined Mossley in the Vauxhall Conference for a while, but the travelling was too much and the directors were not pleased when, without telling them, Curran was interviewed by another club.

Football today for Curran is a memory. Working six days a week from 5.30 am until last orders, in the hotel and transport café he owns off the A1, means he is rarely even a spectator at football.

The decade ended with an event that brought global infamy upon the English game. In April 1989, 96 Liverpool fans attending an FA Cup semi-final against Nottingham Forest at Hillsborough, home of Sheffield Wednesday, were crushed to death after a gate was opened allowing a surge of thousands of fellow fans from outside the ground. The fences at the Leppings Lane End, erected specifically in 1977 prior to an FA Cup fixture between Leeds United and Manchester United, were pulled down. The subsequent enquiry by Lord Justice Taylor was to change the game of football in Britain forever. The demands of the post-Hillsborough era saw United continue their boardroom debacles in a decade that saw the club stagnate amidst suggestions from senior figures that United might cease to exist after 100 years.

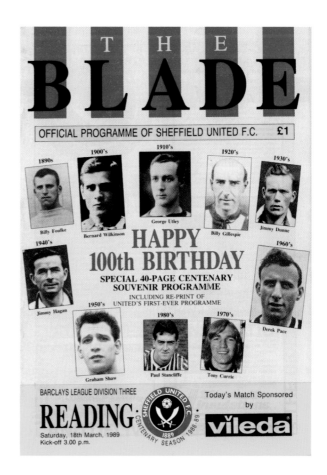

The first one hundred years
Centenary match programme of March 1989

Three Barclay's Bank First Division Performance of the Week trophies awarded to Sheffield United in the 1990s

Paying the Price

In January 1990 the electoral constituency of Sheffield Central, containing Bramall Lane had, at 18.4%, the highest unemployment levels of any equivalent area of Yorkshire. Eight years later, the European Commission gave South Yorkshire 'Objective 1' status, thereby placing the region on the same socio-economic footing as the former East Germany and Sicily. To qualify for this accolade, an area had to have a GDP of less than 75% of the EU average—South Yorkshire's was 70.7%. One might argue the city was not typical of the region, with its cultural industries quarter and the then recently built (at a cost of £15 million) National Centre for Popular Music, Sheffield was trying to reinvent itself as vibrant, creative and slightly avant-garde. Meanwhile the cinema of the era projected the region and city globally as a place where redundant steel-workers wore United shirts when not stripping for a living and unemployed coal miners worked as clowns.

Meanwhile, the unthinkable was debated and deliberated upon. After 100 years of footballing history a report suggested Sheffield's two professional football clubs merge. Written by Deloitte and Touche accountancy analyst, Jonnie Oldham, the document declared that Sheffield was not big enough to sustain two successful football teams. The two Sheffield clubs were the biggest footballing loss-makers in the country in the 1997–98 season. The Owls lost £9.9 million whilst in the Premiership and the Blades lost £6.7 million in Division One. The United chief executive, Derby-born John Thurman, hired in the summer of 1999 following a career in the Royal Marines, was sympathetic to the sentiments but stressed publicly that, as yet, the two clubs had not opened talks.

Leagues Behind

If there was little money in the South Yorkshire region, English football in the 1990s became awash with it by virtue of the creation of the Premiership. In the early 1980s, the big English clubs had considered forming a 'Super League' in their pursuit of avoiding sharing TV income with clubs from all four divisions. In 1983, pressure from the big clubs saw the abolition of gate sharing. The home side now kept all the takings. Further breakaway threats produced the 'Heathrow Agreement' which proposed a new formula for TV money: 50% to the then Division One clubs, 25% to the second and 25% divided between Divisions Three and Four. Even this was not enough for some clubs. In 1992, 22 first division clubs broke away from the Football League and declared a new entity called the FA Premier League. They were to negotiate their own TV deal with Sky and were no longer willing to be part of an equitable share of money to clubs in the lower divisions. Sheffield United and Wednesday were amongst the 22 founder members. United lasted two seasons in the new competition, Wednesday survived until 2000.

From 1993, only 5% of the huge Premiership income went elsewhere to help football. Income stayed with the top 20 clubs, most of which was used to pay players' wages. The changing nature of TV coverage popularised the game, reaching new and generally more affluent audiences. Average crowds in the Premiership rose from 21,000 in 1993 to 34,000 by 2004. The five-year deal that the Premier League signed with Sky for £192 million allowed them to broadcast 60 games a season for five years. The BBC got a *Match of the Day* highlight package. In 1996, Sky and the BBC renegotiated a deal whereby, over a four-year period, the former paid £670 million and the latter £73 million. Teams outside of the Premiership meanwhile, faced financial crisis exacerbated when a Football League deal with OnDigital, which had promised £315 million over three years to the 72 clubs, collapsed with the demise of the company.

The Shoreham End May 1991
The roof was removed in readiness for the new Kop development

The game at the top was all about money. Those without it fell by the wayside. Symptomatic of the era was a March 1999 fixture between Portsmouth and Crystal Palace—the first in the history of the British game played by two clubs in administration. One month earlier a match between Crystal Palace and Sheffield United attracted a TV audience of around one billion viewers in China. Somewhere close to one fifth of the global population tuned in to see Palace's two Chinese players, Fan Zhiyi and Sun Jihai, compete against the Blades. This feat was not lost on United who attempted to exploit the emerging Chinese football market in unprecedented ways.

Money Matters

The Taylor Report sought to ensure that the events of the Hillsborough tragedy would never be repeated. The key recommendation was that football stadiums in Britain should become all-seater. The Football Spectators Act provided the legislation to implement this and across the country football grounds were transformed. In the immediate aftermath United's Shoreham End Kop had its capacity reduced by half to just 9,000. When seats were installed there in 1991 the ground capacity was legally set at just under 30,000. This legislation had huge consequences for United when, between 1994 and 1996, Bramall Lane returned to being a three-sided ground. The John Street terracing and wooden stand was in the post-Taylor report days moribund, even dangerous, and had to go. The stand was pulled down hours after the final game of the 1993–94 season. Another historic symbol of the football ground, the floodlight pylons, also disappeared in 1995 as new lighting technology made such structures superfluous.

A few years later, not only could Blades fans enjoy the match without the discomfort of fellows in close proximity, they could shut them out completely by hiring one of the 31 ten-person private boxes located at the back of the 6,842-seater John Street stand. Complete with glass front, the boxes even sealed its occupants from crowd noise. At the same time the Bramall Lane crowd now spent the game under the gaze of 90 closed-circuit television cameras as the police reduced their visible uniformed presence and instead watched for transgressions in their control room. Ground building was costly, money had to be recouped and football became an expensive leisure pastime. Not everyone saw the benefits of the rising admission costs.

When relegated from the Premiership in 1994, United had one of the smallest wage bills in the division, at just over £3.1 million. The other two low-payers, Oldham and Swindon, were also relegated. By 1995 and now in Division One, United lost £850,000 on the season, had an overall debt of £7.6 million and average crowds of less than 13,000. The decade was to become memorable for all the wrong reasons. Between March 1990 and December 1999, the club saw no fewer than six chairmen, six team-managers, four chief executives between July 1998 and April 1999, and 180 first-team players. One of these, Steven Hawes, became United's youngest Football League first-teamer in September 1995, aged 17 years and 47 days, when he played in a 3–1 defeat at West Bromwich.

One might forget that this decade also saw football played. When Colin Hill was chosen for Northern Ireland in 1990 he became the club's first full international for 15 years. But good players in United's kit were occasionally a product of controversy. In 1991 United supporters 'bought' winger Glyn Hodges for £400,000 after his loan spell from Crystal Palace expired. Via a one-off scheme titled the Grand National Sweepstake, the money raised (in the absence of money in the club's bank account) managed to bring Hodges to the club in circumstances believed to be unique to English football. At times the players bought constituted a team that promised trophies. In 1993 United made it to the FA Cup semi-final, only to lose 2–1 to Wednesday in front of 76,000 at Wembley. Then the financial crises arising out of boardroom idiocy ruined the club's progress. The sale of the top scorer Brian Deane in the summer of 1993 saw a cut-price replacement of sorts in Norwegian Jostein Flo. Forced to buy cheap, the club had to look beyond Britain and more foreign players arrived. Relegated from the Premiership in 1994, United made the first division promotion play-off final at Wembley in 1997 losing 1–0 to Crystal Palace in what was then and still is the most lucrative game in world football by virtue of the winners joining the Premier league. The 1990s was a decade of near misses. In 1998 United lost 1–0 to Newcastle in the FA Cup semi-final at Old Trafford. United never seemed to clear the final hurdle.

Long Throws

An awful start to the 1990–91 season saw United bottom of the first division by Christmas. No manager in United's history, other than Dave Bassett, could not win for 19 games and still not hear a chant calling for his head. Bassett was virtually untouchable at United and respected by all because he was authentic, honest, fun and talked sense. He also turned the season around and United lost only two of their final 20 games and finished in mid-table. The following season United finished a creditable mid-table. Then the 1993–94 season saw United relegated by the last kick of the match at Stamford Bridge. Losing 3–2 was not in itself sufficient to send United down, but all fellow strugglers picked up points—some in dubious circumstances. On the day of relegation, Wimbledon let slip a 2–0 lead at Everton to lose 3–2, in a game notable for the awful goalkeeping of Wimbledon's Hans Segers; a win ensured Everton stayed up and

Sheffield at Wembley 1993
Some 76,000 Sheffielders filled the stadium

sent United down. Allegations that the match was fixed circulated throughout English football. In 1997, Segers appeared in court with the Liverpool goalkeeper, Bruce Grobbelaar, and former Wimbledon and Aston Villa forward, John Fashanu, on accusations of match fixing (going back four years) in return for cash payments of between £40,000 and £225,000 from a Far East betting syndicate which had encouraged the three to throw games in the 1993–94 season. After two trials, the jury could not reach a verdict and the defendants were found not guilty, escaping essentially via a legal technicality. The judge suggested there was evidence to prove their guilt. Segers never played professional football again and was to become a born-again Christian and lay preacher. Meanwhile, Sheffield United needed divine intervention as they sought to resurrect their fortunes amidst a boardroom struggle that descended into a farce.

Courting Disaster

Selling the club was proving difficult for Reg Brealey. In June 1992 Brealey lost a legal dispute with his successor as chairman, Paul Woolhouse, over payments relating to the sale of United, Brealey then sued Woolhouse over breach of contract. In the same year Brealey became a director of Chesterfield FC and brought a High Court writ against United for alleged debts of £3/4 million owed to his brother Len. Woolhouse, meanwhile, agreed to pay the Brealey family's Gibraltar-based company, ELSE (1982) Ltd, in installments for the club shares which, if he defaulted, the Brealey family would reclaim. By August 1992 Woolhouse's arrears were £300,000, so another agreement was negotiated with Reg Brealey's brother— this not only reduced the total price but actually loaned Woolhouse money. Even this arrangement did not work out. In October 1992 Len Brealey began High Court proceedings to reclaim the United shares. Six weeks later Woolhouse's assets were frozen by the High Court as a result of an injunction taken out by five companies.

Former United chairman Paul Woolhouse
Happier times, before becoming a fugitive in the mid-1990s

Things got worse. In October 1992, United were barred by the Premier League from signing players. They had failed to pay Leeds United £25,000 owed to them for the loan of two players. Soon after Woolhouse's problems got worse—his wife left him and was threatening to freeze his assets during the divorce wrangle. Further trouble came from a Belgian company to which Woolhouse had mortgaged his company who claimed he was using company money to pay for United's shares. In October, Woolhouse stepped down 'temporarily' as chairman of United becoming instead a director and 'chief executive' thereby removing Derek Dooley from the job and permitting himself to be paid a salary by the club of £100,000 per year.

Meanwhile, December 1992 saw another High Court hearing as to who owned the club. The court heard how, during a row with Len Brealey, Woolhouse had threatened to publicise the rumour that Reg Brealey was a homosexual, with a flat and 'friend' in Bangkok. This produced a counter-claim that Woolhouse's wife had left him because he was having a homosexual affair with his accountant. The High Court Judge told Woolhouse he was a liar over information he had given Brealey. The court ruled that the shares should return to Len Brealey whose immediate response was to demand an Extraordinary General Meeting of shareholders to force Woolhouse out and then sell the shares. He also handed various documents to the South Yorkshire Police fraud squad.

Two days after the court hearing Woolhouse was relieved of his position as chief executive and left with two years salary. Reg Brealey resigned his position at Chesterfield and returned as United chairman—apparently at the invitation of the new board. Woolhouse was soon back in the familiar surroundings of the High Court being pursued for money by the five companies previously mentioned to the tune of £1 million and threatened with jail due to his contempt of court. Another United director, Stephen Hinchliffe, meanwhile, was preparing to sue Len Brealey for libel regarding allegations of irregularities via a takeover of a Sheffield company of which Hinchliffe was chairman. Amidst all this rancour, £6,500 in cash from match-ticket sales was found to be missing from Woolhouse's office. Weeks later he began a life as a fugitive. Since February 1994 Woolhouse's whereabouts have been known to very few people. He is arrestable on sight and of great interest to Interpol.

Men of Conviction

In this chaos the imposing figure of Stephen Hinchliffe stated in the *Sheffield Star*:

Former United director Stephen Hinchliffe in his prime in the early 1990s

A custodial sentence in 2001 brought both his business empire and his dreams for Sheffield United crashing down

> *My belief is that Sheffield United should be owned by Blades fans. I don't see the point in some outsider who in one breath wants to buy Manchester City and in the next breath Sheffield United.*

Hinchliffe was the club's second biggest shareholder after Reg Brealey. His company Chase Montague controlled 419 shares to Brealey's 1,620. His comments were aimed at Mike McDonald a prospective buyer who was to become the United chairman in autumn 1995. This Manchester-born scrap merchant turned business entrepreneur had, in 1993, tried to purchase two other Premier League clubs and in 1994 attempted to buy his beloved Manchester City. With that avenue no longer available, McDonald sought somewhere else and Sheffield United was available. He in turn told the *Star* of his intentions, 'We have certain plans and ideas that we plan to bring over from the States'. Without naming who else was involved in the take-over, it was revealing how the proposal for Sheffield United was strictly a business deal. The prolonged arrival of McDonald in late September 1995 saw the club unable or unwilling to pay the players' wages the following month. By the middle of October the current (or was it former?) chairman and the intended (or was it new?) one were still sorting out the legal aspects of ownership and on the first day of November the manager was told to abandon his plans to sign two players because no-one knew for certain who owned the club! When Brealey and McDonald shook hands on a deal in November 1995 the price was £2.75 million, which Brealey considered a give-away. After nearly 15 years of being the chairman and, after protracted negotiations, Brealey left United. Reflecting on this time Brealey remembered:

> *It was a brutal ending… you have to accept the club is never yours, it's always theirs [the fans] it's the only thing many of them have in their lives.*

Texan Millions: Mike McDonald

In November 1995 Mike McDonald and his business empire, Texas, which encompassed engineering companies, hotels, property, demolition and metals, agreed to purchase Brealey's shareholding in United. After protracted negotiations, McDonald was to buy a 52% stake. On his first day in charge, he announced; 'I have not bought this club to see it live in the shadow of Sheffield Wednesday'. The monthly wage bill of staff and players was £250,000, but crowds were at the 10,000 mark. The club had to appeal to the Professional Footballer's Association for a loan to pay players' wages. The Football Association threatened to refuse to register any incoming players until United's debts were repaid. Eventually, wages were paid from out of the pockets of directors Alan Laver and Bernard Proctor while McDonald wrote a personal cheque for £200,000. He also promised £1.5 million to strengthen the side. One of his first tasks was to find someone to manage his club.

In December 1995, after eight years in charge, Dave Bassett decided to leave Bramall Lane. Bassett realised the new chairman wanted him out. In his biography, Bassett states, 'I had become a kamikaze pilot—I had taken Brealey out, but taken myself out as well'. He also accused a United player of being a mole in the dressing room for the benefit of the directors. Knowing his intended replacement, Howard Kendall, was in the crowd at a couple of matches before he resigned did not make for a reassuring time. On his final day Bassett found that money owed to him was not to be paid in full. Not taking this lying down, an argument ensued and an invitation to sort it out in the car park was extended by one man. Bassett accepted and walked down the stairs. Realising the likely consequences of the invite, the proposition was withdrawn.

United chairman Mike McDonald with newly-appointed manager Howard Kendall
Looking a little unconvincing as they stress their Blade credentials in 1996

Deciding on a few months off to reflect, Bassett was twice interviewed for the Ireland national team manager's job and was approached by Sheffield Wednesday but accepted a job at Manchester City— only to think about it on the way home and turn it down a few hours later. The thought of another interfering boardroom was too much to contemplate after what he had been through. One chairman who knew him from their days at Wimbledon was Ron Noades who appointed him manager of Crystal Palace in March 1996. This time Bassett lasted longer than three days. After 13 months he left for Nottingham Forest who were relegated from the Premiership as Crystal Palace replaced them by beating United in the 1997 play-off at Wembley. Realising that Forest had no money, Bassett went public with his realisation that clubs only sought him when in trouble. The following season saw Forest go back up as champions of the first division. In 1999 Bassett took the managerial chair at Barnsley. Having shaken hands with the Barnsley chairman in the afternoon, Bassett received a surprise doorstep visit from two United directors in the evening. Whilst flattered, Bassett had to turn down United's offer of the manager's job, arguing that his handshake earlier in the day was binding.

In 2003 a dinner in honour of Bassett's 60th birthday was held at Bramall Lane. Some 400 diners paid tribute, as did two dozen of his former players. In a night that was somewhere between hilarious, scurrilous and slanderous, the microphone was passed around and many rumours were confirmed and secrets revealed. When the floor was Bassett's he announced his great regret in turning down the second chance to manage at Bramall Lane.

McDonald provided Bassett's replacement Howard Kendall with funds to save the club from relegation and assemble a side that reached the first division play-off final. In July 1996 Petr Katchouro (a Belarus international) arrived from Dynamo Minsk for £650,000. After bagging a respectable 20 goals in 52 appearances, he departed holding the record for most appearances as a United substitute, appearing in this role in no less than 58 games. A year later, Greek international Vas Borbokis arrived from AEK Athens for £750,000. Don Hutchison, signed from West Ham in 1996, cost £1.2 million, thereby becoming the club's record signing (and a Scottish international while at Bramall Lane) before being sold to Everton for £650,000. As McDonald stood at Wembley at the 1997 play-off final and sang along to the 'Chip Butty' anthem it looked as if United were in the hands of a saviour. Then Crystal Palace scored a last-minute winner. The back page headline of the *Sheffield Star* lamented the defeat in terms of the £13 million that would have been earned had United been promoted. Having missed out on promotion, Kendall left for Everton. McDonald meanwhile lost interest in United and wanted his money back. His departure, however, was more protracted than his arrival.

Reversing Into Space

United fans learned a new world of business and a new vocabulary as a consequence of McDonald's dealings. In October 1996 Sheffield United Football Club merged with Conrad plc, a Manchester based leisure group, in what was known as a 'reverse takeover'. This put a £20 million valuation on Sheffield United plc and saw the club join the Stock Exchange. United now had two boards of directors—one (the FC) concerned with football, the other (the plc) concerned with finance. For the first time in their history United were vulnerable to a takeover from a total stranger. The chair of both was Mike McDonald, who spoke of his dream of making United financially strong enough to stand alongside any Premiership club. His sidekick and chief executive was South Yorkshire-born Charles Green who explained via a variety of media that the stock market floatation was a way of raising money for a number of projects and that the idea was to sell 50 million shares at 60 pence. The floatation raised £12 million and, on the first day, shares rose to 160 pence, settling at 110 pence. However, at one time in 1998, they fell to as low as 21 pence. McDonald's Texas Group Holdings was the largest shareholder with 13.1%, the rest consisted of small shareholders.

The plc concept theoretically made the club more accountable to shareholders—AGMs would have to be held and accounts presented. Green called it the most significant move in the club's history, and the local newspaper reported that United were perhaps the richest club outside the Premiership. The share floatation saw the club involved in a contest with United's 422 original shareholders. These shares, issued in the 1890s, bought the holders free admission to Bramall Lane for life. Before the new share issue, the originals were valued at £4,000. One such share bought for £500 in the early 1980s could be swapped for £5,540 of Conrad shares in the week of floatation.This share-holding collective refused the terms offered, which provoked McDonald to threaten to quit as chairman if they did not settle on his terms. The dispute provoked those affected to organise themselves in May 1998 into a pressure group. SUISA (Sheffield United Independent Shareholders Association) had a chair and acting chair, and used its powers to scrutinise the activities of the plc and FC. Its membership quadrupled in six months.

Shortly before the reverse takeover McDonald's plans for the Blades Leisure Complex were revealed. Part of this would include a hotel, pub, health centre, sports shop, food outlets and nursing home on land adjacent to Bramall Lane, which had formerly belonged to a wood yard and Sheffield City Council. Another plan was the Blade's Enterprise Centre which, located in the corner of John Street and Bramall Lane, would provide offices for small businesses, a community hall for locals and seven hundred new seats for the Kop. Planning permission for both projects was granted in September 1997. However, the Council owned land was then bought by an entrepreneur who built student accommodation and the ensuing boardroom turmoil meant that construction of the planned hotel did not begin until 2007.

As the 731st richest man in the UK in 1998, according to the *Sunday Times*, McDonald had obviously had financial success in wheeling and dealing elsewhere. McDonald could also point to his footballing successes: relegation that was threatening on his arrival had been avoided, the John Street Stand had been completed at a cost of £6 million and the club had been floated on the Stock Exchange. The floatation raised millions, which went towards high player wages, but the failure to achieve promotion meant the wage bill was untenable and brought the consternation of shareholders. The 1998 AGM saw the 830 shareholders in attendance vote unanimously to throw the absent McDonald off the board. However, the voting power of the board saw him returned. A loss of £6.7 million for the year was reported at the same AGM. Fellow board member Kevin McCabe publicly stated that it was the determination of the board that never again would the club fall under the domination of one shareholder.

The Italian Job

The exotic-sounding Carlo Colombotti took over from McDonald as United chairman in November 1998, declaring he would link his corporate concept of Blades Italia with his extensive contacts with Italian Serie A clubs to exchange players. A practicing solicitor for 30 years and a partner in a London-based law firm, Colombotti was well known for socialising in company that included singers Shirley Bassey and Sinitta. As chairman of the Peter Wood Group, he became a good friend of Phillip Wood, a Sheffielder and lifelong Blades fan, who was the main persuader in his decision to invest in United. When Colombotti took the chair, Wood became executive director. The pair joined forces with Sheffield businessman Stuart Johnson and formed Blades Italia to acquire Mike McDonald's 13% shareholding, advancing an immediate sum of £750,000 and promising £1.25 million in a proposed share issue. There was, however, no money available from Blades Italia for the team manager. For all the talk of links with Serie A, only one Italian player, the 19-year-old Francesco Miacci, arrived at Bramall Lane for a trial in 1999 and left eight weeks later. The boardroom debacle continued when Colombotti could not produce the promised cash to pay for the shares. Colombotti had spoken of slashing the club's wage bill by a third to get wages down to 70% of income. He was unable to achieve this and could not find other investors to help the situation.

Popular democracy saw the car park become the agora for fans' disgust. In March 1999 Kevin McCabe, who had become the football club chairman, addressed a car park demonstration on the same day that Ian Townsend resigned as chief executive after disagreeing with the club's transfer policy. In the furore, and following a year's absence, McDonald returned to board meetings in April 1999. Philip Wood left the position of chief executive—the third in nine months. Weeks later, Derek Dooley was asked to return to the club as acting chief executive to 'mend fences and heal wounds'. In the same month, three United directors met in the absence of Colombotti who blamed his non-appearance on travel difficulties. Colombotti then issued a writ against the three of them.

After repeated public wrangling with McDonald and other board members, Colombotti pulled his money out of United in October 1999. Taking his £750,000 investment (plus £50,000 interest) Colombotti left, accusing McDonald of buying and selling players without consulting the board and obstructing the building of the hotel and Enterprise Centre. Soon after Charles Green resigned and received a £107,000 payoff plus pension contributions. Questions as to why such sums should be paid to a man who resigned were never satisfactorily answered by the board. The search for answers produced unprecedented fan activism.

Blades Italia

Carlo Colombotti and Philip Wood gaze upon all they own in their brief reign at Bramall Lane in 1998

Mergers and Acquisitions

Part of McDonald's return involved a hearts and minds mission, which saw him establish meetings with supporter pressure groups, BIFA (Blades Independent Fans Association) and SUISA, representatives of the official supporter's club and the Senior Blades. Seeking to establish a Fans Forum, McDonald claimed that the entity would have an integral role in policy decisions at the club. His fellow directors initially gave the concept no support and took little part in its early meetings. Interestingly, all attending the Forum had to sign a confidentiality agreement as to the nature of their discussion. At its first meeting the Forum agitated for a 'kids for a quid' scheme with a view to enticing young supporters at massively reduced admission cost. Crowds, however, remained the same and the club even claimed the scheme made them lose tens of thousands in income. It also brought resentment from parents who had paid considerably more for season tickets for their children. In one such meeting with the supporters, McDonald admitted giving his chief executive Charles Green too much leeway in player transfers when, ostensibly, his main task was to oversee the building of the John Street stand. By way of defence, McDonald also emphasised the quality of players he, and not his managers, had brought to the club. He also revealed he had proposed to pay the Colombian international Hamilton Ricard's wages out of his company's funds should he sign for United. This idea was refused by the board and McDonald admitted to brokering the deal that took the player to Middlesbrough.

For the first time in the club's history, selected fans became involved, ostensibly, in the appointment of the team manager. Following the resignation of manager Steve Bruce in 1999, the 100 managerial applicants were reduced by the board to a shortlist of four. A week later, the supporters representatives were permitted to interview one of the four candidates—Sammy McIlroy. He did not get the job and was later to talk publicly about the humiliation of facing questions from fans when other candidates did not face a similar procedure. Regardless of fans' opinions, the board appointed Adrian Heath.

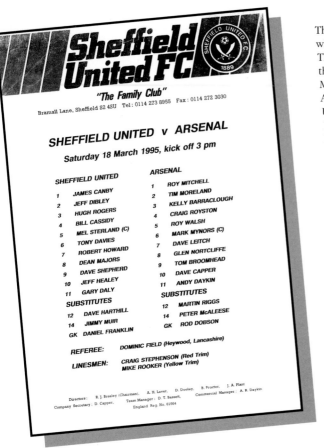

Sheffield United FC

"The Family Club"

Bramall Lane, Sheffield S2 4SU   Tel : 0114 273 8955   Fax : 0114 272 3030

SHEFFIELD UNITED v ARSENAL

Saturday 18 March 1995, kick off 3 pm

SHEFFIELD UNITED		ARSENAL	
1	JAMES CANBY	1	ROY MITCHELL
2	JEFF DIBLEY	2	TIM MORELAND
3	HUGH ROGERS	3	KELLY BARRACLOUGH
4	BILL CASSIDY	4	CRAIG ROYSTON
5	MEL STERLAND (C)	5	ROY WALSH
6	TONY DAVIES	6	MARK MYNORS (C)
7	ROBERT HOWARD	7	DAVE LEITCH
8	DEAN MAJORS	8	GLEN NORTCLIFFE
9	DAVE SHEPHERD	9	TOM BROOMHEAD
10	JEFF HEALEY	10	DAVE CAPPER
11	GARY DALY	11	ANDY DAYKIN
SUBSTITUTES		**SUBSTITUTES**	
12	DAVE HARTHILL	12	MARTIN RIGGS
14	JIMMY MUIR	14	PETER McALEESE
GK	DANIEL FRANKLIN	GK	ROD DOBSON

REFEREE: DOMINIC FIELD (Heywood, Lancashire)

LINESMEN: CRAIG STEPHENSON (Red Trim)
MIKE ROOKER (Yellow Trim)

Directors :   R. J. Brealey (Chairman),   A. H. Laver,   D. Dooley,   B. Procter,   J. A. Plant
Company Secretary : D. Capper.   Team Manager : D. T. Bassett.   Commercial Manager :   A. R. Daykin
England Reg. No. 61564

A prop from the 1996 film When Saturday Comes starring Sean Bean
The Arsenal line-up consists of the names of backroom staff employed at Bramall
Lane at the time. Martin Riggs was Mel Gibson's name in *Lethal Weapon*
and Bean's character was the number 14 for United named Jimmy Muir
The referee was named after United's accountant. One of the linesmen was then
employed as Pools Officer

The Fan Forum collapsed in October 1999 when SUISA pulled out of further negotiations. The following month BIFA left and demanded that McDonald resign. In both instances, McDonald's failure to give money to manager Adrian Heath was cited as a breach of faith. As United lost yet another manager in November 1999, chants of 'Sack the board' were heard. In response, McDonald criticised the fans, citing their inability to reach the 16,000 break-even figure and offering to walk away from the club if someone would take it from him. His statement that the club could only be run by its fans and his promise that the forum would make 90% of decisions concerning the running of the club were hot air. A few weeks later McDonald suggested a merger between United and Wednesday. Using historical reasoning in February 2000 McDonald stated, 'I see Sheffield as the place where football started and it could be the place where football changes'. The club did change when McDonald stood down and left leadership to those more concerned about the legacy of the club.

Literate Fandom

A supporter rebellion at Bramall Lane beginning in the late 1980s reached its apex in the mid-1990s. Fan activism was manifest throughout the country in the post-Hillsborough era and arrived at Bramall Lane in a variety of forms. Initially, opposition came via publication of the fanzine *Flashing Blade*, supplemented later by another, *The Red and White Wizard*. The former was begun in late 1988 and was still going strong at the time of publication, having passed its 100th edition in 2005. The latter, begun in February 1996, lasted for some 17 editions until February 2000 and was bound up with BIFA which had begun two years previously. *Flashing Blade* was started by five enthusiasts who, as well as wishing to inform and entertain, were critical and constructive. The aim as told to readers in the 22-page first edition was to take football out of the hands of property developers and the fist of the hooligan. The first edition cost 30p and the 500 fanzines were sold by enthusiasts outside the ground. Ten editions later, *Flashing Blade* was a 44-page publication and sold over a thousand copies each issue.

Flashing Blade became a forum for opinion, nostalgia and irreverence. The content was, at times, rude, scurrilous and bizarre. The publication's ethos was campaigning, in as much as it permitted debates of both national and local significance around the game. The club had a hands-off policy towards the fanzine and initially refused money earned by it to sponsor players. In later years, the relationship was much better and the fanzine became essential reading for players and some directors. At its peak, *Flashing Blade* produced six editions per season and sold 2000 per edition. *The Red and White Wizard* had similar attributes to *Flashing Blade*, but was more political and campaign-led with articles on racism in football.

It was also particularly antagonistic in its content towards United's dedicated *Sheffield Star* journalist, Tony Pritchett. This publication carried adverts for a solicitor's firm and the *Yorkshire Post*. Those who ran it were involved in the Football Supporters Association fan embassy during the European Championships of 1996 when some of the games were held in Sheffield.

Fan Resistance

It was in the mid-90s, however, that fans' resistance to boardroom controversies reached hitherto unknown levels amongst Blade fans and saw match days subject to a variety of protests. The board of directors were forced onto the back foot when explanations for their decisions and actions were sought from fans. Behind all of this was the Blades Independent Fan Association, an entity begun in 1993 and the brainchild of a Blades' fan and community activist following the sale of Brian Deane. The idea of an independent fan association was not realised until May 1994, when United were relegated from the Premiership and the same instigator, with a few mates, met to brainstorm as to what might be done. One of those present at this inaugural meeting was the editor of *Flashing Blade*. A letter sent by the protagonist to the *Green 'Un* was published and carried the story of the fans discontent and announced a public meeting under the rubric of BIFA in September 1994 for all interested.

BIFA's first meeting was held at Sheffield's Trade and Labour Club, just outside the city centre. The floor was opened to the three hundred supporters. The main issue of concern was seeking an answer from the United board as to what had happened to all the money that had gone into the club. Second to this was the desire for a business plan and a strategy for rebuilding the John Street stand. Seeking to present itself as a partner rather than a threat to the club, the first meeting established a 12-member steering committee.

Blades and Balloons
Blades at Old Trafford Manchester for the April 1998 FA Cup Semi-Final v Newcastle United

The old John Street stand and its replacement built in 1996

The local media dismissed the group as 'rebels' and even suggested their activities could ruin the club. Hundreds more were to sign up to BIFA in the next few weeks, including three former United players and the son of the man who was to become United chairman a few years later. Within ten weeks BIFA had 1,700 members and became the largest 'non-political' gathering in the city for ten years and at one time the largest independent fan association in Britain. With Reg Brealey trying to dismiss them as malcontents and agitators and the club disowning them, BIFA had to create an identity beyond that which they loved and followed and so invented their own insignia, albeit in the club's colours. BIFA then announced a public meeting and invited the United board to answer their questions.

BIFA's aim became primarily one of ridding the club of Reg Brealey, whilst seeking a partnership between fans and club to increase levels of support. It was to be a voice for fans as well as a voice that asked questions at the AGM. By early 1996 BIFA had written rules of association and had involved itself in well-publicised stunts. Thus a dozen members walked 15 miles in 1995 to an away game at Barnsley in an attempt to raise money for the cause. A few months later BIFA funded the unveiling of a plaque in Sheffield city centre at 10 Norfolk Row on the site where United were founded some 106 years previously. Amongst the 150 people in attendance were United's non-executive director Richard Caborn MP and Sheffield's most famous son and Hollywood heart-throb Sean Bean. All players and paid employees of the club were barred from attending by edict from chairman Brealey.

The visible source of BIFA's agitation was the state of the Bramall Lane ground. With the John Street Stand demolished in response to the Taylor Report, the proposed replacement was not built. The match-day atmosphere was poor and aesthetically the club looked third rate. Why, fans asked, would the chairman not build what had been promised? Better still, why didn't he leave the club? To remind him of this possibility BIFA decided to take their protest to a more public and organised level. Insisting on 'peaceful' and 'fun' direct action, members distributed 8,000 'red cards' in surrounding streets before a home game. These cards were then raised shortly after kick-off to show the chairman that they wanted him sent off. The next home game saw a similar number of green cards with the word 'Go!' on them, held aloft for one minute at kick-off.

A contract for the new John Street stand was eventually signed with a Leeds-based building company. Brealey invited the press onto the Bramall Lane pitch along with members of the Supporters Club to witness the signing before the final match of the 1993–94 season. On TV and in the local press Brealey informed fans of the impending start on the new stand. The first day of building was stated as being June 6th, completion would be 32 weeks later, in January 1995. At the AGM in December the revised completion date was specified to be June 1995. In response BIFA organised a June march to the building site to watch the publicised completion date—and found the site deserted and no stand built.

At the December 1994 AGM, the press were excluded for the first time in the club's history on the basis that an item in the accounts was *sub judice*. The meeting revealed an end-of-year operating profit of £1/2 million with debts reduced from £5 million to £3 million, and player assets, as estimated by the manager, of £6.2 million. An unexpected Christmas present came the chairman's way when six BIFA members and two of their children called to his home on Christmas Eve 1994 with 900 BIFA-produced cards bearing a variety of messages. Ever cordial, Brealey invited the callers in, argued his position and accepted their gifts. The card carried a cartoon of Reg Brealey manipulating a tiny figure of journalist Tony Pritchett as he sat on the chairman's knee. The journalist was none too pleased with the depiction. Reports in the *Star* spoke of abusive messages in the cards which infuriated BIFA members who had meticulously censored any abuse. In September of the following year a BBC radio journalist was barred from Bramall Lane by Brealey for reporting stories about the United players not being paid. Unwilling to play along with this situation, manager Dave Bassett held post-match press conferences with the reporter in the club car-park.

Words and Actions

In the battle for hearts and minds, Brealey had the ear of the local newspaper and could produce his own brochure. After 42 editions of the Brealey-inspired *Blades News* between 1981 and 1985, which contained a variety of news and pictures and was given free to fans, the publication disappeared until a special issue in November 1994. In this one-off, diagrams and details appeared of the proposed John Street Stand development. According to Brealey, BIFA was involved in 'anti-Blade behaviour' that 'may well be the ruin of the club'. Brealey blamed such people for the delay in building the new stand, arguing that their activities worried moneylenders, '... snide, cynical comments do nothing other than spread despondency and despair'. Other sources at Brealey's disposal to present his case were the electronic scoreboard at Bramall Lane which Brealey used both to announce the intention to build the new stand and his plan to sell his majority shareholding in January 1995.

In pursuit of getting their views heard, BIFA members sent dozens of letters weekly to the *Green 'Un* letters page in the, usually vain, hope of having them published. Then the newly appointed Publicity Officer encouraged all members to phone him—about anything. The club established a dialogue of sorts when five BIFA members met Derek Dooley. Admitting that there was a lack of communication between club and fans, Dooley refused their request to see the trading accounts. Unable to give any precise details about the proposed new stand, Dooley was forced to admit that he had no idea what the chairman's intentions were, nor could he say whether BIFA would be accepted as a *bona fide* representative organisation of the supporters in further discussion. In early 2000, BIFA published a Fan's Charter influenced, no doubt, by contemporary cross-party ideas that sought to empower individuals in the face of institutions. Seeking the election of a fan onto the board, the charter also sought a vision statement and a partnership with the club. It also proposed a national Football Heritage Centre at Bramall Lane.

Ceremonies and protests were then supplemented by attempts at dialogue. The first meeting between BIFA and Brealey was called by the former for November 1995 and scheduled for the City Memorial Hall hours before a home game. Brealey failed to appear in front of the 300 waiting fans. The agitation of BIFA had struck a chord, and upon replacing Brealey, Mike McDonald, in response to a BIFA invitation, instigated an exploratory meeting in January 1996. Three board members met BIFA, the official supporters' club and Senior Blades in a meeting chaired by local MP and United director Richard Caborn. This meeting of minds was later formalised under the title Fan Forum. A gathering held in January 1997 in the Bramall Lane Executive Club before a home game, saw 200 fans question all board members and the team manager. The dialogue that BIFA established continued for two years. Further Fan Forums were held in late 1997, twice in 1998 and once in 1999. A variety of United personnel attended to answer questions about team strip, ticketing, fan behaviour and building projects. However, in the face of further player sales, such dialogue could not prevent spontaneous pre- and post-match car park demonstrations in March 1998 by United fans, most of whom were not part of the forums.

This footballing glasnost saw vision statements become an integral part of the club's publicity. The sense of partnership with fans remains a debatable topic. A football heritage centre appeared in the shape of the Hall of Fame but this was not of BIFA's making and was built without their involvement. Two further fan bodies began, one, Football Unites, Racism Divides (FURD) was initiated by the same man who had co-founded BIFA. Involved in a variety of projects with minority populations within the vicinity of Bramall Lane, FURD became the first project of its kind to receive European Union funding.

The second half of the decade saw a continuation of the boardroom chaos that characterised the first. Whilst the personnel that constituted the board continued to change, the most visible change from the perspective of the supporters was manifest in the dug-out. Between the departure of Dave Bassett in 1995 and the appointment of Neil Warnock in December 1999, the club saw no fewer than five men hold the manager's job. One lasted weeks, the longest endured just a year. At times the players did not know from week to week who was in charge. That the team made the promotion play-offs and an FA Cup semi-final was credit to both them and their managers who at times worked in spite of the chairman and chief executive.

Howard's Way: Howard Kendall

In seeking to replace Dave Bassett, Mike McDonald brought in a man with impeccable managerial pedigree who had also been a fine footballer. Born in Tyneside in 1946, Howard Kendall had a distinguished career as a midfielder. In 1964 he became the youngest player to appear in an FA Cup Final, in a Preston team that lost 3–2 to West Ham. Moving to Everton in 1967, Kendall won a championship medal in 1970 and, four years later, after 257 League appearances, joined Birmingham for whom he played 115 games before signing for Stoke in 1977. Two years at Stoke saw Kendall then appointed player-manager at Blackburn in 1979. Within a year he got Rovers promoted to Division Two, but had returned to Everton as player-manager by 1981, making only four appearances before concentrating on managing. In 1984 Kendall led Everton out at Wembley on two occasions. Beaten by Liverpool in the League Cup, after a replay at Main Road, Everton won the FA Cup beating Watford 2–0. A year later Everton were League champions, lifted the European Cup Winners' Cup, and Kendall was named Manager of the Year.

The following year Everton finished second in the league, and in their third successive FA Cup Final lost 3–1 to Liverpool. Manager of the Year again in 1987 as Everton won the championship, Kendall's season ended with him seeking new challenges in the shape of Athletic Bilbao. The Spanish journey was brief; he was sacked in 1989. Returning to England, Kendall was appointed manager of Manchester City but resigned after six months to return to Everton. His second spell at Goodison Park was not a success and he left within three years. Six months in Greece preceded his next appointment in England at Notts County, where he lasted just 79 days and departed facing very public allegations of excessive drinking.

Arriving at Bramall Lane in February 1995, aged 49, Kendall inherited a team in free fall, next to the bottom of the league and with only one point from its previous five games. Kendall's arrival produced immediate changes and the club drew five of the next six games. Root and branch reform followed. Kendall signed seven players in seven weeks and implemented the pass-and-move style that typified his management. One of his first moves was to sell the club's only reliable goal scorer, Nathan Blake, to Bolton for £1.5 million. This somewhat controversial move made some financial sense when the money was used to bring in players of Premiership pedigree such as Don Hutchison, David White, Michael Vonk,

United's manager Howard Kendall

Clearly pleased at the new sponsors for the United shirt

Gordon Cowans, Andy Walker and Adrian Heath. The team on its day was a match for anyone in the division. It was an effective unit, but expensive. Losing only one of the season's final fourteen games, United finished a respectable ninth.

One Kendall signing proved very costly. Retiring from the game in late 1998 because of injury, John Ebbrell was at the time the most expensive player in the club's history. Bought from Everton aged 27 in February 1997 for £900,000, Ebbrell had made 265 appearances for Everton in a ten-year career having been originally signed by Kendall. Ebbrell was also a former England under-21 captain. Ebbrell's transfer fee was paid up front and the player given a four-year basic contract of £2,000 per week. His arrival was heralded by the manager as, 'the final piece in the promotion jigsaw'. The club overlooked the fact that Ebbrell had not played football for the previous two months because of an ankle injury. Ebbrell made two appearances for United's reserves before his 45-minute first-team debut ended with the recurrence of an ankle injury. He never played again. United could not make any insurance claim on the player and Ebbrell had his United contract settled at an agreed price of £250,000. This made his playing time whilst at United a remarkable £38,000 per minute.

Some of the money lost on Ebbrell had been earned in a fine 1996–97 season. Kendall took United to the first division play-off final, but a last-second goal saw Crystal Palace promoted at United's expense. This proved to be Kendall's last game in charge of United. His return to Everton for a third managerial stint was not universally welcomed, many Evertonians considered him third choice behind Bobby Robson of Barcelona and Sky television football pundit Andy Gray. Kendall, however, was well remembered for the mid-80s era when he brought glory to Everton and fans also recalled his declaration whilst at Manchester City that managing them was like having an affair whilst his relationship to Everton was akin to a marriage. The final day of the 1997–98 season saw Everton escape relegation. Two months later, the club and manager parted by mutual consent.

United's appointment of Kendall was a gamble, but a calculated one, in as much as Kendall's managerial record was very good. Indeed, Kendall was the second choice of the FA when Graham Taylor was appointed England manager in 1990. His record at United was 34 wins and 21 defeats in 82 games. Many a player in his squad spoke highly of him, he brought a sense of togetherness in a squad that had lost its way. The £1 million compensation that United sought from Everton on his departure, was never paid; any agreement the club entered into was not legally binding. His 18 months at Bramall Lane did see a revival in playing fortunes and Kendall did attract some excellent, if ageing, players. Kendall also commanded a strange adulation from the Bramall Lane faithful. His final game in charge of United saw him wearing a bright lime green shirt, the likes of which Wembley had never before seen on the back of a football manager, having to endure a song in his praise from 30,000 Blades. Drawing on the tune of *Winter Wonderland* it proclaimed:

> *One Howard Kendall,*
> *One Howard Kendall*
> *Whiskey in hand—couple of cans*
> *Walking in a Kendall wonderland.*

His successors had the task of picking up the pieces of a disappointed squad and a huge wage bill that the club could not afford to pay.

Bottling Emotion: Nigel Spackman

Joining United in the summer of 1996 was the 35-year-old Nigel Spackman. Employed as player coach and assistant manager to Kendall, Spackman remained at Bramall Lane for 20 months, before resigning as manager on account of boardroom interference on transfer policy and player selection. Young, intelligent, articulate, frank, and astutely assisted by former Scotland international Willie Donachie, Spackman promoted a passing game, attacking from midfield and encouraging wing-backs to get forward.

A tremendous playing career which began at Bournemouth saw Spackman play at the top level with Chelsea, Liverpool, QPR, Glasgow Rangers (where he won three league championships) and Chelsea again. On joining United, he was still a very capable player and, when Kendall resigned, Spackman in a caretaker capacity, brought in some excellent players—Brian Deane, Paul McGrath, Dean Saunders, and Vas Boborskis. After a few months he was given the managerial position full time.

One match in Spackman's reign brought a controversy not of his making. January 1998 saw Sheffield United become infamous when, for the first time in modern British football history, a linesman was knocked unconscious by a spectator. The perpetrator happened to be a Blade. United were holding hosts Portsmouth 1–1 only for United goalkeeper Simon Tracey to be sent off for handling the ball outside his area. The decision was taken by the referee after discussing the matter with his linesman. Moments later the same linesman was attacked by a United fan, who had clambered over the perimeter wall of the visitors' section. After a 15-minute delay and treatment by the Portsmouth physiotherapist, the linesman was stretchered away. In the resultant media furore, dozens of pundits inevitably clamoured for more restrictive security in the grounds. The assailant was a 34-year-old Sheffield born butcher turned hotel worker living on the south coast. He was not a regular United follower. Pleading guilty to the assault charge, he admitted being drunk and was given a three-month custodial sentence. The 38-year-old linesman was kept in hospital under observation for two days and later claimed to be suffering from stress related disorder. The United manager was also under stress around the same time.

United's manager Nigel Spackman
Looking for the club's two leading goalscorers
sold without his knowledge in February 1998

At the turn of the year, United were third in the table and promotion was within their capabilities. Then in January 1998, chief executive Charles Green sold the club's two leading goalscorers Jan-Aage Fjortoft and Brian Deane on the same day. Soon after, Spackman's assistant Willie Donachie left for a similar position with Joe Royle at Manchester City. As share prices fell to 37p, Spackman was ordered by McDonald to raise £1.5 million in player sales. United still had a chance for promotion, but the powers-that-be at Bramall Lane seemed to be sabotaging Spackman's efforts. Faced with this impossible situation, Spackman resigned a week before the team was due to play an FA Cup quarter-final. In response McDonald labelled Spackman a 'bottler', accusing him further of putting his self-interest ahead of the club. Soon after, McDonald resigned after being barracked by Blades fans in the United car park before and after a match, stating, 'I'm not standing for that after all I've done for this club'. Meanwhile, a figure within the coaching staff took over from Spackman.

Sheffield-born Steve Thompson became the first person born within the city boundaries to hold managerial power at Bramall Lane, albeit in a caretaker capacity. Born in Pitsmoor and having played for Sheffield and Yorkshire schoolboys, Thompson spent six years at Lincoln City before moving to Charlton, then Leicester, arriving at Bramall Lane as a player in 1988 at a cost of £15,000. In 1990, having returned to Lincoln, he had acted as temporary manager and in 1995 held similar positions at Southend and Notts County. Arriving at United in July 1997 as a coach, Thompson assisted Spackman and later Steve Bruce until November 1998 when Bruce decided his services were no longer required. Thompson's temporary stewardship of United between Spackman and Bruce lasted 12 League games and one FA Cup semi-final. The latter saw the Blades lose 1–0 to Newcastle at Old Trafford. The League games saw United confirm their place in the play-offs, but lose to Sunderland on aggregate in the semi-finals. Thompson's League managerial record is thus a creditable won four, lost four. Quick witted and personable, Thompson had the confidence of Charles Green, to whom he had acted as best man at his wedding. Unfortunately for Thompson, he did not have the confidence of the dressing-room. Whilst stating to the local media on taking the caretaker role that he was 'born to manage United', Thompson had to make do and manage with United pre-fixed with Cambridge whom he took charge of briefly in 2005 before they dropped out of the Football League. In the summer of 2006, Thompson was appointed manager of Notts County.

Who's the Boss?: Steve Bruce

Succeeding Thompson as manager was the kingpin of one of England's best ever club sides. In his mid-thirties, Steve Bruce came to Bramall Lane as player-manager in the summer of 1998, in the hope that his captaincy of the great Manchester United side of the mid-1990s might be sufficient to make him a good manager. Chosen ahead of Stuart Houston, Bruce Rioch and Neil Warnock, Bruce decreed to his players on his first day that any mobile phone that rang when he was speaking would merit a fine of £10. Unfortunately, the first tone heard after this decree was that of his own mobile—he duly fined himself. The Newcastle-born Bruce had played for the famous Wallsend Boys Club and represented the city at youth level. However, he had repeated rejections from clubs in the region and in the 1980s found himself seeking a career in football hundreds of miles from home in Gillingham. He stayed with the third division outfit for seven years before moving to Norwich. However, his first season saw Norwich relegated from Division One. A year later he moved to Old Trafford and enjoyed an illustrious career that for some reason never produced full international honours.

In July 1998 Bruce was informed by Mike McDonald that money would be available but the cash was denied to him a month later. In December the club sold its star forward Dean Saunders to Benfica for half a million pounds, none of which was given to Bruce to spend on a replacement. An announcement in March 1999 that the club no longer had to sell to balance the books was followed a week later by the sale of Vas Borboskis for half a million pounds and two players in exchange. A month later, David Holdsworth and Graham Stuart were sold for £1.5 and £1.1 million respectively. Bruce was furious but momentarily placated by the words of McDonald's temporary replacement as chairman, Carlo Colombotti, who promised him two thirds of the net proceeds. In truth it was one tenth. A sum of £275,000 brought in Oliver Tebily. Months later, seeking clarification from the returning McDonald as to what money would be available, Bruce learned that no loan players could be signed and that the wage bill needed cutting by a further £1.5 million. Having reduced the wage bill drastically already and having raised £4.5 million in transfers, Bruce was now being told that his achievements were not enough. At this point, in May 1999, Bruce resigned only one year into his three-year contract. Bruce sought a coherent club policy and a chain of command with which to communicate. When he could not find this, he left. Weeks later he became the manager of Huddersfield Town.

In his time at United, Bruce was to work under no fewer than six chairmen. He remembers the bewilderment of the club's policy:

> *I never knew who the boss was, so when I met Dean Saunders coming out of the ground as I was going in one Saturday afternoon, telling me three hours before kick-off that he had just been sold to Benfica without my knowledge. I didn't even know who to complain to.*

After Huddersfield, Bruce managed Wigan, Crystal Palace and Birmingham. Taking over at Crystal Palace in May 2001, he began his fourth managerial job in 22 months. Bruce also owned a greetings card shop in North Wales and tried his hand at historical soccer-detective fiction, producing three tomes, *Striker!*, *Sweeper!* and *Defender!*

United's Player-Manager Steve Bruce (third left) leading his men in a collective show of annoyance

Cussed Behaviour

Bruce's reign included two incidents that brought global attention to Sheffield United. In February 1999 Arsenal beat United in an FA Cup fifth round tie at Highbury. The Arsenal winner, scored by Dutchman Marc Overmars in the 76th minute, was allowed to stand despite the Nigerian debutant Nwanko Kanu failing to return the ball to United at a throw-in after they had kicked it out of play to allow an injured player to receive attention. United were holding the Gunners 1–1 and were in sight of a replay at Bramall Lane. Some 15 minutes from the end, United's young winger Lee Morris went down with cramp, causing goalkeeper Alan Kelly to punt the ball into touch so he could receive attention. In the customary way following treatment, Arsenal's Ray Parlour, threw the ball towards the United area. However, Kanu gathered it and, going forward, crossed for Overmars to score from close range.

Furious protests followed, which included Bruce signalling to his team to leave the pitch. Police and stewards intervened to prevent Blades fans breaking seats and invading the pitch. The match was held up for eleven minutes. The game ended in a 2–1 Arsenal victory. After the game the United board protested to their Arsenal counterpart. Kanu admitted his error, stating that he had not realised why the throw-in had occurred. In response, the Arsenal vice-chairman David Dein offered to replay the game, as did the Arsenal manager Arsene Wenger. The Arsenal officials met the representatives of the FA and Referees Association, Wenger admitted the result was 'sport-wise, not right'. The FA agreed to the replay which took place in front of 37,000 at Highbury three days later. FIFA became involved and stated that in their opinion, the Football Association had broken its own competition rules, then decided 24 hours before kick off that the game could go ahead. The Premier League's Referees Officer, Phillip Don, said the replay set a dangerous precedent, adding that no laws were broken when the goal was scored. Admission to the replay was half price and all profits were donated to charity. Arsenal won 2–0. Overmars was booed by Blades throughout, as was Kanu when he came off the bench. Arsenal lost in the semi-finals to Manchester United.

It was Bruce's assistant who was responsible for the other incident that brought national attention to United, when his words spoke larger than deeds. In December 1998 United's assistant manager, 41-year-old John Deehan, was arrested during a match at Loftus Road, home of Queens Park Rangers. Shouting instructions to players from the dug-out, he was warned by a nearby woman police constable for his use of language. His continued use of certain words saw him arrested by her during the second half, thereby missing United's victory as he sat in a cell in a West London police station. Released four hours later, he was bailed to appear at Hammersmith police station weeks later where he was cautioned as to his future conduct.

The End of the Century: Adrian Heath

In the summer of 1999 the United share price dropped to 12.5p. Mike McDonald bought another two million, calling it the 'bargain of the century'. Meanwhile, an EGM of the board of directors saw two men leave the meeting to door-step Dave Bassett at his Sheffield home to offer him the manager's chair. He refused the offer, having accepted Barnsley's offer only hours earlier. The United job went instead to Adrian Heath, who became United's third manager in three close seasons and the fifth in thirty months. In the same period, United had managed to lose several directors, the company secretary, the commercial manager, three chief executives, the kit man, the physiotherapist and the promotions manager.

On paper at least, Heath had more experience than his two predecessors. A playing career begun in his home town of Stoke in 1979, had then taken him to Everton under Howard Kendall in the Everton glory years of 1982 to 1989. Heath then moved to Aston Villa following a brief interlude with Spanish club Espanyol. After two years at Manchester City in the early 1990s he returned to Stoke and then enjoyed three years playing at Burnley. Arriving at Bramall Lane in December 1995 as player and assistant manager to Kendall, Heath left in March 1996 to become player-manager of Burnley. When this did not work out, he left Turf Moor in 1997 and was given a coaching job under Howard Kendall at Everton and a year later took charge of the reserves at Sunderland.

On joining United, Heath publicly stated his awareness of the financial problems, adding that he was promised that money generated by outgoing transfers would be his to bring in new talent. Heath had no assistant and no money and his short reign of five months saw the sale of key players of international standing—Alan Kelly, Oliver Tebily, Lee Morris and Marcello, to be replaced by players obtained on free transfers or small fees. After the sale of Alan Kelly, Heath was quoted as saying 'his departure was in the best interests of the club'. But losing a goalkeeper of international quality was not going to convince fans that this was in the club's best interests. The reign of Heath was an unhappy one and his team lost ten and won only four of the games he managed. Heath left in November 1999 when a crowd of less than 9,000 saw United lose 3–1 at home to a Port Vale side that had not won an away game since March. United were 23rd in the table. His assistant Russell Slade took charge for a few games but left banging the door when informed by Derek Dooley in December that the job would not be his.

> **The early years of the decade saw two men in United shirts who whilst drawn from roughly the same neighbourhood were poles apart in character. Whilst both were determined in quite different ways the response they provoked amongst Blades fans was very different. One was to become a fan having left Bramall Lane, the other re-invented himself in a manner unique in the history of the English game.**

Oo—ah: Bob Booker

About once a decade a player becomes the darling of the Sheffield United fans and is remembered with awe and a smile. Usually such players have remarkable footballing ability and usually little is known about them when off the pitch. An exception to this is Bob Booker who was with United for four years from 1988–1992. He arrived in relative silence but left in what was one of the most unusual departures a United player has ever suffered when 25,000 Blades cheered his free transfer to a Second Division side as he stood in the middle of the pitch. This Watford-born battler had modest skills and ambitions but had something many players will never have—an appetite for the game, combined with a love of the club and its fans and an enthusiasm based in the wonderment of being allowed to play football and get paid for it.

Excelling only in running and football at school, Booker left formal education at 16 to begin a four-year apprenticeship in an upholstery warehouse whilst playing for a local Saturday team called Bedmond where he formed a strike force with Derek French. Attracting Watford's interest, Booker attended a couple of training sessions until a director of Brentford invited him to Griffin Park for a trial. Playing centre-forward he scored two goals, and was picked for the next few weeks. Signed on a Thursday, in a deal which saw Bedmond receive a set of tracksuits, Booker made his first team Brentford debut in Division Three two days later against his home town team Watford. He was kicked all over by a centre back called Ian Bolton who was in later years to become his brother-in-law.

Loaned to Barry Fry's Barnet then in the Conference League, Booker scored a few, then in his first game back for Brentford scored a hat-trick. There was no looking back, for the next 10 seasons he was an ever-present playing over 280 league games and scoring 42 goals. Famed for his versatility he alternated between centre-forward, centre-half and right-back. Receiving the supporters' Player of the Year in 1982, Booker had by then played in every position bar goalkeeper. Portsmouth made a bid for him, Dave 'Harry' Bassett, then manager of Wimbledon watched him and having taken over the helm at Bramall Lane in 1988 remembered Booker and got him on a free transfer.

His Brentford career was modest but doing very nicely until a cruciate ligament injury in 1986. Out of the game for 18 months and with a warning from the surgeon that he might not play again, Booker's head dropped. Aged 30, hobbling and in his testimonial year Booker was informed that he was surplus to requirements. His intention was to take the anticipated wedge from the benefit game and sink it into a window cleaning business. Unable to decide he meanwhile got over the injury and was selected for a game against United in October 1988. A 4–1 Blade victory impressed Booker who was touched when wandering around the United dressing room after the game to see that Bassett's flip-chart tactics identified him as the danger man.

Bob Booker
Six foot and cost nothing

Meanwhile the Blades' midfielder, Simon Webster, broke his leg. One Sunday afternoon Derek French, now the physio at Bramall Lane, rang Booker to ask if he fancied a move to United. Within 24 hours of being in the city Booker realised the nature of its football passions. His new tracksuit worn in the pub gave away his new Blade identity and brought him the attention of inquisitive Blades who wanted to know more about him and fill his glass by way of a welcome. Played as an attacking midfielder Booker's main job was to stop the ball when it came from the opposition's defence and knock it forward when it came from United's rearguard, his other task was to win the ball and give it to smaller, cleverer colleagues. It all turned out lovely in the end, but the first few months were distressing. His confidante at the time was Mick Rooker in United's Commercial Department. This Sheffield-born Blade of the same age as Booker knew the fans well and when Booker came to him on a downer after a bad verballing, Rooker gave him the following advice:

Give 100%, don't hide because Blades will suss you; acknowledge them at the end of the match to tell 'em you're here and you're not scared of being seen.

It was sound advice. Booker did as instructed and Blades fans grew to love him.

Memorable performances from Booker soon followed followed. An FA Cup tie victory at Barnsley saw Booker taking the applause and shaking hands with Blades fans 10 minutes after the final whistle. Another cup win at Watford saw him on a one-man lap of honour for both Blades and his family and mates at the other end. There were two Blade chants in honour of the man:

We've got Bobby Booker he's a dirty ——.
He's six foot tall;
He cost —— all

Of wider appeal was the rather daft but infectious,

Oo-ah Bob-Bu-Kah
I said oo-ah Bob-Bu-Kah

which graced nearly every game he played as well as bars and neighbourhoods honoured by beer-soaked Blades.

Booker was a rarity in football. At a loose end after training and with his fiancé still living in Watford, he would take his beloved Rottweiler for walks in the park or seek company back at Bramall Lane. Talking with fans came naturally to him; he would appear at or open supporter functions. A 10-year-old's request to come to the family home for tea saw Booker (and Mick Rooker) turn up, munch meat and potato pie, and stay for two hours. Within a week 50 similar invites arrived at the Lane requesting Booker's presence at various dinner tables.

If that's hard to imagine so is a premiership player who drove a D-reg Sierra estate and who, upon making his premiership debut against Liverpool at the Lane, asked the photographers to take a picture of him in front of the kop for posterity. Modest by nature and modest in what he owns today, Booker appreciates what he earned from the game. It meant a lot to him to be appreciated. He never had an agent, nor as a player did he earn a four-figure weekly wage. Players' contracts were decided by Dave Bassett, but the nitty-gritty was left to the Managing Director, Derek Dooley. The latter and Booker sat and sorted it out and shook on it. His years as a Manager and a Director had resigned Dooley to the knock on the door half an hour after a deal had been agreed, usually disputing clause six and the win bonus or such like. Duly, Booker knocked later in the day but it was to thank Dooley for the extension and the rate and, pledging his devotion to the club, promised to do his best. Never having seen such magnanimity Dooley admitted it brought a tear to his eye.

Booker's life at Bramall Lane ended in late 1991 after 109 League games and 13 goals. Whilst Bassett offered a one-year renewal, Brentford offered a three-year deal. Not wanting to leave but aged 32 and seeking security, Booker made the hardest decision of his life and decided to leave Bramall Lane. It was though in unusual circumstances when, shortly before a United–Wednesday derby and a full-house at Bramall Lane, he said his good-byes:

…I told Harry I was off, he thanked me and we had a cuddle then told me to get out on the pitch. Dave Kilner (the match DJ) announced it and led me out. I saw the John Street boys go into one, but not many saw me bawling my eyes out. I didn't wanna come off…

He watched the match, drank too much in the sponsor's bar after and joined Brentford next day.

The first season back he suffered his first ever relegation. The following season saw promotion, but a renewal of the knee trouble. Told by the surgeon to pack in, Booker cashed in his remaining 18 months of contract and then considered his future. Aimless, difficult and depressed he went off the game. He turned up occasionally at United games and sat with the fans with a club shirt on cheering the team. Periodically he was part of the match commentary team for BBC Radio Sheffield. A Testimonial game saw Brentford play United. This produced a welcome final pay-day and saw 200 Blades travel to out-shout the 4,000 home fans in his praise. He put packs of beer on their coaches by way of thanks.

In 1994 a call came from a Director of Brentford offering Booker the job of youth team coach. In five seasons he won a few trophies and saw a few of his protégées make the first team. Moved up to the position of Assistant manager Booker then moved to Brighton in late 2000 and was assistant to Sheffield-born Micky Adams. Taking over as caretaker manager when Adams left for Leicester, Booker then resumed the position of Assistant to Mark McGhee until September 2006.

The 1988–92 seasons were wonderful years for Blades fans. The commitment of the players was probably unprecedented in the club's history. Known to his team-mates as 'son of' because Bassett excused him from Sunday training sessions to allow him to see his fiancé, Booker could reflect on the unique spirit that was the club in those years:

> *We were a bunch of thugs really, but we worked hard for each other and Harry, and never let ourselves down… Sheffield people can't be fooled. They want a team of eight triers who will give it everything and leave it to three flair players to do the rest. That's what we were…*

United's captain Vinnie Jones
In characteristic mode instructing someone or other as to the benefits of his opinion over theirs

Method acting: Vinnie Jones

One of the more remarkable characters to ever grace Bramall Lane was Vinnie Jones, who arrived from Leeds for a fee of £700,000 in September 1990 and left eleven months later to join Chelsea for £575,000. His 40 first team appearances produced two goals but he can claim one record for United which is unlikely to be beaten—namely being booked after just five seconds at Manchester City in February 1991. A personal best was actually beaten a year later when playing against United for Chelsea. Jones was booked within three seconds. In a career that produced over 486 appearances, he was dismissed 13 times.

Brought to United to captain a failing top division team, Jones proved an inspirational leader, operating in central midfield. He was a non-stop motivator, ball-winner and his long throws were responsible for some crucial United goals. A little-known fact was that before his full United debut at Southampton in September 1990, Jones had actually guested as goalkeeper for a United XI at Bob Booker's testimonial at Brentford.

Born on a Watford council estate, Jones played for Watford Boys but on leaving school washed pots in a boy's public school for four years earning a few pounds to supplement this existence with non-league Wealdstone. His ability saw Dave Bassett pay £10,000 to take him to Wimbledon. In his second game he scored the winner against Manchester United. His debut as Wimbledon captain saw him sent off for brawling. His sense of leadership was about getting the upper hand by any means. In the art of intimidation he was without parallel.

Jones was also a very useful player who provoked some very good managers to pay over £2.6 million for him. He joined Howard Wilkinson's Leeds in June 1989 for £650,000 and won a championship medal. Former Blades' manager Ian Porterfield bought Jones from United for Chelsea and then a year later Wimbledon paid Chelsea £700,000 to facilitate his return to where it all began. He ended his career at Queens Park Rangers, whom he had joined in March 1998 for £500,000.

In his post-football career, Jones was to merit acres of publicity and be a constant figure in all strands of the British media. His transition from footballer to film star had no equal and he was highly acclaimed for his roles in the big-earning films, *Lock, Stock and Two Smoking Barrels*, *Mean Machine*, *Gone in 60 Seconds* with Nicolas Cage and *Snatch*, with Brad Pitt. However not all his celluloid exploits received acclaim. In 1992 he produced a video entitled *Soccer's Hard Men* with the advice to 'follow through with your studs down his Achilles'. The Football Association fined him £20,000 with a six-month suspended sentence.

A one-time satellite TV chat show led to Jones addressing Eton College, the Oxford and Cambridge Unions and acting as coach to the House of Commons football team. In 2001 he relocated to Hollywood, where he captained a team consisting of Rod Stewart, Robbie Williams and Steve Jones of the Sex Pistols. He was the face and body for Yves Saint Laurent clothing and advertised aftershave, vodka and even had his own V-shaped haircut. He also wrote two autobiographies six years apart and, curiously, was Britain's representative to a 1997 Dutch conference on fair play and tolerance in sport.

Jones received international recognition in 1994 by virtue of discovering a Welsh grandmother. After having a Welsh dragon tattooed on his chest, Jones was then sent off on the second of his nine Welsh international appearances.

Antagonism was integral to his game. His first return to Bramall Lane in Chelsea colours provoked an outbreak of booing by Blades fans whenever he touched the ball. When asked about this situation, Jones replied:

> United wanted me off the wage bill. My leaving was nothing to do with me. It just so happened that my first game for Chelsea was Sheffield United away, and they booed me as I walked onto the pitch.

The evening ended in a fracas in a casino with a Blades fan. When United visited Chelsea at Stamford Bridge for an FA Cup fixture Jones gave gestures of abuse to the visiting Blades and made exaggerated claps of appreciation to the Chelsea fans that now cheered him.

Jones was the biggest character in football in his era. His books sold tens of thousands and his legend grows by the year. The hard image he cultivated could not conceal a very useful footballer and the off-pitch antics and controversies both during and post his career should not divert from a character who works endlessly for charity and good causes.

The second half of this decade saw the departure of four men who had made Bramall Lane a happy place. From diverse backgrounds and with diverse abilities they provoke fond memories in Blades who witnessed them at work. One worked for United with no recompense, another left after 30 years of knowledge of the ins and outs of the club and took many secrets to his grave. Yet another left in defiance at the directors who sold him. A final one left Bramall Lane with a limp.

Original and Genuine: Dane Whitehouse

Dane Whitehouse, the most popular locally born United player of the past 20 years, enjoyed a decade of footballing fame from 1988 to 1998 with the club he supported as a boy. The epitome of the local lad made good, Whitehouse's top-of-the-range soft top BMW shouted 'made it', even if it was often parked incongruously in the middle of a tough council estate. But the football cliché that you're only as good as your last game was made painfully true in Whitehouse's career when a challenge from an opponent finished his career at the age of 28.

A schoolteacher had spotted Whitehouse's talent in school-yard kick-abouts and got him a trial with the under-11 city side. He impressed and was selected and remained in the team for the next four years. An extended strike by teachers in the 1980s saw a boycott of extra-curricular activities, which included Saturday football teams. A Sunday team run by a mate's uncle kept Whitehouse busy and talent scouts interested. At the age of 11 he was poached to join the prestigious Sheffield Rangers and eventually the best Sunday boys team, known as Junior Blades; in effect United's nursery team. Scoring up to 30 goals a season whilst playing as a winger made him a valuable commodity. Training twice a week at Bramall Lane and every school holiday, Whitehouse learned the ropes via the three coaching 'Macs': Ray McHale, John McSeveney and, later, Billy McEwan.

Dane Whitehouse

Liking what they saw, United retained Whitehouse under the Youth Training Scheme (YTS) for the princely sum of £27.50 plus travelling expenses. Of this £10 went weekly to his mum and £20 monthly went towards a bus pass. Lunch was crisp sandwiches from 'Bri and Irene's' corner shop adjacent to Bramall Lane. Things improved a little when Dave Bassett took over as manager in 1988—the club fed the youngsters after training. The dismissal of McEwan as manager could have been a major blow because he had managed and nurtured Whitehouse from the age of 15, but Bassett saw something he liked and his youth team coach Keith Mincher made Whitehouse team captain. Continuing to learn and impress, Whitehouse was promoted to the reserves in 1988 and, after only six outings, made it to the first team for a Division Three match at Blackpool.

Whitehouse became a favourite with Blades of all ages. Honest, hard-working, tough-tackling and always liable to score goals, he initially played as a winger. Bassett then told him to 'tuck in' a bit, then back track to close down opposition full-backs. When times demanded it, Whitehouse proved adept in midfield and even at left-back. However, in November 1997 in an away fixture at Port Vale a reckless challenge shattered his knee and all its contents. A four-hour operation was completed two days later and then began a three-day nightmare of pain. The battle of mind-over-matter had only just begun—Whitehouse had a year of basic recovery to endure.

When Port Vale visited the Lane five months after the incident, his father made his move after the match and got onto the visitors' coach looking for the perpetrator. Fortunately for the target two security guards hired for the day by Port Vale in expectation of trouble stood in his way. A week later a letter arrived from the player—it contained an apology, a promise that the tackle was unintentional, and an appeal at empathy having once sustained a broken cheekbone. It had taken five months and a team-coach drama to force him to put pen to paper.

The United side of 1992–93 contained the inseparable triumvirate of local born Blades; Carl Bradshaw, Mitch Ward and Whitehouse, whose on-the-pitch ethos dictated that if one was kicked all three exacted revenge. Known to their predominantly Southern-born team-mates as the 'Three Slap-shots' in honour of the strange brothers in an ice-hockey film starring Paul Newman, only Whitehouse remained at Bramall Lane five years later. A transfer was rumoured, but only one firm offer ever got back to him:

> *I was on holiday in Tenerife and I phoned home and me dad told me I'd signed for Birmingham! When I came home I went straight to Charles Green's office and said 'what's happening?' He tells me they've accepted a £1.5m bid... so I said fair enough, but I want a word with the manager. I said to Nigel Spackman, 'am I in your plans?' He said I was so I told Green I was going nowhere and what did he think he was doing selling me without asking...?*

Whitehouse never recovered from the injury and never played again. United offered him a job coaching the juniors, but Whitehouse went into his own business ventures. His presence at United games and supporters functions still sees him signing autographs and receiving the good wishes of everyone. He may well be the last ever local-born player to serve the club over a decade from youth scheme to professional.

From The Heart: Alan Kelly

After 164 first-team games for Preston North End, Alan Kelly found his way to Sheffield to sign for a team he had never played against. On joining United in July 1992, Kelly became a Premiership player and £100 a week better off than in the second division. He was, in reality, one of the lowest paid players in the new division. The deal for the clubs was £150,000 down, a further £50,000 based on appearances, £10,000 for the first international Cap, and a 20% sell on clause. Signing at 4 am, he met his team mates as they were about to depart for Sweden. Hours later, Kelly was asleep with his head against the coach window. His slumbers were awoken by team mates Carl Bradshaw and David Barnes who, with mock serious faces, offered to fight him. After telling them to go away, he found himself in a headlock and being bitten by Bradshaw while Barnes worked him over from the front. Thinking the assault was real, he managed to throw both his assailants off and in the ensuing scuffle, punched Barnes, who fell down the coach stairway into the toilet. The prostrate Barnes shouted 'Brilliant, brilliant, that will do for me, welcome to Sheffield United'. Next morning his new manager asked him in all innocence: 'Did you get sorted out last night?' Not knowing how to answer, Kelly gave an unconvincing 'Yes', but realised that he passed the test. The fact that he had difficulty moving his neck for the next week was irrelevant to his team mates and manager.

Born in Preston in 1968, Kelly soon realised that his father was a famous local figure. Kelly Senior was a goalkeeper for Preston North End and the Republic of Ireland between 1960 and 1973 and still holds the record number of appearances for the club. Such abilities rubbed off on the three Kelly brothers, all of whom became goalkeepers of varying ability. Two actually made a living from net minding and one had a spell at Bramall Lane in 2003 making one appearance. However, it was as a defender that Kelly represented Preston schools and was signed on schoolboy forms by North End in 1983. A year later he became a goalkeeper when the regular keeper hurt his finger in a practice match. Kelly stood in and played the game of his life. Apprenticed at the nearby Leyland motor factory, Kelly played for Preston's youth team and occasionally the reserves, but found cycling the 11 miles to work at 6 am and finishing at 4 pm to attend away games and returning at midnight hard going. Something had to give and it turned out to be his desire to be an electrician. The joint managerial partnership of Tommy Booth and Brian Kidd offered him a professional contract in September 1985. Breaking into the first team in February 1986, Kelly also represented the Irish youth team in the 1986 European Championship Qualifiers. A full Ireland cap came his way in 1993 and a further 33 were accumulated as well as two World Cup tournaments; in the USA in 1994 and Japan and Korea in 2002, albeit as a squad player in both.

His United home debut came in a 1-1 draw with Arsenal. In the previous week, United's regular goalkeeper Simon Tracey had been sent off at Tottenham, and Kelly made footballing history becoming the first goalkeeping substitute in British football. In his first season at Bramall Lane an injury to his good mate Tracey saw Kelly play 43 games. Because of injuries to Tracey, Kelly played on average two-thirds of each of his seasons at the Lane. Such competition had consequences. Kelly admits he frequently played when not fully fit, but did so to avoid losing his place. He once played a match with a broken finger, assisted by five pain-killing jabs. The season the club were relegated from the Premiership, Kelly played his part in keeping no fewer than nine clean sheets in League games.

Kelly played under five managers at United and a few rows with such men occurred. One took place before the 1994–95 season home opener against Notts County. Kelly explains the circumstances:

> *Harry and me had sorted a contract out Friday night. When I came in to sign it on a Saturday morning, it had been changed. I wouldn't sign it, so he dropped me.*

The incident dragged on. Dropped for the next seven games, Kelly telephoned Bassett to sort out the problem once and for all, face to face. The meeting concluded with the original terms of the contract agreed. In Kelly's opinion the problem lay in the power struggle between Bassett and chairman Brealey.

In 1998, after recovering from a cartilage operation and having played well in his first game for months, he visited the manager Steve Bruce to inform him of how well the knee felt, only to be told that he was on his way out, as part of a player-plus cash deal with Birmingham. Kelly had no say in the matter;

Ireland's number 1
Alan Kelly enjoying a post-match, pre-shower banana after a hard afternoon's keeping in the early 1990s

> *I told him I wanted to stay. He replied that the board would not be offering me a new contract in 18 months. So I went to Birmingham next day, agreed a deal in 90 minutes, and came back to say goodbye. Then Bruce told me the deal was off. I never knew why.*

This event brought a realisation that, despite the good service he had given, he was not going to get a further contract at Bramall Lane, or even be asked where he would like to go. Angry about this, Kelly went public on local radio. This was a conscious decision to let fly about the situation, and afterwards look everybody concerned in the eye. In 1996 Kelly had signed a four-year contract, agreed with chief executive Charles Green. When it came to moving to Blackburn in 1999, Kelly was told again there would be no new offer of a contract by the then manager Adrain Heath. As Kelly explains:

> *I was told before training to get in my car and get to Blackburn's training ground asap, forget what was due in my contract from United or the deal wouldn't happen. I'd been there seven years and cost virtually nothing. That rankled a bit, but you want to leave in the right manner.*

Being right and mannered cost him £50,000 in lost income. A few weeks earlier Aberdeen had offered £575,000, but in a telephone conversation between the player and Dons' chairman, both realised the move would never happen. Two reporters seeking a story, stated the reason Kelly didn't sign was down to his wife and children, this was creative journalism at its worst—Kelly didn't have any children at that time. Days later a story in the *Green 'Un* informed readers of his imminent signing for Aberdeen. In response Kelly did something unique in the history of United players—he logged on to the Blades' Web site and told his story about the goings-on in 300 words.

Blades fans loved Kelly and, whilst the supporters' player of the year just once in seven years, Kelly was never out of the top three nominations in the other years. To those who paid his wages, he gave his time and never refused an autograph. He visited the sick and donated numerous jerseys and gloves to youngsters. The Wembley 1993 FA Cup semi-final was his most memorable and emotional day with United. Not only did United lose to Wednesday, thereby denying Kelly the chance of an FA Cup final appearance, but he played whilst a goalie watched who, while younger than Kelly, died soon after of cancer. A great dressing room character, the powerfully-built 6'4" Mel Rees became a virtual skeleton only four weeks after he had sat on the bench as reserve goalie. At Wembley, Kelly walked off the pitch, crying over the United defeat but stopped his sobbing upon seeing Rees in the tunnel—defeat was put in perspective.

In December 2000, Kelly turned down a loan move to Sheffield Wednesday. With Wednesday's regular keeper Kevin Pressman injured, Owls manager Paul Jewell sought Kelly on loan. This proved a dilemma for Kelly. Whilst Blackburn agreed on the move, Kelly turned down the possibility arguing that, as a Blade, he could never step out in the colours of Wednesday. 'Once a Blade always a Blade', he was quoted as saying at the time. In 2004 Kelly retired as a player and today is goalkeeping coach to the Republic of Ireland national side. In his 255 games with United, Kelly conceded 323 goals in 84 wins and 86 losses. A regular visitor to Bramall Lane, Kelly is still welcomed by hundreds at every home game. He appreciated his time at the Lane:

> *I can honestly say that in a near twenty-year career, the seven years I had at Sheffield United were my best both on and off the pitch. I was fortunate to work, especially in the early years, with a group of people, players and staff, who will stay with me for the rest of my life. The rapport I had then and have still with the fans remains a most treasured memory. For your patience, humour, time and money supporting we lucky few who wore the red and white, I offer my heart-felt thanks and gratitude. Football is not always sweetness and light, there are many ups and downs and, my God, we went through a few in my time at the Lane but you know what? I can think of no other place I would rather have done it.*

The Music Man: Ian Ramsey

Tunes played over the PA system at Bramall Lane are part of the collective memory of all Blades fans over the age of 40. In Ian Ramsey, Sheffield United had a DJ and public address announcer for 32 years, from 1963 to 1995, who without script or interference from the club, made the pre- and post-match music his empire, and coined the phrase 'beautiful downtown Bramall Lane'. His eclectic choice of pop tunes saw a number of records become synonymous with an era and a team.

A life-long Blade, whose grandfather owned one of the original Sheffield United shares, Ramsey was dissatisfied with the music offered in 1963 and wrote to the United manager John Harris suggesting the selection be changed. A reply asked him to make an appointment to discuss matters and two months later while still in his early twenties, Ramsey became Bramall Lane's first DJ. His predecessor remained for the next nine months, announcing pitch side. When he left, Ramsey took over and became the voice of Bramall Lane.

Having raised the issue of musical selection, Ramsey then had the task of finding tunes to please and somehow ease the transition from band music to contemporary pop. The only stipulation from John

Harris was not to alienate older fans with choices that were too modern and too loud. In seeking to please everyone, Ramsey combined the melodies of Matt Monroe and Frank Sinatra with the more uptempo Motown sounds and songs written and produced by Phil Spector. One of the earliest favourites was the 1966 foot tapping *These Boots Are Made For Walking* recorded by Nancy Sinatra. Another was the melodic sing-a-long *Nickelodeon* by Teresa Brewer. The early seventies saw the Bramall Lane broadcast open to *Bad Moon Rising* by Creedence Clearwater Revival. The records came from his personal collection, which numbered 30,000 in 2005, and never cost the club a penny. In his 32 years, Ramsey was never paid for his job, even refusing fees suggested by club secretary Harold Rumsey in the late 1960s because the offer came with a demand he begin his job two hours before kick off. Instead, he was left alone to do what he did best and broadcast 75 minutes before kick-off, in an era when spectators entered the ground early to secure a good view. Crowds of 5,000 were regularly in place on the Kop at 2 pm. Ramsey's job was to entertain them and, in pursuit of the greatest happiness for the greatest number, Ramsey would pan the crowd with his binoculars to see if a tune was liked.

Ramsey inherited the recording of *Ilkla' Moor* which the United team ran out to at Bramall Lane during the previous decade. He kept this tradition alive until the record cracked in the late seventies. Unable to source a replacement, the tradition died with the worn out plastic. He was, however, to create his own musical legends, in particular with two pop records inseparable from memories of early seventies Bramall Lane. These two came from very diverse musical genres, one was the 1970 US country-pop classic *Rose Garden* written and sung by Lynn Anderson who recalls:

> *Between 1970 and 1980 there were only two records bigger than 'Rose Garden'—'Hey Jude' and 'Bridge Over Troubled Water'—it hit the country, pop and R&B charts in 15 countries. For a Nashville created, country produced record to do that back then was phenomenal.*

The other was the 1973 top ten soul tune *You Can Do Magic* performed by the US three piece Limmie and the Family Cookin'. Forever associated with brilliant performances by Tony Currie, the tune was often played after the final whistle of home victories.

Jan Ramsey
Heard but never seen

Privately educated and from a well-to-do Sheffield family that had imported and distributed tea in the city since the 1880s, Ramsey left the family business and become managing director of his own company installing and supplying sound technology. His evenings were spent as Sheffield's first mobile DJ—the first gig being at Sicklehome golf club in 1962. He also managed bands, Danny Harman and the Wildcatz were the first pop band to play Bramall Lane, entertaining fans before a game in late 1963. His company installed the PA system at Bramall Lane in the 1980s. A decade later Ramsey was working in telecommunications. Never missing a match through illness and being absent from only two games in 32 years because of holidays, Ramsey left Bramall Lane in 1995 when the new regime sought to impose a standardised management technique. Demands that he be present each Friday before a home game for a two-hour rehearsal was incompatible with running a business.

The cliché, 'beautiful downtown Bramall Lane' still used by various commentators at the ground was Ramsey's legacy. The phrase was lifted from a BBC TV programme *Rowan and Martin's Laugh-in*. A long running joke involved a report from 'Beautiful downtown Burbank' (in California). Introducing this slightly changed wording to Bramall Lane in the 1960s, Ramsey used at it every home game for the next 30 years. Ramsey never worked to a prescribed play-list and only one record was ever deemed to be unsuitable by the club secretary. This was the 1967 classic *High Ho Silver Lining* by Jeff Beck. Police had requested this 'hooligans record' not be played before a Sheffield derby as they were well aware that both sets of fans changed the wording and celebrated their own fighting ability. A somewhat cussed Ramsey played it anyway—with no consequences. Some 20 years later, as the teams trooped off the pitch after United had defeated Wednesday 2–0, Ramsey put on the Monty Python team's *Always Look on the Bright Side of Life* to the obvious annoyance of the Wednesday fans.

Ramsey ended his broadcasting career at the opposite side of the ground to where he had begun. A new press box built into the rear of the John Street stand in 1966 made a special space for him after his many complaints about the hopeless facilities. However, the opening of the South Stand in 1975 had a purpose built box, offering probably the best view available at Bramall Lane. This lofty position lessened his contact with the players, some of whom had previously dropped by to request he play a tune for them. Only one United manager ever discussed his selection. This was Dave Bassett, who requested that in the half-hour before kick off the music tempo be increased to get the crowd going. Today, Ramsey remains a season ticket holder and accompanies his son to all home games. On his final day as the match announcer, Ramsey left the box to the tune of *Rose Garden*.

Writing Wrongs: Tony Pritchett

The *Sheffield Star* and *Green 'Un* titled him chief sports writer, but Tony Pritchett was called a variety of things by Blades and Owls fans in his three decades of reporting on football in Sheffield until his death aged 69 in 2001. One of four children born to a coal-face worker in the north-east Derbyshire village of Ilkeston, Pritchett took the 11-plus and grammar school route to social mobility. Aged 17 he began life on the local Ilkeston newspaper, covering parish council meetings, church bazaars and court sessions. National Service took him away from this media high life for two years. Resuming the job on his return in 1953, Pritchett then moved a few miles south to Nottingham and worked for the *Evening Post* until 1968. His footballing loyalties, forged from the Derby County side of Raich Carter and Peter Doherty that won the 1946 FA Cup, were superseded by professional loyalties to Nottingham Forest the team he covered for 13 years.

A mate who covered Wednesday for the *Sheffield Star* left to join the *Daily Express* in 1968. Upon his departure he advised his editor to call up Pritchett. The editor duly asked Prichett to the office and a one-hour chat about football got Pritchett the job and a £4 a week pay rise. Moving from Nottingham to the *Sheffield Star* saw him cover all Sheffield Wednesday matches for three years as they fell into the old Division Two. When Peter Howard retired from his job with United, Pritchett was given the job of covering all United's games.

He had no idea that the swap from blue to red would cause controversy. His employers meanwhile encouraged the cult of the personality. Consequently Pritchett had his own columns, the *Green 'Un* had the 'Tell it to Tony' letters page for 15 years. The *Star* gave him a Tuesday 'Talking Sport' column. Each had an accompanying photograph. For this reason he was known and recognised in public. But was to know him, even by face and repute, to love him?

> *The switch from Owls to the Blades was difficult. Sections of the Blades' following made my life a misery; it was unpleasant. I tried to avoid them, but it was only at away games. Years later I was rumoured to be returning to Wednesday, but I said to the gaffers I wouldn't go down that path again...*

Tell it to Tony
The *Star* and *Green 'Un's* chief sports
writer Tony Pritchett ready to write his
words of wisdom in 1984

As chief sports writer from 1969 to1999 and a columnist since 1970, Pritchett had a busy schedule and one in which he could opine on anything sports related. Impartiality was something he had to work towards in choice of letter, he had to negotiate what all readers would consider a fair representation of Blades, Owls and others—an impossible task in Sheffield. At one time his editor implemented a 'marks out of 10' system to grade individual player performances. Surprised at how touchy some players were to such grading, Pritchett found himself on the receiving end of a tongue lashing in the mid-1970s from Mrs Guthrie, upset at the low mark Pritchett afforded her husband. On other occasions, he was befriended by players on the coach home from games seeking reassurance that their performance would not be a '5' or lower.

Accolades came Pritchett's way. Six times winner of the Yorkshire Sports Writer of the Year, he once won the National Provincial Newspaper Sports Writer of the Year for a story that investigated the costs of policing at Bramall Lane. Offers of jobs came from the *London Evening Standard* and the *Daily Mail*. He was once offered a staff job at Bramall Lane. In turn Pritchett offered his services to Reg Brealey as 'Football Advisor', which he explains he became *de facto*. In the year he announced his retirement, the then chief executive of Sheffield United, offered him a role in the PR Department. But he didn't want it—he was retiring. Having 'retired' in 1999, Pritchett worked for nearly two more years on a part-time basis writing match reports on the Blades.

On May 10th 1999, on the Bramall Lane pitch, Derek Dooley presented Pritchett with a silver salver. The onlooking faithful were ambivalent. Some clapped, some booed. When asked about the crowd's reception Pritchett replied, 'It was 'mixed' but it was good humoured. Nobody cheered and nobody wept...I wanted it in the boardroom; Derek insisted it was the pitch'. So why did he never write his memoirs?

> *Why is anyone interested in me, or Sheffield United? They're a middle-of-the-road club and I'm a provincial journalist. Is there really a market in a world saturated in sports books...?*

Some nine months later Pritchett was diagnosed with cancer. Within a year he died. Having had brilliant health until the final 18 months of his life, Pritchett approached death wondering, in his words, 'Why me?' Brought up a Methodist with a strong sense of right and wrong, his dream of retired days playing golf was not to be. Within months of diagnosis the weight fell off and his resistance to infection fell. Two weeks in the solitary confinement of an infection-free cubicle, post-bone-marrow transplant, was an experience hard to take for a gregarious man.

The biggest changes recognised by Pritchett in his years with United were the rise in the cult of the managerial personalities and the dumbing down of reporting. In his early days the conversations he had after games with managers were never considered 'copy'. It was men of a certain age talking of a shared enthusiasm. It went no further. Then the writing on football generally got poorer and for a smaller audience. The contemporary fashion of irreverence and opinion saw too many reporters become the centre of the piece. In his philosophy the reporter was not the story. Avoiding controversy, however, was not easy, particularly when fans of a club were in revolt against the board. Both Chairman and fans wanted their voices heard. Mediating the conflict proved very difficult.

Pritchett's departure from this world in November 2001 saw 500 mourners pack the crematorium. Past players, managers and directors honoured his farewell, which he specified in his will was not to be on the day he and his good mates traditionally met for golf. He had insisted that in his absence the show must go on. As his body left this world to strains of Sinatra's *My Way*, the club and its fans might have reflected how it had lost one of the English game's longest-serving journalists and honoured the only pre-kick-off one minute's silence for a journalist witnessed at an English football ground. Even Pritchett could not have written such an ending.

In December 1999, Mike McDonald severed links to a degree with United when he resigned as chairman and director of the plc. In the same week United's official eight-page brochure, the *Cutting Edge*, informed readers of United's destination and goals. These were to ensure football was affordable to all, to be 'leaders' within the local community, to gain promotion to the Premier League and to promote the Blade's brand. These were fine words but, in the summer of 1999, no-one would sponsor the team shirt and, shortly after, the Commercial Department announced that the shirt's logo was to be paid for by fans' donations having failed to attract an appropriate deal. On the opening day of the 1999–2000 season the United team ran out to a centre circle covered in a huge United shirt held by 20 staff with the logo 'Blades' across its chest. There was less noise to appreciate their performance. Season tickets were down from the previous season's 8,200 to 6,500. The Blades 2000 fundraising scheme had attracted just 120 takers. One consolation was that things were not much happier at Hillsborough. Wednesday were relegated from the Premiership in 2000 and, with players on long-term high paying contracts, were saddled with debt of around £18 million.

In the pre-season before the 1999–2000 kick off, United had budgeted for home crowds of 16,000 and player sales of £1.5 million. The weekly wage bill was £90,000, and chairman Mike McDonald had publicly stated that the club had certain players that were not good enough and earning too much money. The sale of Oliver Tebily in the summer of 1999 to Celtic for £1.2 million, whilst not good for the team was one of the best financial deals the club had ever made. In October 1999 McDonald told of a London-based consortium with US backing, who were interested in buying United. Around the same time the club announced ticket reductions for the Shoreham Kop. A 30% price rise the previous season had badly affected attendances and United's managing director, the same one who saw the advantages of a merger with Wednesday, stated, 'we have alienated the working man and have to do something about it...'. Two months later United were next to bottom of the table. As the new century approached, matters on and off the pitch looked dire. Two men born and bred in the city came to the club's rescue. Another son of the city, famous for his thespian skills, brought global publicity on joining the United board. In less than six years, United were back in the Premiership with a business philosophy that was unique both in the club's history and, indeed, British football.

Christmas Every Day

As the Blades prepared for their first game in the newly formed Premier League, Manager Dave Bassett organised an August 'Christmas Party' for his players, whom he accused the previous season of only starting to play from December onwards

One day, lad, this could all be yours
Sheffield United chairman Kevin McCabe with grandson Charlie,
celebrating United's promotion to the Premiership in April 2006

Sons of the Soil

The match going experience of the new millennium was unlike anything previously known at Bramall Lane. From 2001, Bramall Lane hosted an Enterprise Centre for small businesses. Grant-funded to £1.8 million, the five-storey £3 million complex housed 60 office units and a community hall for local people. Above it were 700 seats for match-goers. Other cash flowing into the club's coffers reflected tradition and modernity. The dugouts were emblazoned with adverts for Sheffield's Assay Office, but the gold and lilac away strip featured colours now chosen by the club's sponsors, computer games makers Midas. This caused a degree of controversy when, in August 2000, rumours circulated that United players had complained that one particular kit design made them look effeminate. In response to the story, United quickly stressed the popularity of the shirt and stated their policy against any form of discrimination. Evidently to emphasise the club's commitment to social inclusion, the official merchandise brochure saw leisurewear modelled in part by teenaged Asian females alongside white grandfathers. Other goods sought to present United as attractive to both man and beast, the solitary and the gregarious—as such, one could buy Sheffield United dog collars, computer games, Sheffield United-branded Highland whisky, mountain bikes, handheld TVs and car accessories. This marketing policy seemed to work. In June 2003, United reported a profit of £1/2 million, having sold 13,500 replica shirts and seen retail income rise 145% to £1.2 million. In 2004, a five-year sponsorship deal was agreed with the HFS Loans finance company, worth seven figures in total to United.

Familiar refrains were heard. In October 2000, United plc chairman Bernard Proctor, announced that only 3,000 extra supporters per home game would remove the need for player sales. In the debacle that was the club at the turn of the century, Proctor was the understated saviour. A long-term director, he grasped the nettle and focused his attention on costs, reducing outgoings in all departments and trying to rebuild the club as a business as he had so successfully done with his own removals and car sales businesses. That said, the traditional route of raising funds by selling young talent continued. The 18-year-old Lee Morris was sold to Derby County in 1999 for what would be a record for the club of £3 million. This was a crucial financial lifeline when the turnstile-paying fan was declining and actually ceased to exist for a time. In the early part of the decade, all match-goers purchased their admission from the ticket office, which they then handed to gate staff. In response to protests, a few cash turnstiles were reinstated in 2002.

Money came into the club by virtue of the return of two backroom employees who were synonymous in the eyes of all supporters with Sheffield United FC. One was Mick Rooker, the other was Andy Daykin. At one time, in 2000, sat three men at Hull City FC in the positions of Chief Executive, Marketing Director and Commercial Officer who had 50 years' experience of running a football club and bringing in funding. All had left Sheffield United in a variety of circumstances not of their own making. In 2000, after nearly 12 years' employment at Bramall Lane, Rooker left and with his departure left a man known to thousands of Blades and a good mate to a multitude of players—usually those new to the city. Beginning life at Bramall Lane as a sales rep, Rooker's portfolio was enhanced to Pools Office Manager and expanded to looking after mascots (and parents)the ticket office, away match coaches for the Travel Club and match-programme sales. At one time Rooker's responsibility was for five full-time office staff, forty programme sellers and 300 sellers of other fundraising schemes. Schemes initiated by Rooker brought in millions to the club's coffers. Under his direction, his staff produced the most efficient lottery scheme in English football. His decision to leave was taken with a heavy heart. Rooker was the commercial hub of Sheffield United alongside Andy Daykin until the latter was removed from his position of Commercial Manager

Andy Daykin
Branding and selling Sheffield United for 25 years

after 16 years in April 1998 for, shall we say, knowing too much. No fewer than seven men held the title of Commercial Manager/ Executive in the thirteen months following Daykin's departure. None were from Sheffield, none were United fans and none had the necessary experience to be United's Commercial Manager. Fortunately for Sheffield United, almost three years to the day of his departure, Daykin returned to Bramall Lane to resume his now-enhanced position. Rooker's exile had lasted less than a year.

In Daykin, Sheffield United had English football's longest-serving Commercial Manager and long-time Chair of the Commercial Manager's Association. Having visited the US in the early 1980s Daykin was inspired by the commercial possibilities that sporting occasions brought to clubs and, under Chairman Reg Brealey, Daykin was given a freedom to expand his ideas. The result was a variety of new revenue streams. The rise in commercial income in the early years of the new millennium was undoubtedly down to the return of Daykin and Rooker and the excellent staff teams they surrounded themselves with. Few clubs in the Football League could find a more personable match-day commercial package than those managed by these two. As both Rooker and Daykin would explain, team-work has to happen off the pitch for a successful football club. Rooker and Daykin were the longest-serving backroom staff of Sheffield United. Their knowledge of the people who paid to watch Sheffield football could not be bettered by anyone in the city.

Sounds and Visions

The club pursued a variety of match-day musical re-brands. The pre-match music at Bramall Lane in 2001 saw the team run out to Tina Turner's anthemic pop classic *Simply the Best*. This slight over-statement was later replaced by the esoteric arrangement of *Also Sprach Zarathustra* written by Richard Strauss and best known from its use in Stanley Kubrick's film, *2001: A Space Odyssey*. This probably was meant as a morale booster for the Nietzschean über-men in red and white stripes. For those attending or playing who could not get their head around the concept, grateful relief, no doubt, came in the shape of the 'Greasy Chip Butty Song', derived from John Denver's 1970's paean to his wife Annie. A 1981 pre-season fixture at Grimsby, heard Blades' fans celebrate their circumstances with changed words to proclaim their football team:

> *You fill up my senses like a gallon of Magnet* (local beer)
> *Like a packet of Woodbines*
> *Like a good pinch of snuff*
> *Like a night out in Sheffield*
> *Like a greasy chip butty*
> *Like Sheffield United—come thrill me again*

The club played the opening lines of the Denver arrangement shortly before kick off. The fans completed the task with their own homage to working class masculine excess. For those needing neither philosophy, romance nor excessive consumption, the 1977 punk foot-stomper, *If the Kids are United* courtesy of Surrey-based band, Sham 69, led the team out for a season. Certain musical arrangements, however, when played by certain people, were not to the liking of the club. In January 2002 before a derby with

Sheffield Wednesday, the visitors' nationally-recognised brass and drum band were denied entry to Bramall Lane, ostensibly due to safety regulations, because, 'music can stimulate co-ordinated crowd motion and induce dynamic excitation' according to the club's citation of a university professor. Perhaps the chance to avoid the irritating refrains of the band was the true cause. Few Blade tears were shed over this decision.

Spectacle and participation were stressed in club publications. The pre kick-off pitch entertainment at the turn of the century came courtesy of, initially, the Midas Interactive Entertainment Groups sponsorship package. They knew their audience; their all-female dancing troupe was more curvaceous and co-ordinated than previous pubescent majorettes who were quietly retired. The more affluent audience reading the match-day programme learned the price of wine and champagne receptions at Bramall Lane and about the possibilities of sponsoring both the ball boys and Captain Blade mascot character, integral to pre-match on-pitch proceedings since his introduction in 1997. The programme had pages titled 'Girls News' and 'Community Blades', the latter telling of United's involvement in various socially responsible projects in the city. The electronic scoreboard broadcast messages against racism. The era's electronic fandom sought a place for itself when

Mick Rooker
Promoting United for 20 years

'Internet Blades' became occasional match sponsors. The pitch flanking the touchline was painted to advertise online ticket purchases. The United players reflected global power shifts when wearing a team strip that advertised a Chinese fruit cordial company. Watching children in the John Street Stand could have their faces painted for free courtesy of the MacDonald's burger empire. For those whose intentions were not always financially driven, or even honourable, the Sheffield United Platinum Suite had attained legendary status by the turn of the century for its Friday night over-25's discos, which attracted hundreds of Sheffield's lotharios and lonely hearts.

Crime and Punishment

Some connected to the club were to have loneliness imposed upon them. In February 2001, United's one-time director and aspiring chairman, Stephen Hinchliffe, received a five-year custodial sentence for defrauding the United Mizrahi Bank of £13 million in loans. Facing ten charges of bribery and one of conspiracy to defraud, Hinchliffe had been the subject of a four-year police inquiry following the collapse of his Facia Group. The latter, established in 2004, sought to buy loss-making companies, but had seen £1.75 million of its funds siphoned off. At an Old Bailey trial lasting seven months Hinchliffe was found guilty of giving £800,000 to a bank employee to obtain £10 million of loans to buy High Street companies. Other former chairmen still played hard to get. In October 2002, some nine years after his disappearance, a BBC *Crimewatch* programme put out a call for information on Paul Woolhouse. Living the life of a fugitive, a suspicion that Woolhouse was attending United's games in London saw plain-clothes police at the visiting fans' turnstiles.

Distress and Disorder

Others perpetrated criminal acts also detrimental to the club's image. The firing of three distress flares from Blades followers in the direction of Wednesday fans in 2003 during a Sheffield derby at Bramall Lane saw United facing an FA inquiry. The outcome was a warning to fans as to their future conduct and the forced closure of two sections of the South Stand, the area from which the projectiles were fired, until the end of 2004. It was ordered that 4,500 seats in the ground be kept closed on the advice of the Safety Advisory Group, consisting of Sheffield councillors and police. This was reduced to 2,000 seats on appeal. When re-opened the area was to be reserved for season ticket holders and subject to extensive improvement and better CCTV surveillance. A £100,000 suspended fine was imposed on the club until the end of the 2004–2005 season to be paid in full if the club was found guilty of similar offences in that period. The club was also ordered to print messages in the match programme for the next three seasons, warning of the consequences of such behaviour. Those who released the missiles received 18-month custodial sentences.

Some individuals received less subtle warnings about their presence. In August 2005 United's visit to Loftus Road, home of Queens Park Rangers, produced the first armed siege at a match in the history of professional football in England. The club's majority shareholder, Gianni Paladini, a former Italian international, had bought into QPR in May of the previous year. A post-playing career saw him act as an agent bringing in seven-figure investments from a Monaco-based consortium. He publicly claimed that his inquiries into a £10 million loan from a Panama-based bank, arranged by pre-existing board members, had provoked hostilities. Minutes before United kicked off the fixture, five men burst into his private box and began beating him. Allegedly facing a gun he was forced to sign a document that declared his resignation from the board. Breaking away from his assailants, he sought sanctuary in the QPR boardroom. Dozens of armed police arrived minutes later and a number of men were arrested in streets surrounding the stadium. The second half was delayed, unofficially, whilst police searched the box that Paladini had occupied. A handgun was reportedly found concealed in the false ceiling. Whilst none of this was of United's doing, it did make for their unwanted involvement in a football 'first'. All the suspects were acquitted in Crown Court in June 2006.

The most formally disciplined player in United's history left Bramall Lane in 2004 after a 16-year career which had produced a club record of five sendings-off. The accolade went to the Woolwich-born goalkeeper Simon Tracey, who arrived at United in October 1988 as a 20-year-old from Wimbledon costing £7,500 (plus a further £5,000 after 15 first-team appearances). Tracey had just two first-team appearances with the Dons but both were memorable. One produced a 5–0 defeat to Arsenal whilst the first was played at Wembley against Liverpool in the Charity Shield. Tracey was an excellent keeper who was called up for the England squad in 1992 but injuries prevented an appearance. A quiet personality and a somewhat stoical playing style once provoked his United manager Dave Bassett to inform fans, by way of a compliment that, 'he hasn't the brain of a rocking horse'. Bassett spoke very highly of Tracey at his Testimonial dinner in 2003. In truth Tracey was one of the best signings of Bassett's managerial career.

The Partisan: Neil Warnock

The appointment of Neil Warnock in December 1999 as the replacement for Adrian Heath heralded a change in managerial policy for United. No longer trusting in young former top-class players, the club had opted instead for a proven, albeit lower division, manager in his early 50s. Warnock had an undistinguished eleven-year playing career (which ended in 1979) at Chesterfield, Rotherham, Hartlepool, Scunthorpe, Aldershot, Barnsley, York, Crewe and Gainsborough, which saw him make 326 league appearances. He moved into management in 1981 with Burton Albion, followed by Scarborough, a team he brought into the Football League in 1987. At Notts County between 1989 and 1993, Warnock took the club up two divisions in successive years and reached Division One in 1991 where they lasted one season. Then followed Torquay before Huddersfield Town, and a two-year stint that ended in 1995 in promotion and Warnock's resignation. Plymouth followed between 1996 and 1997, then Oldham 1997–98 and finally Bury.

The son of a crane operator in Sheffield's steel industry, Warnock's upbringing was not salubrious. In a speech he gave at a benefit dinner in 2000 he told of sleeping 'top to tail' in bed with siblings, of climbing into Bramall Lane to watch games and of being smuggled onto coaches with his father to follow United to away games. Warnock thus came into the Bramall Lane ground, both literally and metaphorically, the hard way.

Controversy was never too far away from Warnock's managerial career. Offered the Chelsea job by chairman Ken Bates in 1991, Warnock turned it down claiming he had no wish to live in London. Falling out with the Huddersfield Town chairman in 1995, Warnock left the club despite having just won promotion. In the mid-90s, despite managing elsewhere, he became a United shareholder and had written to Mike McDonald asking him to keep an eye on him. Even when taking the manager's job at Bury, Warnock spoke of his destiny to one day manage United. Warnock applied to be United manager three times before being appointed. Interviewed for the job in 1998, Warnock told *Sheffield Star* journalist Tony Pritchett, that he could generate £5 million from sales of the current squad and would then work in the 'free market' to replace them. Warnock used Pritchett to remind readers of the *Star* of his achievements and of how, within two years, he had gained a promotion at every club he managed and had won four play-off finals. He felt United and he were made for each other, adding his belief that if he had played for England or in the top flight, the job would now be his. Instead the job went to Steve Bruce. When Bruce's successor, Adrian Heath, resigned in December 1999, Warnock phoned United chairman Kevin McCabe at 7am the next day telling him to give him the vacancy. Warnock was a renowned dressing room ranter, who

Neil Warnock

favoured hard players who were effective rather than delightful in their skills. He was never shy in proclaiming his abilities. Warnock left a Bury team third from bottom of Division Two claiming, 'with the team that we had and the facilities that we had, I think I deserved manager of the year'.

Warnock arrived at Bramall Lane on his 51st birthday to manage a club in turmoil, with a team in the relegation zone and with no money for players. Warnock had to bring in funds to finance the signings he wanted to make. His first message in the match programme, spoke of the need for the players to show 'passion and guts', regardless of technical ability. He sold centre forward Martin Smith to Huddersfield for £350,000 and, two months later, midfielder Sean Derry left for Portsmouth for an initial £300,000. He sold centre-forward Marcus Bent within 11 months for £1.3 million, rising to £2 million on appearances. Warnock's first signing was the Cameroon international Patrick Suffo (an Olympic football gold medal-winner), who cost £150,000 from French club Nantes, but who was banned from football for eight months for spitting at a referee in a reserve game in France. Impressive transfer dealings saw Warnock make the club a profit of close to £4 million between 2000 and mid-2005. A million pounds came into the club's coffers in February 2001, courtesy of the sale of Curtis Woodhouse to Birmingham—United received Zimbabwe international Peter Ndlovu as part of the deal. In the same month, another million arrived in United's account when Wayne Quinn moved to Newcastle. Players on lucrative contracts were released—the Belarus international, Petr Katchouro, sought a new life in China, apparently on a free transfer. The highly paid Jonathan Hunt had his contract paid up.

Appointed over the applications of United heroes Tony Currie, Keith Edwards and local-born managers, Steve Thompson and Gary Megson, Warnock's custody of the club might be considered an end-of-century salute to local origins in the face of the globalisaton of the game. Whatever it symbolised it proved effective. In Warnock's first eleven games, United scored 22, conceded 8 and lost once. Previously, in 21 games, they had scored 24 goals, conceded 38 and had the worst defence in the League. In the next five years, Warnock was able to retain quality players and at last stop United from being considered a selling club. He made United regular challengers for promotion, albeit the club only made the play-offs once in five years, in 2003, before finally attaining promotion in April 2006.

Being local, a qualified chiropodist and owning a greengrocers store in Sheffield, Warnock knew what sold to those he was born amongst. Interviewed on local radio on the Friday night before his first home game, he told listeners, 'It's not a good club but the best club. The only one in the world'. He could reflect on the day that Brian Deane and Jan-Aage Fjortoft were sold as, 'like when President Kennedy was shot—that's how deeply I felt'. Warnock could choose his words to create maximum impact with fans of both Sheffield clubs. Interviewed in the *Four-Four-Two* magazine, he stated his ambition to manage Sheffield Wednesday, whereupon, he would fill the playing squad with 'tosspots' to '— them up' before retiring to Cornwall. Later responding to phone-in criticisms of his managerial ability, he called the disgruntled callers 'morons'. In 2005, a television documentary titled 'Warnock' attempted to portray the man behind the myth. Viewers could witness dozens of oaths in the course of the fifty minutes. Not much else was revealed beyond Warnock owning a tractor. A later print profile revealed a penchant for using moisturiser, making him United's first manager to admit to fighting the ageing process.

Forthright in public, when speaking at the Blades AGM in November 2001, Warnock told the audience that he was frustrated at what other smaller clubs in the division were spending on wages and transfers. Whilst dealing in free transfers was what he had to do, he was public about giving the situation two years before re-considering his position. The commercial income improved considerably. The wage bill at the time of his arrival was £8 million and whilst season tickets brought in £1 million, the turnstile paying fans and related commercial activities brought in only £1.2 million. The TV monies provided more but still left an annual deficit of £1.5 million. Some three years were required before Warnock had a settled team that could unsettle the best in the land on their day. The difference, however, was the wage bill, this was now less than half of what it had been five years previously.

In May 2003 Warnock was runner up to Everton's David Moyes in the Manager of the Year vote by the League Managers' Association. This supreme achievement recognised his team's semi-final appearances in both the League and the FA Cups and United's 3–0 defeat by Wolves in front of 72,000 at the Millennium Stadium, Cardiff, in the Division One promotion play-offs. Warnock took the applause locally when addressing Blades in their thousands at Bramall Lane at the end of the final home game of the 2002–03 season and outside Sheffield Town Hall following an open-top bus parade watched by some 10,000 Blades after the defeat to Wolves. His assistant Kevin Blackwell had worked for Warnock for 16 years, yet weeks later left United to take a similar job at Leeds United. The latter's replacement was eventually found in the former Rangers and Scotland captain, Stuart McCall.

Warnock achieved his stated ambition on being appointed of getting United into the Premiership and filling the Kop. Promotion to the Premiership in April 2006 came with a degree of stealth. Whilst United were never out of the top two positions since the previous August, and never looked like being dislodged by those chasing, a 1–0 victory at Cardiff on Good Friday had put them in a virtually unassailable position. The following day Leeds drew, which made promotion a mathematical certainty for United. A celebration for the Sky TV cameras at the United training ground was combined with a spontaneous gathering of hundreds of fans in the Bramall Lane car park. Days after the Cardiff game, United hosted Leeds in front of 30,000—a full house. A 1–1 draw was overshadowed by the sending off of Warnock from the touchline. His reaction to a challenge on a United player brought about his dismissal and a subsequent FA inquiry.

Despite fulfilling his ambitions, calls for Warnock's resignation or dismissal appeared throughout his six-and-a-half years in various forms, from radio phone-ins to collective chants at the match. Only in his promotion-winning season did Warnock finally gain more than one chant of praise in any game, a fact that he recognised, but could not explain. Halfway through promotion season, Warnock was approached by Premiership strugglers, Portsmouth. Warnock was then involved in brinkmanship with his chairman. The latter had been instrumental in keeping Warnock in the manager's chair in the face of a board divided over his future at the end of the 2004–05 season. Warnock was given a one-year contract with the threat of dismissal if the team were not promotion candidates by Christmas, Warnock resented the threat and opened negotiations with the Portsmouth chairman in late 2005. Warnock spoke of a two-and-a-half times salary increase and a three-and-a-half year contract but, despite describing the offer as a 'super deal', Warnock turned it down because 'it didn't seem right'. Whilst he negotiated, McCabe sounded out prospective replacements. When the issue was resolved and Warnock decided to remain at Bramall Lane, he told the media, 'I know I'll always have a job here even if I get sacked as manager'.

The Battle of Bramall Lane

Bramall Lane attained global infamy under Warnock when it hosted the first game in the history of the Football League that was not completed because the team had insufficient players on the pitch to compete. In December 2000, Warnock stated to the press that his players were too honest for their own good, believing that opponents could have received yellow and red cards in recent weeks had his United team been willing to practise gamesmanship. It was accusations of gamesmanship that brought global notoriety to Bramall Lane. In March 2002, a United–West Bromwich Albion fixture resulted in three United players being sent off. Eight minutes from the final whistle and losing 3–0, another United player limped off with an injury, forcing the referee to abandon the match. The sendings off of Simon Tracey, George Santos, and Patrick Suffo, and the withdrawals of Michael Brown and Rob Ullathorne because of injury, meant United had only six players on the pitch. The West Bromwich manager, Sheffield-born Gary Megson, in an after-match interview accused members of the United staff of encouraging United players to get sent off so as to force an abandonment. The visitors' chairman, Sheffield-born Paul Thompson, said that he did not feel that the United players and officials were committed to finishing the game.

The Battle of Bramall Lane March 2002

The first match in the history of the Football League abandoned because of insufficient players in one team

The fixture had a history. The previous season United had lost 2–1 at West Brom and a late goal by the home team's striker, Lee Hughes, had seen him over-celebrate much to the annoyance of the visiting fans. Earlier in the new season, United had beaten West Brom at the Hawthorns and Hughes suffered constant abuse from the United following. The United defender Shane Nicholson was sent off for a foul tackle on him. Another burning issue concerned United's George Santos who, whilst playing the previous year for West Brom, had suffered an horrific facial injury courtesy of Andy Johnson then of Nottingham Forest. On this day Santos came off the United bench to line up in midfield opposite Johnson—since transferred to West Brom. This was the first occasion the two had met since the injury although the United team had once found itself unwittingly sharing a hotel with the Forest squad—complete with Johnson. Team-mates remember having to restrain Santos from attempting to complete unfinished business with Johnson in the hotel lounge. One final issue of history concerned the respective managers. The managerial vacancy at Bramall Lane in 1999 was narrowed down to two candidates, Neil Warnock and Gary Megson. The latter came second. Both Megson and his father had played for Sheffield Wednesday.

After West Brom's second goal, Warnock made a double substitution bringing on Santos and Suffo. Both were sent off two minutes later. A centre-circle loose ball saw a double-footed Santos challenge on Johnson that sent the latter spinning. The red card was immediate and, whilst Johnson was restrained from retaliating by team-mates, the rest of the players indulged in a free-for-all. The most notable effort was a blatant head-butt by Suffo on West Brom's Derek McInnes. Suffo was off and walked past a visitors' bench that was involved in a heated debate with United fans sitting behind them. Hostilities continued on and off the pitch. Gary Megson's wife, waving a two-fingered gesture at those around her in the director's box, received a telling off from Mrs Derek Dooley. In mitigation, Mrs Megson claimed it was a reminder to the critics of her husband that his team were 2–0 up. United were 3–0 down by the time Michael Brown was withdrawn from the pitch injured. By then United had used all their three substitutes. Minutes later, United's Rob Ullathorne fell over in mid-stride clutching his leg claiming to the referee that he could not continue. The referee realised that, with United down to less than eight players, under the laws of the game he had to abandon the match.

Minutes before Ullathorne's collapse, spectators were surprised to see the team captain Keith Curle doing his damnedest to collect another booking on top of the yellow card he had already received. Blatantly hauling down an attacking opponent he received a telling off from the referee, which he met with a mouthful of invective. The player's tunnel saw a continuation of hostilities at the end of the game as Santos sought to finish business with Johnson. In the ensuing brawl the United club doctor was sent skittling by the players he was attempting to placate. One week later, the club issued a statement that Curle would be out for the rest of the season with pelvic injuries. Soon after Brown had a hernia operation and the other injured player, Rob Ullathorne, did not play any further games that season. Santos and Suffo were sold weeks later.

The football world was appalled. National and local radio phone-ins were jammed with callers criticising the club and Warnock. Accusers and critics called for United to be relegated a division or at least have points deducted. Warnock's response was that he was unaware of the rule regarding the minimum number of players a team needed to continue. An emergency board meeting held immediately after the game realised the vilification being poured on the club and considered Warnock's position. Any ambiguity was resolved after a telephone conversation between Warnock and chairman Kevin McCabe at 10pm that evening: Warnock kept his job.

Accusations levelled against Warnock that this had been a deliberate strategy were never proven. In the FA inquiry neither manager was reported by the referee, but United faced a number of charges; Warnock with improper conduct, Curle with insulting and abusive words to a match official and Suffo with violent conduct. Two charges were placed on Santos, violent conduct for the tackle and threatening behaviour in the tunnel. The Football League inquiry was forwarded to the FA, various parties were interviewed by the FA Compliance Officer. The investigation was overseen by the FA's Chief Executive, Adam Crozier. A month later, punishments were handed out. For his admission of guilt, Curle received a £500 fine and a

Chengdu Blades
Taking the applause from their fans after a game in 2006

two-match ban. Suffo did not enter a plea so received a fine of £3,000 and a three-match ban. Santos received a two-match ban for his tackle, but the tunnel charge was not proven. Warnock was to pay a £300 fine for improper conduct in the technical area and the club were made to pay a small fine for 'failing to ensure that its players conducted themselves in an orderly fashion'. Significantly United were cleared of any charges of cheating. An FA spokesman stated:

> *No independent evidence was forthcoming to indicate that there was a deliberate attempt by any Sheffield United player or official to force the match to be abandoned.*

The wider consequences for United were the cancellation of two season tickets, one prize draw membership and abusive phone-calls to the main reception. Megson added to the controversy months later by claiming that one of the United bench phoned him after the game to apologise for Warnock's behaviour. Megson's proposed biography will apparently reveal more on this infamous day, the publication of which, Warnock suggested, will be good news for insomniacs.

The Languages of Football

In time-honoured fashion, players wages and contracts caused controversies. However, in this new century, contractual disputes were not confined to the dressing room. In September 2001, United's 29-year-old winger Paul Devlin revealed on his personal website (written for his fans) that he had asked the United board for wage parity with other players. When refused, he then accused the club of forcing him out and Warnock of 'throwing him to the wolves'. Days later, after handing in a transfer request, the same website spoke of decisions made in the heat of the moment and later regrets. A month later Devlin's transfer fee was reduced by United from £1.5 million to £500,000. With fans on his back and derogatory comments in the local media, Devlin realised he had to leave and eventually joined Birmingham City and the manager who had signed him to United in the first place. United responded by publicly stating that Devlin's pay rise was refused because he had signed an improved four-year contract only 14 months previously, which would have seen him earn around £1m in that time. The cost of domestic players saw United look to cheaper markets.

By the turn of the century, United were seeking playing talent in three continents as they scouted in China, Vietnam, South Africa, Norway, Morocco and Belgium. Football was now truly global and the United line up reflected this. In January 2002 the team contained surnames such as Suffo, D'Jaffo, Santos, Murphy, Peschisolido and Uhlenbeek. Perhaps the most global of all United teams ran out on December 22nd 2001 for a game at home to Rotherham. The team was: Tracey (England), Uhlenbeek (Holland), Curle (England), Murphy (Australia), Page (Wales), Ndlovu (Zimbabwe), Montgomery (Scotland), Santos (France), Brown (England), Suffo (Cameroon), Peschisolido (Canada) with the following in reserves: Sandford (England), Devlin (Scotland), D'Jaffo (France), Tonge (England) and De Vogt (Holland). There were six foreigners in the line-up three times that season. West Africa became a supplier of United talent, beginning with Oliver Tebily who arrived in 1999 for £275,000 and after only four months and seven appearances was sold to Celtic for £1 million profit. In 2001, East African Peter Ndlovu was signed by United on a part exchange from Birmingham. His goal for Zimbabwe in the Cosafa Castle Cup against Malawi meant he became the leading international goal scorer in the club's history, overtaking the 12 scored by Billy Gillespie for Northern Ireland. The global search, however, was not cheap and United paid £135,000 in agents' fees for 28 transfers in 2005.

In December 2000 two Chinese players, Hao Hai Dong and Wu Cheng Ying, spent 10 days on trial at Bramall Lane. The former had won the Chinese League four times with the Dalian Wanda team and his ability had attracted attention from Crystal Palace following a five-game tour of England with the Chinese national side in 1997. However, Warnock stated that neither would improve his squad but he would continue to seek bargains in the Far East. In December 2004, United signed the 30-year-old Hao Hai Dong on a 30-month contract. Proclaimed as the most famous footballer in China, voted Asian footballer of the year in 1997 and the holder of 102 caps, Hai Dong's role was two-fold—fight for a first team place and learn coaching so as to take up a role in United's proposed China-based academy.

In December 2005 United purchased the Chinese club Chengdu Five Bulls thereby becoming the first club to acquire a team in the Chinese professional leagues. Integral to chairman Kevin McCabe's transformation of Sheffield United, into a football, property and leisure service business, the purchase was part of a strategy to take the name of Sheffield United global and tap into the emerging football market of the world's most populated country.

Academic Issues

At the same time, United sought to produce home-grown players. In 2001, for the first time in its history, the club could say that it owned its own training facilities with the acquisition of a 22-acre site, some 3.5 miles from Bramall Lane. Bought from the Forgemasters steel company, the land included five grass pitches. Opened initially as a youth academy, the complex was later developed for first-team training plus other leisure activities which produced income. Thus, the site witnessed tennis, netball and bowls, and also facilitated a high performance gymnasium and physiotherapy facilities. The building of an indoor sports hall and synthetic pitch allowed the club to attain academy status under FA rules. Youth development saw teams at the academy ranging from under-8s to under-18s which numbered around 150 regular players. The facilities, whilst primarily intended for the use of Sheffield United, were also available for other sporting groups.

The commitment to developing home-grown footballers through the academy was taken by chairman Kevin McCabe both for reasons of economy (it was considered more effective than gambling on expensive signings on the transfer market) and the chairman's belief that the clubs best teams since the war had contained a majority of local-born players. The academy was to supersede United's Centre of Excellence, which had nurtured players who had earned the club combined transfer fees of around £6 million. Before the academy's opening in 2002, United's youth programme had produced players of

A young academy hopeful putting his head in where it hurts and dreaming of a career at Bramall Lane

international quality. Wayne Quinn and Curtis Woodhouse had represented England at under-18 and under-21 level and Lee Morris had made the under-18 squad. Three other players, Phil Jagielka, Michael Tonge and Nick Montgomery, all signed at the age of 16 and went on to become regular first-teamers, and in Jagielka's case, represent England under-21s.

Times and Changes: Kevin McCabe

Kevin McCabe joined the United board in December 1995. Brought up only yards from Bramall Lane in the 1950s, McCabe was by the 1990s, a resident of Scarborough but had moved much further than that geographical distance. Making the *Sunday Times* Rich List in various positions from early 2000, McCabe proved to be a tremendously successful property dealer. Beginning life in the construction industry as a quantity surveyor, McCabe then moved into house building, managing property portfolios and, later, providing office facilities. In the mid-90s he attempted to buy United from Reg Brealey, but was outbid by Paul Woolhouse. McCabe took over as the chairman of the Sheffield United FC Board in March 1998 following the resignation of Mike McDonald. In the tumultuous times of the late 1990s, McCabe resigned from the plc Board, only to return to become acting chairman of both the FC and plc boards in 2002.

Born in Sheffield, but with an ancestry in Armagh, Ulster, McCabe had a modest upbringing. He was provided for by a father employed as a painter and decorator whose claim to fame was that he had once painted the statue of Vulcan on top of Sheffield town hall and played football for an Army XI. McCabe himself was a decent player and represented Sheffield Boys. Initially a striker, he was later a centre-half and, perhaps bizarrely in the 1960s, idolised United's David Munks by virtue of him having been a few years ahead of him at Rowlinson School. Munks managed 124 appearances for United before moving to Portsmouth in 1969. Never making it at the top level of the game, McCabe was happy to represent Old Harrow and later Ranmoor in local leagues. The first match he attended, aged nine in 1958, was a testimonial game for Jimmy Hagan against an All Star XI. Prior to this he had attended United reserve fixtures and watched Yorkshire cricket at Bramall Lane.

Leaving school at 16, McCabe's first job was working on a building site at Sheffield's Masonic Hall. Studying to be a surveyor, he qualified via night school and correspondence courses to work for Ackroyd and Abbot, which when taken over by Bovis, split the business between construction and property. Following the latter pathway, McCabe was sent to manage a project in Edinburgh. Soon after he was moved to Middlesbrough. Married in 1971 to Sandra, a Blades fan from the Hackenthorpe area, their wedding day was memorable for the reception courtesy of the Co-op and for the pair of them missing United's first game (home to Southampton) on the club's return to Division One.

McCabe left the company's payroll in 1976 and branched out into his own business which is loosely defined as 'property development alongside property management'. He based his burgeoning business empire in Scarborough. Self-employed status meant McCabe was no longer able to commit himself to playing football so he turned his attention to squash and represented Scarborough in the Yorkshire league—he plays a mean game to this day. The competitiveness evident in this arena also drove his business concern and, some time in the early 1980s, he made his first million. What McCabe learned in business he transferred in later years to United, most notably that one must learn from those perceived as the opposition and know well those who sit as fellow directors.

The invitation to join the United board in 1993 by then-chairman Paul Woolhouse was a learning process in many ways. Woolhouse approached McCabe who had become known to United for sponsoring matches. Whilst interested in what Woolhouse was suggesting, namely trying to sell the club, McCabe did not strike a deal because the price was too high. Soon after, Len Brealey (Reg's brother) assumed the chairmanship and offered the shares to McCabe which he had obtained, after a court case, from Woolhouse. McCabe admits to never having had an ambition to be chairman and owner of Sheffield United, but was excited by what he could offer the club. He accepted a board position in 1995 but did not last long. Unable to work with Reg Brealey, McCabe resigned but retained an interest in the club, sponsoring games and players.

McCabe returned to the board in 1995 when Mike McDonald had taken over from Brealey. Contacted by McDonald, McCabe bought a 10% shareholding and agreed with McDonald's plan to make United a public company in 1997. He sustained a friendship with McDonald, but did not agree with some of the practices of the board. The variety of goings-on provided him with a number of dilemmas. In the late 1990s he was very close to resigning all office at the club because in his words, 'if I believe it should be done, I feed it and run with it. If it can't be done, I'll step down'. Interestingly, the contract to build the John Street stand was jointly signed by Stephen Hinchliffe and Kevin McCabe and no-one else. McCabe was to have input into the stand's design, notably in function and facilities, based on observations from other stadiums.

For the next few years, McCabe's main tasks as a director centred around property initiatives and commercial usage at Bramall Lane. The ideal models for a football club, in his opinion, were Manchester United, Arsenal, and until they went into receivership a few years ago, Ipswich Town. He was also innovative and instrumental in leaving a legacy to the neighbourhood that produced him. Speaking of a 'moral responsibility' that a football club has to those who live close to its environs, McCabe established the Sharrow Forum and ensured the Enterprise Centre had a remit to encourage local entrepreneurship. Believing that this was the first such football club alliance with its community in the UK, McCabe considered that, as Bramall Lane stood at the heart of Sharrow district, construction jobs and space in the finished entities should be offered first to local people.

McCabe eventually took on a bigger role at United, which saw him become chairman in 2001. Initially he had to compete with a rival approach for the club from Carlo Colombotti and Philip Wood. Under the rubric of *Blades Italia*, they sought to link United with Italian Serie A clubs and proposed to bring in as manager the former Italian full-back Paolo Maldini who at the time of their ambitions was youth team coach at AC Milan. McCabe promised nothing by way of famous playing personnel but set about addressing the club's financial difficulties. A share issue that aimed to raise £14 million (£4 million for the new share issue underwritten by four directors and a £10 million refinancing agreement) was announced by McCabe in 2002. The move required a 75% majority at an EGM. Shares were selling at 7p—lower than the nominal value of the existing ordinary share. The money raised was intended to assist the building and funding of the Academy and finance the off-field income projects based in hotel, leisure and retail. The share issue was defeated 2–1 in 2002, primarily because of the decision of Mike McDonald who refused to back it, combined with the absence of half of all eligible voters. McDonald reasoned that the shareholding promotion would permit the club to fall into the hands of two or three individuals. This was a reasonable argument as the current directors would be expected to underwrite the issue. McDonald, furthermore, did not favour investment in youth, arguing that immediate improvement in the squad was needed, despite his appointing of a director to the United board when he was chairman with the aim of founding an Academy. Had the share issue gone ahead, McDonald's shareholding would have been diluted.

The share issue plan had to be resubmitted and the absent shareholders urged to turn out to vote in favour of McCabe's vision. McCabe won the day and subsequent share issues saw McCabe's control rise to slightly under 60% and saw a downgrading of the shares from the main stock exchange to the Alternative Investment Market. Having invested, by his estimate, £25 million over the previous five years, the club and all its assets were valued at £40 million in May 2006.

The 2005–2006 promotion effort was expensive and part-funded by the share issue. The club's wage bill was one of the highest in the division, up 70% on the previous season. It was a gamble, but it succeeded. Whilst McCabe welcomed promotion, he was disappointed not to have won the title. Believing the club to be badly managed throughout his lifetime, its status, in the eyes of many outsiders, as the city's second club infuriates him. Still believing that the club should not be owned or controlled by one person, McCabe's objective in 2006 is to reduce his majority ownership, which was never his ambition to attain, but happened as a consequence of the rights issue not being taken up by others. Invites to potential investors were extended throughout 2006. His 2006 relocation to Belgium, in his words, should not to be seen as a form of early retirement but a further development of his European interests. The move does mean, however, that McCabe will not be living in the UK for the next five years. For the foreseeable future Sheffield United plc meetings will take place in Brussels.

Away from football, McCabe operates a charitable trust through which he gives to 'good causes'. With a main pastime of reading football programmes and Wisden, McCabe argues that his hobby is Sheffield United. Favouring Bob Dylan and the Rolling Stones to classical sounds, McCabe is an understated personality who, whilst personable, avoids the limelight. A genuinely modest person, he is keen to answer both critics and well wishers and even the curious. He has answered fans' letters personally and, at times, phoned fans to argue the club's position. He has even been known to seek out fans at away games and give them complimentary tickets. Admitting to being non-political and not voting for 15 years, he supported the Duke of Edinburgh scheme, part-funded Football Unites Racism Divides, and in 1998 memorably walked into hundreds of Blades protesting against the management of the club in the usual forum of the car park and addressed their anger.

Like many who have moved away from the city, McCabe rails against what he considers 'the perverse happiness in failure' amongst the ranks of Sheffielders and was forever annoyed by the negativity from which he had escaped by, literally, moving away. In 2001, when making his move to launch a share issue which would see him become chairman and later majority shareholder, McCabe expressed his view to a prospective share buyer that running Sheffield United should be an ambitious project but, if the ambition failed, it was equally crucial to have had some fun along the way. McCabe, capably assisted by Sandra, changed the nature of the boardroom at Bramall Lane and brought the club into the 21st century. That he has had fun himself and put a smile on the faces of the fans is a just reward for a gamble that paid off.

100% Blade: Sean Bean

Joining the United board in 2002 was United's most globally recognised fan and cinema idol Sean Bean. Born in the south east of Sheffield in 1959, Bean came from a dynasty of Blades followers and had watched his team from the Shoreham End since the age of six. His commitment to the club is indelible by virtue of a 1990 tattoo on his left shoulder proclaiming '100% Blade' which cost him £2 in Sheffield's Attercliffe district. After a brief stint as a welder, Bean entered art school in Rotherham where he was fascinated by drama classes to the extent that he swapped courses and proved a natural thespian. He left Sheffield aged 21 to accept a place at the Royal Academy of Dramatic Art in central London, where he was one of 32 entrants out of 11,000 aspirants. He made his professional theatre debut in Glasgow in a production of Shakespeare's *Romeo and Juliet* and made screen appearances in *Stormy Monday*, *Shopping*, *The Field* and *Patriot Games*. His role of 006 in the James Bond movie *Goldeneye* brought him global acclaim and led to further appearances in TV specials with huge audiences, most memorable of which was his role of gamekeeper, Mellors, in *Lady Chatterley's Lover*. The Sunday evening military drama *Sharpe*, made Bean a household name in the UK and, surprisingly, parts of Europe and Australia.

This was followed by acclaimed roles in *Essex Boys*, *Lord of the Rings* and *National Treasure* with Nicolas Cage (in the latter a close up of the crossed swords Blade's insignia which had been felt-tipped onto his arm was captured on celluloid).

A controversy ensued around Bean when, in October 1989, he sent his musings on Sheffield football fandom to a wider audience. United's fanzine, *Flashing Blade*, reproduced a cartoon drawn by Bean. His artistic effort depicted an Owl 'Piggy Jack' being kicked outside a pub by a group called 'Bassetts Allsorts', after the name of the United manager, which ends with the pig being taken away for butchery by a knife-carrying United player. Bean's scribblings and imagination caused consternation in some quarters. A *Sheffield Star* reporter claimed that 'Bassetts Allsorts' was a 'thinly disguised reference to United's troublemakers' and quoted a Police Superintendent describing the cartoon as '…despicable. If it in any way contributes towards violence then this man has done both clubs a big disservice'. The secretary of the Wednesday Supporters Club described it as 'sick humour'. The story was repeated in the *Daily Mirror* and an Irish national daily where Bean was filming. There was nothing more to this cartoon than a bored actor and a witty pen and Bean phoned the *Star* and announced that he would from now on refuse them interviews. The *Star* reporter apologised.

More cerebral pursuits saw Bean realise a long-held ambition to play the role of a footballer. In 1996 Bean played the lead in the feature film, *When Saturday Comes*. Shot entirely in Sheffield, the film contained extensive footage shot in and around Bramall Lane. One scene saw Bean in full United kit score a penalty in front of the Kop in the half-time interval during a United v Manchester United match. The film did not reveal the full circumstances of Bean's repeated inability to score, 'I was trying to put it in the top right hand corner' was his preferred explanation, but the moment was a credit to the thousands of Blades who played their part in simulating the crowd scene. Whilst a resident of London since 1981, Bean never severed his Sheffield connections and is often seen amongst the fans at both home and away games.

Sean Bean
The Board Actor

Bean was always forthright in his philosophy of football fandom. Dismissive of the post-1990's nouveau fans, who appeared to cling to the glories of successful clubs, he stated his hope that the game never turns into a 'fairy middle-class puffball game'. His on-screen persona was invariably action hero, darkly threatening but always seductive to women viewers. For Bean, this was a hazard of the job but the roles and associated images brought him global acclaim and, as he explained, 'I'd rather be an employed sex-symbol than an out of work actor'. Bean's six-figure investment in the club brought United a global profile. Whilst unable to attend many board meetings due to filming commitments, when Bean did attend he was probably the first director in the club's history familiar with the writings of Oscar Wilde and Friedrich Nietzche. Bean is most certainly the only director in the history of the club to attend board meetings in torn tracksuit bottoms, Stone Island labelled jumper and battered training shoes showing evidence of the efforts of the previous day's gardening.

Epilogue: At the End of the Day...

The ultimate aim of a football team and a football club is victory. The shared euphoria this brings to players, owners and fans is what teams exist for. Victories provide for the owners and the players posterity, glorious narratives, and a good income. For the rest the issue is symbolic, encapsulated in glory by association and the chance victory brings to hold or look close-hand at the objects that define footballing glory. These objects are basically cups, caps and medals.

Arriving in Europe in the early 15th century, medals invariably bore a portrait or drawing imitating the coins evident in the Greek and Roman Empires awarded to sporting or warring victors upon which were inscribed the likenesses of powerful rulers. Serving to preserve the posthumous or the revered, medals became a latent way of rewarding the worthy. In Britain, Charles I appointed an official 'medallist' to design and produce such artefacts. Later Oliver Cromwell introduced medals as a form of military reward. In recent times medals, as a symbol, have great potency and create the greatest controversy when withheld or returned. The caps awarded to footballers were a legacy of the origins of the game when teams distinguished themselves by coloured headwear. Such caps do not cover the circumference of the skull sufficiently to be considered a garment. Their symbolism is a derivative of both the public school sporting system and of cricket, which had headgear associated with it from its origins. As for cups—their very design suggests their origin. They were meant to hold a drink that would be passed around. This shared consumption, a libation, was integral to replenishing the body following physical exertion. That cups shine is by virtue of the value placed on the gold and silver precious metals in our culture. The cup symbolises scarcity, that culturally valued, and pays homage to antiquity. It is all very primal and masculine and contains elements of classic religious workings.

Following Religiously

The football ground is, for tens of thousands, part of their personal geography. It is a location they will return to on a bi-weekly basis more than anywhere else in their lives. The trappings of religion are all here—mystery, devotion, occasional revelation, access to a form of ecstasy and a seeking for (a footballing) truth left to trusted guardians. A surprising number of fans visit Bramall Lane in mid-week to take in the emptiness of that which fulfils another purpose on match day. A dozen a year have their final wishes granted and have their ashes scattered pitch side. Like any religion, however, the sceptic cannot see the meaning of its existence. But like all religions, and indeed the currency exchange upon which professional football at Bramall Lane began, football clubs are sustained so long as the people behind it believe in it.

Similar to the Christian church, a football club exists of a holy trinity of players, managers and supporters. So what do Blades followers believe from the club's history? From its players, the devoted can reflect on the longevity of the club's goalkeepers, can ponder why the club's centre-forwards always seem to create controversy of various sorts and wonder why great captains rarely leave happy. They might further reflect as to why big-money signings rarely seem to justify their expense. From the managers, fans can witness their varied eccentricities and either love or loathe them. The High Priests and Elders in the boardroom historically were always boringly dependable and religious in outlook. The men who ran the club for close to 100 years had local horizons and things remained that way until the reign of Reg Brealey, the club's first outsider by virtue of travelling 60 miles from Lincolnshire, whose ideas for the club were a world away from those previously known. The interest he attracted from various legal authorities suggests he did not always follow the straight road. Those that succeeded him, however briefly, similarly did not always follow the road well trodden. A new path was eventually forged and the club's chairman since the beginning of the new century has, somewhat refreshingly, not attracted the attention of the criminal justice system.

The fans remain prone to disorder, are hard to please and according to generations of directors, never turn out in sufficient numbers to balance the budget. The fans faith has not been rewarded in trophies or status but the fans remain remarkably loyal which makes one wonder whether delusion is a kind of belief.

Playing Safe

The tribulations of industrial capitalism brought Sheffield polarities of glut and scarcity. Economic booms and busts produced alternations between awful poverty and full employment. When the good times came they were to be enjoyed. The Empire and the war effort were good for Sheffield, the steel it produced was needed for armoury, but the big guns locally were always small businessmen, solicitors and medics. These sober, plain-speaking men were devoted to good works, be it at the local football clubs or in their Freemason and Rotarian associations. When the steel and coal industries died or left the city and when local and national politicians no longer wished to subsidise ailing or non-profit-making production, Sheffield had to fight for its very survival. Some might say it lost the fight in the 1980s. The city is still seeking to establish a post-industrial identity. Whilst diminished, what remains is the passion from its populace for its two professional football clubs.

Professional football clubs were always commercial entities. The game at elite level was always a business and the pursuit of success was never free of underhand methods. Some clubs attained notoriety for certain questionable practices. For 100 years of their existence United were not one of them. Why they avoided this stigma is interesting. The answer probably lies in the demography of the city. The entrepreneurial cultures of the large insurance and banking companies bypassed the city, as did the regional media. Sheffield thus became provincial in its psyche and inward looking and its populace for decades celebrated the cliché attached to it by its residents as the world's largest village. Its people were always hard working and whilst many of the local worthies declared themselves as devout Methodists, they might more realistically be considered Puritan in outlook. Abstemious, and it might be said, at times humourless, such people tended to shun the bright lights but were not prone to wrong-doing. As Charles Clegg famously stated, 'no-one got lost on a straight road'. The sense of duty and citizenship they held to must have caused them to despair over their fellow citizens who worked hard and drank even harder.

The Real Thing
The promotion medal awarded to the United players in May 2006

Closing the Local?

A fan can romanticise the significance of the local, but the contemporary business world has little respect for emotional attachment. A few reminders might be needed here. History tells us that the original Sheffield United team owed little to local ability. Even in 1919 in a Sheffield derby, only one of the 22 players was locally born. In the inter-war years, some Sheffield derbies did not include a single Sheffield-born player. In recent decades exceptionally talented local players proved to be few and far between. United's record international goal scorer is Zimbabwean, its most capped international and only World Cup player is Norwegian and the record signing is of Jamaican extraction. The most popular team manager in living memory was an archetypal Londoner. The team shirt long ago stopped promoting local products or businesses. Within the next decade a Sheffield United side may well have a foreign-born manager and be made up entirely of players born outside the UK. The club may well be owned in future by foreign interests. What Sheffield United is or represents will be the topic of much debate over the next decade.

The city that gave the game to the world has to accept that the world gave something back. On the final day of the 2005–06 season the team performed its now *de rigueur* pre-kick-off team 'huddle', courtesy of US-inspired team-building psychology. Eleven performances of the 'Mexican Wave' by the 27,000 plus crowd was borrowed from the US college sports days. The match gave way to half-time on-pitch entertainment courtesy of five Chinese musicians and a two-person dancing dragon, obviously to impress those in the ground but more importantly enthral the watching TV audience of hundreds of millions in China. Fireworks and anthemic rhythms over the PA system accompanied the post-match celebration and medal presentation ceremony. Revelry in the boardroom an hour later saw the Sheffield-born Derek Dooley officially retire from the club, departing with his rendition of Frank Sinatra's *New York, New York*. The club chairman returned to his home in Belgium hours later. The 30 days per annum he is allowed in the UK means he will miss at least a quarter of the Premiership season. The global and the local complement one another but the rotating advertising hoardings welcoming a Las Vegas casino chain suggest the big money lies outside the city boundaries.

From Pits to Pitz

Football talent is still evident locally down the pitz. But this Pitz is 'the home of five-a-side football' and not a place that produced coal and dozens of Sheffield United footballers. This American-owned franchise, houses in Sheffield 20 five-a-side artificial football pitches boarded all round with advertisements. Hosting some 400 football teams in the course of a week, it has existed since 1990 and is open seven days a week with games played until 10pm. The facilities offered do not stop at football. The site houses a function room and birthday parties for children. The company's arrival was not welcomed initially by the Sheffield and Hallamshire FA who would not sanction any of their competitions. This changed and Pitz now offer a variety of tournaments for teams drawn from supermarkets, retailers, hotels and catering and a diversity of leagues; 'After-Work', and 'Wednesday and Shift Workers'. No longer do the team names reflect pubs and factories as was largely the case in the 11-a-side leagues of the 1970s and 1980s. The teams that enter its competition can be explicit about their ethnic origins, 'Somali Stars' or their religious affiliation, 'Christians United'. Others enter the pitch with what can only be termed ironic detachment. Referees will thus officiate 'Enter Mi Lamb' v 'Outer Position' or possibly 'Wath Porn Stars' v 'Old Slappers' or even 'Shy Tall Knights' v 'Free Beer'. Such facilities provide good fun and recreation, but they will not produce a footballer for United.

The game is suffering at grass roots. The once-thriving eleven-a-side Saturday leagues begun in the 1950s were down to one league in the late 1990s. The Sunday morning leagues tell a similar story. In 1984 one entity had ten divisions of 12 teams. Twenty years later, only two divisions remain. What exists in recent times, not in existence 20 years previously, are leagues for the under-8s and five divisions of ten teams for the over-35s. The demographics of this is fascinating but beyond this particular text. Referee recruitment, however, is at crisis level because of abuse and violence directed towards them from players and spectators. The costs of hiring football pitches for grass-roots teams have become exorbitant because of the privatisation of the best football facilities and the concomitant neglect of facilities owned by the city council.

Lane Living

All things change. Whilst United still play on the pitch where they began over 115 years ago they are now more than a football club. The city's populace, as well as the fan base, benefits from the wider product they offer and plan to offer, be it the soon to be opened hotel, the impending coffee bar, existing banqueting facilities, the proposed casino, or in its established sponsorship of a local community festival. The streets surrounding Bramall Lane are no longer dominated by the white working class or by the hammering, clanking and shrieking of small steel manufacturing industries. Small enterprises around Bramall Lane are now based on fast food; consumption has largely replaced industrial production. The East End factory site that once employed thousands of men in steel production became, in the early 1990s, Europe's largest shopping mall.

The area around Bramall Lane is increasingly populated by migrants of the former empire. Other recent arrivals come from the 50,000 plus student population studying at the city's two universities. Both sets of outsiders have changed the demography of the city and its voting patterns. The east-west divide, that historically segregated the city, originating out of the prevailing wind that placed the rich in the west and the poor in the east amidst the smoke, smell and grime still remains. But new townships on the city boundaries house both the aspiring and the re-housed in a form of suburban domesticity. The change in industrial relations and new industries combined with the new population have seen the Liberal Democrats assume the position of opposition to Labour formerly held by the minority Tories. The shift is in part a consequence of the city having the highest graduate retention rate of any university in the UK. At the end of the twentieth century, the Liberal Democrats briefly took control of the local council.

The football ground reflects the more privatised, even atomised, domestic consumption that is the new household system. People drink and socialise at home more then they used to. Pubs have closed by the dozens. The domestic is more revered than in times past. The 'community' is more spoken of than a lived reality. Sitting in the Bramall Lane ground, an observer no longer sees out of the corners of the stadium to the skylines of Sheffield or even surrounding streets. The ground is now self-contained. An observer could be anywhere—only the accents of those around and billboards offer a clue. An elevator now exists to travel from Bramall Lane car park to boardroom to eat in its franchised restaurant. For those whose investment is smaller and whose literal and social elevation is not so high, food outlets in the ground permit them to combine the best of the local and traditional, Yorkshire brewed beer with the best of the new, 'Indian' balti pies. The players also combine that recognised for decades with that considered improving. They can pour out their hearts to a 'sports psychologist' who occasionally travels with them and enjoy the benefits of half-time jelly babies, which give them slow release sustenance on top of the isotonic sluicing they seem to spend much of the match involved in. But they know the requirements of the game are time-honoured and simple—keep possession, score goals or at least stop the opponent from doing so.

The United Experience

The recently appointed chief executive of Sheffield United in 2006 stated publicly his aim of improving 'the United experience'. This partly involved providing leisure facilities and retail units for the locale. Sheffield United is no longer just a football club but a leisure, property and services business; the profits from which will sustain the core business—football. The business-speak does not seem to perturb the fans. The 2005–06 season saw United's best average attendance for 32 years at just under 24,000. Season ticket sales for 2006–07, at over 21,000, were the best in the club's history. The combined crowds of both Sheffield teams suggest than one in ten of the city's population remains a match-goer. Their participation is in part financial but once in the ground their main role is to be vocal—preferably in praise. Their chants since the mid-1990s have become increasingly orchestrated by a booming PA system that seeks to prevent the pollution of profanity and mask the danger of the spontaneous which can be irreverent and critical. At each home game, as the players perform their pre-kick-off warm-up, the be-suited on-pitch Master of Ceremonies with a good line in patter rouses the Bramall Lane crowd with a cacophonous backdrop of techno-trance. Those who swear, be it in joy or anger at their own players or to annoy visiting fans and players, risk visits to their homes from police and being banned from the stadium—a process assisted by a confidential hotline that allows an informer to describe the offender and their seat number. One consequence of the desire to stamp out hooliganism has been some 80 Blades fans receiving, through civil law procedures, banning orders preventing them from entering any football ground in the country.

Fans are not dupes, slovenly following a manufactured product. The rendition of 'Sheffield Wednesday's fucked it up again' is still the second loudest chant after the acclamation of a United goal. Blades supporters remain active participants in their own fandom. They can create, subvert and defy the ideas of the football authorities. Football in Sheffield still retains primal qualities. This should come as no surprise when we remember that for some 40 years this fan culture celebrated in its Yorkshire anthem catching pneumonia, dying, rotting and via organic processes being eaten by those who survived them. For the past 25 years the Blades anthem has celebrated excessive nicotine, alcohol and carbohydrate consumption wrapped up in the love of a football club. The beauty the game can provide remains entwined with the unbelievable, the brutal, the sublime and the obscene. As football writer Arthur Hopcraft so famously stated, the game will always be more vinegar than Chanel.

The Local and the Global

A match programme from March 2006 provides some indication of the position of both professional football and Sheffield United in the new millennium. For those seeking a profound or short-term change from the local milieu, jobs are advertised in the armed forces as are holidays in Malta. For those seeking temporary changes to their immediate existence the official SUFC Mastercard credit facility and themed party nights courtesy of the club's Conference and Banqueting Department might help. Instant comfort and solitude is available courtesy of that day's match sponsors, a newly opened city-centre four star hotel. Global finance made the match possible—the match ball was paid for by auditors Grant Thornton. The match programme was part-funded by an urban design consultancy. No fewer than 16 companies part-

Former United director and Minister of Sport Richard Caborn (front row middle) puts his weight behind a national campaign

sponsored the academy players and coaches—ranging from hairdressers to tax consultants and property developers. For those seeking a good walk spoilt, a golf tournament followed by dinner, with tables for eight costing £450 (plus VAT) is promoted. Other adverts promote the Bank of Scotland's corporate facilities and a company named Unite announces itself and its student lodgings. Forms of charity still exist. A £9,000 cheque was donated to financially-stricken near neighbours Rotherham United out of profits from the 'beamed broadcast' at Bramall Lane of a Wednesday v United derby at Hillsborough.

Social concerns are evident amidst the commerce. A staged photo of a blooded and unconscious (dead?) young female passenger, watched by a baseball-capped male of a similar age, informs readers to slow down when driving. The advert comes courtesy of the South Yorkshire Safety Camera Partnership. The disabled enclosure of Bramall Lane is, a reader learns, sponsored by a private health scheme. Youngsters attending the game receive a free wall-chart and player portrait cards which contain safety and anti-crime messages from the Sheffield Safe Communities Partnership as it attempts to resolve crime and anti-social behaviour in the city's young. The officially recognised disaffected youth are now attempting to be re-engaged with the law-abiding, assisted by United's sponsored Academy, under the Vocational Skills Programme, which uses a football-related curriculum to teach basic literacy and numeracy. A photograph of Deputy Prime Minister John Prescott captures him visiting the Chengdu Blades training ground in China's Sichuan province, thereby endorsing United's pioneering purchase of a Chinese team and implicitly football as a marketing vehicle of global significance. A partnership between United and a village in Uganda, begun by an employee of a Sheffield Health Trust, sees United sponsor a football tournament as a facilitator in the prevention of further involvement of young men in warring militias. The game was always the kernel of something greater—but where does it all end?

Football memories can provide a lifetime of significant anchors. At their least they facilitate collective narratives which make life worth living. There is a multitude of delight and life-affirming stories in this tale, alongside desperation, despair and death. That said, for a club of its size and history, Sheffield United is the most under-performing in British football. Since 1925 they have finished, in the footballing sense, nowhere. In defence of this one could argue that, in the footballing sense, even nowhere is somewhere and the ordinary life is, as this text has hopefully revealed, at times equal to that provided by the extraordinary. The words emanating from the United boardroom have not always been informed by reason. The view from the terraces onto the pitch has not always been pretty. But a spirit has struck deep in generations of Blades fans. That spirit remains today and those who have watched, served, managed and administered should, for the most part, be proud of the legacy they left.

The present is where hope and experience meet. The new century sees Sheffield United Football Club looking very different from that which has existed in the previous 117 years. The buzzword in club communiqués is 'diversification'. The chairman, the one man prepared to plough the swamp of the 1990s and make his vision a reality, can now proclaim that Sheffield United has changed from an old-fashioned entity to a modern, progressive football organisation. The gulf between ambition and reality is narrowing.

It is the forward thinking that preserve institutions by inoculating them with future ambitions. Football clubs were not meant to be stagnant entities but to embark on journeys driven by both the conservative and the adventurous. History happens first in the mind. Ideas drive us. In the new millennium dreams have become hopes and the hopes are now to be realised.

The Premiership adventure lasted just one season, United finished third from bottom accumulating 38 points having won just 10 games. One dimensional in playing style and poor away from home, the average home crowd of 31,000 (the highest for over 30 years) enjoyed the occasional glimpse of glory but were back to the more familiar footballing fayre of the Coca Cola Championship. Three days after relegation a press conference saw Neil Warnock and Kevin McCabe inform the world of the former's amicable departure from Bramall Lane as he sought one more managerial challenge. Six days later the Chairman revealed former Manchester United and England captain Bryan Robson as the new manager. No other candidate was interviewed.

The new season went from bad to worse and by February 2008 another press conference saw Robson considering the position of Director of Football whilst the club looked for a replacement coach. Robson turned the offer down, reasoning that the United faithful would not accept him regardless of his status at the club. Replacing Robson was Kevin Blackwell, well known to Blades fans by virtue of his years at Bramall Lane as assistant to Neil Warnock.

The global branding of the club continued apace. 'Link Ups' were entered into with Corinthians of Sao Paulo and Central Coast Mariners of Australia. The Hungarian club Ferencvaros was bought by Kevin McCabe. Potential Blade players were moved from an Ivory Coast academy to further their footballing abilities at United's sister clubs Chengdu of China and White Star of Belgium.

As a new generation sought the right to wear the stripes those who had served so well received recognition of various sorts. In December 2007 Alan Hodgkinson woke to find that his services to football were to be recognised with an MBE in the New Years Honours List. The only man at Bramall Lane with a similar accolade died in March 2008 at the age of 78. The funeral of Derek Dooley received global publicity, Sheffield Cathedral was packed, another 1000 mourners paid their respects outside. A bronze statue will stand at Bramall Lane in Dooley's honour.

The City made by fire out of water changed the world with its ingenuity in steel production and in doing so produced a proud populace who laboured hard to send the steel around the globe. The same people played hard. The soil and sinews, leather and limbs that combined to make football the only global idiom was a product of the same people. It is a heritage many places would cherish and one that should always be celebrated.

All true Blades fans know; support is forever characterised by the heart that aches, the memories that linger and the hope that springs eternal. It will always be so.

'If I can make it there'
The late, great Derek Dooley takes the applause of the Lane faithful following his retirement from United after 33 years of service in 2006.
Derek passed away in March 2008 robbing the City of Sheffield of one of its most loved sons.
Neither United nor Wednesday will see his like again.

Bibliography

Armstrong, G. (1999) *Football hooligans: Knowing the score* Oxford: Berg
Armstrong, G. (2000) *Blade Runners: Lives in football* Sheffield: The Hallamshire Press

Baker, W.J. (1979) *'The making of Working-Class Football Culture in Victorian England'*, Journal of Social History, 13 (2), pp. 241–51
Benton, S. (1976) *'The Strike in the Regions—Sheffield'* in Morris, M. (ed) *The General Strike* London: Journeyman
Bassett, D. (1997) *Harry's Game* Derby: Breedon Books
Birchenall, A. (2000) *Bring back the Birch: The Alan Birchenall Story* Leicester: Polar
Bruce, S. (1994) *Heading for Victory: an autobiography* London: Bloomsbury
Burley, D. (1995) *Playing the Game: Sport and British Society* Manchester: Manchester University Press

Cardinal, R., and Elsner, J. (eds) (1994) *The Cultures of Collecting* London: Reaktion Books
Clarebrough, D. (1989) *The First 100 Years: The Official Century History of Sheffield United.* Sheffield: Sheffield United Publications
Clarebrough, D. (2001) *100 Greats: Sheffield United F.C.* Gloucestershire: Tempus.
Cox, R., Russell, D., Vamplew, W. (eds) (2002) *Encyclopedia of British Football* London: Cass

Davey, R. (1984) *Pubs and people around Sheffield* Manchester: Neil Richardson

Farnsworth, K. (1982) *Wednesday! Sheffield Wednesday. A Complete Record. 1867-1987.* Sheffield: Sheffield City Libraries
Farnsworth, K. (1995) *Sheffield Football: A History. Volume I 1857–1961* Sheffield: The Hallamshire Press
Farnsworth, K. (1995) *Sheffield Football: A History. Volume II 1961–1995* Sheffield: The Hallamshire Press
Fishwick, N. (1986) *From Clegg to Clegg House: The Official Centenary of the Sheffield and Hallamshire Football Association 1886–1986* Sheffield: Sheffield and Hallamshire County Football Association
Fishwick, N. (1988) *A History of Association Football*. Manchester: Manchester University Press
Fishwick, N. (1989) *English Football and Society 1910–1950* Manchester: Manchester University Press
Fox, N. (2003) *Prophet or Traitor? The Jimmy Hagan Story* Manchester: The Parrs Wood Press

Goodman, P. and Hutton, S. (2005) *150 Years of Bramall Lane. Sheffield United F.C..* Sheffield: Northend Limited
Guthrie, J. (1976) *Soccer Rebel: The evolution of the professional footballer* Pinner: Pentagon

Harvey, A. (2005) *Football: The First Hundred Years—The Untold Story* London: Routledge
Hattersley, R. (2004) *The Edwardians* London: Abacus
Holt, R. (1990) *Sport and the Working Class in Britain* Manchester: Manchester University Press
Hopcraft, A (1968) *The Football Man: People and passions in soccer* Middlesex: Penguin
Howard, N.P. (1976) *'Cooling the heat: A history of the rise of trade unionism in the South Yorkshire Iron and Steel Industry from the Origins to the First World War'* in Pollard, S., and Holmes, C. (eds) *Essays in the economic and social history of South Yorkshire* Barnsley: South Yorkshire County Council
Hunt, A. (1956) *'The Morphology and Growth of Sheffield'* in Linton, D. (ed) *Sheffield and its Region: A scientific and historical survey* British Association for the Advancement of Science. Sheffield: Sunley

Inglis, S. (1988) *League Football—and the men who made it* London: Willow Books

James, G. (2000) *Football with a Smile: The authorised biography of Joe Mercer* Leicester: ACL and Polar Publishing
Jenks, C. (ed) (1995) *Visual Culture* London: Routledge
Jones, D. (1975) *Chartism and the Chartists* London: Allen Lane
Jones, G. (1993) *Joe Mercer: Football with a Smile*. Leicester: ACL.
Jones, S. (1988) *Sport, politics and the working class: Organised labour and sport in interwar Britain* Manchester: Manchester University Press
Jones, V. (2001) *A Kick in the Grass*. Front Page Books: London

Kelly, G. (2005) *Terrace Heroes: The life and times of the 1930s professional footballer* Oxfordshire: Routledge

Litster, J. (2000) *The Football Programme: A History and Guide* Gloucestershire: Tempus

Mason, T. (1980) *Association Football & English Society 1863—1915* Sussex: The Harvester Press
McCarthy, T. (1989) *War Games: The Story of Sport in World War Two* London: Queen Anne Press
McKenzie, J. (1987) *Imperialism and Popular Culture* Manchester: Manchester University Press
McVay, D. (2003) *Steak...Diana Ross: Diary of a football nobody* Manchester: The Parrs Wood Press

Owen, A.D.K. (1932) *Unemployment in Sheffield* Sheffield: Sheffield Reference Library

Pelling, H. (1963) *A history of British Trade Unionism* Harmondsworth: Penguin
Pollard, S. (1959) *A History of Labour in Sheffield* Liverpool: University of Liverpool Press
Pollard, S. (1971) *The Sheffield Outrages* Sheffield: Adams and Dart Social Documents
Pollard, S. and Holmes, C. (1976) *Essays in the Economic and Social History of South Yorkshire* Barnsley: South Yorkshire County Council
Phythian, G. (2005) *Colossus: The True Story of William Foulke*. Gloucestershire: Tempus
Pybus, S. (1994) *Damned bad place, Sheffield: An anthology of writing about Sheffield through the ages* Sheffield: Sheffield Academic Press

Raynor, G. (1993) *Football Ambassador at Large*. London: Soccer Book Club.
Rippon, A. (2005) *Gas Masks for Goal Posts: Football in Britain During the Second World War*. London: Sutton
Russell, D. (1997) *Football and the English: A Social History of Association Football in England 1863–1995* Preston: Carnegie Publishing
Russell, D. (2003) *Abiding Memories: The Community Singing Movement and British Social Life in the inter-war period* Unpublished paper: University of Central Lancashire

Saffer, D. (2002) *The Life and Times of Mick Jones*. Gloucestershire: Tempus.
Seddon, P.J. (1999) *A Football Compendium* Wetherby: British Library
Sharpe, G. (1997) *Gambling on Goals: A Century of Football Betting* Edinburgh: Mainstream
Sparling, R.A. (1987) *Romance of the Wednesday*. Southend-on-Sea: Desert Island Books Limited
Steele, J. (1986) *The Countrymen: The story of Hallam FC* Chesterfield: Henry Boot
Studd, S. (1948) *Herbert Chapman: Football Emperor* London: Souvenir Press

Taw, T. (2003) *Football's War and Peace: The tumultuous season 1946–47* Essex: Desert Island Books
The Taylor Report: The Hillsborough Stadium Disaster, Inquiry by Lord Justice Taylor (The Taylor Report) HMSO 1989
Tischler, S. (1981) *Footballers and businessmen. The origins of professional football in England* London: Holmes & Meier
Truman, F. (2004) *As it was: The memoirs of Fred Truman* London: MacMillan

Vamplew, W. (1988) *Pay up and play the game. Professional sport in Britain 1875-1914* Cambridge: Cambridge University Press
Vasili, P. (1998) *The first Black Footballer: Arthur Wharton 1865 – 1930* London: Frank Cass Publishers

Walters, F. (1957) *History of Sheffield Football Club* Sheffield: Allen & Unwin
Walvin, J. (1975) *The People's Game* London: Allen Lane
Westergaard, J., Noble, I., Walker, A. (1989) *After redundancy* Cambridge: Polity Press

Young, P. (1964) *Football in Sheffield* London: The Sportsmans Book Club

Sheffield United Football Club—the future...